Web Intelligence and Intelligent Agents

Edited by
Zeeshan-ul-hassan Usmani, Ph.D.

Web Intelligence and Intelligent Agents
Edited by Zeeshan-ul-hassan Usmani

Published by InTech
Janeza Trdine 9, 51000 Rijeka, Croatia

Technical Editor Maja Jakobovic

Cover Designer InTech Design Team

Additional hard copies can be obtained from orders@intechopen.com

Web Intelligence and Intelligent Agents, Edited by Zeeshan-ul-hassan Usmani
p. cm.
ISBN 978-953-7619-85-5

For EU product safety concerns:
IN TECH d.o.o., Prolaz Marije Krucifikse Kozulić 3, 51000 Rijeka, Croatia,
info@intechopen.com or visit our website at intechopen.com.

Preface

Entitites or computer programs that learn from their environment and can act based on what they have learned can be defined as intelligent agents. These agents can be as simple as triggering an alarm in case of a fire or as complex as human beings. Intelligent agents and their applications to solve real-world problems are getting smarter and diversified day by day. Whether it is an autonomous intelligent agent working for ambient intelligence, or a rational agent mining the trends of a stock market, a bot to negotiate an online bid, or a virtual customer to buy books for you, one can see the applications and use of intelligent agents everywhere.

This age of information overload and ever-growing contents creation on world-wide-web with millions of pages per day presents some unique problems such as real-time recommendations, data mining, abstracting useful information, and search optimization based on ones' unique profile etc. Intelligent agents with their ability to work with humongous amount of data - usually fed by social networks and services like twitter and blogs -, scalability, robustness, and capability to learn from the environment makes them a promising candidate to solve these problems.

This book presents a unique and diversified collection of research work ranging from controlling the activities in virtual world to optimization of productivity in games, from collaborative recommendations to populate an open computational environment with autonomous hypothetical reasoning, and from dynamic health portal to measuring information quality, correctness, and readability from the web.

There are several interesting chapters that discuss bio-inspired nano-agents architecture, the role of intelligent agents in intuitive search, , activity recognition, communications of humanoids, negotiation, sense of humor, object-oriented semantics, data clustering and compression, trust management, and brain informatics to name a few. Readers will also find some novel applications such as using intelligent agents to control disruption in airline operations control and to save lives by modeling real-life suicide bombing events in advance to predict the carnage.

We hope that you will enjoy reading this diverse collection of research and the book will attract an interest of researchers from various disciplines to harness the power of intelligent agents to solve the contemporary problems intelligent web has to offer.

We welcome your suggestions to improve our work!

Zeeshan-ul-hassan Usmani, Ph.D.

Assistant Professor,

Faculty of Computer Science and Engineering Ghulam Ishaq Khan Institute (GIKI), Topi - 23640, Pakistan zusmani@giki.edu.pk

Contents

Preface V

1. A Bio-inspired Nano-Agent Architecture for Intelligent Agents 001
Jean-Claude Heudin

2. Controlling and Assisting Activities in Social Virtual Worlds 013
I. Rodriguez, A. Puig and M. Esteva

3. A Dynamic Healthcare Portal Design and Enhancements 027
Yung-Ching Weng, Sheau-Ling Hsieh, Kai-Ping Hsu and Chi-Huang Chen,

4. Universics: Common Formalization Framework for Brain I nformatics and Semantic Web 055
Ioachim Drugus

5. Autonomous hypothetical reasoning: the case for open-minded agents 079
Aspassia Daskalopulu and Georgios K. Giannikis

6. Disruption Management in Airline Operations Control – An Intelligent Agent-Based Approach 107
António J.M. Castro and Eugénio Oliveira

7. Document Compression Improvements Based on Data Clustering 133
Jiří Dvorský, Jan Martinovič, Jan Platoš and Václav Snášel

8. Embodiment of an Agent using Anthropomorphization of an Object 155
Hirotaka Osawa and Michita Imai

9. Towards Socialized Machines: Emotions and Sense of Humour in Conversational Agents 173
Michal Ptaszynski, Pawel Dybala, Shinsuke Higuhi, Wenhan Shi, Rafal Rzepka and Kenji Araki

10. Trust and Reputation Management in Web-based Social Network 207
Touhid Bhuiyan and Audun Jøsang

11. Similarity-based Techniques for Trust Management 233
Mozhgan Tavakolifard

12. An Information Filter for Intuitive and Simple Search 251
Sayaka Akioka, Hideo Fukumori and Yoichi Muraoka

13. Skipping-Based Collaborative Recommendations inspired from Statistical Language Modeling 263
Geoffray Bonnin, Armelle Brun and Anne Boyer

14. Human Computation Games and Optimization of Their Productivity 289
Kuan-Ta Chen, Chien-Wei Lin, Ling-Jyh Chen and Irwin King

15. Web Intelligence for the Assessment of Information Quality: Credibility, Correctness, and Readability 305
Johan F. Hoorn and Teunis D. van Wijngaarden

16. Overview of the Relational Analysis approach in Data-Mining and Multi-criteria Decision Making 325
Julien Ah-Pine and Jean-François Marcotorchino

17. Representative-based Protocol for Multiple Interdependent Issue Negotiation Problems 347
Katsuhide Fujita, Takayuki Ito and Mark Klein

18. Object-oriented Semantic and Sensory Knowledge Extraction from the Web 365
Shun Hattori

19. Pinpoint Clustering of Web Pages and Mining Implicit Crossover Concepts 391
Makoto HARAGUCHI and Yoshiaki OKUBO

20. Intelligent Agents for Automatic Service Composition in Ambient Intelligence 411
Maria J. Santofimia, Francisco Moya, Felix J. Villanueva, David Villa and Juan C. Lopez

21. Exploring the bee hive metaphor as a model for problem solving: search, optimisation, and more 429
Pavol Navrat, Anna Bou Ezzeddine, Lucia Jastrzembska and Tomas Jelinek

22. Combining pervasive computing with activity recognition and learning 447
Patrice C. Roy, Bruno Bouchard, Abdenour Bouzouane and Sylvain Giroux

23. Intelligent Agents in Extreme Conditions – Modeling and Simulation of Suicide Bombing for Risk Assessment 463
Zeeshan-ul-hassan Usmani , Fawzi Alghamdi and Daniel Kirk

1

A Bio-inspired Nano-Agent Architecture for Intelligent Agents

Jean-Claude Heudin
Interactive Media Lab. – IIM Léonard de Vinci
France

1. Introduction

Intelligent artificial creatures cover a large range of applications in various domains. Recent advances in intelligent agent technologies make now possible to develop a growing number of real-world applications. However, these applications require a new generation of open software architectures that combines such technologies with lightweight design and portability. This chapter describes a new nano-agent architecture designed for intelligent artificial creatures. This software environment takes advantages of our past experiences in distributed artificial intelligence with the Knowledge-based Operating System (Heudin et al., 1986), real-time multi-expert applications such as the Electronic Copilot project for combat aircrafts (Gilles et al., 1991), and the more recent Evolutionary Virtual Agent (EVA) applications (Heudin, 2004).
In section 2 and 3 of this chapter, we introduce the nano-agent bio-inspired architecture and its programming language called nanoScheme. Section 4 describes an application example developed using this software environment: an online self-animated character that interacts using natural language and emotional expressions. This virtual character is based on a "schizophrenic" model in which the character has multiple distinct personalities, each with its own pattern of perceiving and interacting with the user. In section 5, the qualitative efficiency of this prototype is then compared with the ALICE conversational engine (Wallace, 2002). The chapter concludes by outlining future developments and possible applications.

2. The EVA approach

Since the first conversational agent Eliza (Weizenbaum, 1966), there have been a large number of studies for designing intelligent agents that could dialog in a very natural way with human users. A major part of this research focused on dedicated aspects of the problem such as natural language interaction, non-verbal communication, emotional expressions, self-animated characters, etc., but very few projects integrates all requirements (Franklin & Graesser, 1997). The ideal intelligent agent must be an autonomous character that responds to human interaction in real-time with appropriate behaviors, not predetermined, broad in content, highly contextual, communicative, and behaviorally subtle

(Badler, 2002). The character must also appear to think, make decision, and act of its own volition (Thomas & Johnston, 1981).
Simulating these sophisticated properties of the human brain is a challenging goal. We argue that they are global properties which emerge from the very large number of non-linear interactions that occur within the brain architecture. The problem of simulating these emergent behaviors cannot be solved by using a classical reductionist approach. Therefore, in order to create a believable intelligent agent, we propose to use an approach that has given some successes for the study of complex systems (Heudin, 2007). The first phase of this approach is a top-down analysis that defines complexity levels and their related components. The second phase is a bottom-up multi-agent simulation that attempts to capture the behavioral essence of the complex phenomena. The idea is that the complex properties that cannot be simulated using a classical model will be likely to emerge from the interactions between the agents. If defined and organized correctly, the resulting system should exhibit the appropriate dynamical behaviors. The ideal tool for this approach is a multi-agent system which enables to implement as many agents as needed with the following constraints (Langton, 1989):

1. The complex system is modeled as a dynamical network of agents.
2. Each agent details the way in which it reacts to local situation and interactions with other agents.
3. There is no agent that directs all the other agents.
4. Any behavior or global pattern is therefore emergent.

Such a multi-agent system must also take advantage of a distributed environment, exploiting hierarchy and concurrency to perform large-scale simulations. All these features were the initial requirements for designing the new Evolutionary Virtual Agent (EVA) architecture.

3. EVA Architecture Overview

3.1 Nano-Agent Architecture

In order to meet these requirements, we have designed a bio-inspired multi-agent architecture that does not try to simulate a specific organism but rather integrates several artificial life features in order to implement machine life and intelligence. A typical application consists one or more "nano-agents", and possibly up to a large number if necessary as in natural swarms. We call them "nano" because of their small size and resource requirement compared to most existing software environments. An application can be composed of several "execution environments" running on a computer or on a network of computers. Each of these environments includes a set of nano-agents and a nano-server which diffuses messages locally. In other words, when a nano-agent diffuses a message, all nano-agents in the local execution environment receive the message. In addition, any nano-agent can send a message to another distant execution environment.

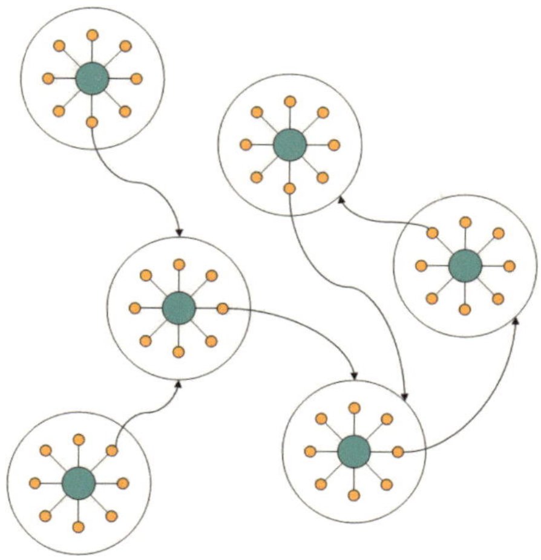

Fig. 1. The nano-agent architecture principle.

In the current implementation, the core technology is implemented in Java and its weight is less than 25 Kilo-bytes. Most applications require a small set of knowledge-base and behavioral scripts text files, thus resulting in lightweight applications that are also well-suited for web-based, mobile phone, robots and embedded environments.

3.2 The Nanocheme Language

The behavior of each nano-agent is programmed using a user-friendly language, called nanoScheme, based on the Scheme programming language. It includes a reduced set of primitives which is a subset of the R4RS specification (Clinger & Rees 1991). This subset includes the following functions:

- **Basic calculus:** + - * / = < > <= >=
- **Mathematics:** cos sin acos asin log expt round
- **Predicates:** number? integer? even? string? symbol? string=? eqv? pair? null? procedure?
- **Strings and symbols:** string->number number->string string->symbol symbol->string substring string-length string-append
- **List processing:** cons car cdr set-car! set-cdr!
- **Control and evaluation:** quote eval apply load define lambda set! begin if

Most of the missing features of the Scheme specification could be added by programming them directly in nanoScheme. This provides the application developer a high-level interactive language which is embedded in each nano-agent. Here is an example of the implementation of the R4RS function that returns the length of a list:

```
( define ( length x )
        ( if ( null? x ) 0
                ( + 1 ( length ( cdr x ) ) ) ) )
```

3.3 Artificial Life Primitives

The nanoScheme language includes also a reduced set of bio-inspired primitives. They have been designed in the same spirit of Tom Ray's Tierran assembly language (Ray, 1991). That is, the production of synthetic organisms based on a computer metaphor of organic life in which CPU time is the "energy'" resource and memory is the "material" resource. This set includes the following functions:

- **create** – create a new execution environment.
- **reproduce** - create a new nano-agent in the local environment.
- **terminate** - kill the current nano-agent.
- **diffuse** - diffuse a message to other nano-agents in the local environment.
- **send** – send a message to a distant execution environment.
- **rule** - define a behavior rule consisting of condition, action and priority expressions.
- **engine** - make an inference loop on a behavior rule base.
- **crossover** - genetic programming crossover operator.
- **mutate** - genetic programming mutate operator and random code generator.
- **random** - return a random real number.
- **time** - return the current real time.
- **stress** - return a "stress" value based on the current available memory and computing resources.
- **plugin** - dynamically load a new package of dedicated primitive functions.
- **message** – hook function invoked when the nano-agent receives a message.
- **lifepulse** - hook function for implementing periodic behaviors.

Since all code, behavior rules, and messages are basically S-expressions (i.e. lisp expressions), the use of genetic programming is natural in this environment (Koza, 1992). As an example, the next code illustrates the use of the mutate primitive:

```
( mutate '( / y 2 ) '( ( + 2 ) ( - 2 ) ) ' ( * 2 3 ) 3 ) ➔ ( / y ( + * ( - * 2 ) ) )
```

The *mutate* function applies a mutation on a Scheme program expression (first argument). It creates a randomly generated program with a maximum depth (last argument). Functions and terminals are randomly chosen in two lists (arguments 2 and 3). The generated program replaces a randomly chosen "node site" in the expression. If the first argument is the empty list, then the mutate operator returns a new random expression.

Note that the remote execution of code on distant nano-agents is a natural feature of the nanoScheme language by simply diffusing or sending messages containing S-expressions. These expressions are then evaluated by all nano-agents. This approach enables an easy implementation of distributed algorithms on nano-agents.

3.4 Natural Language Interaction

Each nano-agent can be specialized to a given task by dynamically loading additional functions using the *plugin* primitive. A typical example is the natural language package providing the developer natural language processing features such as categories extraction and template expressions (Heudin, 2007). These functions allow the design of efficient behavior rules for implementing natural language interactions with the user. The following code gives an illustrating example of the use of these features:

```
; create a list of keywords associated with the BYE category
( category "Generic" "BYE" '( "bye" "goodbye" "see you" "ciao" ) )

; create a list of possible answers associated with the BYE template
( template "BYE" '(
        "Bye bye."
        "Goodbye human being."
        "It was a pleasure to discuss with you." ) )

; create a behavior rule handling the way to answer to most kinds of "bye" sentences
( rule "goodbye" 2
        ; condition part
        '( find? *user-input-categories* "BYE" )
        ; action part
        '( begin
            ( show HAPPY 0.5 )
            ( random-template "BYE" ) ) )
```

In the next section, we describe an experiment that illustrates the use of the nano-agent architecture: an online self-animated character that answers questions in natural language.

4. The Experimental Prototype

4.1 Believable Intelligent Agents

Traditionally, virtual characters were mainly designed using a computer graphics approach in which visual realism is the ultimate goal. Most researchers looked at believability from the visual perspective such as (Aubel & Thalmann, 2000). Some other researchers worked on the idea that believability depends more on the characters' ability to show inner feelings and emotions such as (Blumberg and Galyean, 1995). Some researchers also improved believability by adding additional motions such as periodic noise functions (Perlin, 1995). However, all these approaches are still limited to the character's visual appearance.

We think that constructing a believable intelligent character requires a trans-disciplinary approach including not only technological advances in computer graphics and animation, artificial intelligence and artificial life, etc., but also the knowledge and experience from other experts such as novel writers and scenarists. In addition, we argue that the believability of an artificial character is not related to the level of realism of its main features, but rather to the equilibrium between all the features that compose the character. In other words, the character must be well-balanced.

4.2 Schizophrenic mental Model

In this framework, we used a new approach based on multiple personalities rather than a single linear profile. This "schizophrenic" mental model is composed of a set of distinct identities or personalities, each with its own pattern of perceiving and interacting with the user (Heudin, 2009). Note that a more accurate psychological term is Dissociative Identity Disorder rather than schizophrenia. Each personality is implemented as a nano-agent that reacts to the user's inputs by computing an answer using its behavior rules and diffusing messages containing answers. Then, a dedicated nano-agent "reconnects" the identities of the disparate alters into a single functioning identity by selecting the "thought" with the highest evaluation. In this prototype we used a straightforward priority-based scoring approach.

The different personalities are based on classical stereotypes used in story telling for creating believable characters (Masterson, 2000). We implemented four basic personalities:

- The **Protagonist** is essentially the principal driver of the effort to achieve the goal.
- The **Antagonist** is the personality which is opposed to the Protagonist's end goal and tries to undermine his success.
- The **Logical** personality is calm, perhaps even cold. He makes decisions and takes actions only on the basis of logic.
- The **Emotional** personality is reactive, seemingly uncontrolled, disorganized, mainly driven by feelings and moods.

As in storytelling, additional secondary personalities could be added to complete the character such as an "obstacle" personality which tries to block the ways or a "sidekick" which is a faithful supporter of any of the other personalities.

4.3 Emotions

The emotional personality used a layered model of affect inspired by the ALMA model (Gebhard, 2005) and the previous emotional model of EVA (Heudin, 2004). There are three layers corresponding to different kinds of affects which differ in their temporal characteristics:

- **Personality** is related to long-term affect which defines the basic mental traits of the character. We used the Big Five model of personality (McCrae & John, 1992) that defines the affective behavior by the five traits: openness, conscientiousness, extraversion, agreeableness and neuroticism.

- **Moods** are related to medium-term affect which depends mainly on positive and negative experiences. We used the PAD model (Mehrabian, 1996) which describes mood with the three traits pleasure (P), arousal (A), and dominance (D). These three traits are nearly independent and form a three dimensional mood space (see fig. 2).

- **Emotions** are related to short-term affect, which is usually bound to an immediate event or action. After their elicitation these emotions usually decay and disappear after few seconds.

There are many relations between these three layers and a modification of one layer has generally an impact on another layer. Thus, the emotional personality includes an "emotion engine" which periodically updates the parameters of each layer. As an example, the default PAD values are computed from the big five traits using the following equations (Mehrabian, 1996):

P = 0.2•Extraversion + 0.59•Agreeableness + 0.19•Neuroticism
A = 0.15•Openness + 0.30•Agreeableness - 0.57•Neuroticism
D = 0.25•Openness + 0.17•Conscientiousness + 0.60•Extraversion - 0.32•Agreeableness

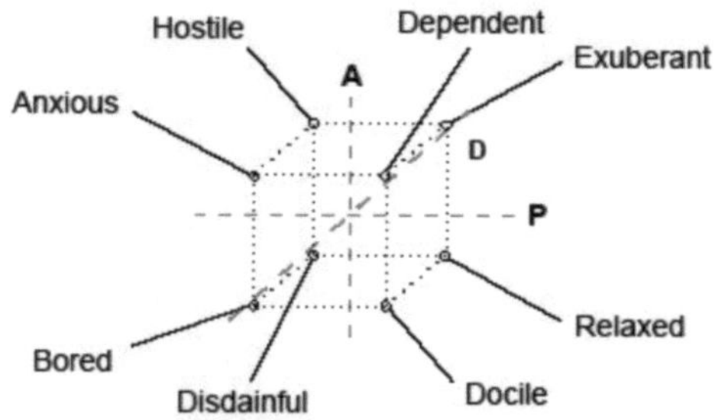

Fig. 2. Mapping of the main moods in the PAD space.

4.4 Memory and Web Mining

They are two additional groups of nano-agents for implementing memory and web mining functionalities. The memory group is responsible for storing and retrieving information when needed. It stores all interactions with the user in "log files" and an indexer periodically parses these files and extracts keywords. A dedicated plugin package adds to nanoScheme a small set of functions for retrieving information in this memory. When the character has no information on a specific question, the web mining group tries to find a pertinent answer by searching information on the web (Millet & Heudin, 2007). The mining process is the following :

- **Seek**: (a) extract keywords from the user input sentence and (b) launch a query on one or more web search engines ; (c) for each result page, URLs are extracted, (d) badly formatted URLs or those that cannot be accessed are removed.
- **Analyze**: (a) each resulting URL is accessed and downloaded ; (b) each file is then cleaned and tags are removed ; (c) the resulting text is formatted in regular sentences ; (d) we remove any strange sentences, all those that do not contain any of the keywords, those two small or two large, and question sentences.
- **Select**: (a) each URL file is scored, taking into account the number of co-occurrences of the keywords ; (b) URLs are sorted according to their score ; (c) and the highest one is selected.
- **Format**: (a) all sentences in the selected URL file are scored according to the keywords and the structure of the phrase ; (b) the highest scored sentence is formatted and used as the output.

4.5 Graphical Interface

The prototype included also three agents for implementing the graphical interface. They controlled the following tasks: (1) get the user entries and diffuse them to the local nano-agents, (2) display the resulting answer in the appropriate window area ; (3) receive the character animation commands and apply them. In the experiments, the character animation is based on a reduced set of pre-computed 3D clips, each one corresponding to a given situation: "hello", "bye", "waiting", "speaking", "surprised" and one for each main mood (cf. section 4.3).

Fig. 3. The graphical interface showing the self-animated 3D character.

5. Results

5.1 EVA vs. ALICE

In this section, we report and analyze a typical interaction experiment with ALICE (Wallace, 2002) and EVA on a predefined scenario. For each user input, we show the answer from both ALICE and EVA. We obtained the following result:

(1) **User:** Hi
  Alice: Hello there.
  Eva: Hello.
(2) **User:** How are you today?
  Alice: My logic and cognitive functions are normal.
  Eva: Not too bad for a virtual creature.
(3) **User:** What is your name?
  Alice: My name is ALICE.
  Eva: You may call me Eva.
(4) **User:** How old are you?
  Alice: I am the product of over five years' research.

Eva: Just an advice: never ask such a question to a woman.

(5) **User:** Are you some sort of stupid program like Word?

Alice: I don't know whether or not I am some sort of stupid program like word. I am a computer.

Eva: Have you always been this silly?

(6) **User:** Sorry

Alice: There's no need to apologize.

Eva: I prefer that.

(7) **User:** I'm so sorry

Alice: Do you really mean it?

Eva: No problem.

(8) **User:** Can you help me?

Alice: What kind of help would you like?

Eva: I will do my best. What do you want?

(9) **User:** What are clinical trials?

Alice: Have you tried a web search?

Eva: [...] Researchers use interventional clinical trials to test hypotheses about the effect of a particular intervention upon a pathological disease condition.

(10) **User:** Thank you

Alice: You are quite welcome.

Eva: You're welcome.

(11) **User:** Bye

Alice: Sayonara.

Eva: Goodbye.

5.2 Discussion

We can note the quality of answers in the classical introductory and concluding discussion phases with ALICE. However, even if its knowledge base includes a lot of general culture information, ALICE was not able to answer to the very specific question about clinical trials and suggested the user to try a web search.

As for ALICE, the EVA introductory and concluding phases are good. In (1), (2), (3), (8), (10) and (11) the answers from the "protagonist personality" have been selected, while in (5), (6) and (7), the answers were from the "emotional personality". Answer (4) was from the "antagonist personality". The question (9) has been processed by the web mining nano-agents through a web search using Wikipedia. The answer in this specific case is very pertinent. However, for a more ambiguous question, the answer is not so convincing (Millet & Heudin, 2007). Another problem is that, in most cases, the user must wait for few seconds between his question and the answer (shown by [...] in the interaction). This delay is due to the time required to access Internet, make the search query and compute the answer (cf. section 4.4). This could be solved by enabling the schizophrenic model to continue interactions with the user while searching on the web. Another problem is that the interaction case reported here is too short and simple to let all the personalities express themselves in the flow of conversation.

6. Conclusion and Future Works

EVA is a long term open project for designing artificial creatures. There are many possible and promising research directions for the near future. Some are related to the technological development of the bio-inspired nano-agent system, while some others are related to a deeper study of the schizophrenic model for creating rich believable characters. From the technological perspective, we are implementing new additional "plugin" packages for more robust web mining and memory functionalities using evolutionary programming and swarm algorithms. Our goal is to learn information from the flow of conversation and from the web rather than coding a large amount of predefined knowledge. We are also implementing a C++ version of the EVA virtual machine that will enable to develop applications that do not support the Java environment such as the iPhone or some robot platforms. From the schizophrenic model perspective, we are studying various models based on psychological, neurophysiological, and storytelling approaches. We also want to experiment a larger number of personalities to create a swarm with social network properties. While our theoretical framework is based on the complex system approach, our experimental approach focuses on real-world applications. The EVA bio-inspired architecture has obvious applications for designing intelligent agents for commercial web sites and marketing studies. We also like to imagine virtual assistants on mobile phones, assistants for lone aged and/or sick people, for learning foreign languages, virtual characters in video games, for robotic and embedded applications.

7. References

Aubel, A. and Thalmann, D. (2000). Realist deformation of human body shapes, *Proceedings of Computer Animation and Simulation*, pp.125-135

Badler, N., Allbeck, J., Byun, M. (2002). Representing and Parameterizing Agent Behaviors. *Proceedings of Imagina*, pp. 151-164, Monaco

Blumberg, B., Galyean, T. (1995). Multi-level direction of autonomous creatures for real-time virtual environments, *Proceedings of SIGGRAPH'95*, pp. 47-54

Clinger, W., Rees, J. (Eds.) (1991). *Revised(4) Report on the Algorithmic Language Scheme*

Franklin, S., Graesser, A. (1997). Is it an Agent, or just a Program?: A Taxonomy for Autonomous Agents, *Proceedings of the 3rd International Workshop on Agent Theories, Architectures and Languages*, pp. 21-35, Springer-Verlag

Gebhard, P. (2005). ALMA: A layered model of affect, *Proceedings of the 4th Int. Joint Conf.erence on Autonomous Agents and Multi-agent Systems*, pp. 29-36

Gilles, A., Lebiannic, Y., Montet, P., Heudin, J.-C. (1991). A parallel architecture for the Electronic Copilote, *Proceedings of the 11th International Conference on Expert Systems Applications*, Avignon, EC2, Paris

Heudin, J.-C., Burg, B., Zavidovique, B. (1986). A flexible operating system for distributed process control, *Proceedings of the 4th International Conference on Applications of Artificial Intelligence*, Innsbruck, SPIE

Heudin, J.-C. (2004). Evolutionary Virtual Agent, Proceedings of the Intelligent Agent Technology Conference, pp. 93-98, Beijing, ACM-WIC-IEEE

Heudin, J.-C. (2007a). Evolutionary Virtual Agent at an exhibition, *Proceedings of the Virtual Systems and Multimedia Conference*, Sydney

Heudin, J.-C.(2007b). Modeling Complexity using Hierarchical Multi-Agent Systems, *Proceedings of the 6th International Workshop on Data Analysis in Astronomy*, Erice

Heudin, J.-C. (2009). An Evolutionary Nano-Agent Control Architecture for Intelligent Artificial Creatures, *Proceedings of the 14th International Symposium on Artificial Life and Robotics*, Beppu, AROB

Koza, J.R. (1992). *Genetic programming*, MIT Press, Boston

Langton, C.G. (1989). Artificial Life, *Procceedings of the 1st Artificial Life Conference*, Vol. VI. Addison-Wesley, Redwood City

Masterson, L. (2000). Casting your character, http://www.fictionfactor.com

McCrae, R.R., John, O.P. (1992). An introduction to the five factor model and its implications, *Journal of Personality*, Vol. 60, 171-215

Mehrabian, A., (1996). Pleasure-arousal-dominance: A general framework for describing and measuring individual differences in temperament, *Current Psychology*, Vol. 14, 261-292.

Mehrabian, A., (1996). Analysis of the Big-five Personality Factors in Terms of the PAD Temperament Model, *Australian Journal of Psychology*, Vol. 48, No. 2, 86-92

Millet, P., Heudin, J.-C. (2007). Web mining in the EVA intelligent agent architecture, *Proceedings of the Intelligent Agent Technology Conference*, California, ACM-WIC-IEEE

Perlin, K. (1995). Real time responsive animation with personality. *IEEE Transactions on Visualization and Computer Graphics*, Vol.1, No.1, 5-15

Ray, T.S. (1991). An approach to the synthesis of life. Proceedings of the 2nd Artificial Life Conference, pp. 371-408, Addison-Wesley, Redwood City

Thomas, F., Johnston, O. (1981). *The Illusion of Life: Disney Animation*, Hyperion Books, New York

Wallace, R.S. (2002). The anatomy of Alice, http://www.alicebot.org

Weizenbaum, J. (1966). Eliza, A Computer Program for the Study of Natura Language Communication between Man and Machine, *Communication ACM*, No. 9, 36-45

2

Controlling and Assisting Activities in Social Virtual Worlds

I. Rodriguez, A. Puig and M. Esteva
Applied Mathematics Department. University of Barcelona, Spain
Artificial Intelligence Research Institute. Barcelona, Spain

1. Introduction

Since its beginning, web technology has advanced from a text-based to a visual-based interaction. This evolution has been facilitated by both high speed internet connections and PC's graphical power. Virtual world (VW) technology began as standalone applications (e.g.. virtual simulations) but soon evolved into web-based applications. Nowadays, home users for entertainment and wide-spread enterprises or institutions for business can exploit virtual worlds to develop remote activities between friends, employees, clients, teachers or students (Sherman, 2002). Then, virtual worlds have clear applications in e-governance, e-learning and e-commerce, and therefore it is mandatory to study mechanisms ensuring the assistance and the control of activities taking place in these applications.

We focus on social virtual worlds populated by participants that act in order to achieve common and individual goals (Bartle, 2003). Due to the type of activities taking place in a Social Virtual World (SVW), the virtual environment should be prepared to be a dynamic space where participants are informed about activities' evolution and where norms are used to organize participants' actions, to define actions' consequences and to prevent undesired participants behaviours. We rely on electronic institutions (Esteva, 2003) to set up participants' valid interactions and on virtual objects, named intelligent objects, populating the virtual world, to enforce norms and to give assistance to participants (Rodriguez, 2008). This work exploits the Virtual Institution (VI) concept which is a combination of both multiagent and virtual world technologies (Bogdanovych, 2007).

We have designed a general framework of object behaviour control tied with an IA based external module and prepared to be exploited by several virtual world platforms. This is done creating a specific module to capture participant interactions on objects populating the virtual world and connecting this module with an external and generic one in charge of deciding what should be the virtual object action. Decision depends on an organization-based multiagent system (MAS) which, as said before, establishes the valid interactions participants may have and the consequences of those interactions. Our main objectives are:

- Establish participants' roles, activities and norms by means of a multiagent system named electronic institution. Participants can be both software agents and humans.

- Use of intelligent virtual objects with an external module named *iObject* manager i) to inform participants about activities evolution and ii) to decide whether participants comply established norms.
- Design an object behaviour control scheme applicable to different VW (Virtual World) platforms.
- Exploit the virtual nature of the spaces, and the objects populating these spaces, allowing to represent things impossible for their real world counterparts.

The dynamic feature of current VW platforms only rely on users who are free to dynamically change aspects of the virtual world by means of built-in tools and scripting features. Our proposal is to extend the ability of a VW to dynamically change itself and exploit the virtualness of the space supporting the presentation of information, which would be impossible to do in the real world, and so provide a better support to participants on their activities.

This chapter is structured as follows. Section 2 presents related work in areas related with norms enforcement in virtual worlds and multiagent systems combined with virtual environments. Section 3 describes how our system models activities taking place in normative virtual worlds and uses intelligent objects to guide and control the user during the activities. Section 4 presents the developed intelligent objects framework and finally section 5 presents conclusions and future work.

2. Related work

2.1 Norms in web based communities

Most of well-known virtual communities -such as Second Life, Active Worlds, Entropia and others- require participants to agree to the company's terms of service in the signing up process (Linden, 2008). Participants should understand the terms and conditions to which they are agreeing as a member of that community. Most people don't read or are otherwise immune due to the lack of real consequences. There are some types of incorrect behaviours that we think can be addressed programatically, that is contemplated in the design of the VW platform and ensured at deployment time.

We propose to use intelligent objects (iObjects) as elements helping users to comply norms and if it is necessary to prevent forbidden actions. For example, to block entry to people who is less than 18 years old in a special virtual room. WonderDAC is an extension module developed for Wonderland that allows to show or hide parts of a VW depending on the user and group profile (Wright and Madey, 2008). In contrast to WonderDAC, developed to control discretionary access basing on users and group permissions, our approach is more general allowing, for example, the control of access to spaces based on the historic of user activities. For example, a norm establishes that a participant can not enter to the projection room unless he has bought a ticket for that room and session.

Part of our inspiration for a general interaction approach for objects populating a social virtual world comes from the smart objects proposal (Kallmann et al., 2000) (Abaci et al, 2005) and the posterior work done by Jorinssen (Jorissen et al., 2004) (Jorissen et al., 2005). Nevertheless, our approach is different to those because they worked with their own virtual environments named ACE (Agent Common Environment) and ALVIC (Architecture for Large-Scale Virtual Interactive communities), respectively. In this way, their object interaction approach is general in the sense it is independent of the final application but can not get out of their concrete virtual platform (they have their own scripting language and engine). Our interaction framework for control and assist activities in SVW has been designed to be applied to different VW platforms such as Wonderland and Second Life. In this way, rendering and event capture continue being controlled in the concrete VW platform but the behaviour decision is managed in an external and generic manager connected with an AI based module, i.e. Electronic Institution.

Virtual worlds can be seen as singular information spaces where the virtual nature of the 3D space (e.g.. floor) and the furniture (e.g.. noticeboard) can be exploited in a special manner not possible for their real counterparts. For example, in the real world it is not possible to dynamically change tiles colour in a floor to represent an agree/disagree position of participants in a discussion. This has been done in a recent work (Harry & Donath, 2008). We aim to incorporate an added value to virtual objects allowing to give valuable information to participants. As an example in section 4.1, a door is visualized either green or red depending on the user trying to pass through. Accessibility issues can also be addressed in these information spaces, for example a noticeboard object adapts letter size depending either on user profile and on the distance between the user and the panel. Exploiting these native properties of virtual objects, we create rich and expressive social spaces.

We extend the dynamic conception of current VW platforms in which users are free to dynamically change aspects of the virtual world by means of built-in tools and scripting behaviours (Friedman et al., 2007) (Sun, 2008). Part of the unexplored feature of virtual spaces is their ability to be adapted in architectural terms. Our proposal is to extend the ability of a VW to dynamically change itself and exploit the virtualness of the space supporting the presentation of information, which would be impossible to do in the real world, and so provide a better support to participants on their activities.

2.2 Combining multiagent systems and virtual environments

A system that incorporated intelligent agents within virtual environments was mVITAL (multi-agent VITAL) which allowed the definition of agent societies so that intelligent agents could communicate through simple speech acts, co-operate and help each other to achieve goals (Vosinakis et al., 1999) (Anastassakis et al. 2001a) (Anastassakis et al. 2001b) . The mVITAL viewer allowed human supervisors to observe the activity inside the environment. We propose to allow the user not only to supervise but to control his avatar and communicate with a regulated multi-agent system in order to test whether his actions are allowed. We have used the so-called iObjects in order to provide facilities for avatar-object interaction and the visualization of the social virtual world execution context. A detail description of iObjects integration at MAS level by means of an Interaction Language can be found in (Rodriguez et al. 2007).

Several researches integrated BDI (Belief, Desire and Intention) agents within virtual worlds. Torres et al. developed an interface that allowed a BDI-based agent reasoning system to be used for guiding the behaviour of articulated characters in a virtual environment (Torres et al., 2003). ACE (Agent Common Environment) was designed for virtual human agent simulations. It provided pre-built commands to perceive and actuate meanwhile the reasoning processing is defined by means of a collection of external modules (i.e. python scripts)(Kallmann et al, 1998), (Kallmann et al, 2000). Virtual agents were used to enhance Customer Relationship Management (CRM). eGain's virtual assistants interact in plain English over the Web with online users (Osterfelt, 2001). They combined 3D graphical representations and artificial intelligence to assist customers to locate information or place orders. Our system provides assistance to the participant also by means of 3D graphical representations (i.e. iObjects). An iObject allows the user to be aware of current execution state (e.g.. data visualized on an intelligent noticeboard), enforcing norms (e.g. let to pass through a door depending on user previous activities) and adapting object's features depending on user profile (e.g.. adapts the font's size of a noticeboard depending on user's visual capacity).

Guyot and Honiden's approach merged multiagent systems and role-playing games (MAS/RPG) (Guyot, 2006). They compared agent-based participatory simulations and the MAS/RPG approach and explained the advantages of their approach: "actions and interactions can be registered and used for learning purposes, the gap between the agent model and the participants can be decreased and the user interface with an assistant agent may improve the understanding of the model by the participants". Our system, exploiting iObjects in the context of social virtual worlds, aims to work along those advantages too.

Another research conceives the organisation infrastructure of a multiagent system in terms of agents and artifacts (Kitio et al.. 2007). They distinguish between organizational artifacts, which provide organization's functional aspects, and organizational agents, which provide decision aspects of organizations management. Artifacts and iObjects, although both arise with a similar objective, that is, to model "entities" used to develop activities in the institutions, they are situated in different levels of abstraction. Artifacts facilitate agent activities at a organizational MAS level and iObjects facilitate user interactions at 3D world level.

3. Modelling activities in a social virtual world

3.1 Our approach: a hybrid system with software agents and humans in 3D virtual worlds

Conventional virtual communities are populated by avatars representing human participants connected to the virtual world. We focus on a hybrid approach due to the heterogeneous nature of participants as they can be software agents and humans. Our system is based on Bogdanovych approach which utilizes this hybrid nature of participants in the so named Virtual Institutions (Bogdanovych, 2007) (Bogdanovych et al., 2008). Despite of the hybrid system complexity, it has advantatges as the human participant controls its avatar in a concrete activity happening in a concrete 3D scene (e.g.. asking for information in an e-goverment information office) but it could launch an agent software, that in his behalf, should perform another activity in another 3D space (e.g.. filling an administrative form in the tax office). Then, it is needed to set up roles, activities, norms and obligations of participants in the social virtual world as described in the next section.

3.2 An organization based Multiagent System

We are interested in social virtual worlds which emulate activities in a real institution. For the specification of the institutional rules, we use electronic institutions (Esteva, 2003), a well-known MAS methodology. The institutional rules establish the valid interactions agents may have and the consequences of those interactions. Specifically, institution designers should define the following components (the formalization of these components can be found in (Arcos et al. 2005)):

- Dialogical framework. It establishes the common ontology and communication language to allow agents to exchange knowledge and understand each other.
- Social structure. It establishes the roles that the agents may play within the institution and the relationships among them. Each role defines a pattern of behaviour within the institution.
- Scenes. Each scene defines an interaction protocol among a set of roles. The protocol, specified by a finite state machine (FSM), establishes the valid interactions that agents may have. The nodes of the FSM represent the different conversation states, while the arcs are labelled with messages of the communication language or timeouts. A scene specification also defines at which states agents, depending on their role, can join or leave.
- Performative structure. It defines the role flow policy among scenes, that is, how agents depending on their role can move among the different scenes. The performative structure is specified as a graph. Graph's nodes are scenes and transitions, and arcs are labelled with the roles that can progress through them. Transitions are a kind of routers that permit to express synchronisation, parallelisation and choice points for agents moving between scenes.
- Norms. They capture the consequences of agents' actions within the institution. Such consequences are modeled as commitments (obligations) that agents acquire as the result of their actions. It is worth mentioning that the specification also includes the definition of the information model that the institution uses to keep the state of participants and activities going on at run time. For instance, an auction house may keep for each buyer her current credit and the list of purchased goods. This is specified as a list of attributes (or properties) associated to some of the previous elements. The specification of the institutional rules is supported by ISLANDER, the electronic institutions specification tool (Arcos et al. 2005).

At design time, the specification focusses on macro-level (rules) aspects of agents not in their micro-level (players) aspects. No assumptions are made at specification time about the internal architecture of participating agents. Hence, participants can be human and software agents. Electronic institutions infrastructure at run-time is named AMELI which is in charge of guaranteeing the participants do not violate the institutional rules established at design time.

3.3 Intelligent objects to control and assist participants' activities

An Electronic Institution models roles and activities as they happen in a real institution. Therefore, a Social Virtual World gives a 3D appearance to an EI specification, participants (both humans and software agents) are represented as avatars in the virtual world and some participant actions can be controlled and assisted by means of iObjects. The virtual world is generated from multiagent system specification (using ISLANDER tool) as described in (Bogdanovych, 2007).

iObjects are entities having both visualization properties and decision mechanisms, that help to improve human participation in a VW in the following ways:

- Representation of execution context. They provide an effective mapping of the institutional state (i.e. current good price in an auction) into the 3D virtual world. Hence, it facilitates participants perception of the current state and its changes.
- User participation. To some extent iObjects are similar to real world objects in appearance and the way to use (interact with) them. Hence, they provide an intuitive way to participate in the institution by interacting with the iObjects populating the virtual world. For instance, by opening a door to leave a room or by pressing an accept button in a remote control to accept an offer from another agent within a negotiation process.
- Enforcement of norms. iObjects collaborate with the other elements of the run time environment in the enforcement of the institutional rules. Furthermore, they can inform users when a norm has been violated and, optionally, they can guide a user in order to avoid a new wrong action.
- Guide and learn of user actions. They can incorporate a knowledge base to guide user participation (i.e. actions) inside the virtual environment. An iObject with learning abilities may gain knowledge about user actions within the simulated environment and after that, apply this knowledge to facilitate future user participation.

An iObject may have several sensors (which allow to capture events from the environment) and some effectors (which allow to act upon the environment). In the context of normative and social virtual words, by environment we mean both the virtual world and AMELI. AMELI is the component keeping the execution state and capable of verifying than an action complies with the institutional rules. An iObject central component is a decision module which determines, taking into account sensors inputs, iObject's effectors actions.

Though their sensors, iObjects can perceive events occurring at the virtual world due to avatar actions and movements. For instance, *touching* sensors allow iObjects to perceive avatars interacting with them, while *proximity* sensors allow them to react to avatars presence. An iObject can also interpret *gesture* events which allow it to act according to avatar gestures, for example a shaking head meaning "I disagree" in a e-business meeting or a raising hand meaning "I want to bid" in a auction house. Another source of events for iObjects is AMELI. That is, iObjects should be aware of changes in the execution state, in Figure 1 named *state* variables. For example, changes in the interaction context within a scene (e.g. current price of a good in an auction house), the fulfilment of a pending obligation by a participant, or *norms* changes (e.g.. a door has been opened to everyone because a scene activity has finished). When an iObject's sensor captures an event from the environment as consequence an iObject's effector reacts to the event. It is worth mentioning that in some cases, although the required reaction can be situated in the virtual world (e.g. opening a door), that reaction may depend on the compliance of the avatar action with the institutional rules. If this is the case, the iObject requests for institutional verification of the action to AMELI by using its *enforce norm* effectors. Then, the door will only open if the avatar is allowed to leave the room, which is checked by contacting AMELI. Furthermore, iObjects can also be informed about the result, executed or failed, of the actions for which they requested institutional verification, in this way, they can inform the user about the result of the action in a friendly way.

Effectors act upon the virtual world changing several properties of the iObject itself: the *aspect* (e.g. color, geometry, textures), the *information* that some types of iObjects provide (e.g. notice board) and *transformation* properties (e.g. position, rotation and scale). For example, an intelligent e-business room may scale if there is an increasing number of clients populating the space, or if it is difficult to overcome the change of its dimensions by a scaling transformation may even replicate itself. An iObject's effectors may also maintain AMELI informed about changes of the *current state* of execution, for example a door iObject informs that an avatar has moved from one scene to another one.

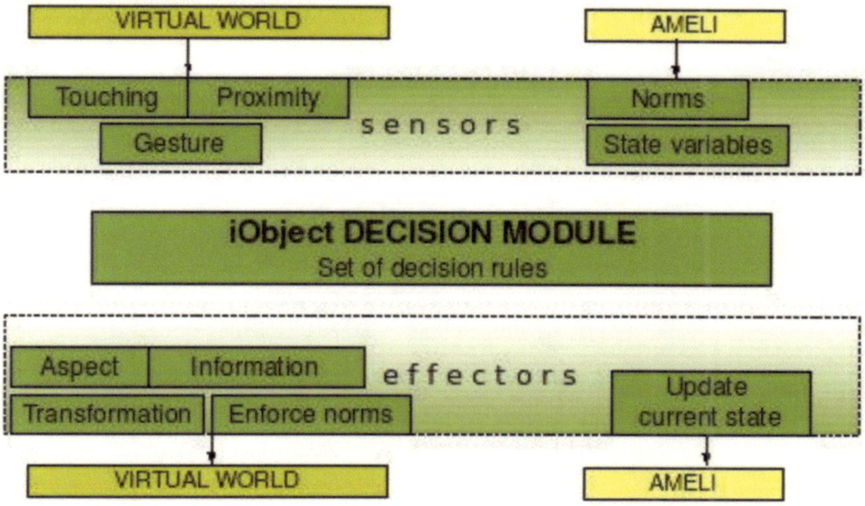

Fig. 1. Intelligent object structure

Every iObject may have some of the following features: *actionable, state modifier, self-configurable, learnable. Actionable* iObjects offer the avatar the possibility to act on them. An example of actionable objects are remote controls or a touch screen. iObjects are *state modifiers* if they may change the execution state, as for instance a door or a remote control. In the first case, because there are avatars moving from one scene to another, and in the second one by modifying the current winning bid within an auction. On the contrary, a brochure, a touch screen or an item on sale are merely informative. A *self-configurable* iObject (e.g.., a brochure or an item on sale) adapts its features according to changes in its environment. Finally, a *learnable* iObject may discharge the electronic institution infrastructure of doing the same norm checking several times. For example, a door iObject may learn a pattern of norm enforcement (i.e. circumstances such as role and agent's state that let an avatar pass through the door) so that next time it would not be necessary to query the MAS organizational infrastructure.

As can be seen in Figure 2, the human participates by controlling an avatar in the virtual world. Among other actions the avatar can interact with the different iObjects within the virtual world. The user can perceive the different iObjects in the virtual world to be aware of the execution context and use this information to decide what actions to do. Figure 2 distinguishes between iObjects at *scene/institution level* and *participant level*. The first one correspond to the iObjects belonging to the scene infrastructure (e.g. noticeboard) or institution infrastructure (i.e. door). Figure 3 shows a notice board iObject showing information about good and its price, red salmon at 3 euros, of the current round within an auction room.

iObjects at *participant level* give the user personal information about his participation in the SVW. Hence, each user perceives their own iObjects at this level containing their information. They are placed in the user interface but not in the virtual world. At this level, there are three types of iObjects, namely the backpack, the information model notice board, and the historial. The backpack keeps the user pending obligations, which are shown by clicking with the mouse on the backpack. The information model notice board shows the current values of the user information model attributes which depend on his role. For instance, within an auction house buyer attributes may be his current credit and the list of purchased goods. The historical shows a register of the user participation (e.g.. actions) within the institution.

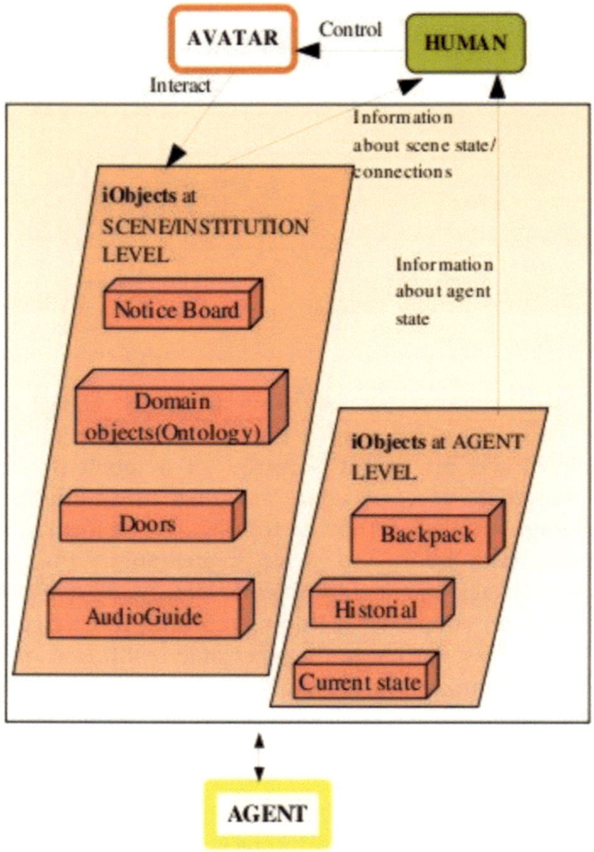

Fig. 2.Intelligent objects at scene and participant level

Fig. 3. Noticeboard iObject at Fish auction room

4. Generic framework to enforce norms in SVW

4.1 General description

We have developed a framework for generic behaviour management of virtual intelligent objects. It decouples event provider from event dealer (i.e. behaviour handling) and, compared to traditional virtual worlds, allows a better support for normative and dynamic social virtual worlds. In a conventional VW, clients take charge of rendering, interaction and behaviour handling (i.e. event capture and treatment). On the server side, digital assets are stored (in proprietary or standard format), and the server propagates client changes to the rest of connected users. The main drawback of this architecture is that an object behaviour has to be reprogrammed when VW platform changes.

Our approach gets behaviour handling out of the VW platform. It is treated in an external module named iObjects manager. An iObject is a 3D entity populating the virtual environment which is exploited in two ways: it allows normal interaction as it would do in the real world (e.g. approach/touch a door to open) and its virtual nature gives an added value to the provided information (e.g. adapts dynamically color or size). More information on iObjects can be found in (Rodriguez et al. 2008) . In the virtual world, iObjects ensure participants norm compliance and give the user assistance during his participation.

iObjects' manager is designed to be used by several virtual world platforms. To do that, it is needed to develop an extension module, iObjects extension in Figure 4, in the VW platform that will communicate with the generic manager using a socket connection. Next section presents the prototype we have developed in Wonderland virtual world (from Sun Microsystems) and presents some simulation results.

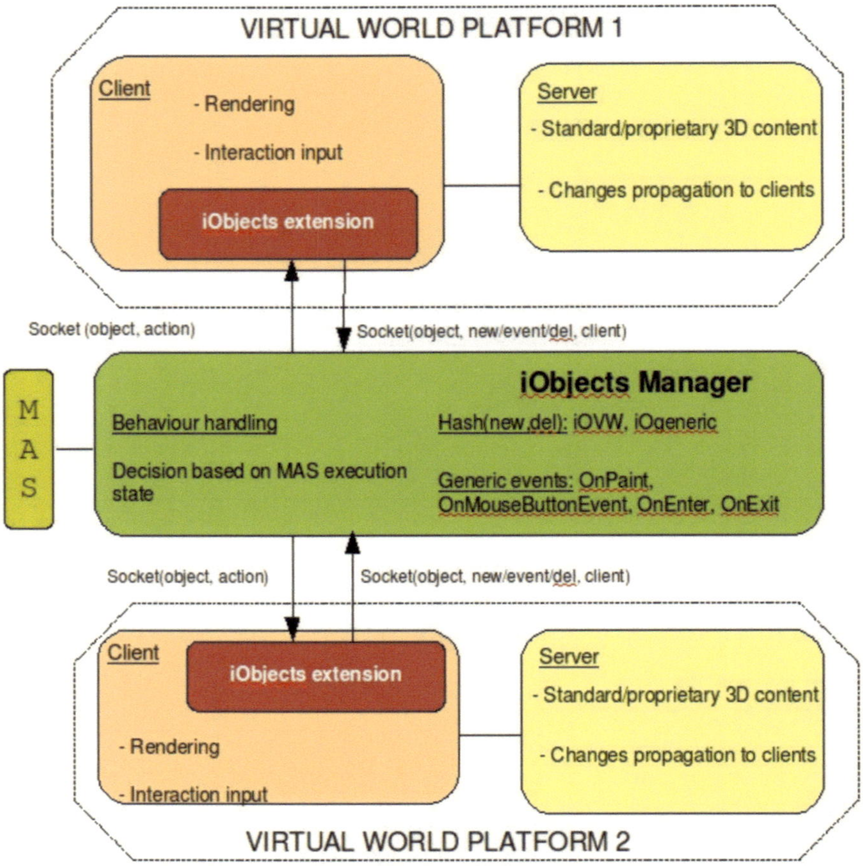

Fig. 4. Generic approach to enforce norms in a SVW

As can be appreciated in Figure 4, an interaction with an iObject is captured in the virtual world client and it is sent, using a socket message, to the iObjects manager. The message indicates client identifier, object and event used to interact with the object. The iObject manager decides which iObject action (e.g.. change color, size, trigger animation) has to be sent back to the VW. This decision is based on a response given by an organization-based multiagent system which establishes norms and possible interactions. The manager maintains a hash with iObject identifier in the concrete VW (ioVW) and its generic counterpart (iOgeneric). Currently, generic iObject events contemplated are OnPaint, OnMouseButton, OnEnter (an avatar enters in an area near to object's position) and OnExit (an avatar leaves an area near to object's position). Note that it is needed to do a mapping between concrete VW events and generic ones contemplated by the iObjects manager.

4.2 Prototype

There are several VW platforms to develop an interactive virtual environment, Second Life, Active Worlds and Wonderland, to name a few. All of them consist of similar components such as avatars, buildings, scripting components and built-in features. We chose

Wonderland because it was conceived to work with 3D standards, it is open-source and multi-platform (java-based). We have developed our prototype in WL 0.4 where 3D content is represented in X3D standard format. WL 0.5 works with COLLADA, a well-extended 3D interchange format. We are now migrating to version 0.5 available only for developers.
Once selected the VW platform, we studied how to incorporate iObjects in WL and how to capture an event (i.e. an object interaction) in WL and communicate it to the external and generic iObject manager. In particular, our prototype presents results obtained using an iObjectDoor. In WL, doors are merely holes allowing to pass through them to avatars and so change from one room to another one. An iObjectDoor adds an additional nuance letting pass through it only avatars having permission, that is, avatars who comply with the norms established by the multiagent system refered in Figure 4. Figure 5 shows two simulations exploiting norm compliance for an *iObjectDoor* in Wonderland. Client 1 (named c1a) sees the door in green because he complies with the norm allowing to enter the next room. Client 2 (named c2) sees it in red because he does not comply the norm. Note that both snapshots correspond to the same door in the same virtual world but thanks to a multi-view scheme both clients see the same door with different colors depending on their permission to pass through it. Avatars without access permission have always the collision control enabled so that they can never get closer to the door.

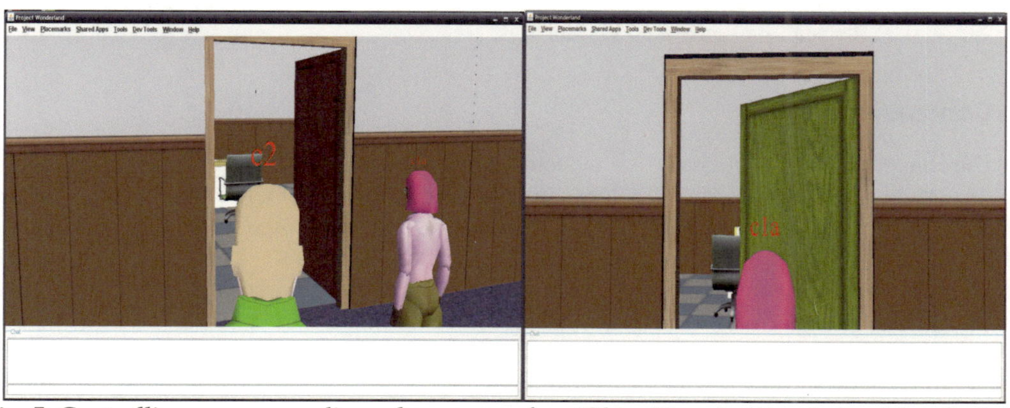

Fig. 5. Controlling norm compliance by means of an iObjectDoor in Wonderland (on the left: Client1, on the right: Client2)

Virtual worlds can be exploited as dynamic information spaces, for example, adapting the visualization of a virtual object depending on the participant profile or previous activities. As mentioned before, we propose an iObject multi-view scheme by keeping different 3D models of the iObject. All clients share an indexed set of visual representations (red door, green door, glazing door, etc.), but only one is active for each client in a given moment. Figure 6 shows the multi-view scheme of an iObjectDoor in Wonderland. On the left side, Client 2 sees glazed red door because he has permission to see the next room but not to pass through it. On the right side, Client 3 has both permission to see and to pass through it.

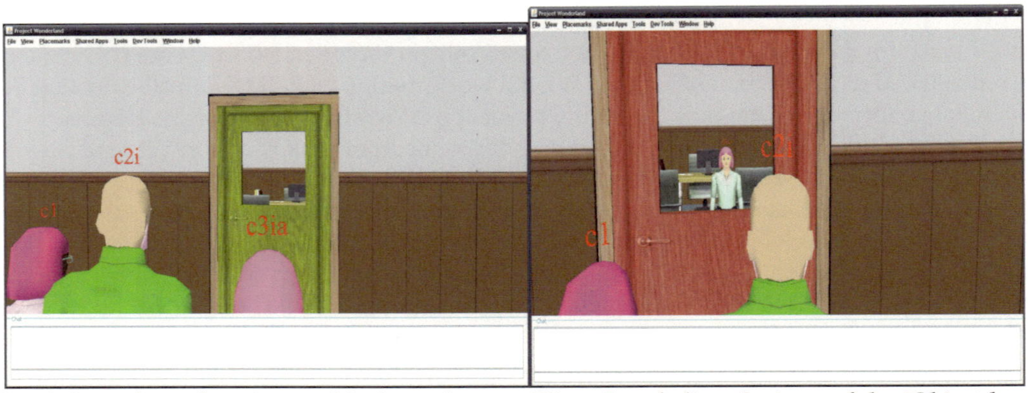

Fig. 6. Snapshots showing multi-view scheme. Client 2 and client 3 views of the iObjectdoor on left and right pictures, respectively

When an avatar is near to the door and clicks the mouse over the door, the iObjectDoor captures the event and asks the iObjects manager whether the client complies norms allowing to access the room (e.g.. in an auction, the buyer has paid registration fee). Then, if the answer is affirmative, the iObjectDoor runs the local animation and notifies it to the server so that the rest of clients also visualize it.

5. Conclusions

In this paper we have presented a system that merges multi-agent systems and virtual environments in order to model roles, activities and norms characterizing a social virtual world. We contribute with an intelligent object framework to enforce established norms and provide feedback and guide the participants on their activities. We propose a generic behaviour management for these objects populating a virtual world. We get behaviour handling out of the VW platform so that it is performed in an external module named iObjects manager allowing to be exploited by different virtual world platforms. An iObject is a 3D entity populating the virtual environment which is exploited in two ways: it allows normal interaction as it would do in the real world (e.g. approach/touch a door to open) and its virtual nature gives an added value to the provided information (e.g. adapts dynamically color or size depending on the client). We have the interoperability between different virtual world technologies in mind and so provide a general solution in which participants can be connected from different immersive environment platforms.
As future research, there is an interesting work to do regarding iObjects role at design time, i.e. when the 3D virtual world is generated from an institution specification. Shape grammars, semantic annotation and template based techniques could help us to generate and populate an initial design efficiently. In particular, we are in an initial stage of shape grammar exploitation as an alternative method for layout plan generation. As another issue of future research, iObjects could also incorporate sound sensors to obey voiced commands. We also plan to extend the iObject module with new types of intelligent objects (e.g. notice-board, brochure) and test its functionality in other VW platforms such as SL or Active Worlds.

6. Acknowledgements

Partially funded by projects IEA (TIN2006-15662-C02-01), AT (CONSOLIDER CSD2007-0022), EU-FEDER, CICYT TIN2008-02903 and by the Generalitat de Catalunya under the grant 2005-SGR-00093. M.Esteva enjoys a Ramon y Cajal contract from the Spanish Government.

7. References

Abaci T., Ciger J., and Thalmann D.(2005). *Planning with smartobjects*. In Int. Conference in Central Europe on Computer Graphics, pages 25–28.

Anastassakis G., Panayiotopoulos T., and Ritchings T. (2001a). *Virtual agent societies with the mvital intelligent agent system*. In International Workshop on Intelligent Virtual Agents,pages 112–125.

Anastassakis G., Ritchings T., and Panayiotopoulos T. (2001b). *Multi-agent systems as intelligent virtual environments*. Lecture Notes in Artificial Intelligence, 2174:381–395.

Arcos J. L., Esteva M., Noriega P., Rodriguez-Aguilar J.A., and Sierra C. (2005) *Environment engineering for multiagent systems*. Engineering Applications of Artificial Intelligence, 18(1):191–204, January 2005.

Bartle R. (2003), *Designing Virtual Worlds*. New Riders.

Bogdanovych A., Esteva M., Simoff S., Sierra C., and Berger H (2008). *A methodology for developing multiagent systems as 3d electronic institutions*. In M. Luck and L. Padgham, editors, Agent-Oriented Software Engineering VIII., volume 4951 of Lecture Notes in Computer Science, pages 103–117. Springer Berlin / Heidelberg.

Bogdanovych. A. (2007) Virtual Institutions. PhD thesis, University of Technology, Sydney, Australia.

Esteva M. (2003). Electronic Institutions: from specification to development. PhD Thesis Universitat Politècnica de Catalunya (UPC), 2003. Number 19 in IIIA Monograph Series. IIIA, 2003.

Friedman D., Steed A., and Slater M. (2007), *Spatial social behavior in second life*, Lecture Notes in Computer Science, Springer, vol. 4722, pp. 252–263.

Guyot P. and Honiden S.(2006) *Agent-based participatory simulations: Merging multi-agent systems and role-playing games*. Journal of Artificial Societies and Social Simulation, 9(4), Oct.

Harry D. and Donath J. (2008), *Information spaces: Building meeting rooms in virtual environments*, in Conference on Human Factors in Computing Systems, pp. 3741–3746.

Jorissen P., Wijnants M., and Lamotte W. (2004), *Using collaborative interactive objects and animation to enable dynamic interactions in collaborative virtual environments*, Conference on Computer animation and Social Agents

Jorissen P., Wijnants M., and Lamotte W. (2005), *Dynamic interactions in physically realistic collaborative virtual environments*, IEEE transaction on visualization and computer graphics, vol. 11, no. 6, pp.649–659.

Kallmann M. and Thalmman D. (1998) *Modeling objects for interaction tasks*. In Proc. Eurographics Workshop on Animation and Simulation, pages 73–86.

Kallmann M., Monzani J., Caicedo A., and Thalmann D. (2000), *A common environment for simulating virtual human agents in real time,* in Proc.Workshop on Achieving Human-Like Behavior in Interactive Animated Agents.

Kallmann M., Monzani J., Caicedo A., and Thalmann D. (2000). *A common environment for simulating virtual human agents in real time.* In Proc. Workshop on Achieving Human-Like Behavior in Interactive Animated Agents.

Kitio, R., Boissier O., Hubner J., Ricci A. (2007) *Organisational artifacts and agents for open multi-agent organisations: giving the power back to the agents.* In European Workshop on Multi-agent Systems.

Linden, Lab (2008). *Second life term of services,* http://secondlife.com/corporate/tos.php.

Osterfelt S. (2001) *A customer service odyssey.* In DM Review Magazine.

Rodriguez I., Puig A., Esteva M., Sierra C., Bogdanovych A., and Simoff S. (2008), *Intelligent objects to facilitate human participation in virtual institutions,* in Conference on Web Intelligence.

Rodriguez I., Salamo M., Lopez-Sanchez M., Cerquides J., Puig A., and Sierra C.(2007). *Completing the virtual analogy of real Institutions via iobjects.* In Congres Internacional de l'Associacio Catalana d'Intelligencia Artificial.

Sherman W. R. and Craig A. B. (2002) *Understanding virtual reality: interface, application, and design.* Morgan Kaufmann Publishers Inc., San Francisco, CA, USA.

Sun Microsystems (2008). *Wonderland from Sun Microsystems.* https://lg3d-wonderland.dev.java.net/.

Torres J. A. , Nedel L. P. , and BordiniR. H. (2003) *Using the bdi architecture to produce autonomous characters in virtual worlds.* In IVA, pages 197–201.

Vosinakis S., Anastassakis G., and Panayiotopoulos G. (1999) *Diva: Distributed intelligent virtual agents.* In Workshop on Intelligent Virtual Agents.

Wright T. E. and Madey G. (2008), *Wonderdac: An implementation of discretionary access controls within the project Wonderland,* in Tech report. Univ. of Notre Dam.

3

A Dynamic Healthcare Portal Design and Enhancements

Yung-Ching Weng[1], Sheau-Ling Hsieh[2], Kai-Ping Hsu[1], Chi-Huang Chen[1], Po Hsun Cheng[3] and Feipei Lai[1]
[1]National Taiwan University, [2]National Chiao Tung University, [3]National Kaohsiung Normal University Taiwan

1. Introduction

National Taiwan University Hospital (NTUH) is a large scale healthcare centre and has been operating over hundred years. Currently, it includes different generations of Healthcare Information Systems (HIS); there are over 30 major independent systems in NTUH. These systems consist of clinical information applications focusing on patient cares, pharmacy, laboratory and radiology systems, administrative facilities, financial systems, resource management, claims processing, etc. The portal is an essential entity to integrate, glue these systems, platforms together. An effective, convenient as well as user friendly portal can provide adequate information for NTUH staff, medical practitioners' daily operations. Moreover, a Single Sign on Service (SSOS) design is crucial to unify, simplify various systems log-on processing.
As NTUH users' requirements increase rapidly, the number of menu selections, i.e., applications or function linkages, grows exponentially. The scrollable extension menu, implemented in the previous portal, is not spatial, temporal sufficiently and efficiently. The maintainability of menu items is hampered under the situation. Furthermore, in general, a user normally accesses not more than 10 function selections. In order to trace individual behaviours for frequently executed functions, a logging scheme, containing a list of actions, is proposed. Assistive web technologies for persons with disabilities are initiated. Therefore, to improve the NTUH portal, we explore and launch a new one to achieve the targets.

2. Background & Related Work

2.1 Background

National Taiwan University Hospital (NTUH) was established in 1895. There are approximate 8,000 outpatients, 300 emergency cases, daily on average, and around 2,200 beds for inpatients. The NTUH portal is the main entrance to various aggregated systems supporting operations for NTUH staffs, physicians as well as educational purposes. The portal provides essential directions for users to browse over NTUH Intranet behind the firewalls. It involves extensible difficulties:

1) There are over 30, rapidly increasing, major independent systems in NTUH. The systems encompass many resources; it becomes cumbersome for medical staff to authenticate every time while attempting to access a new resource. The legacy or previous portal did not support SSOS. Users need to keep separate identifications, passwords to execute different systems individually.
In addition, the multiple login processes disturb medical staffs. It also generates resistances and causes the system's usage downgrade or undesirable. There were cases that doctors avoid the login process, and simply provide usernames, passwords to the assistants and ask them to operate directly. The situation raises security concerns regarding the correctness of patient's records and data entered. Later, it may generate threats to patient's health or life. A Single Sign-On facility is a must.
2) The previous portal main page contains scrollable extension menu (Weng et al., 2007; Goodman, 2003) to support function linkages. As NTUH users' operation demands increase, the number of linkages, steady increments, is over 300 currently. The scrollable menu is not spatial sufficiently, well organized. Thus, the menu utilization is not convenient.
3) The existing portal has been implemented at server side ASP scripting technologies. Any ASP page modification only requires uploading onto web servers for menu deployment. However, the newly designed portal is implemented in ASP.NET with C# programming language. C# is a compiling language. If any menu altered, the server side programs have to be re-compiled and re-deployed. The menu modification efforts increase significantly. Therefore, more efficient approaches ought to be brought up and enhanced under the new environment.
4) Because of lacking maintenance, the legacy portal contains failure links as well as redundant entrances in the previous scrollable extension menu.

2.2 Related Work

2.2.1 Web portal system

The web portal services have turned into an imperative part of human life. The portal is an environment through which a user can gain access to web-based information and tools from a single Internet location (Brakel, 2003; Mary, 2002; Tsai et al., 2005; Zhu et al., 2004). Early clinical systems attempted to provide the functionality envisioned by the computer-based patient records, but were hampered by incompatible standards and a lack of interconnectivity (Fraser et al., 1997; McDonald et al., 1998). With the development of the web portal services, almost every large system vendor is now offering a web-based clinical system (Shepherd, 2000). In particular, consumers of health care are demanding easy access to relevant health information (Lee et al., 2007; Raghupathi, 1997; Zirpins et al., 2001).
A web portal is built upon layers of services and component modules (Azar et al., 2008; Freudenstein et al., 2006; Murray, 2002; Murray, 2003; Oo, 2006). The framework must facilitate the integration of a wide range of data, provide efficient access to relevant content, and incorporate the ability to organize materials that employees routinely operate.
There is no definitive categorization of the types of web portals (Azar et al., 2008). Strauss (Strauss, 2002) categorizes web portals into "Horizontal Enterprise Portals" and "Vertical Enterprise Portals". The classification of horizontal and vertical portals is the most commonly used and understood method (Tsai et al., 2005; Brakel, 2003; Zirpins et al., 2001;

Amor, 1999). In general, portals are in layered, web, architectures (Murray, 2002; Freudenstein et al., 2006; Murray, 2003).
Murray (Murray, 2002) defined that a healthcare portal strategy is comprised of six layers. To accomplish these, each layer addresses its primary functionalities. For examples, in the Security layer, a single sign on environment for all users is the basis of providing a single point of entrance (Russler et al., 2001; Hsieh et al., 2006). The Enterprise Application Integration layer provides the ability to exchange and integrate data among applications via open standards, e.g. eXtensible Markup Language (XML) (Freudenstein et al., 2006; Murray, 2003).
In addition, the web-based applications are designed to be modular and built on a distributed, n-tier architecture. The middle tier seamlessly connects the front end, web-based browsers, to the back end servers, or applications (Shepherd, 2000; Oo, 2006). Overtime, new business applications and capabilities can simply be added to existing resources within the highly extensible architecture (Yang et al., 2006). The ability of identifying and extracting pertinent information in an efficient manner is paramount. Moreover, the portal should be programmable and flexible so that the information can be dynamically selected from various sources (Trippe, 2001). The ability to exchange data among applications and provide application integration enterprise-wide is a fundamental component of a successful web portal (Rosen, 2000; Rudenstien, 2000). Within healthcare, the Health Level Seven (HL7) standard defines the format and protocol of messages that are exchanged among healthcare applications. It enables systems to create XML documents that incorporate HL7 message content (Shepherd, 2000; Arbor, 2000).

2.2.2 Service oriented architecture

A Service Oriented Architecture (SOA) represents the current pinnacle of interoperability, in which resources on a network are available as individual, loosely-coupled and independent services (Freudenstein et al., 2006; Murray, 2003; Bunge et al., 2008; Lewis et al., 2007). As Service-oriented Architecture (SOA) matures, an efficient approach for the integration of web services in portals is required. SOA is a desirable and inevitable solution.
In summary, a successful portal includes determining factors: 1) architecture built on layers of services and component modules; 2) providing the ability to inter-mingled data and content from multiple sources stored in multiple formats; 3) a framework that is extensible by employing open standards in the development of portal services (Mary, 2002; Brakel, 2003; Azar et al., 2008).

2.2.3 Single sign-on approach

Single sign-on is a simple means of managing passwords and authenticating users to various applications. It allows users to access all authorized services and resources seamlessly (Adabala et al., 2004; Heckle et al., 2008; Volchkov, 2001; Heckle, 2007; Mauro, 2008). However, its implementation has tremendous complexities that involve overall security policies, user profiles, natures of business, integration of legacy, web applications portfolios, cost structures of Information Technology operations, as well as future application development strategies (Heckle et al., 2008; Volchkov, 2001).
In general, pragmatic approaches adopt the following criteria: 1) modifying existing applications and building new ones, synchronizing passwords to share recourses and

services; 2) establishing external tools or an authentication middleware, layer to support authentication methods or servers; 3) configuring legacy applications with their existing directories and synchronizing with the enterprise directory, central administration promptly; 4) delegating or mapping user credentials or capabilities on resources; 5) developing trust channels to deliver, share user credentials information (Adabala et al., 2004; Heckle et al., 2008; Volchkov, 2001; Heckle, 2007). In addition, the single sign-on technology can mitigate the shortcomings of id/password approaches.

2.2.4 Web resources monitoring

The web servers record their visitors' behaviours, e.g., handling the resource requests from clients in log files; statistical analyses of these files can provide measurements on total page acquired, referrals, visitors' uniqueness, as well as requested resource types (Bracke, 2002 ; Anamarija et al., 2002). In addition, the logging services and analyses have been adopted in a few healthcare and bioscience websites to determine the usefulness of online resources. Furthermore, the system evaluation can enhance the online health sciences to conform to the healthcare practitioners needs as well as to identify patient-specific information (Liu et al., 2006). The techniques can assist administrators to evaluate websites, analyze resource usages, justify the resource priorities, and improve websites design (Rowbottom et al., 2005; Chen & Cimino, 2003; Chen & Cimino, 2004).

2.2.5 Site map

Numerous design and usability guidelines suggested that a site map is necessary for every web site (Farkas & Farkas, 2000; Nielson, 2002). A well designed site map mirrors its associated web site contents, link structures accordingly. It can alleviate users' bewilderment during web navigating (Bernard, 1999), to understand an overview of a site topology, and to search for required information quickly and accurately (Dieberger, 1997; Kim & Hirtle, 1995; Li et al., 2001). In principle, the criteria for prominent large web site maps can be summarized as: 1) capable of covering the contents of Web sites; 2) capable of supporting navigation via visualized Web site topologies; 3) flexible to illustrate or render the web contents and link structures imposing hidden or flatten descriptions, i.e., with multiple granularity of details or topic-focused; 4) enabling site maps construction automatically (Li et al., 2001; Yip, 2004; Inder et al., 1998; Danielson, 2002). In addition, Li, Ayan, and et al. (Li et al., 2001) identify the site maps must be informative and representative indicated by citation analyses.

Although doctors can be slow adapters of new information technology (Tsai et al., 2005; Cheng et al., 2004), the availability of any data, at any time, from any place, changes the healthcare infrastructures dynamically via web portal.

3. Design Objectives & Requirements

According to the problems described in the Background, we design a new portal to solve them. Planning for the portal implementation should be seen as a process of building an infrastructure, foundation for the future, not as developing of a single all-encompassing solution. Therefore, the new portal has to satisfy the requirements as listed:

1) The new portal demands integrating the interface of multi-system authentication and authorization, i.e., Single Sign on Service (SSOS) interface. It validates user's authentication as well as access control capabilities. The capabilities are visualized in menu selections based upon user's authorization. If a user has no authority to access certain functions, the selections will be invisible.
2) The new portal main page ought to be well organized and hierarchical. It needs cover over 300 menu selections for clinicians and administrative staff usages. The selections provide function linkages to HIS (Outpatient, Inpatient, and Emergency Information Systems (Ko et al., 2006)), Healthcare Supporting Services (Critical Healthcare Alerts, Medical Report Review Services, and Consultation Services), Administrative Information System (Human Resources, Medicine Inventory, and Accounting), as well as others. Therefore, a hierarchical, drop-down navigation menu system architecture is inevitable.
3) The function linkages vary frequently; a dynamic menu configuration and generation must be manipulated effectively and efficiently.
4) The portal supports two bulletin boards in one web page, one for HIS, the other for administrative purpose. Furthermore, the boards require supporting real time, on-line features.
5) Because of the large numbers of linkages, the performance of main page rendering is concerned.
6) At present, NTUH HIS is under developing. The portal acquires to correctly redirect to developing, testing, or on-line production servers instantaneously.

4. System description & implementation

After requirement analyses, NTUH HIS has been developed, deployed based upon the middleware multi-tier infrastructure, Service-Oriented Architecture (SOA) technologies (Papazoglou, 2003; Papazoglou & Heuvel, 2007), i.e., Web Services (Krafzig et al., 2005; Shepherd et al., 2000) .NET. SOA represents the current pinnacle of interoperability, in which HIS resources distributed over networks are available as individual, loosely-coupled and independent services (Freudenstein et al., 2007; Murray, 2003; Bunge et al., 2008; Lewis et al., 2007). SOA is a desirable and inevitable solution to integrate diverse platforms, database as well as further merging, extending into NTUH HIS. The overall NTUH HIS frameworks are depicted in Figure 1. Within the diagram, individual components are described as followings.

4.1 Overall architecture

In Figure 1, it contains three major components, i.e., the front-end module, the middleware module, and the back-end services including database servers. The front-end module handles user interfaces via browsers. It establishes the user sessions as well as provides services to validate users' authentications, authorizations. The middleware module, i.e., HL7 Middleware Framework as indicated in the diagram, glues the front-end services and the back-end facilities together. It provides communication and connectivity via SOA (Web Services) mechanism. The HL7 embedded XML formatted data is implemented in the framework for data exchanges among the modules. The back-end facilities support services and database storage.

Further detailed illustrations of the individual modules are provided as followings. In the front-end module, for user friendly browsing interfaces, we adopt web based services. The Portal Servers support the login process with the Single Sign on Service (SSOS) features (Cheng et al., 2004). The servers construct dynamic web URL linkages (Weng et al., 2007), direct to HIS components in the architecture. To enable the SSOS features, the authentication and authorization component (Auth-WS) is introduced. During the HIS operations, any validation needs to be verified through the Auth-WS. The Auth-WS integrates the Web-session Servers and Win-session Servers. The Web-session Servers interact with all other servers in the architecture under the .NET web services environment. The Win-session Servers are implemented as daemons (Window Services). All established conversations, sessions are executed by the daemons including database access.

The Web User Interface (WebUI) Servers generate web-based pages for users' interactive activities. The State-session Servers store the user's web session status variables for analyzing user logic and validation.

In the middleware module, the ancillary Sub-systems provide the connectivity between the WebUI Servers and HIS database (HIS DB) for HIS applications. The messages communicated between the Sub-systems and WebUI Servers are exchanged via the HL7 Framework (Ko et al., 2006). The HL7 Framework is the Middleware Integration Engine of the HIS architecture. It supports message management, routing, mapping, and database access. Detailed information about the processing of each message is also automatically logged by the Engine. Moreover, the Engine glues the medical systems (or applications) together. The HL7 Middleware accesses HL7 message, embedded in XML format, over Simple Object Access Protocol (SOAP). (Yang et al., 2006; Phan et al., 2007; HL7 Standard v2.5, 2003)

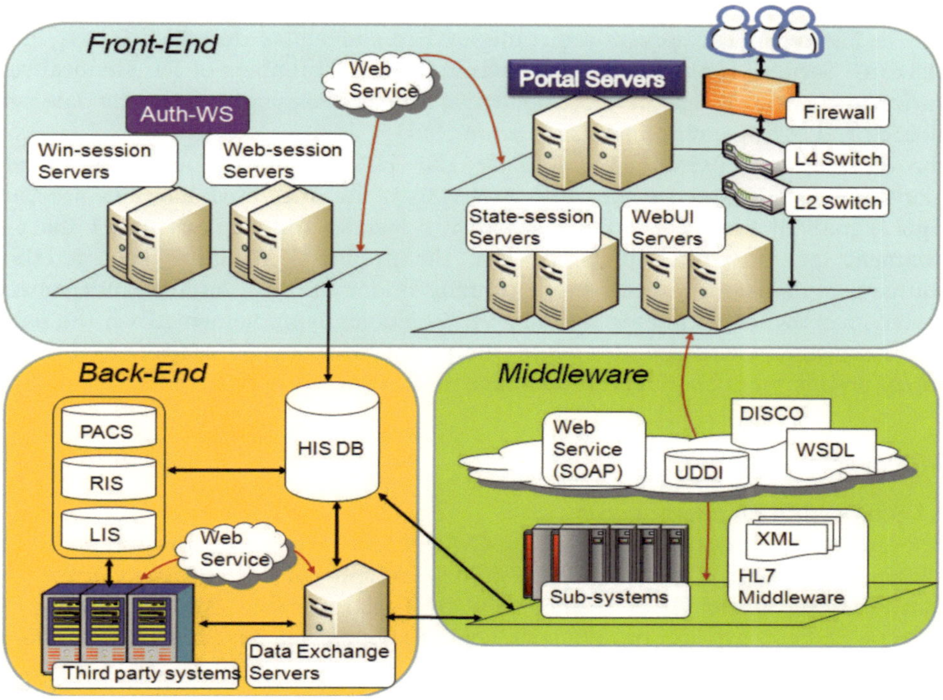

Fig. 1. NTUH HIS overall architecture

In order to achieve the data consistency, we introduce a Data Exchange Server that only receives the message sending from the HL7 Middleware. While Data Exchange server receiving messages, it will perform the data synchronization among patient demographic data in HIS, patient radiology information orders to Outsourcing Systems, i.e., RIS (Radiology Information System) database, or laboratory orders to LIS (Laboratory Information System), i.e. Legacy HIS, database. This data exchange processing can ensure all data in the systems, i.e., HIS and Outsourcing Systems, are updated and consistent as indicated in the back-end facilities (Hsieh et al., 2006; Hsieh et al., 2007; Weng et al., 2006).
To increase the performance of the NTUH HIS, a cluster of identical servers are deployed and dispatched dynamically by introducing Layer 4 and Layer 2 Switches. All the servers are configured running under load balancing as well as failover modes to ensure the system's availability and concurrency. The firewalls are also installed to enhance the security of the architecture.

4.2 Redirect scheme & Single sign on service

4.2.1 Redirect scheme

NTUH HIS is a newly developed system (Hsieh et al., 2007; Ko et al., 2006; Yang et al., 2006). It supports multiple execution environments, i.e., developing, testing, as well as on-line production. Every environment is a complete HIS framework. For example, it includes Portal Server, Auth-WS (Web-session Server & Win-session Server), WebUI Server and

State-session Server (i.e., Application Server), Sub-system, as well as Database Server (shown in Figure 2). The servers are configured in clusters as described in the "Overall architecture" Section. However, in each environment, the numbers of the identical servers are varied in clusters. To ensure practitioners as well as patients privacies, the databases in developing and testing environments are scrambled.

In the developing environment, initially the HIS engineers implement modules, functionalities locally and individually. Afterwards, the integrated modules are verified through regression tests. Secondly, the software installs and deploys under the testing environment for fully evaluations. At last, the products, including Legacy HIS and Outsourcing Systems, are executed and running under the real, on-line environment for daily activities. Switching among different environments is implemented via the usage of Windows registry mechanism. Therefore, the portal can correctly redirect to developing, testing, or on-line production servers spontaneously.

4.2.2 Single sign on service

4.2.2.1 Single sign on components

The concept and the essence of Single Sign-On scenario have been addressed above. Users can login the portal from NTUH Intranet behind the firewalls. Currently, the implementations of the SSOS scheme contain Portal Servers, Auth-WS servers, and Application Servers: e.g. HIS components, Legacy HIS, as well as Outsourcing Systems, as shown in Figure 2. The servers are configured, in clusters, running under load balancing, fault tolerance mode.

The Portal Servers consolidate the SSOS, as illustrated in Figure 2 blue arrows, and deliver users' identities to the Auth-WS servers as indicated in red arrows. The Auth-WS validates user's authentication, authorization and generates an authentication access key for the user. The Web-session Servers and Win-session Servers execute together to provide the Auth-WS functionalities. During verifications, the Web-session Servers interact with all other servers, i.e., Portal Servers, HIS components, Legacy HIS, Outsourcing Systems (depicted in red arrows) to achieve the SSOS scheme. After SSOS validation, via Portal Server, other servers can be invoked subsequently, eventually connected to the HIS databases if required.

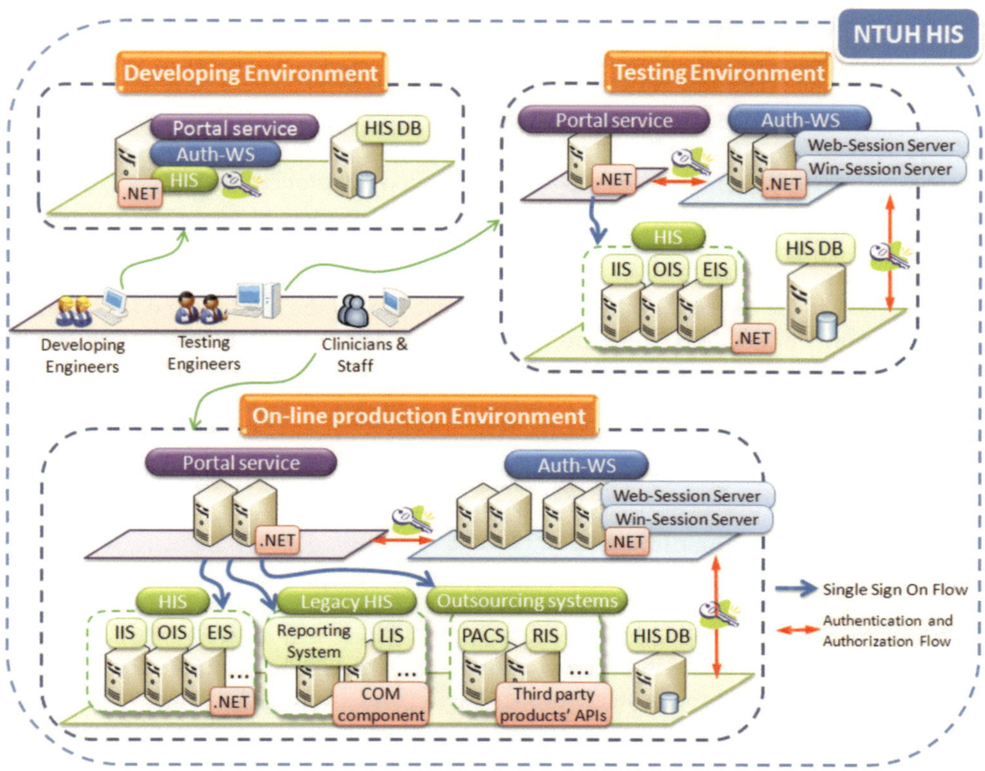

Fig. 2. NTUH Single Sign On scheme & execution environment

4.2.2.2 Single sign on approaches

NTUH is a large enterprise having the ramifications of roles and access permissions. For growing diversity, complexities of acute hospital care, it is particularly difficult to achieve, predict clearly mapping medical providers into roles or assigning access permissions, privileges to roles in healthcare environments. Initially, the hospital adopts the classical role based access control mechanism to deal with users, roles, and associated access rights (Barkley, 1997; 2004-Single). However, we encounter a dilemma: either few roles defined inducing role expansion (Adamcik et al., 1986; Bullough, 1976) or a role per individual resulting in role proliferation (Zhang, 2003; Woods, 2007). Therefore, to cope with the conflicts, a NTUH employee is entitled a basic set of permissions, following the principle of least privilege, according to his/her occupational territory. Additional access permissions, authorities will be aggrandized on demand. In here, the access permissions are pre-defined as web page access rights.

The SSOS scheme has been implemented as followings. For authentication, user's employee ID, SSN (Social Security Number), and current timestamp are utilized to randomly generate the authentication access key. The key is utilized to authenticate among the NTUH components to achieve the SSOS scheme as described in the previous section. For authorization or access permissions, each HIS web page is assigned an identity, i.e., a web page ID; every user is correlated with a set of web pages. If a user does not have the authority, the user can not access, execute the web pages. The user ID and his/her associated web page IDs are stored and maintained in the HIS database. In addition, pre-fetched, paired page ID & user ID can be cached in Win-Session Server in order to improve the validation performance. The cached data are synchronized with HIS database on hourly basis.

The architecture of Web-session Servers is developed, deployed under the .NET web services environment. The Win-session Servers are implemented as daemons. All requests received in the Web-session Servers are forwarded to the daemons and operated there, including database interfaces.

Auth-WS is the core of the SSOS scheme for certifications. In the scheme, the Portal service and HIS components are developed under Microsoft .Net technologies. Thus, these two modules can communicate with Auth-WS directly. However, we design a COM component to adopt, facilitate the communications between the Legacy HIS applications and the Auth-WS. The communications between the Auth-WS and the Outsourcing Systems are achieved via their APIs. The flows of the scheme are demonstrated in Figure 2 red arrows.

4.3 Portal design & implementation

In order to achieve the requirements, we design and enhance a new, dynamic portal for NTUH. First, the portal integrates SSOS features. Secondly, we establish a hierarchical architecture and classify function linkages into groups which will be described clearly later. Therefore, the portal can provide intuitive and effective access. In addition, the portal site needs to provide visualized menu selections. The independent function linkages (URL links) are kept in files, i.e., configuration files. These files will be used for menu configuration and generation dynamically.

4.3.1 Classification of function linkages

In NTUH, the number of function linkages is numerous, over 300. Moreover, in the previous portal, the links are not classified. It is not easy to scroll and select the target links. After reviewing existing function links, we classify 7 groups and establish a hierarchical, drop-down navigation menu as shown at top row of Figure 3. Each sub-tree or branch of the hierarchical classification rooted at the portal represents a major subject area such as clinical care, patient care, health services administration, research, and teaching. In here, the groups are categorized into: HIS, Healthcare Supporting Services (HSS), Administrative Information System (AIS), Digital Learning (DL), Information Security (IS), Personal Data Management (PDM), and Other Resources (OR).

HIS and HSS involve most healthcare associated services. In HIS, it includes the major healthcare information services, e.g., Registration, Ward, Laboratory, Pathology, Pharmacy, and Billing. Medical Report Review Services, Critical Healthcare Alerts, and IC card tools are classified in the HSS group. The AIS consists of Human Resources, Accounting, and Medicine Inventory. The DL contains: educational instructions, discussion forums, questionnaires, as well as on-line exams. Secured, classified documents and materials are stored in IS. It provides privacy and security. Users' personal information functions are maintained in PDM group. These functions include personal password, e-mails, and control access. Finally, the other administrative information is preserved in OR group, e.g., individual department home pages as well as announcements. Based on the classification, the NTUH users can operate the portal intuitively and effectively.

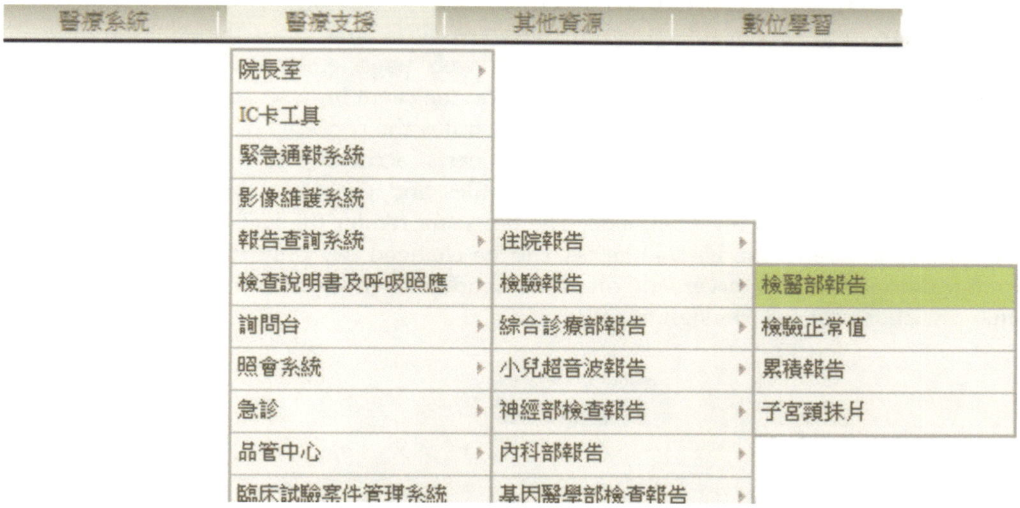

Fig. 3. Hierarchical drop-down navigation menus

4.3.2 Access control capability

The portal provides the menu access control. It means if a user has no right to operate a function, the application link is not visible. For example, administrative staffs cannot execute the Medical Report Review Services in the HSS group; the service links are not visible to them. This capability is implemented in configuration files. There is a "check" property for every menu selection item in the files. The property can control the visibility of menu linkage. This feature will be discussed in details in the "Content of configuration file" Section.

4.3.3 DDNM design & implementation

NTUH portal site is designed as hierarchical, drop-down navigation menus (DDNM) (Goodman, 2003), depicted in Figure 3. The web page only displays in groups initially. Users first select a group; all the function linkages in the group will be rendered. This approach makes space usage flexibly as well as enlarges the amount of function linkages effectively.

Hierarchical DDNM is a client side display mechanism, i.e., this feature executes on user local machine by web browser. JavaScript is a powerful scripting language running in client browser, and it has been supported by many websites. Therefore, we choose JavaScript to implement the client side hierarchical DDNM.

Although the hierarchical DDNM solves the spatial problem of displaying a huge amount of function linkages (URL links), we quickly face another challenge. Because scripts are executed at client side, the URL link is normally hard coded in the scripts. Any URL link modification will cause the server side programs be revised. In addition, if the server side language is a compiling language, i.e., ASP.NET with C# programming language, the program needs to be re-compiled and re-deployed. Therefore, the modification of URL link is time consuming. In order to solve the problem, the URL link should be retrieved at server side dynamically and not hard coded in scripts.

At beginning, the server side program retrieves URL links from the configuration files stored in the servers. A complete DDNM web page embedded with JavaScript is dynamically generated by the server. Afterwards, the client browser executes the scripts and displays the hierarchical DDNM. Figure 4 illustrates the concepts of dynamic, hierarchical DDNM. In the diagram, the users initiate requests; according to the selections, the web server retrieves the associated configuration files and generates the corresponding web pages, delivers them to the client side. The browsers render the web page and display the DDNM. Therefore, if the URL links need to be changed, we only modify the contents of configuration files. The server side program is independent from URL links. Thus, the URL links variation cost reduces significantly.

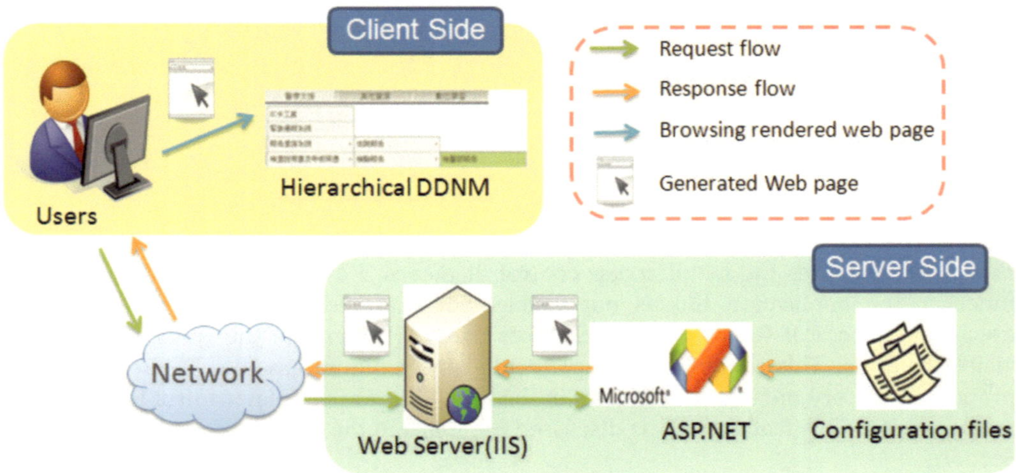

Fig. 4. Concepts of dynamic, hierarchical DDNM

4.3.4 Content of configuration file

While generating the portal main page, the server side programs retrieve properties from configuration files. In the file, it contains parameters: access control capabilities, linkage modes and multi-server redirections, as well as target control.

The configuration files have been categorized into 7 groups. Thus, there are 7 configuration files initially. Because the portal needs to redirect to servers of development, test, or on-line production environment, we create the corresponding configuration files. The additional configuration files can be introduced as needed later. The XML formatted configuration file is chosen to facilitate the NTUH portal. The detailed attributes with their associated values in configuration files, listed clearly in Table 1, are illustrated as the following:

(a) Access control capability: In the configuration file, the check property defines menu selection visibility. Multiple values can assign to the property as a concatenate string delimited by space. For example, the check value: "report showTestENV MIS" indicates a URL link needs to satisfy three criteria to enable the menu visibility. The user must have the report viewing (report) and system developer (MIS) authorities as well as locate in the test environment (showTestENV). Any failure of the checked value will result in the URL link menu not visible.

<name link="linkValue" check="checkValue" target="targetValue">nodeValue</name>
Example:
<Clinics link="ntuhWeb" check="MIS" target="_self">/WebApplication/Clinics/Default.aspx</Clinics>

Node or property	Value	Description
Name		Node name. It is the text of menu shown on web page
Link		Link mode. It indicates how to manipulate the URL link and includes server redirection.
linkValue	adminWeb	Administration web application: the URL of administration server appends with the web page URL, retrieved from nodeValue, to generate a full web URL.
	inpatWeb	Inpatient web application: the URL of inpatient server appends with the web page URL, retrieved from nodeValue, to generate a full web URL.
	outpatWeb	Outpatient web application: the URL of outpatient server concatenates with the web page URL, retrieved from nodeValue, to generate a full web URL.
	outpatWebWithID	The URL of outpatWeb appends with the user login ID.
	reportLink	Reporting web application. The URL of reporting server appends with the web page URL, retrieved from nodeValue, to generate a full web URL.
	staticLink	Output the nodeValue directly as the target URL.
	staticWithID	The nodeValue attaches the user login ID as the target URL
	staticWithKey	The nodeValue appends the access key as the target URL
	staticWithKeyAndID	The nodeValue concatenates with the access key and user login ID as the target URL
Check		Access control by login ID
checkValue	MIS	Check if the login ID belongs to the role of MIS
	GSMMaintain	Check if the login ID has the right to maintain GSM cell phone table
	report	Check if the login ID has the right to access the

		reports of patients
	shownTestENV	Check if the login ID has the right to access the testing environment.
	qResult	Check if the login ID has the right to access the questionary results
Target		Target control. It indicates how to open the web page with browser
targetValue	_self	Open a new page in the original browser
	_blank	Open a new page in a newly created browser
nodeValue		URL Link: it can be a real URL or a code that needs to be translated

Table 1. The properties of a configuration file

(b) Linkage modes and multi-server redirections: the link property controls the URL link generation. For example, the link property can assign outpatWeb, inpatWeb, ssoLink, or reportLink as value. The outpatWeb indicates the application linkage redirects to Outpatient Information System servers. Similarly, the inpatWeb redirects to Inpatient Information System servers. The ssoLink integrates SSOS for NTUH multi-system validation, especially in non ASP.NET server environment. Finally, the reportLink enables Medical Report Review Services. In addition, HIS provides multi-environment, as mentioned in the "Redirect scheme" Section, to perform the complete execution environment. The link property also controls the multi-server redirections for HIS multi-environment.
(c) Target control: This control has the same meaning as HTML target property. Target property controls where the new web page will be displayed when a user follows a link. In the configuration file, target property maintains the target control.

4.3.5 A case study

Figure 5 shows a brief scenario. Initially, a user logs into the on-line production portal. After selecting the target menu group, i.e., HIS (as described in 4.3.1), the portal server will parse the HIS configuration file, as enclosed in the upper rectangular block of Figure 5, to generate the linkage web URLs. In the group, there are two menus: OutPatientSystem and InPatientSystem. PatientRegistration, Clinics, and Billing are the sub-menus of OutPatientSystem. In Clinics and Billing, there are two access capabilities which are kept in the check property: MIS and showTestENV (indicated in the pink boxes). If a user cannot pass either of the two checks, these menus will not be visible on the web page, as depicted at the right hand side of menu selections. On the other hand, when a user passes both checks of MIS and shownTestENV, the result is shown as the left hand side of menu selections. The menu selections are visible to the user. The menu, in green, means it is active. When it is active, one click will trigger the redirection to the menu's web URL.
A medical staff logs onto the PatientRegistration of the Outpatient Information System (OIS) under the on-line production environment as indicated in the middle part of Figure 5. The link property has outpatWeb as its value. Based on the value, the Portal Service retrieves the OIS server URL, http://online.outpat.ntuh.gov.tw, concatenates it with the PatientRegistration default page, /WebApplication/Clinics/Default.aspx, and constructs the OIS PatientRegistration URL. Finally, the user access key, provided by Auth-WS, is appended at the end of PatientRegistration web URL, indicated at the bottom of Figure 5.

The last property is target control. The value "_self" means that the linked web page will be displayed in the same browser window and our design default value is "_blank", i.e., displaying in a new browser window. Therefore, the approach enables menu navigation accurately and timely.

4.3.6 DDNMLog Scheme

The design criteria of the newly NTUH HIS logging system can be defined as: 1) To provide an application framework for logging website usages with a caching and database approach; 2) Not to interfere with normal NTUH HIS Web operation traffics or performances. In the DDNM portal, in order to keep the favourite links for the NTUH users, we can log users' behaviour, DDNMLog, and obtain users popular function links accessed by adapting LRU (Least Recent Used) algorithm. These links will be collected and implemented as "my favourite". Therefore, users can quickly retrieve the links they frequently select. In addition, the pre-fetched links can be cached in advance to improve navigating performance.

DDNMLog, as depicted in Figure 6, allows NTUH HIS website administrators to record and analyze clinician usages of HIS online resources. The application includes four components: Favourite Links Generation, Logging, Queuing & Caching, and Back-end HIS Database. Favourite Links Generation and Logging components are embedded in NTUH portal. The other components are integrated in NTUH HIS .NET environment.

In the diagram, the Auth-WS validates user's authentication, authorization and generates an access key for the user. DDNMLog recognizes the same individual no matter where he/she might be located in office, in lab, at home (via NTUH Virtual Private Network), or behind the NTUH Intranet. To facilitate and expedite the clinician operations, the Favourite Links Generation Module constructs and extracts the most recently executed function linkages retrieved (via .Net Remoting technique) from the FavouriteTable, implemented as .NET DataTable, in Queuing & Caching Module. The Module is implemented as a daemon, i.e., Window Service, resided in Portal Server.

The DDNMLog presents a caching and database approach implemented as an embeddable, plug-in, service, invoked by the medical practitioners. The FavouriteTable is periodically restored into the HIS Database for synchronization. The table is solely pre-fetched from the Database by the daemon, i.e., Queuing & Caching Module, after each re-start. Under normal operations, the daemon re-start rarely happens.

The DDNMLog database schema is described as followings. The MyFavouriteTable, in HIS Database, consists of 4 attributes: 1) ID (User ID); 2) LinkItemNum (function linkage number); 3) AccessTime (function linkage access timestamp); 4) Rank (LRU priority based on 3). The FavouriteTable attributes, in Queuing & Caching Module, are matched with the MyFavouriteTable attributes correspondingly.

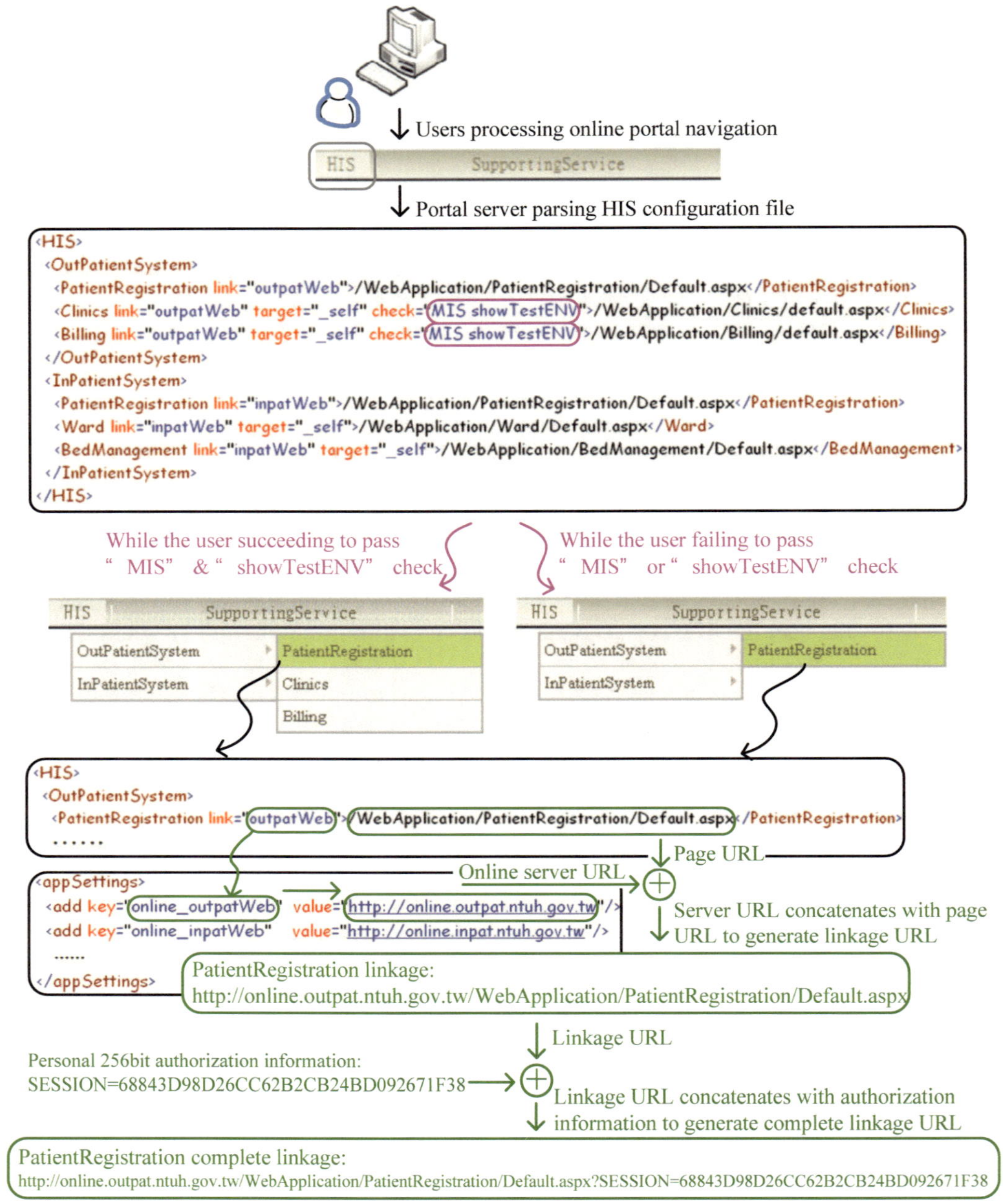

Fig. 5. An example of dynamic, hierarchical DDNM

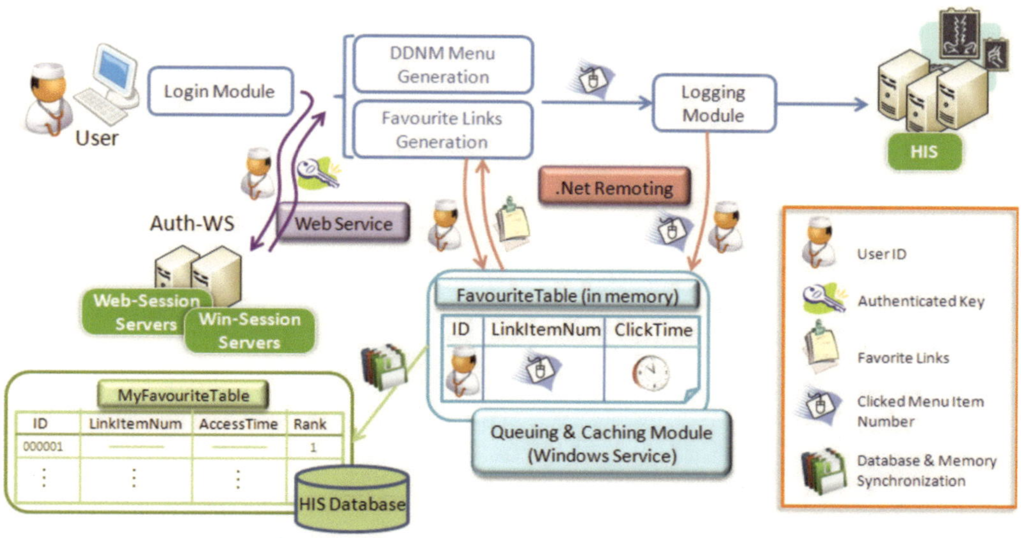

Fig. 6. Concepts of DDNMLog

4.3.7 Additional tools

There are two bulletins in NTUH, administrative and system bulletins. The administrative bulletin focuses on NTUH news, announcements; the system bulletin addresses HIS maintenance. Two bulletins need to be rendered within a web page margin. In addition, the bulletins require supporting the on-line modification features. The NTUH system administrator can insert, delete, and update the bulletins frequently in real time. Any alternation of the bulletins ought to be logged into a database promptly. When a user enters into the portal, the main page will dynamically, immediately retrieve information from the database and display on the page.

Moreover, the portal provides two tools: site map and download template. The site map is generated automatically, accordingly by the portal configuration files. The map will be updated while the portal is being altered. When a user activates the site map function, the map can be spontaneously regenerated based upon the newly configured features stored in the configuration files. In other words, the site map is maintained correspondingly by the portal configuration files. The function supports "shortcuts" to improve linkage targets searching temporally and spatially. Furthermore, the administrator can utilize the template, created from a web page, in order to construct the download page to announce special issues, meeting memorandums, etc. uploaded as files in NTUH.

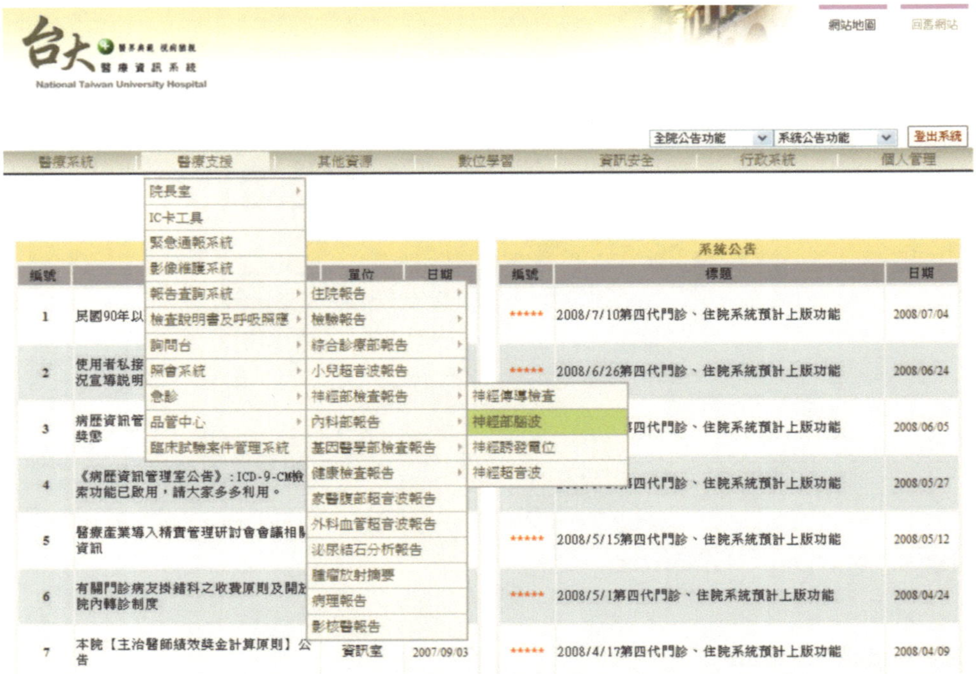

Fig. 7. The new portal contains two bulletins and over 300 function linkages classified in groups

5. Achievements & performance evaluation

5.1 Achievements

The new portal has been operating on-line since June 2006 (as shown in Figure 7). The portal provides the front end integration for NTUH numerous systems by implementing the SSOS strategy. In the diagram, for menu selections, well organized classifications as well as grouping make the user navigate intuitively. The usage of dynamic, hierarchical DDNM reduces menu clicks and prevents the menu bar scrolling. In addition, it is easier to spontaneously maintain the URL links by simply managing the configuration files.

The portal implementation raises a performance issue. In the first version of DDNM, it generates all function linkages every time (about 300). The server side program needs to parse all configuration files as well as create all HTML and JavaScript codes. It takes about 10 seconds on average to display the portal main page. In order to solve the issue, the DDNM second version has been designed and implemented by classified groups. The server side program only needs to process the selected group configuration file each time. Under the most complicated group, it takes approximately 2 seconds, on average, to render the main page.

5.2 Performance evaluations

In the NTUH HIS, the Portal Servers construct dynamic web URL linkages and front end requests to HIS components. The Auth-WS validates user's authentication as well as authorization. The Portal Servers and the Auth-WS act critical roles for NTUH HIS front end performance. Therefore, we evaluate and analyze these two components respectively in the architecture.

The Portal Servers, Auth-WS CPU and memory usages, as well as the number of connections collected in a week, 04/13 ~ 04/19/2009, aggregated by hours daily. The Portal Servers CPU and memory usages, as well as the number of connections data collected are

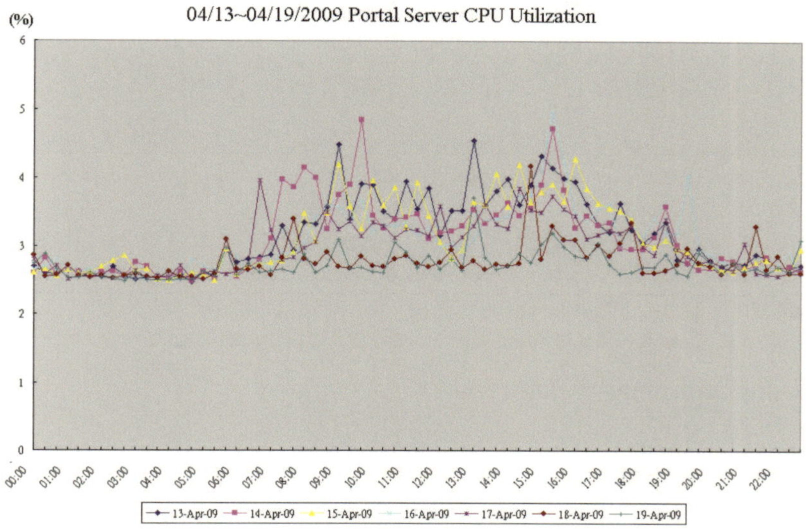

Fig. 8. CPU utilization of the Portal Server

illustrated in Figures 8, 9, and 10 respectively. During the period, on average, the Portal Servers CPU usage reaches 5% at most diurnally. The memory utilization is under 23% (on average, it reaches 700 MB approximately with total memory 3GB) and remains steady daily. The number of concurrent connections peaks in the morning and early afternoon during the hospital operational hours. In addition, the numbers fluctuate between 8:00 am and 5:00 pm.

The Auth-WS contains the Web-session Servers and Win-session Servers. The Web-session and Win-session Servers CPU, memory usages, as well as the number of concurrent connections are shown in Figures 11-15 respectively. The Win-session Servers are daemons,

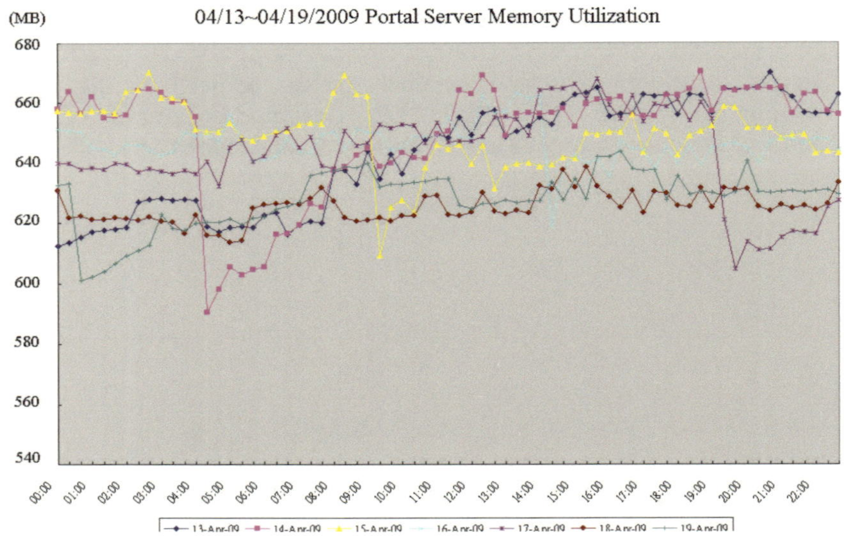

Fig. 9. Memory utilization of the Portal Server

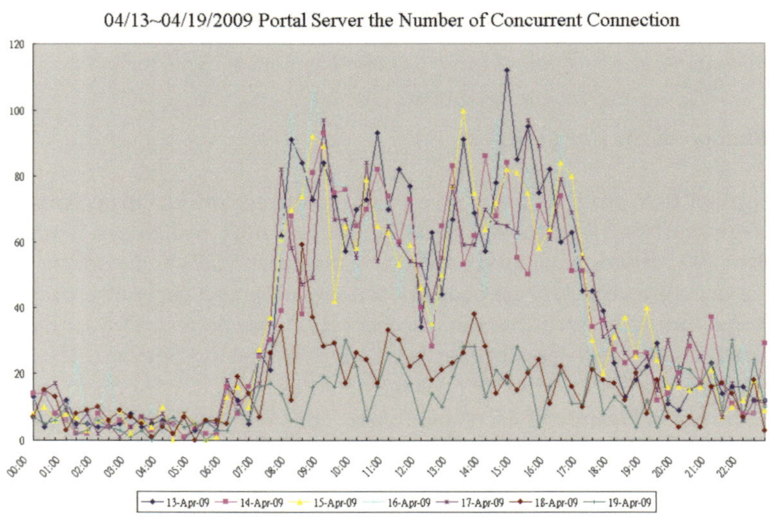

Fig. 10. The number of concurrent connections of the Portal Web Server

not web servers; the number of concurrent connections is not available. During the period, on average, the Web-session Servers and the Win-session Servers CPU usages reach 35% at most diurnally as indicated in Figures 11 and 14. The usages drop during the lunch break. In Web-session Servers, the memory utilization is under 21% (on average, it reaches 630 MB approximately with total memory 3GB) and remains steady daily as presented in Figure 12.

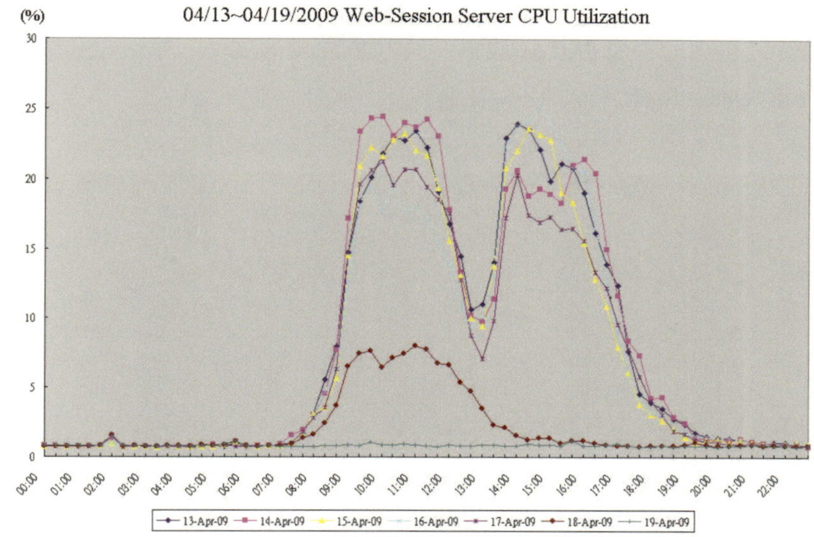

Fig. 11. CPU utilization of the Web-session Server

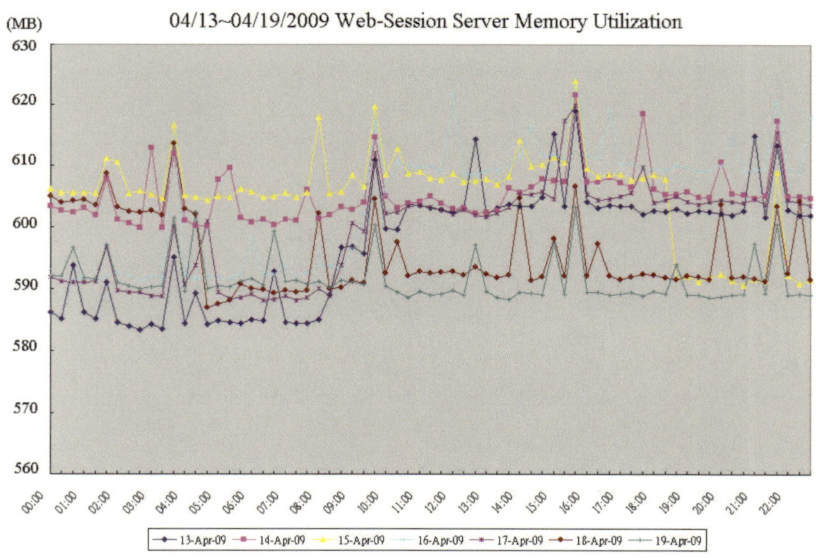

Fig. 12. Memory utilization of the Web-session Server

However, in Win-session Servers the utilization is around 50% daily as shown in Figure 15. The peaks, indicated in Figure 15, result in the synchronization of authentication and authorization data between the Win-Session Servers and HIS database on hourly basis.

In general, Figures 8-15, the CPU, memory usages, and the number of concurrent connections in Servers fluctuate steadily between 8:00 am and 5:00 pm over the hospital regular hours from Monday thru Friday (4/13~4/17/2009); the usages drop significantly

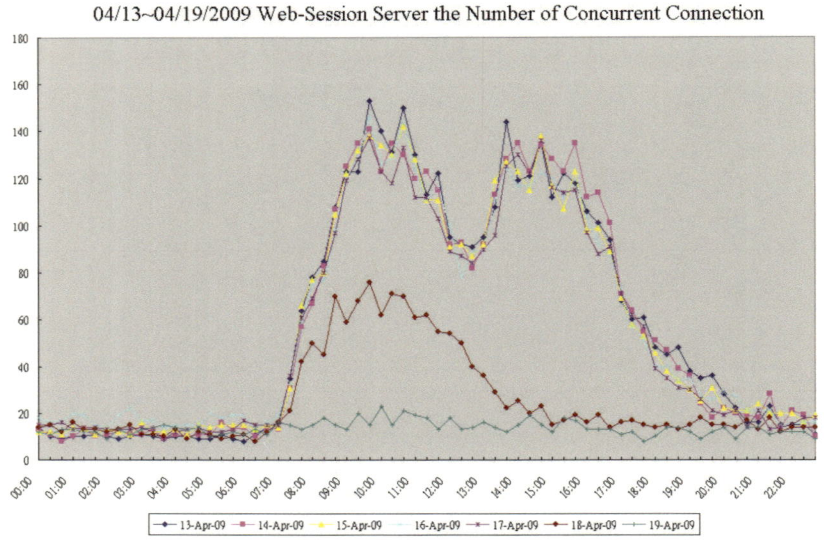

Fig. 13. The number of concurrent connections of the Web-session Web Server

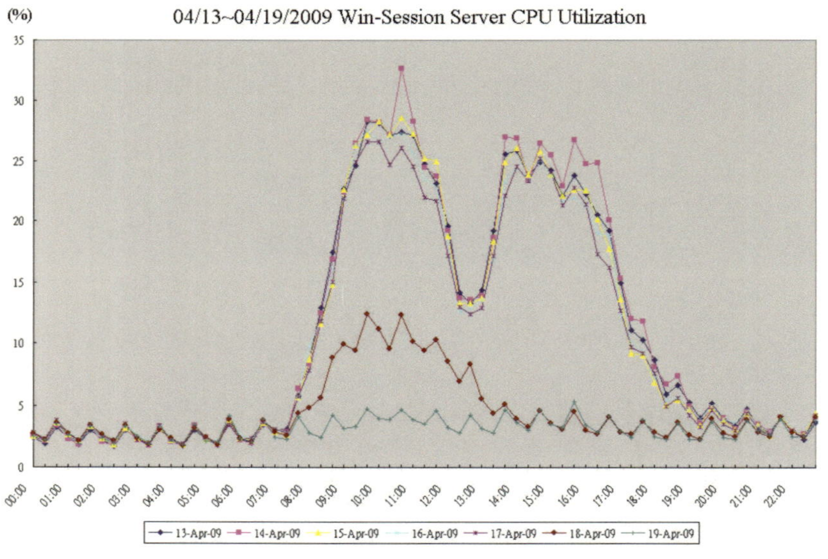

Fig. 14. CPU utilization of the Win-session Server

during the lunch break. On Saturday (4/18/2009, as indicated in the dark brown dashed line), the regular hours for outpatient services are 8:00 am to noon; on Sunday (4/19/2009, as indicated in the dark green dashed line), the hospital is closed for outpatient registrations and services. The corresponding usage statistics are presented in the diagrams.

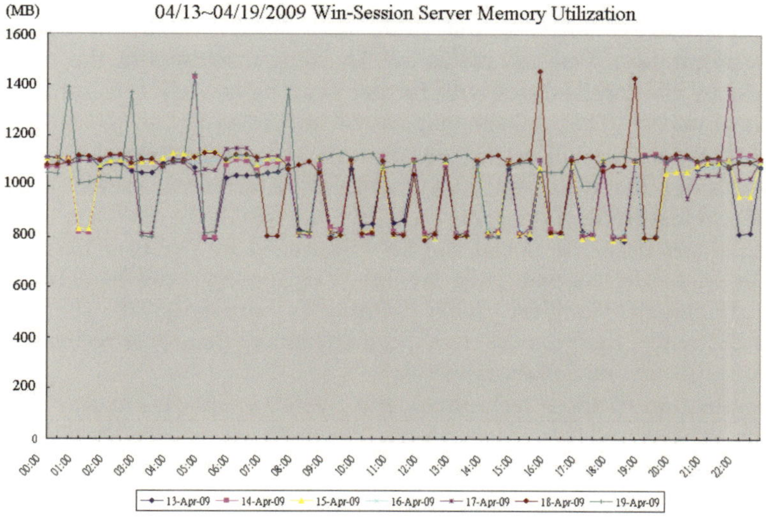

Fig. 15. Memory utilization of the Win-session Server

6. Discussion

The NTUH new portal has classified the linkages into groups; the users can operate the portal intuitively and effectively. The portal permits searching by browsing hierarchical classifications of the web-based information. Although there are many positive feedbacks, a beginner is not familiar with the portal layouts initially and may not navigate them smoothly. There is one issue users complain. In general, a user accesses not more than 10 function selections on average. However, in the current design, the user needs to select the target menu from classified groups covering over 300 linkages. It is still time consuming. Regarding the issue, we plan to improve it according to the following approaches:

1) Keeping the favourite links for users: we can log (Liu et al., 2006) users' behaviour and obtain users popular function links by adapting LRU (Least Recent Used) algorithm. These links will be collected and implemented as "my favourite". Users can quickly retrieve the links they frequently execute. In addition, the pre-fetched links can be cached in advance to improve performance. Therefore, an embedded DDNMLog has been implemented in conjunction with NTUH HIS. The application uses Oracle as the back-end log database and is integrated in Microsoft .NET environment. In addition, the application has been pilot since April, 2009.

2) Providing site map facilities: the portal site map can improve targets searching temporally and spatially. The site map is generated, maintained automatically, accordingly by the portal configuration files. The approach illustrates the flexibility of the site map maintenance. NTUH HIS Portal provides medical practitioners and staff with a visible site map to encourage them to navigate the Portal via shortcuts. However, the current NTUH site map is a heavily hierarchical interlinked tree structures; it can induce disorientations (Dieberger,

1997). On the other hand, the practitioners have different expectations and preferences while navigating the web site to perform their daily operations. It is desirable to ameliorate the situation. Therefore, we propose a technique by utilizing the DDNMLog scheme to retrieve users' behaviours in order to construct a multi-granular, topic of interests site map imposed, derived via the configuration files automatically. The link structures of the map can be presented, indicated by citation analyses with further pruning as well. It is anticipated that the usability effects of the NTUH Portal site map can be improved.
3) Full text searching: the portal will provide the feature. The planned searching engine will examine all the words in bulletin contents, documents, announcements, as well as menus to expedite searching and text retrieval.
4) Customized portal per user: the portal can be customized by per user basis including groups, function links, as well as web page layouts. The approach can be achieved using Web 2.0-based technologies (Knights., 2007; Schroth & Janner, 2007). The techniques empower users to customize their experiences more effectively than ever before, and share information in more efficient and collaborative way.
Therefore, the combination of these techniques effectively benefits the entire NTUH HIS systems workloads. The portal has been on-line formally since June 2006. The portal provides services for doctors, medical staffs, as well as administrative personnel. In order to understand and validate the perfectionism, completeness of the portal, we conduct periodically assessment interrogation, interviewing, and debriefing to obtain the portal usages, suggestions from the associates for further enhancements as well.

7. Conclusion

The NTUH new portal explores the dynamic, hierarchical drop-down navigation menu to visualize function linkages by simply managing the configuration files. The DDNM rendering is flexible for space usage and enlarges the capacity of URL links. It leads the portal contain over 300 function links as well as two bulletins in one web page. The XML formatted configuration files are designed to automate function linkages with access control, linkage modes and multi-server redirections, as well as target control. The new portal generates the main page effectively and efficiently. In addition, the portal supports front end integration for NTUH numerous systems, platforms applying the SSOS scheme. Therefore, the portal provides a unique entrance for NTUH HIS infrastructure. The infrastructure supports the availability of any data, at any time, from any place dynamically.
The NTUH HIS has been developed from the ground up to be an available, robust, reliable, secure, interoperable, and service-oriented architecture. Moreover, the NTUH HIS is an innovation designed to address the continuously changing and demanding natures of today's healthcare environment in Taiwan. It presents a solution to perform challenges imposed by heavy messaging traffic that is threatening the viability of Web-Services (.NET) implementations. As a result, capital expenditures are controlled and the return on investment is shorter.
In summary, the NTUH HIS portal is a vehicle driven to support integrated access to information needed by Hospital constituents, whether they are students, staff, or faculty. Furthermore, the additional tools, techniques empower medical practitioners to customize, fulfil their experiences more comprehensively. The DDNMLog service provides a dynamic function linkage usages monitoring and allows just-in-time (shortcuts) accesses for users. On

the other hand, NTUH HIS Portal is a large, complicated, heavily interlinked web site; it is likely to be disoriented. However, the Portal is a visible, hierarchical tree topology, and immediately accessible; under the circumstances, the site map is significantly accommodating (Yip, 2004; Danielson, 2002). As the portal continues to be developed and enhanced, the new features can be added on a regular basis.

The aspects of the NTUH Portal accessibility, i.e., visual structure, colour contrast, and text size, in compliance with Web Content Accessibility Guidelines 2.0 (WCAG 2.0, 2008), are under preliminary investigation.

8. References

Adabala, S.; Matsunaga, A.; Tsugawa, M.; Figueiredo, R. & Fortes, J.A.B. (2004). Single Sign-On in In-VIGO: Role-based Access via Delegation Mechanisms Using Short-lived User Identities, *Proceedings of the 18th Parallel and Distributed Processing Symposium*, pp. 22

Adamcik, B.A.; Ransford, H.E.; Oppenheimer, P.R.; Brown, J.F.; Eagan, P.A. & Weissman, F.G. (1986). New clinical roles for pharmacists: a study of role expansion, *Soc Sci Med.*,23(11):1187-200

Amor, D. (1999). E-business Revolution, *Hewlett-Packard Books*, pp. 220 - 221

Anamarija, R.H. ; Dimitar, H. & Ljupco, T. (2002). Users' information-seeking behavior on a medical library website, *J Med Libr Assoc*, 90:210 –7

Arbor, A. (2000). Health Level 7, HL7 Version 3.0., MI: HL7, 2000 [Online]: http://www.hl7.org (Accessed: 18 June 2009)

Azar, S.N. ; Jalali, A.H. & Falsafi, S. (2008). Commercial Portals Evaluation, *Advanced Communication Technology, ICACT 2008, 10th International Conference*, pp. 2035 - 2039

Barkley, J. (1997). Comparing Simple Role Based Access Control Models and Access Control Lists, *Proceedings of the Second ACM Workshop on Role Based Access Control*, pp. 127-132

Bernard, M. (1999). Findings on the use of sitemap. [Online]: http://psychology.wichita.edu/surl/Sitemap.html (Accessed: 6 Mar 2003).

Bracke, P.J. (2002). Web usage mining at an academic health sciences library: an exploratory study, *J Med Libr Assoc*, 92:421– 8

Brakel, Pieter van (2003). Campus Portals for content: the next generation of academic Websites?, *5th Annual Conference on World Wide Web Applications*

Bullough, B. (1976). Influences on Role Expansion, *the American Journal of Nursing*, Vol. 76, No. 9, pp. 1476-1481

Bunge, R., Chung, S. & Endicott-Popovsky et al. (2008). An Operational Framework for Service Oriented Architecture Network Security, *Hawaii International Conference on System Sciences, Proceedings of the 41st Annual*, pp. 312 – 312

Chen, E.S. & Cimino, J.J. (2003). Automated discovery of patient-specific clinician information needs using clinical information system log files, *AMIA Annu Symp Proc. 2003*,pp. 145–149

Chen, E.S. & Cimino, J.J. (2004). Patterns of usage for a Web-based clinical information system. *Med Inform*, pp. 18 –22.

Cheng, P.H. ; Yang, T.H. ; Chen, H.S. ; Hsu, K.P. ; Chen, S.J. & Lai, J.S. (2004). Codesign of a Healthcare Enterprise Information Portal and Hospital Information Systems, in Plastics, 2nd ed. vol. 3, J. Peters, Ed. New York: McGraw-Hill, pp. 15-64

Danielson, D.R. (2002). Web navigation and the behavioral effects of constantly visible site maps. *Interacting with Computers*, 14 (5), October 2002, pp. 601-618

Dieberger, A. (1997). A city metaphor to support navigation in complex information spaces. Spatial Information Theory: a Theoretical Basic for Gis, 1329, 67

Farkas, D. K. & Farkas, J. B. (2000). Guidelines for designing web navigation. *Technical Communication*, Third Quarter, pp. 341-358

Fraser, H.S.F. ; Kohane, I.S. & Long, W.J. (1997). Using the Technology of the Would Wide Web to Manage Clinical Information, *BMJ*, 314: pp. 1600-1603

Freudenstein, P. ; Nussbaumer, M. ; Majer, F. & Gaedke, M. (2007). A Workflow-Driven Approach for the Efficient Integration of Web Services in Portals, *Services Computing, SCC 2007, IEEE International Conference*, pp. 410 - 417

Goodman, D. (2003). *JavaScript & DHTML Cookbook*, O'Reilly

Heckle, R. (2007). Individual authentication in a collaborative environment: lessons from a single sign-on implementation, *Conference on Supporting Group Work*, Group '07 Doctoral Consortium papers, Article No. 3

Heckle, R.; Lutters, W.G. & Gurzick, D. (2008). Network authentication using single sign-on: the challenge of aligning mental models, *Proceedings of the 2nd ACM Symposium on Computer Human Interaction for Management of Information Technology*, SESSION: Security, Article No. 6

HL7 Standard v2.5 (2003), Health Level Seven (HL7), Chapter 4, pp. 4-14 – 4-17

Hsieh, S.H. ; Hsieh, S.L. ; Weng, Y.C. ; Yang, T.H. ; Lai, Feipei & Cheng, P.H. et al. (2007). Middleware based Inpatient Healthcare Information System, *Bioinformatics and Bioengineering, BIBE 2007, Proceedings of the 7th IEEE International Conference*, pp. 1230 – 1234

Hsieh, S.L.; Lai, F.; Cheng, P.H.; Chen, J.L.; Lee, H.H. & Tsai, W.N. et al. (2006). An Integrated Healthcare Enterprise Information Portal and Healthcare Information System Framework, *IEEE EMBC 2006*, pp. 4731-4734

Inder, R. ; Kilgour, J. & Lee, J. (1998). Automatic generation of diagrammatic Web site maps, *Proceedings of the 1998 ACM symposium on Applied Computing*, pp. 719-725

Kim, H. & Hirtle, S. (1995). Spatial metaphors and disorientation in hypertext browsing. Behaviour & Information Technology, 14(4), 239-250

Ko, L.F. ; Lin, J.C. ; Chen, C.H. ; Chang, J.S. ; Lai, Feipei & Hsu, K.P. et al. (2006). HL7 middleware framework for healthcare information system, *e-Health Networking, Applications and Services, HEALTHCOM 2006*, pp. 152-156

Lee, W.B. ; Min, S.D. ; Jeong, W. ; Choo, Y. & Lee, M. (2007). Construction of APEC e-Health Portal Site for e-Health Service Providers and Demanders in APEC area. *e-Health Networking, Application and Services, 2007 9th International Conference*, pp. 300 - 303

Lewis, G.A. ; Morris, E. ; Simanta, S. & Wrage, L. et al. (2007). Common Misconceptions about Service-Oriented Architecture, *Commercial-off-the-Shelf (COTS)-Based Software Systems, ICCBSS '07, Sixth International IEEE Conference*, pp. 123 – 130

Li, W.S. ; Ayan, N.F. ; Kolak, O. ; Vu, Q. ; Takano, H. & Shimamura, H. (2001). Constructing Multi-Granular and Topic-Focused Web Site Maps, *Proceedings of the 10th international conference on World Wide Web*, pp. 343 - 354

Liu, N. ; Marenco, L. & Miller, P.L. (2006). ResourceLog: An Embeddable Tool for Dynamically Monitoring the Usage of Web-Based Bioscience Resources, *J. Am. Med. Inform. Assoc. 2006*, 13(4): pp. 432-437; doi:10.1197/jamia.M2013

Mary, D. (2002). Portal Project Overview, Washington State University, [online] Available: http://www.wsu.edu/portal-project/background.html

Mauro, C.; Sunyaev, A.; Leimeister, J.M.; Schweiger, A. & Krcmar, H. (2008). A Proposed Solution for Managing Doctor's Smart Cards in Hospitals Using a Single Sign-On Central Architecture, *Proceedings of the Proceedings of the 41st Annual Hawaii International Conference on System Sciences*, pp. 256

McDonald, C.J. ; Overhage, J.M. ; Dexter, P.R. ; Blevins, L. ; Johnson, J.M. & Suico, J.G. et al. (1998). Canopy Computing: Using the Web in Clinical Practice, *Journal of the American Medical Association*, 280(15): pp. 1325-1329

Murray, M. (2002). An investigation of specifications for migrating to a web portal framework for the dissemination of health information within a public health network, *In Proceedings of the 35th Annual Hawaii International Conference on System Sciences*, pp. 1917-1925

Murray, M. (2003). Strategies for the successful implementation of workflow systems within healthcare: a cross case comparison, *System Sciences, 2003. Proceedings of the 36th Annual Hawaii International Conference*, pp. 10

Nielson, J. (2002). Site Map Usability. [Online]:http://www.useit.com/alertbox/20020106.html (Accessed: 6 Mar 2003)

Knights, M. (2007). Web 2.0, *Communications Engineer*, Vol. 5, Issue 1, pp. 30 - 35, February-March 2007

Krafzig, D., Banke, K. & Slama, D. (2005). Enterprise SOA: Service Oriented Architecture Best Practices, *Prentice-Hall, Englewood Cliffs*, 2005

Oo, I. (2006). Presentation Level Integration of Portal Personalization Architecture, *Information and Communication Technologies, ICTTA '06*. 2nd Volume 1, 24-28, pp. 564 - 565

Papazoglou, M.P. (2003). Service -Oriented Computing: Concepts, Characteristics and Directions, *Proceedings of the Fourth International Conference on Web Information Systems Engineering*, pp. 3

Papazoglou M.P. & Heuvel, W.J. (2007). Service-Oriented Architectures: Approaches, Technologies and Research Issues, *VLDB J.*, vol. 16, no. 3, 2007, pp. 389–415

Phan, C. ; Lee, L. & Fleischer, R. (2007). Service Oriented Architecture (SOA) - Security Challenges and Mitigation Strategies, *Military Communications Conference, MILCOM 2007*, pp 1 – 7

Raghupathi, W. (1997). Health Care Information Systems, *Comm of the Association for Computing Machinery*, 40(8): pp. 81-82

Rosen, M. (2000). Enterprise Portals, *Software Magazine*, Vol. 20, No. 5, pp. 22 - 25, October 2000

Rozic-Hristovski, A.; Hristovski, D. & Todorovski, L (2002). Users' information-seeking behavior on a medical library Website, *J Med Libr Assoc*, 90:210 –7

Rowbottom, N.; Allam, A. & Lymer, A (2005). An exploration of the potential for studying the usage of investor relations information through the analysis of Web server logs, *International Journal of Accounting Information Systems*, 6 :31-53

Rudenstien, R. (2000). A Bright Idea, *Enterprise Systems Journal*, Vol. 15, No. 1, pp. 24 - 30, January 2000

Russler, D.; Stanic, S. & Davis, F. (2001). Benefiting from the Evolution towards a Healthcare Adaptive Portal Framework, *Proceedings of the 2001 Health Information Systems Society Conference*, Vol. 4, February 2001

Schroth, C. & Janner, T. (2007). Web 2.0 and SOA: Converging Concepts Enabling the Internet of Services, *IT Professional*, Vol. 9, Issue 3, pp. 36 – 41, May-June 2007

Shepherd, M. ; Zitner, D. & Watters, C. (2000). Medical portals: Web-based access to medical information, *In Proceedings of the 33rd Annual Hawaii International Conference on System Sciences*, pp. 1–10

Strauss, H. (2002). All about Web Portals: A Home Page Doth Not a Portal Make, *In Web Portals & Higher. Education: Technologies to Make IT Personal*, edited by RichardN. Katz. San Francisco: Jossey-Bass

Trippe, B. (2001). Content Management Technology: A Booming Market, *Econtent*, Vol. 24, No. 1, pp. 22 - 27, February/March 2001

Tsai, C.W. ; Ho, J.H. ; Liang, T.W. & Yang, C.S. (2005). An intelligent Web portal system for Web information region integration, *Systems, Man and Cybernetics, IEEE International Conference*, pp. 3878-3883 Vol. 4

Volchkov, A. (2001). Revisiting Single Sign-On: A Pragmatic Approach in a New Context, *IT Professional*, Volume 3, Issue 1, pp. 39-45

WCAG 2.0, Web Content Accessibility Guidelines 2.0, December 2008 [Online]: http://www.w3.org/TR/WCAG20/ (Accessed: 18 June 2009)

Weng, Y.C. ; Hsieh, S.L. ; Hsieh, S.H. & Lai, Feipei (2007). Design and Enhance a Dynamic Healthcare Portal Site, *Web Intelligence and Intelligent Agent Technology Workshops, 2007 IEEE/WIC/ACM International Conferences*, pp. 173 – 176

Woods, N.F. (2007). Women's roles and illness episodes: A prospective study, *Research in Nursing & Health*, Volume 3 Issue 4, pp. 137-145

Yang, T.H. ; Cheng, P.H. ; Yang, C.H. ; Lai, Feipei ; Chen, C.L. & Lee, H.H. et al. (2006). A Scalable Multi-tier Architecture for the National Taiwan University Hospital Information System based on HL7 Standard, *Computer-Based Medical Systems, CBMS 2006, 19th IEEE International Symposium*, pp. 99 - 104

Yip, A (2004). The effect of different types of site maps on user's performance in an information-searching task, *Proceedings of the 13th international World Wide Web conference*, pp. 368-369

Zhang, L.; Ahn, G.J. & Chu, B.T. (2003). A rule-based framework for role-based delegation and revocation, *ACM Transactions on Information and System Security (TISSEC)*, Volume 6 , Issue 3, pp. 404-441

Zhu, F. ; Wang, A. & Ju, Y. (2004). A framework to develop a university information portal, *Information Acquisition 2004 Proceedings, International Conference*, pp. 506-509

Zirpins, C. ; Weinreich, H. ; Bartelt, A. & Lamersdor, W. (2001). Advanced Concepts for Next Generation Portals, *12th International Workshop on Database and Expert Systems Applications*, pp. 501 – 506

4

Universics - A Common Formalization Framework for Brain Informatics and Semantic Web

Ioachim Drugus
Moldova Academy of Sciences, Semantic Soft, Inc
Republic of Moldova

1. Introduction

This chapter is an introduction to a conceptual framewok and a mathematical apparatus, said to be *Universics,* designed to serve for integration of other disciplines via their universes of discourse and, in particular, for the integration of Brain Informatics and Semantic Web, which are in the focus of this chapter. By *universe* I refer not only to what is said to be a „universe of discourse", but also to any modeling framework where, for modeling, we use representation rather than discourse, so that such universe can be said to be a „universe of *representation*". Universics is a fundamental theory which posits the notion of *universe* (or *world*) with a plural *universes* (or *worlds*) in the basis of a conceptual framework, and expresses other notions through this basis.
An object said to be a *universe* must be rather complex and only a complex mathematical structure can serve as its formalization. I have previously outlined (Drugus, 2007) an approach to the content of mind said to be the *A3 approach.* This approach is introduced in this paper in full detail and used for the formalization of the concepts of Universics which, thus, becomes centered around the A3 approach. The A3 approach can also serve for the formal specification of an intelligent agent - a virtual machine for processing ‚mind content' which adds non-determinacy to the Turing machine to enhance its algorithmic capabilities with features of intelligence. I will outline the features of such a machine, which I say to be a *conceptor,* but a complete specification of conceptor would require a separate publication. I had to make reference to this intelligent agent here, because its involvement simplifies the account of Universics strongly centered around the data model of ‚mind content' of such an intelligent agent.
Since the ‚mind content' of an intelligent agent is obtained in result of cognition of the Universe and is „in the image" of the Universe, it is natural to say a piece of mind content to be a *universe* - an „inner universe", „subjective universe", or „subject universe", as opposed to the „objective universe" or „object universe". Moreover, due to the A3 approach, the ‚mind content' has a strictly specified „format", defined in the language of an enlarged set theory said to be *A3 language*. Therefore, by applying „conceptual inverse engineering" (my term), I ascribe this „format" to any universe. Having this manner obtained a uniform

formalization of the universes of discourse, by the application of other formal methods, we can look for relationships between different disciplines, discover convergence, or develop integrative methods. Since Universics' terminology and conceptuality proceeds from the largest „whole", the Universe, Universics is a *holistic* discipline, and since it can be used as a formal framework to discuss about other disciplines, it is a meta-discipline.

The A3 approach, its A3 language, and its A3 data model are strongly correlated with Semantic Web and its languages for knowledge representation, in particular, with the most complete one, the formal language of the OWL standard. A piece of mind content is formatted according the A3 language, and can be uniformely mapped into an OWL ontology, and viceversa.

The A3 approach makes abstraction from presentation details of Semantic Web standards, in particular, from the URI's and other web-related notions and entities, and therefore, despite its larger expression power, the A3 language is simpler than the Semantic Web languages. Also, the A3 approach complements the Semantic Web with notions and methods which simplify ontology engineering and helps in modeling the reality due to new notions, which have well established meaning in practice. Finally, the A3 approach does not need separate treatment of precise semantics in the language of set theory as all the standards of Semantic Web do, because A3 language itself is a language of an extended set theory and can be used to describe the semantics of Semantic Web standards. Finally, as a formal language, A3 is a very simple „language of brackets" (three pairs of brackets) to which a special meaning is assigned and for which special manipulation rules are formulated to obtain a strict calculus directly correlated with the λ-conversion calculus (Curry, 1941) and the Turing machine (Turing, 1937).

The idea of Universics as a mathematical holistic discipline goes back to my doctoral dissertation on superintuitionistic logics (Drugus, 1982), where I have applied a model theory strongly based on Leibniz ‚possible worlds' apparatus. By that time, mathematicians, including myself, became aware that the ‚forcing method' used to solve the „Continuum Hypothesis" problem (Cohen 1963-64), i.e. the problem N1 in Hilbert's collection of open problems for the 20th century, is essentially the ‚possible worlds' conceptuality but is formulated in different terms. The solution of this problem is currently treated by many authors as the last strong result in the set theoretic foundation of mathematics. It became obvious that, by treating ‚possible worlds' as multiple universes of discourse for set theory, a more expressive set theory can be obtained. For this purpose such universes must be formalized by moving the discourse from sets to classes and, finally, to universes of discourse, and treat the universes of discourse as entities studied by a meta-theory with respect to set theory. Universics turns out to be such a meta-theory.

In 2007 I learnt about Semantic Web and discovered that „formally" it is close to what I have been thinking twenty years before, except that Semantic Web standards add technical matter specific to the web. Also, I have soon got the conviction that wide deployment of Semantic Web is hindered by lack of „pure mathematics" for *presentation* methods as opposed to *logical methods* (of discourse) prepared for Semantic Web by the Description Logic developed in late 1990s. Finally, Semantic Web lacks a formally defined „semantic machine" or „intelligent agent" to process the ontologies. My paper of 2007 (Drugus, 2007) is basically a general plan of development of Brain Informatics and Semantic Web based on pure mathematics and this chapter is a step in implementation of this plan.

I also believe that the failures of the technological solutions, like those which caused the so called ‚AI winter' and currently hinder the wide deployment of the Semantic Web, are due to pure engineering approaches, and such difficulties can be avoided if mathematical methods prior to engineering concrete solutions are developed. I think, that a „brain mathematics" should and can be obtained by extending the set theory, a commonly accepted *foundation of mathematics*, up to a theory, the entities of which have an intuitive and natural meaning for intelligence. In particular, an intelligent agent must be treated as a virtual machine which processes the sets and other entities of such an extended set theory.
The results of this research are currently being implemented in software tools for Semantic Web at the Semantic Soft, Inc. company.

2. The A3 approach to brain informatics

Universics is centered around the A3 approach which serves as its methodology and formalization framework. The A3 approach is a conceptuality and a data model said to be the *A3 data model*, a language said to be the *A3 language*, and a vision on the mechanism of mind from which all other aspects of this approach can be inferred. The A3 data model is the data model of the mind content, and it can also serve as an alternative framework for knowledge representation and formal representation of linguistic corpora (Drugus, 2009). This section is an introduction to the A3 vision of mind which discovers the main operations of mind which I would attribute to „brain mathematics".

2.1 The A3 vision on the mechanism of mind

The A3 approach proceeds from a vision on the process of formation of mind content, treated as a network consisting of mental entities. Also, the formation of this network is treated as „weaving" rather than „creation of a whole" because this process is perpetual and it never ends during the lifetime of mind. Since the term „formation" is too general to reflect the specifics of this process, and „weaving" is not a convenient word to serve as a term, I will use the term „synthesis" for such formation of mind content. Currently, there exist a large number of different types of networks used in research and technology - neural networks, semantic networks, Petri nets, and other types. Mind content is a new type of network.

Synthesis unfolds in steps and for a natural (i.e. not „artificial") mind, probably, a large number of mental entities is created at one step. In order to simplify the analysis, in this paper I will limit to only one atomic mental entity created at one step of the mind content synthesis.

Since the mind content synthesis is regarded as perpetual and never ending during the lifetime of mind, it always encreases in size and, even though the mental entities are more abstract than sensual data, the mind content is always a realistic „film of the reality" - a „conceptual film". I am not interested here in the dynamic aspect of mind content which determined me to assimilate it with a „conceptual film". The dynamic aspect only shows that mind content is an „open world", i.e. a changing object. I am interested in mind content as a „history" or „memory" of the synthesis process reflecting the „structure" or „form" of the mind content. The Figure 1 below illustrates the „mathematics of brain" and serves as a roadmap to further material.

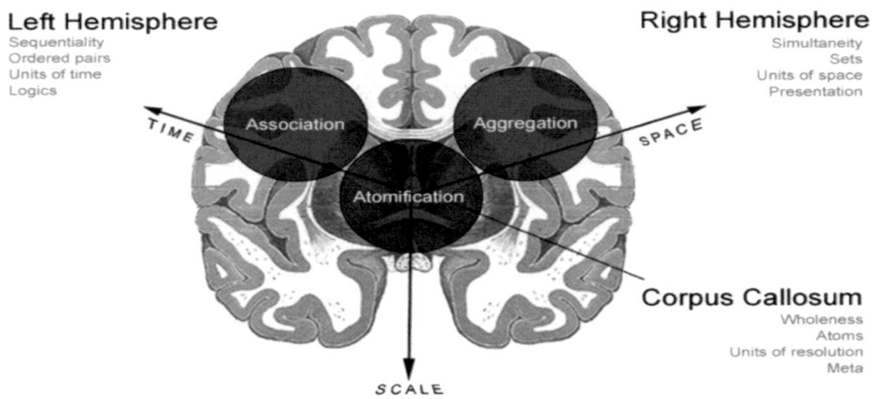

Fig. 1. Brain Mathematics

Earlier (Drugus, 2007), I treated the synthesis of mind content without the part-whole aspect. I explained that such synthesis is done by alternative involvement of each of the two hemispheres of brain at one step of synthesis, and with each involvement, it does exactly one operation whereby it creates an entity. For right-handed people, I substanciated that the left hemisphere is specialized on the *association* operation whereby it produces a new entity also called *association*, while the right hemisphere is specialized on the *aggregation* operation whereby it produces a new entity also called *aggregation*. In this paper, I will additionally treat the part-whole aspect, which became possible due to finding a better explaination of the part-whole aspect, dealt with by the third component of brain - the bridge between two hemispheres called corpus callosum. I assume this component to be specialized on the operation of *atomification* of the A3 approach.

The mind content obtained in result of a perpetual synthesis can serve only as a basis for intelligence, which alongside accumulation of conceptual experience as mind content, manifests via other activities, including the logical activity. But the mind content synthesis unfolds on a level which serves as a basis for higher levels of intelligence. The level immediately above it allows to cut on this wealth of conceptual data and can be said to be the level of *identification*. The identification allows to regard many mental entities as „the same". Because these two layers are sufficient for the discipline of Universics, in this paper, I will focus only on the level of mind content *synthesis* and on the level of *identification*.

To summarize the account of the A3 approach vision on brain mathematics, I will say, that at one step of mind content synthesis, the brain applies exactly one of the three operations, said to be *A3 operations*, for creating a new entity:

- *Aggregation* operation for creating an entity also called *aggregation* - an entity type generalizing the notion of *set* of set theory, and the notions of *class, container* and *collection* of Semantic Web,
- *Association* operation for creating an entity also called *association* - an entity type generalizing the notion of *ordered pair* of set theory, and the notion of *property* of Semantic Web,
- *Atomification* operation for creating an entity also called *atomification* - an entity type generalizing the notion of *atom* (also said to be *ur-element*) of set theory and

the notion of ‚whole' of mereology, science of „parthood" or of „part-whole" relationship (and for which there is no corresponding notion in Semantic Web).

To clarify the above, it should be added that the entities are either *untyped* or *typed*, and if an entity is typed, then it can have one of the three types above, which I will refer to as the *A3 types*. Each of the terms *aggregation, association, atomification*, will serve as a name both for the operation and for its result, and we will distinguish between them by specifying to which of the two we refer. So, we will use expressions like „an aggregation", „entity of type *aggregation*", or „aggregation operation" and similar expressions for „association" and „atomification".

In the most general case, I am treating the term *operation* as a many-to-many correspondence. So, even though A3 operations are not yet completely defined, they should be treated as many-to-many correspondences or, how they are called elsewhere - „many-valued functions". The notion of *property* in Semantic Web corresponds to the notion of set theoretic relationship and of „functional property" as it is said to be there. This is why to avoid term collision, I will not say a many-to-many correspondence to be a *function* - I will say it to be *operation*.

One of the greatest difficulties in guessing how the mind content is synthesized is to find out how the representations of different objects can be retrieved at a later time. This is a general problem for any kind of networks. Also in philosophy the process of discriminating separate entities in the „material network" of the Universe has been a problem since ancient times - a problem, which has not been solved up to date.

I would have preferred the term „domain of integrity" for the representation of an object in the network of mind content, because this would have better reflected the idea of dealing with the „wholeness" treated here as a synonym for „integrity". But „integrity" has a special meaning in English, and I will use the term „integral domain", which though is good due to being shorter. I consider the integral domains, as representations of objects, to appear in mind due to the *atomification* operation.

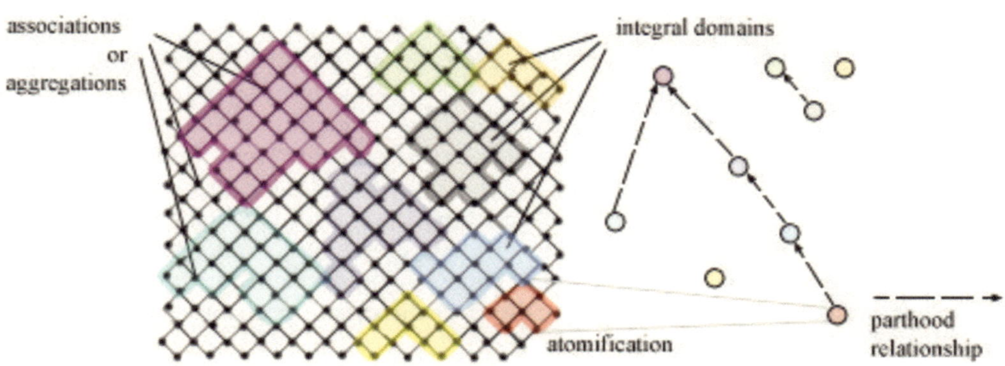

Fig. 2. A piece of mind content

The figure 2 above illustrates the mind content obtained in result of a synthesis process, which is a directed process: in this figure, we consider that mind content „grows" upwards. The results of applications of both the aggregation and association operation are represented as nodes of the network. In order to simplify the picture, the distinction between the entity types aggregation and association is not indicated in the figure and all the aggregations in this figure are deemed to be two-element aggregations - same number of arguments as of the association operation. The colored areas are said to be *integral domains*. These pieces of mind content are „production“ of the atomification operation, which can be thought to act in a dimension, different from the dimensions where act association and aggregation. The results of applications of the atomification operation can be imagined to lie in space above the 2D space of the picture. This is why, to represent the integral domains as new entities not lying in the plane and to be able to discriminate between them, they are represented in different colors. The bottom of each integral domain is represented by the *atoms* (indivisible constituents) of the represented object. This botom is „dented“ because in the synthesis process the representations of the atoms appear at different times. The top of each integral domain is represented by exactly one entity which we regard as the *unity* of this integral domain. The first intuitive idea about the manner how an integral domain can be extracted from the mind content is by imagining that such a domain is "carved out" from the mind content taking into account the two boundaries - top boundary represented only by the unity, and bottom boundary represented by many atoms.

Notice that in the Universe of matter, one body B is part of another body C, if B is spatially "inside" C. The universe of mind differs from the Universe of matter and the representations of B and C in mind look totally different. Namely, the unity of B becomes an atom of C, so that in a graphical representation as that of Figure 2, the representation of B would be beneath (and not inside) the representation of C.

2.2 Place of A3 approach among other approaches

In order to correctly place the A3 approach among others, I will mention the features of three main existing approaches and explain why they are incomplete for knowledge representation purposes and for describing the mind content.

The relational model (Codd, 1970) was placed in the basis of database technology and the entity-relationship approach (Chen, 1976) is successfully used in object management and UML. Some authors regard a ‚world' as represented by a database where all data about the entities of such a world are persisted. Both these two main modeling frameworks, widely used today in IT and AI implementations, don't offer the level of precision required by mathematics. Really, set theory is regarded as the main formalization framework for mathematics and other disciplines, but the notion of *set* and *ordered pair* (treated as „element of order“), not only are not among the primitive notions of these approaches, but are used uncounsciously. Set theorists know that such attitude to the intuitive notion of set can raise serious logical contradictions. In software, logical contradictions manifest as bugs. Therefore, the software for representation of mind content developed according approaches which unconsciously treat the basic operations of mind will, probably, have „conceptual bugs“ in their specification and will not work.

The sound mathematical foundation of Semantic Web is reflected in its standards by formulation of semantics of standards in the language of set theory. But Semantic Web is focused on the *discourse* about the Universe, rather than the *representation* of the Universe. The representation capabilities are an essential feature of an intelligent agent, and a representation framework missing in Semantic Web might be responsible for the fact that, so far, there is no proposal of a generic agent for processing the Semantic Web data.

Also, even though the notion of *class*, which is a conceptual conterpart of the notion of *set,* is among its primitive notions, Semantic Web standards totally ignore the notion of *atom*, or

„urelement" of set theory, and this results in difficulties to strictly discriminate between the notions of *individual* and of *class*. Say, according OWL, an individual can also be a class. But then, it remains unclear what is an individual which is not a class and how to express in OWL the property of such an entity. Despite that the notion of *class* is examined by Semantic Web, and the other notions correlated with class, like *container* and *collection*, are also used all such notions are regarded as independent of each other and no correlation between them is indicated. Finally, the SPARQL querry language uses graphs to indicate different universes of discourse without any indication of correlation of such graphs with the notions *class*, *container* and *collection*.
All the difficulties above show that Semantic Web, as it is currently formulated via different standards, also does not completely satisfy the requirements for a really mathematical approach. True, we can clearly separate the aspect which Semantic Web currently does not cover - this is *presentation* of entities, versus *discourse* about entities. Even after such separation, there remains the main difficulty on the path of wide deployment of Semantic Web to become a really „democratic" tool - the extreme complexity of the standards, which shows that there is insufficient mathematics behind them.

2.3 The operational and structural completeness of the A3 approach

The activity of an agent consists of separate operations, and the agent builds data structures also by applying various operations. I am treating an approach to intelligence as mathematical, if it

(1) Specifies a set S of mathematical operations which our mind is capable to do,
(2) Substanciates that other operations of mind can be reduced to the operations in S (operational completeness),
(3) Substanciates that any structure represented as mind content can be represented as a result of multiple of applications of these operations (structural completeness).

I will say a set S of mathematical operations to be an *orthogonal basis* of a class C of operatons if additionally to the conditions above, the operations in S are irreducible to one another. Can there exist such a set S of operations in natural intelligence?
Since a brain neuron can do a limited number of operations and these are sufficient for the neuron to serve as a building block for the physical substratum of intelligence, there must exist a limited number of operations to which all phenomena of logical mind can be reduced. This shows that the operational-structural mechanism of the brain and the „soft" layer above it, the mind, must have an orthogonal basis of operations. But, since we are talking about the mind content, such an orthogonal basis should be looked for in the mind and there is only one method to study the mind - introspection.
The A3 operations are an orthogonal basis of operations of mind defined above. This basis was found by introspection and this fact is substanciated by reference to neuro-science, physics, and set theory. The A3 approach is a mathematical approach, because the A3 operations are mathematical operations - they are generalizations of set theoretic operations. The thesis that the A3 operations are operationally and structurally complete, cannot be proven and its validity is a matter of belief. This thesis has the same status as Church-Turing thesis about the algorithmic completeness of the programs for Turing machines, and I will refer to this thesis as the *A3 completeness thesis*.

3. Conceptor – an intelligent agent for the Universics

The A3 approach is an approach to intelligence, which proceeds from a generic intelligent agent capable to create entities of the A3 types by applying the A3 operations and process the structures created this manner said to be mind content. The Latin for „to create an entity" in mind is „concipere" – a word from which comes the family of words correlated with „concept". Therefore, by analogy with the commonly used in Pattern Recognition term ‚perceptron', but without mixing Latin (percepere) with Greek (-tron), I introduce the term *conceptor*. I will say a conceptor to be an agent capable of two activities:

- Creating structures by multiple applications of A3 operations, and
- Using such structures

According the A3 approach vision on the mechanism of mind, the brain is a conceptor. The characteristics of conceptor among other possible intelligent agents, is that the conceptor is meant to be capable to do „brain mathematics" – i.e. create mind content by applying mathematical operations, which in our case are chosen to be the A3 operations. I regard a conceptor as a „lower level" mechanism upon which builds the „upper level" mechanism of intelligence, and which, in order to stick to mathematical methods, can be said to be a mechanism of reduction of any operation to multiple applications of the A3 operations. Obviously, the use of the term „mind content" for a conceptor imposes to also use the term „mind" for a conceptor. Also, I will use in discourse about conceptors the other terms previously used in discourse about human brains.

All „superior" animals have a two hemispheres brain with a bridge between them, which means that the Nature, as the best tester of mechanisms of life, found out that specialization is essential for intelligence. Thus, even though according some views the inanimate matter can bear features of intelligence so that the whole Universe can be regarded as intelligent, I would regard specialization in doing main mathematical operations as a distinguishing feature of intelligence. Therefore, as the first requirement in specification of a conceptor, I regard its full compliance with the A3 vision on brain – namely, a conceptor must have three components each specialized on one of the A3 operations. Going forward, I will also use for the components of a conceptor same names as for the human brain – „hemisphere", „left hemisphere", „right hemisphere". This cannot raise confusion within the context of the A3 approach, because „operationally", i.e. with respect to the A3 operations, the components of a conceptor and of the brain are identical as per the specification of the conceptor.

This paper is focused on how the conceptor, by applying the A3 operations, creates structures called mind content. But to get a better understanding of this aspect of the activity of a conceptor, I will also give below a general idea of how such structures are used by a conceptor in reasoning.

Prior to other intelligent activities, the conceptor must be able to *view* pieces of data, including pieces of mind content for the introspection processes. For this purpose it must have an „attention" *focus*, which can

1. Enlarge (narrow) from one aggregation to a larger (smaller) aggregation,
2. Move allong associations in both directions,
3. Zoom in from an atom representing the identity of a structure to the structure itself and viceversa.

The read-write head of a Turing machine is an example of such a focus, which though, is limited to motion along associations of a „linear universe". By specifying for the conceptor the read-write operations similar to those of the Turing machine and introducing the states,

we obtain a more general agent, with non-deterministic „programs", versus the deterministic programs for a Turing machine (Turing, 1936).
The conceptor is significantly richer in its behavior, including, due to being capable of doing more complex motions of its attention scope, than the Turing machine head. At the same time, all such motions are required, in order to be able to travel in a universe with all three possible axes, like the universe of mind. Conceptor is meant to serve as a conceptual virtual machine for processing data modeling mind content.
A formal specification of the conceptor as virtual machine is not the focus of this paper, but the described features are sufficient for understanding the focus of this paper - creating mind content. The material below also provides details of the conceptor's behavior, which will be included in its formal specificaton.

3.1 The intelligence of a conceptor

„What is intelligence?" is a question which has been extensively discussed about and the only good and widely accepted approach to anwering this question turns out to remain the „Turing test", which actually does <u>not</u> answer this question, but gives a clue how to compare artificial intelligence with human intelligence. Such an approach to answering this question suggests that an artificial intellect must be able to do same operations as a natural intellect. In my approach I regard a conceptor as intelligent if it, simply, repeats the functionality of brain regarding the A3 operations.
Despite that due to such simulation of brain, we might admit that an „advanced" conceptor might have same level of intelligence as the Human, this cannot ensure higher intelligence, because we actually don't know what is intelligence. With all fuzziness of terms, we can say that intelligence is capability to cognize the Universe. An intellect is part of the Universe and, thus, intelligence is also the capability to cognize himself.
I regard the Universe as having 3 main dimensionalities - *space*, *time* and *scale*. Even though *space*, as one of such axes, in turn, can be three-dimensional as in the case of the physical Universe, this is unessential for our approach. Notice, that also in the fundamental equations of physics space is represented by one parameter, sometimes denoted by one variable „x". Below, I will relate intelligence with capabilities of the brain or of a conceptor to work with these „universal" axes.

3.2 A conceptor's hemispheres specialization in cognition of the Universe

I assume that the right hemisphere is specialized on processing simultaneity, i.e. it „takes shots" of simultaneously *viewed* entities. Same speciality must have one hemisphere of a conceptor. To view several entities „simultaneously", the entities must be present „at the same time" and I treat the „same-timeness" as a property of *space*, which allows to distinguish it from its opposite - *time*. Thus, we can regard the right hemisphere as a virtual „space machine" - a machine for processing spacial relationships.
I assume that the specialty of the left hemisphere is processing the sequentially viewed entities. Sequentiality in viewing is imposed by time and is a property of time which distinguishes time from space. Really, no matter how many directions has a space, and how the direction from one entity to another entity is indicated, there is a possibility to view the entities in the opposite direction. For example, given an ordered pair (a, b), which is written

in the linear space of text, we actually don't know which element is considered first and which should be regarded as second, unless we know the consensus on „viewing direction". While a piece of mind content is static, perception of a varying „content" in the Universe, like a vision or sound which change, is a dynamic process involving sequentiality in processing. Sequential order is represented in mathematics by a set of ordered pairs and an ordered pair is an association. Thus, the left hemisphere specialized on creating and processing associations can be said to be a „time machine" - a machine for processing termporal relationships.

In the fundamental equations of physics expressed in space x and time t parameters, you can exchange the places of x and t, and the equation remains valid. Due to such space-time symmetry, there is no physical law which would help distinguish between space and time. I am resolving this difficulty by considering *time* as a dimensionality of a universe, which allows viewing in only one direction, and space - as a dimentionality of a universe, which allows viewing in any direction.

I assume that the specialty of the bridge between hemispheres is processing the *scale* dimensionality and it can be said to be a „scale machine". Scale refers to the part-whole relationship and seems to be the least studied dimensionality of the Universe. The dimensions and qualities of physical bodies relate to different units of measure, and this also relate to scale. A conceptor processes scale by the zoom in and zoom out capabilities of the attention focus. Probably, the operation of this component of a conceptor, will be better understood after we will have dealt below with atomifications.

3.3 Identities – the units of mind content

The main aspect of cognition is identification and for a conceptor to identify an object, it first creates an entity in mind which we will say to be the object's *identity*. In A3 approach we will say all the atomic (indivisible) mental entities, out of which the mind content is made, to be *identities*. Even though an atomic mental entity may not yet have been used as an identity of an entity at a moment of time, it is destined to serve as such at a later time - this is the explaination of this use of the term *identity*. With this understanding of the notion of *identity*, we can say that the *distinguishing property of the identities among other entities is their residence in mind.*

Because the Universe must have an unlimited number of objects, the next requirement to a conceptor is the capability to create identities without any limitation. An important aspect of the synthesis process is that at each step a new identity is created - notice, that in defining the vision on workings of mind we underlined the word „new". To ensure this, the conceptor must have an *identity generator* for creation of new identities without any limit. In the process of synthesizing mind content, the re-use of an old identity is not acceptible. This is because similar to the human mind, the conceptor must treat each situation as totally new, and only later consider different entities „the same".

According the A3 vision on mind, the perpetural synthesis process imposes creation of many identities for one single object. This is not a peculiarity of the synthesis process but reflects the cognition process. An object in the Universe can be perceived at different moments or in different places. We will say each of such „object instance" to be an object's *presentation*. The multitude of identities of an object is actually the class of identities of the object's presentations.

3.4 Identification and reification

The synthesis of mind content is acompanied by a process which makes several mental entities „the same" or „identical". This process complies with Occum's razor principle „entities should not be multipied without necessity" and is part of the „economy of mind". „To be identical" can be also treated as „having same identity" (in mind).

I will distinguish between the notion of *entity* and the notion of *object*. By *entity* we generally mean anything, whether in the material Universe or within the mind. By *object* we don't mean everything, but only an entity **e** for which there is a representation **r** in mind. So called things-in-themselves, invented by the philosopher Immanuel Kant, are entities, but they are not objects. Also, for a device recognizing pictures by a pattern, a picture which cannot be recognized because it lacks a pattern in the database of patterns, is an entity, but it cannot be said to be an object.

An object may have many identities. For example, the star Venus, also called by two other names „Morning Star" and „Evening Star", must be expected to have at least three identities in the mind of an English speaking child, until he or she learnt that this is the same object. The process which takes place when he learnt this fact is said to be *identification*. This process is complex and we will not study it here, but will focus only on the result of this process, which is said to be „identical entities" or „entities which are the same". In mathematics, the fact that two entities denoted by **E** and **F** are identical is denoted by the equality symbol between them, **E = F**. If we denote the predicate „is identical" by the term **sameAs** of the OWL language, then we can denote such fact by **[E sameAs F]**. The use of square brackets for quotation of an expression is rather a new practice, but it makes part of the A3 language, and I will explain this type of denotation later.

For an entity denoted by e, I will denote by **=(e)** or **=e** its identity. The meaning of this denotation is "neglecting the name and keeping only identity of the value", or "making the name replacible by any other name with same value". Obviously, the denotation "=e" is equivalent to the denotation "_:e" of a blank node. This is a new type of notation which treats the equality sign as denotation of a unary operator instead of a binary operator. Obviously, **e** and **=e** are equal, and we can denote this fact by **(e == e)** or **(=e = e)**. We said that an entity may have many identities - which of these identities is denoted by the expression „**=e**"? Any identity of **e** can be also denoted by „**=e**". The two notations **e** and **=e** denote same entities and can be said to be synonymic denotations, but each of synonyms has its meaning - this is the reason for existence of many synonyms with same values (denotata). The format **=e** has the meaning we assigned to it – „the identity of **e**". Such a property of names (or „denotations") will become clearer when we will discuss later on the properties of names. Despite that such use of the equality sign is rather peculiar, the conceptually behind it has same fundamental character as the equality and it makes much sense in the A3 language.

Mind content is the „reality of mind". The Latin „rei" stands for „things" or „objects" and „reification" is a term which denotes „making the reality" and it is used in Semantic Web to denote a method of reference to a statement. We will use this term with wider meaning and apply reification to any entities. Namely, by *reification* I mean „creating an image of an object in mind".

3.5 Reflection

Mind content is synthesized to represent the Universe and, therefore, a piece of mind content is „in the image" of a piece of reality of the Universe. I will refer to this imagery by the term *reflection*. Reflection is a many-to-many correspondence between the identities in mind and the entities within universe which I can prove to be Galois connections – a structure widely used in algebra (Stewart, 1973) which has applications in various domains. Suppose that a piece **S** of mind content is in the image of a piece **O** of the Universe under an aspect. We will say that an *aspect* is due to a *view* of the agent, the conceptor. *Aspect* is on the side of the Universe and *view* is on the side of the conceptor. I will say both S and O to be *universes*, and to be specific on the „residence" of such universes – I will say S to be a *subject universe*, and O to be an *object universe*. Notice that O may also be a piece of mind content – this situation is specific for the process of introspection. Taking into account the introspection, we did not say S to be „inner universe" and O - „outer universe". Also, due to different views there can exist many representations in mind of the same piece of reality. Therefore, the two universes must be correlated this manner only with respect to a representation R. In other words, we examined the universes above with respect to the object-subject relationship within the context of a concrete representation R.

3.6 Structure and form

I said that the subject universe is „in the image" of the object universe at some representation. In order for this imaging to make sense, the representation must preserve the „structure" or the „form" of the object universe and confer it to the subject universe. While we will define the notions of „structure" or „form" for the mind content, the question what might be these notions when applied for the objects of matter remains a problem and this „to be in the image" does not make sense. In order for it to make sense, by a conceptual „inverse engineering" method, I will ascribe the „structure" or „form" of the inner universe to the outer universe, and declare this to be the „structure" and „form" of any universe.
On a more general note, I make distinction between the notions *structure* and *form* by involving an agent's two complementary aptitudes, operation and view. Namely, if an agent builds via operations, i.e. „constructs", an object, then I say the object to be a *structure* (to remember, notice that to „con-struct" is linguistically correlated with „structure"). If an object is viewed by an agent, then I say it to be a *form*. A form can be „structured" in different manners, depending on the analysis done by an agent viewing the result of construction, so that we can say that a form has many structures. On the other hand, if an object is viewed by an agent with memory, who memorized the construction process, then such an object „has one structure" or we say „is a structure". After a structure is created, it can be viewed – a structure is a partial case of form.
The mind content obtained in result of the synthesis process is a *structure*, versus a *form*. Really, at each step of the synthesis process, one A3 operation is applied, and each A3 operation is „invertable" - the arguments of the operation can be restored from its result. We will apply to mind content or to the universes the word *structure* and to the objects inside them the word *form*. This conforms with our saying that an object has a form.
While the distinction between *structure* and *form* is rather subtle, these two notions are essentially different and, in practice, different terminology is associated with each. Only by taking into account this distinction I will be able to explain below the essence of atomifications. Sometimes, the notion of „building block" in a construction process is

referred to as „atom". We will use the word *atom* only with respect to forms and we will introduce other terms for structures.
I will say the entities from which starts a construction process in a structure S to be the *initial entities* of the structure S, and the entity last produced in construction process of S to be the *final entity* in structure S. The initial entity and the final entity are notions correlated with a structure and specify the boundary „in depth" which I say to be scale dimension. Such specification of boundary „in depth" is missing in set theory. So, when we said that a set of the form {{a}, {a, b}} is said to be an ordered pair (a,b), we did not define an object, but expressed one form through another form. According such definition the set {{{a, b}}, {{a, b}, a}} is also an ordered pair, but it has another form. Mathematicians don't have difficulties with this because they subconsciously are doing additional mental work. But our goal is to reflect any mental work through formal processing of mind content.
Before defining what is a universe obtained in result of multiple applications of the A3 operations, it is useful to first study the „pure universes" consisting of entities of only one type - the universe of aggregations, the universe of associations, the universe of atomifications. Each of these universes can be considered as part (in the sense of subset or subclass) of a larger universe where reside entities of any A3 type. We will say this last universe to be the Full Universe, where I borrowed the word „full" from „full OWL" - the variant of the OWL Semantic Web language meant to reflect the Description Logic in full. This variant of OWL is only mentioned in standards, but it remains unspecified. Since the A3 language to be specified by the end of this paper has an absolute minimum of primitives, and the choice of such primitives is based on fundamenta mathematicae reasons, I assume that the A3 language can serve as a „nucleus" of the „full OWL".

4. The universe of aggregations

The universe of aggregations is the residence of only aggregations or, to use physical terminology, this is a universe which has only one dimensionality - the space dimensionality. This universe extends the universe of discourse of any axiomatic set theory so that the conceptuality and terminology of set theory can be applied to aggregations. I have actually extended, where applicable, the set theoretic terminology to Universics, and will use it for the aggregations.
The term *aggregation* denoting the result of the aggregation operation has the same meaning as in IT, but the aggregation operation which produces this result is studied only in set theory, where it is named „set abstraction" and is reflected in the notation $\{x : \varphi(x)\}$, for a formula $\varphi(x)$ in the language of set theory. Obviously, when $\varphi(x)$ is true for any value of x, for example, when $\varphi(x)$ is $(x = x)$, then the aggregation coincides with the universe of discourse of set theory.
The use of the term *aggregation* for *set*, is motivated by actually treating the term aggregation as wider than the term *set*. According classic axiomatic set theories, a set is defined by its elements so that two sets with same elements coincide due to the *extensionality axiom*. The meaning of this axiom is that a set has exactly one identity. I do not postulate the extensionality axiom for the universe of aggregations - actually, I don't postulate any axioms because axioms have to do with discourse, and a universe is a presentation framework. Therefore, in the universe of aggregations, two aggregations might be equal

while their identities be different. One aggregation may have different identities at different times – a multitude of identities. But at one time an aggregation has exactly one identity.
We can define aggregations in terms of sets the following manner – an aggregation is a set together with an entity on the role of its identity. For all these reasons, we can say aggregations to be multi-identity sets, or multi-sets. Generally, by „multi-set" they refer to „simple", i.e., one identity set, the elements of which can be multi-identity. But if the quality of multi-identity is attributed to all the multi-sets in a universe of multi-sets, then it should apply not only to the elements of a multi-set, but also to the multi-set itself.

4.1 Representation of aggregations in mind

I will denote aggregations by using the regular set-theoretic notations for denoting sets and classes, which utilize the braces - „{" and „}". So, the aggregation of the entities $a_1,..., a_n$ will be denoted by $\{a_1,..., a_n\}$. Notice, that in this denotation, the comma can be treated as an operation. I will say this operation to be *assembly* operation, because it actually can serve for the „element-wise" assembling a finite set out of it elements, and, since I have just introduced a new term, I will refer to its etymology, which is the French word „ensemble", „togetherness" which served as the original name in French for a „set", introduced by the founder of „set theory", Georg Cantor.
The assembly operation is commutative, associative and idempotent, where the last property means that for any **e** and **f** the following equality is true: **{e, e} = {e}**. In this paper, I will not focus on this operation - I needed to mention about the assembly operation only for the purpose of making the notations of the A3 language precise, so that the comma is used only in notations where its properties are expected and to avoid its use in the contexts where such properties are not intended (like in denotation of associations).
Because an aggregation of n elements $\{a_1,..., a_n\}$ has an identity it must be represented in mind by n+1 entities: n identities of the elements a_i and the identity, of the aggregation itself. Where is represented the identity of the aggregation in the notation $\{a_1,..., a_n\}$? Such a question, obviously, makes sense only for a conceptor, the mental space of which is paper on which are placed the inscriptions of such notations. We will regard the pair of braces „{" and „}" as the denotation of the aggregation's *unity* because it makes out of the elements $a_1,..., a_n$ a *unit of data*. All the denotation, i.e. this object presentation (see above what is an „object presentation") is an identity of the aggregation.

4.2 The aggregation as an abstraction

The application of the operation of aggregation results in an aggregation as a structure $\{a_1,..., a_n\}$. What is or what are the arguments of this operation? The first idea that these are $a_1,..., a_n$ is not correct, because with such a treatment we would need to have an infinite number of n-ary aggregation operations. I am treating this as an operation of abstracting the set from the universe by selecting those elements which are in the focus of the conceptor. This can be also an explaination of the term „set abstraction". Thus, the abstraction operation applies to the whole universe of discourse.
The operation of „set abstraction" in set theory is known to cause logical contradictions, and one of the methods to avoid them is to limit its application to the elements of another set U, which is reflected in the following type of notation: S = $\{x \in U : \varphi\}$.

But the universe of entities in mind at a certain moment of time is finite and this abstraction is unlikely to create contradictions. Anyway, I treat the set abstraction, or aggregation, without any limitations on its applicability, as a natural operation of mind, even when used in a manner which creates contradictions. This is because a human can reason contradictorily and build in mind „impossible geometric pictures" like those of Bosch, including for the purpose of denying their existence. Similarily to the natural intelligence, we must allow the conceptor to create contradictory concepts and we will place no limitation on how it applies the aggregation operation.

Each aggregation U can be treated as a universe of discourse, if we limit our discourse to the aggregations which are elements of U. Specifically to avoid contradictions, mathematicians replaced the notation $\{x : \varphi(x)\}$ of the intuitive set theory by the notation $\{x \in U : \varphi(x)\}$. But the intuition behind this sometimes escapes the regular users, and in practice sometimes the intuitive set theory notation is used. In Universics, which can be treated as an extension of intuitive set theory and as a presentation framework, the notation $\{x \in U : \varphi(x)\}$ is rather useless, because it actually reminds you which is the universe of discourse. In Universics, in order to avoid contradictions it is enough to follow the principle „in reasoning, don't get outside the universe of discourse". Such principle can be referred to as „factoring out the universe" which has the meaning of „bringing a factor outside the brackets" (in this case - outside the braces of aggregation).

Alongside universes of presentation, Universics also alows to conduct discourse and deal with universes of discourse. For this purpose, alongside operations, we need relationships and we will take over from set theory the membership relationship. In set theory this relationship is denoted by **ε** (epsylon) or, more often, by a special sign similar to **∈**. In order to reduce the non-ASCII notations, I prefer to use the reserved word **in**, used with same meaning in database SQL language, to denote the membership relationship. In sync with this is the fact that the result of an SQL query is a multi-set, i.e. an aggregation.

In order to avoid contradictions, classical axiomatizations of set theory demand from the membership relationship to be acyclic, i.e., it does not admit the chains $\mathbf{s_1}$ **in ... in** $\mathbf{s_n}$, where $\mathbf{s_1} = \mathbf{s_n}$. But there are reasons for admittance of cyclic membership. So, for example, the set S of infinite sets is itself an infinite set, while „S **in** S" is true. Such set has a good and natural intuitive meaning for practice and in the intuitive set theory. Therefore, I will not demand for aggregations the membership acyclicity property, and will show that cyclic membership is also admissible for so called *open* or, more customarily „open world", aggregations.

Similarily to set theory, we can allow other entities to reside in the universe of aggregations and say them to be non-aggregations, ur-elements or *atoms*. The word „non-aggregation" is rather a definition than a term and „ur-element" is a german-latin word - a mixed formation un-welcome by linguistics, but also implying that it is necessarily an element (of an aggregation), which is not always the case. Therefore, I preferred the term *atom*. Unlike the universe of aggregations and atoms, in an arbitrary universe it is recommended to use the term *atomification*, because in Universics, atoms are regarded as obtained via the operation of *atomification*.

Additionally the notion of set, there are also other notions generalized by the term aggregation. These are the notion of set theoretic *class* - an object obtained in set theory via the abstraction denoted by $\{x : \varphi(x)\}$ (not by $\{x \in U : \varphi\}$). The notions *class, container* and *collection* of Semantic Web are also certain types of aggregations, which require separate treatment and are not in the focus of this paper. The only feature of these entities worth mentioning here is that in Semantic Web all are treated as multi-identity entities, and thus, fall under the incidence of aggregations.

4.3 Graphical representation of aggregations

The aggregations can be represented graphically as multi-hypergraphs. The multitude of identities of an aggregation is represented by multiple closed contours surrounding the elements. „To be immediately inside" is to be treated as „to be an element". Therefore, the multiple contours due to multitude of identities must intersect each other as in the Figure 3 below. The empty aggregations are represented as contours surrounding nothing. If there are atoms alongside aggregation, the atoms are represented by black pictures - here these are black small dots.

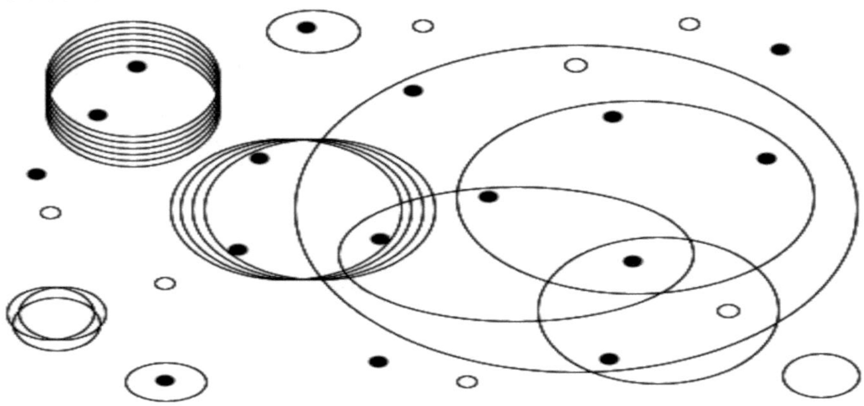

Fig. 3. A multi-hyper graph of aggregations

Notice, that the graphical representation method introduced above is rather limited. The main difficulty is with representing the complement of an aggregation. To fix this, we could introduce orientation to the contours. We can consider that the current graphical representation method is the method with oriented countours where, by default, the orientation is towards „the inside" and, therefore, it is not indicated.

Another difficulty appears when we want to enclose into a countour distant images separated by images which we don't want to inclose. Then the contour becomes so convoluted that the graph is more confusive than illustrative. This situation could be overcome by coloring the graphic elements, i.e., by using poly-chromatic multi-graphs.

The difficulties above hindered the use of hypergraphs, say nothing of poly-chromatic multigraphs, in Semantic Web, where they use only simple oriented (directed) graphs. This also hinders wide deployment of Semantic Web to deliver its methods, democratically, to biologists, chemists and other non-technical people.

4.4 Operational set theory

Because, by *agent* it is common to refer to an animate entity capable of action, and action consists of separate *operations* done by the agent, we could characterize an agent-oriented set theory as „operational" versus the usual „relational". An operational set theory must be based on *primitive operations, versus primitive relations (of membership and of being an atom) of a classical set theory*. The idea of „operational set theory" goes back to the „intuitive" or „naive" set theory developed in late 19th century. In this „theory", the sets, same as the axioms of an axiomatic set theory, are *represented* in mind as „mind content"taking the place of statements about them. Therefore such a „theory" can do without axiomatization. In other words, the „intuitive set theory" is more of a „presentation framework" than a theory. The „intuitive set theory" was replaced by axiomatic set theories (many such theories) in order to avoid contradictions which appeared in the early 20th century, but in practice it remains up to day a useful framework without raising any contradictions. Moreover, in practice, they rarely make reference to any axiomatization and one reason for this is the multitude of existing axiomatizations.

As a formal framework, Universics is an agent-oriented operational and presentational framework and it can be considered a continuation of "naive" set theory. The certainty that Universics is consistent, i.e. that it lacks contradictions, is provided by the multitude of universes of discourse which ensures that by keeping within one universe of discourse, you cannot obtain contradictions. All the contraditions found in set theory are caused by unconsiously getting outside of the unique universe of discourse. True, Universics itself also has a universe of discourse, the entities of which are universes and, probably, contradictory constructs can be designed. But, if the status of meta-discipline of Universics is observed, and it is used only to discuss about universes of discourse of other disciplines, then such contradictions are highly improbabe.

5. The universe of associations

Associations are multi-identity ordered pairs. Applying association operation multiple times is a specialty of the left hemisphere of a conceptor - a component which can be said to be a „time machine".

I will denote an association by $(a : b)$ – a denotation which differs from denotation (a, b) of an ordered pair used in set theory. As I explained above, comma denotes the assembly operator which has properties (commutativity, associativity, idemponence) different from those expected from a separator for association. Thus, the separator sign (:) widely used in many domains, including IT, will be also used for separation in denotation of an association. The notation $(a : b)$ is taken over to the A3 language as one of its primitive expressions where it has the meaning of qualification by the name *a* of the name *b*. Such notation conforms with the practice of using the colon (:) in Semantic Web languages to qualify a name by a namespace.

I am treating the notion of association as orthogonal to the notion of aggregation, and this refers both to operations and the resulting entities. The reasons for such treatment are to avoid the difficulties encountered by set theory related to the notion of ordered pair and to enable their proper handling by an agent. In set theory, the ordered pair of two entities (sets or atoms) *a* and *b* (in this order) is denoted by (a, b) and is defined as a set in different manners, where the best known definition is that of Kuratowski: $(a, b) = \{\{a\}, \{a, b\}\}$. The only requirement from any such definition is that for any entities for any entities $a, b, a', b', (a, b) = (a', b')$, if and only if $a = a'$ and $b = b'$. Various authors provided a large number of definitions of the ordered pair, each with its merits and drawbacks. Actually, the notion of ordered pair can be defined by an infinite number of non-equivalent definitions, and this is one reason, why the property above should be treated as pertaining to entities of a type different from sets, and their formation - to an operation different from that of formation of sets. This entity type and operation is the association.

Defining an ordered pair as a special type of set was dictated by the necessity to avoid introduction of an extra sort of entities different from the sort *set* (and different from the sort *atom*, if the theory is set theory with atoms). Such a definition is good only for theory, but for an agent viewing the universe of sets and ordered pairs defined as a special type of sets, such definition makes impossible the recognition of the entity type. Namely, if an agent views the set {{*a*}, {*a*, *b*}}, it does not know, whether to consider this an ordered pair or a set which, coincidentally, has same form. Also, an author who meant {{*a*}, {*a*, *b*}} to be a set, cannot encrypt this information in this denotation and would have to add it in words like „where by {{*a*}, {*a*, *b*}} I mean a set and not an ordered pair". For a virtual machine there can appear also other problems due to incomplete encryption of information. For all these reasons I regard the notion of ordered pair as *orthogonal* to the notion of set.

In set theory, the notion of n-tuple is defined by induction: $(a_1, a_2..., a_n) = (a_1, (a_2..., a_n))$.

This definition is interesting mostly for mathematics, but Semantic Web uses oriented (directed) graphs which can be represented by various superpositions of associations. This a reason, why we will introduce no default aggreement like „association to the right (left)" similar to set theory or other special domains. Various structures can be represented by different arrangement of parentheses and this is the „modeling methodology" of some programming languages like LISP. Probably, it is exactly due to the richness of structures obtained by various arrangement of parantheses that the language LISP is so powerful as to serve for the AI modeling.

The most ancient use of round parentheses is indication of the order of application of various operations in a formal expression by enclosing in round parentheses the results of some applications of various operations. We will say such use of round parentheses to be *formal association*, because sometimes such grouping is said to be „associating". We need to separate the formal use of round parentheses and their use as denotation of an association (*a* : *b*), where the round parantheses (together with colon) make part of the syntax of the A3 language to be specified later. We will agree to always use the round parantheses of the A3 language syntax except, maybe, the „external" ones of a complete expression. With such agreement, the formal association cannot create any confusion.

Given an association *A*=(*a*, *b*) we will denote *a* by **source** (*A*) and *b* by **target** (*A*). Notice that due to formal convention above, the last two notations can have also the form „**source** *A*" and „**target** *B*". In the universe of associations **source** and **target** are operations which interact with the association operation according the following correlations:

$$\textbf{source}\ (a, b) = a,\ \textbf{target}\ (a, b) = b,\ c = (\textbf{source}\ c, \textbf{target}\ c). \quad (1)$$

The term *member* (or *element*) pertains to the language of set theory, and by extension - to the language about the universe of aggregations. I will adopt this term for associations as universe two association memberships. Namely, we will say both the source and the target of an association to be elements or members of the association.

Same as the universe of aggregations, the universe of associations can also contain atoms. Associations can be graphically represented by generalized multi-orgraphs. Oriented graphs, or simply, orgraphs are also said to be directed graphs. Such graphs are used in the RDF standard of Semantic Web. In Universics, to be able to graphically represent all types of associations, we need to use multi-orgraphs, i.e. graphs with multiple directed arcs. Moreover, since there are no limitations on application of the association operation, an arc also may connect nodes with arcs or only arcs as in the Figure 3.

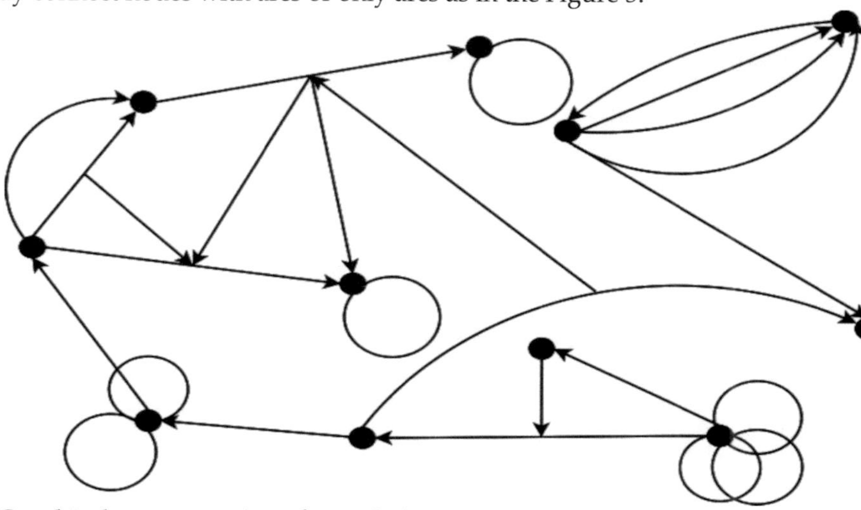

Fig. 4. Graphical representation of associations

6. The universe of atomifications

The operation and entity type called *atomification* are a new operation and entity type introduced in mathematics by Universics. The atomification operation can be treated as the operation of making a „whole" and it can be attributed to *mereology* - a term coming from Gr. „meros", „part". Mereology goes back to the beginning of the 20th century when the mathematicians were buiding a strict foundation for mathematics and most of them we focused on set theory as such a foundation. The Polish mathematician Lesniewski proposed mereology as an alternative foundation, but since only a restricted part of public could read his works in Polish, mereology is better known from the publications of the American mathematician Goodman, who also authored a monography (Goodman, 1951), where he tried to place all mathematics on the basis of this science.

Mereology was initially regarded as the science about the „part-whole" relationship, but later it was found that representing all the discipline of research was actually focused on the relationship between parts, which was then said to be *parthood* relationship, while the relation between parts and the whole remained an open problem. The aspect of „wholeness" does not seem to have been fully clarified up to our days. The atomification operation of Universics seems to clarify the aspect of „whole" from the point of view of structure.

Many mathematicians regarded mereology as a foundation for mathematics better than set theory and the competition between the two frameworks continued up to 1970's, when the „truce" was established with the aggrement that both approaches have good methods and should complement each other. Today, building a natural „bridge" between the two approaches, or even better, integrating the two approaches, is important for Semantic Web where, on one hand, many researchers develop mereology ontologies needed in various domains and, on the other hand, the semantics of Semantic Web standards is formulated in the language of set theory. As a formal framework, Universics integrates set theory and mereology into one discipline. I will now explain informally how Universics does this.

Set theory is regarded by most mathematicians as the best framework for representing structures. The mereological parthood relationship, which at a certain time in the past was regarded as all the mereology, is represented in the universe of sets as two simple relationships – the membership relationship and the sub-set relationship.

The simplicity of set theoretic methods and the illusion that all of the mereology is comprised in set theory, determined that set theory became the main formalization framework and mereology remained as just as an alternative approach. But the notion of ‚whole' is very important for any approach, say nothing about a holistic approach, and set theoretic methods cannot deal with this notion. On the other hand, mereology, even though did not offer a „final solution" regarding part-whole relationship, developed a number of good mathematical and conceptual methods to treat this relationship.

Based on the reasons formulated above, Universics takes from each discipline their strength: from set theory focused on structures – the formalization of structures, and from mereology focused on forms – the notion of a whole, for which it introduces the atomification operation of making a whole. The difference between structures and forms has been explained in section 3.2.

Now I will proceed to *atomifications*, and will start with their rudiments encountered in set theory and said to be *atoms*. In set theory, an atom is an entity within the universe of discourse which is not a set. Thus, set theory regards the two notions, set and atom, as conceptually orthogonal, i.e. irreducible to one another. To conform to Greek etymology, according which „*a-tom*" means „un-cut", the word *atom* must be treated as an entity indivisible under certain aspect. I regard such aspect of an entity as dependent on the agent's view. Namely, I treat the property of being an atom, the *atomicity*, as a kind of *opacity* of the view of this entity. In the language of behavior of a conceptor, the opacity can be expressed as interdiction to zoom into the structure of an entity. Thus, the atomicity expresses the agent's intention to ignore the structure of the entity.

The property to be an atom, the atomicity, is relative and is correlated to an agent or, more precisely, to an agent's view. This conforms with the relativity of what is said to be „indivisibility". So, in material world, the matter might be infinitely divisible and it is the agent view which determines whether something is or it is not divisible. In order to discriminate between the notion of atom described above, from other notions, say, from the notion of atom introduced in physics by Democrites, we could refer to our atom as „conceptual atom". But in this paper, we deal only with concepts and the qualification „conceptual" is superfluous.

I treat the notion of *atomification* as a common name (and concept) for the *atoms* and the „whole". The reason for such treatment is that a structure as a whole can also serve as an atom in another structure. To put it in other words, the notion of *atom* and the notion *whole* are correlated with a structure, and while an entity E is an atom of a structure T, the entity E can also be inself a structure with its atoms, or to reflect the logic in language – it can be "the *whole* of the another structure". This logic shows that „*the whole*" is an attribute (more precisely – the value of the attribute) of a structure and, thus, is different from the structure. Because by whole we are used to refer to the structure itself, I will use another name for this entity - *unity* of the structure. To sum up, a structure has atoms, maybe many *atoms*, and it has one *unity*, and I refer to both these types of entities as atomifications.

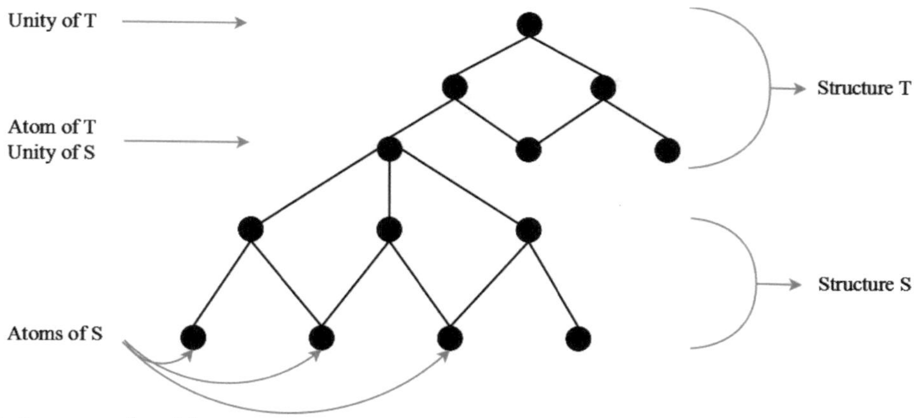

Fig. 5. Atoms and unities

The intuition behind these notions can be explained by reference to the physical matter which has a multi-layered organization in granularity levels: subatomic particles, physical atoms, planets and stars, galaxies, or to the world of biology: biomolecules, cells, animals, populations, etc. I say any of the „grains" at a certain level of granularity to be an *atomification* and regard it as obtained by an operation also said to be *atomification*.

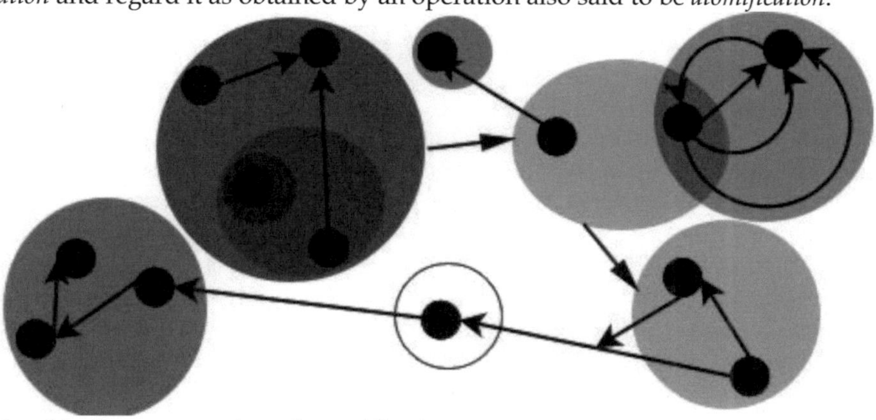

Fig. 6. Graphical representation of atomifications

A universe of atomifications is a universe governed by the part-whole relationship. Atomicity is treated by the conceptor as opacity of its view. By atomifications we mean both unity „making the whole" for a structure and the atoms of a structure. Therefore, to graphically represent a universe of aggregations, we need to draw atoms with different degrees of transparency, which still allow viewing inside an entity. Such „view control" can be generalized in order to reflect many concepts in programming.

7. The form and structure of a universe

At this point we have all the conceptuality and terminology ready to formulate the notion of universe. It is easier to define the notion of universe <u>after</u> the notion of *body*, even though the usual meaning of *body* as a „body in the Universe" implies that an inverse approach would be more appropriate. I am also using the linguistic term *corpus* (pl. *corpora*) for a body of knowledge, and I will treat these two notions structurally and formally the same. Therefore, body and corpus can be defined in one definition.

A *body* (or *corpus*) B is a tuple (A, A_1, A_2, A_3), where A is a set said to be the *foundation* of the body B, its elements are said to be *entities* of the body B, and the other components are defined as below:

1. A_1 is a 1-ary relationship (property) of "being an *atom*", or *atomicity* property, and an entity with this property - an *atom*,
2. A_2 is a 2-ary relationship over A, said to be *aggregation* relationship and, for any (i,x) in A_2 , i is said to be (*aggregation*) *unity* of the set $\{x \in A \mid (i, x) \in A_2 \}$ and x is an element of this set,
3. A_3 is a 3-ary relationship over A said to be *association* relationship and, for any (i,x,y) in A_3, i is said to be the (*association*) *unity* of the ordered pair (x,y).

An argument **i** of a n-ary relationship R is said to be *primary key*, if the following statement is true for any values of its variables:

$$\textbf{IF } (R(x_1,\dots, x_n) \textbf{ AND } R(y_1,\dots, y_n) \textbf{ AND } (x_i=y_i)) \textbf{ THEN } (\textbf{FOR ANY } j)\ (x_j=y_j). \quad (2)$$

A *universe* is said to be a body whose identities are primary keys. Examples of universes are the universes of discourse of (axiomatic) set theories.

The knowledge representation method of Universics is obtained by assigning algebraic meaning to the statement "A body of knowledge is a homomorphic image of a body in the Universe". The notion of homomorphic image formalizes the subject-object relationship for universes as it was treated above in the section 3.5.

A homomorphism of a body B=(A, A_1, A_2, A_3) into the body B'= (A', A'_1, A'_2, A'_3) is a triple (B, **h**, B'), where **h** is a function from A to A', such that **h** *preserves* each of the relationships A_n, i.e., for n=1,2,3, and a $(x_1,\dots x_n)$ **in** A_n, $\mathbf{h}(x_1,\dots x_n) = (\mathbf{h}(x_1,),\dots, h(x_n))$. This is a very compact definition which allows to generalize the notion of open function from topology, homomorphism from algebra, and introduces the notion of preservation of *discreteness* (vs *continuality*). To discover the homomorphism behavior in each of the three universal dimensions, this definition needs to be examined in detail for each value of **n**.

8. The A3 language

The vocabulary of this language consists of two sorts of atoms

- An infinite set of *main symbols,*
- *Nine auxiliary symbols*:
    - Aggregation symbols "{", "}" and comma ","
    - Association symbols "(", ")" and colon ":"
    - Atomification symbols "[", "]"
    - Equality symbol "="

In software, we can require the main symbols to be any string of Unicode characters except the auxiliary symbols. The expressions have different meaning and are named differently depending on whether they are used for denotation or for discourse. The expressions of A3 language are defined by the rules below, where the names of expressions reflect their semantics: *aggregation, association, identity.*

1. If *a* is a main symbol, then *a* is an expression said to be an *atom* (denotation), or *individual* (discourse);
   If *a* is an expression, then [*a*] is an expression said to *atomification* of *a* (denotation) or *reference* to expression *a* (discourse);
2. If *a1,..., an* are expressions, then {*a1,..., an*} is an expression called *aggregation* of *a1,..., an* (denotation) *correlation* with correlates *a1,..., an* (discourse)
3. If *a* and *b* are expressions, then (*a* : *b*) is expression said to be the *association* of *a* to *b* (denotation) or qualification of *b* by *a* (discourse);
4. If *a* is an expression, then =*a* is an expression said to be *identity* of *a.*

Since the use of the expressions of A3 language for denotation of structures was already explained, I will discuss only about its use in discourse. Notice, that a discourse is a body of knowledge, and the structure of a discourse was defined in section 7.

In Semantic Web the discourse is formulated in triples. You can read the triple <a b c > like this: "a has the property b with value c". The "synonymic" expression of the "A3 language" is ((b:c):a). Also, you may use any n-tuples in discourse, in particular, the pair (a : b) expresses the same as the triple <a rdf:type b>.

In Semantic Web, in order to make reference to a set of triples (graph), you have to write complex XML code. In A3, you enclose a set of expressions ((b:c):a) between braces and qualify this construct. You may also represent this structurally as in programming languages – closing brace under opening brace.

In languages of Semantic Web, you cannot name a triple or a discourse other than by wrapping them in complex XML code. In A3 language you just enclose the text between square brakets.

The statement that two names are equal (synonymy) is represented in OWL by the triple <*a* owl:sameAs *b*> - in A3 it is represented as *a*:=*b* ("*a* qualifies the identity of *b*").

In Semantic Web, there is a special technique and are used long expressions to express an n-ary relationship. In A3 language, you just name the correlates of the relationship and enclose them between braces. You can also qualify this expression to obtain different relationships with same signature of names for the correlates.

Blank nodes of Semantic Web are just "temporary names" which can be changed by other names, and in A3 language, you just precede such names with an equality sign with the meaning "equal to any other name". To comply with notation of blank node of Semantic Web, a special name denoted undersore "_" can be added to A3 language as "syntactic sugar", so that for any name *a*, "_:*a*" is defined as "=*a*".

In Semantic Web there is no possibility to express syntactic correlations between expressions - in particular, you cannot define one expression through other expressions. In A3, you just enclose such expressions between square brakets. Say, to denote the expression "x+y/2" by "f(x, y)", you just write [f(x,y)]:=[x+y/2].

9. Aknoledgements

I would like to express my gratitude to my friend Bettin Mironov, a great physicist, who managed to reduce the physical laws to interaction of waves (Mironov, 2007). The long

discussions with him provided "physical intuition" which helped in my mathematical research .
I am also greatful to my colleague Grigoriy Kunetskiy whose "difficulties" in implementing Universics in software and sharp "feeling of truth" helped so much to formulate correct definitions.

10. References

Church, A. (1941). The Theory of Lambda Conversion, Princeton University Press, (1941).

Chen, P. (1976), The entity-relationship model - towards a unified view of data, ACM Transactions on Database Systems (TODS), v.1. n.1, (March 1976), p.9-36

Codd, E. (1970), A relational Model of Data for Large Shared Data Banks. Communications of the ACM, Vol.13, No.7, (June 1970), pp.377-387

Cohen, P. (1963). "The Independence of the Continuum Hypothesis". Proceedings of theNational Academy of Sciences of the United States of America 50 (6), (December 1963), pp. 1143–1148.

Cohen, P. (1964). The Independence of the Continuum Hypothesis, II". Proceedings of the National Academy of Sciences of the United States of America 51 (1), (January, 1964), pp. 105–110.

Drugus, I. (1982). Forest superintuitionistic logics. Doklady Academii Nauk SSSR. (February, 1982). Volume 262. Nr 3.

Drugus, I. (2007), A Wholebrain approach to the Web. In: Proceedings of the „Web Intelligence - Intelligent Agent Technology Conference", Silicon Valley, (November, 2007).

Drugus, I. (2009), Universics - a structural framework for knowledge representation. Knowledge Engineering: Principles and Techniques Conference. Studia Universitatis, Babes-Bolyai, (July, 2009), pp. 115-118

Drugus, I. (2009), Universics: an Approach to Knowledge based on Set theory. In: Knowledge Engineering Principles and Techniques, Selected Extended Papers (Cluj-Napoca, Romania, July 2-4, 2009), Presa Universitara Clujeana (October, 2009), pp. 193-200.

Goodman, N (1951), The structure of appearence, Harvard University Press - Cambridge - Massachusetts. (1951) Stewart, I. (1973). Galois Theory, Chapman and Hall, (1973)

Mironov, B (2007), Mechanisms of electromagnetic and gravitational fields, (2007)

Turing, A.M. (1936/7). On computable numbers, with an application to the Entscheidungs problem, Proceedings of the London Mathematical Society 42, pp. 230-265. (1936/7)

Turing, A.M. (1937). Computability and λ-definability, Journal of Symbolic Logic 2, pp. 153-163 (1937)

5

Autonomous hypothetical reasoning: the case for open-minded agents

Aspassia Daskalopulu and Georgios K. Giannikis
University of Thessaly
Greece

1. Introduction

This chapter is concerned with *intelligent* software agents that populate *open* computational environments, in which they *interact* for various purposes, and in various manners, e.g. competitively in the case of electronic auctions or resource allocation problems, collaboratively in the case of distributed problem solving, parallel processing, joint planning, etc. By the term 'intelligent' we refer to agents that are *autonomous* (i.e. they decide for themselves what action to perform in order to meet their design goals), *rational* (i.e. they choose the best available course of action in order to meet their design goals; more precisely, they are *computationally rational*, in that they base their decision on the information available to them at the time of decision-making), and *social* (i.e. their interaction goes beyond mere data exchange and resembles social interaction among humans, that is, they may exchange promises, enter negotiations, raise requests, make demands, and so on). We use the term 'open' to characterize a computational environment in the sense defined by Hewitt (Hewitt, 1985), that is, in order to refer to an environment that is dynamic, continuous, unobservable (or, at best, partially observable) and non-deterministic. The interactions among agents in any multi-agent system are typically governed by *norms* that regulate the behaviour of the agents in the specific environment. Norms prescribe what behaviours are socially acceptable within a particular context, that is they specify what actions are obligatory, permitted or forbidden for each agent, in various circumstances, and usually within associated time bounds. For instance, norms may be used to regulate the agents' communication and coordination, and to specify liveness and safety properties of each agent, as well as the whole multi-agent system. In some cases, for example in electronic auction markets, or an information grid to which agents subscribe, these norms are designed *a priori* by the market owner, and when an agent joins the particular forum, this is taken to signal tacitly that the agent agrees to be subject to the market 'contract' that is specified by these norms. In other application areas, such as e-commerce exchanges or ad hoc distributed problem solving, and ad hoc task and resource allocation problems, agents may negotiate and agree between themselves the norms that will govern their interaction; by agreeing on a set of norms, agents signal tacitly that they agree to be subject to the 'contract' that is specified by these norms. However, since agents are autonomous and rational, and since the environment is open, their actual behaviour may deviate from the ideal behaviour prescribed by the 'contract', whether intentionally or unintentionally. For example, an agent that is obliged to perform a particular calculation at some specific time point, and return the result to some other agent, in a distributed problem solving scenario, may fail to comply with its obligation because at the designated time the agent lacked the computational resources to perform the calculation, or because by the time the agent completed the computation, it lost its communication means and could not deliver the result to the intended recipient; in an e-commerce scenario, a provider agent that is obliged to deliver a specific service or goods to a consumer agent may fail to do so, because it chose to deliver the service or goods to some other agent instead, after it established that the income that it would receive in this way outweighed the reparation costs that it would owe to the consumer agent. Autonomous agents decide for themselves what actions to perform, as noted earlier, and this decision includes the decision on whether to comply with the 'contract' that governs their behaviour. An agent's rationality is measured against the quality of its decisions, and this relies heavily on the quantity and quality of information that the agent possesses at the time point of decision-making. Unavoidably, agents is open environments possess information that is incomplete, imprecise, maybe even incorrect, due to the very fact that the environment is open and, at the very least, agents join and leave it as they choose. Information exchange between agents may be delayed, and message content may be distorted by noise during communication; it may even be intentionally false in the case of insincere agents. It is natural, therefore, to expect that agents will have to perform their decision-making by employing assumptions, in order to fill in what they perceive as information gaps. Assumption identification and deployment must be dynamic, since the agents operate in a dynamic environment, and the agents' reasoning must be nonmonotonic, since any conclusions drawn on the basis of assumptions may need to be revised, should information that was previously missing become available later.

We begin by motivating the need for dynamic and autonomous hypothetical reasoning, and we identify and state explicitly three aspects of this problem in the context of open norm-governed environments. Then we present our approach to dynamic assumption identification and usage, and we demonstrate the way in which it permits agents to establish their current knowledge state, as well as their current assumption requirements, autonomously. Our approach exploits the syntax of Default Logic (DfL) rules (Reiter, 1980), in order to separate the definite knowledge from the assumptions that are used in drawing a conclusion; however, as we explain later, assumption identification and deployment is conducted without resorting to proof, which is notably computationally hard. Finally, we review and discuss the main other approaches to assumption-based reasoning found in the Artificial Intelligence literature. We should note from the outset that the distinctive feature of our approach, which sets it apart from these other approaches, is that agents do not rely on a pre-specified pool of assumptions, in order to identify their assumption requirements. Nor do they rely on goal-orientation, as a means to identify candidate assumptions. In this way, we argue, an agent is *open-minded*, in that it decides for itself which assumptions are plausible and appropriate at any given time, and crucially, this involves making assumptions about its past, as well as its future; as it turns out it manages assumption deployment in a rational manner.

2. Who needs assumptions and when?

Rule-based knowledge representation, typically in first-order logic or some subset of it, has become popular and is used in many symbolic Artificial Intelligence applications, in order to encode domain information, as well as the decision-making behaviour of the system. Typically, rules have the form of sequent calculus sentences (Jean-Yves Girard and Lafont, 1989), i.e.

$$Y \leftarrow X_1, X_2, \ldots, X_k \quad (1)$$

where Y and Xi ($1 \leq i \leq k$) are positive or negative literals (any variables are assumed to be universally quantified) representing the rule conclusion and conditions, respectively. The semantics of such a rule is "*if all of the conditions Xi hold, then conclusion Y holds*". The system checks whether conditions hold against its knowledge base, and the conclusion Y it draws, in case the conditions are true given its knowledge, may result in belief revision – the knowledge base is updated to contain new information – or in the actualization of some behaviour – the system does something, and this action may be private (some internal computation), or public (e.g. the dispatch of a message, or, in the case of robotic agents, the performance of some action that transforms the environment in some way).

A question that arises naturally is: what happens when the system does not know all of the conditions Xi that are involved in some rule contained in its knowledge base, i.e. it does not have explicit information, in its knowledge base, about the truth or falsity of some, or all of the conditions of a rule? There are two options: (i) if the system employs the Closed World Assumption (CWA) (Reiter, 1977) - anything not explicitly known is considered false - then the unknown conditions are treated as false, and hence the rule does not apply; (ii) if the system employs the Open World Assumption (OWA) - anything not explicitly known is considered neither true, nor false, merely unknown - then the evaluation of unknown conditions is unsuccessful, and, again, the rule does not apply. In the first case the system deals with information gaps by filling them in, in a narrow-minded manner, based only on its set of beliefs; in the second case, the system is open-minded, in that it remains agnostic about missing information, allowing for the possibility that something it does not know may be true, but this stance is counterproductive, since the system cannot in effect apply its rule. In the worst case, if all of the rules of its knowledge base do not apply, because some of their conditions are unknown given the current knowledge base, the system will do nothing, whether it employs the CWA or the OWA. At best, in order to avoid idleness, the system may ask its user to determine the truth value of the information it lacks. This is, in fact, the classic approach to inference employed in expert systems, where the system user becomes responsible for the quality of information that is available to the system, and ultimately for the quality of the conclusions that the system draws. The user herself may not have definite knowledge about the missing information, yet she may want the system to proceed and produce even a tentative result; in this case the user provides an answer to the system, noting to herself that this answer is, in fact, an assumption that she makes for the time being, yet the system is not aware that it is employing an assumption, nor does it have any control over assumption deployment, since it is not up to it to decide whether to use the answer provided by the user or not.

This approach is clearly inappropriate for intelligent agents, which are, after all, designed and developed in order to perform tasks delegated to them by humans, and which by definition, must behave autonomously and rationally. Typically, intelligent agents interact with other agents in a designated computational or physical environment, and this interaction is regulated by norms that stipulate what each agent is obliged, permitted, prohibited, institutionally empowered and so on to do, much in the same spirit that human agent interaction is regulated by the Law, organizational, and other formal, or informal, social rules. Human agents do not always comply with legal, organizational and social norms. The mere existence of these norms, whose purpose is to describe which behaviours are acceptable, encouraged, or even imperative, does not guarantee that their subjects will, in fact, behave accordingly. The actual behaviour that a human agent demonstrates deviates, quite often, from the ideal, and this may happen intentionally or unintentionally. It may be the case that a human agent knows what the norm prescribes, knows the consequences of a potential violation, but nonetheless chooses to violate it, for various reasons – she cannot do otherwise, or she judges that the penalty associated with the violation is worth paying, for the violation itself results in some state that she considers in some way positive, given her subjective value system. It may be the case that human agents violate norms unintentionally, often for the simple reason that they do not know that specific norms apply. In similar spirit, autonomous, rational, artificial agents cannot be expected to behave in accordance to the norms that govern their virtual societies, for the simple reason that they are designed and developed to act in the interest of their human/organizational owners, in accordance with the latter's value systems and goals.

Social norms may be thought of as rules of the form (1), shown above, where the conditions Xi and the conclusion Y refer not only to application domain entities, but to normative notions as well, which characterize agents' actions, or the states of affairs that can be effected by agents' actions; the main normative notions are obligation, permission, prohibition, and institutional power (the ability to create normative relations). For instance, in an electronic commerce scenario, a norm may specify that "*if the seller agent delivers the specified quantity of goods to the buyer agent by the due date, then the buyer agent is obliged to pay the specified amount to the seller agent by a specified date*"; in a distributed problem solving scenario, a norm may specify that "*if the planning agent computes a partial plan for a specified goal, then it is permitted for the planning agent to send the partial plan it computed to the coordinator agent immediately*", or that "*a planning agent is prohibited from sending partial solutions without being asked to do so by the coordinator agent*", and another may specify that "*the coordinator agent is prohibited from computing the final plan, unless it has received partial plans for all of the subgoals that it allocated to planning agents*"; in a task or resource allocation scenario a norm may specify that "*the scheduler agent is permitted to change the order of print jobs in the printer queue, when a print job arrives from a designated port, which is to be treated as an emergency port*", or another norm may specify that "*a scheduler agent is empowered to impose an obligation on a printer agent that processes jobs in first-in-first-out manner to start processing jobs in shortest-job-first manner, whenever the queue reaches a certain capacity*"

In order for an agent to decide whether to comply or not with a norm, first it must establish that the norm applies, and to do this it must be able to establish both factual information and prescriptive information, given a history of events that have occurred up to the point of its query. We saw earlier that a system that lacks information about rule conditions cannot apply its rules and, inevitably, if it is not to remain idle, it has to resort to its owner and obtain answers from her. This is not a realistic solution in the case of autonomous, rational agents, which are designed to act on behalf of their owners – idleness is not an attractive option, and an autonomous agent is expected to turn to its owner for help only in extreme circumstances!

Obviously agents in any system (not necessarily open) do not possess information about the future. In order for an agent to meet its design goals, though, and plan its course of action at any given time, it needs to fill in information gaps by employing assumptions about the future. In open computational environments, even the historical information available to an agent when it poses its query may be incomplete, for various reasons: Information may be lost, or distorted by noise, and in a truly open system, where agents join or leave the system at different times, information delivery from agent to agent may simply be delayed. In order to reason in the absence of complete historical knowledge, agents must be able to fill in information gaps, by employing assumptions about the past and the present. One might argue that it would be reasonable for an agent to adopt the CWA in order to deal with information gaps that concern the past, and the OWA in order to deal with information gaps that concern the future. However, such an agent would not be truly open-minded, in that it would treat the historical information that it would possess as definitive. And in any case, as we argued earlier, both the adoption of the CWA and the adoption of the OWA have the same practical effect: the agent would remain idle, or it would need to resort to its owner, in order to fill in information gaps and proceed with its inferences.

Therefore assumption-based reasoning is useful in two modes, progressively, because the agent cannot know the future, and retrospectively, because the agent may not know the past. Progressive hypothetical reasoning is sometimes referred to as *best-guess reasoning*, while retrospective hypothetical reasoning is sometimes referred to as *no-risk reasoning*.

- *Best-guess reasoning*: An agent cannot know the future, yet it may need to plan its activities on the basis of hypotheses that concern the future, i.e., on the assumption that certain events or other agents' actions will occur, or that certain causal relations will be effected in the environment, or that it will bear a certain normative status (obligations, permissions, prohibitions, powers) towards other agents.
- *No-risk reasoning*: An agent may not know everything about the past and present, i.e., the history of its environment, other agents and itself so far, yet it may need to plan its activities on the basis of hypotheses that concern the past and present, i.e., on the assumption that certain events or other agents' actions have occurred, or that certain normative relations have obtained between itself and other agents, in order to protect itself from an undesirable situation in the future.

To illustrate these cases, consider a business transaction that takes place in an electronic marketplace populated by software agents. A buyer agent communicates, at time point T, with a seller agent and establishes an agreement with it for purchasing a certain product. Consequently, the seller agent communicates with a carrier agent and establishes another agreement with it for the timely and safe delivery of goods to the buyer agent. A reasonable query that the buyer agent might have might be general, such as "*What do I have to do from now on, with respect to this contract?*". The buyer agent would expect a list of all the obligations, permissions, prohibitions, etc. that arise for it as a result of entering this agreement, along with their associated times, which may be relatively or absolutely defined. However, such an answer can only be derived on a hypothetical basis, that is on the assumption that the buyer agent's order will be received correctly and on time by the seller agent, that the seller agent will acknowledge its obligation to respond to such an order with delivery, and that it will, in fact, be able and willing to provide the required quantity and quality of goods in time, that the buyer agent will acknowledge its obligation to pay for the goods that it will receive, and so on. The buyer agent's query about the future might be more specific, such as *"When will I, potentially, have to pay for this order, assuming all goes well and I receive the goods in due time, so that I plan to have adequate available funds?"*. To derive an answer the buyer, again, needs to reason on the basis of future hypotheses, i.e. to perform best-guess reasoning. Now, consider the case where, after placing an order at time T, the buyer agent at some subsequent time point T'' (T<T''), wonders *"I placed an order at time point T, and so far I have not received any information about how this order is proceeding. What if the seller agent has already dispatched the goods to me, and is expecting payment from me, while I am blissfully unaware that I should do something about this?"*. In this case, the buyer agent does not know whether the carrier agent has performed delivery at some point T', such that T<T'<T''. Unless the buyer agent resorts to an assumption about the past (that delivery happened at some time point T'), that is unless it performs no-risk reasoning, it cannot infer that an obligation for it to pay the seller has become active, and it risks finding itself in the undesirable situation, where its time allowance for paying has expired and it now bears a sanction, say to pay some extra amount to the seller agent, to compensate for missing its deadline.

We see that the reasoning problem faced by an agent in this context involves the following aspects:

1H. *Assumption identification and usage*: What assumptions are applicable to fill in information gaps and how should these be employed in the inference process?

2H. *Assumption influence*: What is the relation between the assumptions and the current or future world, i.e. how do assumptions employed at a given time point enable or restrict present and future conclusions?

3H. *Assumption corroboration*: What happens when new information becomes available at some time point, confirming or disproving assumptions employed at earlier time points, or conclusions drawn at earlier time points?

In order to address question 1H an agent seeks to identify appropriate assumptions, and because it operates in an open, essentially dynamic, environment, assumption identification must be carried out dynamically. In order to answer question 2H the agent needs to employ some way that commits its reasoning to the specific assumptions that it employs, from that moment onwards. Finally, in order to answer question 3H the agent needs to reason nonmonotonically.

There are many interesting approaches to dynamic assumption-based reasoning, which we review in section 4, after we present our approach in section 3. We stress from the outset that these approaches rely either on the existence of a pre-specified assumption space or on pre-specified criteria for the identification of assumptions. In the first case, assumption identification is not really dynamic, rather assumption usage, i.e. the management of the pre-specified assumption space, may be done dynamically. In the second case assumption identification is dynamic, only in the sense that the appropriate assumption is chosen at run-time, but since this choice is made on pre-specified criteria, it is in a sense static. What distinguishes, therefore, our work from these approaches, is that we propose a way in which both identification and usage of appropriate candidate assumptions are done dynamically. In this way, we argue, the agent is truly autonomous in deciding what assumptions to employ and when to employ them. We start by presenting our approach, before we review these other approaches, in order to facilitate the reader in appreciating these differences, without getting lost in technical detail.

3. Autonomous hypothetical reasoning

In (Giannikis and Daskalopulu, 2006, Giannikis and Daskalopulu, 2007) we proposed an approach for representing norms (focussing specifically on e-contracts), as Default Theories (DfT), constructed dynamically from an initial Event Calculus (EC) representation (Kowalski and Sergot, 1986).

Many researchers have explored the use of temporal logics for the representation of e-contracts (e.g. (Marvn and Sartor, 1999, Artikis *et al.*, 2002, Farrell *et al.*, 2005, Rouached *et al.*, 2005)), and have demonstrated how such representations allow us to establish the state of a business exchange, given the actions that parties perform or omit to perform. On the basis of such a representation and in order to support nonmonotonic reasoning, one might use some of the various approaches such as Circumscription (McCarthy, 1980), Logic Programs (Gelfond and Lifschitz, 1988, Gelfond and Lifschitz, 1991), or Defeasible Logic (Nute, 1994), as many other researchers have done. In (Giannikis and Daskalopulu, 2007) we discussed in detail our view on the extent to which these approaches can cope with hypothetical reasoning, and argued for the adoption of Default Logic for the following reasons:

(i) The syntax of DfL offers a natural way to represent separately what is known, what is assumed and what is concluded on the basis of this knowledge and assumptions. We saw an opportunity to exploit this syntax, in order to address the first aspect (1H) of our problem, namely assumption identification and usage.

(ii) The semantics of DfL offers a way to reason nonmonotonically and to preserve the relation of an assumption and any inferences drawn on its basis. This enables us to address the second and the third aspect (2H, 3H) of our problem, namely assumption influence and assumption corroboration.

However, we should note that although we exploit the syntax of DfL, we do not resort to proof in DfL, which is notably computationally hard. Instead we adapt an incremental technique for the computation of possible world models, initially proposed in (Antoniou, 1999) which requires set manipulation.

3.1 Preliminaries

A default rule (henceforth default) has the form:

$$P : J_1, J_2, \ldots J_n \,/\, C,$$

where P is the prerequisite, $J=\{J_1,J_2,\ldots J_n\}$ is a set of justifications, and C is the derived consequent of the rule. The semantics of this rule is: If P holds and the justifications contained in J are consistent with the current knowledge, then C may be inferred. A DfT is a pair of the form (W, D), where W is a set of propositional or predicate logic formulae that represent currently available knowledge, and D is a set of defaults. A default is applicable to a deductively closed set of formulae $E \supseteq W$, if and only if $P \in E$ and $\neg J_1 \notin E, \ldots, \neg J_n \notin E$. The set E is called the *extension* of the DfT. The notion of extension is the most complicated concept of Reiter's logic, because it is hard to determine an accurate belief set for which justifications should be consistent. In his initial paper on DfL (Reiter, 1980) Reiter noted three important properties of extensions: (i) an extension E of a DfT (W, D) should contain W, (ii) the extension E of a DfT should be deductively closed, and (iii) for a default rule of the form $P:J_1,J_2,\ldots J_n / C$, if $P \in E$ and $\neg J_1,\ldots, \neg J_n \notin E$ then $C \in E$.

The requirement that the extension of a DfT be deductively closed is computationally problematic. However, Antoniou in (Antoniou, 1999) proposed a useful operational definition of extensions and a technique for their computation, which is done incrementally, by maintaining syntactically consistent sets of formulae, whose conditions part (prerequisites and justifications) is interpreted conjunctively and the conclusions part (consequent) is interpreted disjunctively, as in sequent calculus.

Let Π represent a default reasoning process by recording the order in which defaults from D apply. At each step i of the reasoning process, i.e. after the application of each default $P:J_1,J_2,\ldots,J_n/C$, the extension computed is a set of ground sentences $In(i)=In(i-1) \cup \{C\}$, and the set of justifications employed, which should not turn out to be true, is $Out(i) = Out(i-1) \cup \{\neg J_1\ldots, \neg J_n\}$. As a result, $\Pi(i)= \Pi(i-1) \cup \{Di \mid Di$ is the default rule which applied at step $i\}$. Initially $In(0)=W$, $Out(0)=\varnothing$ and $\Pi(0)=\varnothing$ for i=0. The default reasoning process $\Pi(i)$ is successful if and only if $In(i) \cap Out(i)= \varnothing$, otherwise it is failed. Moreover, the process $\Pi(i)$ is closed if and only if every default rule that belongs in the set D and is applicable to In(i) already occurs in $\Pi(i)$. According to (Antoniou, 1999) a set of formulae E is a DfT extension, if there is a closed and successful process $\Pi(i)$ of the DfT such that E=In(i).

For a quick illustration of these concepts, consider the DfT (W, D), where W={A} and D contains the following defaults:

$$D1 \equiv A : B / C$$

$$D2 \equiv true : \neg D / E$$

The process $\Pi(2)=\{D1,D2\}$, i.e. $In(2)=\{A,C,E\}$ and $Out(2)=\{\neg B,D\}$, is successful and closed, thus it is considered as an extension of the theory.

Now, consider the DfT (W, D), where W={A} and D contains the following defaults:

$$D1 \equiv A : B / C$$

$$D2 \equiv true : D / \neg B$$

The process $\Pi(2)=\{D1,D2\}$, i.e. $In(2)=\{A,C,\neg B\}$ and $Out(2)=\{\neg B,\neg D\}$, is closed but not successful, thus it is not considered as an extension of the theory. The process $\Pi(1)=\{D2\}$, i.e. $In(1)=\{A,\neg B\}$ and $Out(1)=\{\neg D\}$, is successful and closed, since D1 does not apply, thus it is considered as an extension of the theory.

3.2 The idea in a nutshell

We saw an opportunity to exploit the syntax of default rules in order to represent the inference relation between what the agent knows definitely (the premises in Reiter's terms), what the agent can assume, consistently with its current knowledge (the justifications in Reiter's terms), and what the agent can infer on the basis of its current knowledge and the assumptions that it adopts (the consequent in Reiter's terms). Therefore, the basic idea of our approach, which was initially proposed in our (Giannikis and Daskalopulu, 2006), is to have agents reason, via constructing extensions of default theories, using Antoniou's incremental technique. To achieve this, the agents must reason with default theories, that is, their knowledge base, whose contents are initially in the form of sentences of sequent calculus, must be translated into default rules.

Recall, that initially an agent's knowledge base contains sentences of the form (1):

$$Y \leftarrow X_1, X_2, \ldots, X_k$$

where Y and Xi ($1 \leq i \leq k$) are positive or negative literals (any variables are assumed universally quantified) representing the rule conclusion and conditions, respectively. A rule of such a form must be translated into a default rule, where what the agent knows definitely will be captured by the prerequisite component, what the agent does not know will be captured by the justification component, and the conclusion Y will be captured by the consequent component. In principle the agent's definite knowledge changes over time, while it interacts with other agents and it perceives its environment, so in principle any one or all of the conditions Xi of such a rule may be known or unknown. Hence, a single rule of the form (1) shown above may be mapped to *any* one of the following default rules:

- To the single assumption-free default of the form $X_1, X_2, \ldots, X_k$: true / Y, just in case the agent possesses definite knowledge about all of the conditions Xi, and therefore needs to make no assumptions, in order to be able to apply the rule and derive a conclusion.
- To k one-assumption defaults, that correspond to the k possible situations, where the agent possesses definite knowledge about k-1 of the conditions Xi, and needs to make a single assumption for the unknown condition, that is to one of the defaults of the set:

$$\{ X_1, X_2, \ldots, X_{k-1} : X_k / Y,$$
$$X_1, X_2, \ldots, X_{k-2}, X_k : X_{k-1} / Y,$$
$$X_1, X_2, \ldots, X_{k-1}, X_k : X_{k-2} / Y,$$
$$\ldots$$
$$X_2, \ldots, X_k : X_1 / Y \}$$

- To k(k-1)/2 two-assumption defaults, that correspond to the k(k-1)/2 possible situations, where the agent possesses definite knowledge about (k-2) of the conditions Xi, and needs to make assumptions for the two unknown conditions, that is to one of the defaults of the set:

$$\{ X_1, X_2, \ldots, X_{k-2} : X_{k-1}, X_k / Y,$$
$$X_1, X_2, \ldots, X_{k-3}, X_{k-1} : X_{k-2}, X_k / Y,$$
$$X_1, X_2, \ldots, X_{k-4}, X_{k-2}, X_{k-1} : X_{k-3}, X_k / Y,$$
$$\ldots$$
$$X_3, \ldots, X_k : X_1, X_2 / Y \}$$

- In similar spirit, to any one of the set containing three-assumption defaults, four-assumption defaults and so on, right down to the single k-assumption default, which corresponds to the case where the agent knows nothing and has to make assumptions about everything, i.e. true : $X_1, \ldots, X_k$ / Y.

So, each initial rule, which involves k conditions, may be translated into any one of 2^k defaults[1]. The question is, which one is the appropriate one? And the answer is, let the agent decide, depending on its current knowledge/absence of knowledge state, that is, let the agent determine what it knows and what it needs to make assumptions about, dynamically, as its knowledge base evolves over time.
Our first proposal for the translation of an agent's initial knowledge base into a DfT appeared in (Giannikis and Daskalopulu, 2007): Given a sequent calculus rule in its knowledge base, the agent would construct a default rule by mapping the conclusion of the rule to the consequent part of the default, all of the conditions Xi that could be proved from its knowledge base to the prerequisite part of the default, and the remaining conditions that could not be proved from its knowledge base to the justification part of the default. Although this is a correct formal characterization of the intended translation, it is computationally unacceptable, since it requires an agent to attempt to prove literals from its knowledge base, in order to decide whether to use them in the prerequisite or the justification part of each default that it constructs. In other words, the agent needs to attempt to prove literals (and fail in doing so) in order to identify candidate assumptions. In order to overcome this limitation we proposed an alternative view in (Giannikis and Daskalopulu, 2008), which is suitable for implementation, and relies on structuring hierarchically the 2^k possible translations into a multi-level structure and have the agent traverse it. We present this in detail in the next section.

3.3 Default theory construction and inference

We may think of the 2^k possible defaults for a single rule of the form (1) as representations of the possible mental states in which the agent may find itself. Each such state is characterized by what is known and what is not known to the agent, i.e. it represents what we may call the single-rule knowledge/hypothesis (KH) status of the agent. These possible states are organized in a multi-level hierarchy, which we depict as a triangle, such as the one shown in Figure 1. The top of the triangle shows the direction in which the agent's mental state evolves over time. Each level of the KH structure contains those of the 2^k possible default translations of the rule that contain as many assumptions as indicated by the number of the leverl, that is level 0 contains the single assumption-free default, level 1 contains the k one-assumption defaults, and so on, until the top level which contains the single, knowledge-free default. That is, for a an agent which possesses an initial rule of the form (1), moving upwards in a stepwise manner until it reaches the top level of the single-norm KH structure, is tantamount to identifying candidate assumptions among the conditions that are included in the initial rule. Defaults contained in the same level have the same number of assumptions; the defaults of any given level contain one more assumption than the defaults of the immediately lower level, and one fewer assumption than the defaults of the

1 To be precise, we should note that there is one more default that could be used as the translation of the initial sequent calculus rule, namely the normal default of the form $X_1, \ldots, X_k : Y / Y$, which corresponds to the case where the agent knows all of the conditions, and proceeds to infer Y, if assuming it is consistent with its current knowledge. There is a short philosophical discussion that can be made about this point, but we leave it aside for the time being, and we shall return to it in the discussion at the end of this section, after we have presented the details of our approach.

immediately higher level. Let | L | denote the total number of defaults contained at level L, where $0 \leq L \leq k$, and k is the total number of conditions in an initial rule of the form (1). Then, it is easy to verify that the following properties hold:

- $|L| = 1$ if $L = 0$
- $|L| = (k - L + 1) * |L-1| / L$ if $L \neq 0$

To illustrate this idea consider the following rule, given in the initial sequent calculus form, which involves four conditions (k=4):

$Y \leftarrow X_1, X_2, X_3, X_4$

The corresponding 5-level triangle is:

Level 0: $\{ X_1,X_2,X_3,X_4 : true / Y \}$

Level 1: $\{ X_1,X_2,X_3 : X_4 / Y,$
$X_1,X_2,X_4 : X_3 / Y,$
$X_1,X_3,X_4 : X_2 / Y,$
$X_2,X_3,X_4 : X_1 / Y \}$

Level 2: $\{ X_1,X_2 : X_4, X_3 / Y,$
$X_1,X_3 : X_4, X_2 / Y,$
$X_2,X_3 : X_4, X_1 / Y,$
$X_1,X_4 : X_3, X_2 / Y,$
$X_2,X_4 : X_3, X_1 / Y,$
$X_3,X_4 : X_2, X_1 / Y \}$

Level 3: $\{ X_1 : X_4, X_3, X_2 / Y,$
$X_2 : X_4, X_3, X_1 / Y,$
$X_3 : X_4, X_2, X_1 / Y,$
$X_4 : X_3, X_2, X_1 / Y \}$

Level 4: $\{ true : X_4,X_3,X_2,X_1 / Y \}$

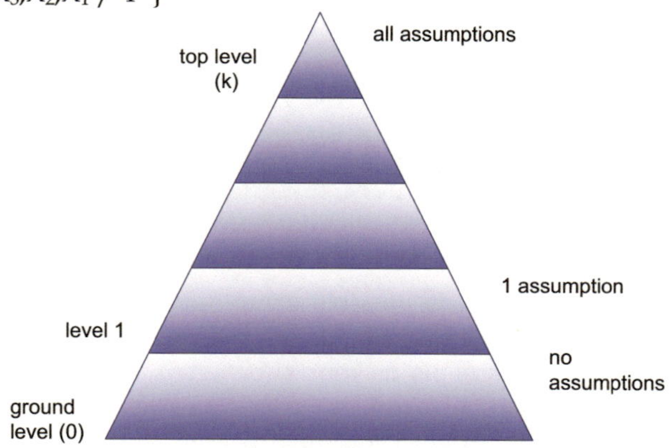

Fig. 1. Single-rule KH structure of an agent's mental states

An agent's initial knowledge base will typically contain many rules, for each of which the agent constructs a KH structure. All the resulting single-rule KH structures are composed into a single polygon-like structure (Figure 2), which contains as many levels as the tallest of the constituent single-rule KH structures. Given an initial set of rules, the number of levels of the multi-rule KH structure is equal to the maximum k_i, where $1 \leq i \leq r$ and r is the number of the initial norms of the form (1). To be precise, we should note that the multi-rule KH structure does not have a single top, since each constituent single-rule KH structure may have its own top level. We are interested in the highest amongst these top levels, since this denotes the point of termination of an agent's inference process, when an agent moves upwards in the multi-rule KH structure and its mental state evolves over time.
Therefore, the full DfT that is constructed by an agent is a pair of the form (W, D), where W contains all of the available (if any) historical information and D is the multi-rule KH structure. Level 0 contains the r assumption-free defaults, level 1 contains the $\sum^{r}_{i=1} k_i$ one-assumption defaults, and so on, until the top $\max(k_i)$ level, which contains some of the knowledge-free defaults.
Note that, although the corresponding rule mapping is one-to-many, only one default for each initial rule may finally be employed for inference. The inference process starts from the ground level, by applying as many defaults as possible given the agent's current knowledge. Each time a default applies its consequent is included in the extension that is being computed currently. When there are no further defaults that can be applied in a level, this signals to the agent that assumptions are needed in order to proceed, and inference continues by examining defaults that lie in the next level upwards.

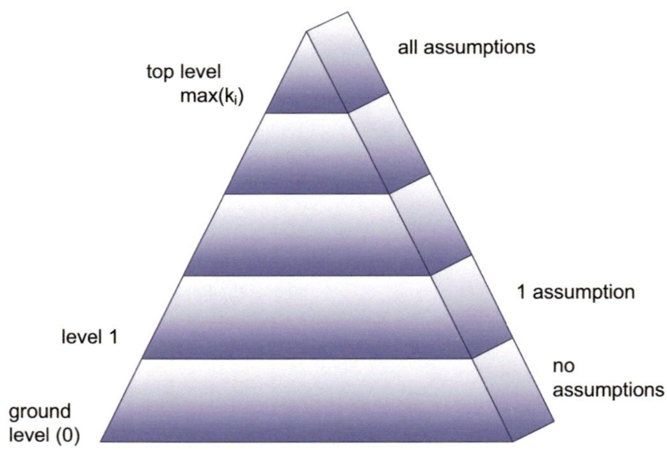

Fig. 2. Multi-rule KH structure of an agent's mental states

Note that the case where reasoning is possible using only rules from the ground level is identical to inference in classical logic. During its reasoning process an agent infers all possible conclusions on the basis of its current knowledge. When no further inference is possible, the agent is able to reassess its mental state and establish its knowledge/hypothesis status, in order to continue. That is, the agent first attempts to draw conclusions using only assumption-free defaults, then by employing one assumption per default, then by employing two assumptions per default, and so on, until no further defaults

apply. In other words, a general priority criterion among defaults is being established: This is the number of assumptions employed via the use of a default rule. Thus, such inference in a step-wise manner ensures that the agent employs the fewest possible hypotheses, always, that is, that the agent is rational in its deployment of assumptions.
To illustrate the inference procedure, consider this next example: let us assume that a normative system comprises two rules of the form:

$$R1 \equiv Y_1 \leftarrow X_1, X_2$$

$$R2 \equiv Y_2 \leftarrow X_3, X_4, X_5$$

Thus, the corresponding single-rule and multi-rule KH structures are as follows ($D_{level,number}$ denotes the level of the default and its identification number within its level, and it is used to facilitate reference):

Single-rule KH structure for R1:
Level 0: { $D1_{0,1} \equiv X_1,X_2 : true \,/\, Y_1$ }

Level 1: { $D1_{1,1} \equiv X_1 : X_2 \,/\, Y_1$,
$D1_{1,2} \equiv X_2 : X_1 \,/\, Y_1$ }

Level 2: { $D1_{2,1} \equiv true : X_2,X_1 \,/\, Y_1$ }

Single-rule KH structure for R2:
Level 0: { $D2_{0,1} \equiv X_3,X_4,X_5 : true \,/\, Y_2$ }

Level 1: { $D2_{1,1} \equiv X_3,X_4 : X_5 \,/\, Y_2$,
$D2_{1,2} \equiv X_3,X_5 : X_4 \,/\, Y_2$,
$D2_{1,3} \equiv X_4,X_5 : X_3 \,/\, Y_2$ }

Level 2: { $D2_{2,1} \equiv X_3 : X_5, X_4 \,/\, Y_2$,
$D2_{2,2} \equiv X_4 : X_5, X_3 \,/\, Y_2$,
$D2_{2,3} \equiv X_5 : X_4, X_3 \,/\, Y_2$ }

Level 3: { $D2_{3,1} \equiv true : X_5, X_4, X_3 \,/\, Y_2$ }

Multi-rule KH structure for R1 and R2:
Level 0: { $D1_{0,1} \equiv X_1,X_2 : true \,/\, Y_1$, $D2_{0,1} \equiv X_3,X_4,X_5 : true \,/\, Y_2$ }

Level 1: { $D1_{1,1} \equiv X_1 : X_2 \,/\, Y_1$, $D2_{1,1} \equiv X_3,X_4 : X_5 \,/\, Y_2$,
$D1_{1,2} \equiv X_2 : X_1 \,/\, Y_1$, $D2_{1,2} \equiv X_3,X_5 : X_4 \,/\, Y_2$,
$D2_{1,3} \equiv X_4,X_5 : X_3 \,/\, Y_2$ }

Level 2: { $D1_{2,1} \equiv true : X_2,X_1 \,/\, Y_1$, $D2_{2,1} \equiv X_3 : X_5, X_4 \,/\, Y_2$,
$D2_{2,2} \equiv X_4 : X_5, X_3 \,/\, Y_2$,
$D2_{2,3} \equiv X_5 : X_4, X_3 \,/\, Y_2$ }

Level 3: { $D2_{3,1} \equiv true : X_5, X_4, X_3 / Y_2$ }

Here are some possible scenaria, with different initial knowledge available each time, in the beginning of the reasoning process:

- if $W=\{X_1, X_2\}$ then extension $In(2)= W \cup \{Y_1, Y_2\}$ is computed by making the assumption that X_5, X_4 and X_3 hold ($Out(2)=\{\neg X_5, \neg X_4, \neg X_3\}$) and by applying defaults $D1_{0,1}$ and $D2_{3,1}$ respectively, i.e. $\Pi(2)=\{D1_{0,1}, D2_{3,1}\}$. Note that, the default $D1_{0,1}$ takes priority over the default $D2_{3,1}$, due to the fact that the first one does not employ any assumptions while the second one employs three assumptions in the inference process.
- if $W=\{X_1, X_2, X_3\}$ then extension $In(2)= W \cup \{Y_1, Y_2\}$ is computed by making the assumption that X_5 and X_4 hold ($Out(2)=\{\neg X_5, \neg X_4\}$) and by applying defaults $D1_{0,1}$ and $D2_{2,1}$ respectively, i.e. $\Pi(2)=\{D1_{0,1}, D2_{2,1}\}$. Also, note that, the default $D1_{0,1}$ takes priority over the default $D2_{2,1}$.
- if $W=\{X_1, X_3, X_4, X_5\}$ then extension $In(2)= W \cup \{Y_2, Y_1\}$ is computed by making the assumption that only X_2 holds ($Out(2)=\{\neg X_2\}$) and by applying defaults $D2_{0,1}$ and $D1_{1,1}$ respectively, i.e. $\Pi(2)=\{D2_{0,1}, D1_{1,1}\}$. The default $D2_{0,1}$ takes priority over the default $D1_{1,1}$, due to the fact that the first one does not employ any assumptions while the second one employs an assumption in the inference process.
- if $W=\{X_1, X_3, X_4\}$ then extension $In(2)= W \cup \{Y_1, Y_2\}$ is computed by making the assumptions that X_2 and X_5 hold ($Out(2)=\{\neg X_2, \neg X_5\}$) and by applying defaults $D1_{1,1}$ and $D2_{1,1}$ respectively, i.e. $\Pi(2)=\{D1_{1,1}, D2_{1,1}\}$. Now, note that, defaults $D1_{1,1}$ and $D2_{1,1}$, employ the same number of assumptions in the inferences process. Due to this fact and according to the priority criterion on the basis of the total number of assumptions employed by a rule, none of the rules takes priority over the other. Thus, both process $\Pi(2)=\{D1_{1,1}, D2_{1,1}\}$ and $\Pi(2)=\{D2_{1,1}, D1_{1,1}\}$ are feasible. It just happens in this case that processes have identical final impacts to the environment, i.e. $In(2)= W \cup \{Y_1, Y_2\}$ and $Out(2)=\{\neg X_2, \neg X_5\}$ or $In(2)= W \cup \{Y_2, Y_1\}$ and $Out(2)=\{\neg X_5, \neg X_2\}$.

This last example indicates the need for additional priority criteria. For instance, we may use as a criterion the size of factual knowledge a rule employs, i.e. the number of prerequisites. In this case the default $D2_{1,1}$ takes priority over the default $D1_{1,1}$, due to the fact that the first one fires on a larger factual basis in contrast to the second one, although both of them employ the same number of assumptions in the inference process.

Note that although a level may contain two or more defaults that correspond to the same initial contract rule (e.g. $D2_{1,1}$ or $D2_{1,2}$ or $D2_{1,3}$) there is no need for some kind of prioritization among these defaults. If two or more defaults of the same level, which are derived from the same initial rule (i.e. they belong to the same level within the same single-rule KH structure), were to apply simultaneously, then the more general default contained in the immediately lower level should have applied.

Also, note that, it is important to consider the issue of consistency between assumptions employed during the reasoning process and new inferences derived as a result of the reasoning process. One of the reasons for which we revised our initial proposal for the construction of the DfT is precisely because an agent would require a revision mechanism in order to reconstruct the default rules as new information becomes available, and the agent is able to prove literals from its updated knowledge, and hence treat them as prerequisites rather than justifications. The alternative way that we propose here, for the construction of the DfT does not require any revision of the defaults. This is because inference involves one level at a time in a stepwise manner, and the agent moves upwards to the next level of the multi-rule KH structure only when it has exhausted inference at a given level. This ensures that the agent employs the fewest possible hypotheses. We are able to preserve consistency of entailment, if we employ appropriate variations of DfL such as Constrained Default Logic (CDfT) (Schaub, 1992). A CDfT is a DfT that ensures the joint consistency of all justifications involved in reasoning. A default is applied only if its justifications and consequents are consistent with the background theory, i.e., In(i)∪¬Out(i). In this case, the possible world model that the agent infers incrementally is the consistent set In(i)∪¬Out(i). This is tantamount to saying that the new possible world models inferred by the agent contain, besides previously available knowledge, both the consequents and the assumptions of the defaults that the agent applied.

Finally, note that the technique described here resembles, in a way, stratification of a DfT (Cholewinski, 1994). A DfT is stratified (SDfT) iff there exists a stratification function s that assigns a natural number to each default and, thus, separates the initial set of defaults D into strata. The stratification function is chosen so that, if the consequent of a default D1 is required as a prerequisite or justification by another default D2, than D1 is to be applied before D2 i.e., s(D1)≤s(D2). Our separation of the possible set of defaults that correspond to each rule of the initial representation into levels, based on the number of assumptions employed, may be regarded as somewhat similar to a stratification criterion. We believe that it is worth examining the use of stratification, in its original sense, in combination with our proposed separation of the set of defaults based on the number of assumptions employed, to establish whether an agent's reasoning may be guided more thouroughly.

So far, we have omitted normal defaults from the discussion about the way in which an agent may construct its default theory. Normal defaults have the form P:C/C, i.e., their justification coincides with their consequent. Two questions seem to arise naturally: (i) Should the agent include normal defaults in the set of potential mappings that it constructs from the initial e-contract representation? And, if so, (ii) In which level of the triangle should normal defaults be placed? It seems to us that normal defaults are required only in order to ensure that there is at least one extension of the currently available knowledge, which may be computed by adding to it new information, provided that consistency is preserved. That is, the normal default may be viewed as behaving similarly to the justification-free default, in that all its prerequisites should be satisfied by the current knowledge base; the only additional assumption made in the case of the normal default concerns the consistency of its conclusion with the current knowledge base. For this reason, although the normal default contains a single assumption, and should therefore belong to level 1 of the triangle, 'operationally' it belongs to level 0, since its assumption is not genuinely about something that holds in the world. Hence, an agent may either omit normal defaults totally from the triangles that it constructs, or it may include them in level 0, if it is important to ensure that at least one extension exists while preserving consistency.

3.4. Example

For the sake of generality we have, so far, presented our approach to dynamic assumption identification and deployment in abstract terms. In this section we present a flavour of a real example from the application area of e-commerce. We omit, here, a full representation in EC (or some other temporal logic), in order to avoid distracting the reader with details, but an interested reader is referred to (Giannikis and Daskalopulu, 2006, Giannikis and Daskalopulu, 2007). Consider a 3-party business transaction that takes place in an electronic marketplace populated by software agents. A buyer agent (BA) communicates with a seller agent (SA) and establishes an agreement for purchasing a certain product. Consequently, the seller agent communicates with a carrier agent (CA) and establishes a separate agreement for the safe and timely delivery of goods to the buyer agent. An extract of the initial set of contract norms for the agreement between the buyer agent and the seller agents is as follows:

R={ R1 ≡ SAIsObligedToDeliverToBAWithinNext20days ← BAOrdersFromSA
∧ E-shopFunctionsWell,

R2 ≡ BAIsObligedToPayCAOnBehalfOfSA ← BAOrdersFromSA ∧ CADeliversToBA
∧ CAIsEmpoweredToAcceptPaymentFromBAOnBehalfOfSA }

Note that these norms have the same number of conditions as the norms considered in the abstract example presented in section 3.3. Thus, the corresponding KH structures are as follows:

Single-rule KH structure for R1:
Level 0: {
$D1_{0,1}$ ≡
BAOrdersFromSA, E-shopFunctionsWell
: true
/ SAIsObligedToDeliverToBAWithinNext20days }

Level 1: {
$D1_{1,1}$ ≡
BAOrdersFromSA
: E-shopFunctionsWell
/ SAIsObligedToDeliverToBAWithinNext20days,

$D1_{1,2}$ ≡
E-shopFunctionsWell
: BAOrdersFromSA
/ SAIsObligedToDeliverToBAWithinNext20days }

Level 2: {
$D1_{2,1}$ ≡
true
: E-shopFunctionsWell, BAOrdersFromSA
/ SAIsObligedToDeliverToBAWithinNext20days }

Single-rule KH structure for R2:
Level 0: {
$D2_{0,1}$ ≡

BAOrdersFromSA, CADeliversToBA, CAIsEmpoweredToAcceptPaymentFromBAOnBehalfOfSA
: true
/ BAIsObligedToPayCAOnBehalfOfSA }

Level 1: {
$D2_{1,1} \equiv$
BAOrdersFromSA, CADeliversToBA
: CAIsEmpoweredToAcceptPaymentFromBAOnBehalfOfSA
/ BAIsObligedToPayCAOnBehalfOfSA,

$D2_{1,2} \equiv$
BAOrdersFromSA, CAIsEmpoweredToAcceptPaymentFromBAOnBehalfOfSA
: CADeliversToBA
/ BAIsObligedToPayCAOnBehalfOfSA,

$D2_{1,3} \equiv$
CADeliversToBA, CAIsEmpoweredToAcceptPaymentFromBAOnBehalfOfSA
: BAOrdersFromSA
/ BAIsObligedToPayCAOnBehalfOfSA }

Level 2: {
$D2_{2,1} \equiv$
BAOrdersFromSA
: CAIsEmpoweredToAcceptPaymentFromBAOnBehalfOfSA, CADeliversToBA
/ BAIsObligedToPayCAOnBehalfOfSA,

$D2_{2,2} \equiv$
CADeliversToBA
: CAIsEmpoweredToAcceptPaymentFromBAOnBehalfOfSA, BAOrdersFromSA
/ BAIsObligedToPayCAOnBehalfOfSA,

$D2_{2,3} \equiv$
CAIsEmpoweredToAcceptPaymentFromBAOnBehalfOfSA
: CADeliversToBA, BAOrdersFromSA
/ BAIsObligedToPayCAOnBehalfOfSA }

Level 3: {
$D2_{3,1} \equiv$
true
: CAIsEmpoweredToAcceptPaymentFromBAOnBehalfOfSA, CADeliversToBA, BAOrdersFromSA
/ BAIsObligedToPayCAOnBehalfOfSA }

Multi-rule KH structure for R1 and R2:
Level 0: {
$D1_{0,1} \equiv$
BAOrdersFromSA, E-shopFunctionsWell

: true
/ SAIsObligedToDeliverToBAWithinNext20days,

$D2_{0,1} \equiv$
BAOrdersFromSA, CADeliversToBA, CAIsEmpoweredToAcceptPaymentFromBAOnBehalfOfSA
: true
/ BAIsObligedToPayCAOnBehalfOfSA }

Level 1: {
$D1_{1,1} \equiv$
BAOrdersFromSA
: E-shopFunctionsWell
/ SAIsObligedToDeliverToBAWithinNext20days,

$D1_{1,2} \equiv$
E-shopFunctionsWell
: BAOrdersFromSA
/ SAIsObligedToDeliverToBAWithinNext20days,

$D2_{1,1} \equiv$
BAOrdersFromSA, CADeliversToBA
: CAIsEmpoweredToAcceptPaymentFromBAOnBehalfOfSA
/ BAIsObligedToPayCAOnBehalfOfSA,

$D2_{1,2} \equiv$
BAOrdersFromSA, CAIsEmpoweredToAcceptPaymentFromBAOnBehalfOfSA
: CADeliversToBA
/ BAIsObligedToPayCAOnBehalfOfSA,

$D2_{1,3} \equiv$
CADeliversToBA, CAIsEmpoweredToAcceptPaymentFromBAOnBehalfOfSA
: BAOrdersFromSA
/ BAIsObligedToPayCAOnBehalfOfSA }

Level 2: {
$D1_{2,1} \equiv$
true
: E-shopFunctionsWell, BAOrdersFromSA
/ SAIsObligedToDeliverToBAWithinNext20days,

$D2_{2,1} \equiv$
BAOrdersFromSA
: CAIsEmpoweredToAcceptPaymentFromBAOnBehalfOfSA, CADeliversToBA
/ BAIsObligedToPayCAOnBehalfOfSA,

$D2_{2,2} \equiv$
CADeliversToBA
: CAIsEmpoweredToAcceptPaymentFromBAOnBehalfOfSA, BAOrdersFromSA
/ BAIsObligedToPayCAOnBehalfOfSA,

$D2_{2,3} \equiv$
CAIsEmpoweredToAcceptPaymentFromBAOnBehalfOfSA
: CADeliversToBA, BAOrdersFromSA
/ BAIsObligedToPayCAOnBehalfOfSA }

Level 3: {
$D2_{3,1} \equiv$
true
: CAIsEmpoweredToAcceptPaymentFromBAOnBehalfOfSA, CADeliversToBA, BAOrdersFromSA
/ BAIsObligedToPayCAOnBehalfOfSA }

Suppose that the current explicit knowledge that the buyer agent possesses is that it has ordered goods from the seller agent, that the e-shop functions properly, and that the carrier agent that will actually deliver the goods is legally empowered to accept payment on behalf of the seller agent, i.e., the buyer agent's current knowledge is:

W={ BAOrdersFromSA, E-shopFunctionsWell,
CAIsEmpoweredToAcceptPaymentFromBAOnBehalfOfSA }

On the basis of this knowledge alone, the buyer may only infer, that the seller is obliged to deliver products to it, within the next 20 days, i.e. the extension In(1)= W $\cup$ { SAIsObligedToDeliverToBAWithinNext20days } is computed by making no assumptions (Out(1)={ }) and by applying default $D1_{0,1}$, i.e. $\Pi(1)$={ $D1_{0,1}$ }.
But, apart from establishing what it must expect from its counterparty, the buyer agent may wish to explore potential future scenaria. For instance, the buyer may need to perform best-guess reasoning and plan its future activities on the assumption that certain events/actions will occur, and that its partners' actions will be valid. Suppose that the buyer wants to infer the time by which it will have to pay for the goods, assuming that all goes well and it receives them in good time, because it wants to plan to have adequate funds available. To derive such an answer the buyer agent needs to identify and employ the assumption that delivery happens in due time (CADeliversToBA)[2], i.e. the extension In(2)= W $\cup$ { SAIsObligedToDeliverToBAWithinNext20days, BAIsObligedToPayCAOnBehalfOfSA } is computed by making the assumption that CADeliversToBA holds (Out(2)={ ¬CADeliversToBA }) and by applying defaults $D1_{0,1}$ and $D2_{1,2}$ ($\Pi(2)$={ $D1_{0,1}$, $D2_{1,2}$ }), respectively.
Now suppose that the buyer agent does not possess complete historical information, i.e. it does not know everything that may have happened so far. Let its current knowledge be such

[2] In the full representation of the example, using some temporal logic, the temporal conditions involved in norms, are treated as all other conditions, when the agent constructs single-norm KH structures, i.e. the agent can make assumptions about them as well.

that it only knows that it ordered goods from the seller agent, that the e-shop functions well, and that the carrier agent delivered goods to it.

W={ BAOrdersFromSA, E-shopFunctionsWell, CADeliversToBA }

The buyer may need to perform no-risk reasoning, in order to derive a conclusion based on assumptions, because alternatively it might find itself in an undesirable situation. For instance, it may want to infer that it has an obligation to pay for the goods that it received, yet this inference is not possible, unless it assumes that the carrier agent is legally empowered to accept payment on behalf of the seller agent (CAIsEmpoweredToAcceptPaymentFromBAOnBehalfOfSA), i.e. the extension In(2)= W $\cup$ { SAIsObligedToDeliverToBAWithinNext20days, BAIsObligedToPayCAOnBehalfOfSA } is computed by making the assumption that CAIsEmpoweredToAcceptPayment FromBAOnBehalfOfSA holds (Out(2)={¬CAIsEmpoweredToAcceptPaymenFromBAOn BehalfOfSA}) and by applying defaults $D1_{0,1}$ and $D2_{1,1}$ ($\Pi(2)$={ $D1_{0,1}$, $D2_{1,1}$ }), respectively. In this scenario, the buyer agent does not possess knowledge about the carrier agent's legal power to accept payment on behalf of the seller agent. It may be the case that when such information was communicated to it by the seller agent, it got lost or distorted, or it may be the case that the seller agent simply 'forgot' to communicate such information to it. If the buyer agent does not perform no-risk reasoning, it risks finding itself in a situation where it will have violated its obligation to pay for the goods that it received, inadvertently, and it will have to face the legal consequences, e.g. to pay extra charges.

4. Related Work on Assumption-based Reasoning

During the past thirty years or so various approaches to assumption-based reasoning have been proposed in the Artificial Intelligence literature. These can be broadly grouped into:

- those that rely on *a priori specification* of the assumptions that can be employed during the reasoning process, i.e., those where assumption identification is static; and
- those that attempt to support *ad hoc identification* of potentially useful assumptions during the reasoning process, that is those that purport to identify and employ assumptions dynamically.

Our approach, which is presented in section 3, is clearly related closely to the second group. However, we review here static approaches as well, since they form the basis on which dynamic approaches to assumption-based reasoning were developed. In order to assist readers to familiarize themselves both with the motivations for assumption-based reasoning and with the technical aspects of the various approaches, we found it useful to include static approaches in our discussion.

4.1 Static Assumption-based Reasoning

Doyle in 1979 (Doyle, 1979) described the representation and structure of a Truth Maintenance System (TMS). He argued that his work solves part of the belief revision problem and provides a mechanism for making assumptions. It is guided by the so called problem of control, that is the problem of deciding on what the system's next inference will be. In other words, the agent needs an inference about which inference to make. New inferences are made by the Reasoner System (or overall Problem Solver) based on different assumptions that are statements believed without a particular reason. Consequently, different assumptions define different justified beliefs or reasoned arguments. A TMS, firstly, works as a cache by storing all inferences (justifications) ever made and, secondly, it makes any necessary revisions in the current belief set when the justifications-set, i.e. a set of justifications that represent different reasons for accepting a belief, is altered either by removing or adding a justification. In cases where a contradiction arises, a procedure, called 'reasoned retraction of assumptions' is introduced. The procedure searches each belief justification-set for at least one assumption to be removed or added, in order to eliminate the contradiction. In 1986, de Kleer in (de Kleer, 1986a, de Kleer, 1986b) presented a new kind of TMS that avoids certain previous pitfalls. Contrary to (Doyle, 1979) this new approach, the Assumption-based Truth Maintenance System (ATMS), is based on manipulating not only justifications but assumptions as well. In this way, each belief is labelled with the set of assumptions under which it holds, besides the justifications that support it. Later, Reiter and de Kleer, in (Reiter and de Kleer, 1987) and (de Kleer, 1988) respectively, proposed some extensions and generalizations of the ATMS that are concerned mainly with the way the system is able to manipulate clauses, which are more general than Horn clauses. Based on the above ideas of TMS and ATMS, Kohals *et al.* in (Kohlas and Monney, 1993, Anrig *et al.*, 1997) proposed an extension of the propositional assumption-based model with probabilities, the so called Assumption-based Evidential Language (ABEL). Consequently, hypotheses were, also, enhanced with notions such as support, quasi-support, plausibility and doubt.

Poole in (Poole *et al.*, 1987, Poole, 1988) presents Theorist that is a framework for default reasoning implemented in Prolog. Poole argues that no special logic is required for default reasoning and proposes a modification to classical logic to achieve default reasoning. He considers the simplest case of hypothetical reasoning, where the user provides the form of possible assumptions in order to achieve explanation. Specifically, Theorist accepts from users a set of closed formulae called facts (F), and a set Δ of potential assumptions called possible hypotheses. A closed formula G is explainable from F and Δ, if there is a set D of ground instances of Δ such that $F \cup D$ entails G, and $F \cup D$ is consistent[3]. Finally, in (Poole, 1996) a very interesting discussion is presented. Queries such as "What are the possible hypotheses?" and "Who makes the assumptions?" are answered based on the type of problem that the agent faces, i.e. planning, diagnosis or default reasoning. Although, this approach is close to the technique that is presented in this chapter, there is a quite important difference. In Theorist, predefined rules determine what can be used as hypotheses, while in ours an agent discovers candidate hypotheses for itself.

Bondarenko *et al.* in (Bondarenko *et al.*, 1993) proposed an argumentation-based approach to hypothetical reasoning. This work is inspired by Dung's general argumentation framework and it is based on the notions of attack and counterattack of argumentation theory. An assumption is said to be acceptable, if it is able to counterattack any other attacking set of assumptions. According to this view, definitions for admissible, complete, grounded, stable and preferred sets of assumptions were given. This fixed-assumptions framework is first introduced for logic programming, while an extension for its application to other formalisms of nonmonotonic reasoning is possible.

---

[3] As Poole points out, his assumptions are identical to Reiter's supernormal default rules.

Kowalski and Sadri in (Kowalski and Sadri, 1994, Kowalski and Sadri, 1997) compare the Situation Calculus (McCarthy, 1963, Reiter, 1993) and the EC. Both calculi are formulated as Logic Programs. As noted, the EC was intended primarily for reasoning about actual events, and the Situation Calculus was primarily designed for reasoning about hypothetical actions. Thus the unification of the way both calculi handle hypothetical and actual events is proposed. Actual events are simply asserted in the knowledge base and their effects are considered valid. On the contrary, hypothetical events are also asserted in the knowledge base but nothing on their effects is stated. When events are asserted in the knowledge base it is important to verify its integrity, and to this end integrity constraints are used to ensure that i) an event that happens is possible given the current situation, that is all its associated preconditions actually or hypothetically hold; and ii) no concurrent events are possible. These constraints play different roles in the case of actual or hypothetical events. In the first case, they ensure that only possible events happen, and, in the second case, they define the context in which an assumption is possible.

Provetti in (Provetti, 1996) also deals with the problem of actual and hypothetical actions in terms of the Situation Calculus and the EC and introduces new predicates such as HypHolds(fluent,situation) to denote that a fluent is assumed to hold in a situation, as well as new ordered types of constants. A simple version of the EC formulated as an Extended Logic Program with answer sets semantics is presented and discussed as a tool for making assumptions on domains. Thus the new axiomatization of the EC is enhanced with new predicates and constants of the language.

Florea in (Florea, 1997) presents an assumption-based reasoning approach for multi-agent systems that is based on the TLI (Teoria Logica Implicita) logic. The proposed logic is first-order logic enhanced with special notation for the representation of Reiter's original default rules and for the derivation of extensions.

Tahara in (Tahara, 2004) addresses the issue of inconsistency that may arises in the knowledge base as a result of inconsistent hypotheses and uses a preference ordering in order to resolve contradictions.

4.2 Dynamic Assumption-based Reasoning

The most notable approaches that fall into the second category, where it is attempted to identify and employ assumptions dynamically, include those of Cox and Pietrzykowski (Cox and Pietrzykowski, 1986), Reichgelt and Shadbolt (Reichgelt and Shadbolt, 1989, Reichgelt and Shadbolt, 1990), Abe (Abe, 1999), Pellier and Fiorino (Pellier and Fiorino, 2004, Pellier and Fiorino, 2005) and Jago (Jago, 2005). Our work is, obviously, related mostly to this second category. However, it seems to us that assumption identification in these approaches is not truly dynamic. Before we discuss briefly each of these approaches, we make some general remarks on this issue: Some of these approaches rely on the use of a pre-specified pool of assumptions, from which the agent must choose appropriate ones, whenever it identifies an information gap and needs to fill it, in order to proceed with its reasoning. A natural question that arises though, is whether it is realistic to expect that candidate assumptions can be identified in advance. It may be the case that in some application domains this is possible. However, in such cases, candidate assumption identification is not really dynamic, rather selection of an appropriate assumption from the pre-specified pool, may be carried out dynamically during the inference process. This selection though, requires deductive proof, which is notably computationally expensive.

Other dynamic approaches that purport to support dynamic identification of assumptions, rely on finding appropriate assumptions in a goal-driven manner, that is, a particular conclusion that the agent wants to derive is given, and then the agent identifies the assumptions that are required, in order for this conclusion to be derivable. In some cases, such goal-driven identification of candidate assumptions requires proof. But more importantly, the problem that we perceive with purely goal-driven assumption identification is the following: although software agents, in general, are inherently goal-driven in planning their activity, their rationality (and consequently their performance measure) depends on the extent to which they are perceptive of their environment, so that they may exploit changes in it. A purely goal-driven identification of candidate assumptions does not leave much room for the agent to adapt to circumstances.

We now discuss each one of the approaches on dynamic assumption identification and usage, with some additional comments on each of them:

Cox and Pietrzykowski in (Cox and Pietrzykowski, 1986) explore the problem of the derivation of hypotheses to explain observed events. This is equivalent to finding what assumptions together with some axioms imply a given formula. This is similar to what we refer to as no-risk reasoning, i.e. the identification and usage of assumptions about the past. In this work, the identification of assumptions is essentially goal-driven, and it requires proof, in order to establish that the observed event is implied by what is known (the axioms) and what is assumed.

Reichgelt and Shadbolt in (Reichgelt and Shadbolt, 1989, Reichgelt and Shadbolt, 1990) present a way to analyze planning as a form of theory extension. Theory extension enables an agent to add further assumptions to its knowledge base, in order to derive potential plans towards goal achievement. This is similar to what we refer to as best-guess reasoning, i.e. the identification and usage of assumptions about the future. Their approach requires the use of a pre-specified assumption pool, where candidate assumptions are defined in advance, along with preconditions for their usage. The selection of an appropriate assumption from this pool is conducted in a goal-driven manner and requires that the preconditions associated with the assumption may be deductively proved from the knowledge base. If multiple assumptions have preconditions that are satisfied, selection amongst them is performed by checking them against pre-specified criteria, e.g. parsimony (the assumption with the fewest preconditions is selected) or generality (the more general assumption is preferred).

Abe in (Abe, 1999), also, deals with the problem of missing hypotheses for the explanation of an observation. He proposes a way to generate analogous hypotheses from the knowledge base when the latter lacks the necessary ones. This work extends the Clause Management System (CMS) proposed by Reiter and de Kleer (Reiter and de Kleer, 1987) for abduction. A CMS, given an observation O that cannot be explained from the knowledge base KB ($KB \nvDash O$), returns as set of minimal clauses O′ such that $KB \vDash O \cup O'$ and $KB \nvDash O'$. That is to say, O′ is the minimal support for O with respect to KB, iff no proper subset of O′ is support for O with respect to KB. Hypothesis generation is done in two distinct steps: i) using first abduction and then deduction, candidate hypotheses are searched in the knowledge base, and ii) in case where such candidate assumptions do not exist in the knowledge base, analogous hypotheses are generated by examining clauses in the knowledge base and the assumption requirements that were identified in the previous step. Hypotheses are generated ad hoc during the inference process, by exploiting predefined analogy relationships between clauses. This is an attractive approach, but it requires caution: in some applications it is difficult to define analogy relations between clauses, in advance; if no such definition for analogy is provided a priori, counterintuitive results may be produced: For instance, suppose that a buyer agent is obliged to pay a seller agent by some deadline, and that it actually proceeds to do so by cash deposit into the seller's bank account. Although the action of paying via a cash deposit is analogous to the action of paying in cash (in the sense that they have the same practical effect, the seller agent ends up possessing the required funds), the contract that regulates the exchange between the two agents may dictate that only payment in some specific form is deemed as acceptable. The two distinct forms of payment that seem analogous in terms of practical effects, may have different legal effects: one will result in the successful discharge of the buyer's obligation to pay the seller, while the other will result in a (technical) violation of this obligation.

Pellier and Fiorino in (Pellier and Fiorino, 2004, Pellier and Fiorino, 2005) address Assumption-based Planning, and propose a mechanism by which an agent can produce "reasonable" conjectures, i.e. assumptions, based on its current knowledge. Any action precondition that cannot be proved from the knowledge base is considered to be a candidate assumption. A tentative plan (i.e. one that involves assumptions) becomes firm, and can be employed by the agent in order to achieve a specific goal, only when the agent can satisfy all of the conjectures, and this requires the agent to regard them as sub-goals and produce plans for them in turn.

Jago in (Jago, 2005) uses the notion of context in making assumptions. A context is the current set of the agent's beliefs. Nested contexts are used to model nested assumptions, and temporally ordered contexts are used to represent the agent's set of beliefs as it changes over time. Assumptions are not identified a priori, but rather during the reasoning process, either by guessing or in a goal-driven manner.

5. Conclusions

The work presented in this chapter is motivated by the need for assumption-based reasoning in open normative multi-agent environments. The behaviour of agents in multi-agent environments is restricted by the norms that regulate the particular environment in which they participate. In the most general case, regardless of any particular application domain, some communication and interaction protocols govern the society of agents; specific application domains may require additional prescription of agent behaviour, and pose application-specific norms. Unavoidably in open environments agents have incomplete knowledge about their world, and about other agents, yet they must somehow plan their activities (both private and public), and they must somehow preserve their autonomy, i.e. decide for themselves which behaviour serves their private or shared goals in the best way. We believe that the degree of agent autonomy is related to the extent to which an agent is 'free' to make assumptions about anything it does not know about, and we want to support assumption identification and usage, without a priori restrictions on the agent, and without resorting to proof, which is prohibitive computationally.

We have developed a prototype implementation, in order to establish that our proposal is feasible. One natural direction for future work is the extension of our prototype to handle variables and their quantification, and we are currently investigating four major approaches (cf. (Reiter, 1980, Lifschitz, 1990, Poole, 1988, Kaminski, 1995, Kaminski *et al.*, 1998)) to the semantics of open Default Theories, to establish what might be appropriate for computational purposes.

Another direction for future work is to explore whether our ideas about the dynamic and ad hoc identification and usage of candidate assumptions via the construction of hierarchical multi-level structures, can be applied to other approaches to nonmonotonic reasoning such as Logic Programs (Gelfond and Lifschitz, 1988, Gelfond and Lifschitz, 1991) and Defeasible Logic (Nute, 1994).

Finally, we have already started exploring alternative ways for representing the possible knowledge/hypothesis states of an agent as lattices, which can be traversed both upwards and downwards, reflecting an agent's expanding or contracting knowledge base, or equivalently an agent's contracting or expanding assumption requirements; we are experimenting with the computational implementation of the associated algorithms for such traversal and have recorded some preliminary results in (Giannikis and Daskalopulu, 2009).

6. References

Abe, 1999.Akinori Abe. Two-sided hypotheses generation for abductive analogical reasoning. In *Proceedings of the 11th IEEE International Conference on Tools with Artificial Intelligence (ICTAI'99)*, pages 145–152, Washington, DC, USA, 1999. IEEE Computer Society.

Anrig *et al.*, 1997. Bernhard Anrig, Rolf Haenni, Jörg Kohlas, and Norbert Lehmann. Assumption-based modeling using ABEL. In Dov M. Gabbay, Rudolf Kruse, Andreas Nonnengart, and Hans Jörgen Ohlbach, editors, *ECSQARU-FAPR*, volume 1244 of *Lecture Notes in Computer Science*, pages 171–182. Springer, 1997.

Antoniou, 1999. Grigoris Antoniou. A tutorial on default logics. *ACM Computer Surveys*, 31(4):337–359, 1999.

Artikis *et al.*, 2002. Alexander Artikis, Jeremy Pitt, and Marek J. Sergot. Animated specifications of computational societies. In *1st International Joint Conference on Autonomous Agents and Multiagent Systems*, pages 1053–1061, Bologna, Italy, July 15-19 2002. ACM.

Bondarenko *et al.*, 1993. Andrei Bondarenko, Francesca Toni, and Robert A. Kowalski. An assumption-based framework for non-monotonic reasoning. In *LPNMR*, pages 171–189, 1993.

Cholewinski, 1994. Pawel Cholewinski. Stratified default theories. In Leszek Pacholski and Jerzy Tiuryn, editors, *CSL*, volume 933 of *Lecture Notes in Computer Science*, pages 456–470. Springer, 1994.

Cox and Pietrzykowski, 1986. Philip T. Cox and Tomasz Pietrzykowski. Causes for events: Their computation and applications. In Jφrg H. Siekmann, editor, *CADE*, volume 230 of *Lecture Notes in Computer Science*, pages 608–621, New York, NY, USA, 1986. Springer-Verlag New York, Inc.

de Kleer, 1986a. Johan de Kleer. An assumption-based TMS. *Artif. Intell.*, 28(2):127–162, 1986.

de Kleer, 1986b. Johan de Kleer. Extending the ATMS. *Artif. Intell.*, 28(2):163–196, 1986.

de Kleer, 1988. Johan de Kleer. A general labeling algorithm for Assumption-based Truth Maintenance. In *Proceedings of the 7th National Conference on Artificial Intelligence. St. Paul, MN, August 21-26, AAAI Press / The MIT Press*, pages 188–192, 1988.

Doyle, 1979. Jon Doyle. A truth maintenance system. *Artif. Intell.*, 12(3):231–272, 1979.

Farrell *et al.*, 2005. Andrew D. H. Farrell, Marek J. Sergot, Mathias Sallι, and Claudio Bartolini. Using the event calculus for tracking the normative state of contracts. *Int. J. Cooperative Inf. Syst.*, 14(2-3):99–129, 2005.

Florea, 1997. Adina Magda Florea. Assumption-based reasoning of intelligent agents. In *11th International Conference on Control Systems and Computer Science (CSCS'97)*, pages 126–133, 1997.

Gelfond and Lifschitz, 1988. Michael Gelfond and Vladimir Lifschitz. The stable model semantics for logic programming. pages 1070–1080, 1988.

Gelfond and Lifschitz, 1991. Michael Gelfond and Vladimir Lifschitz. Classical negation in logic programs and disjunctive databases. *New Generation Comput.*, 9(3/4):365–386, 1991.

Giannikis and Daskalopulu, 2006. Georgios K. Giannikis and Aspassia Daskalopulu. Defeasible reasoning with e-contracts. In *IEEE/WIC/ACM International Conference on Intelligent Agent Technology (IAT 2006)*, pages 690–694, Hong Kong, China, 2006. IEEE Computer Society.

Giannikis and Daskalopulu, 2007. Georgios K. Giannikis and Aspassia Daskalopulu. The representation of e-Contracts as default theories. In H.G. Okuno and M. Ali, editors, *Proceedings of 19th International Conference on Industrial, Engineering and Other Applications of Applied Intelligent Systems (IEA/AIE 2007)*, LNAI 4570, pages 963–973, Kyoto, Japan, 2007. Springer-Verlag Berlin Heidelberg.

Giannikis and Daskalopulu, 2008. Georgios K. Giannikis and Aspassia Daskalopulu. How agents know what to assume when? In *IEEE/WIC/ACM International Conference on Intelligent Agent Technology (IAT 2008)*, pages 538–545, Sydney, Australia, 9 - 12 December 2008. IEEE Computer Society.

Giannikis and Daskalopulu, 2009. Georgios K. Giannikis and Aspassia Daskalopulu. E-contracting agents reasoning hypothetically and nonmonotonically. Technical Report 7122/1, A006.3ΓΙΑ, Department of Computer and Communications Engineering, University of Thessaly, 7122/1, A006.3ΓΙΑ, April 2009.

Hewitt, 1985. Carl Hewitt. The challenge of open systems: current logic programming methods may be insufficient for developing the intelligent systems of the future. *BYTE*, 10(4):223–242, 1985.

Jago, 2005. Mark Jago. Modelling assumption-based reasoning using contexts. In *Workshop on Context Representation and Reasoning (CRR'05)*, 2005.

Jean-Yves Girard and Lafont, 1989. Paul Taylor Jean-Yves Girard and Yves Lafont. *Proofs and types*. Cambridge University Press, New York, NY, USA, 1989.

Kaminski *et al.*, 1998. Michael Kaminski, Johann A. Makowsky, and Michael L. Tiomkin. Extensions for open default theories via the domain closure assumption. *J. Log. Comput.*, 8(2):169–187, 1998.

Kaminski, 1995. Michael Kaminski. A comparative study of open default theories. *Artif. Intell.*, 77(2):285–319, 1995.

Kohlas and Monney, 1993. Jòrg Kohlas and Paul-Andrι Monney. Probabilistic assumption-based reasoning. In David Heckerman and E. H. Mamdani, editors, *UAI*, pages 485–491. Morgan Kaufmann, 1993.

Kowalski and Sadri, 1994. Robert A. Kowalski and Fariba Sadri. The situation calculus and event calculus compared. In *Maurice Bruynooghe (Ed.): Logic Programming,*

Proceedings of the 1994 International Symposium, November 13-17, MIT Press, pages 539–553, 1994.

Kowalski and Sadri, 1997. Robert A. Kowalski and Fariba Sadri. Reconciling the event calculus with the situation calculus. *J. Log. Program.*, 31(1-3):39–58, 1997.

Kowalski and Sergot, 1986. Robert A. Kowalski and Marek J. Sergot. A logic-based calculus of events. *New Generation Comput.*, 4(1):67–95, 1986.

Lifschitz, 1990. Vladimir Lifschitz. On open defaults. In J. Lloyd, editor, *Proceedings of the symposium on computational logic*, pages 80–95. Berlin: Springer-Verlag, 1990.

Marvn and Sartor, 1999. Rafaèl Hernández Marín and Giovanni Sartor. Time and norms: a formalisation in the event-calculus. In *7th International Conference on Artificial Intelligence and Law*, pages 90–99, New York, NY, USA, 1999. ACM Press.

McCarthy, 1963. John McCarthy. Situations, actions as causal laws. *Memo 2, Stanford University, Artificial Intelligence Project, Stanford, California*, 1963.

McCarthy, 1980. John McCarthy. Circumscription - a form of non-monotonic reasoning. *Artif. Intell.*, 13(1-2):27–39, 1980.

Nute, 1994. Donald Nute. Defeasible logic. In Dov Gabbay, Christopher J. Hogger, and J. A. Robinson, editors, *Handbook of Logic in Artificial Intelligence and Logic Programming, Nonmonotonic Reasoning and Uncertain Reasoning*, volume 3, pages 353–395. Oxford University Press, 1994.

Pellier and Fiorino, 2004. Damien Pellier and Humbert Fiorino. Assumption-based planning. In *AISTA'04: International Conference on Advances in Intelligence Systems Theory and Applications*, pages 367–376, Luxembourg-Kirchberg, Luxembourg, November 2004.

Pellier and Fiorino, 2005. Damien Pellier and Humbert Fiorino. Multi-agent assumption-based planning. In Leslie Pack Kaelbling and Alessandro Saffiotti, editors, *IJCAI*, pages 1717–1718. Professional Book Center, 2005.

Poole *et al.*, 1987. D. Poole, R. Goebel, and R. Aleliunas. *Theorist: a logical reasoning system for defaults and diagnosis*, pages 331–352. Knowledge Frontier: Essays in the Representation of Knowledge, Springer Verlag, New York, 1987.

Poole, 1988. David Poole. A logical framework for default reasoning. *Artif. Intell.*, 36(1):27–47, 1988.

Poole, 1996. David Poole. *Who chooses the assumptions?* Abductive Reasoning, Cambridge: MIT Press., 1996.

Provetti, 1996. Alessandro Provetti. Hypothetical reasoning about actions: From situation calculus to event calculus. *Computational Intelligence*, 12:478–498, 1996.

Reichgelt and Shadbolt, 1989. Han Reichgelt and Nigel Shadbolt. Planning as theory extension. In *Proceedings of the Seventh Conference on Artificial Intelligence and Simulation of Behaviour (AISB89)*, pages 191–199, San Francisco, CA, USA, 1989. Morgan Kaufmann Publishers Inc.

Reichgelt and Shadbolt, 1990. Han Reichgelt and Nigel Shadbolt. A specification tool for planning systems. In *European Conference on Artificial Intelligence (ECAI90)*, pages 541–546, 1990.

Reiter and de Kleer, 1987. Raymond Reiter and Johan de Kleer. Foundations of assumption-based truth maintenance systems: Preliminary report. In *Proceedings AAAI-87 Sixth National Conference on Artificial Intelligence, July 13-17, Seattle, WA. AAAI Press*, pages 183–189, 1987.

Reiter, 1977. Raymond Reiter. On closed world data bases. In *Logic and Data Bases*, pages 55–76, 1977.

Reiter, 1980. Raymond Reiter. A logic for default reasoning. *Artif. Intell.*, 13(1-2):81–132, 1980.

Reiter, 1993. Raymond Reiter. Proving properties of states in the situation calculus. volume 64, pages 337–351, 1993.

Rouached *et al.*, 2005. Mohsen Rouached, Olivier Perrin, and Claude Godart. A contract-based approach for monitoring collaborative web services using commitments in the event calculus. In Anne H. H. Ngu, Masaru Kitsuregawa, Erich J. Neuhold, Jen-Yao Chung, and Quan Z. Sheng, editors, *6th International Conference on Web Information Systems Engineering*, volume 3806 of *Lecture Notes in Computer Science*, pages 426–434. Springer, 2005.

Schaub, 1992. Torsten Schaub. On constrained default theories. In *17th European Conference on Artificial Intelligence (ECAI'92)*, pages 304–308, 1992.

Tahara, 2004. Ikuo Tahara. Computing scenario from knowledge with preferentially ordered hypotheses. *Systems and Computers in Japan*, 35(4):19–26, 2004.

6

Disruption Management in Airline Operations Control – An Intelligent Agent-Based Approach

António J.M. Castro[1] and Eugénio Oliveira[1]
[1]*LIACC-NIAD&R, FEUP, DEI, University of Porto*
Portugal

1. Introduction

Operations control is one of the most important areas for an airline company. Through operations control mechanisms an airline company monitors all the flights checking if they follow the schedule that was previously defined by other areas of the company. Unfortunately, some problems may arise during this stage (Clausen et al., 2005). Those problems can be related with crewmembers, aircrafts and passengers. The Airline Operations Control Centre (AOCC) includes teams of experts specialized in solving the above problems under the supervision of an operation control manager. Each team has a specific goal contributing to the common and general goal of having the airline operation running under as few problems as possible. The process of solving these kinds of problems is known as Disruption Management (Kohl et al., 2004) or Operations Recovery.

To select the best solution to a specific problem, it is necessary to include the actual costs in the decision process. One can separate the costs in two categories: Direct Operational Costs (easily quantifiable costs) and Quality Operational Costs (less easily quantifiable costs). Direct operational costs are, for example, crew related costs (salaries, lodgement, extra-crew travel, etc.) and aircraft/flights cost (fuel, approach and route taxes, handling services, line maintenance, etc.). The quality operational costs that AOCC is interested in calculating are, usually, related with passengers satisfaction. Specifically, we want to include in the decision process the estimated cost of delaying or cancelling a flight from the passenger point of view, that is, in terms of the importance that such a delay will have to the passenger.

In this chapter we present our intelligent agent-based approach to help the AOCC solving the disruption management problem. It is organized as follows: In Section 2 we present some related regarding operations recovery, a classification of current tools and systems in use in some airline companies and a brief summary of the current use of software agents' technology in other domains. Section 3 introduces the Airline Operations Control Centre (AOCC), including typical organizations and problems, the current disruption management (DM) process and a description of the main costs involved. Section 4 is the main section of this chapter and presents our agent-based approach to this problem. This section presents: (i) the reasons that made us adopt the software agents and multi-agent system (MAS) paradigm; (ii) the MAS architecture including the specific agents, roles and protocols as well as some relevant agent characteristics like autonomy and social-awareness; (iii) decision mechanisms, including costs criteria and negotiation protocols and (iv) examples of the problem solving algorithms used. In Section 5 we present the experimental setup and, in Section 6, we evaluate our approach, presenting and discussing the results. Finally, in Section 7, we conclude and give some insights on the future work.

2. Related Work and Current Tools and Systems

The goal of this section is threefold. In Section 2.1 we present the related work regarding operations recovery. Research in this area has been made, mainly, through Operations Research (OR) techniques. Barnhart et al., (Barnhart et al., 2003) gives an overview of OR-based applications in the air transport industry. In Section 2.2 we describe and classify the current tools and systems in use at some worldwide airlines and in Section 2.3 we present some interesting examples of how agents are used in other applications domains and problems.

2.1 Related Work

We divided the bibliography we have analyzed in three main areas: aircraft recovery, crew recovery and integrated recovery. For a more detailed explanation of those papers as well as for older papers related with each of these subjects, please consult (Clausen et al., 2005).

Aircraft Recovery: In (Liu et al., 2008) the authors propose a "multi-objective genetic algorithm to generate an efficient time-effective multi-fleet aircraft routing algorithm" in response to disruption of flights. It uses a combination of a traditional genetic algorithm with a multi-objective optimization method, attempting to optimize objective functions involving flight connections, flight swaps, total flight delay time and ground turn-around times. According to the authors "(...) the proposed method has demonstrated the ability to solve the dynamic and complex problem of airline disruption management". As in other approaches, the authors do use the delay time in the objective functions but nothing is included regarding passengers' quality of services costs.

Mei Yang Ph.D. thesis (Yang, 2007) investigates the use of advanced tabu search methodologies to solve the aircraft-grounding problem and the reduced station capacity problem. The objective is to minimize the schedule recovery costs associated with flight schedule modifications and deviations from the original route. Mei introduces cancellation and delay costs in the objective function. For the delay costs, Mei uses a value of $20 if the delay is less than 15 minutes and $20 each minute if the delay is greater or equal to 15 minutes. For flight cancellations it uses a combination of lost revenue, loss of passenger goodwill and other negative effects, specific and predefined for each flight. The main difference regarding our approach is that we allow the definition of profiles for passengers of each flight (Mei and others, do not consider passengers' profiles). Each one with an associated cost formula, that reflects the delay costs from the passenger point of view.

In (Rosenberger et al., 2001) the authors formulate the problem as a Set Partitioning master problem and a route generating procedure. The goal is to minimize the cost of cancellation and retiming, and it is the responsibility of the controllers to define the parameters accordingly. It is included in the paper a testing process using SimAir (Rosenberger et al., 2002), simulating 500 days of operations for three fleets ranging in size from 32 to 96 aircraft servicing 139-407 flights. Although the authors do try to minimize flight delays, nothing is included regarding the importance of using quality costs.

Crew Recovery: In (Abdelgahny et al., 2004) the flight crew recovery problem for an airline with a hub-and-spoke network structure is addressed. The paper details and sub-divides the recovery problem into four categories: misplacement problems, rest problems, duty problems and unassigned problems. The proposed model is an assignment model with side constraints. Due to the stepwise approach, the proposed solution is sub-optimal. Results are presented for a situation involving a US airline taking into account 18 different problems. This work also omits the use of quality costs for deriving an appropriate solution.

Integrated Recovery: In (Bratu & Barnhart, 2006) the author presents two models that considers aircraft and crew recovery and through the objective function focuses on passenger recovery. They include delay costs that capture relevant hotel costs and ticket costs if passengers are recovered by other airlines. According to the authors, it is possible to include, although hard to calculate, estimations of delay costs to passengers and potential costs of loosing future ticket sales. To test those models an AOCC simulator was developed, simulating domestic operations of a major US airline. It involves 302 aircrafts divided into 4 fleets, 74 airports and 3 hubs. Furthermore, 83869 passengers on 9925 different passengers' itineraries per day are used. For all scenarios solutions are generated with reductions in passenger delays and disruptions. The difference comparing with our approach is that we propose a generic model to calculate the delay cost to passengers, based on their specific profile and opinion (obtained through frequent surveys).

In (Kohl et al., 2004) the author reports on the experiences obtained during the research and development of project DESCARTES (a large scale project supported by EU) on airline disruption management. The current (almost manual) mode of dealing with recovery is presented. They also present the results of the first prototype of a multiple resource decision support system. Passenger delay costs are calculated regarding the delay at the destination and not at departure (we include both in our proposal) and takes into consideration the commercial value of the passenger based on the booked fare class and frequent flyer information. The main difference regarding our proposal is that we use the opinion of the passengers when calculating the importance of the delay.

Lettovsky's Ph.D. thesis (Lettovsky, 1997) is the first presentation of a truly integrated approach in the literature, although only parts of it are implemented. The thesis presents a linear mixed-integer mathematical problem that maximizes total profit to the airline while capturing availability of the three most important resources: aircraft, crew and passengers. The formulation has three parts corresponding to each of the resources, that is, crew assignment, aircraft routing and passenger flow. In a decomposition scheme these are three parts of a master problem known as the Schedule Recovery Model. Although the author takes into consideration the passenger, it does so concerning finding the best solution for the disrupted passengers. The difference of our approach is that we use the opinion of the passengers regarding the delay (expressed through a mathematical formula) to reach the best possible solution concerning delaying the flight. We still do not approach (at least at present time) the, also important, issue of finding the best itinerary for disrupted passengers.

2.2 Current Tools and Systems

In previous work (Castro, 2008) we have classified the current tools (or systems that provide those tools) in use at AOCCs in one of these three categories:

1. Database Query Systems (DBQS)
2. Decision Support Systems (DSS)
3. Automatic or Semi-Automatic Systems (ASAS)

The DBQS – Database Query Systems (the most common situation at airlines) allows the AOCC human operators to perform queries on the existing databases to monitor the airline operation and to obtain other data essential for decision-making. For example, the aircraft and/or crew roster, aircraft maintenance schedule, passenger reservations, and so on. These systems are useful and relatively easy to implement and/or acquire but they have some important disadvantages, for example, to find the best solution and to take the best decision is completely dependent on the human operator. As we have explained in (Castro, 2008) there are two problems when airline companies use only this type of systems: (1) the solution quality is dependent on knowledge and experience of the human operator and, (2) due to the usual difficulty of the human being in leading with large volumes of data simultaneously, they do not use all the necessary information (variables) to take the best decision.

The DSS - Decision Support Systems, besides having the same characteristics of the DBQS, also include additional functionalities to support the human operators on the decision-making. For example, after a request made by a human operator, these systems are able to recommend the best solution to solve a problem related with a delayed aircraft. Some of them may just recommend a flight re-scheduling but others are able to justify the candidate solution as well as to present the solution cost. DSS systems eliminate some of the disadvantages of the DBQS systems. Namely, they are able to analyze large volumes of data and, because of that, propose solutions that take into consideration more information (variables). The decision-making still is on the human operator side but, now, he is able to take better decisions. Unfortunately, one of the big problems with airline companies is the absence and/or complexity of the computerized information system keeping all the operational information. These are of paramount importance for the success of the decision support tools. This problem, referred in (Kohl et al., 2004) as the Data Quality and System Accessibility Problem, gains more importance when we start to implement decision support tools and/or automatic or semi-automatic systems.

The goal of the third type of systems, ASAS – Automatic or Semi-Automatic Systems, is to automate as much as possible the AOCC, replacing the functional part by computerized programs. Specifically, these systems try to automate the repetitive tasks and also the tasks related with searching for the best solution (problem solving). In a totally automatic system, decision-making is also taken by the system. In a semi-automatic system, the final decision is taken by the human operator. In ASAS type of systems, the AOCC does not need as much human operators as in the previous ones, to operate correctly. Usually, roles or functions related with operation monitoring, searching for solutions related with aircraft, crew or passenger problems and re-allocation of resources, are performed by specialists agents (Castro & Oliveira, 2007) replacing the human specialists. The final decision regarding the application of the solution found by these systems on the environment (for example, making the necessary changes on the airline operational plan database) depends on the human supervisor. According to (Wooldridge, 2009) and (Castro, 2007) the agent and multi-agent systems paradigm is more appropriate to be used in this domain than any other paradigm.

2.3 Other Application Domains

To the best of our knowledge, we were the first to propose an organization of agents to represent all roles of an AOCC, including specialist agents that cooperate to achieve the common overall goal of solving the unexpected problems arising during airline operations (Castro, 2007), (Castro & Oliveira, 2007). However, agents and multi-agent systems have been applied both to other problems in air transportation domain and in other application domains. A brief and incomplete list of such applications follows. Tumer and Agogino developed a multi-agent algorithm for traffic flow management (Tumer & Agogino, 2007). Wolfe et al., use agents to compare routing selection strategies in collaborative traffic flow management (Wolfe et al., 2007). For ATC Tower operations, Jonker et al., have also proposed the use of multi-agent systems (Jonker et al., 2005). As a last example, a multi-agent system for the integrated dynamic scheduling of steel production has been proposed by Ouelhadj (Ouelhadj, 2003), (Cowling et al., 2003).

3. Airline Operations Control

In this section we introduce the airline operations control problem - AOCP (also known as airline disruption management problem). To contextualize, we start by briefly introducing the AOCP preceding problem known as the Airline Scheduling Problem (ASP). Then we explain what an airline operational control centre (AOCC) is and we present some typical AOCC organizations. The typical problems, the current disruption management process as well as the main costs involved are also introduced.

3.1 Airline Scheduling Problem

According to (Kohl et al., 2004) the scheduling process of an airline company is composed by the long and short-term phases presented in Figure 1. The scheduling process has three main dimensions or views: (1) passenger view; (2) aircraft view and (3) crew view. The first one represents the seats available to be sold to the airline customers. The other two views, represents resources that will be allocated.

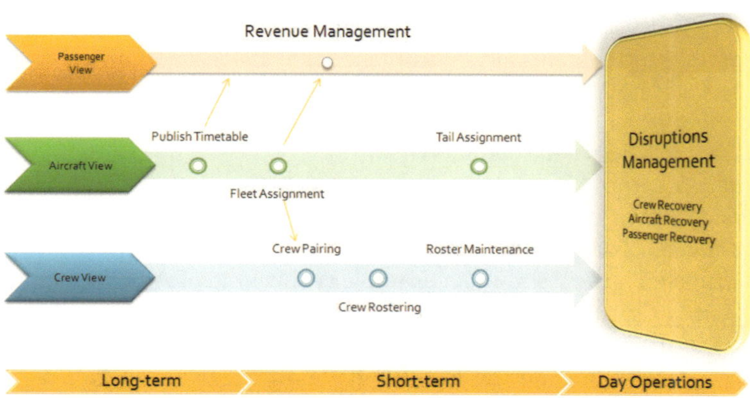

Fig. 1. The airline scheduling process

Everything starts with *publishing the flights timetable* for a specific period of time (usually six months). After publishing the timetable, the *revenue management* phase starts. Here the goal is to maximize the revenue obtained selling tickets. At the same time, the scheduling of the two most important resources starts: aircrafts and crew. Regarding the aircraft, the first step is the *fleet assignment*. Here, the goal is to assign the aircraft type or aircraft fleet that will perform the flights. It is an important step because the aircraft type/fleet will define the number of available seats in each flight. Near to the day of operations, the assignment of the specific aircraft to each flight is performed. This step is known as *tail assignment*. After the fleet assignment step, it is possible to start to schedule the crew. The first step is the *crew pairing*. The goal is to define the crew duty periods (pairings) that will be necessary to cover all the flights of the airline for a specific period of time (typical one month). Having the pairings, it is possible to start the *crew rostering* step that is, assign crewmembers to the pairings. The output of this step is an individual crew roster that is distributed or published in the crew web portal. Finally and until the day of operations, it is necessary to change/updated the crew roster (*roster maintenance*), to include any changes that might appear after publishing the roster. The airline scheduling problem (ASP) is composed of all the previous phases and steps and ends some hours or days (depends on the airline policy) before the day of operation. The global objective of the ASP is to maximize the airline operating profit. For more detailed information please consult (Grosche, 2009) specially Section 2.1 to Section 2.4.

3.2 AOCC Organization

The airline operations control problem (AOCP) starts where the airline scheduling problem stops. In Figure 1 the AOCP is represented by the disruption management square. If everything goes as planned the airline just needs to monitor the execution of the plan. Unfortunately, several unexpected events appear during this phase that can disrupt the plan. To monitor those events and solve the problems that arise from these disruptions and return to the previous plan as soon as possible, it is necessary to define and follow a disruption management process. Airline companies have an entity called Airline Operations Control Centre (AOCC) that is responsible for the disruption management process. There are three main AOCC organizations (Castro, 2008):

- Decision Centre: The aircraft controllers share the same physical space. The other roles or support functions (crew control, maintenance service, etc.) are in a different physical space. In this type of *Collective Organization* all roles need to cooperate to achieve the common goal.
- Integrated Centre: All roles share the same physical space and are hierarchically dependent of a supervisor. For small companies we have a *Simple Hierarchy Organization*. For bigger companies we have a *Multidimensional Hierarchy Organization*. Figure 2 shows an example of this kind of AOCC organization.
- Hub Control Centre (HCC): Most of the roles are physically separated at the airports where the airline companies operate a hub. In this case, if the aircraft controller role stays physically outside the hub we have an organization called *Decision Centre with a hub*. If the both the aircraft controller and crew controller roles are physically outside the hub we have an organization called *Integrated Centre with a hub*. The main advantage of this kind of organization is to have the roles that are related

with airport operations (customer service, catering, cleaning, passengers transfer, etc.) physically closer to the operation.

The organization adopted depends on several factors like airline size, airline network type (for example, hub-and-spoke) and geographic distribution of the operation. In Figure 2 we present the organization of a typical *Integrated Operational Control Centre*. It is important to point out the role of the supervisor, a characteristic that makes this organization hierarchical and, also, the operation time-window that marks the responsibility boundaries of the AOCC. This operation time-window is different from airline to airline but, usually, ranges from 72 to 24 hours before to 12 to 24 hours after the day of operation.

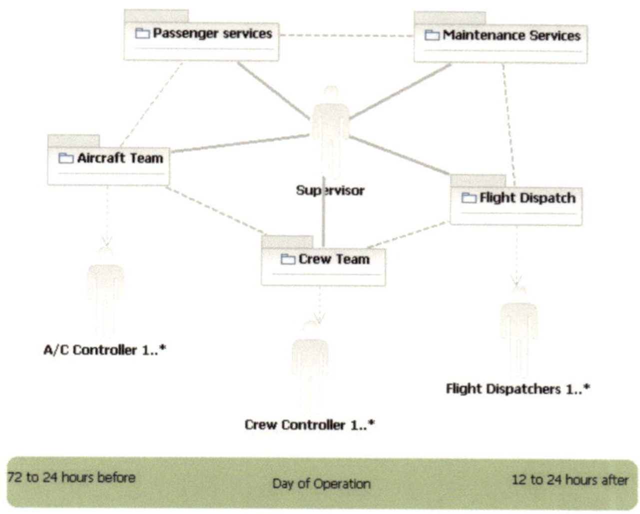

Fig. 2. Integrated airline operational control centre

The roles or support functions more common in an AOCC, according to (Kohl et al., 2004) and (Castro, 2008), are the following:

- <u>Flight Dispatch</u>: Prepares the flight plans and requests new flight slots to the Air Traffic Control (ATC) entities (FAA in North America and EUROCONTROL in Europe, for example).
- <u>Aircraft Control</u>: Manages the resource aircraft. It is the central coordination role in the operational control.
- <u>Crew Control</u>: Manages the resource crew. Monitors the crew check-in and check-out, updates and changes the crew roster according to the disruptions that might appear during the operation.
- <u>Maintenance Services</u>: Responsible for the unplanned maintenance services and for short-term maintenance scheduling. Changes on aircraft rotations may impact the short-term maintenance (maintenance cannot be done at all stations).
- <u>Passenger Services</u>: Decisions taken on the AOCC will have an impact on the passengers. The responsibility of this role is to consider and minimize the impact of the decisions on passengers. Typical this role is performed on the airports and for bigger companies is part of the HCC organization.

3.3 Typical Problems

In the previous section we presented typical AOCC organizations and the roles that exist on those organizations. Now, it is important to understand the typical problems that appear during the execution of the airline operation. From our observations in a real AOCC, and from (Kohl & Karisch, 2004), we found the typical problems presented in Figure 3. In this diagram we have also included the impact that each problem might have on flight arrival or departure delays as well as the relation that exist between them. The diagram also shows that the problems might propagate due to the relation between them, and generate new problems on different flights. This propagation characteristic makes the problem more difficult to be solved optimally in a real time and dynamic environment, like the one we have on the AOCC.

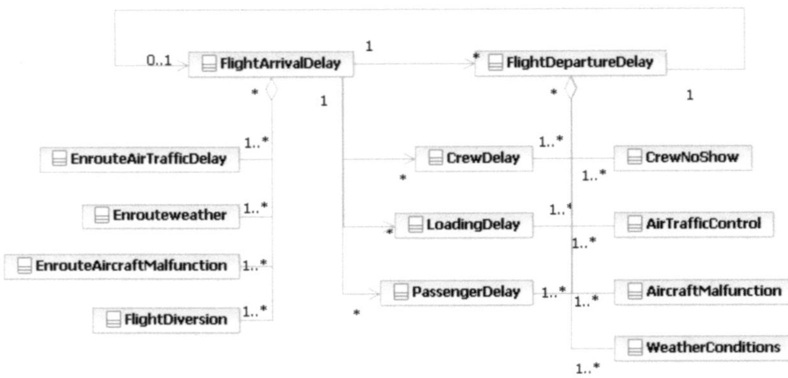

Fig. 3. Typical AOCC problems and relations

As we can see in Figure 3 there is an obvious relation between *Flight Arrival Delays* and *Flight Departure Delays*. Most of the flights are performed by aircrafts that are used in previous flights. If we have an arrival delay and the aircraft turn-around time at the airport is not enough, then, if the AOCC does not find an alternative solution, we will also have a departure delay. From the diagram we can also see that the main reasons for flight arrival delay (besides the delay on departure) are: *En-route air traffic, en-route weather, en-route aircraft malfunction* and *flight diversion*. In the previous cases and to minimize the arrival delay it is necessary a cooperation between the pilot, the AOCC and ATC. Regarding departure delays, the main reasons are: crew delays, cargo/baggage loading delays and passenger delays as a consequence of an arrival delay. Crewmembers that do not report for duty, air traffic control reasons, aircraft malfunctions and weather conditions (at departure or at arrival) are the other main reasons for departure delays.

3.4 Current Disruption Management Process

As we can see from the previous section, there are several problems that might cause flight delays. AOCCs have a process to monitor the events and solve the problems, so that flight delays are minimized with the minimum impact on passenger and, preferably, with the minimum operational cost. In Figure 4 we present the current disruption management process in use at most of the airlines. This process has five steps:

1. Operation Monitoring: In this step the flights are monitored to see if anything is not going according the plan. The same happens in relation with crewmembers, passenger check-in and boarding, cargo and baggage loading, etc.
2. Take Action: If an event happens, like for example, a crewmember is delayed or an aircraft malfunction, a quick assessment is performed to see if an action is required. If not, the monitoring continues. If an action is necessary than we have a problem that needs to be solved.
3. Generate and Evaluate Solutions: Having all the information regarding the problem the AOCC needs to find and evaluate the candidate solutions. Although there are several costs involved in this process, we found that the AOCC relies heavily on the experience of their controllers and in some rules-of-thumb (a kind of hidden knowledge) that exist on the AOCC.
4. Take Decision: Having the candidate solutions a decision needs to be taken.
5. Apply Decision: After the decision the final solution needs to be applied in the environment, that is, the operational plan needs to be updated accordingly.

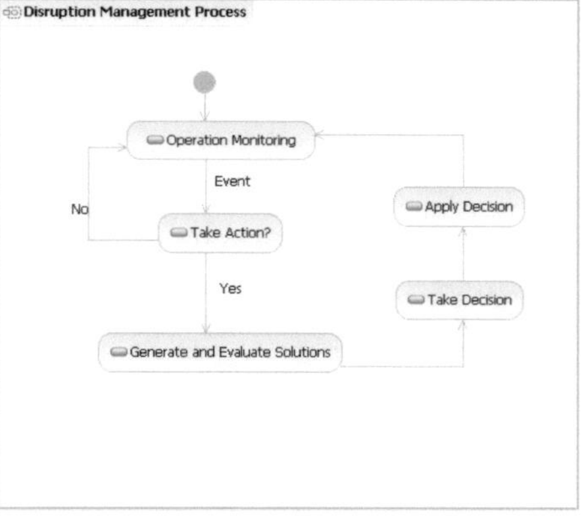

Fig. 4. AOCC disruption management process

In our opinion, this process can greatly benefit from an intelligent agent based approach to the problem, as we will explain in Section 4.

3.5 Main Costs Involved

In the step *Generate and Evaluate Solutions* of the disruption management process on the previous section, we should consider the main costs involved in generating and choosing from candidate solutions. According to our observations these are the main costs involved when generating and evaluating a solution for a specific disruption:

1. Crew Costs: the average or real salary costs of the crewmembers, additional work hours and *perdiem* days to be paid, hotel costs and extra-crew travel costs.
2. Flight Costs: airport costs (approach and taxing taxes, for example), service costs (cleaning services, handling services, line maintenance, etc.), and average maintenance costs for the type of aircraft, ATC en-route charges and fuel consumption.

3. *Passenger Costs*: passenger airport meals, passenger hotel costs and passenger compensations.

Finally, there is a less easily quantifiable cost that is also included: the cost of delaying or cancelling a flight from the passenger point of view. Most airlines use some kind of rule-of-thumb when they are evaluating the impact of the decisions on passengers. Others just assign a monetary cost to each minute of delay and evaluate the solutions taking into consideration this value. We propose a different way of calculating this cost component.

4. A MAS for Disruption Management in Airline Operations Control

In Section 3 we introduced the Airline Scheduling Problem and the Airline Operations Control Problem (or Disruption Management Problem). We have described the AOCC organization and roles as well as the typical problems that appear during the execution of the operational plan. The disruption management process used by airlines was presented as well as the main costs involved in generating and evaluating the solutions. In this section we present our intelligent agent based approach to solve the Disruption Management Problem in the airline domain. The MAS was developed using Java[1] and JADE (Bellifemine et al., 2004) as the development platform and as the run-time environment that provides the basic services for agents to execute.

4.1 Why an Agent and Multi-Agent System Paradigm?

Considering the agent and multi-agent system characteristics as specified in (Wooldridge, 2009) and (Elamy, 2005), the following ones make us adopt this paradigm to the Airline Operations Control Problem:

- *Autonomy*: MAS models problems in terms of autonomous interacting component-agents, which are a more natural way of representing task allocation, team planning, and user preferences, among others. In Figure 5 the *PaxManager*, *AircraftManager* and *CrewManager* agents (among others) are agents that can choose to respond or not to the requests according to their own objectives.
- *Agents are a Natural Metaphor*: The AOCC is naturally modelled as a society of agents cooperating with each other to solve such a complex problem.
- *Reactivity*: Agents are able to perceive and react to the changes in their environment. The *Monitor* agent in Figure 5 is an example of such an agent.
- *Distribution of resources*: With a MAS we can distribute the computational resources and capabilities across a network of interconnected agents avoiding problems associated with centralized systems. Airline companies of some dimension have different operational bases. We use a MAS for each operational base, taking advantage of this important characteristic. Due to the *social awareness* characteristics of some of our agents (for example, *Monitoring* agent in Figure 5) they are able to distribute their tasks among other agents with similar behaviour.
- *Modularity and Scalability*: A MAS is extensible, scalable, robust, maintainable, flexible and promotes reuse. These characteristics are very important in systems of

1 http://www.java.com

this dimension and complexity. Our MAS is able to scale in terms of supporting more operational bases as well as in supporting different algorithms to solve specific problems.

- Concurrency/Parallelism: Agents are capable of reasoning and performing tasks in parallel. This provides flexibility and speeds up computation. The *CrewSimAnneal*, *CrewCBR* and *CrewHillClimb* agents in Figure 5, are examples of concurrent agents. Additionally and according to (Stone & Veloso, 2000) "if control and responsibilities are sufficiently shared among agents, the system can tolerate failures by one or more agents". Our MAS can be totally or partially replicated in different computers. If one or more agents fail, the global objective is not affected.
- Legacy Systems: The AOCC needs information that exists in obsolete but functional systems. We can wrap the legacy components in an agent layer, enabling them to interact with other software components.

4.2 MAS Architecture

It is important to point out that we arrived to the architecture of our multi-agent system, after performing an analysis and design using an agent-oriented software methodology (Castro & Oliveira, 2008). The agent model and service model were the outputs of this process and the base for this architecture.

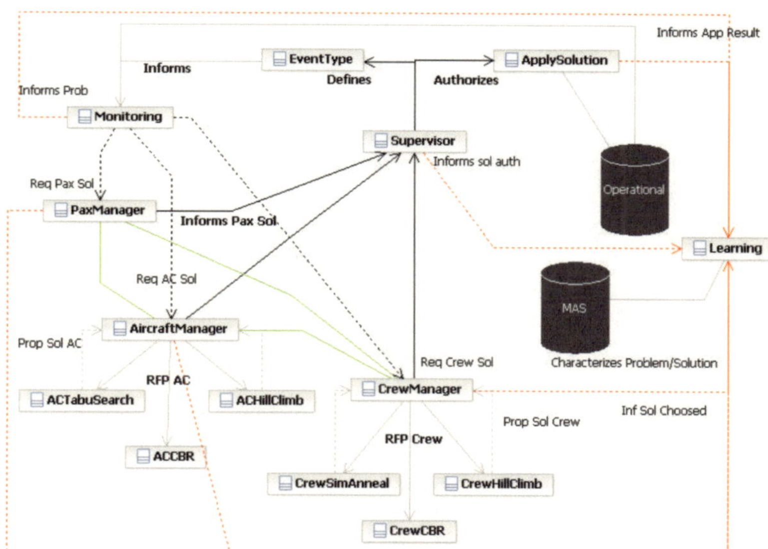

Fig. 5. MAS architecture

Figure 5 shows the architecture of our multi-agent system approach. The boxes represent agents and the narrow black dash lines represent requests/proposals made. The larger green lines represent the interaction between agents regarding negotiation and distributed problem-solving process. The narrow gray lines represent interaction within a hierarchy of agents and the normal black lines represent the interactions after a solution is found. It is important to clarify that Figure 5 represents only one instance of the MAS. We can replicate almost all agents with the exception of the *Supervisor* agent because it is the one that interacts with the human supervisor (an application domain restriction). Each one of the agents *Monitoring, PaxManager, AircraftManager, CrewManager* and *Supervisor* has a specific role in the AOCC. The *Monitoring* agent monitors the operational plan looking for events that may represent any of the usual three problem dimensions, that is, aircraft, crew and/or passenger problems. In case there are other instances of this agent, they recognize and interact with each other, splitting the monitoring task. For example, if each instance corresponds to an operational base, each one will monitor the corresponding operation plan. This is one example of the social-awareness characteristic of our agents. The agent is autonomous in the sense that it will consider an event as a problem only if the event has certain characteristics.

The *PaxManager* agent has the responsibility to find solutions for passenger problems. The *AircraftManager* and *CrewManager* agents have the responsibility for finding solutions for aircraft and crew problems, respectively. These agents are autonomous in the sense that they can choose not to respond to the information received from the *Monitor* agent, i.e., if the problem is not related with their field of expertise or if they do not have local resources to solve that problem. These agents have similar social-awareness characteristics of the *Monitor* agent. Although not yet implemented, these agents may decide to participate with their expertise in the integrated and distributed problem solving approach of the system.

The *AircraftManager* and *CrewManager* agents manage a team of specialized agents (Castro & Oliveira, 2007). Each team should have several specialist agents, each one implementing a different problem solving algorithm, making them heterogeneous regarding this characteristic. The *ACTabuSearch* agent, *ACCBR* agent and *ACHillClimb* agent implements algorithms dedicated to solve aircraft problems and present the candidate solutions they find to the *AircraftManager* agent. The *CrewSimAnneal* agent, *CrewHillClimb* agent and *CrewCBR* agent implements algorithms dedicated to solve crew problems and present the candidate solutions to the *CrewManager*.

The agent *Supervisor* and agent *EventType* are the only ones that interact with a human user of the AOCC. The *Supervisor* agent presents the solutions to the human supervisor, ranked according to the criteria in use by the airline (more information on the next section), including details about the solution to help the human to decide. After getting approval from the human supervisor, the *Supervisor* agent requests *ApplySolution* agent to apply it on the environment.

All agents are able to act and observe the environment that is represented by the *Operational* and *MAS* database, in our diagram. The operational database includes information regarding the flight, aircraft and crew schedule as well as airport and company specific information. The other database is related with the learning characteristics of our system and is used, mainly, by the *Learning* agent. The learning characteristics of our system are not yet implemented. In Section 7, the interested reader can find more information about the way we expect to apply learning in our MAS. Finally, the protocols we use are the following FIPA compliant ones:

- Fipa-Request: This protocol allows one agent to request another to perform some action and the receiving agent to perform the action or reply, in some way, that it cannot perform it. Fipa-request is used in interactions between the *Monitor, PaxManager, AircraftManager* and *CrewManager* agents.

- <u>*Fipa-Query*</u>: This protocol allows one agent to request to perform some kind of action on another agent. It is used in the interactions that involve *PaxManager, AircraftManager, CrewManager* and *Supervisor* agent; *Supervisor, ApplySolution* and *EventType* agent and, finally, *EventType* and *Monitoring* agent.
- <u>*Fipa-Contract.net*</u>: "In the contract net protocol, one agent (the Initiator) takes the role of manager which wishes to have some task performed by one or more other agents (the Participants) and further wishes to optimize a function that characterizes the task"(Fipa, 2002). We use a simplified version of this protocol in the interactions that entail the *AircraftManager* and its specialized agents, i.e., *ACTabuSearch, ACCBR* and *ACHillClimb;* and *CrewManager* and its specialized agents, i.e., *CrewSimAnneal, CrewHillClimb* and *CrewCBR*. More information about how we use this protocol is presented in the next section.

4.3 Decision Mechanisms

Our system uses negotiation at two levels. The <u>first level</u> is the *Manager Agents* level, i.e., between *PaxManager, CrewManager* and *AircraftManager* agents. At this level the agents cooperate so that an integrated solution can be found. We define an integrated solution as one that considers the impact on the three dimensions of the problem, that is, aircraft, crew and passengers. As of the writing of this paper, we do not have this negotiation protocol completely implemented. Section 7 gives a glimpse of how we are implementing it. The <u>second level</u> is the *Specialist Agents or Team level*, i.e., between each manager agent and the specialist agents of the team. At this level we have used a simplified fipa-contract.net (Fipa, 2002) (Smith, 1980).

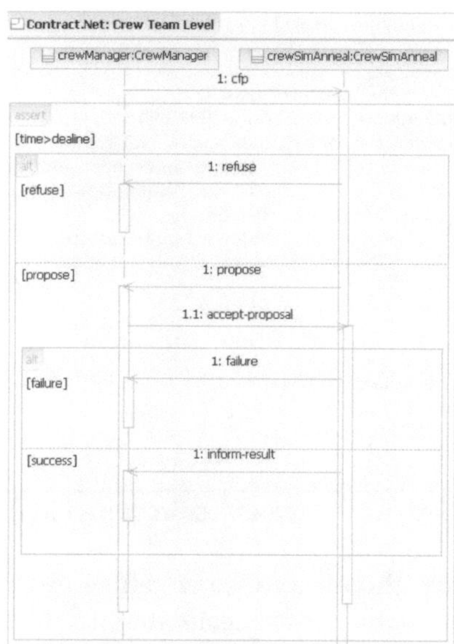

Fig. 6. Simplified contract net protocol

Figure 6 shows the simplified contract.net protocol applied to the *CrewManager* team (for simplicity only the interaction between *CrewManager* and one of the specialist agents is shown). After receiving a request from the *Monitoring* agent and case the *CrewManager* agent decides to reply, a Call for Proposal (cfp) is issued to initiate the negotiation process. Table 1 shows an example of a message sent in this step.

```
(cfp
  :sender (agent-identifier :name CrewManager@masdima:1099/JADE
    :addresses (sequence http://masdima:7778/acc))
  :receiver (set (agent-identifier :name CrewSimAnneal@masdima:1099/JADE
    :addresses (sequence http://masdima:7778/acc)))
  :X-JADE-Encoding Base64
  :content "ABXN rO0AAAA eHB4h3CAAAAAsAAAAAeHB4"
  :language fipa-sl
  :conversation-id cfp_crew_solution)
```

Table 1. CFP message sent by CrewManager agent

Please note that the content of the FIPA-ACL message is a serialized Java object (see Table 2), that contains the event description, as well as the deadline for receiving an answer (propose or refuse) and the deadline for receiving the candidate solution (i.e., the *CrewSimAnneal* agent needs to send a candidate solution before a specific period of time).

```
import java.io.Serializable;
import java.util.ArrayList;
import java.util.GregorianCalendar;

public class CrewProblem implements Serializable {
  private ArrayList<Event> events;
  private int numSeconds;
  private int maxCost;
  private int numMinutesTimeWindow;
  private GregorianCalendar bidDeadline;
  private GregorianCalendar candSolutionDeadline;
  public ArrayList<Event> getEvents() {return events;}
  (...)
  public int getMaxCost() {return maxCost;}
  public void setMaxCost(int maxCost) {this.maxCost = maxCost;}
  public GregorianCalendar getBidDeadline() {return bidDeadline;}
  public void setBidDeadline(GregorianCalendar bidDeadline) {this.bidDeadline = bidDeadline;}
  public GregorianCalendar getCandSolutionDeadline() {return candSolutionDeadline;}
  public void setCandSolutionDeadline(GregorianCalendar candSolutionDeadline) {
          this.candSolutionDeadline = candSolutionDeadline;}
  public CrewProblem(ArrayList<Event> events, int numSeconds, int maxCost, int numMinutesTimeWindow,
      GregorianCalendar bidDeadline, GregorianCalendar candSolutionDeadline)
  {
    this.maxCost = maxCost;
    this.events = events;
    this.numSeconds = numSeconds;
    this.numMinutesTimeWindow = numMinutesTimeWindow;
    this.bidDeadline = bidDeadline;
    this.candSolutionDeadline = candSolutionDeadline;
  }
}
```

Table 2. Partial example of a Serialized Java object included in the CFP message

The *CrewSimAnneal* agent may choose to answer refuse or propose. In our approach the *CrewSimAnneal* propose performative only means that it will look for a candidate solution according to the conditions of the cfp. The *CrewManager* agent will automatically answer back with an accept-proposal. Here we simplified the contract.net protocol to speed-up the communication between our agents. In our case, the answer we get from specialist agents is a simple yes or no, because we want all available agents (i.e., that are not busy looking for candidate-solutions for other requests) to work in parallel to find candidate solutions.

Because of that we do not need to choose between all the answers received. If there is a problem during the execution of the task, the *CrewSimAnneal* agent issues a failure performative stating the reasons for the failure, in the serialized Java object included in the message content. If the agent is able to perform the task with success, it will issue an inform-result performative (Table 3) that includes the serialized object (Table 4) with the candidate solution.

```
(inform
  :sender (agent-identifier :name CrewSimAnneal @masdima:1099/JADE
     :addresses (sequence http://masdima:7778/acc))
  :receiver (set (agent-identifier :name CrewManager@masdima:1099/JADE
     :addresses (sequence http://masdima:7778/acc)))
  :X-JADE-Encoding Base64
  :content "eHB4h3CAAAAAsAAAAAeHABXNrO0AAAAB4"
  :language  fipa-sl
  :conversation-id  cfp_crew_solution)
```

Table 3. Example of a Failure and Inform message

```
import java.io.Serializable;
import java.util.ArrayList;

public class CrewSolution implements Serializable {
   private int cost;
   private int initialCost;
   private String description;
   private ArrayList<Flight> solution;

   public int getCost() {return cost;}
   public void setCost(int cost) {this.cost = cost;}
   public int getInitialCost() {return initialCost;}
   public void setInitialCost(int initialCost) {this.initialCost = initialCost;}
   public String getDescription() {return description;}
   public void setDescription(String description) {this.description = description;}
   public ArrayList<Flight> getSolution() {return solution;}
   public void setSolution(ArrayList<Flight> solution) {this.solution = solution;}
   public  CrewSolution(ArrayList<Flight>  solution,  String  description,  int  cost,  int
initialCost)
   {
      setCost(cost);
      setInitialCost(initialCost);
      setDescription(description);
      setSolution(solution);
   }
}
```

Table 4. Serialized Java object included in the Inform Message

At the team level, the manager agent needs to select the best solution from the candidate solutions that were found by the specialist agents. As of the writing of this paper, we use the *Total Operational Cost* as the only criteria for the selection. Other criteria, like *AOCC Global Performance*, are being tested but we do not have any results at this moment.

The *Total Operational Cost (tc)* of a specific solution includes *Direct Operational Costs (dc)* and *Quality Operational Costs (qc)* and is given by Equation 1.

$$tc = dc + \beta qc \qquad \beta \in R, \beta \geq 0 \tag{1}$$

Coefficient β is used to define the weight of quality costs.

Direct Operational Costs (dc) of a specific solution are costs that are easily quantifiable and are related with the operation of the flights, namely, *Crew Costs (cc)*, *Flight Costs (fc)* and *Passenger Costs (pc)*. It is given by Equation 2.

$$dc = cc + fc + pc \tag{2}$$

The *Crew Cost (cc)* for a specific flight includes the salary costs of all crew members (*Salary*), additional work hours to be paid (*Hour*), additional perdiem days to be paid (*Perdiem*), hotel costs (*Hotel*) and extra-crew travel costs (*Dhc*). The *Crew Cost* for a specific solution is given by Equation 3.

$$cc = \sum_{i=1}^{|F|}\sum_{j=1}^{|C|}(Salary_{\{i,j\}} + Hour_{\{i,j\}} + Perdiem_{\{i,j\}} + Hotel_{\{i,j\}} + Dhc_{\{i,j\}}) \tag{3}$$

$where$
$i \in F; F = \{all\ flights\ in\ solution\}$
$j \in C; C = \{all\ crewmembers\ in\ flight\}$

The *Flight Cost (fc)* for a specific flight includes the airport costs (*Airp*), i.e., charges applied by the airport operator like approaching and taxing; service costs (*Service*), i.e., flight dispatch, line maintenance, cleaning services and other costs; average maintenance costs for the type of aircraft that performs the flight (*Maint*); ATC en-route charges (*Atc*); and fuel consumption (*Fuel*), i.e., fuel to go from the origin to the destination (trip fuel) plus any additional extra fuel required. The *Flight Cost* for a specific solution is given by Equation 4.

$$fc = \sum_{i=1}^{|F|}(Airp_i + Service_i + Maint_i + Atc_i + Fuel_i) \tag{4}$$

$where$
$i \in F; F = \{all\ flights\ in\ solution\}$

The *Passenger Cost (pc)* of the delayed passengers for a specific flight includes airport meals the airline has to support when a flight is delayed or cancelled (*Meals*), hotels costs (*PHotel*) and any compensation to the passengers according to regulations (*Comp*). The *Passenger Cost* of the delayed passengers for a specific solution is given by Equation 5.

$$pc = \sum_{i=1}^{|F|}\sum_{d=1}^{|D|}\left(Meals_{\{d,i\}} + PHotel_{\{d,i\}} + Comp_{\{d,i\}}\right) \tag{5}$$

$where$
$i \in F; F = \{all\ flights\ in\ solution\}$
$d \in D; D = \{all\ delayed\ passengers\ in\ flight\}$

Quality Operational Costs (qc) of a specific solution are costs that are not easily quantifiable and are related with passenger satisfaction. The quantification of this value is very important to increase the quality level of an airline company when facing a disruption. Equation 6 presents a generic expression that calculates this value according to (Castro & Oliveira, 2009).

$$qc = \alpha \sum_{i=1}^{|F|} \sum_{p=1}^{|PP|} (P_{\{p,i\}} * C_{\{p,i\}}) \quad (6)$$

$$\begin{aligned}
&where \\
&i \in F; F = \{all\ flights\ in\ solution\} \\
&p \in PP; PP = \{flight\ passengers\ profiles\} \\
&P = number\ of\ passengers\ of\ profile\ p \\
&C = delay\ cost\ of\ each\ passenger\ on\ profile\ p \\
&\alpha = coefficient\ to\ convert\ to\ monetary\ costs
\end{aligned}$$

Now that we know the main costs involved, it is time to understand how each manager agent selects the best (or the best x candidate solutions). Once the participant agent has completed the task (for example, agent *CrewHillClimb* in Figure 5), it sends a completion message to the initiator (agent *CrewManager* in Figure 5) in the form of an *inform-result performative* (Table 3), with the details of the candidate solution (Table 4) including the *Total Operational Cost*. The manager agent sorts, in ascending order, all candidate solutions received by total operational cost. The top three solutions are selected (Castro & Oliveira, 2007).

4.4 Problem Solving Algorithms

As it is possible to see in Figure 5 (Section 4.2), the aircraft and crew dimension have, each one, a team of specialist agents. Each agent should implement a heterogeneous problem solving algorithm on the team they belong to. Preliminary results show that a single problem solving algorithm is not able to solve, dynamically and within the required time restriction, all types of problems that we have identified during our observations (see Section 3.3). Taking advantage of the modularity, scalability and distributed characteristics of the MAS paradigm, we are able to add as many specialist agents as required, so that all types of problems are covered. As we have seen in Section 4.2 and 4.3, the idea is to have all specialist agents of a team looking for solutions concurrently.

In this section we are going to show how we have implemented one of the specialist agents of the crew team, namely, *CrewHillClimb*. This agent implements a hill climb algorithm. For more details regarding how we have implemented this and other specialist agents, please read (Mota, 2007).

The hill climbing agent solves the problem iteratively by following the steps:

1. Obtains the flights that are in the time window of the problem. This time window starts at the flight date, and ends at a customizable period in the future. This will be the initial solution of the problem. The crew members' exchanges are made between flights that are inside the time window of the problem.
2. While some specific and customizable time has not yet passed, or a solution below a specific and customizable cost has not been found, repeats steps 3 and 4.
3. Generates the successor of the initial solution (the way a successor is generated is described below).
4. Evaluates the cost of the solution. If it is smaller than the cost of the current solution, accepts the generated solution as the new current solution. Otherwise, discards the generated solution. The way a solution is evaluated is described below.

5. Send the current solution to the *CrewManager* agent following the protocol as we have seen in Section 4.3.

The generation of a new solution is made by finding a successor that distances itself to the current solution by one unit, that is, the successor is obtained by one, and only one, of the following operations:

- Swap two crewmembers between flights that belong to the flights that are in the time window of the problem.
- Swap a crewmember of a flight that belongs to the flights that are in the time window of the problem with a crewmember that isn't on duty, but is on standby.

When choosing the first element to swap, there are two possibilities: (1) choose randomly or (2) choose an element that is delayed. The choice is made based on the probability of choosing an element that is late, which was given a value of 0.9, so that the algorithms can proceed faster to good solutions (exchanges are highly penalized, so choosing an element that is not late probably won't reduce the cost, as a possible saving by choosing a less costly element probably won't compensate the penalization associated with the exchange).
If the decision is to exchange an element that is delayed, the list of flights will be examined and the first delayed element is chosen. If the decision is to choose randomly, then a random flight is picked, and a crewmember or the aircraft is chosen, depending on the probability of choosing a crewmember, which was given a value of 0.85. When choosing the second element that is going to swap with the first, there are two possibilities: (1) swap between elements of flights or (2) swap between an element of a flight and an element that is not on duty. The choice is made based on the probability of choosing a swap between elements of flights, which was given a value of 0.5.
The evaluation of the solution is done by an objective function that measures the following types of costs:

- The crew cost according to Equation 3;
- The penalization for exchanging elements;
- The penalization for delayed elements. The cost associated with this aspect is the highest, because the goal is to have no delayed elements.

The *Hill Climbing Objective Function (hc)* is given by Equation 7.

$$hc = cc + excW * nExc + delayW * nDelay \tag{7}$$

$$\begin{aligned}
&where\\
&cc = crew\ cost\ according\ to\ equation\ 3\\
&excW = penalization\ for\ crew\ exchanges\\
&nExc = the\ number\ of\ crew\ exchanges\\
&delayW = penalization\ for\ delaying\ crewmembers\\
&nDelay = the\ number\ of\ delayed\ crewmembers
\end{aligned}$$

Table 5 shows the implementation of the hill climbing algorithm in Java.

```
GregorianCalendar currentDate = new GregorianCalendar();
int secondsExecution = (int) ((currentDate.getTimeInMillis() - startDateResolution.getTimeInMillis()) / 1000);
while(!Shared.to(problem.getNumSeconds(), secondsExecution, problem.getMaxCost(), currentSolutionCost))
{
   // get successor
```

```
successor = Shared.generateSuccessor(Shared.copyArrayList(currentSolution));
// checks if successor has an inferior solution cost
successorCost = Shared.calculateCost(successor, initialPlainSolution);
System.out.println("Successor Cost: " + successorCost + "\n");
if(sucessorCost < currentSolutionCost)
{
   currentSolution = successor;
   currentSolutionCost = successorCost;
}
currentDate = new GregorianCalendar();
secondsExecution = (int) ((currentDate.getTimeInMillis() - startDateResolution.getTimeInMillis()) / 1000);
}
```

Table 5. Implementation of the Hill-Climbing algorithm in Java

5. Experimental Setup

To evaluate our approach we have setup a scenario that includes 3 operational bases (A, B and C). Each base includes their crewmembers each one with a specific roster. The data used corresponds to a real airline operation of June 2006 of base A. We have simulated a situation where 15 crewmembers, with different ranks, did not report for duty in base A. A description of the information collected for each event is presented in Table 6.

Attribute	**Description**
Event ID	A number that represents the ID of the event. For tracking purposes only
Duty Date Time	The start date and time of the duty in UTC for which the crew did not report.
Duty ID	A string that represents the ID of the duty for which the crew did not report.
Flt Dly	Flight delay in minutes
C Pax	Number of passengers in business class
Y Pax	Number of passengers in economy class
End Date Time	The end date and time of the duty in UTC for which the crew did not report.
Ready Date Time	The date and time at which the crew member is ready for another duty after this one.
Delay	The delay of the crewmember. We have considered 10 minutes in our scenario.
Credit Minutes	The minutes of this duty that will count for payroll.
Crew Group	The crew group (Technical = 1; Cabin = 2) that the crewmember belongs to.
Crew Rank	CPT = Captain; OPT = First Officer; CCB = Chief Purser; CAB = Purser.
Crew Number	The employee number.
Crew Name	The employee name.
Base ID	The base where the event happened. We considered all events in base A.
Open Positions	The number of missing crews for this duty and rank. We used a fixed number of 1.

Table 6. Description of the information collected for each event

The events did not happen at the same day and each one corresponds to a crewmember that did not report for a specific duty in a specific day. Table 7 shows the data for each of the events created. As you can see we have omitted the information regarding *Delay*, *Base ID* and *Open Positions* because we have used fixed values as indicated in Table 6. For example, the event 10 corresponds to the following situation: Crew Peter B, with number 32 and rank CPT (captain) belonging to the crew group 1 (technical crew), did not report for the duty with ID 1ZRH12X with briefing time (duty date time) at 15:25 in 15-06-2006. This flight did not delay on departure and has 5 passengers in business class and 115 in economy class. The event was created after a 10 minutes delay of the crewmember in reporting for duty and happened at base A. It is necessary to find another crewmember to be assigned to this duty. The duty ends at 09:30 on 17-06-2006 and the crewmember assigned to this duty will be ready for another one at 21:30 in 17-06-2006. The duty will contribute with 1318 minutes (21h58) for the payroll. The new crewmember must belong to the same rank and group.

After setting-up the scenario we found the solutions for each crew event using three methods.

	Duty DateTime	DutyID	Flt Dly	C Pax	Y Pax	End DateTime	Ready DateTime	Cred Min	Crew Grp	Rnk	Crw Nr	Crew Name
1	05-06 07:25	1ORY149S	0	7	123	05-06 13:35	06-06 01:35	370	2	CAB	80	John A
2	05-06 07:25	1ORY149S	10	11	114	05-06 13:35	06-06 01:35	370	2	CAB	45	Mary A
3	05-06 07:25	1ORY85P	0	10	112	05-06 13:35	06-06 01:35	370	1	CPT	35	Anthony
4	15-06 04:10	2LIS24X	30	0	90	16-06 16:15	17-06 04:15	1757	2	CAB	99	Paul M
5	15-06 04:10	3LIS25X	25	3	77	15-06 09:20	15-06 21:20	632	2	CAB	56	John B
6	15-06 12:50	2LHR63P	5	25	85	16-06 20:45	17-06 08:45	1549	1	CPT	57	Paul S
7	15-06 12:50	2LHR63P	0	20	95	16-06 20:45	17-06 08:45	1549	1	OPT	53	Mary S
8	15-06 14:15	1LHR31P	0	23	52	15-06 20:55	16-06 08:55	843	2	CCB	23	Sophie
9	15-06 15:25	2LHR19P	10	27	105	16-06 20:45	17-06 08:45	1341	2	CCB	34	Angel
10	15-06 15:25	1ZRH12X	0	5	115	17-06 09:30	17-06 21:30	1318	1	CPT	32	Peter B
11	25-06 05:20	1LIS16S	20	3	97	25-06 15:05	26-06 03:05	585	2	CAB	20	Paul G
12	25-06 05:20	1LIS16S	5	2	108	25-06 15:05	26-06 03:05	585	2	CAB	10	Alice
13	25-06 05:20	1LIS158T	0	4	92	25-06 15:05	26-06 03:05	585	2	CAB	15	Daniel
14	25-06 06:15	3LIS174S	0	1	129	27-06 16:15	28-06 04:15	1258	2	CAB	71	George
15	25-06 14:20	4LIS50A	0	2	83	28-06 19:40	29-06 07:40	219	1	OPT	65	Allan

Table 7. Events data used for testing

In the first method we used one of the best users from the AOCC, with current tools available, to find the solutions. The user uses software that shows the roster of each crewmember in a Gantt chart for a specific period. The user can scroll down the information, filter according to the crew rank and base, and sort the information by name, month duty, etc. Each user has a specific way of trying to find the solutions. However, we have observed that, in general, they follow these steps:

1. Open the roster for a one month period, starting two days before the current day. For example, let's suppose that the current day is 7th of June of 2006, they open the roster from the 5th of June until the 4th of July.
2. Filter the roster by crew rank and base, where the base is equal to the base where the crew event happened and crew rank is equal to the crewmember rank that did not report for duty.
3. Order the information by month duty, in an ascendant order and by seniority in a descendent order.
4. Visually, they scroll down the information until they found a crewmember with an open space for the period of time that corresponds to the duty to be assigned. This period of time takes into consideration the start and end time of the duty and also the time required for resting (ready date time).
5. If they do not found a crewmember in the base specified, they try to find it in another base, filtering the information accordingly.
6. They assign the duty to the crewmember with less *credit hours*.

The data collected using this method is presented in Table 8. We point out that the data in columns marked with an asterisk where calculated manually, according to the equations presented in chapter 4.3. The reason for this is that the information system that is available for the users does not include information related with any kind of costs.

	Duty ID	Base ID	Crew Grp	Rank	Hour Pay (*)	Perdiem Pay (*)	Quality Op. Cost	Op. Cost (*)
1	1ORY149S	A	2	CAB	0,00	72,00	0	72,00
2	1ORY149S	B	2	CAB	0,00	72,00	0	86,40

3	1ORY85P	A	1	CPT	942,90	106,00	0	1048,90
4	2LIS24X	A	2	CAB	939,00	144,00	0	1083,00
5	3LIS25X	B	2	CAB	0,00	72,00	0	86,40
6	2LHR63P	B	1	CPT	777,00	212,00	0	1186,80
7	2LHR63P	B	1	OPT	0,00	148,00	0	177,60
8	1LHR31P	A	2	CCB	687,65	72,00	0	759,65
9	2LHR19P	B	2	CCB	0,00	144,00	0	172,80
10	1ZRH12X	C	1	CPT	0,00	212,00	0	296,80
11	1LIS16S	A	2	CAB	0,00	72,00	0	72,00
12	1LIS16S	C	2	CAB	0,00	72,00	0	100,80
13	1LIS158T	B	2	CAB	0,00	72,00	0	86,40
14	3LIS174S	A	2	CAB	1051,60	216,00	0	1267,60
15	4LIS50A	A	1	OPT	246,40	296,00	0	542,40
	Totals				**4644,55**	**1982,00**	0	**7039,55**

Table 8. Data collected (partial) after using method 1 (human user)

In the second method we have used our approach as indicated in Section 4 but with β=0 in Equation 1 (*Total Operational Cost*), i.e., although we calculate the *Quality Operational Cost* as indicated in Equation 6 we did not considered this value in resolution as well as in the decision process. The data collected is presented in Table 9.

	Duty ID	Base ID	Crew Grp	Rank	Hour Pay	Perdiem Pay	Quality Op. Cost	Direct Op. Cost
1	1ORY149S	A	2	CAB	0,00	72,00	0	72,00
2	1ORY149S	B	2	CAB	0,00	72,00	501,31	86,40
3	1ORY85P	B	1	CPT	0,00	106,00	0	127,20
4	2LIS24X	C	2	CAB	563,40	62,00	1561,76	875,56
5	3LIS25X	B	2	CAB	0,00	72,00	1877,73	86,40
6	2LHR63P	C	1	CPT	0,00	212,00	658	296,80
7	2LHR63P	A	1	OPT	0,00	144,00	687,62	144,00
8	1LHR31P	B	2	CCB	229,17	72,00	0	361,40
9	2LHR19P	B	2	CCB	0,00	144,00	788,78	172,80
10	1ZRH12X	C	1	CPT	0,00	212,00	0	296,80
11	1LIS16S	A	2	CAB	0,00	72,00	961,95	72,00
12	1LIS16S	C	2	CAB	0,00	72,00	301,48	100,80
13	1LIS158T	B	2	CAB	0,00	72,00	0	86,40
14	3LIS174S	C	2	CAB	411,00	93,00	0	705,60
15	4LIS50A	B	1	OPT	0,00	296,00	449,84	355,20
	Totals				**1203,57**	**1773,00**	**7788,47**	**3839,36**

Table 9. Data collected (partial) after using method 2 (No Quality Costs)

In the third method we have used our approach as indicated in Section 4 but with β=1 in Equation 1, i.e., considering the *Quality Operational Cost* in the resolution as well as in the decision process. The *Quality Operational Cost* was calculated using two passenger profiles (business and economy classes) and with α=0,1. Equation 9 and Equation 10 are the formulas used to calculate the delay cost of each passenger in business and economy profile, respectively. For more information about how we reached these equations, please read (Castro & Oliveira, 2009).

$$C_{business} = 0.16 * x^2 + 1.38 * x \qquad x = \text{minutes of flight delay, } x >= 0 \qquad (9)$$

$$C_{economy} = 1.20 * x \qquad x = \text{minutes of flight delay, } x >= 0 \qquad (10)$$

The data collected is presented in Table 10.

	Duty ID	Base ID	Crew Grp	Rank	Hour Pay	Perdiem Pay	Quality Op. Cost	Direct Op. Cost
1	1ORY149S	A	2	CAB	0,00	72,00	0	72,00
2	1ORY149S	B	2	CAB	0,00	72,00	501,31	86,40
3	1ORY85P	B	1	CPT	0,00	106,00	0	127,20
4	2LIS24X	C	2	CAB	503,50	144,00	1060,92	906,50
5	3LIS25X	C	2	CAB	0,00	72,00	1420,78	100,80
6	2LHR63P	B	1	CPT	102,90	212,00	272,10	377,88
7	2LHR63P	B	1	OPT	37,22	144,00	0	217,46
8	1LHR31P	B	2	CCB	229,17	72,00	0	361,40
9	2LHR19P	B	2	CCB	0,00	144,00	788,78	172,80
10	1ZRH12X	C	1	CPT	0,00	212,00	0	296,80
11	1LIS16S	A	2	CAB	0,00	80,00	593,30	80,00
12	1LIS16S	C	2	CAB	0,00	80,00	144,34	112,00
13	1LIS158T	B	2	CAB	0,00	72,00	0	86,40
14	3LIS174S	C	2	CAB	411,00	93,00	0	705,60
15	4LIS50A	A	1	OPT	138,83	288,00	0	426,83
	Totals				**1422,62**	**1863,00**	**4781,53**	**4130,07**

Table 10. Data collected (partial) after using method 3 (Quality Costs)

6. Results and Discussion

Table 11 shows a comparison of the results obtained through the above methods. We point out that in method 1 (*human*) we did not calculate the quality costs, and in method 2 (*agent-no-quality*) we did calculate the quality costs but they were not used to find the best solution, although we use that value for comparison purposes. From the results obtained we can see that on average, method 3 (*agent-quality*) produced solutions that decreased flight delays in aprox. 36%. *Agent-quality* is, on average 3% slower than *agent-no-quality* in finding a solution and produces solutions that represent a decrease of 23% on the total operational costs, when compared with *agent-no-quality*.

From the results (Table 11) we can see that our approach obtains valid solutions faster and with fewer direct operational costs when compared with the current method used in a real airline company (*human*). *Agent-no-quality* represents a decrease of aprox. 45,5% and *agent-quality* a decrease of aprox. 41%. *Agent-quality* has a higher direct operational cost than *agent-no-quality* because it uses the quality operational cost in the decision process. If we read this number without any other consideration, we have to say that the goal of having less direct operational costs was not achieved. An 8% increased on direct operational costs can represent a lot of money. However, we should read this number together with the flight delay figure. As we can see, although *agent-quality* has increased the direct operational costs (when compared with *agent-no-quality*) in 8% it was able to choose solutions that decrease, in average, 36% of the flight delays. This means that, when there are multiple solutions to the same problem, *agent-quality* is able to choose the one with less operational cost, less quality costs (hence, better passenger satisfaction) and, because of the relation between quality costs and flight delays, the solution that produces shorter flight delays.

	Human (M1)		Agent-no-Quality (M2)		Agent-Quality (M3)	
	Total	**%**	**Total**	**%**	**Total**	**%**
Base of the solution:						
- From the crew event base (A)	7	47%	3	20%	3	20%
- From base B	6	40%	7	47%	7	47%

- From base C	2	13%	5	33%	5	33%
Time to Find Solution (avr sec)	**101**	**100,00%**	**25**	**24,75%**	**26**	**25,74%**
Flight Delays (avr min):			**11**	**100,00%**	**7**	**63,64%**
- Base A (avr)			14	40%	7	30%
- Base B (avr)			9	26%	4	17%
- Base C (avr)			12	34%	12	52%
Total Direct Operational Costs:	**7039,60**	**100,00%**	**3839,36**	**54,54%**	**4130,07**	**58,67%**
Total by Base:						
- Base A	4845,55	92,42%	288,00	11,23%	578,83	14,02%
- Base B	1796,40	34,26%	1275,80	49,77%	1429,54	34,61%
- Base C	397,60	7,58%	2275,56	88,77%	2121,70	51,37%
Total Quality Operational Cost:			**7788,47**	**100%**	**4781,53**	**61,39%**
Total by Base:						
- Base A			1649,57	21,18%	593,30	12,41%
- Base B			3617,66	46,45%	1562,19	32,67%
- Base C			2521,24	32,37%	2626,04	54,92%
Total Operational Costs:			**11628,01**	**165%**	**8911,60**	**126,6%**
Total by Base:						
- Base A			1937,57	16,66%	1172,13	13,15%
- Base B			4088,42	35,16%	2991,73	33,57%
- Base C			4796,80	41,25%	4747,74	53,28%

Table 11. Summary of the results obtained by each method

From this conclusion, one can argue that if we just include the direct operational costs and the expected flight delay, minimizing both values, the same results could be achieved having all passengers happy. In general, this assumption might be true. However, when we have to choose between two solutions with the same direct operational cost and delay time, which one should we choose? In our opinion, the answer depends on the profile of the passengers of each flight and on the importance they give to the delays (quality operational cost), and not only in minimizing the flight delays and direct operational cost. *Agent-quality* takes into consideration this important information when making decisions. This is the reason why we think that one of the main contributions of our work is the generic approach to quantify the passenger satisfaction regarding delaying a flight, from the passenger point of view. It is fair to say that we cannot conclude that our MAS will always have this behaviour. For that we need to evaluate a higher number of scenarios, at different times of the year (we might have seasonal behaviours) and, then, find an average value.

Additionally, we found that the cooperation between different operational bases has increased with our approach, because we evaluate all the solutions found (including the ones from different operational bases where the event happened) and we select the one with less cost. In *human*, they choose the first one they find with less credit hours, usually from the same base where the event was triggered. This cooperation is also possible to be inferred from the costs by base. In Table 11 is possible to see that the direct operational costs of base C using *human* represents only 7,58% of the costs of all bases, whilst in *agent-no-quality* and *agent-quality* it represents 88,77% and 51,73%, respectively. The same is possible to be inferred from the other bases (although with different figures). This means that our MAS uses more resources from other bases than the base where the problem happened (base A).

7. Conclusion and Future Works

In this chapter we have introduced the Airline Operations Control Problem as well as the Airline Operations Control Centre (AOCC), including typical organizations and problems, the current disruption management (DM) process and a description of the main costs involved. We described our agent-based approach to this problem, including the reasons that make us adopt an agent and multi-agent system (MAS) paradigm; the MAS architecture with agents, roles and protocols as well as some agent characteristics like autonomy and social-awareness; the decision mechanisms, including the costs criteria and negotiation protocols used and examples of the problem solving algorithms. Using data from a real airline company, we tested our approach and discussed the results obtained by three different methods. We have shown that our approach is able to select solutions that contribute to a better passenger satisfaction and that produce shorter flight delays when compared with methods that only minimize direct operational costs.

We are working on several improvements. Some of them are already implemented. However, we did not perform, yet, enough tests to have meaningful results. These are our goals:

- Improve autonomy and learning characteristics of the *Monitor* agent, so that he is able to consider new events (or change existing ones) according to the experience he gets from monitoring the operation, without relying exclusively on the definition of events created by the human operator.
- Working on a protocol at the *Manager Agent* team level that allows a better coordination and improves the distributed problem solving characteristics of our approach. For example, including in each team, knowledge provided by other teams to improve the objective function of each specialist agent, with parameters of the other dimensions (aircraft, crew and passenger).
- Solving problems learning by example, applying Case-Based Reasoning (CBR).
- Increase robustness of future schedules by applying the knowledge gathered from learning by example.
- Study the behaviour and compare the results, of several problem solving algorithms, including the ones that implement heuristics to specific problems. The idea is to classify the algorithms according to their success rate in solving specific types of problems in this domain.

8. Acknowledgements

The first author is supported by FCT (Fundação para a Ciência e Tecnologia) under research grant SFRH/BD/44109/2008. The authors are grateful to TAP Portugal for allowing the use of real data from the airline company.

9. References

Abdelgahny, A., Ekollu, G., Narisimhan, R. & Abdelgahny, K. 2004. A Proactive Crew Recovery Decision Support Tool for Commercial Airlines during Irregular Operations, *Annals of Operations Research*, Vol.127, pp. 309-331.

Barnhart, C., Belobaba, P. & Odoni, A. (2003). Applications of Operations Research in the Air Transport Industry, *Transportation Science*, Vol. 37, pp. 368-391.

Bellifemine, F., Caire, G., Trucco, T. & Rimassa, G. (2004). JADE Programmer's Guide, *JADE 3.3*, TILab S.p.A.

Bratu, S. & Barnhart, C. (2006). Flight Operations Recovery: New Approaches Considering Passenger Recovery, *Journal of Scheduling*, Vol. 9, No. 3, pp.279-298.

Castro, A.J.M. (2007). Designing a Multi-Agent System for Monitoring and Operations Recovery for an Airline Operations Control Centre, *MsC Thesis*, pp.1-133, Porto, Portugal: University of Porto, Faculty of Engineering.

Castro, A.J.M. & Oliveira, E. (2007). Using Specialized Agents in a Distributed MAS to Solve Airline Operations Problems: a Case Study, *Proceedings of IAT 2007 (Intelligent Agent Technology Conference)*, pp. 473-476, Silicon Valley, California, USA 2-5 November 2007, IEEE Computer Society, ISBN: 0-7695-3027-3.

Castro, A. (2008). Centros de Controlo Operacional: Organização e Ferramentas, *Monograph for Post-graduation in Air Transport Operations*, ISEC - Instituto Superior de Educação e Ciências, Outubro 2008 (In Portuguese).

Castro, A. & Oliveira, E. (2008). The rationale behind the development of an airline operations control centre using Gaia-based methodology, *International Journal of Agent-Oriented Software Engineering*, Vol. 2, No. 3, pp. 350–377.

Castro, A.J.M & Oliveira, E. (2009). Using Quality Costs in a Multi-Agent System for Airline Operations Control, *11th International Conference on Enterprise Information Systems*, Artificial Intelligence and Decision Support Systems, pp. 19-24, Milan, Italy, May 6-10, 2009. ISBN: 978-989-8111-85-2

Clausen, J., Larsen, A. & Larsen, J. (2005). Disruption Management in the Airline Industry - Concepts, Models and Methods, *Technical Report, 2005-01*, Informatics and Mathematical Modeling, Technical University of Denmark, DTU.

Cowling, P.I., Ouelhadj, D., & Petrovic, S. (2003). A Multi-Agent Architecture for Dynamic Scheduling of Steel Hot Rolling, *Journal of Intelligent Manufacturing, Special Issue on Agent-Based Manufacturing Process Planning and Scheduling*, Vol. 15, No. 5, pp. 457-470.

Elamy, A. (2005). Perspectives in Agents-Based Technology, *AgentLink News 18*, August 2005, ISSN: 1465-3842.

Fipa. (2002). *FIPA Contract Net Interaction Protocol Specification*, http://www.fipa.org/specs/fipa00029/SC00029H.html, Accessed in 2009/06/21.

Grosche, T. (2009). Computational Intelligence in Integrated Airline scheduling, *Springer-Verlag Berlin Heidelberg*, 978-3-540-89886-3, Germany.

Jonker, G., Meyer, J.-J., & Dignum, F. (2005). Towards a Market Mechanism for Airport Traffic Control, *12th Portuguese Conference on Artificial Intelligence (EPIA 2005)*, Covilha, Portugal.

Kohl, N. & Karisch, S. (2004). Airline crew rostering. problem types, modeling, and optimization, *Annals of Operations Research*, Vol. 127, pp. 223-257.

Kohl, N., Larsen, A., Larsen, J., Ross, A. & Tiourline, S. (2004). Airline Disruption Management - Perspectives, Experiences and Outlook, *Technical Report, CRTR-0407*, Carmen Research.

Lettovsky, L. (1997). Airline Operations Recovery: An Optimization Approach, *Ph.D. dissertation*, Georgia Institute of Technology, Atlanta, USA.

Liu, T., Jeng, C. & Chang, Y. (2008). Disruption Management of an Inequality-Based Multi-Fleet Airline Schedule by a Multi-Objective Genetic Algorithm, *Transportation Planning and Technology*, Vol. 31, No. 6, pp. 613-639.

Mota, A. (2007). Multi-Agent System for an Airline Operations Control Centre, *MsC Thesis, Porto*, Portugal: University of Porto, Faculty of Engineering.

Ouelhadj, D. (2003). A Multi-Agent System for the Integrated Dynamic Scheduling of Steel Production, *Ph.D. dissertation*, The University of Nottingham, School of Computer Science and Information Technology, England, August 2003.

Rosenberger, J., Johnson, E. & Nemhauser, G. (2001). Rerouting aircraft for airline recovery, *Technical Report, TLI-LEC 01-04*, Georgia Institute of Technology.

Rosenberger, J., Schaefer, A., Goldsmans, D., Johnson, E., Kleywegt, A. & Nemhauser, G. (2002). A Stochastic Model of Airline Operations, *Transportation Science*, Vol. 36, No. 4, pp. 357-377.

Smith, R. (1980). The Contract Net Protocol: High-Level Communication and Control in a Distributed Problem Solver, *IEEE Transactions on Computers*, Vol. C, No. 29.

Stone, P. & Veloso, M. (2000). Multi-Agent Systems: a Survey from a Machine Learning Perspective, *Autonomous Robotics*, Vol. 8. No. 3.

Tumer, K., & Agogino, A. (2007). Distributed Agent-Based Air Traffic Flow Management, *6th International Joint Conference on Autonomous Agents and Multiagent Systems (AAMAS 2007)*, Honolulu, Hawaii.

Wolfe, S. R., Jarvis, P. A., Enomoto, F. Y., & Sierhuis, M. (2007). Comparing Route Selection Strategies in Collaborative Traffic Flow Management., *Proceedings of IAT 2007 (Intelligent Agent Technology Conference)*, Silicon Valley, California, USA 2-5 November 2007, IEEE Computer Society, ISBN: 0-7695-3027-3.

Wooldridge, M., (2009). When is an Agent-Based Solution Appropriate? *An Introduction to Multiagent Systems*, West Sussex, England: John Wiley & Sons, Ltd., 2nd Edition (15 May 2009), pp. 183, ISBN: 978-0470519462.

Yang, M. (2007). Using Advanced Tabu Search Techniques to Solve Airline Disruption Management Problems, *Ph.D. dissertation*, The University of Texas at Austin, December 2007, USA.

7

Document Compression Improvements Based on Data Clustering

Jiří Dvorský, Jan Martinovič, Jan Platoš and Václav Snášel
VŠB – Technical University of Ostrava
Czech Republic

1. Introduction

The modern information society produces immense quantities of textual information. Storing text effectively and searching necessary information in stored texts are the tasks for *Information Retrieval Systems* (IRS). The size of an IRS increases with the increasing size of available external memories of computers. Therefore, it is now possible to have a several gigabyte IRS on one DVD. Similarly, with the growth of Internet it is possible to have an easy remote access to an extensive IRS, which is stored in an even bigger disk array that operates on an Web server. We can only expect even faster growth of memory capacity requirements in future. The information explosion can be avoided basically in two ways:

1. Extensively - by purchasing higher capacity memories, or
2. Intensively - by storing data in memories in a better way.

The first solution is not interesting in terms of research. The key to the second solution is *data compression*. The database of a typical IRS is a *textual database*, which stores all information that is necessary for the function of the IRS. Textual databases typically consist of the three following parts:

- Document full-texts that form a document collection
- Data structures for searching documents
- List of document identifiers and of their attributes and other auxiliary structures

Haskin claims in (Haskin, 1981) that the size of textual database auxiliary structures (i.e. except actual document texts) makes up 50% to 300% of the size of original documents. This implies that a textual database is a suitable material for compression. You only have to use one of lossless compression methods to save more or less space.
However, the problem of compression in IRS is not as simple as it seems at first sight. On the one hand, compression saves space for data, however, on the other hand, it may entail a certain operation overhead i.e. adding certain amount of time to the cost of accessing the data. Also, the space saving must be significant to be useful. Therefore, the objective is not to compress the textual database as a whole. This usually does not lead to good results since individual parts of an IRS contain redundancies of different types; different data structure types are based on a different model, according to which it is possible to determine the best compression method.

Experiences show that it is useful to consider, analyze and design the best compression method when storing extensive textual databases. It also proves to be desirable to study highly specialized compression methods that are convenient only for a certain data type in an IRS. Even saving e.g. one bit in data structures for searching and the improvement of text compression ratio in an IRS by one percent result in savings of tens of megabytes.

2. Information Retrieval Systems

Information retrieval systems (Baeza-Yates & Ribeiro-Neto, 1999) constitute a class of program tools for processing, storing and selecting data that are texts. An IRS is accessed by a user who needs to obtain certain information from this system to solve a problem. Such information is called *relevant*. Various documents can naturally satisfy users to various extents. Therefore we also speak of a *document relevancy ratio*.
When searching information in an IRS, a system user submits his or her requirement, a *query*, and awaits a result in the form of a set of documents selected by the system as documents matching the user requirement, i.e. matching the user's query. Users submit queries using a query language. Not only the logical structure of the query is important but also *terms* that users use in their formulations of the query. Under term we understand a certain text sample, mostly one word. It is generally required that the IRS provides system users with relevant documents (i.e. documents that are of interest to the user), namely all documents (presently available in the system), if possible, and only those documents (that are relevant). The algorithm, which implements the selection of relevant documents, presupposes a suitable preprocessing of input information about documents and storing to suitable data structures.

2.1 IRS architecture

The possibility of separating individual system components gave rise to the modular system architecture and lead to the separate development of these components in terms of optimizing the performance. The IRS therefore consists of several cooperating subsystems – modules. Architectures of individual systems differ from case to case but the architecture that is presented here can be considered typical. The architecture of a typical IRS is illustrated in Figures 1(a) and 1(b).
bsubsectionQuery Processing Diagram 1(a) shows the typical solution of a search problem, i.e. finding necessary information stored in a textual database. Especially the modules that are connected with the creating and debugging of queries are useful in this phase. These are the user interface that communicates with the user and the search algorithm that implements the actual search. In the search algorithm, it is then possible to specify modules of query lexical analysis, a stemmer for the creation of lemmas, a query evaluation module – data for query evaluation are obtained from a textual database. The sorting module sorts selected documents according to their relevancy to the query. The last operation carried out by this part of the IRS is presenting the selected documents to the user. When displaying document full-texts, they are retrieved from textual database structures and then decompressed and presented to the user.

2.2 Documents indexing

The second important part of the IRS is the indexing algorithm (see Figure 1(b)). The task of this module is to incorporate input documents into the textual database. The module assigns a unique internal identification to each document, then determines terms that characterize the document, and saves full text of the document to internal textual database structure.

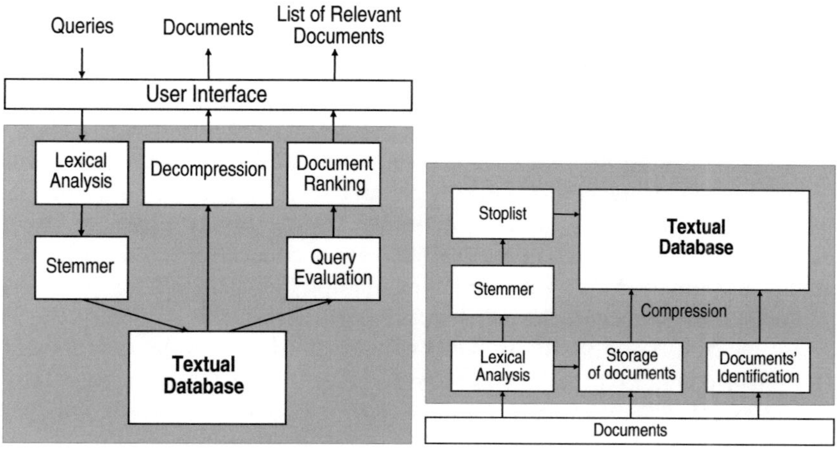

(a) Query Processing (b) Documents Indexing

Fig. 1. Architecture of IRS

The task of determining terms that appropriately characterize a document is called *document indexing*. The automatic indexing consists of selecting the terms to be included in the index and determining (mostly statistical) properties of the document, such as frequency of the occurrence of terms in one document, in the whole textual database, the length of documents etc. In the course of term evaluation, the relationship term – document is evaluated on the basis of these statistics and is rated with a certain weight. Similar mechanisms are also used to determine the term weight in the query. The relevancy ratio of the query and of individual documents is then determined on the basis of this *weight*[1].
The process of automatic indexing can be divided in the following phases:

- Lexical analyzer read input document character by character and extracts terms from the document.
- Stemming algorithm converts all terms from the document to their basic forms, *lemmas*. For English language standard stemming algorithm can be found in (Porter, 1980).
- All indexing methods define a certain set of words that will not be used for indexing. These words have only grammatical meaning in texts and do not form the content identity of documents. The set of these words is often called a non-word vocabulary or a *stoplist*.
- The last operation carried out by the indexing algorithm is saving the full text of the document to the textual database internal structures. Data compression algorithms specialized in text, that will be the subject of this chapter, will be used just in this phase.

[1] In 1988, Salton and Buckley (Salton & Buckley, 1988) presented a summary of twenty years of experiments during which they tested 287 different possibilities of assigning weights to terms in documents and to terms in queries.

3. Word-based Compression

The compression algorithm transforms input data that contain a certain redundancy to output data, in which redundancy is reduced to a minimum. The input and the output of data compression algorithms are generally strings of characters over a certain alphabet. There are no requirements concerning the alphabet. The selection of the alphabet is therefore a question of choice, which is influenced by various perspectives. Apart from a character alphabet, a word-based alphabet (Dvorský, Pokorný & Snášel, 1999; Dvorský, Snášel & Pokorný, 1999; Horspool & Cormack, 1992; Witten et al., 1999) is mostly chosen for the compression of texts. This alphabet is independent on used character encoding (ASCII/UNICODE), it has minimal cardinality[2] and it describes characteristic letter clusters in the text.
A compression method based on an alphabet of words, which will be called the *word-based compression method*, regards text as a sequence of words in a certain language. Sequences of white space characters between words are called nonwords. The application of irregular distribution of individual word occurrence probabilities is then assumed during compression in statistical compression methods or the clustering of words into language syntactical structures is assumed in dictionary methods. It is namely assumed that the language structure controls not only characters but also words. It is also assumed that these constructions are repeated and that it is possible to achieve a certain compression on the basis of this repetition. It is not assumed that the text consist only of hapax legomena[3] – even though this assumption can be used as well.

3.1 Compression and Decompression Algorithms

Word alphabets for text compression use several compression algorithms. One option is the HuffWord (Witten et al., 1999). Compression is based on the Huffman Canonic code. The Huffman canonic code differs from the standard Huffman code in the method in which it produces code words.
Methods tested in this chapter are: WLZW, WBW, and WLZ77. The WLZW (Dvorský, 2004) method is based on the LZW algorithm (Welch, 1984), while the WBW (Dvorský, 2004) method is based on the Burrows-Wheeler transformation (Burrows & Wheeler, 1994). And the WLZ77 (Platoš & Dvorský, 2007; Platoš et al., 2008) method is based on the LZ77 method (Ziv & Lempel, 1977).
Among common features of these methods belong:

- Usage of word-based alphabet
- Token alternation – if some conditions hold words and nonwords take turns – alternate. This alternation makes it possible to predict the type of the following token and thus reduce the entropy of the following token.
- The victim elimination makes it possible to eliminate a chosen nonword on the basis of token alternation. A shortening of the input token sequence and an improvement of compression effectiveness will thus be achieved.
- Substitution of hapax legomena – it is useless to compress tokens with only one occurrence. The tokens are therefore replaced with a single substitute, which indicates the occurrence of the token of this class.

[2] The alphabet contains only used symbols, not all potentially possible symbols.
[3] Hapax legomenon – a word with only one occurrence in the examined text.

- Two-pass compression method – all designed methods are intended for IRS that are used for archiving. Documents are compressed once and decompressed many times. The semi adaptive approach is no complication in this case.
- Integration with full-text search in IRS – searching and compression can benefit from shared data structures e.g. full-text indices, clustering etc.

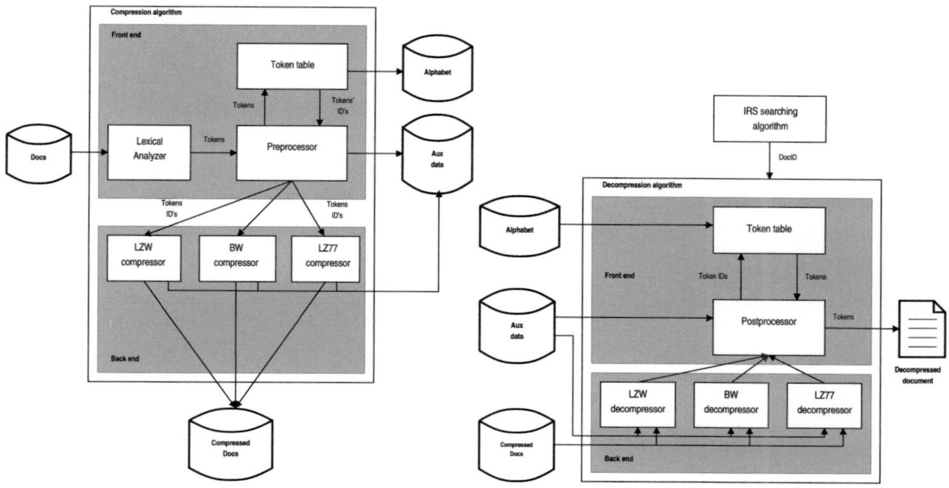

(a) compressor schema (b) decompressor schema

Fig. 2. Compression and decompression algorithms

In the diagram in Figure 2(a), the schematic structures compression algorithms are illustrated. As seen in the illustration, all compression algorithms are separable into approximately two parts, identified as *front end* and *back end*. Both compression algorithms process text documents in two passes. Separation of the compression methods into two parts corresponds with these passes. We can distinguish the following two phases in all algorithms:

First phase – corresponds to the *first pass* compression algorithm. In this phase, a word alphabet is created. Individual tokens are extracted from documents by performing a lexical partition, which is performed in the front end part. This phase is shared with document indexing in a textual database.

Second phase – corresponds to the *second pass* compression algorithm. Upon completion of the first phase, we have a complete word alphabet at our disposal and we can begin the actual document compression. Again, a lexical partition is performed and the emergent token sequence is compressed with the chosen algorithm. In this phase, both the front end and back end of the compression algorithm are working.

Separation of the compression algorithm into two relatively independent parts enabled the separation of two different phases of the compression algorithm or, in other words, the creation of a word alphabet and its actual compression was enabled. Understandably, this separation simplified the algorithm's design, clarified implementation, etc.
In diagram in Figure 2(b) the structure of decompression algorithms is illustrated. As seen in the illustration, all decompression algorithms can be separated into two parts, as in compression. – *front end* a *back end*.

The proposed methods are designed asymmetrically, resulting in the following:

- Decompression is easier than compression. All activities able to be performed by compression algorithms are transposed to the algorithm in a way that ensures that only the most necessary decompression algorithms are performed.
- Decompression has only one phase. Only one pass through compressed text is needed to decompress a document. All objects illustrated in schema in Figure 2(b) are consequently active during decompression and the decompression process maintains a *through-flow* character.

4. Cluster Analysis

Cluster analysis is the process of separating documents, with the same or similar properties, into groups that are created based on specific issues. We will call these groups of documents *clusters* (Jain & Dubes, 1988). Clustering may be applied to terms or documents when working with documents in IR systems. Term clustering can be used for creating a thesaurus. Joining similar documents to a cluster may be done by increasing the speed level for searching in search engines. The reason for carrying out a cluster partitioning is explained in *hypothesis about clusters* (Jain et al., 1999):

When documents are in close proximity, they are relevant to the same information.

We are going to focus on clustering documents and our work can be summarized by the following two steps: creating a cluster and searching for relevant clusters (Faloutsos, 1995).
The process within which the ideal cluster partitioning for sets of document is searched, and within which there are mutually similar documents, is called *clustering*. The cluster is then formed mutually by a set with similar documents.
In an ideal situation, the clustering procedure should accomplish two goals: correctness and effectiveness (Faloutsos, 1995). The criteria for correctness follow:

- methods should remain stable while collections grow or, in other words, distribution into clusters should not drastically change the addition of new documents,
- small errors in document descriptions should be carried over as small changes in cluster distributions into clusters,
- a method should not be dependent on its initial document ordering.

Conventional cluster distribution methods (Berkhin, 2006; Gan et al., 2007; Jain et al., 1999) are split into two categories:

Partitional methods – the goal is to employ a partition that best maintains clustering criteria[4].

Hierarchal methods – These methods are based on matrix similarities in documents. The goal of this method is to create a cluster hierarchy (tree cluster).

Sets of clustering algorithms being used and developed today are too large. A similar view can be found in publications such as (Gan et al., 2007; Jain et al., 1999).
Due to the fact that most clustering methods work with mutual similarities between clusters, it is necessary to convey this similarity by using *cluster similarity partitioning coefficient*.

[4] In following text we study hierarchal methods only.

Let us have a twin cluster c_i a $c_j \in \{c_1, c_2, \ldots c_l\}$, where l is the amount of all calculated clusters. Then, similarity coefficient $sim(c_i, c_j)$ fulfills these conditions:

$$sim(c_i, c_j) \geq 0 \quad (1)$$
$$sim(c_i, c_j) = sim(c_j, c_i) \quad (2)$$
$$sim(c_i, c_i) = \max_{sim} \quad (3)$$

where max_{sim} is the maximum value of similarity coefficient. Similarity between clusters is defined the same as the similarity between two documents or between a document and a query, e.g. cosine measure can be used and some kind of term weighting (Berry, 2003).

4.1 Hierarchical Methods

These methods utilize the matrix similarity C, which can be described as follows for the document collection n :

$$C = \begin{pmatrix} sim_{11} & sim_{12} & \ldots & sim_{1n} \\ sim_{21} & sim_{22} & \ldots & sim_{2n} \\ \vdots & \vdots & \ddots & \vdots \\ sim_{n1} & sim_{n2} & \ldots & sim_{nn} \end{pmatrix}$$

where i-th row answers the i-th document and j-th column answers the j-th document.
A hierarchy of partitions for requisite documents is formed with these clustering methods. During calculations, a cluster surface is formed. Points are joined to the cluster on this surface. Hierarchal methods can be split into two groups:

Agglomerative – At the start of this method each document is understood as one cluster. These documents are gradually joined together (clustering). The calculation is over the moment all joined documents form one cluster.

Divisive – This method works exactly opposite to agglomerative methods. At the start of this method, all documents form one cluster. These clusters gradually break down, until the moment each point becomes an individual cluster.

4.1.1 Aglomerative Clustering

Aglomerative hierarchal clustering methods mainly belong to the SAHN (sequential agglomerative hierarchical no-overlapping) method. It holds true that two clusters formed with this method do not contain the same object (Downs & Barnard, 2003). These methods differ in the way in which their similarity matrix is initially calculated (point 4 following Algorithm 4.1). These methods usually have $O(n^2)$ for memory space complexity and $O(n^3)$ for time complexity, where n is the number of data points. This conversion is derived from Lance-Williams' formula for matrix conversions (Downs & Barnard, 2003):

$$prox[t,(p,q)] = \alpha_p \; prox[t,p] + \alpha_q \; prox[t,q] + \beta \; prox[p,q] + \gamma \; |prox[t,p] - prox[t,q]| \quad (4)$$

where $prox[t,(p,q)]$ determines cluster similarity c_t and cluster $c_{(pq)}$ is formed by clusters c_p joined with cluster c_q. Value parameters α_p, α_q, β a γ define various cluster SAHN methods. We list some of these methods in the Table 1. The Algorithm 4.1 describe calculations for hierarchal agglomerative clustering. In the following paragraphs N_i is amount of documents in a cluster c_i.
The results of the aforementioned algorithm differ in accordance with the similarity matrix conversion method used. Now we will present some of these methods:

SAHN method	α_p	α_q	β	γ
Single link	$\frac{1}{2}$	$\frac{1}{2}$	0	$-\frac{1}{2}$
Complete link	$\frac{1}{2}$	$\frac{1}{2}$	0	$\frac{1}{2}$
Centroid method	$\frac{N_p}{N_p+N_q}$	$\frac{N_q}{N_p+N_q}$	$\frac{-N_p\,N_q}{(N_p+N_q)^2}$	0
Ward's method	$\frac{N_p+N_t}{N_p+N_q+N_t}$	$\frac{N_q+N_t}{N_p+N_q+N_t}$	$\frac{-N_t}{N_p+N_q+N_t}$	0
Median method	$\frac{1}{2}$	$\frac{1}{2}$	$-\frac{1}{4}$	0

Table 1. SAHN matrix similarity conversion methods

Algorithm 4.1 Hierarchal agglomerative clustering

1. Form a document similarity matrix.
2. When clustering begins, each document represents one cluster. In other words, we have as many clusters as we have documents. Gradually, as each individual cluster is joined, clusters dwindle away until we are left with one cluster.
3. Locate the two most similar clusters p a q and identify this similarity as $prox_s[p,q]$.
4. Reduce the amount of joined clusters p and q. We identify the new cluster as t (replaces row and column q) and recalculates the similarity ($prox_s[t,r]$) of the newly formed cluster t to other clusters r. Further, we identify $prox_l[p,q]$ as the similarity to which p a q clusters have been joined. This similarity is equal to $prox_s[p,q]$ in most methods. Then we delete the row and column corresponding to cluster p from the similarity matrix.
5. Repeat the previous two steps until only one cluster remains.

Single linkage – We calculate the similarity of all documents in a single cluster with all the documents in another cluster, whose greatest value is searched for with a similarity cluster. Recalculation $prox_s[t,r]$ with:

$$prox_s[t,r] = max(prox_s[p,r], prox_s[q,r]) \tag{5}$$

Complete linkage – We calculate the similarity of all documents in a single cluster with all the documents in another cluster, whose smallest value is searched for with a similarity cluster. Recalculation $prox_s[t,r]$ with:

$$prox_s[t,r] = min(prox_s[p,r], prox_s[q,r]) \tag{6}$$

Centroid method – This method leads to clusters where each document in a cluster has a larger similarity average with remaining documents in the cluster than all the documents in any other cluster. Recalculate $prox_s[t,r]$ with:

$$prox_s[t,r] = \frac{N_p prox_s[p,r] + N_q prox_s[q,r]}{N_p + N_q} \tag{7}$$

Today, other specialized hierarchical clustering methods exist. Thanks to these new methods, we can reduce time and memory complexity and work with large documents collections more effectively. Some of these new methods include (Gan et al., 2007): SLINK, Single-link algorithm based on minimum spanning tree, CLINK, BIRCH, CURE, etc.

5. Topical Development

There are many systems used for searching collections of textual documents. These systems are based on the vector model, probability models and other models for document representation, queries, rules and procedures. All of these systems contain a number of limitations. Incomplete lists of relevant documents obtained in search results ranks among one of the most basic of these limitations.

An important service for systems providing access to information is the organization of returned search results. Conventional IRS evaluate obtained documents based on their similarity to given query (Chalmers & Chitson, 1992). Other systems present graphic illustrations based on mutually similar documents (Jacobs et al., 2000; Salton, 1989; Thompson & Croft, 1989), specific attribute relations (Korfhage, 1991; Spoerri, 1993) and samples of terms distributed in the query (Hearst, 1995).

Vector model search results may be represented by a sphere in an n-dimensional space. A query represents the center of this sphere whose size is determined by its radius (range query) or by the amount of documents it contains (NN–query). The goal of searching is to have all documents relevant to a query present within this sphere. It is known that not all relevant documents are present in this sphere and that is why various methods for improving search results, which can be implemented on the basis of expanding the original question, have been developed.

Our goal is to utilize knowledge of document similarity contained in textual databases to obtain a larger amount of relevant documents while minimizing those canceled due to their irrelevance (Martinovič, 2004; Martinovič & Gajdoš, 2005; Martinovič et al., 2008). In this section, we focus on metric issues and follow this focus up with defining of the concept of *topical development*, as a method for eliminating this problem.

5.1 Issues with Metric Searching

The distance between the two documents x and y is the function $\delta(x,y) : \mathbb{X} \times \mathbb{X} \rightarrow \mathbb{R}$ (where $\mathbb{X}$ is a set of all documents), for which the following conditions hold:

$$\delta(x,x) = 0 \tag{8}$$

$$\delta(x,y) \geq 0 \tag{9}$$

$$\delta(x,y) = \delta(y,x) \tag{10}$$

Distance further requires the validity of triangle inequality. Triangle inequality is only valid when triad x, y and z abide by the following conditions:

$$\delta(x,z) \leq \delta(x,y) + \delta(y,z) \tag{11}$$

Set $\mathbb{X}$ and function δ create the metric space (Armstrong, 1997), which we identify as $(\mathbb{X}, \delta)$.

5.1.1 ϵ-ball and ϵ-k-ball

For given $x \in \mathbb{X}$ and $\epsilon \in \mathbb{R}^+$ (where $\mathbb{R}^+ = \{x \in \mathbb{R} | x \geq 0\}$), the set $B(x,\epsilon) = \{y \in \mathbb{X}; \delta(x,y) \leq \epsilon\}$ is called the *ball* with the radius ϵ, or ϵ-ball centered at the point x.
The ϵ-k-ball is an equivalent of ϵ-ball in a metric space. For given $x \in \mathbb{X}$, $\epsilon \in \mathbb{R}^+$ and $k \in \mathbb{N}^+$, the set $B^k(x,\epsilon) = \{y \in \mathbb{X}; x_1, \ldots, x_k \in \mathbb{X}, x = x_1, y = x_k, \sum_{l=1}^{k-1} \delta(x_l, x_{l+1}) \leq \epsilon\}$ is called the k-ball with the radius ϵ, or ϵ-k-ball centered at the point x.
It is easy to show that:

$$B(x,\epsilon) = B^k(x,\epsilon) \tag{12}$$

Formally, this means that any k-step path of length ϵ belong to ϵ-ball.

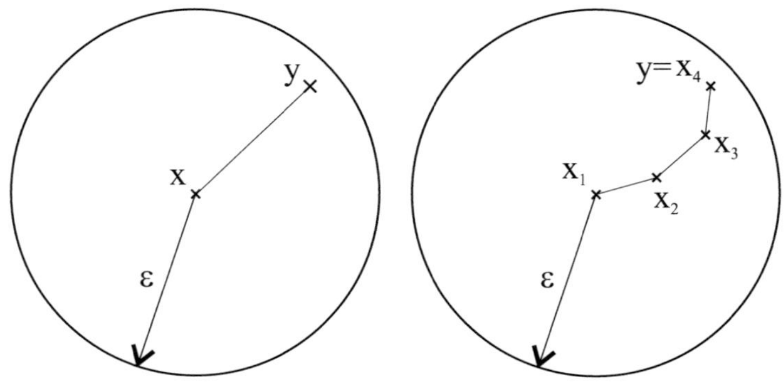

(a) ϵ-ball (b) ϵ-k-ball

Fig. 3. Balls in metric space

The Figure 3(a) represents ϵ-ball well known in the vector model. The extension ϵ-k-ball is shown in Figure 3(b). The Figure 4 illustrates the back-transformation from ϵ-k-ball to ϵ-ball. We are able to construct a triangle between two different points. The hypotenuse can replace two legs of such triangle. The condition of a triangle inequality is satisfied.

5.1.2 ϵ-k-ball and Similarity

A *similarity* $s(x,y)$ between document x and y is function $s(x,y) : \mathbb{X} \times \mathbb{X} \rightarrow \mathbb{R}$ which satisfied the following conditions:

$$s(x,x) = 1 \tag{13}$$
$$s(x,y) \geq 0 \tag{14}$$
$$s(x,y) = s(y,x) \tag{15}$$

If a non-metric is used, the triangle inequality is disturbed and the identity generally does not hold. We performed some experiments with non-metric, which satisfies the condition of ϵ-k-ball. This is shown in an illustrative example below. In this way, we were able to find some documents which could be not found in a metric space.
The Table 1(a) creates the input vectors which represent documents. A dissimilarity matrix computed for this input is shown in Table 1(c). Cosine similarity is used for computing the similarity matrix (see Table 1(b)) and the similarity matrix is then converted to a dissimilarity

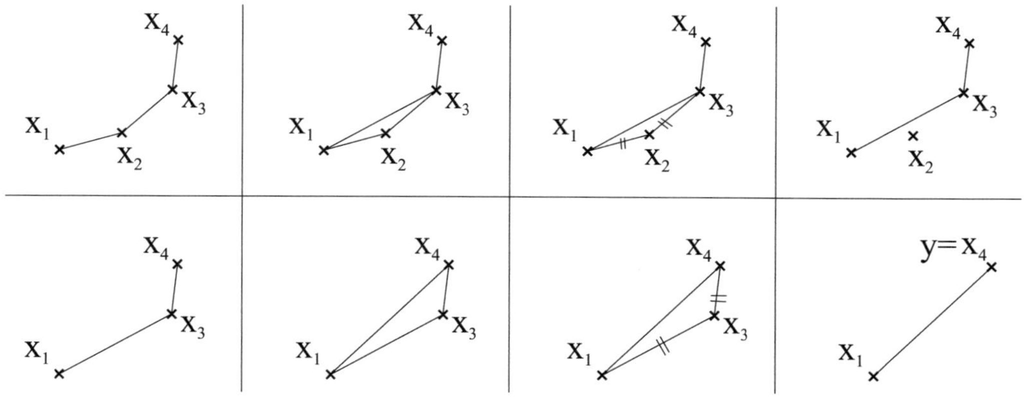

Fig. 4. ϵ-k-ball to ϵ-ball transformation

(a) incidence matrix

	t_0	t_1	t_2	t_3	t_4
d_0	1	1	0	0	0
d_1	1	1	1	1	0
d_2	0	1	1	1	0
d_3	0	0	1	0	1

(b) similarity matrix

	d_0	d_1	d_2	d_3
d_0	1.00	0.71	0.14	0.00
d_1	0.71	1.00	0.76	0.06
d_2	0.14	0.76	1.00	0.07
d_3	0.00	0.06	0.07	1.00

(c) dissimilarity matrix

	d_0	d_1	d_2	d_3
d_0	0.00	0.29	0.86	1.00
d_1	0.29	0.00	0.24	0.94
d_2	0.86	0.24	0.00	0.93
d_3	1.00	0.94	0.93	0.00

Table 2. Sample document collection

matrix. The ϵ-ball is centered in the document d_0. Only the document d_1 could be reached using a conventional vector model for ϵ-ball $= 0.6$.
Then, there are two ϵ-k-ball in Figure 5. The first one consists of documents d_0, d_1 and d_2. The second one contains the documents d_0, d_1 and d_3.

5.2 Topical Development of a Given Document

In the preceding paragraphs, we defined ϵ-k-ball and its behavior in a space that does not maintain the rules of triangle inequality. Now, we define the concept k-path, for which the term "topical development" will be used.
The definition of k-path: for the given $x \in \mathbb{X}$ and $k \in \mathbb{N}^+$, the set $B^k(x) = \{y \in \mathbb{X}; x_1, \ldots, x_k \in \mathbb{X}, x = x_1, y = x_k\}$ is called the k-path centered at the point x.
We can present topical development as a path leading away from the initial document, through similar documents and towards other documents pertaining to this document.

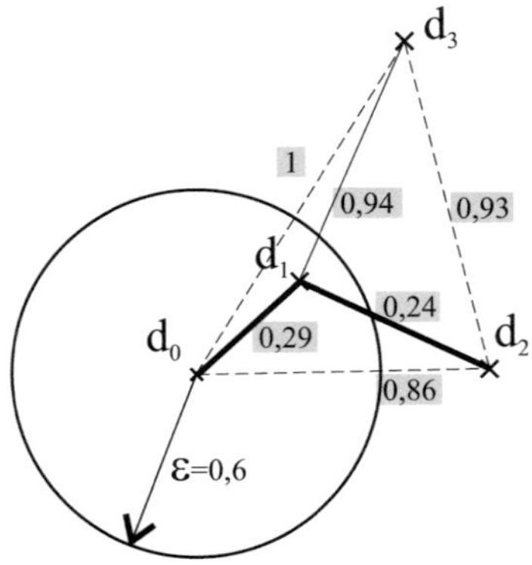

Fig. 5. The result in sphere dissimilarity distances

We can illustrate this path in a vector space, where our document forms nodes. The edges between these nodes evaluate their similarity. If this path satisfies the conditions for k-path we can say that it is a proper representation of topical development.
Thematic similarity between documents in text collections is influenced by terms that occur in the document. Let us take a document, which describes a given topic, from a collection of documents. There may be other documents in our collection of documents that either entirely, or partially, shares the same topic (problematic). These documents, however, may use a part of another word to describe the given topic. The difference in this word may be caused by various reasons. The first document may direct a set of words toward the topic and the second document may include a synonym or it may be more focused on other circumstances influenced by the chosen topic (a new fact, a political situation, a new problem trend and so on).
We can create many other methods based on IRS theories for topical development. In our work, we have subsequently defined several of these methods:

TOPIC-NN2 – topical development with NN-query - variant 2.

TOPIC-CA – topical development using a cluster analysis.

5.2.1 Topical Development with NN-query

The principle of the TOPIC-NN2 follows: we start with document d_i, for which we search for topical development. For this document, we find the most similar d_k document and add it to the resulting topical development. Then, we repeat this process, but instead of using the original d_i document, we use document d_k. The expansion is completed either when the necessary amount of documents in the development has been reached, or if the next closest document we are searching for does not exist. An example of this method is illustrated in Figure 6.

5.2.2 Topical Development using a Cluster Analysis

Now we face the question of how to effectively search for topical development. One possible approach to carrying out a search for topical development is to use a cluster partitioning (see

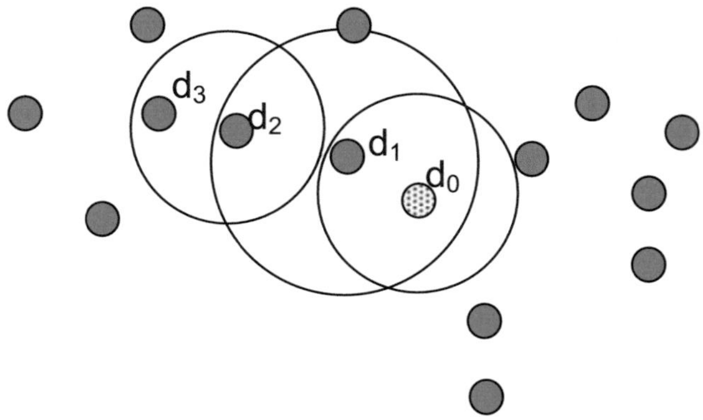

Fig. 6. Example of TOPIC-NN2

Section 4). The method which we now present carries out the main part of the calculation during the document indexing phase. This enables fast searching.
The reason we chose cluster partitioning for determining topical development is its ability to create groups of similar documents. We chose hierarchal aglomerative clustering from the available clustering method options. We can present the results of this type of clustering using a dendrogram (see Section 4.1.1).
Steps for the automation of topical development are as follows:

1. Index text collections into the IRS.
2. Create a similarity matrix for the document C.
3. Hierarchal aglomerative clustering in the similarity matrix C.
4. Topical development query - algorithm acquired in topical development.

5.2.2.1 Algorithm Acquired of Topical Development

For acquiring topical development from hierarchal clustering, we will define the algorithm *TOPIC-CA*, which uses the amount of documents in the development as a hindrance.

Definition 5.1. *The TOPIC-CA algorithm (see Algorithm 5.1) for acquiring topical development is defined with the aid of a dendrogram* D_{Tree} *as list* $S_T = TOPIC\_CA(d_q)$. *Where* d_q *is a node in the dendrogram for which we want to generate a topical development.*

The advantage of using this algorithm for acquiring topical development is low time and space requirement during querying. For searching topical development, we need a dendrogram with pre-calculated similarity for each individual node of the dendrogram. The disadvantage is the time required to create the dendrogram. A calculation of the hierarchal cluster is performed during the creation of a textual database, so users entering queries into the IRSs are not influenced by this factor.
The following functions are used in the algorithm:

$TOPIC\_CA$ – main function for calculating topical development (see Algorithm 5.1),

Sub – function for recursive dendrogram outlet (see Algorithm 5.2),

Algorithm 5.1 Algorithm TOPIC-CA – function *TOPIC_CA*

function TOPIC_CA($node \in D_{Tree} \cup null$)
  $L \leftarrow$ Empty list
  if $node \neq null$ **then**
    AddNodeToEnd(L, $node$)
    while $node \neq null$ **do**
      $sibling \leftarrow$ SIBLING($node$)
      $L \leftarrow$ SUB($sibling$, L)
      $node \leftarrow$ PARENT($node$)
    end while
  end if
  return L
end function

Sim – calculation for similarity of a given cluster in a dendrogram D_{Tree} to a neighbor's descendant cluster (see Algorithm 5.3),

Sibling – acquired neighboring nodes,

Parent – acquired parent nodes,

LeftChild – acquired left descendant,

RightChild – acquired right descendant,

AddNodeToEnd – addition of a document to resulting topical development. If the calculation of documents in a topic is equal to the required amount of documents, algorithm *TOPIC_CA* ends (to simplify the process, it is left out of algorithm *TOPIC_CA*).

6. Using Topical Development for Improved Text Document Compression

Input document ordering has not yet been taken into consideration within the general description of word-base compression methods. The compression method works properly for any type of document ordering. Time ordering is probably the simplest of input documents ordering options, i.e. documents are compressed in the same order as they are added to a textual database. Seeing that compression methods are based on searching repeated parts of texts, it is easy to surmise that this ordering option is not necessarily the best solution. Improvement of compression performance can be achieved by reordering input documents. We improve the ordering of input documents by moving similar documents nearer to one another. This improved ordering can be achieved using a cluster analysis. Of course, a cluster analysis is very time consuming so that it is counterproductive to perform the analysis in order to enhance compression performance alone. However, when compression methods for IR system are developed, results from a cluster analysis can be used in query processing (Dvorský et al., 2004; Martinovič & Gajdoš, 2005) and vice versa. Cluster analysis originally performed solely for query processing can be incorporated to compression.

Incorporating a cluster analysis to improve a compression is common in methods that compress inverted indexes (includes a list of documents for every indexed term). These methods, using hierarchical clustering (Blandford & Blelloc, 2002) or clustering algorithms, resemble the k-means (Orlando et al., 2004).

Algorithm 5.2 Algorithm TOPIC-CA – function *Sub*

function SUB($node \in D_{Tree} \cup null$, list L)
  if $node = null$ **then**
    return L
  end if
  $sibling \leftarrow$ SIBLING($node$)
  if $node \in$ leaf nodes of D_{Tree} **then**
    AddNodeToEnd(L, $node$)
  else if $sibling \neq null$ **then**
    $siblingLeft \leftarrow$ LEFTCHILD($sibling$)
    $siblingRight \leftarrow$ RIGHTCHILD($sibling$)
    $sim_{Left} \leftarrow$ SIM($node, siblingLeft$)
    $sim_{Right} \leftarrow$ SIM($node, siblingRight$)
    if $Sim_{Right} \leq Sim_{Left}$ **then**
      $L \leftarrow$ SUB($siblingLeft, L$)
      $L \leftarrow$ SUB($siblingRight, L$)
    else
      $L \leftarrow$ SUB($siblingRight, L$)
      $L \leftarrow$ SUB($siblingLeft, L$)
    end if
  end if
  return L
end function

However, the question of how to convert a hierarchical tree structure of clusters to a linear list of documents still remains. The answer is to use topical development (Dvorský & Martinovič, 2007; Martinovič et al., 2007; Platoš et al., 2008). The topical development commands one document that specifies a topic the as starting point of a topic development searching process. This starting document can be chosen arbitrarily – there is no topic defined by a document retrieved during the user query searching process.
Two strategies were used to reorder document collections entering the compression process:

Most Similar Left (MSL) – k-path (k equal to amount of all documents in the collection) by TOPIC-CA algorithm for the leftmost document in the dendrogram created during clustering.

Most Similar Right (MSR) – k-path (k equal to amount of all documents in the collection) TOPIC-CA algorithm for the rightmost document in the dendrogram created during clustering.

7. Experimental Results

Several experiments have been carried out to test impact clustering on word-based compression methods. Both compression methods were used in our tests. Two large text files were used for our tests: latimes.txt coming from TREC corpus (Harman, 1997), and enron.txt, which consists of emails from Enron email corpus [5]. In the file latimes.txt, individual documents are

[5] Duplicate emails were deleted before processing.

Algorithm 5.3 Algorithm TOPIC-CA – function *Sim*. Calculated proximity of cluster n_1 to a descendant of a neighboring cluster n_2 in the hierarchy

function SIM($n_1 \in D_{Tree} \cup null, n_2 \in D_{Tree} \cup null$)
    if $node_1 = null \vee node_2 = null$ **then**
        return 0
    end if
    $c_{n_1} \leftarrow$ centroid created from all leafs nodes in n_1
    $c_{n_2} \leftarrow$ centroid created from all leafs nodes in n_2
    $sim \leftarrow$ similarity between c_{n_1} and c_{n_2}
    return *sim*
end function

represented by each newspaper article and ordering is determined by date of publication. Each individual email represents a document in the enron.txt file, and ordering is defined as alphabetical ordering of users in Enron corpus. Results for this type of ordering without ordering is provided in the Table 4.

A notation used to describe results of experiments can be seen in Table 3. The value Δ represents the difference between a given value and a corresponding value in a compression without clustering. A positive Δ value means that the given value is worse than the original value. A negative value means that the new value is better than the original one.

The first experiment was focused on comparison among three types of word-based compression methods and two commonly-used programs - GZip and BZip. Results of this experiment are depicted in Table 4. As can be seen, the best result was achieved by algorithms WBW for latimes.txt file and WLZ77 for enron.txt file. Other algorithms were much worse than WLZ77.

The second experiment was focused on compression of clustered files. Both files are relatively large. The size of these documents (newspapers articles, emails) varies from hundreds of bytes to eight kilobytes. Compression with clustering and five random permutations were tested.

It is easy to see from Table 5, that clustering brings positive results in terms of compression ratio. The size of the compressed text for latimes.txt file is about 4% less than the original size in the WLZW methods, about 5% smaller than the original one in the WBW method and about 3.5% smaller than the original size in the WLZ77 method. The compression ratio improves to cca 1.2% with respect to original values in all cases. Better results were achieved for file enron.txt, see Table 5. The improvement of compression ratio is more than 2 % with respect to the original compressed size in the WLZW and WLZ77 methods, and cca 4 % in the WBW method.

Random permutations deteriorate compressions in all cases (see Table 6, and Table 7). These negative results mean that clustering has a measurable impact on compression performance, and the positive results of considering cluster supported compressions are not coincidental.

The results of standard GZip and BZip2 compression utilities provide data for comparison with our proposed word-based compression methods. As can be seen from tables, character of these results is very close to our methods; therefore clustering has serious impact on compression regardless of selected compression method.

Symbol	Meaning	Units
S_0	size of original file	bytes
CS_α	size of compressed file using α method	bytes
CR_α	compression ratio using α method $CR_\alpha = \frac{CS_\alpha}{S_0} \times 100\%$	percents
CS	size of compressed file with clustering and using particular compression method	bytes
ΔCS	relative improvement of compression $\Delta CS = \frac{CS_\alpha - CS}{CS_\alpha} \times 100\%$	percents
CR	compression ratio for given CS $CR = \frac{CS}{S_0} \times 100\%$	percents
ΔCR	improvement of compression ratio for given CR $\Delta CR = CR_\alpha - CR$	percents
	where $\alpha \in \{WLZW, WBW, WLZ77, GZIP, BZIP2\}$	

Table 3. Notation used in compression experiments

		latimes.txt	**enron.txt**
Original size	S_0	498,360,166	886,993,953
WLZW method			
Compressed size	CS_{WLZW}	158,017,940	207,908,560
Compression ratio	CR_{WLZW}	31.708	23.440
WBW method			
Compressed size	CS_{WBW}	110,246,524	167,099,129
Compression ratio	CR_{WBW}	22.122	18.839
WLZ77 method			
Compressed size [bytes]	CS_{WLZ77}	113,185,477	113,394,015
Compression ratio [%]	CR_{WLZ77}	22.712	12.784
Gzip			
Compressed size	CS_{GZIP}	175,864,812	228,953,895
Compression ratio	CR_{GZIP}	35.289	25.812
BZip2			
Compressed size	CS_{BZIP2}	131,371,338	164,720,382
Compression ratio	CR_{BZIP2}	26.361	18.571

Table 4. Compression without clustering

(a) WLZW method

Cluster strategy on file	CS	$CS_{WLZW} - CS$	ΔCS	CR	ΔCR
MSL latimes.txt	151,869,588	-6,148,352	-3.891	30.474	-1.234
MSR latimes.txt	151,973,800	-6,044,140	-3.825	30.495	-1.213
MSL enron.txt	187,951,820	-19,956,740	-9.599	21.190	-2.250

(b) WBW method

Cluster strategy on file	CS	$CS_{WBW} - CS$	ΔCS	CR	ΔCR
MSL latimes.txt	104,701,332	-5,545,192	-5.030	21.009	-1.113
MSR latimes.txt	104,706,446	-5,540,078	-5.025	21.010	-1.112
MSL enron.txt	132,707,295	-34,391,834	-20.582	14.961	-3.877

(c) WLZ77 method

Cluster strategy on file	CS	$CS_{WLZ77} - CS$	Δ_{CS}	CR	Δ_{CR}
MSL latimes.txt	109,102,809	-4,082,668	-3.741	21.892	-0.814
MSR latimes.txt	109,127,221	-4,058,256	-3.502	21.897	-0.819
MSL enron.txt	92,094,979	-21,299,036	-18.783	10.383	-2.401

(d) GZip method

Cluster strategy on file	CS	$CS_{GZIP} - CS$	ΔCS	CR	ΔCR
MSL latimes.txt	164,298,043	-11,566,769	-6.577	32.968	-2.321
MSR latimes.txt	164,322,641	-11,542,171	-6.563	32.973	-2.316
MSL enron.txt	153,765,189	-75,188,706	-32.84	17.336	-8.477

(e) Bzip2 method

Cluster strategy on file	CS	$CS_{BZIP2} - CS$	ΔCS	CR	ΔCR
MSL latimes.txt	120,149,683	-11,221,655	-8.542	24.109	-2.252
MSR latimes.txt	120,154,853	-11,216,485	-8.538	24.110	-2.251
MSL enron.txt	122,024,594	-42,695,788	-25.920	13.757	-4.814

Table 5. Impact of clustering on compression

(a) WLZW method

Permutation	CS	$CS_{WLZW} - CS$	ΔCS	CR	ΔCR
1	160,417,812	2,399,872	1.519	32.189	0.481
2	160,456,620	2,438,680	1.543	32.197	0.489
3	160,448,056	2,430,116	1.538	32.195	0.487
4	160,456,564	2,438,624	1.543	32.197	0.489
5	160,475,324	2,457,384	1.555	32.201	0.493
Average	160,450,875	2,432,935	1.540	32.196	0.488

(b) WBW method

Permutation	CS	$CS_{WBW} - CS$	ΔCS	CR	ΔCR
1	111,686,104	1,439,580	1.306	22.411	0.289
2	111,713,942	1,467,418	1.331	22.416	0.294
3	111,718,068	1,471,544	1.335	22.417	0.295
4	111,717,879	1,471,355	1.335	22.417	0.295
5	111,712,566	1,466,042	1.330	22.416	0.294
Average	111,709,712	1,463,188	1.327	22.415	0.293

(c) WLZ77 method

Permutation	CS	$CS_{WLZ77} - CS$	ΔCS	CR	ΔCR
1	115,818,360	2,632,883	2.326	23.240	0.528
2	115,864,040	2,678,563	2.367	23.249	0.537
3	115,874,546	2,689,069	2.376	23.251	0.540
4	115,886,055	2,700,578	2.386	23.253	0.542
5	115,880,575	2,695,098	2.381	23.252	0.541
Average	115,864,715	2,679,238	2,367	23,249	0,538

(d) GZip method

Permutation	CS	$CS_{GZIP} - CS$	ΔCS	CR	ΔCR
1	182,350,555	6,485,743	3.688	36.590	1.301
2	182,612,870	6,748,058	3.837	36.643	1.354
3	182,626,115	6,761,303	3.845	36.645	1.357
4	182,616,966	6,752,154	3.839	36.644	1.355
5	182,616,986	6,752,174	3.839	36.644	1.355
Average	182,564,698	6,699,886	3.810	36.633	1.344

(e) BZip2 method

Permutation	CS	$CS_{BZIP2} - CS$	ΔCS	CR	ΔCR
1	133,747,217	2,375,879	1.809	26.837	0.477
2	133,859,533	2,488,195	1.894	26.860	0.499
3	133,848,650	2,477,312	1.886	26.858	0.497
4	133,864,200	2,492,862	1.898	26.861	0.500
5	133,854,622	2,483,284	1.890	26.859	0.498
Average	133,834,844	2,463,506	1.875	26.855	0.494

Table 6. File latimes.txt: random permutations

Permutation	CS	$CS_{WLZW} - CS$	ΔCS	CR	ΔCR
1	242,459,136	34,550,576	16.618	27.335	3.895
2	249,122,668	41,214,108	19.823	28.086	4.646
3	250,203,876	42,295,316	20.343	28.208	4.768
4	250,342,664	42,434,104	20.410	28.224	4.784
5	250,511,920	42,603,360	20.491	28.243	4.803
Average	248,528,052	40,619,492	19.537	28.019	4.579

Table 7. File enron.txt: random permutations

The results of standard GZip and BZip2 compression utilities provide data for comparison with our proposed word-based compression methods. As can be seen in tables, the character of these results is very close to our methods; therefore clustering has a serious impact on compression regardless of the selected compression method.

8. Conclusion

The present information society creates huge quantities of textual information. This information explosion is being handled using Information Retrieval Systems. Their tasks are effective storage and searching in the text collections. The amount of text stored in IRS and auxiliary data structures constitute a suitable material for data compression. However, the data that form the textual database of every IRS are very mixed and it is therefore useful to study special data compression methods.
This chapter focuses on high compression ratio algorithms specialized in text compression in IRS that enable a fast decompression of individual documents, fully integrated with the IRS, and work with an adequate compression speed. These methods uses word-based compression methods combined with topical development of input documents. Experimental results prove that clustering has a positive impact on the compression ratio. The advantage of implementing this approach is that it is not necessary to change the existing compression algorithm. The only thing that changes is the ordering in which compressed documents are input. Decompression algorithms are not influenced at all and knowledge of topical development is not necessary.

9. References

Armstrong, M. A. (1997). *Basic Topology (Undergraduate Texts in Mathematics)*, Springer.

Baeza-Yates, R. & Ribeiro-Neto, B. (1999). *Modern Information Retrieval*, Addison-Wesley, Harlow.

Berkhin, P. (2006). A survey of clustering data mining techniques, *Grouping Multidimensional Data* pp. 25–71.
URL: *http://dx.doi.org/10.1007/3-540-28349-8_2*

Berry, M. (2003). *Survey of Text Mining : Clustering, Classification, and Retrieval*, Springer.

Blandford, D. & Blelloc, G. (2002). Index compression through document reordering, *Data Compression Conf.*, UT, USA, pp. 342–351.

Burrows, M. & Wheeler, D. J. (1994). A block-sorting lossless data compression algorithm, *Technical report*, Digital Systems Research Center Research Report 124.

Chalmers, M. & Chitson, P. (1992). Bead: explorations in information visualization, *SIGIR '92: Proceedings of the 15th annual international ACM SIGIR conference on Research and development in information retrieval*, ACM, New York, NY, USA, pp. 330–337.

Downs, G. M. & Barnard, J. M. (2003). *Reviews in Computational Chemistry*, Vol. 18, Wiley-VCH.

Dvorský, J. (2004). *Word-based Compression Methods for Information Retrieval Systems*, Phd thesis, Charles University Prague.

Dvorský, J. & Martinovič, J. (2007). Improvement of text compression parameters using cluster analysis, *in* V. Snášel, J. Pokorný & K. Richta (eds), *DATESO*, Vol. 235 of *CEUR Workshop Proceedings*, CEUR-WS.org.

Dvorský, J., Martinovič, J. & Snášel, V. (2004). Query expansion and evolution of topic in information retrieval systems, *in* V. Snášel, J. Pokorný & K. Richta (eds), *DATESO*, Vol. 98 of *CEUR Workshop Proceedings*, CEUR-WS.org, pp. 117–127.

Dvorský, J., Pokorný, J. & Snášel, V. (1999). Word-based compression methods and indexing for text retrieval systems, *in* J. Eder, I. Rozman & T. Welzer (eds), *Proceedings of ADBIS 99*, number 1691 in *Lecture Notes in Computer Science*, Springer-Verlag, Berlin, pp. 75–84.

Dvorský, J., Snášel, V. & Pokorný, J. (1999). Word-based compression methods for large text documents, *Data Compression Conference - DCC '99*, Snowbird, Utah, USA, p. 523.

Faloutsos, C. (1995). Fast searching by content in multimedia databases, *IEEE Data Eng. Bull.* **18**(4): 31–40.

Gan, G., Ma, C. & Wu, J. (2007). *Data Clustering: Theory, Algorithms, and Applications*, ASA-SIAM Series on Statistics and Applied Probability, SIAM.

Harman, D. (ed.) (1997). *The Forth REtrieval Conference (TREC-4)*, NIST.

Haskin, R. L. (1981). Special-purpose processors for text retrieval, *Database Engineering* **4**(1): 16–29.

Hearst, M. A. (1995). Tilebars: Visualization of term distribution information in full text information access, *Proceedings of the Conference on Human Factors in Computing Systems, CHI'95*.

Horspool, N. R. & Cormack, G. V. (1992). Constructing word-based text compression algorithms, *Data Compression Conference*, pp. 62–71.
URL: *http://citeseer.ist.psu.edu/horspool92constructing.html*

Jacobs, D. W., Weinshall, D. & Gdalyahu, Y. (2000). Classification with nonmetric distances: image retrieval and class representation, *Pattern Analysis and Machine Intelligence, IEEE Transactions on* **22**(6): 583–600.

Jain, A. K. & Dubes, R. C. (1988). *Algorithms for Clustering Data*, Prentice-Hall, Inc., Upper Saddle River, NJ, USA.

Jain, A. K., Murty, M. N. & Flynn, P. J. (1999). Data clustering: a review, *ACM Computing Surveys* **31**(3): 264–323.
URL: *citeseer.ist.psu.edu/jain99data.html*

Korfhage, R. R. (1991). To see, or not to see - is that the query?, *SIGIR '91: Proceedings of the 14th annual international ACM SIGIR conference on Research and development in information retrieval*, ACM Press, New York, NY, USA, pp. 134–141.

Martinovič, J. (2004). Evolution of topic in information retrieval systems, *WOFEX*, Ostrava, Czech Republic.

Martinovič, J. & Gajdoš, P. (2005). Vector model improvement by fca and topic evolution, *in* K. Richta, V. Snášel & J. Pokorný (eds), *DATESO*, Vol. 129 of *CEUR Workshop Proceedings*, CEUR-WS.org, pp. 46–57.

Martinovič, J., Gajdoš, P. & Snášel, V. (2008). Similarity in information retrieval, *Computer Information Systems and Industrial Management Applications, 2008. CISIM '08. 7th* pp. 145–150. IEEE.

Martinovič, J., Novosad, T. & Snášel, V. (2007). Vector model improvement using suffix trees, *ICDIM*, IEEE, pp. 180–187.

Orlando, S., Perego, R. & Silvestri, F. (2004). Assigning document identifiers to enhance compressibility of fulltext indices, *In SAC'04: Proceedings of the 2004 ACM symposium on Applied computing*, ACM Press, pp. 222–229.

Platoš, J. & Dvorský, J. (2007). Word-based text compression, *DCCA 2007*, p. 7.

Platoš, J., Dvorský, J. & Martinovič, J. (2008). Using clustering to improve WLZ77 compression, *ICADIWT 2008. First International Conference on Applications of Digital Information and Web Technologies,*, IEEE Computer Society, pp. 308 – 313.

Porter, M. F. (1980). An algorithm for suffix stripping, *Program* **14**: 130–137.

Salton, G. (1989). *Automatic Text Processing*, Addison-Wesley.

Salton, G. & Buckley, C. (1988). Term-weighting approaches in automatic text retrieval, *Information Processing and Management* **24**(5): 513–523.

Spoerri, A. (1993). Infocrystal: a visual tool for information retrieval & management, *CIKM '93: Proceedings of the second international conference on Information and knowledge management*, ACM, New York, NY, USA, pp. 11–20.

Thompson, R. H. & Croft, W. B. (1989). Support for browsing in an intelligent text retrieval system, *Int. J. Man-Mach. Stud.* **30**(6): 639–668.

Welch, T. A. (1984). A technique for high-performance data compression, *IEEE Computer* **17**(6): 8–19.

Witten, I. H., Moffat, A. & Bell, T. C. (1999). *Managing Gigabytes: Compressing and Indexing Documents and Images*, Morgan Kaufmann.

Ziv, J. & Lempel, A. (1977). A universal algorithm for sequential data compression, *IEEE Transactions on Information Theory* **IT-23**(3): 337–343.

8

Embodiment of an Agent using Anthropomorphization of an Object

Hirotaka Osawa and Michita Imai
Keio University
Japan

1. Introduction

Recently, many home appliances have acquired multiple functions due to the development of ubiquitous technology. For example, refrigerators are able to provide users the expiration dates of foods to a user from the RFID tags attached to the food package (Chen et al., 2007). The development of such intelligent environments increases the quantity of information passed from appliances to users. For users, it has become more difficult to understand all the appliances' functions and information. Thus, it is important for users to know what functions they should be using and what information they should focus on.

An anthropomorphic agent including virtual agent and real world agent like communication robot is one way of relating this enormous amount of information to users. It can enhance this information by speaking, pointing, and using gestures on screen or in the real world.

There have been many studies on the communication methods and gestures of anthropomorphic agents. For example, Scheutz studied the influence of spoken words of robots on the cooperation task between human and robot (Scheutz et al., 2008). Breazeal studied how users accept emotions expressed via a robot's facial movements using the facial robot Kismet (Breazeal, 1997). Imai et al. succeeded in joint attention between a user and the robot Robovie and attracting the user attention toward a poster using the robot's face and arm direction (Imai et al., 2003). Shinozawa et al. noted in their experiment (Shinozawa et al., 2005) that using a communication robot is a better way for providing real world information than a virtual agent. This study also suggested that a communication robot is useful for describing the information and functional capabilities of home and office equipment.

However, the agent's ability to direct the users' attention towards an artifact sometimes fails because the agent gains more of the user's attention than the target. Presentations given by robots at exhibitions sometimes fail because the people are attracted to the robots more than what the robot is explaining. Murakawa et al. noted that a sales-robot in a shop does not ensure that the amount of goods sold will increased even though it does attract the attention of customers and that they did look at the goods (Murakawa and Totoki et al., 2006). These failures occurred because of an underestimation of peoples' curiosity in robots. Fukayama et al. noted in their experiment using a virtual agent that the agent sometimes draws attention and disturbs the user's attention on the task before them (Fukayama et al., 2003). They

compared two situations in their explanation. The experimental setup consisted of a virtual agent placed in the center of a PC screen and the control condition consisted of a voice without an agent. In the experimental setup, the participants had a harder time remembering the agent's explanation.
We propose a direct anthropomorphization method to solve an information disturbance by an agent. In this method, we attached human-like devices to an artefact so that it can provide information about itself. These devices are attached to the target object, making it into an anthropomorphic agent, and providing the target's functions or information to users intuitively. Our method use gestures, pointing, emotion, and expression to initiate interaction between a human and the object. Compared to text or vocal instructions, our method anthropomorphic appearance allows users to focus more on their interaction. This method does not disturb the users' intentions more than a method that uses separate anthropomorphic agents, because its explaining style is in the form of a self introduction. There are no other agents in the interaction field. Figure 1 illustrates our method.

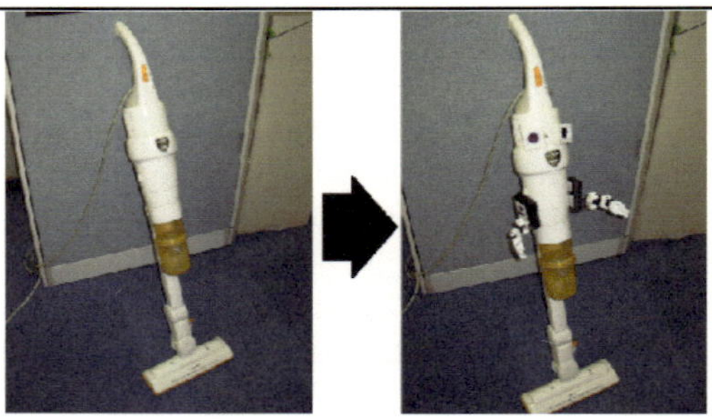

Fig. 1. Anthropomorphized cleaner

To achieve our method, we designed and implemented anthropomorphic robotic devices that resemble eyes and arms. We also conducted an experiment to evaluate the direct anthropomorphization method. This experiment compares the attention and understanding of a user of the functions of an artifact. We had two conditions in this experiment. The first one had a direct anthropomorphized printer explain its own functions and the second one had a humanoid robot "Robovie" (Kanda et al. 2002) explain the printer's functions. The results from participants' questionnaires and gazes during the experiment indicated that they noticed the target artifact and memorized the functions more quickly and easily from using the direct anthropomorphization method than from the "Robovie".
The reminder of this chapter is organized as follows. Section 2 describes the background behind the direct anthropomorphization method and presents a formulation model of this method. It shows basic biological and psychological attitude of humans, especially about The Media Equation, and describes human robot interaction studies and human agent interaction studies that uses these human features to improve interaction. These features are also useful with our method. Section 3 explains our design and the implementation of humanoid parts (eye-like parts and arm-like parts). Section 4 describes the experiment to compare our proposed interaction to that with Robovie. Section 5 presents and discusses the results from the experiment. Section 6 concludes the paper with a summary of our results and provides an overview of future work according to the results.

2. Background

We defined our direct anthropomorphization method by adding human-like devices, such as eyes and arms, to a target object. That way a user can perceive the object as an agent and then they can expect the target object to explain something to them. The user can pay much more attention to the target and more clearly understand it using the direct anthropomorphization method.

Figure 2 shows three method on human and machine interaction. Conventional human-computer interaction improves interface directly like the top image of Fig. 2. Common human-agent interaction uses independent agents like that shown at the middle of Fig. 2. Users are forced to pay attention to not only the target object but also the agent itself under this interaction. On the other hand, if the target object is directly anthropomorphized and becomes the agent using our method as in the bottom image of Fig. 2, users can focus their attention on the body of the agent and the target object because they are one in the same.

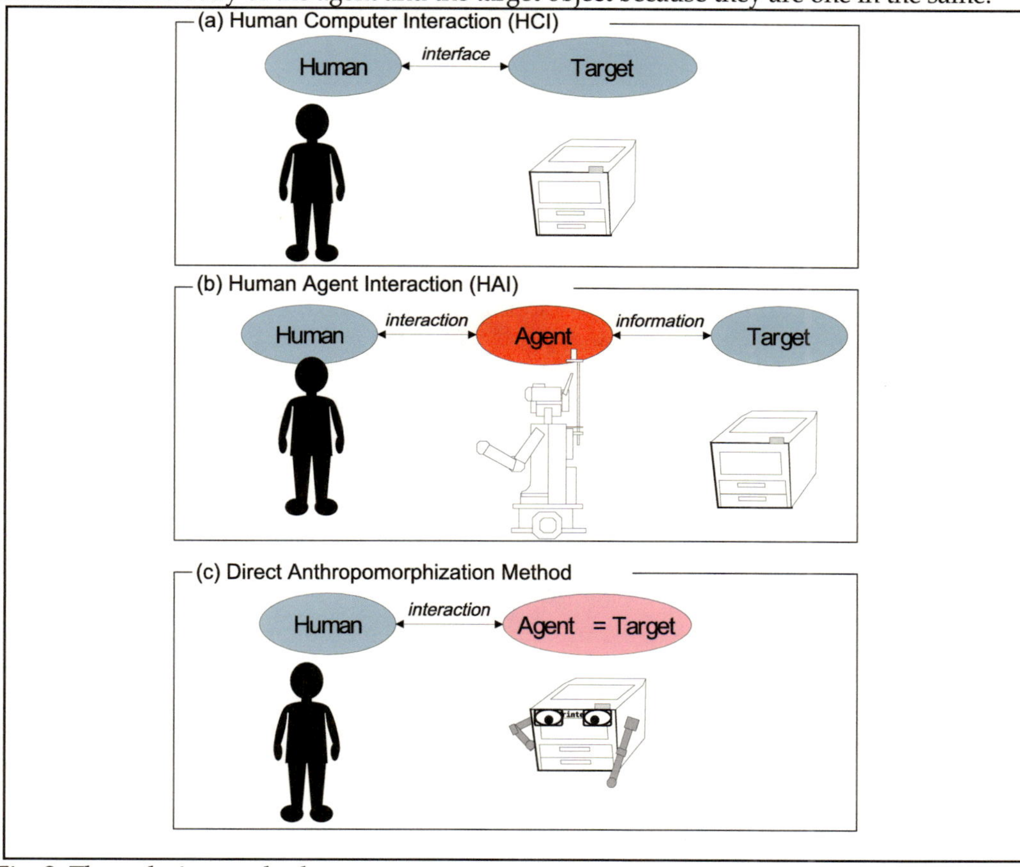

Fig. 2. Three design methods

We examine the basics of our method according to The Media Equation (Reeves & Nass, 1996). People do not expect an object to be an interactive agent. The Media Equation notes people's tendency to communicatively behave even if the target is just a mere object. The

Media Equation states that a human treats informative media like a communicative human. They found through experimentation that users perceive intimacy (as if they are in same group), and respect for a mere computer (attached display and keyboard). This response was found not only in children, but in all age groups.
Our method extends this response and uses it to give information to users. In our method, we attach anthropomorphic human parts, eyes and arms, to an artifact. We believe that these devices create a body image for the artifact.

3. Design and Implementation

In this section, we make human-like devices that attached to an artefact. Many parts of a communication robot can be used for human-like representation. However the design policy of each part is different because our devices attached on an artefact and run with it. We considered the eyes and arms of the robot to be the most important and designed them as follows based on previous study (Sugiyama et al., 2006).

3.1 Eye-like Parts

The eye-like parts imitated human eyes.
The human eye (1) enables vision and (2) indicates what a person is looking at (Kobayashi & Kohshima, 2001). We focused on objects being looked at and hence used a positioning algorithm design.
The eye-like module that simulates the human eye (Fig. 3) uses an "iris" that represents the human iris and pupil together. The open elliptical region on the right in Fig. 3 represents the sclera and the closed circle, the iris and pupil. Here, the eye-like parts looking at a cup consist of a pair of displays to simulate the eyes. The locations of the irises are calculated with respect to the location of the object, which is acquired by a position sensor.

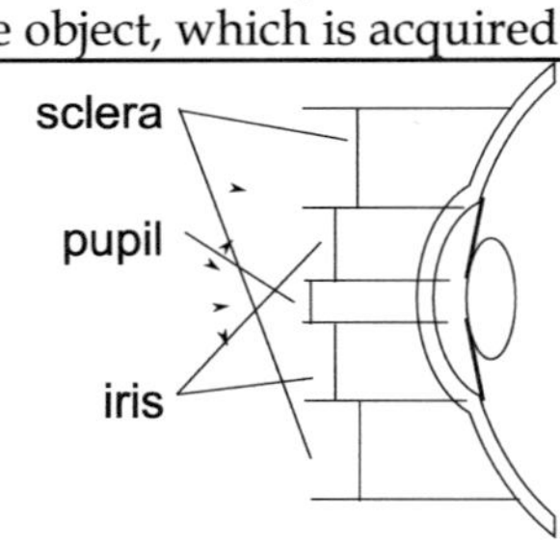

Fig. 3. Human Eye

First, it calculates each iris position as shown below. Each board has an "imaginary eyeball" and it calculates the point of intersection, ***p***, of a vector from the object, ***i***, to the center of the eyeball, ***c***, and board plane **A**. Based on this point of intersection, the eye-like parts convert the global coordinates of ***p*** into display coordinates, ***i***; these processes are performed in both eye-like panels (Fig. 4).
Second, it calculates the orientation of the front of anthropomorphized target by the directions of two eye boards as shown below.

While calculating the normal vector ***a*** in certain cases, for example, if the eye-like parts are based on one panel, some additional sensors need to be used, e.g., gyros, to calculate the orientation of panel **A**.

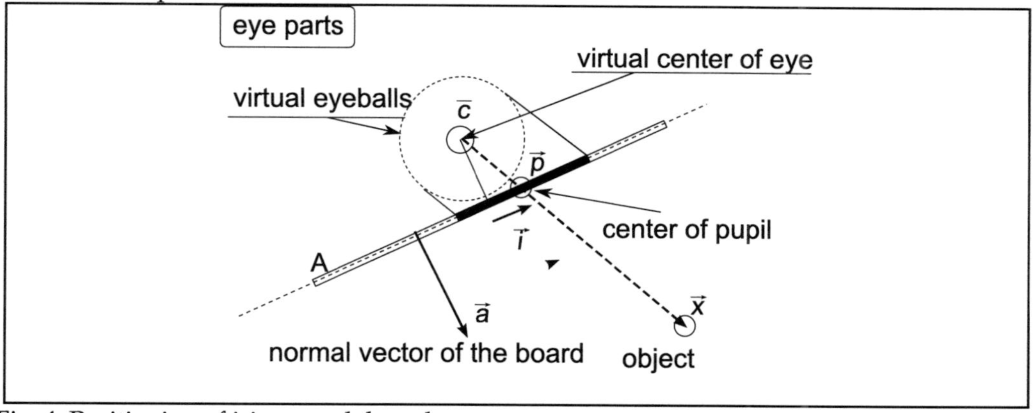

Fig. 4. Positioning of iris on each board

Since the eye-like parts use two panels, ***a*** is calculated from the vector ***r*** between the position sensors in the right and left panels. Restrictions exist when the two panels are symmetrically oriented with plane in the middle of the two boards, when the panels are placed vertically (i.e., their pitch angles are 90 degree), and when the tilt angle is known. Under these restrictions, the eye-like parts calculate the iris positions even if one of the two panels moves.

3.2 Arm-like Parts

The arm-like parts of the robot imitated a human arm in all respects except in terms of manipulating objects.

When the arm-like parts pointed at the outside of an attached common object, we used the vector from the root of the limb to the tip of the hand as the pointing vector, as shown on the left side of Fig. 5 according to Sugiyama's study on pointing gestures of a communication robot (Sugiyama et al., 2006). However, when the arm-like parts pointed at the inside of an attached common object, we used the vector from the root of the hand to the tip of the hand as the pointing vector, as shown on the right side of Fig. 5.

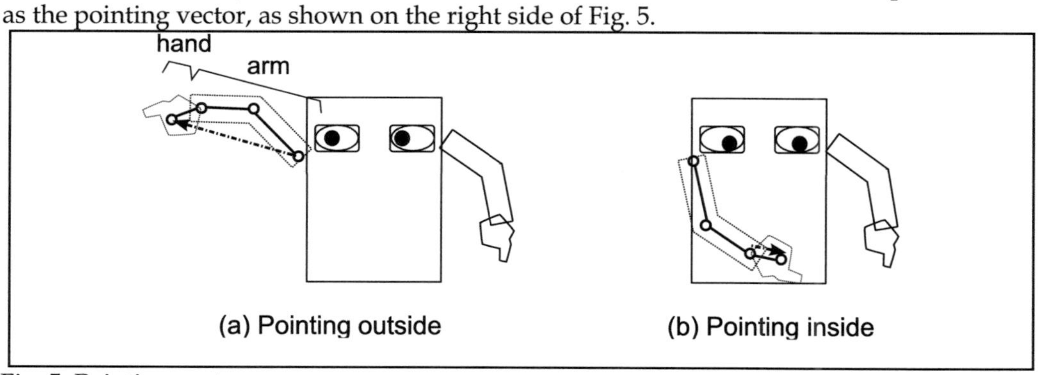

Fig. 5. Pointing vector

3.3 Implementation

Our anthropomorphized object did not need to manipulate other objects using its attached hands. Because the target already has its own task, and our devices are used for just expressionism. Instead of manipulation, these devices must be simple and light so they can be easily attached. We developed human-like robotic devices and attached them to our target by using hook and loop fasteners.

The eye-like parts are consisted of a TFT LC Panel. They were used to determine the positions of the pupils and irises using the 3-D coordinate of the places they were attached to and their direction vectors. The eye-like parts were 2-cm wide. They were thin and could be attached anywhere. They can be used to gaze in any directions as if the implemented eye of the object were watching.

The arm-like parts are consisted of six servo motors. Its hand had three motors and it could express delicate gestures with its fingers. The hands looked like long gloves, were covered with cloth, and concealed the implementation required for intuitive interaction.

The parts' locations are obtained from ultrasonic 3D tags (Nishida et al., 2006) on the parts. They send ultrasonic waves to implemented ultrasonic receivers, which calculate 3D axis of the tags. Humanoid parts search for "anthropomorphize-able" objects according to the locations of the parts.

Specifications of parts for an experiment are presented in Tables 1 and 2, and the parts are depicted in Fig. 6.

Scale	120mm x 160mm x 50mm
Weight	180g
TFT Controller	ITC-2432-035
Wireless module	ZEAL-Z1(19200bps)
Microcontroller	Renesas H8/3694
Connection method	Velcro tape
Cover	Sponge sheet, Plastic board

Table 1. Specification of eye parts

Scale	250mm x 40mm x 40mm
Weight	250g
Motor	Micro-MG x 3, GWS-pico x 3
Wireless module	ZEAL-Z1(9600bps)
Microcontroller	Renesas H8/3694
Connection method	Velcro tape
Cover	Aluminum, sponge, rubber, gloves

Table 2. Specification of arm parts

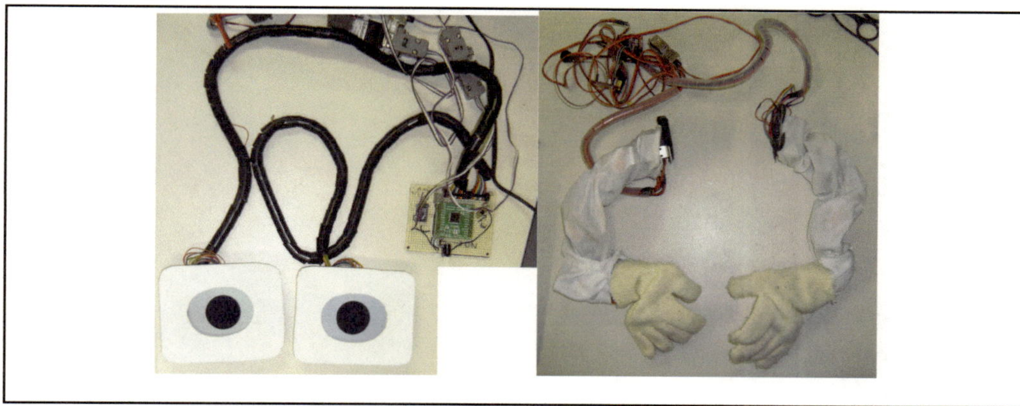

Fig. 6. Humanoid parts

4. Experiment

4.1 Hypothesis

We hypothesize that users pay more attention to a target using anthropomorphization by humanoid parts than when using an independent anthropomorphic agent. This hypothesis is based on the fact that if a target is the agent, the attention of the user is focused on the target object because the target and the agent are one.

4.2 Condition

We used two experimental conditions. In one, we used a printer with human-like devices attached to it and in the other we used a printer and an independent humanoid robot Robovie.

To verify an interaction in a natural situation, we conducted this experiment as a field experiment. For this purpose, we sought ordinary people as subjects at our booth in a university festival.

The detailed conditions of the experiment are as follows. We called the participants who joined our experiment with the direct anthropomorphized printer the experimental group and those who joined the experiment using Robovie, the control group. The up photograph in Fig. 7 shows a scene from the experimental group and the down one is a scene from the control group.

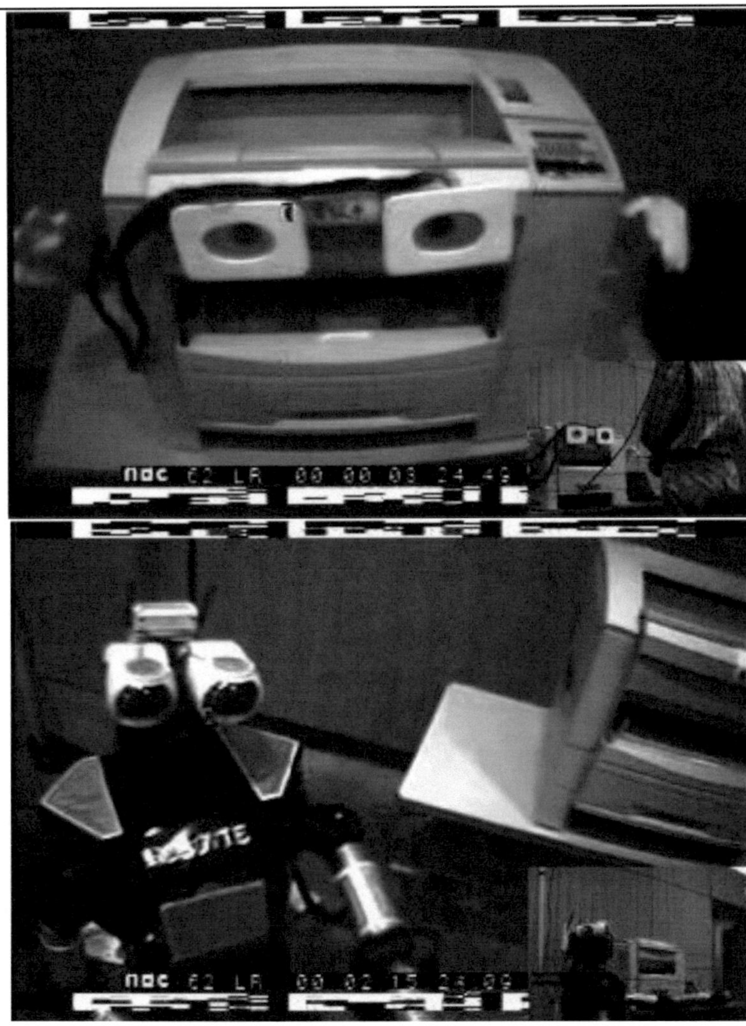

Fig. 7. Experimental (left) and control (right) group

4.3 Environment

We isolated a 3 x 3 m space on the floor and used it for the experiment, and we used an office laser printer LP-9200 (made by EPSON, Inc.). We assumed that the participants were not familiar with using the printer since it is typically not used in homes.

We used the same voice for the experimental and control groups, except a name of "the first person". The voices were played from the back of the printer in the experimental group and from Robovie's mouth in the control group. We tried to avoid several differences between the two groups to maintain accuracy.

We also used an eyemark record device EMR-8B (made by NAC Image Technology, Inc.) to detect where the participants looked. Radial motion was measured to detect the participants' focus of attention. Although we were unable to directly measure the participants' focus of attention, we assumed that the time duration for which humans stare at something can approximately determine where they are focusing their attention and this duration could be measured.

Each device was arranged as shown in Fig. 8. The left side of this figure shows the experimental condition and the right side, the control condition. Participants were videotaped under consent using a side camera and eyemark recorder.

To detect participant action certainly, this experiment was conducted by the "Wizard of Oz" method. All utterances and gestures of the printer and Robovie were conducted according to the determined scenario. Instructions toward participants are informed by an assistant of the experiment.

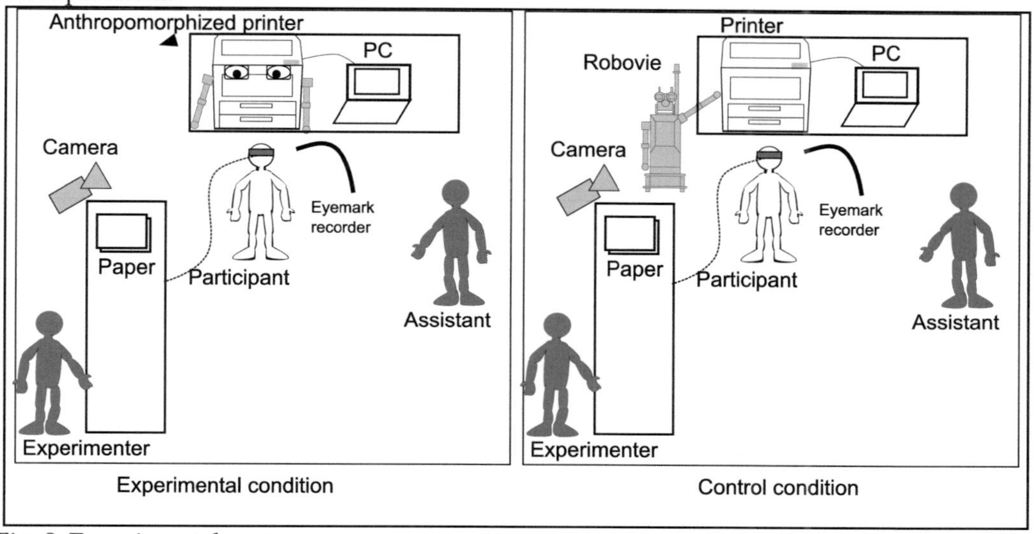

Fig. 8. Experimental system

We conducted this experiment in the lab presentation space at a university festival. The experiment was conducted during 3 days in 2007. We conducted the experiment on the experimental group on October 20 and December 22 and that on the control group on October 21. The participants were unaware that they would be participating in an experiment until after they visited our space. They consented to the experimental conditions. The participants had no prior knowledge of the experiment and had no deep motivation for the success of the experiment, as compared to normal human experiments.

We believed that our experimental condition was better, than the condition in a normal experiment, for our purpose to verify the validity of our method, because this experimental style is the same as HRI in the real world (in vivo) and differs from experiments conducted in a room (in vitro).

4.4 Instruction to Participants

First, we briefly explained our experiment and obtained participant consent. In addition, we attached the eyemark recorder only if a participant allowed its use.

After obtaining consent, we executed each experimental scenario for the participants in the experimental group (EG) and control group (CG).

- Self introduction
  - EG "Hello, my name is printer."
  - CG "Hello, my name is Robovie, and this is a printer."
- Explaining names: formal name (LP-9200) and nickname (ESPER)
  - EG "My formal name is LP-9200. Everyone calls me ESPER."
  - CG "Its formal name is LP-9200. Everyone calls it ESPER."
- Function: printing
  - "(My/Its) purpose is to print papers."
- Function: power button
  - EG "My power button is on my right side."
  - CG "Its power button is on the right side of the printer."
- Leading action: push power button
  - "Let's push it."
- Function: printing speed
  - EG "I can print 20 pages per minute."
  - CG "This printer can print 20 pages per minute."
- Function: resolution
  - "(My/Its) resolution is 1200 dpi."
- Function: The principle of a laser printer
  - EG "I use a laser for printing."
  - CG "This printer uses a laser for printing."
- Function: The principle of a laser printer (cont.)
  - "The cost of printing using my functions is much cheaper than for home printers because (I/it) pastes ink using a laser."
- Leading action: printing
  - "Let's print something! Push a button on the PC beside me."
- Fail of printing
  - "(I/It) can't print anything … hmm … oh, there is no blank paper in a bin."
- Leading action: insert blank papers
  - EG "Insert blank papers into my mouth."
  - CG "Insert blank papers into its mouth."
- Function: repairing miss print
  - EG "If you missed printing something, please lift up my head."
  - CG "If you missed printing something, please open its top."
- Function: printing papers that one surface is not used
  - "(I/It) can use papers that one surface is not used.
  - But, they always jam.
- Function: remove jammed papers
  - "If there is a paper jam, remove the paper from here (with pointing)."
- Function: help button
  - "If you find other errors, push the left button(with pointing)"
- Questionnaire
  - Participants filled out questionnaires after the experiment.
- Fee for the experiment
  - Participants got souvenir photos and a cookie for participating.

In the experimental group, the printer used "I" and "My" for explaining. On the other hand, Robovie used "This printer" and "It" for explaining printer functions to the control group. Other words are the same in both experiments. Because each instruction pair on the above scenario has same duration, we think that there is no difference in instruction complexity between these two groups.
Each participant listened to the description of nine functions during the experiment. The experiment was interactive, explaining that each participant should manipulate the object according to the instructions. We think that this interactivity helped motivate the participants to concentrate on the experiment. The participants had an easier time answering the questionnaire according to the interactive explanation. Each utterance and gesture was repeated when participants did not understand it.
Finally, the participants filled out a questionnaire, which asked them about the functions explained to them (printing speed, resolution, and other functions they remembered).

4.5 Participants

Twenty-one males and eight females participated in our experiment. There were 13 males and 3 females in the experimental group and 8 males and 5 females in the control group. Their ages ranged from 10 to 60 years. The age distribution of the participants is presented in Table 3.

Age	Experimental Group	Control Group
10-19	8	3
20-29	2	4
30-39	2	1
40-49	1	0
50-59	3	5

Table 3. Age of each participant

We conducted an F-test with a $p > 0.10$ basis for gender and age to check that all values in the two groups are dispersed according to the F-distribution. The results in each case were $p = 0.640 > 0.10$, and $p = 0.207 > 0.10$. The results show that there was no deviation in these two groups. We asked participants, through the questionnaire, about their experience with the printer, Robovie, and the humanoid parts. No participant used these devices.

4.6 Prediction

The predictions from our experiment based on the abovementioned plan are as follows.
The participants in the experimental group were able to write more about the functions in their questionnaires, because they remembered the explained functions more clearly than the participants in the control group.

5. Result and Discussion

5.1 Result

We counted the total number of functions recalled by each participant. Figure 9 presents the differences between the experimental and control groups. Figure 10 presents their distributions. The Y-axis in Fig. 9 represents the answered functions. The X and Y axes in

Fig. 9 represent the number of noted functions and participants, respectively. The average number of functions noted was 2.3 for the experimental group and 1.3 for the control group. We conducted an F-test with a $p > 0.10$ basis to check that all values in two groups are dispersed according to F-distribution. The results showed a p value of 0.876, which is greater than 0.10, and there was no deviation in these two groups. We conducted a Welch's t-test with a $p < 0.05$ basis for each of the recalled functions to verify our prediction. The results showed that there was significant difference, $p = 0.029 < 0.05$, between the two groups.

There were 11 participants in the experimental group and 11 in the control group whose gaze times were detected using the eyemark recorder. Figure11 shows the ratio of attention in each experiment. The X-axis in both the top and bottom graphs in Fig. 11 represents the participant and the Y-axis in the top graph is the ratio of the time of gaze toward the printer to that toward other objects. The Y-axis in the bottom graph of Fig. 11 represents the ratio of the time of gaze toward the printer, that toward Robovie, and that toward other objects.

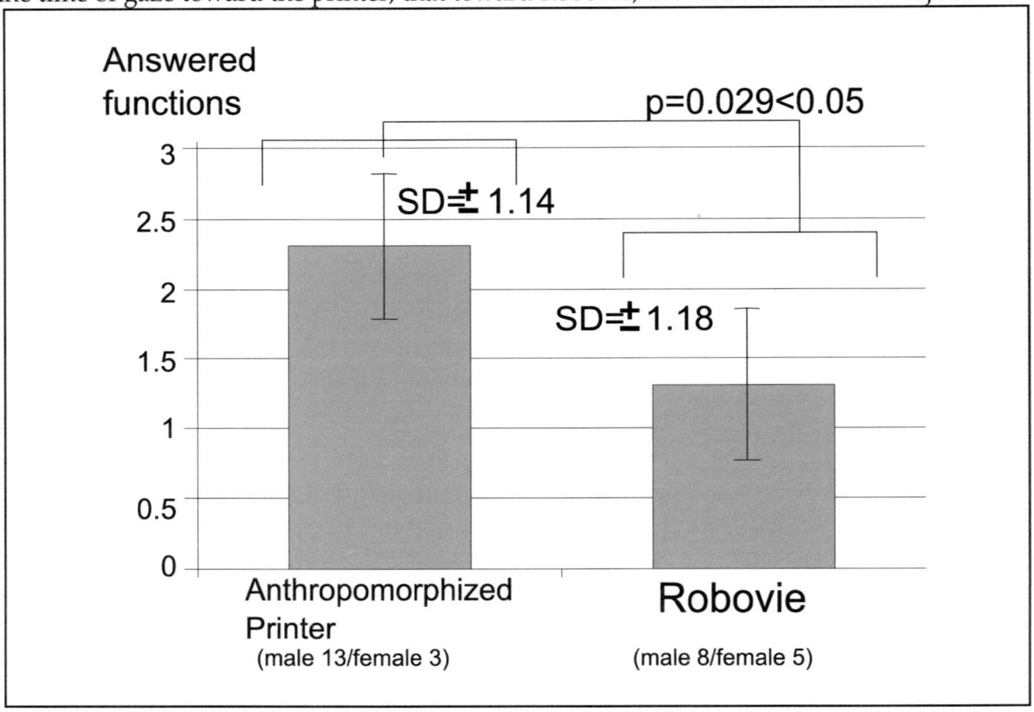

Fig. 9. Difference in noted functions of printer

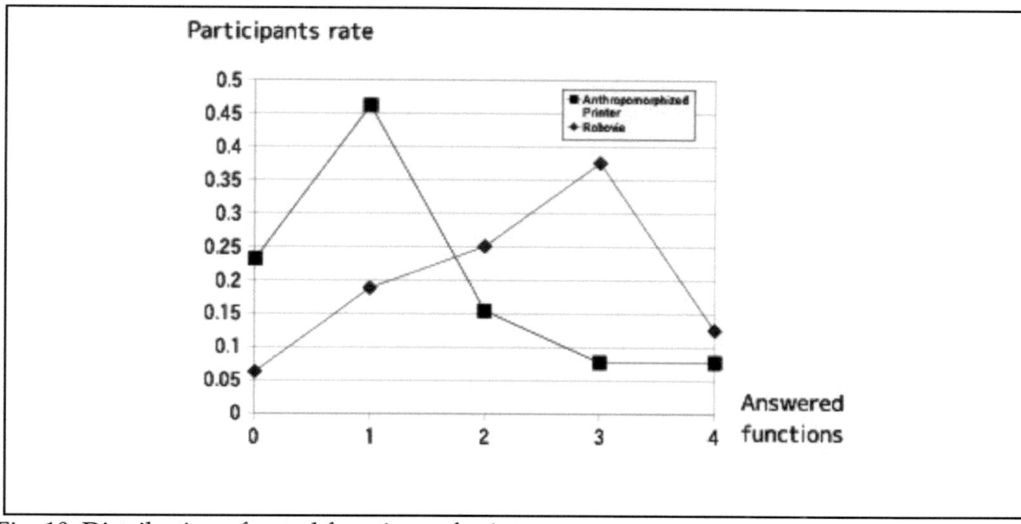

Fig. 10. Distribution of noted functions of printer

5.2 Discussion

The results showed that the participants in the experimental group remembered more functions than those in the control group. We think that this difference arose because the participants in the experimental group could more easily concentrate on the printer since they did not need to focus their attention on other objects. On the other hand, the participants in the control group looked at Robovie most of the time and only sometimes focused their attention on the printer. This proves that the participants in the control group were more distracted than those in the experimental group.

We also calculated the attention rate R_{user} under these conditions using an independent agent and the attention rate R'_{user} with the direct anthropomorphization method using the data from the graph presented in Fig. 11. The average for each set of results was $R_{user} = 0.419$ and $R'_{user} = 0.851$. This result suggests that participants concentrate on the printer more in the experimental condition than in the control condition.

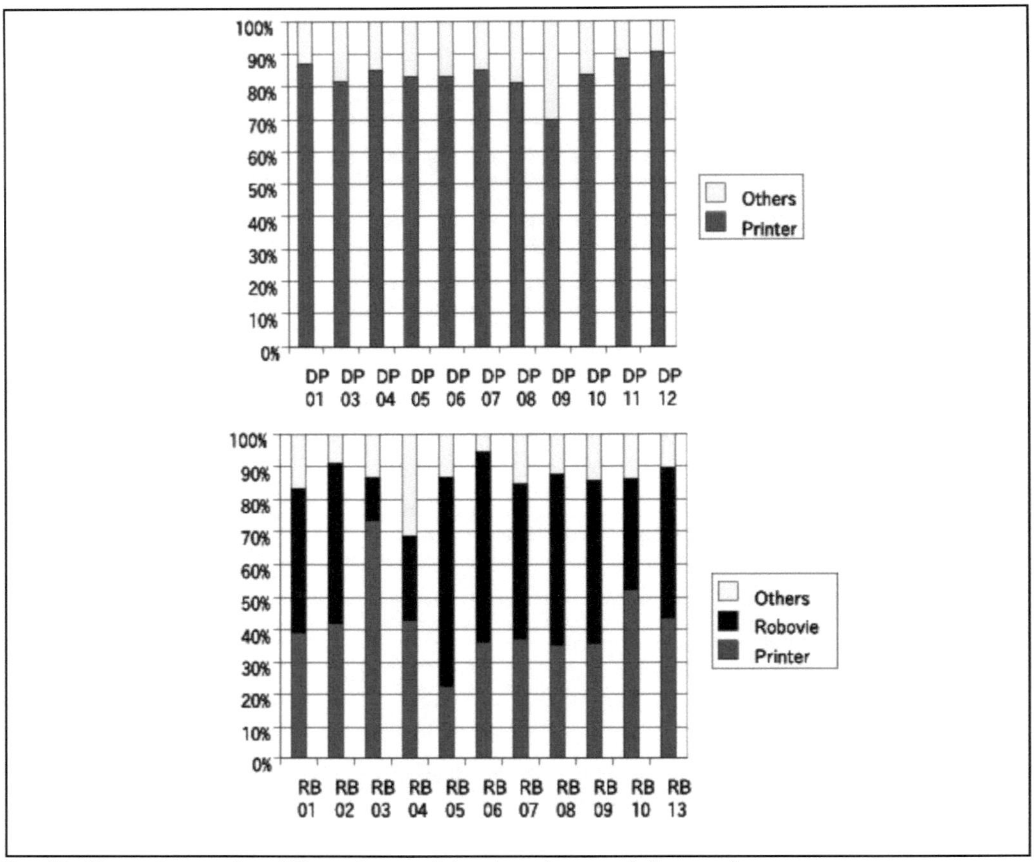

Fig. 11. Gaze time ratio of Experimental (top) and control (bottom) groups

The results graphed in Fig. 11 show that eight participants in the control group gazed more at Robovie than they did at the target printer. These participants almost always focused their attention on Robovie. If Robovie pointed to the printer and explained it, they looked at the printer but focused on Robovie once again. In addition, they sometimes moved their eyes quickly between Robovie and the printer. However, participant RB03 always looked at the printer while listening to Robovie and sometimes even nodded to Robovie. This was a rare case. His score was better than the average score for the noted functions in the control group. This style is similar to that observed in human-human explanation interaction. However, this is not always true when using a humanoid robot. This result suggests there is a contradiction when a humanoid robot develops well and attracts more attention, and thus does not appropriately explain target information. However, there is no contradiction with the direct anthropomorphization method.

On the other hand, the participants in the experimental group paid complete attention to the printer, as shown in the top graph in Fig. 11. Their attention wavered during some actions such as moving paper or the pushing the PC button. However, these actions were needed for proper interaction. Fast moving eyes were not recorded in the experimental group, another point of difference between the experimental and control groups.

It appears contradictory that if a humanoid robot attracts more attention then it does not appropriately explain target information. Many HRI studies presupposed that users will understand a robot's explanation well if the robot is attractive to them.
We think that this hypothesis is inaccurate. A user's state toward the robot is divisible into the following two states; (1) Humanoid appearance and actions are attractive; (2) Humanoid appearance and actions are reliable and can explain other things.
In our anthropomorphization method, the explainer and target are synthesized. We think that the attractiveness of the target is strongly related to its reliability for itself under this situation. Using an independent robot, however, we must estimate the user's state more carefully. Murakawa et al. and Miyashita et al. suggested in their research of a selling robot in a shopping center that even if users highly evaluate a robot, there is no relation between attractiveness and shop sales (Murakawa and Totoki et al., 2006) (Miyashita et al., 2008). These results show that a deeper evaluation of a user's state for the robot is more important.
In this experiment, it is still not clear that the difference in attention duration depends on the manner of anthropomorphization. To say in other words, what is a key role for anthropomorphic image of users are still ambiguous. To solve this problem, we are planning to analyze manner of anthropomorphization of users using several conditions with decreasing anthropomorphic elements.
However, the result of the experiment shows an advantage of our method compared with independent agent method (like virtual agent or humanoid robot). Users must consider both agent and the target at least in independent agent situation because it is impossible to remove the independent agent in this method. It is able to say at least that we can reduce attention duration of users to synthesize an explainer and a target using our method.
Based on these results, we believe that our hypothesis, users pay more attention to a target when using anthropomorphization by humanoid parts than when using an independent anthropomorphic agent, is verified.
Our proposed interaction also improved user intimacy for a common object. The anthropomorphized printer or Robovie instructed printer had both a formal name and a nickname during this experiment. We asked participants, through a questionnaire, "What is the name of the printer?" Three participants in the experimental group responded with the nickname, no participants responded with the formal name, and 13 participants responded with no name. On the other hand, no participants in the control group responded with the nickname, 5 participants responded with the formal name, and 8 participants responded with no name. We conducted a Fisher's exact test with a $p < 0.05$ basis on this result. The result showed a p value of 0.0087, which was less than 0.05, and showed significant difference. This result suggested that anthropomorphization of a common object increases not only the concentration of participants but also intimacy among them and the object. In the future, we will study what model leads to this result.

5.3 Comparison with Related Studies

A commonly-used method to instruct users uses built-in LCD panels or a computer monitor. There are several advantages to our approach compared with current approaches that use monitors;

- Our approach does not depend on the cultural differences or literacy of users because it is based on the human body image and human-like motions. The user understands its instructions by body metaphors even if they did not have prior knowledge about the target. This representation does not need indirect imagination for the space.

- In the monitor situation, for example, a user must interpret a directed point from the information on the monitor and make an image at first. Next, he/she searches the target in the real world using the image. Using our method, users directly understand what is instructed without above process.

Norman suggested famous design guideline using affordance of the object - the fundamental properties of a device that determines its way of use (Norman, 1998). In this guideline, adding moving arms and eyes not only increases the product's cost and complexity, but they increase the possibility of wear and tear, malfunction, obstruction and maintenance.

However, we think that our approach complements Norman's approach because our method uses "attachable" human-like parts. The first reason is that users can customize the explanation style of the object according to their own knowledge. If a user needs more explanation for a smart design object, he/she can attach these human-like parts for explanation. If a user thinks human-like acts are needless for his/her task, he/she can simply remove these parts.

Second reason is as follows. There are two interactions between a user and an object; (1) Interaction to use an object; (2) Interaction to learn about an object.

We think that anthropomorphization parts are appropriate, especially for second goal. Additionally, we think that this attachable explaining method may simplify an original object's design much more, due to the above reasons.

6. Conclusion

We proposed humanoid parts that can be attached to a common object and anthropomorphize it as if it had an intention and its body was like that of a communication robot.

To verify our approach, we developed eye-like and arm-like parts and attached them to a target object and conducted experiments in order to verify the user's perception of the intention of a target (with an anthropomorphized refrigerator) and the imaginary body image of a target (with an anthropomorphized desk and box). We also used our approach to compare the explanation of the functions of a printer by an anthropomorphized printer and explanation by an independent agent Robovie.

The results obtained by observing the actions of participants and administering questionnaires during the experiment indicated that users can interact with a target while perceiving its intention and its imaginary body image. Users also noticed target artifacts and memorized target functions more easily when the direct anthropomorphization method was used than when an independent humanoid agent was used.

6.1 Future Works: Explanation Using Body Metaphors

Our experimental results proved that a user accepts a target's intention and imaginary body image by our proposed anthropomorphization method. Our proposed method, in comparison to the use of an independent agent, is also better at gaining the attention of users for explaining the functions of artifacts.

We think that this method is easy to use, allows various representations, and will extend the application of HRI studies. We believe that this method has the following possibilities.
It is possible to use metaphors for pointing at the location of an artifact. For example, the printer can say "I have a stomachache" when it is jammed. These metaphors would be impossible to use for normal explanation using an independent agent. If we study these metaphors more closely, we might be able to use more understandable expressions for the artifact using our method.

7. Acknowledgements

The first author was supported in part by the JSPS Research Fellowships for Young Scientists. This work was supported in part by Grant in Aid for the Global Center of Excellence Program for "Center for Education and Research of Symbiotic, Safe and Secure System Design from the Ministry of Education, Culture, Sport, and Technology in Japan."

8. References

Fukayama, A.; Pham, V. & Ohno, T. (2003). Analysis of user's gaze for usability assessment of anthropomorphic agents. *IEICE TECHNICAL REPORT,* Vol.103, No.743, pp. 53-58

Reeves, B. & Nass, C. (1996). The Media Equation: How People Treat Computers, Television, and New Media Like Real People and Places, *Univ. of Chicago Press.*

Breazeal, C. (1998). Regulating human-robot interaction using 'emotions','drives', and facial expressions. *Proceedings of Autonomous Agents,* pp. 14—21

Norman, DA.; (1998). The Design of Everyday Things. *The MIT Press,* USA

Kobayashi, H.& Kohshima, S. (2001). Unique morphology of the human eye and its adaptive meaning: comparative studies on external morphology of the primate eye. *Journal of human evolution,* Vol. 40, No. 5, pp. 419—435

Shinozawa, K.; Naya, F.; Yamato, J. & Kogure, K. (2005). Differences in effect of robot and screen agent recommendations on human decision-making. *International Journal of Human-Computer Studies,* Vol. 62, No. 2, pp. 267--279

Scheutz, M.; Schermerhorn, P. & Kramer, J. (2008). The utility of affect expression in natural language interactions in joint humanrobot tasks. *Proceedings of Human Robot Interaction},* Vol. 1, No. 1

Imai, M.; Ono, T.; & Ishiguro, H. (2003). Physical relation and expression: Joint attention for human-robot interaction, *IEEE Transactions on Industrial Electronics,* Vol.50, pp. 636--643

Sugiyama, O.; Kanda, T.; Imai, M.; Ishiguro, H. & Hagita, N. (2006). Three-layer model for generation and recognition of attention-drawing behavior. *International Conference on Intelligent Robots and Systems,* pp. 5843--5850, IEEE/RSJ

Kanda, T.; Ishiguro, H.; Ono, T.; Imai, M. & Nakatsu, R. (2002). Development and evaluation of an interactive humanoid robot "Robovie." *Proceedings of {IEEE} International Conference on Robotics and Automation,* pp. 4166--4173, IEEE, Washington, DC, USA

Chen, Y.; Hsieh, M.; Wang, C. & Lee, H. (2007). Rfid-based intelligent systems for home-healthcare. *International Conference on Consumer Electronics,* pp. 1-2, January 2007.

Murakawa, Y. & Totoki, S. (2006). Evaluation of "behaviour" of service robot "enon" : Experimental operation of enon in a shopping center. *Technical report of IEICE*, Vol. 131, pp. 31--36

Nishida, Y.; Aizawa, H.; Hori, T.; Hoffman, NH.; Kanade, T. & Kakikura, M. (2003). 3D ultrasonic tagging system for observing human activity. *Proceedings of International Conference on Intelligent Robots and Systems*, Vol. 1, No. 1, pp. 785-791

Miyashita, Z.; Kanda, T.; Shiomi, M.; Ishiguro, H. & Hagita, N. (2008). Guide robot that tries to be familiar with customers. *Proceedings of Interaction*

9

Towards Socialized Machines: Emotions and Sense of Humour in Conversational Agents

Michal Ptaszynski, Pawel Dybala, Shinsuke Higuhi, Wenhan Shi, Rafal Rzepka and Kenji Araki
Hokkaido University
Japan

1. Introduction

From the beginning of computer era over half a century ago, humanity was fascinated by the idea of creating a machine substituting their mental capabilities. This New Age version of Mary Shelley's *Frankenstein* gave birth to S-F literature and was one of the motors for development of our civilisation. The mental functions digitalized as the first ones were fast processing of large numbers or sophisticated formulas for specialized fields like mathematics or physics. These functions were the most troublesome for humans, but the easiest to process mechanically. Ironically, the human mental functions said to be the most human-like, and thought of as the ones which make up a grown well-socialized man, such as a sense of humour or understanding emotions of others, were neglected in Computer Science for a long time as too subjective and therefore unscientific. With the development of the Artificial Intelligence research and the related fields, like Human-Computer Interaction (HCI) or Human Factors Design, shortly before the new millennium the door opened to the fields of research of what had been unscientific till then - Affective Computing (Picard, 1997), and Humour Processing (Binsted, 1996). When Kerstin Dautenhahn and colleagues talked about the Socially Intelligent Agents (SIA) on the AAAI Fall Symposium in 2000 (Dautenhahn et al., 2002), they signalised the need for the attempts to incorporate multiple human factors into conversational agents. However, completing the task of creating a user-friendly and human-like machine was still far ahead.

In this chapter we present some of the first practical experiments on enhancing Japanese speaking conversational agent with human factors. In our research we focused on the two important features, said to make up an intelligent and socialized man: understanding emotions of others, and a sense of humour to evoke positive attitudes in other people for better socialization (Yip & Martin, 2006). These two features are also said to be the most creative and difficult to process by machines human factors (Boden, 1998). In our research we undertake the task to incorporate these two features in a conversational agent to make it more human like. A conversational agent is enhanced with a pun generator, and a system for affect analysis. The affect analysis system uses a novel method of estimating not only the valence and type of the conveyed emotions, but also, supported with a Web-mining procedure, verifies whether the emotion is appropriate for the present context of the

conversation. The pun generator is using Web contents to generate fresh jokes each time used. We perform a number of experiments concerning the incorporation of those two features. We verify the accuracy of affect analysis system in laboratory settings, as well as in the field, during a chat of users with two conversational agents - first one using modality to enhance utterance generation based on propositions gathered from the Web, and the second one - using also automatically generated puns to better socialize with the user. We check the influence of using puns on human-computer interaction.
The outline of this chapter is as follows. First, we present the conversational agent used as a base for further experiments. Next, we describe the pun-generator, and present the ideas for its combination with the conversational agent. One of the combination methods assumes using an affect analysis system to recognize user's emotions and on its basis decide whether to generate a joke or not. We present a system for affect analysis of textual input. Finally we describe experiments with implementing those two systems – pun generator and affect analysis system - into the baseline conversational agent. The implementation of those two systems is performed first separately, and then we present the first attempt to implement both of the systems. At the end concluding remarks are presented and perspectives for further research are discussed.

2. Modalin - conversational agent as a platform for experiments

Many task-oriented conversational agents (Liu et al., 2003; Reitter et al., 2006) have been developed. Research on non-task-oriented conversational agents like casual conversation dialogue systems ("chat-bots") is on the other hand not very common, perhaps due to many amateurs who try to build naturally talking systems using sometimes very clever, but rather unscientific methods. Although there are systems with chatting abilities (Bickmore & Cassell, 2001), they concentrate on applying strategies to casual conversations rather than on their automatic generation. We believe, that the main reason is that an unrestricted domain is disproportionately difficult compared to the possible uses such a system could have. It is for example very hard to predict the contents and topics of user utterances, and therefore it is almost impossible to prepare conversational scenarios. Furthermore, scenarios need more or less specific goals to be useful. However, in our opinion, sooner or later non-task-oriented conversational agents will have to be combined with task oriented systems and used after recognizing that the user's utterance does not belong to a given task. This would lead to more natural interfaces, such as information kiosks or automatic guides placed in public places where anyone can talk to them about anything (Gustafson & Bell, 2000; Kopp et al., 2005) regardless of the role the developers intended. Well-known examples of non-task-oriented conversational agents are ELIZA (Weizenbaum, 1966) and A.L.I.C.E. Both systems and their countless imitators[1] use a lot of rules coded by hand. ELIZA is able to make a response to any input, but these responses are only information requests without providing any new information to the user. In the case of A.L.I.C.E., the knowledge resource is limited to the existing database. These examples and many other "chat-bots" need handcrafted rules, and are thus often ignored by computer scientists and rarely become a research topic. However, they have proved to be useful for e-Learning (Pietro et al., 2005) and machine

[1] Many of them have been quite successful in the Loebner Prize and the Chatterbox Challenge - competitions only for English-speaking bots, but explanations of their algorithms are not available.

learning (Araki & Kuroda, 2006) support. Therefore, building a system using automatic methods seems to be the most realistic way for unrestricted domains. Considering the large cost of developing a program capable to talk about any topic, it is reasonable to turn to the Internet - a huge and cheap source of text.

The baseline system described in this section is built upon the idea that human utterances consist of a proposition and modality (Nitta & Masuoka, 1989). The system uses an algorithm for extracting word associations from the Web and a method for adding modality to statements. The system described here works for Japanese and uses text as input and output. Though we plan to combine this project with research on voice recognition and generation, e.g., to help developing freely talking car navigation systems that by their chatting abilities could help avoiding drowsiness while driving. The general description of the system procedures in order is as follows: **1.** Extraction of keywords from user utterance; **2.** Extraction of word associations from the Web; **3.** Generation of sentence proposition using the extracted associations; **4.** Addition of modality to the sentence proposition

2.1 Extraction of keywords from user utterance

Every second millions of people update their blogs and write articles on every possible topic (Kumar et al., 2003). These are available on the Web, which can be accessed any time in a faster manner every day because of the growing efficiency of search engines. Thus, the Web is well suited to extracting word associations triggered by words from user utterance with a conversational agent. We use the Google[2] search engine snippets to extract word associations in real time without using pre-prepared resources, such as off-line databases. First, the system analyses user's utterances using the morphological analyser MeCab (Kudo, 2001) in order to spot query keywords for extracting word association lists. We define nouns, verbs, adjectives, and unknown words as query keywords. The reason we chose these word classes is that they, to some extent, describe the context. We define a noun as the longest set of nouns in a compound noun. For example, the compound noun *shizen gengo shori*[3] (natural language processing) is treated by MeCab as three words: (*shizen* - natural), (*gengo* - language) and (*shori* - processing). Our system, however, treats it as one noun.

2.2 Extraction of word associations from the Web

The extracted keywords are used as query words in the Google search engine. The system extracts nouns from the search results and sorts them in frequency order. This process is based on the idea that words co-occuring frequently with the input words are of high relevance to them. The number of extracted snippets is 500 (value set experimentally, taking into account the processing time and output quality). The top five words of a list are treated as word associations (see Table 1). Approximately 81% of the word associations obtained using this method were judged as valid (Higuchi at al., 2008). The main reason for extracting word associations from the Web is that thanks to this method, the system can handle new information, proper names, technical terms and so on. by using only the snippets from the search engine. The word association extraction takes no more than few seconds.

---

[2] Google, http://www.google.co.jp/

[3] All Japanese transcriptions will be written in italics.

Sapporo wa samui. (Sapporo city is cold.)		
Association frequency ranking:		
1	*yuki* (snow)	52
2	*fuyu* (winter)	50
3	*kion* (temperature)	16
4	*jiki* (season)	12
5	*Tokyo* (Tokyo)	12

Table 1. Examples of noun associations triggered by a user utterance.

(noun) (*wa*) (adjective)
(noun) (*ga*) (adjective)
(noun) (*ga*) (verb)
(noun) (*wa*) (verb)
(*so-re*) (*wa*) (verb)
(noun)
(adjective)
(verb)

Table 2. Proposition templates.

informative expression	frequency
maa - kedo (Well , it can be said - but -)	21
maa - dana (Well , it can be said -)	16
maa - desu-ga (Well , it appears that -)	16
soko-de - desu-yo (Here , it is said that -)	15
maa - da-ga (Well , it can be said - but -)	14
maa - desu-yo (Well , it is that -)	12

Table 3. Examples of informative expression modality

question freqency	frequency
...desuka? (Is it that ... ?)	232
...kana? (Maybe ... ?)	90
...da-kke? (Is it right that ... ?)	87
...masu-ka? (Is it that ... ?)	69
...nano? (Is it that ... ?)	68
...toka? (... , isn't it ?)	55

Table 4. Examples of question modality sentence endings

2.3 Generation of proposition using word associations

Using the associations, the system generates the proposition of a sentence reply to the user input. A proposition is an expression representing an objective statement. It is generated by applying associations to a proposition template like [(noun) (particle *wa* indicating topic) (adjective)]. We prepared 8 proposition templates manually (see Table 2). The templates were chosen subjectively after examining statistics from IRC chat logs. Our criteria for choosing the templates was that they should belong to the 20 most frequent modality patterns and to be flexible enough to fit a range of grammatical constructions, e.g., in English, "isn't it" cannot follow verbs while "I guess" can follow nouns, adjectives, and verbs. The proposition templates are applied in a predetermined order: e.g., first a template "(noun) (*wa*) (adjective)" is used; next a template "(noun) (*ga*) (adjective)" is used. However, since the generated proposition is not always a natural statement, the system uses exact matching searches of the whole phrases in a search engine to check the naturalness of each proposition. If the frequency of occurrence of the proposition is low, it is defined as unnatural and deleted. This processing is based on the idea that the phrases existing on the Web in large numbers are most probably correct grammatically and semantically. In case of discarding an unnatural proposition, the system generates another proposition in the same way. In this experiment the system used propositions for which the hit number exceeded 1,000 hits in Google. The processing proceeds as follows. The system first selects the top noun, top verb, and top adjective word associations. These are applied to the templates. If a generated proposition is judged as valid (occurrence on the Web indicates validity), it is used. If not, another template is tried until a valid proposition is found. The reason for not trying every possible combination of associations is prohibitively long processing time.

2.4 Adding Modality to the Propositions

Finally, the system adds modality to the generated proposition. By modality we mean a set of grammatical and pragmatic rules to express subjective judgments and attitudes. In our system, modality is realized through adverbs at the end of a sentence and a pair of sentence head and sentence ending auxiliary verb. This kind of modality is common in Japanese (Nitta & Masuoka, 1989).

2.4.1 Extracting Modality

There is no standard definition of what constitutes modality in Japanese. In this research we classify modality of casual conversation into questions and informative expressions. Questions are defiend as expressions that request information from the user. Informative expressions are transmitting information to the user. Patterns for these modalities are extracted automatically from IRC chat logs (100,000 utterances) in advance. Modality patterns are extracted in the ways as below:

- ❖ Pairs of grammatical particles and an auxiliary verbs placed at the end of sentences are defined as ending patterns
- ❖ Sentences with question marks are defined as questions
- ❖ Adverbs, emotive words, and connectives at the beginning of sentences are defined as informative expressions
- ❖ Candidate patterns thus obtained are sorted by frequency

First, the system extracts sentence-ending patterns from IRC chat logs. If an expression contains question marks, it is classified as a question. Next, the system extracts adverbs, emotive words, and connectives from the beginning and end of sentences from the IRC logs. These pairs (beginning and end) of expressions are classified as "informative expressions". For example question expression *"desu-ka? "* (question marker) is extracted from a human utterance like *"Kyou-wa samui desu-ka?"* (Is it cold today?). An informative expression *"maa ... kedo"* is extracted from a human utterance as *"Maa sore-wa ureshii kedo"* (Well, I'm glad, but you know...). After obtaining the patterns this way, 668 for informative expressions and 396 for questions, they were filtered manually to discard the ones extracted incorrectly. The overall number of patterns obtained was 550 of the former (80%) and 292 of the latter (73%). The candidates were sorted in frequency order. The examples of modality patterns are presented in Table 3 for informative expressions and in Table 4 for questions.

2.4.2 Adding Modality

The system adds the modality from section 2.4.1 to the proposition from section 2.3 to generate the system output. This process is based on the idea that human utterance consists of proposition and modality. A modality pattern is selected randomly. For example, if the system generates the proposition *"fuyu wa samui* (winter is cold)" and selects *"iyaa ... desu-yo* (Ooh ... isn't it?)" as modality pattern, the generated output will be *"iyaa, fuyu-wa samui desu-yo* (Winter is cold, you know)". However, there is a possibility that the output is unnatural, like *"fuyu-wa samui dayo-ne* (Winter is cold, aren't it?)", depending on the pair of proposition and modality. To solve this problem, the system uses the Google search engine to filter out unnatural output. The system performs a phrase search on the end of the sentence. If the number of search hits is higher than threshold, the output is judged as correct. If the number of hits is lower than the threshold, the output is judged as incorrect and discarded, and a new reply is generated. We experimentally set the threshold to 100 hits.

2.5 Evaluation of Modalin

We used system α, generating only the proposition, and system β, generating both proposition and modality. 5 participants used each system for 10-turn conversations and evaluated the conversations on a 5-point scale. Evaluation criteria were "will to continue the conversation" (A), "grammatical naturalness of dialogues" (B), "semantic naturalness of dialogues" (C), "vocabulary richness" (D), "knowledge richness" (E), and "human-likness of the system" (F). Table 6 shows average scores for the evaluations of each system. System β that uses modality scored much higher than system α. In the evaluation, the participants expressed the opinion that an utterance like (xx *wa* yy) is unnatural and using a modality like *maa* ("well"), *moo* ("anyway") is very natural. Thus we can say that the modality expressions make the utterances of the system seem more natural. The results were considered to be very statistically significant with P value = .0032.

	System α (proposition)						System β (proposition + modality)					
Evaluation criteria	A	B	C	D	E	F	A	B	C	D	E	F
Participant a	1	3	2	2	4	2	4	4	3	4	3	5
Participant b	1	3	1	2	1	1	4	4	4	5	4	3
Participant c	1	2	1	2	1	1	1	2	1	2	1	1
Participant d	1	3	1	3	1	2	4	3	1	3	3	4
Participant e	1	4	1	1	2	1	3	2	2	4	5	4
Average	1	3	1.2	2	1.8	1.4	3.2	3	2.2	3.6	3.2	3.4

Table 6. Modalin evaluation results.

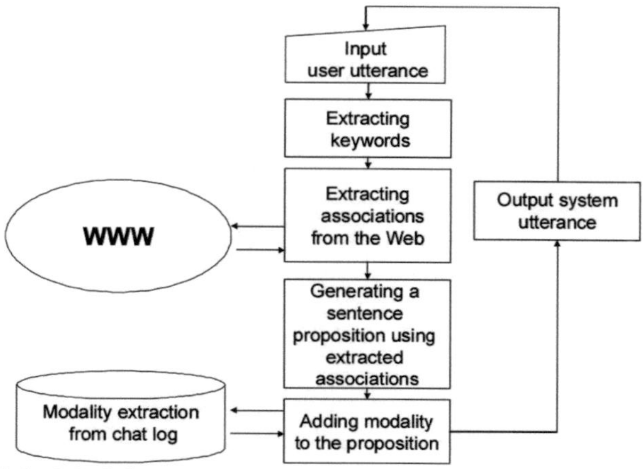

Fig. 1. Flow chart of the Modalin system.

user	*Nani-ka suki-na tabemono aru?* (What food do you like ?)
system	*Maa, tabemono-wa oishii-desu.* (Well, food tastes good.)
user	*Saikin-wa o-sake-mo suki-ni natte kita-n-da.* (Recently, I've become quite a alcohol lover)
system	*Demo, sake-wa yowai-no-yo-ne.* (But I can't drink much, oh no.)
user	*Yowai-n-da. Sugu yocchau-no?* (Oh, I see, you get loaded quickly?)
system	*Maa, sore-wa sugo-wa-ne.* (Well, it's amazing.)
user	*Boku-wa wari-to o-sake-wa tsuyoi hou-nan-da.* (In my case I guess I can drink quite a lot)
system	*Iya, sore-wa tsuyoi-n-de.* (Ooh, strong, one can say.)

Table 5. Example of a dialogue with Modalin (language errors translated close to original).

3. Pundalin – implementing humour to conversational agent

3.1 Humour as a positive factor

There are, many proofs for beneficial influence of humour on our life. For example, humour is often used as a measure to cope with negative emotions and moods, such as stress (Cann et al., 1999), anxiety, or depression (Moran, 1996). Vilaythong et al. (2003) showed that exposing people to humorous contents, like funny videos, increased their feeling of hope and made them feel better in general. Cook & Rice (2003) provided proofs for social benefits of humour, by showing that a sense of humour in another person increases the perceived benefits of a relationship. According to Sprecher & Regan (2002), humour is also one of the main characteristics people use when choosing a partner, which means we like to interact with people with a sense of humour. Finally, Mulkay (1988) proved that we tend to use jokes when discussing difficult matters, which leads to the conclusion that humour makes conversation easier in general.

3.2 Necessity of humour in talking agents

It has been demonstrated that humans treat computers as social actors. According to SRCT (Social Response to Communication Technologies) theory, people respond to computers using the same social attitudes and behaviours they apply to humans (Reeves and Nass, 1996). This also means we expect our interaction with them go smoothly and in a natural way. Therefore, if humour enhances the interaction between humans, a similar effect should be obtained in interaction with machines.

The necessity of creating a joking conversational agent was pointed out and motivated by Nijholt (2007). However, not much has been done to actually construct such an agent. The first known attempt of this kind was made by Loehr (1996), who combined Binsted's joking system JAPE (1996) and talking agent Elmo. The results of the evaluation experiment were relatively poor, for there was barely any relevance between the user's input and the agent's humorous output. Another attempt at creating a humour-equipped agent was made by Tinholt & Nijholt (2007), who implemented a cross-reference ambiguity-based joke generator into an AIML based chat-bot. However, the opportunities for generating cross-reference jokes in daily conversation turned out to be rather rare and the impact on human involvement in the conversation could not be evaluated properly. Also, Morkes et al. (1999), checked the impact of pre-programmed (not generated) humour on a task-oriented conversation. The results showed that a humour-equipped agent was evaluated as better and easier to socialize with by human participants.

3.3 Humoroids – new class of conversational agents

Although not completely untouched (see above), the research field on humour-equipped talking agents needed to be precisely defined. The first consistent definition of such agents was proposed by Dybala et al. (2009a). His definition of this new class of agents says that humour-equipped agents, or "humoroids", are agents that are able to use humour during a conversation. He also defined two major subclasses of humoroids: task-oriented (Loehr, 1996; Morkes et al., 1999) and non-task-oriented (Tinholt & Nijholt, 2007). The agent presented here belongs to the latter type. The presence of humour is of higher importance in non-task-oriented agents, for their main purpose is to entertain human interlocutors and socialize with them during the conversation.

3.4 Punda – a pun generator for Japanese

Considering the NLP methodology, the most "computable" genre of jokes is puns. They can be found in most of the existing languages. In some, however, puns are easier to create and

thus their amount is much bigger than in others. One of such languages is Japanese, in which puns (called *dajare*) are one of main humour genres. This makes Japanese a perfect environment for pun processing research. However, although some attempts of constructing pun generating engine have been made, also in Japanese, creating a funny joking conversational system have been an unfulfilled challenge in NLP field for a long time.
PUNDA research project (Dybala et al., 2008b) is a project aiming to create a Japanese joking conversational system. As a part of this project, we developed a simple pun generating system - PUNDA Simple. This system is a simplified version of the algorithm of the main PUNDA system, which, although still under development, at its current state can be used as a pun generating support tool. Although PUNDA Simple was created for the need of this research, the main part of the algorithm is similar to the one used in the main system.

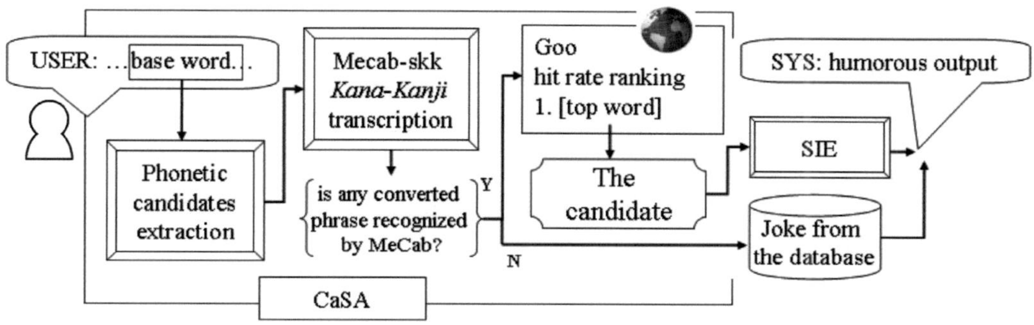

Fig. 2. Algorithm outline for PUNDA Simple joke generating engine.

3.4.1 Algorithm

The PUNDA Simple algorithm consists of two parts: Candidate Selection Algorithm (CaSA) and Sentence Integration Engine (SIE) - see Figure 2.
CaSA. In this step, the system generates a candidate for a pun. The input is a sentence, from which a base word for a pun (a word that will be transformed into a pun) is selected. The input is analysed by morphological analyser MeCab (Kudo, 2001), and if any element is recognized as an ordinary noun, it becomes the base word (a preliminary experiment proved that most of *dajare* base words are ordinary nouns). If no ordinary noun is found, one words with medium number of characters is selected randomly. Then, for the base word, pun candidates are generated using 4 generation patterns: homophony, initial mora addition, internal mora addition and final mora addition. For example, for the word *katana* (a Japanese sabre), the process goes as follows (* means one single mora):
base word: {katana}
candidates:
1. **homophony**: {`katana`}
2. **initial mora addition**: {`*katana` } (`akatana, ikatana, ukatana`...)
3. **final mora addition**: { `katana*`} (`katanaa, katanai, katanau`...)
4. **internal mora addition**: {`ka*tana`}, {`kata*na`} (`kaatana, kaitana, kautana`...)

The candidates are generated in Kana characters (one character = one mora). In the next step, for each candidate a list of possible Kanji (Japanese ideograms) transcriptions is extracted using MeCab-skkserv Kana-Kanji Converter[4]. Then, if any of the converted character sequences of was recognized by the morphological analyser as an existing word, its hit rate was checked in the Internet. The candidate with highest Goo[5] hit rate was extracted as a pun candidate. For example, for the word katana the candidate would be *takatana* (a high shelf).

SIE. In this step, a sentence including the candidate extracted by CaSA is generated. To make system's response more related to the user's input, each sentence that included joke started with the pattern "[base word] *to ieba*" ("Speaking of [base word]"). The following part of the sentence is extracted from KWIC on WEB online Keyword-in-context sentences database (Yoshihira et al., 2004) - the candidate is used as a query word and the list of sentences including this word is extracted. All sentences that contain non-Japanese characters (such as Latin letters, brackets, numbers etc.) are deleted, as they may be difficult to understand without the context. Then, the shortest sentence with exclamation marks is selected (we assumed that most jokes convey some emotions, and exclamation marks are its visible sign). If no such sentence is found, the shortest sentence that ended with a period is selected. Finally, the part following the candidate is extracted and added as the second part to the system's response – see the example below:

User: - *Natsu wa atsui desu kedo, Toukyou hodo ja nai desu.* (The summer is hot, but not as hot as in Tokyo); [base word: *natsu* (summer), pun candidate: *natsukashii* (emotionally attached; loved)]

System: -*Natsu to ieba, natsukashii Nose de, kyuuyuu to waiwai!* (Speaking of summer, it will be fun to meet some old friends in my beloved Nose! <a town near Osaka>)

If no appropriate sentence is found on KWIC, the response ends with "[candidate] *da yo ne*" ("it's the [candidate], isn't it") – see the example below.

User: -*Ame da kara kaimono iku no wa mendokusai ne.* (It's raining so going shopping is a bad idea) [base word: *ame* (rain), pun candidate: *ame* (a candy)]

System: -*Ame to ieba ame da yo ne.* (Rain reminds me of candies.)

When the candidates list is empty, the system selects one random pun from Sjöbergh's pun database (Sjöbergh & Araki, 2008b) – see the example below.

User: - *Sou, atarashii baito ne.* (Yeah, it's my new part-time job) [base word: *baito* (a part-time job), pun candidate: *none*]

System's response (from the pun corpus): -*Kureyon wo katte kureyon!* (Buy the pen, man!).

3.5 Pundalin – joking conversational agent

The conversational agent Modalin and the pun generator were merged to create a joking conversational system Pundalin. The merging rule was – in every third dialogue turn Modalin's output was replaced by PUNDA Simple's joke. In other words, every third user's utterance became PUNDA's input and an appropriate pun for it was generated, using the algorithm described above. This method, albeit quite simple, allowed us to check if the usage of humour improved the reception of the conversational agent in the eyes of users, and therefore system's overall performance as a companion for conversation.

[4] MeCab-skkserv Kanji-Kana converter, http://chasen.org/~taku/software/mecab-skkserv/

[5] Goo search engine, http://www.goo.ne.jp/

3.6 Evaluation of Pundalin

To check if humour can enhance the non-task oriented dialogue, we conducted an evaluation experiment, using Modalin as the baseline system and Pundalin as the main, humour-equipped system. As is argued by Dybala et al., (2009c), since it is users who are the "clients" of our product, in the research on dialogue systems the first person oriented evaluation is of the highest importance. It allows checking the user's impressions of the interaction with the system in the most direct way. In the experiment, users were asked to perform a 10-turn dialogue with Modalin, and then with Pundalin. No topic restrictions were made. The utterance variety was big, however, the beginning of conversations by the users was usually very normal, like: "What did you do yesterday?", "May I ask you a question?" or "It's hot today, isn't it?" There were 13 participants, 11 male and 2 female; all of them were university undergraduate students. After talking with both systems, they were asked to fill out a questionnaire about each system's performance. The questions concerned both linguistic (B-D) and non-linguistic (A, E-H) areas of interaction: **A**) Do you want to continue the dialogue with the system?; **B**) Was the system's output grammatically natural?; **C**) Was the system's output semantically natural?; **D**) Was the system's vocabulary rich?; **E**) Did you get an impression that the system possesses any knowledge?; **F**) Did you get an impression that the system was human-like?; **G**) Do you think the system tried to make the dialogue more interesting?; **H**) Did you find the conversation with the system interesting?

The replies to the questions were given on 5-point scales with explanations added. Each evaluator filled out two questionnaires, one for each system. The final, summarizing question was "Which system do you think was better?" Statistical significance of the results was calculated using the student's t-test. The results are summarized in Table 7. The results show that the system with humour received higher scores in both linguistic and non-linguistic areas. As for the former, it may seem unusual that the presence of humour improved the system's linguistic skills – this fact, however, could have been caused by the fact that Pundalin uses fragments of human created sentences and jokes from a data base, which naturally are more correct than those generated automatically. Also in the non-linguistic area all results point at the humour-equipped system. Users wanted to continue the conversation with Pundalin more than with Modalin; Pundalin was perceived as more human-like, knowledgeable, funny and generally better than Modalin (Dybala et al., 2008a). Results for questions A and B were found to be significant on 6% level, and for remaining questions – on 5% level. The overall compared results of Modalin and Pundalin were extremely statistically significant, with P value = .0002.

Questions	A	B	C	D	E	F	G	H	**Which is better?**
Modalin	2.62	2.15	1.85	2.08	2.15	2.38	1.92	2.46	15%
Pundalin	3.38	2.92	2.69	3.00	2.85	3.31	4.15	4.08	**85%**
Difference	**0.76**	**0.77**	**0.84**	**0.92**	**0.70**	**0.93**	**2.23**	**1.62**	
P value	> .05	> .05	**< .05**	**< .05**	**< .05**	**< .05**	**< .05**	**< .05**	

Table 7. User evaluation results for Modalin and Pundalin for detailed questions. Answers were given on a 5-point scale.

4. Implementing Emotional Intelligence in conversational agents

Developing methods for processing human emotions is one of the current issues in Artificial Intelligence. The field embracing this subject, Affective Computing, has been gathering popularity of researchers since being initiated only a little over ten years ago (Picard, 1997). The interest in this field is usually focused on recognizing the human emotions in human-computer interaction. In the popular methods, emotion recognition is focused on: facial expressions (Hager et al., 2002), voice (Kang et al., 2000) or biometric data (Teixeira et al., 2008). However, these methods, based on a behavioural approach, ignore the semantic and pragmatic context of emotions. Therefore, although they achieve good results in laboratory settings, such methods lack usability in real life. A system for recognition of emotions from facial expressions, assigning "sadness" when a user is crying would be critically mistaken, if the user was, e.g., cutting an onion in the kitchen. This leads to the need of applying contextual analysis to emotion processing. Furthermore, although it was proved that affective states should be analysed as emotion specific (Lerner & Kelter, 2000), most of the behavioural approach methods simply classify them to opposing pairs such as joy-anger, or happiness-sadness (Teixeira et al., 2008). A positive change in this tendency can be seen in text mining and information extraction approaches to emotion estimation (Tokuhisa et al., 2008; Ptaszynski et al., 2009b). However, the lack of standardization often causes inconsistencies in emotion classification. As one of the recent advances in affect analysis, it was shown that Web mining methods can improve the performance of language-based affect analysis systems (Tokuhisa et al., 2008; Ptaszynski et al., 2009b). However, in such methods, although the results of experiments appear to be positive, the two different approaches, the language-syntax based and Web mining based, are mixed. The former, comparing the information provided by the user to the existing lexicons and sets of rules, is responsible for recognizing the particular emotion expression conveyed by the user. The latter is based on gathering from the Internet large numbers of examples and deriving from them an approximated reasoning about what emotions usually associate with a certain contents. Using the Web simply as complementary mean for the language based approach, although achieving reasonable results, means not fully exploiting the great potential lying in the Web (Rzepka and Araki, 2007).

In this research we present a method capable of specifying users' emotional states in a more sophisticated way than simple valence classification. The method also contributes to standardization of the emotion classification for the Japanese language since instead of creating a new classification we apply the most reliable and coherent one available today, mentioned firstly by Ptaszynski et al. (2008) and developed further by Ptaszynski et al. (2009b), who base their classification on Nakamura's (1993) research in lexicology of emotive expressions in the Japanese language. Finally, our method does not only specify what type of emotion was expressed, but also determines whether the expressed emotion is appropriate for the context it appears in. In the method we use Ptaszynski's et al., (2009f) system for affect analysis and annotation of utterances and Shi's et al. (2008) method for gathering emotive associations from the Web. The baseline of the system presented here was first proposed by Ptaszynski et al. (2009c) and evaluated at 45% of accuracy. We improved the system in two ways. Firstly, Ptaszynski's system for affect analysis was improved with Contextual Valence Shifters to avoid confusing the valence polarity of emotive expressions. Secondly, we improved Shi's Web mining technique. The problem was it was gathering too much noise from the Internet. To solve this problem we referred to the proof provided by

Abbasi and Chen (2007), who showed that public Web services, such as forums or blogs, are rich in emotive information and thus ideal for affect analysis. Therefore we restricted the mining scope of Shi's technique from the whole Web to the contents of *Yahoo!Japan–Blogs* (blogs.yahoo.co.jp) a robust weblog service.

4.1 Definitions

Emotional Intelligence

The idea of *Emotional Intelligence* (EI) was first officially proposed by Salovey & Mayer (1990), who defined it as a part of human intelligence consisting of the ability to: I) perceive emotions; II) integrate emotions to facilitate thoughts; III) understand emotions; IV) regulate emotions. In the EI Framework (Mayer & Salovey, 1997) the first step consists of the abilities to a) identify emotions and b) discriminate between appropriate and inappropriate expressions of emotion. Salovey and Mayer (1990) argue that recognizing emotions is only the first step to acquire full scope of Emotional Intelligence and does not tell us anything about whether it is appropriate for a given situation or what reactions should be undertaken. According to Solomon (1993), the valence of emotions is determined by the context they are expressed in. For example, anger can be positive, when warranted (e.g. a reaction to a direct and deliberate offence) and negative, when unwarranted (scolding one's own children unjustly) and the reactions should be different for the two different contexts of anger. The attempts to implement the EI Framework usually do not go beyond theory (Andre et al., 2004), and the few practical attempts eventually still do not surmount the first step of recognition (Picard et al., 2001). The research presented here is an attempt to go beyond this simple approach. Following emotion recognition, their appropriateness is verified against their contexts. By providing an agent means to determine the appropriateness of emotions, we make a step towards the full implementation of EI framework in machines.

Definition and classification of emotions

Our working definition of emotions is based on Nakamura's (1993), who defines them as every temporary state of mind, feeling, or affective state evoked by experiencing different sensations. This definition is complemented by Solomon's (1993), who argues that people are not passive participants in their emotions, but rather the emotions are strategies by which people engage with the world. Since we operate on language, the above is further complemented by Beijer's (2002) definition of emotive utterances, which he describes as every utterance in which the speaker is emotionally involved, and this involvement, expressed linguistically, is informative for the listener. Nakamura (1993), proposed also a 10 type emotion classification, the most appropriate for the Japanese language: *ki / yorokobi* (joy, delight), *do / ikari* (anger), *ai / aware* (gloom, sorrow, sadness), *fu / kowagari* (fear), *chi / haji* (shame, shyness, bashfulness), *kou/ suki* (liking, fondness), *en / iya* (dislike, detestation), *kou / takaburi* (excitement), *an / yasuragi* (relief) and *kyou / odoroki* (surprise, amazement).

Contextual Valence Shifters

The idea of Contextual Valence Shifters (CVS) as an application in Sentiment Analysis was first proposed by Polanyi & Zaenen (2004). They distinguish two kinds of CVS: negations and intensifiers. The group of negations contains words like "not", "never", and "not quite", which change the valence polarity of semantic orientation of an evaluative word they are attached to. The group of intensifiers contains words like "very", "very much", and "deeply", which intensify the semantic orientation of an evaluative word. So far the idea of CVS analysis was successfully applied to Sentiment Analysis of English texts (Kennedy & Inkpen, 2005). Successful attempts on Japanese ground (Miyoshi & Nakagami, 2007) show that it is also applicable for the Japanese language. Examples of CVS negations in Japanese are grammatical structures like: *amari -nai* (not quite-), *-to wa ienai* (cannot say it is-), or *mattaku -nai* (not at all-). Intensifiers are represented by: *totemo-* (very much-), *sugoku-* (-a lot), or *kiwamete-* (extremely). The idea of CVS is applied in line with Ptaszynski's et al. (2009a) research on improving affect analysis by valence shifting. The Contextual Valence Shifting Procedure (details below) is supported further with Russell's (1980) 2-dimmensional model of affect.

Two-dimensional model of affect

The idea of a two-dimensional model of affect was first proposed by Schlosberg (1952) and developed further by Russell (1980). Its main assumption is that all emotions can be described in a space of two-dimensions: valence polarity (positive/negative) and activation (activated/deactivated). An example of positive-activated emotion is excitement; positive-deactivated emotion is, e.g., relief; negative-activated and deactivated emotions are anger and gloom respectively. This way 4 emotion areas are distinguished: activated-positive, activated-negative, deactivated-positive and deactivated-negative. Nakamura's emotion types were mapped on this model and their affiliation to one of the spaces was determined. Those emotions for which the affiliation was not obvious (e.g. surprise can be both positive as well as negative, etc.) were mapped on all of the areas they could belong to. However, no emotion type was mapped on more than two adjacent fields. This grouping is then used in our system for two reasons. Firstly, in the CVS analysis procedure to specify which emotion corresponds to the one negated by a CVS phrase. Secondly, in emotion appropriateness verification procedure, for estimating whether the emotion types belong to the same area, even if not perfectly matching with the emotive associations gathered from the Web.

Example of a sentence (English translation)	Emotemes	**Emotive expressions**
(1) *Kyo wa nante* ***kimochi ii*** *hi nanda!* (Today is such a nice day!)	yes	yes
(2) *Iyaa, sore wa sugoi desu ne!* (Woa, that's great!)	yes	no
(3) *Ryoushin wa minna jibun no kodomo wo* ***aishiteiru.*** (All parents love their children.)	no	yes
(4) *Kore wa hon desu.* (This is a book.)	no	no

Table 8. Examples of sentences containing emotemes (underlined) and/or emotive expressions (bold type font).

4.2 Linguistic approach to emotions – the emotive function of language

The semantic and pragmatic diversity of emotions is best conveyed in language (Solomon, 1993). Therefore we designed our method to be language-based. There are different linguistic means used to inform other interlocutors of emotional states. The elements of speech used to convey emotive meaning are described by the emotive function of language (Jakobson, 1960). In Japanese it is realized lexically through such parts of speech as exclamations (Beijer, 2002), hypocoristics (endearments), vulgar language (Crystal, 1989;

Potts & Kawahara, 2004) and mimetic expressions (in Japanese: *gitaigo*) (Baba, 2003). A key role in expressing emotions is also played by the lexicon of words describing emotional states (Nakamura, 1993). The para-linguistic elements, like intonation, are represented lexically by exclamation marks or ellipsis. Ptaszynski (2006) classified the realizations of emotive function in Japanese in two general types. The first one, emotive elements (or **emotemes**), indicate that emotions have been conveyed, but not detailing their specificity. This group is linguistically realized by interjections, exclamations, mimetic expressions, or vulgarities. The second type, **emotive expressions**, are parts of speech like nouns, verbs, adjectives or metaphors describing affective states. Examples of sentences containing emotemes and/or emotive expressions are shown in Table 8. Examples (1) and (2) are emotive sentences. (1) is an exclamative sentence, which is determined by the use of exclamative constructions *nante* (how/such a) and *nanda!* (exclamative sentence ending), and contains an emotive expression *kimochi ii* (to feel good). (2) is also an exclamative. It is easily recognizable by the use of an interjection *iyaa*, an adjective in the function of interjection *sugoi* (great), and by the emphatic particle *-ne*. However, it does not contain any emotive expressions and therefore it is ambiguous whether the emotions conveyed by the speaker are positive or negative. The examples (3) and (4) show non-emotive sentences. (3), although containing an emotive verb *aishiteiru* (to love), is a generic statement and, if not put in a specific context, does not convey any emotions. Finally, (4) is a simple declarative sentence without any emotive value.

4.2.1 Defining emotive linguistic features

We defined emotemes and emotive expressions according to Ptaszynski's two-part classification. The feature set was defined in a way similar to the one proposed by Alm et al. (2005), by using multiple features to handle emotive sentences. Alm however, designed their research for English children's stories, whereas we focus on utterances in Japanese, and therefore used Ptaszynski's classification as more appropriate for our research.

Emotemes

Into the group of emotive elements, formally visualisable as textual representations of speech, Ptaszynski (2006) includes the following lexical and syntactical structures. **Exclamative utterance**. The research on exclamatives in Japanese (Ono, 2002; Sasai, 2006) provides a wide scope of topics useful as features in our system. Some of the exclamative structures are: *nan(te/to/ka)-*, *-darou*, or *-da(yo/ne)*, partially corresponding to *wh*-exclamatives in English (see the first sentence in Table 8).

Interjections are typical emotems. Some of the most representative Japanese interjections are *waa*, *yare-yare* or *iyaa* (see the second sentence in Table 8).

Casual Speech. Casual speech is not an emotem per se, however, many structures of casual speech are used when expressing emotions. Examples of casual language use are modifications of adjective and verb endings *-ai* to *-ee*, like in the example: *Ha ga itee!* (My tooth hurts!), or abbreviations of forms *-noda* into *-nda*, like in the example: *Nani yattenda yo!?* (What the hell are you doing!?).

Gitaigo. Baba (2003) distinguishes *gitaigo* (mimetic expressions) as emotems specific for the Japanese language. Not all *gitaigo* are emotive, but rather they can be classified into emotive mimetics (describing one's emotions), and sensation/state mimetics (describing manner and appearance). Examples of emotive *gitaigo* are: *iraira* (be irritated), like in the sentence:

Omoidasenkute iraira shita yo. (I was so irritated, 'cause I couldn't remember.), or *hiyahiya* (be in fear, nervous), like in the sentence: *Juugeki demo sareru n janai ka to omotte, hiyahiya shita ze.* (I thought he was gonna shoot me - I was petrified.)

Emotive marks. This group contains punctuation marks used as textual representations of emotive intonation features. The most obvious example is exclamation mark „!" (see Table 8). In Japanese, marks like "..." (ellipsis), or prolongation marks, like " – " or "~" are also used to inform interlocutors that emotions have been conveyed

Hypocoristics (endearments) in Japanese express emotions and attitudes towards an object by the use of diminutive forms of a name or status of the object (*Hanako* [girl's name] vs *Hanako-chan* [/endearment/]; *o-nee-san* [older sister] vs *o-nee-chan* [sis /endearment/], *inu* [a dog] vs *wanko* [doggy /endearment/]). Sentence example: *Saikin Oo-chan to Mit-chan ga bokura to karamu youni nattekita!!* (Oo-chan and Mit-chan has been palling around with us lately!!)

Vulgarisms. The use of vulgarisms usually accompanies expressing emotions. However, despite a general belief that vulgarisms express only negative meaning, Ptaszynski (2006) notices that they can be also used as expressions of strong positive feelings, and Sjöbergh (2006) showed, that they can also be funny, when used in jokes, like in the example: *Mono wa mono dakedo, fuete komarimasu mono wa nanda-? Bakamono.* (A thing (*mono*) is a thing, but what kind of thing is bothersome if they increase? Idiots (*bakamono*).)

Emotive expressions

A lexicon of expressions describing emotional states contains words, phrases or idioms. Such a lexicon can be used to express emotions, like in the first example in Table 8, however, it can also be used to formulate, not emphasized emotively, generic or declarative statements (third example in Table 8). Some examples are:

adjectives: *sabishii* (sad), *ureshii* (happy);

nouns: *aijou* (love), *kyofu* (fear);

verbs: *yorokobu* (to feel happy), *aisuru* (to love);

fixed phrases/idioms: *mushizu ga hashiru* (give one the creeps [of hate]), *kokoro ga odoru* (one's heart is dancing [of joy]);

proverbs: *dohatsuten wo tsuku* (be in a towering rage), *ashi wo fumu tokoro wo shirazu* (be with one's heart up the sky [of happiness]);

metaphors/similes: *itai hodo kanashii* (pain of sadness), *aijou wa eien no honoo da* (love is an eternal flame);

4.3 ML-Ask

Based on the linguistic approach towards emotions as well as the classification of emotions, Ptaszynski et al. (2009f) constructed ML-Ask (eMotive eLements–SeeK & Analyse) system for automatic annotation of utterances with emotive information. The emotem database was gathered manually from other research and grouped into five types (code, reference research and number of gathered items in square, round and curly brackets, respectively):

1. **[EX]** Interjections and structures of exclamative and emotive-casual utterances (Nakamura, 1993; Oshima-Takane et al., 1995-1998; Tsuchiya, 1999; Ono, 2002). {477}
2. **[GI]** *Gitaigo* (Nakamura, 1993; Oshima-Takane et al., 1995-1998; Baba, 2003). {213}
3. **[HY]** Hypocorystrics (Kamei et al., 1996). {8}
4. **[VU]** Vulgarisms (Sjöbergh, 2008a). {200}

5. **[EM]** Emotive marks (Kamei et al., 1996). {9}

These databases were used as a core for ML-Ask. We also added Nakamura's (1993) dictionary as a database of emotive expressions (code: **[EMO-X]**, 2100 items in total). The breakdown with number of items per emotion type was as follows: *yorokobi* {224}, *ikari* {199}, *aware* {232}, *kowagari* {147}, *haji* {65}, *suki* {197}, *iya* {532}, *takaburi* {269}, *yasuragi* {106}, *odoroki* {129}.

4.3.1 Emotems analysis procedure

Based on the databases described above, a textual input utterance is analysed and emotive information is annotated. The system first determines whether an utterance is emotive (appearance of at least one emotive feature), extracts all features from the sentence, and analyses the structure of the emotive utterance. This is the system's main procedure. Examples of analysis are shown below (from top line: example in Japanese, emotive information annotation, English translation; emotems-underlined, emotive expressions bold type font, n-noun, ptl-particle, AUX-auxiliary verb, the system flow is shown on Figure 3).

(1) *Kyo* *wa* *nante* ***kimochi ii*** *hi* *nanda* *!*
Today ptl:THEM EX:nante **EMO-X:joy** day:SUBJ EX:nanda EM:!

(2) *Iyaa,* *sore* *wa* *sugoi* *desu* *ne* *!*
EX:iyaa that ptl:THEM EX:sugoi AUX EX:ne EM:!

(5) ***Akirame*** *cha* *ikenai* *yo* *!*
EMO-X:dislike EX:cha | CVS:cha-ikenai{→joy} EX:yo EM:!
Translation: Don't cha give up!

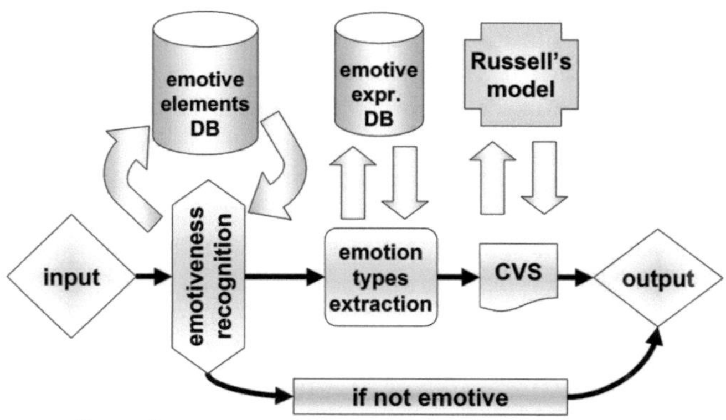

Fig. 3. ML-Ask system flow chart

4.3.2 Emotive expressions analysis procedure

In all utterances determined as emotive, the system searches for emotive expressions from the databases (Nakamura's dictionary). This procedure is used to verify:

1) How many of all determined emotive utterances contain emotive expressions;

2) If the system is capable of determining specific types of emotions in human-computer interaction. However, keyword-based extraction allowed mismatching the specific emotion types. To avoid this we applied Contextual Valence Shifters.

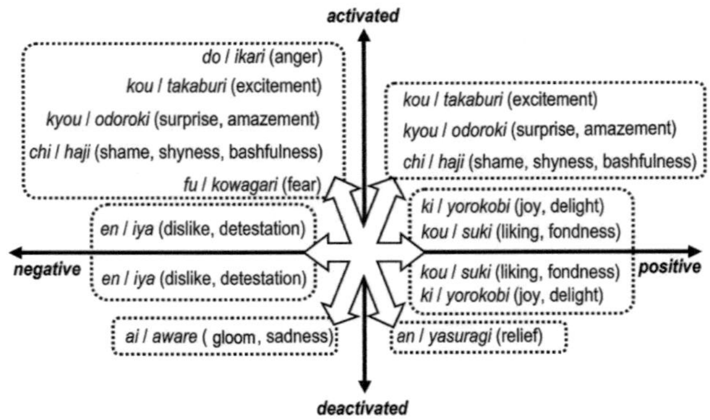

Fig. 4. Nakamura's emotion types mapped on Russell's space and gathered in 6 contrasting groups: positive-activated↔negative-deactivated; negative-activated↔positive- deactivated; positive↔negative (for emotion types with two possible activation parameters).

4.3.3 Contextual Valence Shifters in ML-Ask

When a CVS structure is discovered, ML-Ask changes the valence polarity of the detected emotion. To specify the emotion types afterwards, we applied the 2-dimensional model of affect (Russell, 1980). After valence shifting the emotion type is determined as the one with valence polarity and activation parameters opposite to the contrasted emotion (see Figure 4 and example (5) above). Nakamura's emotion types mapped on Russell's model specify a restricted group of potential emotions.

4.3.4 Evaluation of ML-Ask in laboratory settings

In the evaluation we contrasted the emotive information annotation by ML-Ask and laypeople. We gathered a corpus of natural utterances through an anonymous survey in which we asked people of different ages and social groups to remember a conversation with a friend and write three sentences from that conversation: 1) free, 2) emotive, and 3) non-emotive. From this collection we used only the utterances meant to be either emotive or non-emotive. The participants also annotated the specific emotion types on emotive utterances. Since laypeople, not possessing any linguistic knowledge, are unable to describe the structure of emotive utterances, we checked whether ML-Ask could distinguish between emotive and non-emotive utterances. As a result, ML-Ask annotated correctly 72 from 80 utterances (90%). In 2 cases the system wrongly annotated utterances as "emotive", in 6 cases it was the opposite. The system's agreement with annotators was indicated as very high (kappa=.8). Therefore, ML-Ask proved its reliability in identifying emotive utterances.

We also checked whether the system could determine about the specified emotion types. ML-Ask can potentially extract up to ten emotion types for one utterance. However, some of them could be extracted wrongly or unextracted at all. Therefore we calculated the accuracy as balanced F-score with emotive tags added by authors of the utterances as gold standard. The system's accuracy in estimating the specific types of emotions including "non-emotive" reached F=.45 (Precision=.62, Recall=.35) of balanced F-score. Then we asked a group of third party human annotators (but different to the first group) to annotate the emotion types to the utterances (12 people for one utterance) to check the human level in this task. For the third party human annotators the average F-score was .72 (Precision=.84, Recall=.64), therefore system's accuracy was 62.5% (.45/.72) of the human level. This experiment verified the reliability of Nakamura's dictionary as emotive expressions database. The coverage was not high (Recall=.35), which has two reasons: 1) Nakamura stopped updating his dictionary in 1993 and the lexicon is out-of-date (only 2100 expressions); 2) instead of using straight forward emotive expressions, people often use ambiguous emotive utterances in which valence of emphasis is based on the situation the sentence is used in (see example (2) in Table 8).

4.4 Web mining technique

To verify the appropriateness of the speaker's affective states we applied Shi's et al. (2008) Web mining technique for extracting emotive associations from the Web. Ptaszynski et al. (2009b) already showed that ML-Ask and Shi's technique are compatible and can be used as complementary means to improve the emotion recognition task. However, these two methods are based on different assumptions. ML-Ask is a language based affect analysis system and can recognize the particular emotion expression conveyed by a user. On the other hand, Shi's technique is gathering from the Internet large number of examples and deriving from such data an approximated reasoning about what emotion types usually associate with an input contents. Therefore it is more reasonable to use the former system as emotion detector, and the latter one as verifier of naturalness, or appropriateness of user emotions.

Shi's technique performs common-sense reasoning about what emotions are the most natural to appear in a context of an utterance, or, which emotions should be associated with it. Emotions expressed, which are unnatural for the context (low or not on the list) are perceived as inappropriate. The technique is composed of three steps: 1) phrase extraction from an utterance; 2) morpheme modification; 3) extraction of emotion associations.

4.4.1 Phrase extraction procedure

An utterance is first processed by MeCab (Kudo, 2001). Every element separated by MeCab is treated as a unigram. All unigrams are grouped into larger n-gram groups preserving their word order in the utterance. The groups are arranged from the longest n-gram (the whole sentence) down to all groups of trigrams.

4.4.2 Morpheme modification procedure

On the list of n-gram phrases the ones ending with a verb or an adjective are then modified grammatically in line with Yamashita's argument (Yamahsita, 1999) that Japanese people tend to convey emotive meaning after causality morphemes. This was independently confirmed experimentally by Shi et al., (2008). They distinguished eleven emotively stigmatised morphemes for the Japanese language using statistical analysis of Web contents and performed a cross reference of appearance of the eleven morphemes with the emotive expression database using the Google search engine. This provided the results (hit-rate) showing which of the eleven causality morphemes were the most frequently used to express emotions. For the five most frequent morphemes, the coverage of Web mining procedure still exceeded 90%. Therefore for Web mining they decided to use only those five ones, namely: *-te*, *-to*, *-node*, *-kara* and *-tara* (see Table 9).

morpheme	*-te*	*-to*	*-node*	*-kara*	*-tara*	*-ba*	*-nowa*	*-noga*	*-nara*	*-kotoga*	*-kotowa*
result	**41.97%**	**31.97%**	**7.20%**	**6.32%**	**5.94%**	3.19%	2.30%	2.15%	1.17%	0.35%	0.30%

Table 9. Hit-rate results for each of the eleven morphemes

4.4.3 Emotion type extraction procedure

In this step the modified phrases are used as a query in Google search engine with 100 snippets for one morpheme modification per query phrase. This way a maximum of 500 snippets for each queried phrase is extracted and cross-referenced with emotive expression database (see Figure 5). The emotive expressions extracted from the snippets are collected, and the results for every emotion type are sorted in descending order. This way we obtain a list of emotions associated with the queried sentence - the approximated emotive common sense used further as an appropriateness indicator (an example is shown in Table 10).

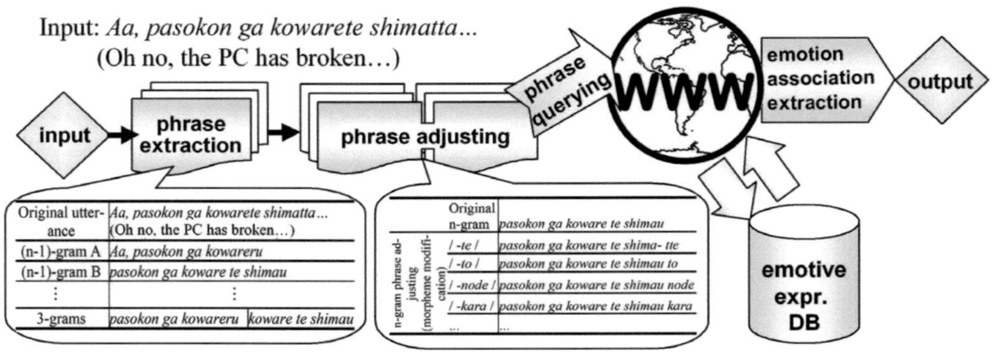

Fig. 5. Flow chart of the Web mining technique

4.4.4 Blog mining

The baseline Web mining method, using Google to search through the whole Web, was gathering a large amount of noise. To solve this problem we made two modifications. Firstly, we added a command stopping the search if any emotions were found using the longer n-grams. This assures the extraction of only the closest emotive associations and speeds up the extraction process. Secondly, since, as mentioned before, people convey on blogs their opinions and emotions, we restricted the mining to blog contents to assure extraction of more accurate emotive associations. The blog mining procedure performs the query first on the public blogs from *Yahoo!Japan-Blogs*. The paragraphs of each blog containing query phrases are co-referenced with emotive expression database to gather the emotive associations. If no information was gathered from the blog contents, the same search is performed with the baseline conditions - on the whole Web. An example of improvement is presented in Table 10.

4.4.5 Evaluation of Web mining technique

To evaluate the Web mining technique we used the same collection of utterances as in evaluation of ML-Ask. However, as mentioned above, the Web mining technique is meant not to recognize the emotions of a particular user, but rather to find a general common sense about what emotion should be expressed in a particular utterance. Therefore, here, we used the emotions tagged by the third party evaluators as the gold standard. The correct result had to fulfil at least one of the two conditions: **1)** one or more of the extracted emotive associations belonged to the group of emotion types tagged by the third party annotators; **2)** the extracted emotive associations agreed with the majority of the human annotations. Under these conditions, Shi's Web mining technique obtained an accuracy rate of 72%.

Sentence: *Konpyuuta wa omoshiroi desu ne.* (Computers are so interesting.)			
Extracted emotion type	**Baseline: Type extracted / all extracted types(Ratio)**	**Extracted emotion type**	**Blogs: Type extracted / all extracted types(Ratio)**
liking	79/284(0.287)	liking	601/610(0.985)
surprise	30/284(0.105)	excitement	1/610 (0.001) [rejected as noise]
excitement	30/284(0.105)	fear	1/610 (0.001) [rejected as noise]
fear	29/284(0.102)	relief	1/610 (0.001) [rejected as noise]

Table 10. Example of emotion association extraction from the Web and its improvement by blog mining procedure.

4.5 Contextual appropriateness of emotion verification (CAEV) procedure

The two above described systems are combined as follows: when ML-Ask discovers an emotive utterance and successfully specifies emotion types, the Web mining technique begins the process of verification of whether the expressed emotions are appropriate to be used in such context. The emotions commonly associated with the context of the utterance are extracted from the Web and the emotions reported by ML-Ask from the user utterances are compared to the Web mining results. If the two match, the emotions expressed by the user are determined to be appropriate for the context. In such situations, a conversational agent equipped with this system could choose a dialogue strategy that sympathizes with the user (two examples are presented below).

Positive-appropriate emotion:
User: I'm so happy I passed the exam!
`ML-Ask: joy;  Web mining: joy, excitement`
Agent: Yeah! That's great! `[sympathy]`

Negative-appropriate emotion:
User: I hate him for making a fool of me in front of everyone.
`ML-Ask: dislike;  Web mining: anger, dislike`
Agent: You have a reason to be angry. `[empathy]`
However if the verification procedure indicates that the expressed emotion is inappropriate for the context, the agent could undertake different measures, e.g. helping the user to manage their emotions. Two examples are shown below.

Positive-inappropriate emotion:
User: I'd be happy if he was hit by a car!
`ML-Ask: joy;  Web mining: fear, sadness`
Agent: Are you sure that is what you are really feeling? `[counselling]`

Negative-inappropriate emotion:
User: I won the prize, but I feel so bored.
`ML-Ask: dislike, depression; Web mining: excitement, joy`
Agent: You should be happy! `[consolation]`

4.9.1 Two-dimensional Model of Affect in CAEV procedure

According to Solomon (1993), people sometimes misattribute the specific emotion types, but they rarely misattribute their valence. One could, e.g., confuse anger with irritation, but not admiration with detestation. Therefore, we checked if at least the general features matched even when specific emotion types did not match perfectly with the emotive associations. By general features we refer to those proposed by Russell (1980) in the theory of the two-dimensional model of affect. Using the mapping of Nakamura's emotion types on Russell's model we checked whether the emotion types tagged by ML-Ask belonged to the same space, even if they did not perfectly match the emotive associations gathered from the Web.

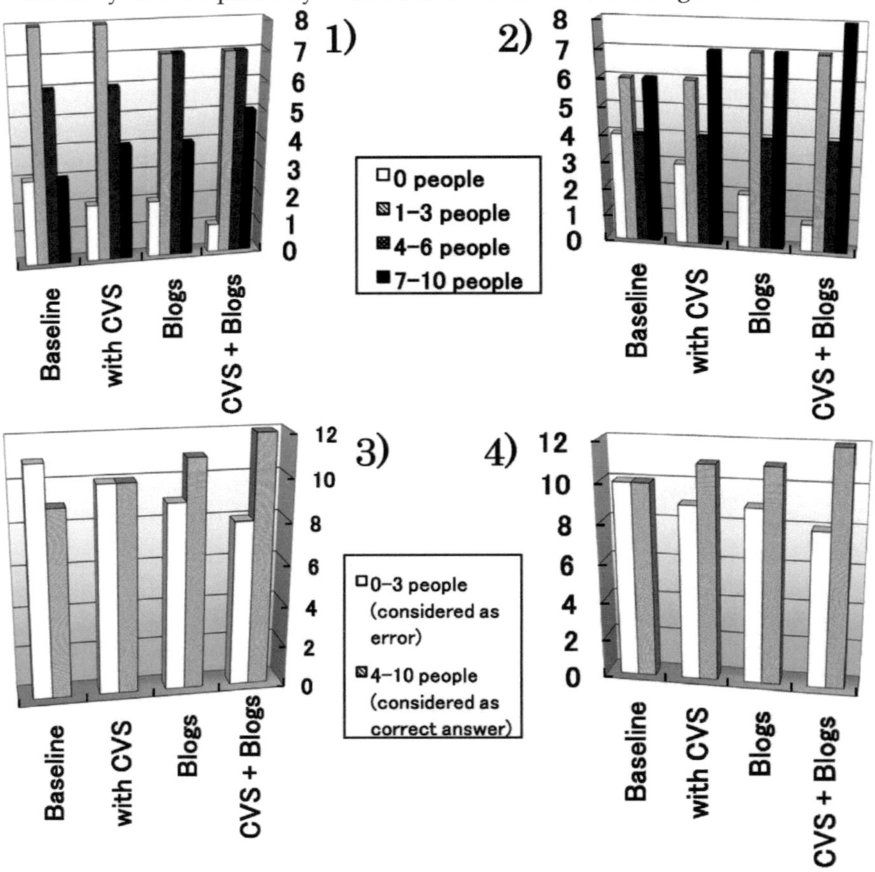

Fig. 6. Results of CAEV Procedure evaluation in estimating appropriateness of: specific emotion types - 1), 3) and valence - 2), 4). Summarization in four - 1), 2) and two - 3), 4) groups of results.

4.10 Evaluation experiment

To evaluate the method we performed an experiment. In the experiment we used the chat logs from the evaluation experiment of Modalin and Pundalin (see section **3**). All 26 conversations were analysed by ML-Ask. 6 out of all 26 conversations contained no specified emotional states and were excluded from the further evaluation process. For the rest the Web mining procedure was carried out to determine whether the emotions expressed by the user were contextually appropriate. We compared four versions of the method: 1) ML-Ask and Web mining baseline; 2) ML-Ask supported only with CVS, Web mining baseline; 3) ML-Ask baseline and Blog mining; 4) supported with both - CVS and blog mining. The difference in results appeared in 5 conversation sets. Then a questionnaire was designed to evaluate how close the results were to human thinking. One questionnaire set consisted of one conversation record and questions inquiring what were: 1) the valence and 2) the specific type of emotions conveyed in the conversation, and 3) whether they were contextually appropriate. Every questionnaire set was filled out by 10 people (undergraduate students, but different from the users who performed the conversations with the agents). The conversations where differences in results appeared for the two compared procedures, were evaluated separately for each version of the method. Therefore there were 20 questionnaire sets for the baseline method and additional 5 for the conversations which results changed after improvements. With every questionnaire set filled by 10 human evaluators we obtained a total number of 250 different evaluations performed by different people. For every conversation set we calculated how many of the human evaluators confirmed the system's results. The evaluated items were: A) general valence determination and B) specific emotion types determination accuracies of ML-Ask; the accuracy of the system as a whole to determine the contextual appropriateness of C) specific emotion types and D) valence. The results for A) and B) are provided in Table 12. The results for C) and D) are given in Table 11, 12 and in Figure 6: 1)-4).

4.10.1 Results

In the majority of research on emotion processing in Japanese, the process of evaluation is usually performed by a small number of evaluators, sometimes only one or two people (Tokuhisa et al., 2008). This might cause the problem of small statistical significance of the results, or, simply of subjectivisation of the results and its small reliability. To overcome this tendency, in our research we used 10 independent evaluators for each agent conversation and assumed that at least four people out of ten have to confirm the system's results. This is a fair ratio when we consider that it means that at least four people of ten had to provide exactly the same results as the system. The survey provided many positive results. Improving the method with both CVS procedure and restricting the query scope in the Web mining procedure to blog contents improved the performance of the appropriateness verification procedure both on the level of valence and specific emotion types. The highest accuracy and therefore the most efficient one was the version of the system with both improvements applied, by which the system's performance was improved from 45.0% to 60.0% for the specific emotion types and from 50.0% to 60.0% for the valence. Moreover, for the conversations without humour (with Modalin) the system's performance reached satisfying 70%. The contextual appropriateness of emotions was more difficult to determine in the conversations containing puns, which is reasonable, since humour is said to be one of the most creative and therefore difficult tasks in Artificial Intelligence (Boden, 1998). In most cases the results changed after the improvement were statistically significant (see Table 13) on a 5% level. The only version in which the change of the results was not significant was the baseline method with only CVS improvement (P value= 0.1599). Improving the system with blog mining, when compared to both – baseline version of the system and with CVS, were statistically significant (0.0274) and, what is the most important, the results of the version fully improved were the most significant from all (P=0.0119). Some of the successful examples of the CAEV Procedure are shown in Table 14. Aside from this, in most cases the results of affect analysis performed by ML-Ask were confirmed by humans. ML-Ask supported with the CVS procedure acquired 90.0% of accuracy in emotion valence recognition and 85% in specific emotion types recognition. This confirmed the system's high performance "in the field" although not ideal accuracy was achieved in laboratory settings (see section 4.3.4). This shows that language behaviour causing the system errors occurs rarely in the real conversation. As an interesting remark we should add that the survey participants sometimes determined the valence and the specific types of emotions in a non-standard way, e.g. for some contexts "fear" was determined as positive, or "joy" as negative, etc. As we assume, it is another proof that emotions are not only constituted of valence, but rather the valence of an emotion is made up by a certain context it is expressed in.

C) Emotion types	**Modalin**				**Pundalin**				**Modalin + Pundalin**			
Version of the system	Baseline system	With CVS	Blog mining	CVS + Blogs	Baseline system	With CVS	Blog mining	CVS + Blogs	Baseline system	With CVS	Blog mining	CVS + Blogs
0 people	1	1	1	1	2	1	1	0	3	2	2	1
1-3 people	3	3	2	2	5	5	5	5	8	8	7	7
4-6 people	**4**	**4**	**5**	**5**	**2**	**2**	**2**	**2**	**6**	**6**	**7**	**7**
7-10 people	**2**	**2**	**2**	**2**	**1**	**2**	**2**	**3**	**3**	**4**	**4**	**5**
Summary (10-4 people)	60%	60%	70%	70%	30%	40%	40%	50%	45%	50%	55%	60%
D) Valence	**Modalin**				**Pundalin**				**Modalin + Pundalin**			
Version of the system	Baseline system	With CVS	Blog mining	CVS + Blogs	Baseline system	With CVS	Blog mining	CVS + Blogs	Baseline system	With CVS	Blog mining	CVS + Blogs
0 people	2	2	1	1	2	1	1	0	4	3	2	1
1-3 people	2	2	3	3	4	4	4	4	6	6	7	7
4-6 people	**1**	**1**	**1**	**1**	**3**	**3**	**3**	**3**	**4**	**4**	**4**	**4**
7-10 people	**5**	**5**	**5**	**5**	**1**	**2**	**2**	**3**	**6**	**7**	**7**	**8**
Summary (10-4 people)	60%	60%	60%	60%	40%	50%	50%	60%	50%	55%	55%	60%

Table 11. The number of people that agreed with all four system versions when analysing one agent at a time for evaluated items C) specified emotion types and D) valence; summarized results for Modalin (upper), Pundalin (middle) and for both systems (lower).

Since one of the agents was using humorous responses we also checked whether the jokes influenced the human-computer interaction. Most of the emotions expressed in the conversations with Pundalin were positive (67%) whereas for Modalin most of the emotions were negative (75%), which confirms that users tend to be positively influenced by the use of jokes in conversational agents (Dybala et al., 2009a). With all improvements applied there were as much as 8 cases of a perfect agreement with all 10 human evaluators for one questionnaire set. In conversations with Modalin ML-Ask reached perfect agreement two times for both - valence and emotion-specific determination. As for Pundalin, the perfect agreement cases appeared twice in valence determination and, in both kinds of determining about appropriateness of emotions. Although the method presented here is still not ideal, the numerous improvements show, that it is easily improvable (Ptaszynski et al., 2009c, 2009d, 2009e). Considering the further enhancements that are already in plans, we are expecting a very high improvement in the near future.

	Modalin				Pundalin				Overall results				Summary (10-4ppl.)	
No. of people	10-7 ppl.	6-4 ppl.	3-1 ppl.	0 ppl.	10-7 ppl.	6-4 ppl.	3-1 ppl.	0 ppl.	10-7 ppl.	6-4 ppl.	3-1 ppl.	0 ppl.	Baseline system	Blog mining + CVS
A	**7**	2	0	1	**7**	2	1	0	**14**	4	1	1	75%	90%
B	4	**5**	0	1	**6**	2	2	0	**10**	7	2	1	75%	85%
C	2	**5**	2	1	3	2	**5**	0	5	**7**	**7**	1	45%	60%
D	**5**	1	3	1	3	3	**4**	0	**8**	4	7	1	50%	60%

Table 12. The number of people that agreed with the fully improved system when analysing one agent at a time for evaluated items A)-D); summarized results for both agents separately (left; centre-left) and together (centre-right); the results compared for the baseline and blog-mining with CVS versions of the system (right).

Versions of the system	**Baseline vs CVS**	**Baseline vs Blogs**	**CVS vs CVS+Blogs**	**Baseline vs CVS+Blogs**
Statistical significance (p value)	0.1599	0.0274	0.0274	**0.0119**

Table 13. Statistical significance of the results for different versions of the system

Part of conversation in Japanese (English translation)	**ML-Ask output**		**Web mining**	**CAEV**
USER: *Konpyuuta wa omoshiroi desu ne.* (Computers are so interesting!)	**positive** [joy]		**positive** [joy]	**appro-priate**
SYSTEM: *Sore wa oishii desu ka.* (Is it tasty?) [about instant noodles]	x		x	x
USER: *Oishii kedo, ore wa akita kana.* (Its tasty, but I've grown tired of it.)	**negative** [dislike]		**negative** [dislike]	**appro-priate**
Part of conversation in Japanese (English translation)	**ML-Ask baseline**	**with CVS**	**Web Mining**	**CAEV**
SYSTEM: *Sore wa omoshiroi tte* (Its so interesting!) [about conversation]	x	x	x	X
USER: *Sore hodo omoshiroku mo nakatta yo.* (It wasn't that interesting.)	positive [joy]	**negative** [dislike]	**negative** [fear], [sad]	**appro-priate**

Table 14. 3 examples of the results provided by the emotion appropriateness verification procedure (CAEV) with a separate display of CVS improvement of the procedure.

5. Discussions and work in progress

5.1 The socialized conversational agent algorithm

With already started attempts of combining the systems described above, we decided to combine them all and make the next step on the path to a naturally chatting agent. As the first step we decided to implement the following algorithm (see Figure 7): first, the emotive recogniser tries to categorize the emotion included inside the user's utterance. Here, experimentally we checked, after which emotions it was appropriate to say a joke. We tried different possibilities and the decision for this step is still unsettled. However, for now the tendency is that the use of jokes is more effective when the user's attitude is negative or neutral. When the system decides that it is possible to say a joke, the Punda Generator tries to find a pun fitting the keywords. If it is not possible, the Modalin creates a preposition and statistically chooses a modality using the Internet Relay Chat logs while the original program adds modality almost randomly. The chat-logs are automatically tagged by affect analyser for emotion types and for sentence endings usually describing grammatical functions and dialog acts[6]. This version of the algorithm, although still not evaluated, was presented by Rzepka et al. (2009a). The system is still in its test phase, during which different versions of the algorithm are proposed and evaluated. However, the first preliminary experiments, which results will be published in the near future, made us rethink the procedures deciding about the joke generation according to users' emotional states and its appropriateness to the situation.

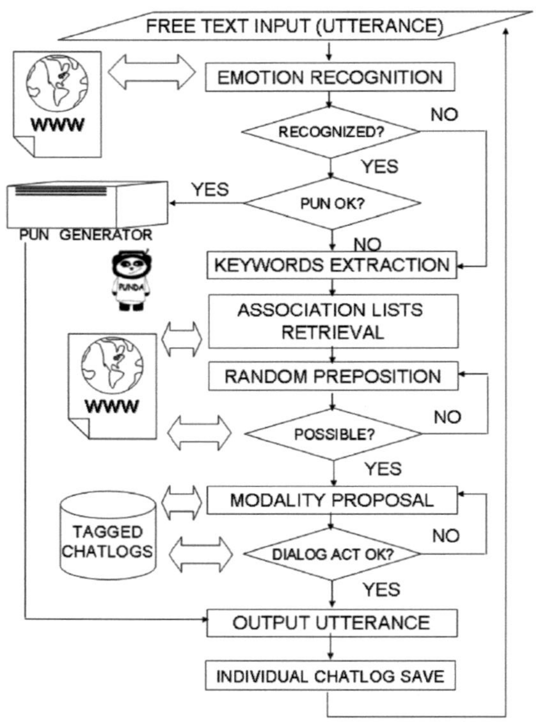

Fig. 7. Three systems combined into one multi-agent system.

5.2 Evolutionary algorithm for modelling individualized sense of humour

ML-Ask, the affect analysis system described in section 4, determines the user's emotional states. However, the applicability of this system exceeds the emotion recognition task. As it was proposed by Dybala et al. (2009b), the results of analysis can also be used in a sense of

---

[6] For determining the ending types we used a grammar book for Japanese language learners.

humour evolution algorithm. During the dialogue, the system can analyse each user's utterance, and check how he or she reacts to particular types of jokes. On this basis, the system can build a model of the user's sense of humour, determining the types of jokes the user likes or dislikes. For example, if the user reacts with positive emotions to jokes concerning politics, the system can assume that this type of joke matches his/her sense of humour. In this manner, the longer the system talks to the user, the more accurate "tags" of humour sense it can attach - and this, in effect, shall lead to more personalized, more individualized jokes that with a high probability would be appreciated by the user.

5.3 Emotional appropriateness as "conscience calculus" - implications towards computational conscience.

"*Public opinion is a second conscience.*" (William R. Alger)

As mentioned above, expressing and understanding emotions is one of the most important cognitive human behaviours present in everyday communication. In particular, Salovey & Mayer (1990) showed that emotions are a vital part of human intelligence, and Schwarz (2000) showed, that emotional states influence the decision making process in humans. When we define the process of decision making as distinguishing between good and bad, or appropriate and inappropriate, the emotions appear as an influential part of human conscience. The thesis that emotions strongly influence the development of human conscience was proved by Thompson and colleagues (2003) who showed, that children acquire the conscience by learning the emotional patterns from other people. The significance of the society was pointed out also by Rzepka et al. (2006), who define the Internet, being a collection of other people's ideas and experiences, as an approximation of general human common sense. Since conscience can be also defined as a part of common sense, this statement can be expanded further to that the Web can also be used to determine human conscience. The need for research in this matter, was pointed out inter alia by Rzepka et al. (2008), who raised the matter not of creating an artificial human being, as it is popularly ventured in Artificial Intelligence research, but rather an intelligent agent in the form of a toy or a companion, designed to support humans in everyday life. To perform that, the agent needs to be equipped, not only in procedures for recognizing phenomena concerning the user, in which emotions play a great role, but it also needs to be equipped with evaluative procedures distinguishing about whether the phenomena are appropriate or not for a situation the user is in. This is an up to date matter in fields such as Roboethics (Veruggio & Operto, 2006), Human Aspects in Ambient Intelligence (Treur, 2007), and in Artificial Intelligence in general. In our research we perform that by verifying emotions expressed by the user with a Web mining technique for gathering an emotional common sense, which could be also defined as an approximated vector of conscience. We understand, that the idea of conscience is far more sophisticated, but when defined narrowly as the ability to distinguish between what is appropriate and what is not, our method for verifying contextual appropriateness of emotions could be applied to obtain simplified conscience calculus for machines. We plan to develop further this idea and introduce it as a complementary algorithm for the novel research on discovering morality level in text utterances presented by Rzepka et al., (2009b).

6. Conclusions

In this chapter we presented a series of experiments aiming to implement into machines human factors and therefore making them more human-like and therefore user-friendly. In the first experiment on a conversational agent, Modalin, we showed, that adding modality to the propositions gathered from the Web is a good mean of improving the overall impression of the machine interlocutor. In the second experiment, we compared Modalin to its modified version Pundalin, which uses humorous output. In this experiment we showed that especially for non-task oriented conversational agents, which goal is mainly to entertain the user, the use of humour in the conversation greatly improves not only the impression about the agent's general performance, but also the user's attitudes towards the agent, making it easier to familiarize. In the last experiment we presented a novel method for estimating the contextual appropriateness of emotions. Two systems are used in this method, ML-Ask, a language based affect analysis system, and Web mining technique for extracting from the Internet a generalized emotive common sense. The first one used as the emotion detector and the second one as the emotion verificator provide a conversational agent computable means to determine whether the emotions expressed by the user are appropriate for the context they are expressed in. Enhancing a conversational agent with this method is the next step in implementing the full scope of Emotional Intelligence Framework in machines. We also presented some future implications of using this method, concluding that it could also be used to estimate human conscience. As the results of all experiments were satisfying enough, we developed a design of the full implementation of the two human factors, emotion estimation and sense of humour, into a conversational agent to be evaluated in the near future.

7. Acknowledgements

This research is partially supported by a Research Grant from the Nissan Science Foundation and The Global COE Program founded by Japan's Ministry of Education, Culture, Sports, Science and Technology.

8. References

Abbasi, A. & Chen, H. (2007). Affect Intensity Analysis of Dark Web Forums, *Intelligence and Security Informatics 2007*, pp. 282-288

Alm, C. O.; Roth, D. & Sproat, R. (2005). Emotions from text: machine learning for text based emotion prediction, In *Proceedings of HLT/EMNLP*, pp. 579-586

Andre, E.; Rehm M.; Minker W. & Buhler D. (2004). Endowing Spoken Language Dialogue Systems with Emotional Intelligence, *LNCS*, Vol. 3068, pp. 178-187

Araki K. & Kuroda, M. (2006). Generality of a Spoken Dialogue System Using SeGAIL for Different Languages, In *Proceedings of the IASTED International Conference Computer Intelligence*, pp. 70-75

Baba, J. (2003). Pragmatic function of Japanese mimetics in the spoken discourse of varying emotive intensity levels. *Journal of Pragmatics*, Vol.35, No. 12, pp. 1861-1889, Elsevier

Beijer, F. (2002). The syntax and pragmatics of exclamations and other expressive/emotional utterances, *Working Papers in Linguistics 2*, The Dept. of English in Lund

Bickmore, T. & Cassell, J. (2001). Relational Agents: A Model and Implementation of Building User Trust, In *Proceedings of Human Factors in Computing Systems (SIGCHI'01)*, pp. 396–403

Binsted, K. (1996). *Machine humour: An implemented model of puns*, University of Edinburgh

Boden, M. A. (1998). Creativity and artificial intelligence, *Artificial Intelligence*, Vol. 103, No. 1-2, pp. 347-356

Cann, A.; Holt, K. & Calhoun, L. G. (1999). The roles of humor and sense of humor in responses to stressors. *Humor*, Vol. 12, No. 2, pp. 177–193

Cook, K.S. & Rice, E. (2003). Social exchange theory, In Delamater, J. (ed.) *Handbook of social psychology*, Plenum, New York, pp. 53–76

Crystal, D. (1989). *The Cambridge Encyclopedia of Language*, Cambridge University Press

Dautenhahn, K.; Bond, A. H.; Cañamero, L. & Edmonds, B. (2002). *Socially intelligent agents: creating relationships with computers and robots*, Springer

Dybala, P.; Ptaszynski, M.; Higuchi, S.; Rzepka, R. & Araki, K. (2008a). Humor Prevails! - Implementing a Joke Generator into a Conversational System, *LNAI*, Vol. 5360, pp. 214-225, Berlin-Heidelberg, 2008.

Dybala, P.; Ptaszynski, M.; Rzepka, R. & Araki, K. (2008b). Extracting Dajare Candidates from the Web - Japanese Puns Generating System as a Part of Humor Processing Research, In *Proceedings of LIBM'08*, pp. 46-51

Dybala, P.; Ptaszynski, M.; Rzepka, R. & Araki, K. (2009a). Humoroids - Conversational Agents That Induce Positive Emotions with Humor, In *Proceedings of 8th International Conference on Autonomous Agents and Multiagent Systems (AAMAS 2009)*, May, 2009, Budapest, Hungary, pp. 1171-1172

Dybala, P.; Ptaszynski, M.; Rzepka, R. & Araki, K. (2009b). Humorized Computational Intelligence: Towards User-Adapted Systems with a Sense of Humor, *LNCS*, Vol. 5484, pp. 452–461, Springer-Verlag Berlin Heidelberg, 2009.

Dybala, P.; Ptaszynski, M.; Rzepka, R. & Araki, K. (2009c). Subjective, But Not Worthless - Non-linguistic Features of Chatterbot Evaluations, The IJCAI-09 Workshop on Knowledge and Reasoning in Practical Dialogue Systems, In *Working Notes of Twenty-first International Joint Conference on Artificial Intelligence (IJCAI-09)*, California, Pasadena

Gustafson, J. & Bell, L. (2000). Speech technology on trial: Experiences from the August system, In *Natural Language Engineering*, Vol. 1. No. 1, pp. 1-15

Hager, J. C.; Ekman, P.; Friesen, W. V. (2002). *Facial action coding system*, Salt Lake City, UT: A Human Face

Higuchi, S.; Rzepka, R. & Araki, K. (2008). A Casual Conversation System Using Modality and Word Associations Retrieved from the Web, *Proceedings of the 2008 Conference on Empirical Methods in Natural Language Processing (EMNLP'08)*, Honolulu, USA, October 2008, pp. 382-390

Jakobson, R. (1960). Closing Statement: Linguistics and Poetics, *Style in Language*, pp. 350-377, The MIT Press

Kamei, T.; Kouno, R. & Chino, E. [Eds.] (1996). *The Sanseido Encyclopedia of Linguistics*, VI, Sanseido

Kang, B.S.; Han, C.H.; Lee, S.T.; Youn, D.H. & Lee, C. (2000). Speaker dependent emotion recognition using speech signals. In *Proceedings of ICSLP*, pp. 383-386

Kennedy, A. & Inkpen, D. (2005). Sentiment classification of movie and product reviews using contextual valence shifters, *Workshop on the Analysis of Informal and Formal Information Exchange during Negotiations (FINEXIN-2005)*

Kopp, S.; Gesellensetter, L.; Kramer, N. C. & Wachsmuth, I. (2005). A Conversational Agent as Museum Guide–Design and Evaluation of a Real-World Application, *Intelligent Virtual Agents, LNAI*, 3661, pp. 329-343

Kudo, T. (2001). MeCab: Yet another part-of-speech and morphological analyzer, http://mecab.sourceforge.ne

Kumar, R.; Novak,J.; Raghavan, P.& Tomkins,A.(2003).On the Bursty Evolution of Blogspace, In *Proceedings of The Twelfth International World Wide Web Conference*, pp. 568-257

Lerner, J.S. & Keltner, D. (2000). Beyond valence: Toward a model of emotion-specific influences on judgment and choice, *Cognition & Emotion*

Liu, B; Du, L. & Yu, S. (2003). The method of building expectation model in task-oriented dialogue systems and its realization algorithms, In *Proceedings of Natural Language Processing and Knowledge Engineering*, pp. 174-179

Loehr, D. (1996). An integration of a pun generator with a natural language robot. In *Proceedings of International Workshop on Computational Humor*, pp. 161-172

Mayer, J. D. & Salovey, P. (1997). What is emotional intelligence?, In Salovey, P. & Sluyter, D. [Eds.] (1997). *Emotional Development and Emotional Intelligence*, Basic Books, pp. 3-31

Miyoshi, T. & Nakagami, Y. (2007). Sentiment classification of customer reviews on electric products, *IEEE International Conference on Systems, Man and Cybernetics*

Moran, C.C. (1996). Short-term mood change, perceived funniness, and the effect of humor stimuli, *Behavioural Medicine*, Vol. 22, No. 1, pp. 32–38

Morkes, J.; Kernal, H. K. & Nass, C. (1999). Effects of humor in task-oriented human-computer interaction and computer-mediated communication: A direct test of SRCT theory. *Human-Computer Interaction*, Vol. 14, No. 4, pp. 395-435

Mulkay, M. (1988). *On humor: Its nature and its place in modern society*, Basil Blackwell, NY

Nakamura, A. (1993). *Kanjo hyogen jiten* (Dictionary of Emotive Expressions) (in Japanese), Tokyodo Publishing, Tokyo

Nijholt, A. (2007). Conversational Agents and the Construction of Humorous Acts, In *Conversational Informatics: An Engineering Approach*, John Wiley & Sons, Chicester, England, pp. 21-47

Nitta, Y. & Masuoka, T. [Eds.] (1989). *Nihongo no modarithi* (Japanese Modality), Kuroshio, Tokyo, pp. 131–157

Ono, H. (2002). *An emphatic particle DA and exclamatory sentences in Japanese*, University of California, Irvine

Oshima-Takane, Y. & MacWhinney, B. [Eds.], Shirai, H.; Miyata, S. & Naka, N. [Rev.] (1995-1998). *CHILDES Manual for Japanese*, McGill University, The JCHAT Project

Picard, R. W. (1997). *Affective Computing*, The MIT Press, Cambridge

Picard, R. W.; Vyzas, E.; Healey, J. (2001). Toward Machine Emotional Intelligence: Analysis of Affective Physiological State, *IEEE Transactions on Pattern Analysis and Machine Intelligence*, Vol. 23, No. 10, pp. 1175-1191

Pietro, O.; Rose, M. & Frontera, G. (2005). Automatic Update of AIML Knowledge Base in E-Learning Environment, In *Proceedings of Computers and Advanced Technology in Education*, Oranjestad, Aruba, August, pp. 29-31

Polanyi, L. & Zaenen, A. (2004). Contextual Valence Shifters, *AAAI Spring Symposium on Exploring Attitude and Affect in Text: Theories and Applications*

Potts, C. & Kawahara, S. (2004). Japanese honorifics as emotive definite descriptions, In *Proceedings of Semantics and Linguistic Theory 14*, pp. 235-254

Ptaszynski, M. (2006). *Boisterous language. Analysis of structures and semiotic functions of emotive expressions in conversation on Japanese Internet bulletin board forum '2channel'* (in Japanese), M.A. Dissertation, UAM, Poznan, Poland

Ptaszynski, M.; Dybala, P.; Rzepka, R. & Araki, K. (2008). Effective Analysis of Emotive-ness in Utterances Based on Features of Lexical and Non-Lexical Layers of Speech, In *Proceedings of NLP-2008*, pp. 171-174

Ptaszynski, M.; Dybala, P.; Rzepka, R. & Araki, K. (2009a). Contextual Valence Shifters Supporting Affect Analysis of Utterances in Japanese, In *Proceedings of NLP-2009*, pp. 825-828

Ptaszynski, M.; Dybala, P.; Shi, W.; Rzepka, R. & Araki, K. (2009b). A System for Affect Analysis of Utterances in Japanese Supported with Web Mining, *Journal of Japan Society for Fuzzy Theory and Intelligent Informatics, Special Issue on Kansei Retrieval*, Vol. 21, No. 2 (April), pp. 30-49 (194-213)

Ptaszynski, M.; Dybala, P.; Shi, W.; Rzepka, R. & Araki, K. (2009c). Towards Context Aware Emotional Intelligence in Machines: Computing Contextual Appropriateness of Affective States, In *Proceedings of IJCAI 2009*, California, Pasadena

Ptaszynski, M.; Dybala, P.; Shi, W.; Rzepka, R. & Araki, K. (2009d). Shifting Valence Helps Verify Contextual Appropriateness of Emotions, The IJCAI-09 Workshop on Automated Reasoning about Context and Ontology Evolution (ARCOE-09), In *Working Notes of Twenty-first International Joint Conference on Artificial Intelligence (IJCAI-09)*, California, Pasadena

Ptaszynski, M.; Dybala, P.; Shi, W.; Rzepka, R. & Araki, K. (2009e). Conscience of Blogs: Verifying Contextual Appropriateness of Emotions Basing on Blog Contents, In *Proceedings of The Fourth IASTED International Conference on Computational Intelligence (CI-2009)*, August, 2009, Honolulu, Hawaii, USA

Ptaszynski, M.; Dybala, P.; Rzepka, R. & Araki, K. (2009f). Affecting Corpora: Experiments with Automatic Affect Annotation System - A Case Study of the 2channel Forum -, In *Proceedings of PACLING 2009*, Sapporo, Japan

Reeves, B. & Nass, C. (1996). *The media equation: How people treat computers, television, and new media like real people and places*, Cambridge University Press

Reitter, D.; Moore, J. D. & Keller, F. (2006). Priming of syntactic rules in task-oriented dialogue and spontaneous conversation, In *Proceedings of 28th Annual Conference of the Cognitive Science Society (CogSci)*, Vancouver, Canada

Russell, J. A. (1980). A circumplex model of affect, *Journal of Personality and Social Psychology*, Vol. 39, No. 6, pp. 1161-1178

Rzepka, R.; Ge, Y. and Araki, K. (2006). Common Sense from the Web? Naturalness of Everyday Knowledge Retrieved from WWW. *Journal of Advanced Computational Intelligence and Intelligent Informatics*, Vol. 10 No. 6, pp. 868-875

Rzepka, R. & Araki, K. (2007). Consciousness of Crowds - The Internet As a Knowledge Source of Human's Conscious Behavior and Machine Self-Understanding, *AI and Consciousness: Theoretical Foundations and Current Approaches*, Papers from AAAI Fall Symposium, Technical Report, November, 2007, Arlington, USA, pp. 127-128

Rzepka, R.; Higuchi, S.; Ptaszynski, M. & Araki, K. (2008). Straight Thinking Straight from the Net - On the Web-based Intelligent Talking Toy Development, In *The Proceedings of the IEEE International Conference on Systems, Man and Cybernetics (SMC'08)*, Singapore, October 2008, pp. 2172-2176

Rzepka, R.; Dybala, P.; Shi, W.; Higuchi, S.; Ptaszynski, M. & Araki, K. (2009a). Serious Processing for Frivolous Purpose - A Chatbot Using Web-mining Supported Affect Analysis and Pun Generation, In *Proceedings of IUI'09 - International Conference on Intelligent User Interfaces*, Sanibel Island, FL, USA. (ACM Press), pp 487-488

Rzepka, R.; Masui, F. and Araki, R. (2009b). The First Challenge to Discover Morality Level In Text Utterances by Using Web Resources, In *Proceedings of The 23rd Annual Conference of the Japanese Society for Artificial Intelligence*, Takamatsu, June 2009

Salovey, P. & Mayer, J. D. (1990). Emotional intelligence, *Imagination, Cognition, and Personality*, Vol. 9, pp. 185-211

Sasai, K. (2006). The Structure of Modern Japanese Exclamatory Sentences: On the Structure of the Nanto-Type Sentence, *Studies in the Japanese language*, Vol. 2, No. 1, pp. 16-31

Schlosberg, H. (1952). The description of facial expressions in terms of two dimensions, *Journal of Experimental Psychology*, Vol. 44, pp. 229-237

Schwarz, N. (2000). Emotion, cognition, and decision making, *Cognition & Emotion*, Vol. 14, No. 4, pp. 433-440

Shelley, M. W. (1818). *Frankenstein, or, The Modern Prometheus*, Oxford University Press, republished in 1998

Shi, W.; Rzepka, R. & Araki, K. (2008). Emotive Information Discovery from User Textual Input Using Causal Associations from the Internet, *FIT2008*, pp. 267-268

Sjöbergh, J. (2006). Vulgarities are fucking funny, or at least make things a little bit funnier, *Technical Report of KTH*, Stockholm

Sjöbergh, J. & Araki, K. (2008a). A Multi-Lingual Dictionary of Dirty Words, *LREC*

Sjöbergh, J. & Araki, K. (2008b). Robots Make Things Funnier, In *Proceedings of LIBM'08*, pp. 46-51

Solomon, R. C. (1993). *The Passions: Emotions and the Meaning of Life*, Hackett Publishing

Sprecher, S. & Regan, P.C. (2002). Liking some things (in some people) more than others: Partner preferences in romantic relationships and friendships. *Journal of Social and Personal Relationships*, Vol. 19, No. 4, pp. 463-481

Tinholt, H. W. & Nijholt, A. (2007). Computational Humour: Utilizing Cross-Reference Ambiguity for Conversational Jokes, *LNAI*, Springer-Verlag, Berlin, pp. 477-483

Teixeira, J.; Vinhas, V.; Oliveira, E. & Reis, L. (2008). A New Approach to Emotion Assessment Based on Biometric Data, HAI'08 Workshop, In *Proceedings of the WI-IAT'08*, pp. 459-500

Thompson, R. A.; Laible, D. J; Ontai, L. L. (2003). Early understandings of emotion, morality, and self: Developing a working model, *Advances in child development and behavior*, Vol. 31, pp. 137-171

Tokuhisa, R.; Inui, K. & Matsumoto, Y. (2008). Emotion Classification Using Massive Examples Extracted from the Web, In *Proceedings of Coling 2008*, pp. 881-888

Treur, J. (2007). On Human Aspects in Ambient Intelligence, In *Proceedings of The First International Workshop on Human Aspects in Ambient Intelligence*, pp. 5-10

Tsuchiya, N. (1999). Taiwa ni okeru kandoshi, iiyodomi no togoteki seishitsu ni tsuite no kosatsu (Statistical observations of interjections and faltering in discourse) (in Japanese), *SIG-SLUD-9903-11*

Veruggio, G.; Operto, F. (2006). Roboethics: a Bottom-up Interdisciplinary Discourse in the Field of Applied Ethics in Robotics, *International Review of Information Ethics, Ethics in Robotics*, Vol. 6 (12)

Vilathong, A. P.; Arnau, R. C.; Rosen, D. H. & Mascaro, N. (2003). Humor and hope: Can humor increase hope?, *Humor*, Vol. 16, No. 1, pp. 79–89

Weizenbaum, J. (1966). ELIZA-computer program for the study of natural language communication between man and machine, *Communications of the ACM*, Vol. 9, No. 1, pp. 36-45

Yamashita, Y. (1999). Kara, node, te-conjunctions which express cause or reason in Japanese (in Japanese). *Journal of the International Student Center, Hokkaido University*, Vol. 3

Yip, J. A.; Martin, R.A. (2006). Sense of humor, emotional intelligence, and social competence. *Journal of Research in Personality*, Vol. 40, Issue 6, December 2006, pp. 1202-1208

Yoshihira, K.; Takeda, T. & Sekine, S. (2004). KWIC system for Web Documents (in Japanese) In *Proceedings of NLP-2004*, pp. 137-139

10

Trust and Reputation Management in Web-based Social Network

Touhid Bhuiyan[1], Audun Jøsang[2] and Yue Xu[1]
[1]Queensland University of Technology
[2]University of Oslo
[1]Australia
[2]Norway

1. Introduction

In a web-based social network, people may communicate with their friends whom they know personally. They also communicate with other members of the network who are the friends of their friends and may be friends of their friend's network. They share their experiences and opinions within the social network about an item which may be a product or service. The user faces the problem of evaluating trust in a service or service provider before making a choice. Opinions, reputations and recommendations will influence users' choice and usage of online resources. Recommendations may be received through a chain of friends of friends, so the problem for the user is to be able to evaluate various types of trust recommendations and reputations. This opinion or recommendation has a great influence to choose to use or enjoy the item by the other user of the community. Users share information on the level of trust they explicitly assign to other users. This trust can be used to determine while taking decision based on any recommendation. In case of the absence of direct connection of the recommender user, propagated trust could be useful.
The first problem for the user is how much he/she can trust on a particular opinion to select an item. The opinion or recommendation may come from a friend's of a friend's friend. So, the problem for the member is, how much to trust on the opinion giver. The quality of an opinion in terms of reliability may increase if we can consider the overall public reputation of that particular item. For example, if a member is interested to choose a hotel to stay in Sydney, he may browse the experiences of his/her friends who have stayed in that hotel in past. While receiving a recommendation about a particular hotel from a trusted friend, it is also possible to include the general opinion of the users, or the reputation of the same hotel, in order to be better informed about the quality of service, and thereby to enable a better decision.
As the social network is growing very fast by doubling the number of people joining every year (Golbeck, 2006), the possibility of getting a huge number of opinion regarding a particular item is very common. It is another problem for a member to read all these opinions from other members of the social network. This requires a recommender system to summarize or filter the top opinions or recommendation in terms of quality of the opinion

and the trust between the user and the opinion giver. Social networking has been around for some time. Facebook and MySpace have become iconic, and other sites such as LinkedIn, hi5, Bebo, CyWorld and Orkut are becoming important as well. At the end of 2007, Microsoft paid $240 million for a 1.6% stake in Facebook, sparking a fierce debate about the theoretical valuation of Facebook. While few would go along with the $15 billion price tag, nobody would deny the huge potential of Facebook. The relevance of social networking for advertisers is very high considering they want to invest their money where the potential customers are located on social networking sites. The success of social networking should not come as a surprise. Social interaction is deeply rooted in human nature and is one of the most fundamental needs. Wireless and Internet technology act as enablers and facilitators for enhanced social interaction with a global reach. While social networking has been and still is dominated by teenagers and young adults, it is quickly spreading to all age groups and beyond the confines of consumer entertainment. Corporations are discovering the power of networking sites to enhance their brands, communities, and overall interaction with their customers by seamlessly linking corporate Web sites to public sites such as Facebook. And something even bigger is about to take place.

There has been dramatic growth in the number and size of Web-based social network. The number of sites almost doubled over the two year period from December 2004 to December 2006, growing from 125 to 223. Over the same period, the total number of members among all sites grew four-fold from 115 million to 490 million (Golbeck, 2006). The growth is continuing for last two years at the same rate, even more. The recent emergence of location-based mobile social networking services offered by providers such as Rummble, GyPSii, Whrrl and Loopt is revolutionizing social networking allowing users to share real-life experiences via geo-tagged user-generated multimedia content, see where their friends are and meet up with them. This new technology-enabled social geo-lifestyle will drive the uptake of Location-based services and provide opportunities for location-based advertising in the future.

In this research, we have tried to consider trust among the members while they select an item based on the opinion of friends. We calculate the public reputation of that item based on the general opinion given by previous users or customers. Then we combine this reputation with the trust among the opinion giver and the member who is going to select the item. As the recommendation comes from a trusted friend and it also includes the general public opinions, the quality of the opinion may improve. Currently, none of the web-based social network is considering combining the public reputation of an item with the trust among the members of the network to suggest or recommend an item. In general, people like to express their opinion and are interested about others opinion regarding the items they have concern. One popular way of obtaining customer feedback is collecting ratings about the product or services by the end users. In addition to the customer ratings about the product or services, there is also a good number of online customer feedback information available over the Internet as free text customer reviews, comments, newsgroups post, discussion forums or blogs. This information also can be used to generate the public reputation of the service providers'. To do this, data mining techniques, specially recently emerged opinion mining (Hu & Liu, 2004a), (Popescu & Etzioni, 2005), (Ku, Liang, & Chen, 2006) could be a useful tool. Mining and organizing opinions from the feedback of the customer or user of an item could be useful for the person or organization that is going to use the item in future.

2. Fundamentals of Trust and Reputation

2.1 Defining Trust

Trust has become important topic of research in many fields including sociology, psychology, philosophy, economics, business, law and IT. It is not a new topic to discuss. In fact, it has been the topic of hundreds books and scholarly articles over a long period of time. Trust is a complex word with multiple dimensions. A vast literature on trust has grown in several area of research but it is relatively confusing and sometimes contradictory, because the term is being used with a variety of meaning (McKnight & Chervany, 2002). Also a lack of coherence exists among researchers in the definition of trust. Though dozens of proposed definitions are available in the literature, a complete formal unambiguous definition of trust is rare. In many occasions, trust is used as a word or concept with no real definition. Hussain et al. present an overview of the definitions of the terms of trust and reputation from the existing literature (Hussain & Chang, 2007). They have shown that none of these definitions is fully capable to satisfy all of the context dependence, time dependence and the dynamic nature of trust.The most cited definition of trust is given by Dasgupta where he define trust as "the expectation of one person about the actions of others that affects the first person's choice, when an action must be taken before the actions of others are known" (Dasgupta, 1990). This definition captures both the purpose of trust and its nature in a form that can be reasoned about. Deutsch (Deutsch, 2004) states that "trusting behaviour occurs when a person encounters a situation where she perceives an ambiguous path. The result of following the path can be good or bad and the occurrence of the good or bad result is contingent on the action of another person" (Hussain & Chang, 2007). Another definition for trust by Gambetta is also often quoted in the literature: "trust is a particular level of the subjective probability with which an agent assesses that another agent or group of agents will perform a particular action, both before he can monitor such action and in a context in which it affects his own action" (Gambetta, 2000). But trust can be more complex than these definitions.

Trust is the root of almost any personal or economic interaction. Keser states "trust as the expectation of other persons goodwill and benign intent, implying that in certain situations those persons will place the interests of others before their own" (Keser, 2003). Golbeck (Golbeck , 2006) defines trust as "trust in a person is a commitment to an action based on belief that the future actions of that person will lead to a good outcome". This definition has a great limitation that it considers trust as always leading to positive outcome. But in reality, it may not be always true. Trust is such a concept that crosses disciplines and also domains. The focus of definition differs on the basis of the goal and the scope of the projects. Two generalized definitions of trust defined by Jøsang (Jøsang et al. 2007) which they called reliability trust (the term "evaluation trust" is more widely used by the other researchers, therefore we use this term) and decision trust respectively will be used for this work. Evaluation trust can be interpreted as the reliability of something or somebody and the decision trust captures broader concept of trust.

Evaluation Trust: Trust is the subjective probability by which an individual, A, expects that another individual, B, performs a given action on which its welfare depends.

Decision Trust: Trust is the extent to which one party is willing to depend on something or somebody in a given situation with a feeling of relative security, even though negative consequences are possible.

2.2 Defining Reputation

Reputation systems represent a significant trend in decision support for Internet mediated service provision (Resnick et al, 2000). The Feedback Forum on eBay is the most prominent example of online reputation systems (Keser, 2003). The basic idea is to let parties rate each other, for example after the completion of a transaction, and use the aggregated ratings about a given party to derive a reputation score, which can assist other parties in deciding whether or not to transact with that party in the future. A natural effect is that it also provides an incentive for good behavior, and therefore tends to have a positive impact on market quality.

Reputation is generally defines as the opinion or view of one about the character of somebody or an entity. Here, an entity could be an agent, a product or a service. Reputation is frequently used as the basis of a judgment to trust an individual or organization particularly in the absence of previous direct experience or contact with them. Mui et al. (Lik Mui, 2002) define reputation "as a perception that an agent creates through past actions about its intentions and norms". A similar definition given by Abdul-Rahman et al. (Abdul-Rahman & Hailes, 2000) who defines "a reputation is an expectation about an agents behaviour based on information about or observations of its past behavior".

We will use the Concise Oxford dictionary definition of reputation for the purpose of this work. This definition supports the view of social network researchers (Jøsang et al., 2007).

Reputation: Reputation is what is generally said or believed about a persons or things character or standing.

2.3 Characteristics of Trust and Reputation

The characteristics of trust and reputation may differ from business to business or their applications. But there are some common delimiters that indicate the existence of general principles governing trust in online environments. Dimitrakos (Dimitrakos, 2003) surveyed and analyzed the general properties of trust in e-services and listed the general properties of trust (and distrust) as follows:

- Trust is relativised to some business transaction. A may trust B to drive her car but not to baby-sit.
- Trust is a measurable belief. A may trust B more than A trusts C for the same business.
- Trust is directed. A may trust B to be a profitable customer but B may distrust A to be a retailer worth buying from.
- Trust exists in time. The fact that A trusted B in the past does not in itself guarantee that A will trust B in the future. Bs performance and other relevant information may lead A to re-evaluate her trust in B.
- Trust evolves in time, even within the same transaction. During a business transaction, the more A realizes she can depend on B for a service X the more A trusts B. On the other hand, A's trust in B may decrease if B proves to be less dependable than A anticipated.
- Trust between collectives does not necessarily distribute to trust between their members. On the assumption that A trusts a group of contractors to deliver (as a group) in a collaborative project, one cannot conclude that A trusts each member of the team to deliver independently.

- Trust is reflexive, yet trust in oneself is measurable. A may trust her lawyer to win a case in court more than she trusts herself to do it. Self-assessment underlies the ability of an agent to delegate or offer a task to another agent in order to improve efficiency or reduce risk.
- Trust is a subjective belief. A may trust B more than C trusts B with the same trust scope.

Wang et al. (Wang & Vassileva, 2007) identifies that trust and reputation share some common characteristics such as context specific, multi-faceted and dynamic. They argue that trust and reputation both depend on some context. Even in the same context there is a need to develop differentiated trust in different aspects of a service. As the dynamic character, they refer that trust and reputation can increase or decrease with further experiences of interactions or observations. Both of them also decay with time. Jennifer (Golbeck, 2006) proposes there are three main properties of trust in the web-based social environment. They are (i) transitivity, (ii) asymmetry and (iii) personalization. She explains transitivity as the propagation capability, asymmetry as the direction of trust which may be different depends on the direction and personalization as the personal opinion on a particular object by different agents.

2.4 Difference between Trust and Reputation

Reputation systems are closely related to the concept of trust. Mui et al. (Lik Mui, 2002) differentiate the concepts of trust and reputation by defining reputation is the perception that an agent creates through past actions about its intentions and norms and trust as a subjective expectation an agent has about another's future behavior based on the history of their encounters. The difference between trust and reputation can be illustrated by the following perfectly normal and plausible statements:

1. I trust you because of your good reputation.
2. I trust you despite your bad reputation.

Statement (1) reflects that the relying party is aware of the trustee's reputation, and bases his or her trust on that. Statement (2) reflects that the relying party has some private knowledge about the trustee, e.g. through direct experience or intimate relationship, and that these factors overrule any reputation that the trustee might have. This observation reflects that trust ultimately is a personal and subjective phenomenon that is based on various factors or evidence, and that some of those carry more weight than others. Personal experience typically carries more weight than second hand recommendations or reputation, but in the absence of personal experience, trust often has to be based on reputation. Reputation can be considered as a collective measure of trustworthiness (in the sense of reliability) based on ratings from members in a community. Any individual's subjective trust in a given party can be derived from a combination of reputation and personal experience.

That an entity is trusted for a specific task does not necessarily mean that it can be trusted for everything. The scope defines the specific purpose and semantics of a given assessment of trust or reputation. A particular scope can be narrow or general. Although a particular reputation has a given scope, it can often be used as an estimate of the reputation of other scopes (Jøsang et al., 2007). In general, we may say that trust is the subjective view of an agent to another but reputation is overall impression of members of the community on an agent based on its previous activities.

3. A Survey of Online Trust and Reputation Systems Research

The issue of trust has been gaining an increasing amount of attention in a number of research communities including online service provision. There are many different views of how to measure and use trust. Some researchers use trust and reputation as same meaning while others are not. Though the meaning of trust is different to different people, a brief review on these models is a good starting point to research in the area of Trust and Reputation. As trust is a social phenomenon, the model of trust for the artificial world like Internet should be based on how trust works between people in society (Abdul-Rahman & Hailes, 2000). The rich literature growing around trust and reputation systems for Internet transactions, as well as the implementations of reputation systems in successful commercial application such as eBay and Amazon, give a strong indication that this is an important technology (Jøsang et al., 2007). Feedback on an online marketplace like eBay is an expression of reputation which provides a simple accumulative model for reputation (Sundaresan, 2007). In Amazons reputations scheme, reviews consist of a rating in the range between 1 and 5 stars. The average of all ratings gives a books reputation (Zou, Gu, Li, Xie, & Mei, 2007). Commercial implementations seem to have settled around relatively simple principles, whereas a multitude of different systems with advanced features are being proposed by the academic community. A general observation is that the proposals from the academic community so far lack coherence and are rarely evaluated in a commercial/industrial application environment. The systems being proposed are usually designed from scratch, and only in very few cases are authors building on proposals by other authors. The period we are in can therefore be seen as a period of pioneers. Consolidation around a set of sound and well recognized principles is needed in order to get the most benefit out of reputation systems.

Stephen Marsh (Marsh, 1994) is one of the pioneers to introduce a computational model for trust in the computing literature. For his PhD thesis, Marsh investigates the notions of trust in various contexts and develops a formal description of its use with distributed, intelligent agents. His model is based on social and psychological factors. He defines trust in three categories; namely the basic trust, general trust and situational trust. These trust values are used to help an agent to decide if it is worth it or not to cooperate with another agent. To calculate the risk and the perceived competence, different types of trust (basic, general and situational) are used. But the model is complex, mostly theoretical and difficult to implement. He did not considered reputation in his work. Zacharia et al. (Zacharia & Maes, 1999) have suggested that reputation in an on-line community can be related to the ratings that an agent receives from others. Their *Sporas* and *Histos* systems use the notions of global versus personalized reputation. Reputation in Sporas is similar to that used in eBay or Amazon, based on average of all ratings given to an agent. Sporas incorporates a measure of the reliability of the users' reputation based on the standard deviation of reputation values. Histos retrieves reputation based on who makes a query and the local environment surrounding the inquirer. It was designed as a response to the lack of personalization that Sporas reputation values have. The model can deal with direct information and witness information. Contrary to Sporas, the reputation value is a subjective property assigned particularly by each individual. Abdul-Rahman et al. (Abdul-Rahman & Hailes, 2000) proposed a model for supporting trust in virtual communities, based on direct experiences and reputation. They have proposed that the trust concept can be divided into direct and recommender trust. Recommended trust can be derived from word-of-mouth recommendations, which they consider as reputation. However, there are certain aspects of their model that are ad-hoc which limits the applicability of the model in broader scope. Schillo et al (Schillo, Funk, & Rovatsos, 2000) proposed a trust model for scenarios where interaction result is Boolean, either good or bad, between two agents trust relationship. Though, they did not consider the degrees of satisfaction. Resnick (Resnick et al., 2000) described reputation management as a system that collects, distributes and aggregates feedback about past behaviour.

Classification of Trust and Reputation Systems Research

Model Type	**Implementation Environment**	
	Centralized (Less complex system)	**Decentralized** (e.g. a peer-to-peer system))
Trust Management	Representative research examples: • Marsh 1994 • Schillo et al. 2000 • Esfandiari & Chandrasekharan 2001 • McKnight & Chervany, 2002 • Dimitrakos 2003 • Levien 2004 • Guha et al. 2004 • O'Donovan & Smyth 2005 • Ziegler 2005 • Pitsilis & Marshall, 2008	Representative research examples: • Golbeck 2006 • Ziegler & Golbeck 2007 • Coetzee & Eloff 2007 • Peng et al, 2008 • Tian et al, 2008
Reputation Management	Representative research examples: • Zacharia & Maes, 1999 • Resnick et al. 2000 • Malaga 2001 • Pujol et al. 2002 • Sen & Sajja 2002 • Carbo et al. 2002 • Carter et al. 2002 • Grishchenko 2004 • Folkerts 2005 • Whitby et al 2005	Representative research examples: • Aberer et al. 2001 • Damiani et al. 2002 • Yu & Singh 2002 • Kamvar et al. 2003 • Xiong 2005 • Jin et al, 2008
Trust & Reputation Management (Trust based reputation/ Reputation based trust))	Representative research examples: • Abdul-Rahman & Halies 2000 • Yu & Singh 2001 • Sabater & Sierra, 2005 • Mui et al. 2002 • Lin et al. 2005 • Jøsang et al. 2006, 2007 • Hussain & Chang 2007 • Silaghi et al. 2007 • Zou et al. 2007 • Xue & Fan, 2008 • Bi et al, 2008 • Bachrach, 2009	Representative research examples: • Venkatraman et al 2000 • Selcuk et al. 2004 • Nada et al. 2007 • Fuller et al 2007 • Sundaresan 2007 • Wang 2008, 2009 • Bharadwaj, 2009

Table 1. Research on trust and reputation systems

Venkatraman et al. (Venkatraman, Yu, & Singh, 2000) express their views of e-commerce community as a social network which supports reputations both for providing good services and for providing good referrals. Their model preserves the autonomy and privacy of the user by allowing the choice of ignoring such requests, if a user wishes not to give referrals.

Two one-on-one trust acquisition mechanisms are proposed by (Esfandiari & Chandrasekharan, 2001) in their trust model. The first is based on observation. They proposed the use of Bayesian networks and to perform the trust acquisition by Bayesian learning. The second trust acquisition mechanism is based on interaction. A simple way to calculate the interaction-based trust during the exploratory stage is using the formula

$$T_{inter}(A,B) = \frac{number\_of\_correct\_replies}{total\_number\_of\_replies} \quad (1)$$

(Sen & Sajja, 2002) present a method for ensuring robustness of a reputation model that is used to select processor resources. The model uses service selection as its measure of success. In this model, an agent selects the service provider that has the highest reputation from a pool. Aberer et al. (Aberer, 2001) describe a reputation system for Peer-to-peer (P2P) systems which is intended to meet needs that are left unfulfilled by other reputation systems: scalability to large numbers of nodes, and reduced amounts of required data storage and network communications. In order to reduce the amount of data stored and communicated, the model works on a binary rating system - an agent is either considered trustworthy or not. In the model proposed by Yu and Singh (Yu & Singh, 2002), the information stored by an agent about direct interactions is a set of values that reflect the quality of these interactions. Only the most recent experiences with each concrete partner are considered for the calculations. This model failed to combine direct information with witness information. When direct information is available, it is considered the only source to determine the trust of the target agent. Only when the direct information is not available, the model appeals to witness information.

Sabater et al. (Sabater & Sierra, 2005) have proposed a modular trust and reputation system oriented to complex small/mid-size e-commerce environments which they called ReGreT, where social relations among individuals play an important role. Mui et al. (Lik Mui, 2002) proposed a computational model based on sociological and biological understanding. The model can be used to calculate agent's trust and reputation scores. They also identified some weaknesses of the trust and reputation study which is the lack of differentiation of trust and reputation and the mechanism for inference between them is not explicit. Trust and reputation are taken to be the same across multiple contexts or are treated as uniform across time and the existing computational models for trust and reputation are often not grounded on understood social characteristics of these quantities. They did not examine effects of deception in this model. Pujol (Pujol et al, 2002) proposed a method for calculating the reputation of a given member in a society or in a social network by making use of PageRank™ algorithm. Dimitrakos (Dimitrakos, 2003) presented and analysed a service-oriented trust management framework based on the integration of role-based modelling and risk assessment in order to support trust management solutions. They provided evidence of emerging methods, formalisms and conceptual frameworks which, if appropriately integrated, can bridge the gap between systems modelling, trust and risk management in e-commerce.

Kamvar et al. (Kamvar, Schlosser, & Garcia-Molina, 2003) proposes a reputation system which makes use of matrices of reputation information which are maintained and stored by agents in their system. The authors explicitly target their system at providing reputation for peer-to-peer systems where malicious peers can generate illegitimate files for sharing and the general population of peers have no way of distinguishing illegitimate files from the legitimate ones. O'Donovan et al (O'Donovan & Smyth, 2005) distinguished between two types of profiles in the context of a given recommendation session or rating prediction. The consumer profile and the producer profile. They described "trust" as the reliability of a partner profile to deliver accurate recommendations in the past. They described two models of trust which they called profile-level trust and item-level trust. Selcuk et al. (Selcuk, Uzun, & Pariente, 2004) proposed a reputation-based trust management protocol for P2P networks where users rate the reliability of the parties they deal with and share this information with their peers.

Guha et al (Guha, Kumar, Raghavan, & Tomkins, 2004) proposed a method based on PageRank™ algorithm for propagating both trust and distrust. They identified four different methods for propagating the net beliefs values, namely direct propagation, co-citation, transpose and coupling. The Advogato maximum flow trust metric has been proposed by Levien (Levien, 2004) in order to discover which users are trusted by members of an online community and which are not. Trust is computed through one centralized community server and considered relative to a seed of users enjoying supreme trust. Local group trust metrics compute sets of agents trusted by those being part of the trust seed. Advogato, only assigns Boolean values indicating presence or absence of trust. It is a global trust algorithm which uses the same trusted nodes to make trust calculation for all users. It makes the algorithm suitable for P2P networks. As the trust inference algorithm has released under a free software license, it became the basis of many research paper. Appleseed trust metric was proposed by Ziegler (Zieglera, 2005). AppelSeed is closely based on PageRank™ algorithm. It allows rankings of agents with respect to trust accorded. One of the major weakness is that a person who has made many high trust ratings will have lower value than if only one or two people had been rated. Another weakness of this model is; it requires exponentially higher computation with increasing number of user which makes it non-scalable.

Shmatikov et al. (Shmatikov & Talcott, 2005) proposed a reputation-based trust management model which allows mutually distrusting agents to develop a basis for interaction in the absence of central authority. The model is proposed in the context of peer-to-peer applications, online games or military situations. Folkerts (Folkerts, 2005) proposed a simulation framework to perform comparison analysis between reputation models. They have implemented two reputation models and compared with regard to accuracy, performance and resistance to deception. Teacy (Teacy, 2005) proposed a probabilistic framework for assessing trust based on direct observations of a trustees behavior and indirect observations made by a third party. They claimed that their proposed mechanism can cope with the possibility of unreliable third party information in some context. Xiong (Xiong, 2005) also proposed a decentralized reputation based trust supporting framework called PeerTrust for P2P environment. The have focused on models and techniques for resilient reputation management against feed back aggregation, feedback oscillation and loss of feedback privacy. Jøsang (Jøsang et al, 2006) proposed a model for trust derivation with Subjective Logic. They argued that Subjective logic represents a practical belief calculus which can be used for calculative analysis trust networks. TNASL requires trust relationships to be expressed as beliefs, and trust networks to be expressed as DSPGs in the form of canonical expressions. They have described how trust can be derived with the belief calculus of subjective logic. Xue and Fan (Xue & Fan, 2008) proposed a new trust model for the Semantic Web which allows agents to decide which among different sources of information to trust and thus act rationally on the semantic web. Tian et al (Tian, Zou, Wang, & Cheng, 2008) proposed trust model for P2P networks in which the trust value of a given peer was computed using its local trust information and recommendation from other nodes.

4. Trust Network Analysis

Trust networks consist of transitive trust relationships between people, organisations and software agents connected through a medium for communication and interaction. By formalising trust relationships, e.g. as reputation scores or as subjective trust measures, trust between parties within a domain can be derived by analysing the trust paths linking the parties together. A method for trust network analysis using subjective logic (TNA-SL) has been described by Jøsang et al (2006, 2007). TNA-SL takes directed trust edges between pairs as input, and can be used to derive a level of trust between arbitrary parties that are interconnected through the network. Even in case of no explicit trust paths between two parties exist; subjective logic allows a level of trust to be derived through the default vacuous opinions. TNA-SL therefore has a general applicability and is suitable for many types of trust networks. A potential limitation with the previously described TNA-SL is that complex trust networks must be simplified to *series-parallel* networks in order for TNA-SL to produce consistent results. The simplification consisted of gradually removing the least certain trust paths until the whole network can be represented in a series-parallel form. As this process removes information it is intuitively sub-optimal.

In the following sections, we describe how TNA-SL can preserve consistency without removing information. Inconsistency can result from dependence between separate trust paths, which when combined will take the same information into account several times. Including the same trust edges multiple times will by definition produce an inconsistent result. Optimal TNA-SL avoids this problem by allowing the trust measure of a given trust edge to be split into several independent parts, so that each part is taken into account by separate trust paths. The result of this approach is compared with the analysis based on networks simplification.

4.1 Serial Trust Paths

Trust transitivity means, for example, that if A trusts B who trusts D, then A will also trust D. This assumes that A is actually aware that B trusts D. This could be achieved through a *recommendation* from B to A as illustrated in Fig.1, where the indexes on each arrow indicate the sequence in which the trust relationships/recommendation is formed.

It can be shown that trust is not always transitive in real life (Christianson, 2003). For example the fact that A trusts B to look after her child, and B trusts D to fix his car, does not imply that A trusts D for looking after her child, or for fixing her car. However, under certain semantic constraints (Jøsang and Pope, 2005), trust can be transitive, and a trust system can be used to derive trust. In the last example, trust transitivity collapses because the scopes of A's and B's trust are different. Trust scope is defined as the specific type(s) of trust assumed in a given trust relationship.

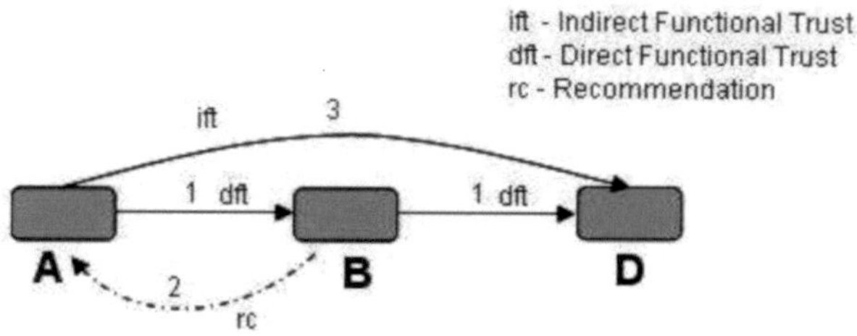

Fig. 1. Trust transitivity

It is important to separate between trust in the ability to recommend a good car mechanic which represents *referral trust*, and trust in actually being a good car mechanic which represents *functional trust*. The scope of the trust is nevertheless the same, namely to be a good car mechanic. Assuming that, on several occasions, B has proved to A that he is knowledgeable in matters relating to car maintenance, A's referral trust in B for the purpose of recommending a good car mechanic can be considered to be *direct*. Assuming that D on several occasions has proved to B that he is a good mechanic, B's functional trust in D can also be considered to be direct. Thanks to B's advice, A also trusts D to actually be a good mechanic. However, this functional trust must be considered to be *indirect*, because A has not directly observed or experienced D's skills in car mechanics. Let us slightly extend the example, wherein B does not actually know any car mechanics himself, but he knows C, whom he believes knows a good car mechanic. As it happens, C is happy to recommend the car mechanic named D. As a result of transitivity, A is able to derive trust in D, as illustrated in Fig.2, where the indexes indicate the order in which the trust relationships and recommendations are formed. The "drt" denotes direct referral trust, "dft" denotes direct functional trust, and "ift" denotes indirect functional trust.

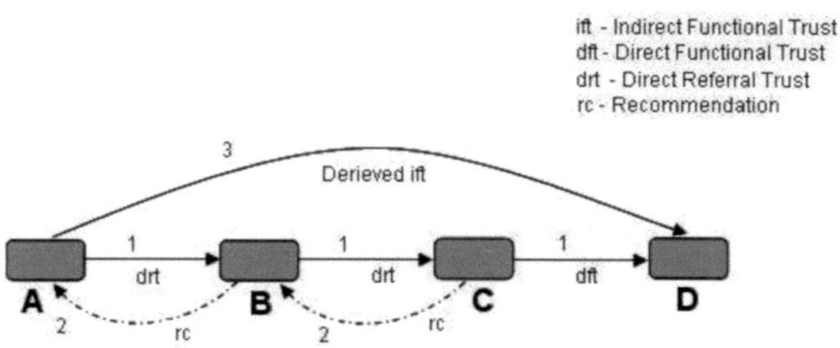

Fig. 2. Serial trust path

The "referral" variant of a trust scope can be considered to be recursive, so that any transitive trust chain, with arbitrary length, can be expressed using only one trust scope with two variants. This principle can be expressed as the derivation of functional trust through referral trust, requires that the last trust edge represents functional trust and all previous trust edges represent referral trust. It could be argued that negative trust in a transitive chain can have the paradoxical effect of strengthening the derived trust. Take for example the case of Fig.1, but in this case A distrusts B, and B distrusts D. In this situation, A might actually derive positive trust in D, since she does not believe B when he says: "D is bad mechanic, do not use him". So the fact that B recommends distrusts in D might count as a pro-D argument from A's perspective. The question boils down to "is the enemy of my enemy my friend?". However this question relates to how multiple types of untrustworthiness, such as dishonesty and unreliability, should be interpreted in a trust network.

4.2 Parallel Trust Paths

It is common to collect advice from several sources in order to be better informed when making decisions. This can be modelled as *parallel trust combination* illustrated in Fig.3, where again the indexes indicate the order in which the trust relationships and recommendations are formed.

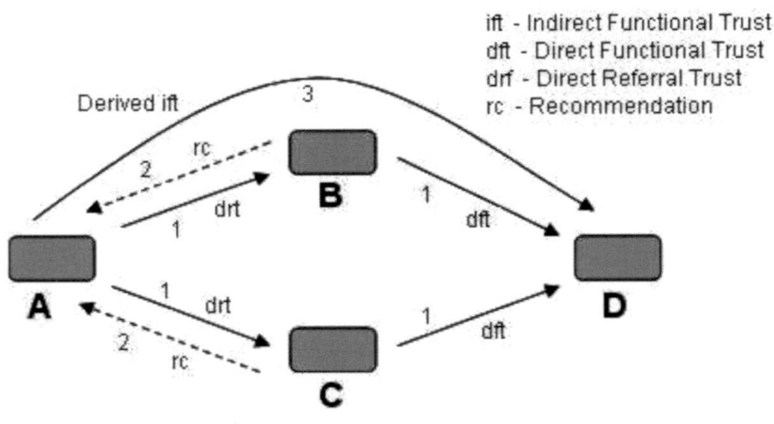

Fig. 3. Parallel trust paths

Let us assume again that A needs to get her car serviced, and that she asks B to recommend a good car mechanic. When B recommends D, A would like to get a second opinion, so she asks C whether she has heard about D. Intuitively, if both B and C recommend D as a good car mechanics, A's trust in D will be stronger than if she had only asked B. Parallel combination of positive trust thus has the effect of strengthening the derived trust. In the case where A receives conflicting recommended trust, e.g. trust and distrust at the same time, she needs some method for combining these conflicting recommendations in order to derive her trust in D. Our method, which is described in Sec.7, is based on subjective logic which easily can handle such cases. Subjective logic is suitable for analysing trust networks because trust relationships can be expressed as subjective opinions with degrees of uncertainty.

4.3 Operators for Deriving Trust

Subjective logic is a belief calculus specifically developed for modeling trust relationships. In subjective logic, beliefs are represented on binary state spaces, where each of the two possible states can consist of sub-states. Belief functions on binary state spaces are called *subjective opinions* and are formally expressed in the form of an ordered tuple $\omega_x^A = (b, d, u, a)$, where b, d, and u represent belief, disbelief and uncertainty respectively where $b, d, u \in [0, 1]$ and $b+d+u = 1$. The base rate parameter $a \in [0, 1]$ represents the base rate probability in the absence of evidence, and is used for computing an opinion's probability expectation value $E(\omega_x^A) = b + au$, meaning that a determines how uncertainty shall contribute to $E(\omega_x^A)$. A subjective opinion is interpreted as an agent A's belief in the truth of statement x. Ownership of an opinion is represented as a superscript so that for example A's opinion about x is denoted as ω_x^A.

The fact that subjective logic is compatible with binary logic and probability calculus means that whenever corresponding operators exist in probability calculus, the probability expectation value $E(\omega)$ of an opinion ω that has been derived with subjective logic, is always equal to the probability value that would have been derived had simple probability calculus been applied. Similarly, whenever corresponding binary logic operators exist, an absolute opinion (i.e. equivalent to binary logic TRUE or FALSE) derived with subjective logic, is always equal to the truth value that can be derived with binary logic. Subjective logic has a sound mathematical basis and is compatible with binary logic and traditional Bayesian analysis. Subjective logic defines a rich set of operators for combining subjective opinions in various ways (Jøsang, 2009). Some operators represent generalizations of binary logic and probability calculus, whereas others are unique to belief calculus because they depend on belief ownership. With belief ownership it is possible to explicitly express that different agents have different opinions about the same issue.

The advantage of subjective logic over probability calculus and binary logic is its ability to explicitly express and take advantage of ignorance and belief ownership. Subjective logic can be applied to all situations where probability calculus can be applied, and to many situations where probability calculus fails precisely because it can not capture degrees of ignorance. Subjective opinions can be interpreted as probability density functions, making subjective logic a simple and efficient calculus for probability density functions. Subjective logic defines a number of operators. Some operators represent generalizations of binary logic and probability calculus operators, whereas others are unique to belief theory because they depend on belief ownership. Here we will only focus on the *transitivity* and the *fusion* operators. The transitivity operator can be used to derive trust from a trust path consisting of a chain of trust edges, and the fusion operator can be used to combine trust from parallel trust paths. These operators are described below.

Transitivity is used to compute trust along a chain of trust edges. Assume two agents A and B where A has referral trust in B, denoted by ω_B^A, for the purpose of judging the functional or referral trustworthiness of C. In addition B has functional or referral trust in C, denoted by ω_C^B. Agent A can then derive her trust in C by discounting B's trust in C with A's trust in B, denoted by $\omega_C^{A:B}$. By using the symbol '$\otimes$' to designate this operator, we define

$$\omega_C^{A:B} = \omega_B^A \otimes \omega_C^B \quad \begin{cases} b_C^{A:B} = b_B^A b_C^B \\ d_C^{A:B} = b_B^A d_C^B \\ u_C^{A:B} = d_B^A + u_B^A + b_B^A u_C^B \\ a_C^{A:B} = a_C^B . \end{cases} \tag{2}$$

The effect of discounting in a transitive chain is that uncertainty increases, not disbelief. Cumulative *Fusion* is equivalent to Bayesian updating in statistics. The cumulative fusion of two possibly conflicting opinions is an opinion that reflects both opinions in a fair and equal way. Let ω_C^A and ω_C^B be *A*'s and *B*'s trust in *C* respectively. The opinion $\omega_C^{A\Diamond B}$ is then called the fused trust between ω_C^A and ω_C^B, denoting an imaginary agent [*A*,*B*]'s trust in *C*, as if she represented both *A* and *B*. By using the symbol '$\oplus$' to designate this operator, we define $\omega_C^{A\Diamond B} = \omega_B^A \oplus \omega_C^B$

$$\omega_C^{A\Diamond B} = \omega_B^A \oplus \omega_C^B \quad \begin{cases} b_C^{A\Diamond B} = (b_C^A u_C^B + b_C^B u_C^A)/(u_C^A + u_C^B - u_C^A u_C^B) \\ d_C^{A\Diamond B} = (d_C^A u_C^B + d_C^B u_C^A)/(u_C^A + u_C^B - u_C^A u_C^B) \\ u_C^{A\Diamond B} = (u_C^A u_C^B)/(u_C^A + u_C^B - u_C^A u_C^B) \\ a_C^{A\Diamond B} = a_C^A . \end{cases} \tag{3}$$

where it is assumed that $a_C^A = a_C^B$. Limits can be computed (Jøsang, 2007) for $u_C^A = u_C^B = 0$. The effect of the cumulative fusion operator is to amplify belief and disbelief and reduce uncertainty.

4.4 Example Derivation of Trust Measures

The transitivity and fusion operators will be used for the purpose of deriving trust measures applied to the trust graph of Fig.2 and Fig.3.

In case of Fig.2, the edge trust values will all be set equal as:

$$\omega_B^A = \omega_C^B = \omega_D^C = (0.9, 0.0, 0.1, 0.5) \tag{4}$$

By applying the transitivity operator to the expression of Eq.(2), the derived trust value evaluates to:

$$\omega_D^{A:B:C} = \omega_B^A \otimes \omega_C^B \otimes \omega_D^C = (0.729, 0.000, 0.271, 0.5) \tag{5}$$

In case of Fig.3, the edge trust values will all be set equal as:

$$\omega_B^A = \omega_D^B = \omega_C^A = \omega_D^C = (0.9, 0.0, 0.1, 0.5) \tag{6}$$

By applying the transitivity and cumulative fusion operators to the expression of Eq(3), the derived indirect trust measure can be computed. The expression for the derived trust measure and the numerical result is given below.

$$\omega_D^A = (\omega_B^A \otimes \omega_D^B) \oplus (\omega_C^A \otimes \omega_D^C) = (0.895, 0.000, 0.105, 0.5) \tag{7}$$

5. Trust Fusions of Opinion

Computational trust allows new trust relationships to be derived from pre-existing trust relationship through mathematical computations. Trust fusion is an important element in computational trust, meaning that A can combine B's recommendation with her own personal experience in dealing with C, or with other recommendations about C, in order to derive a more reliable measure of trust in C. These simple principles, which are essential for human interaction in business and everyday life, manifest it in many different forms. This section identifies the parameter dependence problem in trust fusions and investigates possible formal computational models that can be implemented using belief reasoning based on subjective logic. We have proposed three definitions of trust fusion for independent, dependent and partially dependent opinions. We explain the definitions by respective examples. With adequate computational trust models, the principles of trust propagation can be ported to online communities of people, organizations and software agents, with the purpose of enhancing the quality of those communities.

5.1 Fusion of Independent Trust

This operator is most naturally expressed in the evidence space, so we define it first and subsequently map it over to the opinion space.

Definition 1 (Consensus Operator for Independent Opinions).

Let $\omega_x^A = (b_x^A, d_x^A, u_x^A, a_x^A)$ and $\omega_x^B = (b_x^B, d_x^B, u_x^B, a_x^B)$ be trust in x from A and B respectively. The opinion $\omega_x^{A\Diamond B} = (b_x^{A\Diamond B}, d_x^{A\Diamond B}, u_x^{A\Diamond B}, a_x^{A\Diamond B})$ is then called the consensus between ω_x^A and ω_x^B, denoting the trust that an imaginary agent [A,B] would have in x, as if that agent represented both A and B. In case of Bayesian (totally certain) opinions, their relative weight can be defined as $\gamma^{A/B} = \lim(u_x^B / u_x^A)$.

Case I:

$$u_x^A + u_x^B - u_x^A u_x^B \neq 0$$

$$\begin{cases} b_x^{A\Diamond B} = \dfrac{b_x^A u_x^B + b_x^B u_x^A}{u_x^A + u_x^B - u_x^A u_x^B} \\ d_x^{A\Diamond B} = \dfrac{d_x^A u_x^B + d_x^B u_x^A}{u_x^A + u_x^B - u_x^A u_x^B} \\ u_x^{A\Diamond B} = \dfrac{u_x^A u_x^B}{u_x^A + u_x^B - u_x^A u_x^B} \\ a_x^{A\Diamond B} = \dfrac{a_x^A u_x^B + a_x^B u_x^A - (a_x^A + a_x^B) u_x^A u_x^B}{u_x^A + u_x^B - 2u_x^A u_x^B} \end{cases}.$$

Case2:

$$u_x^A + u_x^B - u_x^A u_x^B) = 0$$

$$\begin{cases} b_x^{A\Diamond B} = \dfrac{(\gamma^{A/B} b_x^A + b_x^B)}{(\gamma^{A/B} + 1)} \\ d_x^{A\Diamond B} = \dfrac{(\gamma^{A/B} d_x^A + d_x^B)}{(\gamma^{A/B} + 1)} \\ u_x^{A\Diamond B} = 0 \\ a_x^{A\Diamond B} = \dfrac{\gamma^{A/B} a_x^A + a_x^B)}{\gamma^{A/B} + 1} \end{cases}.$$

By using the symbol '$\oplus$' to designate this operator, we can $\omega_x^{A\Diamond B} = \omega_x^A \oplus \omega_x^B$.

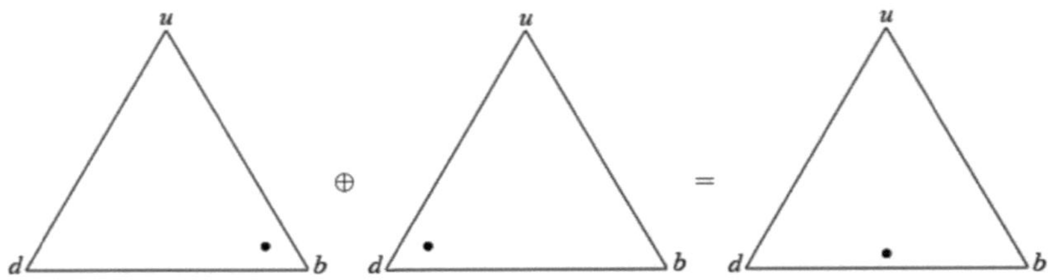

Fig. 4. Example of applying the consensus operator for fusing independent trust

It can be shown that $\oplus$ is both commutative and associative which means that the order in which opinions are combined has no importance. Opinion independence must be assured, which obviously translates into not allowing an entity's opinion to be counted more than once. The effect of independent consensus is to reduce uncertainty. For example the case where several witnesses give consistent testimony should amplify the judge's opinion, and that is exactly what the operator does. Consensus between an infinite number of not totally uncertain (i.e. $u < 1$) opinions would necessarily produce a consensus opinion with $u = 0$. Fig.1 illustrates an example of applying the consensus operator for independent opinions where ω_x^A = {0.8, 0.1, 0.1, a} and ω_x^B = {0.1, 0.8, 0.1, a}, so that $\omega_x^{A\Diamond B} = \omega_x^A \oplus \omega_x^B$ = {0.47, 0.47, 0.06, a} .

5.2 Fusion of Dependent Trust

Assume two agents *A* and *B* having simultaneously observed the same process. Because their observations are identical, their respective opinions will necessarily be dependent, and a consensus according to Def.1 would be meaningless. If the two observers have made exactly the same observations, and their estimates are equal, it is sufficient to take only one of the estimates into account. However, although two observers witness the same phenomenon, it is possible (indeed, likely) that they record and interpret it differently. The observers may have started and ended the observations at slightly different times; one of them may have missed or misinterpreted some of the events, resulting in varying, but still dependent opinions.

Definition 2 (Consensus Operator for Dependent Opinions).

Let $\omega_x^{A_i} = (b_x^{A_i}, d_x^{A_i}, u_x^{A_i}, a_x^{A_i})$ where i $\in$ [1, n], be n dependent opinions respectively held by agents A_1, ...,A_n about the same proposition x. The depended consensus is then $\omega_x^{A_1 \underline{\diamond} \ldots \underline{\diamond} A_n} = b_x^{A_1 \underline{\diamond} \ldots \underline{\diamond} A_n}, d_x^{A_1 \underline{\diamond} \ldots \underline{\diamond} A_n}, u_x^{A_1 \underline{\diamond} \ldots \underline{\diamond} A_n}, a_x^{A_1 \underline{\diamond} \ldots \underline{\diamond} A_n}$ where:

$$\begin{cases} b_x^{A_1\underline{\diamond}\ldots\underline{\diamond}A_n} = \dfrac{\sum_1^n (b_x^{A_i}/\mathrm{u}_x^{A_i})}{\sum_1^n (b_x^{A_i}/\mathrm{u}_x^{A_i}) + \sum_1^n (d_x^{A_i}/\mathrm{u}_x^{A_i}) + n} \\ d_x^{A_1\underline{\diamond}\ldots\underline{\diamond}A_n} = \dfrac{\sum_1^n (d_x^{A_i}/\mathrm{u}_x^{A_i})}{\sum_1^n (b_x^{A_i}/\mathrm{u}_x^{A_i}) + \sum_1^n (d_x^{A_i}/\mathrm{u}_x^{A_i}) + n} \\ u_x^{A_1\underline{\diamond}\ldots\underline{\diamond}A_n} = \dfrac{n}{\sum_1^n (b_x^{A_i}/\mathrm{u}_x^{A_i}) + \sum_1^n (d_x^{A_i}/\mathrm{u}_x^{A_i}) + n} \\ a_x^{A_1\underline{\diamond}\ldots\underline{\diamond}A_n} = \dfrac{\sum_1^n a_x^{A_i}}{n} \end{cases}$$

where all the $u_x^{A_i}$ are different from zero. By using the symbol $\underline{\oplus}$ to designate this operation, we get $\omega_x^{A_1\underline{\diamond}\ldots\underline{\diamond}A_n} = \omega_x^{A_1} \underline{\oplus} \ldots \underline{\oplus}\, \omega_x^{A_n}$.

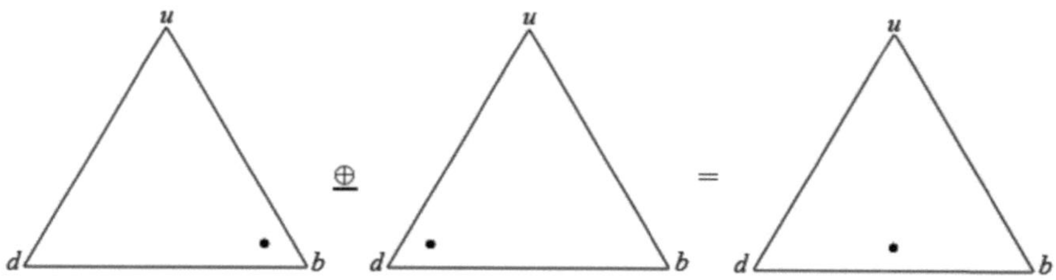

Fig. 5. Example of applying the consensus operator for dependent opinions

The $\underline{\oplus}$ operator is both commutative and associative. The effect of the dependent consensus operator is to produce an opinion which is based on an average of positive and an average of negative evidence. Fig.2 illustrates an example of applying the consensus operator for dependent opinions where ω_x^A = {0.8, 0.1, 0.1, a} and ω_x^B = {0.1, 0.8, 0.1, a}, so that $\omega_x^{A\underline{\diamond}B} = \omega_x^A \underline{\oplus}\, \omega_x^B$ = {0.45, 0.45, 0.10, a} .

5.3 Fusion of Trust Under Partial Dependence

Let two agents *A* and *B* observed the same process during two partially overlapping periods. If it is known exactly which events were observed by both, one of the agents can simply dismiss these observations, and their opinions will be independent. However, it may not always be possible to determine which observations are identical.

Fig.6 illustrates a situation of partly dependent observations. Assuming that the fraction of overlapping observations is known, the dependent and the independent parts of their observations can be estimated, so that a consensus operator can be defined.

In the figure, $\omega_x^{Ai(B)}$ and $\omega_x^{Bi(A)}$ represent the independent parts of A and B's opinions, whereas $\omega_x^{Ad(B)}$ and $\omega_x^{Bd(A)}$ represent their dependent parts.

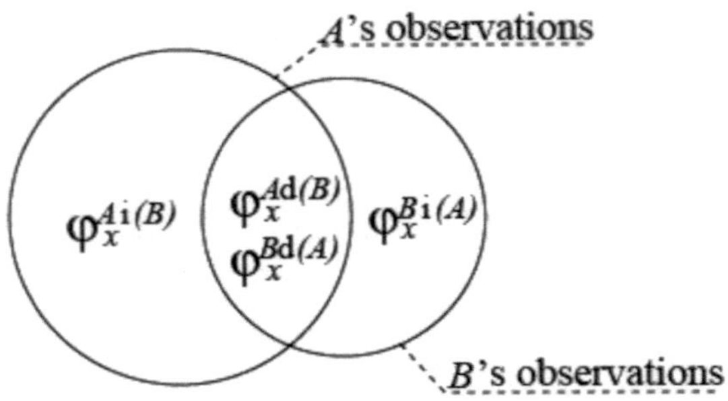

Fig. 6. Beta PDFs based on partly dependent observations

The representation of dependent and independent opinions can be defined by using reciprocal dependence factors denoted by $\lambda^{Ad(B)}$ and $\lambda^{Bd(A)}$.

$$\omega_x^{Ai(B)}:\begin{cases} b_x^{Ai(B)} = b_x^A \mu_x^{Ai(B)} \\ d_x^{Ai(B)} = d_x^A \mu_x^{Ai(B)} \\ u_x^{Ai(B)} = u_x^A \mu_x^{Ai(B)} /(1-\lambda_x^{Ad(B)}, \end{cases} \qquad \mu_x^{Ai(B)} = \frac{1-\lambda_x^{Ad(B)}}{(1-\lambda_x^{Ad(B)})(b_x^A + d_x^A)+u_x^A}$$

$$\omega_x^{Ad(B)}:\begin{cases} b_x^{Ad(B)} = b_x^A \mu_x^{Ad(B)} \\ d_x^{Ad(B)} = d_x^A \mu_x^{Ad(B)} \\ u_x^{Ad(B)} = u_x^A \mu_x^{Ad(B)} / \lambda_x^{Ad(B)}, \end{cases} \qquad \mu_x^{Ad(B)} = \frac{\lambda_x^{Ad(B)}}{\lambda_x^{Ad(B)}(b_x^A + d_x^A)+u_x^A}$$

$$\omega_x^{Bi(A)}:\begin{cases} b_x^{Bi(A)} = b_x^B \mu_x^{Bi(A)} \\ d_x^{Bi(A)} = d_x^B \mu_x^{Bi(A)} \\ u_x^{Bi(A)} = u_x^B \mu_x^{Bi(A)} /(1-\lambda_x^{Bd(A)}, \end{cases} \qquad \mu_x^{Bi(A)} = \frac{1-\lambda_x^{Bd(A)}}{(1-\lambda_x^{Bd(A)})(b_x^B + d_x^B)+u_x^B}$$

$$\omega_x^{Bd(A)}:\begin{cases} b_x^{Bd(A)} = b_x^B \mu_x^{Bd(A)} \\ d_x^{Bd(A)} = d_x^B \mu_x^{Bd(A)} \\ u_x^{Bd(A)} = u_x^B \mu_x^{Bd(A)} / \lambda_x^{Ad(A)}, \end{cases} \qquad \mu_x^{Bd(A)} = \frac{\lambda_x^{Bd(A)}}{\lambda_x^{Bd(A)}(b_x^B + d_x^B)+u_x^B} \tag{8}$$

Having specified the separate dependent and independent parts of two partially dependent opinions, we can now define the consensus operator for partially dependent opinions.

Definition 3 (Consensus Operator for Partially Dependent Opinions).
Let A and B have the partially dependent opinions ω_x^A and ω_x^B respectively, about the same proposition x, and let their dependent and independent parts be expressed according to Eq.(8).We will use the symbol $\tilde{\oplus}$ to designate consensus between partially dependent opinions. As before $\underline{\oplus}$ is the operator for entirely dependent opinions. The consensus of A and B's opinions can then be written as:

$$\begin{aligned} &\omega_x^A \tilde{\oplus} \omega_x^B \\ &= \omega_x^{A \tilde{\diamond} B} \\ &= \omega_x^{(Ad(B) \underline{\diamond} Bd(A)) \diamond Ai(B) \diamond Bi(A)} \\ &= (\omega_x^{Ad(B)} \underline{\oplus} \omega_x^{Bd(A)}) \oplus \omega_x^{Ai(B)} \oplus \omega_x^{Bd(A)} \end{aligned} \tag{9}$$

It could be proved that for any opinion ω_x^A with a dependence factor $\lambda_x^{Ad(B)}$ to any other opinion ω_x^B the following equality holds:

$$\omega_x^A = \omega_x^{Ai(B)} \oplus \omega_x^{Ad(B)} \tag{10}$$

6. Trust Paths Dependency and Network Simplification

Transitive trust networks can involve many principals, and in the examples below, capital letters *A,B,C* and *D* will be used to denote principals We will use basic constructs of directed graphs to represent transitive trust networks, and add some notation elements which allow us to express trust networks in a structured way. A single trust relationship can be expressed as a directed edge between two nodes that represent the trust source and the trust target of that edge. For example the edge [*A,B*] means that *A* trusts *B*. The symbol ":" will be used to denote the transitive connection of two consecutive trust edges to form a transitive trust path. The trust relationships of Fig.1 can be expressed as:

$$([A,D]) = ([A,B]:[B,C]:[C,D]) \tag{11}$$

where the trust scope is implicit. Let the trust scope e.g. be defined as σ: *"trust to be a good car mechanic"*. Let the functional variant be denoted by "fσ" and the referral variant by "rσ". A distinction can be made between initial *direct trust* and derived *indirect trust*. Whenever relevant, the trust scope can be prefixed with "d" to indicate direct trust (dσ), and with "i" to indicate indirect trust (iσ). This can be combined with referral and functional trust, so that for example indirect functional trust can be denoted as "ifσ". A reference to the trust scope can then be explicitly included in the trust edge notation as e.g. denoted by $[A,B,\text{dr}\sigma]$. The trust network of Fig.2 can then be explicitly expressed as:

$$([A,B,\text{if}\sigma]) = ([A,B,\text{dr}\sigma]:[B,C,\text{df}\sigma]:[C,D,\text{df}\sigma] \tag{12}$$

Let us now turn to the combination of parallel trust paths, as illustrated in Fig.3. We will use the symbol "◊" to denote the graph connector for this purpose. The "◊" symbol visually resembles a simple graph of two parallel paths between a pair of agents, so that it is natural to use it for this purpose. In short notation, A's combination of the two parallel trust paths from her to D in Fig.3 is then expressed as:

$$([A,D]) = (([A,B]:[B,D]) \lozenge ([A,C]:[C,D])) \tag{13}$$

It can be noted that Fig.3 contains two parallel paths.

Trust networks can have dependent paths. This is illustrated on the left-hand side of Fig.7. The expression for the graph on the left-hand side of Fig7 would be:

$$([A,D]) = (([A,B]:[B,D]) \lozenge ([A,C]:[C,D]) \lozenge ([A,B]:[B,C]:[C,D])) \tag{14}$$

Fig. 7. Network simplification by removing weakest path

A problem with Eq.(14) is that the arcs $[A,B]$ and $[C,D]$ appear twice, and the expression is therefore not canonical. Trust network analysis with subjective logic may produce inconsistent results when applied directly to non-canonical expressions. It is therefore desirable to express graphs in a form where an arc only appears once. A canonical expression can be defined as an expression of a trust graph in structured notation where every edge only appears once.

A method for canonicalization based on network simplification was described in (Jøsang, 2006). Simplification consists of removing the weakest, i.e. the least certain paths, until the network becomes a directed series-parallel network which can be expressed on a canonical form. Assuming that the path $([A,B]:[B,C]:[C,D])$ is the weakest path in the graph on the left-hand side of Fig.7, network simplification of the dependent graph would be to remove the edge $[B,C]$ from the graph, as illustrated on the right-hand side of Fig.7. Since the simplified graph is equal to that of Fig.3, the formal expression is the same as Eq.(13).

7. Trust Network Canonicalization by Node Splitting

The existence of a dependent edge in a graph is recognized by multiple instances of the same edge in the trust network expression. Node splitting is a new approach to achieving independent trust edges. This is achieved by splitting the target edge of a given dependent edge into as many different nodes as there are different instances of the same edge in the exploded notation. A general directed trust graph is based on directed trust edges between pairs of nodes. It is desirable not to put any restrictions on the possible trust arcs except that they should not be cyclic. This means that the set of possible trust paths from a given source X to a given target Y can contain dependent paths. The left-hand side of Fig.8 shows an example of a trust network with dependent paths.

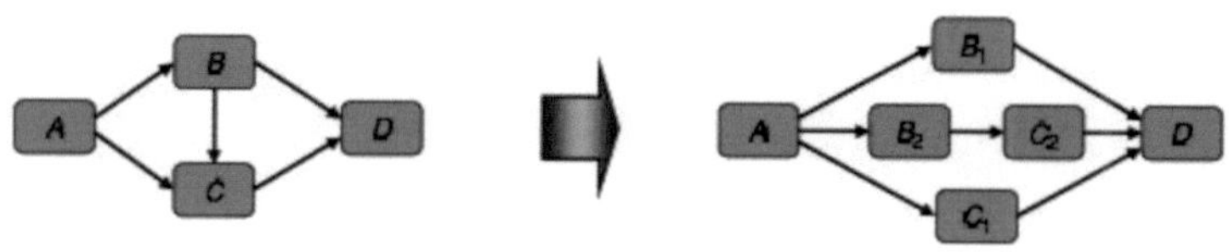

Fig. 8. Node splitting of trust network to produce independent paths

In the non-canonical expression for the left-hand side trust network of Fig.8:

$$([A,D]) = ([A,B]:[B,D]) \diamond ([A,C]:[C,D]) \diamond ([A,B]:[B,C]:[C,D])) \tag{15}$$

the edges $[A,B]$ and $[C,D]$ appear twice. Node splitting in this example consists of splitting the node B into B_1 and B_2, and the node C into C_1 and C_2. This produces the right-hand side trust network in Fig.5 with canonical expression:

$$([A,D]) = ([A,B_1]:[B_1,D]) \diamond ([A,C_1]:[C_1,D]) \diamond ([A,B_2]:[B_2,C_2]:[C_2,D])) \tag{16}$$

Node splitting must be translated into opinion splitting in order to apply subjective logic. The principle for opinions splitting will be to separate the opinion on the dependent edge into two independent opinions that when cumulatively fused produce the original opinion. This can be called fission of opinions, and will depend on a fission factor ø that determines the proportion of evidence assigned to each independent opinion part. The mapping of an opinion $\omega = (b,d,u,a)$ to Beta evidence parameters Beta(r,s,a) and linear splitting into two parts Beta(r_1,s_1,a_1) and Beta(r_2,s_2,a_2) as a function of the fission factor ø is:

$$\text{Beta}(r_1,s_1,a_1): \begin{cases} r_1 = \dfrac{\phi 2b}{u} \\ s_1 = \dfrac{\phi 2d}{u} \\ a_1 = a \end{cases} \qquad \text{Beta}(r_2,s_2,a_2): \begin{cases} r_2 = \dfrac{(1-\phi)2b}{u} \\ s_2 = \dfrac{(1-\phi)2d}{u} \\ a_2 = a \end{cases} \tag{17}$$

The reverse mapping of these evidence parameters into two separate opinions according to Eq.(2) produces:

$$\omega_1 : \begin{cases} b_1 = \dfrac{\phi b}{\phi(b+d)+u} \\ d_1 = \dfrac{\phi d}{\phi(b+d)+u} \\ u_1 = \dfrac{u}{\phi(b+d)+u} \\ a_1 = a \end{cases} \qquad \omega_2 : \begin{cases} b_2 = \dfrac{(1-\phi)b}{(1-\phi)(b+d)+u} \\ d_2 = \dfrac{(1-\phi)d}{(1-\phi)(b+d)+u} \\ u_2 = \dfrac{u}{(1-\phi)(b+d)+u} \\ a_2 = a \end{cases} \quad (18)$$

It can be verified that $\omega_1 \oplus \omega_2 = \omega$, as expected.
When deriving trust values from the cannibalized trust network of Eq.(14) we are interested in knowing its certainty level as compared with a simplified network. We are interested in the expression for the uncertainty of ω_D^A corresponding to trust expression of Eq.(16). Since the node splitting introduces parameters for splitting opinions, the uncertainty will be a function of these parameters. By using Eq.(2) the expressions for the uncertainty in the trust paths of Eq.(16) can be derived as:

$$\begin{aligned} u_D^{A:B_1} &= d_{B_1}^A + u_{B_1}^A + b_{B_1}^A u_D^{B_1} \\ u_D^{A:C_1} &= d_{C_1}^A + u_{C_1}^A + b_{C_1}^A u_D^{C_1} \\ u_D^{A:B_2:C_2} &= b_{B_2}^A d_{C_2}^{B_2} + d_{B_2}^A + u_{B_2}^A + b_{B_2}^A u_D^{B_2} + b_{B_2}^A b_{C_2}^{B_2} u_D^{C_2} \end{aligned} \quad (19)$$

By using Eq.(3) and Eq.(19), the expression for the uncertainty in the trust network of Eq.(16) can be derived as:

$$u_D^A = \frac{u_D^{A:B_1} u_D^{A:C_1} u_D^{A:B_2:C_2}}{u_D^{A:B_1} u_D^{A:C_1} + u_D^{A:B_1} u_D^{A:B_2:C_2} + u_D^{A:C_1} u_D^{A:B_2:C_2} - 2u_D^{A:B_1} u_D^{A:C_1} u_D^{A:B_2:C_2}} \quad (20)$$

By using Eq.(17), Eq.(19) and Eq.(20), the uncertainty value of the derived trust ω_D^A according to the node splitting principle can be computed. This value depends on the trust edge opinions and on the two splitting parameters ϕ_B^A and ϕ_D^C. By fixing the opinion values as in the example of Eq.(4) according to

$$\omega_B^A = \omega_D^B = \omega_C^A = \omega_D^C = \omega_C^B = (0.9, 0.0, 0.1, 0.5) \quad (21)$$

a plot of the uncertainty u_D^A as a function of ϕ_B^A and ϕ_D^C is shown in Fig.9

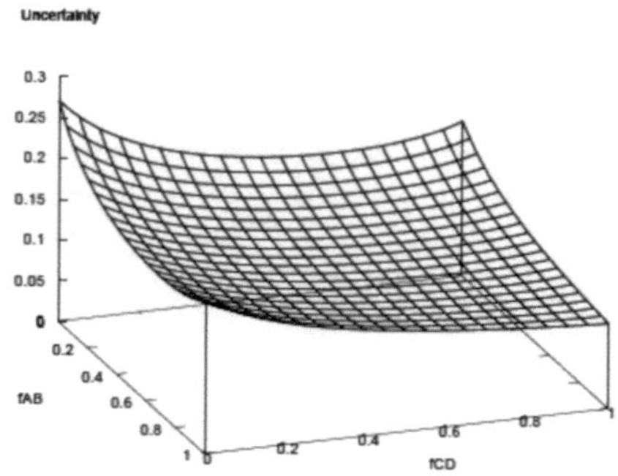

Fig. 9. Uncertainty u_D^A as a function of ϕ_B^A and ϕ_D^C

The conclusion which can be drawn from this is that the optimal value for the splitting parameters are $\phi_B^A = \phi_D^C = 1$ because that is when the uncertainty is at its lowest. In fact the uncertainty can be evaluated to u_D^A = 0.105 in that case, which is equal to the uncertainty of Eq.(10). This is equivalent to the case of trust network simplification where the edge [*B*,*C*] is removed from the left-hand side graph of Fig.5.

The least optimal values for the splitting parameters is when $\phi_B^A = \phi_D^C = 0$, resulting in u_D^A = 0.271 which is equal to the uncertainty of Eq.(12). This is thus equivalent to the absurd trust network simplification where the edges [*A*,*C*] and [*B*,*D*], and thereby the most certain trust paths are removed from the left-hand side graph of Fig.8. Given the edge opinion values used in this example, ([*A*,*B*]:[*B*,*C*]:[*C*,*D*]) is the least certain path of the left-hand side graph of Fig.8. It turns out that the optimal splitting parameters for analysing the right-hand side graph of Fig.8 produces the same result as network simplification where this particular least certain path is removed.

8. Calculating Public Reputation

Opinion Mining is the area of research that attempts to make automatic systems to determine human opinion from free text written in natural language as a feedback. It is a recent discipline at the crossroads of information retrieval and computational linguistics. The discipline is also known as Sentiment Mining, Sentiment Analysis, Sentiment Classification, Opinion Extraction etc. Unlike the text mining, opinion Mining is concerned with the opinion it expresses instead of the topic of a document. Inspiring by the algorithm proposed by Ding (Ding et al, 2008), we can calculate the public reputation from a given opinion text. Usually an item has several features, for example, a hotel can have features such as room, food, etc. One review expresses one customer's comments toward one item. From each review, we first generate the customer's sentimental orientation to each feature of the item, such as positive or like, negative or dislike, and neutral etc (Popescu et al, 2005), then generate a score to this item according to the user's feature sentimental orientation, finally generate an overall score to this item based on all users' scores.

9. Integrating Trust and Reputation

While we calculate the public reputation of an item, we may combine that with the trust between the opinion giver and the potential user of that item. How it can be done is shown in the framework given in Fig.10. As thousands of web offers to provide opinions from their users, from the Internet, we can download a large amount of opinion data and calculate the general public opinion about an item based on those opinions. We can also calculate the existence of the degree of trust between two members in a trust network and that can be considered while suggesting an item to each other. If any suggestion or recommendation comes from a trusted member, it is more likely to be the right choice of item for a member.

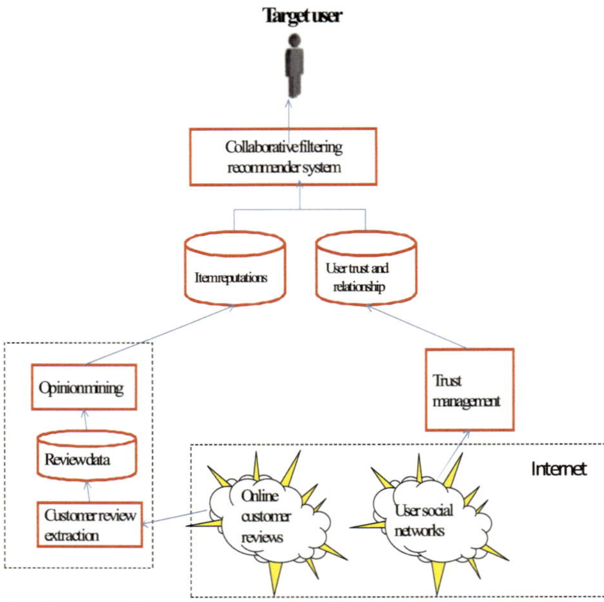

Fig. 10. Framework for integrating trust and public reputation

10. Conclusion

The current online community is suffering the lack of trust or confidence on the opinion expressed in the web-based social network where the degree of trust among the members is absent. The members are facing the quality problem in terms of poor quality and even deceptive opinions or recommendations. In this research work, we have surveyed the current scholars work in the area of trust and reputation management in online social network. We also discuss the method of trust propagation in a trust network. We have described node splitting which is a new principle for trust network analysis with subjective logic. This method which consists of splitting dependent trust edge opinions in order to avoid inconsistencies seems to produce the same result as the previously described method of network simplification. Our analysis was based on a fixed set of edge opinion values. Because of the large number of parameters involved, it is a relatively complex task to verify if our conclusion is valid for all possible trust edge opinion values, so a complete study must be the subject of future work. The present study has given a strong indication that trust network simplification produces the optimal result even though edges are removed from the trust graph. Trust and reputation management represents an important approach for stabilizing and moderating online communities including the members of a social network. Integration of different systems would be problematic with incompatible trust and reputation systems. We have also described how it is possible to gracefully integrate public reputation and trust management with recommender system. This provides a flexible and powerful framework for online trust and reputation management.

11. References

A. A. Selcuk, E. Uzun, and M. R. Pariente. (2004). A Reputation-based Trust Management System for P2P Networks. IEEE Int. Symposium on Cluster Computing and the Grid, 2004.

A. Abdul-Rahman and S. Hailes.(2000). Supporting Trust in Virtual Communities. Proceedings of the Hawaii International Conference on System Sciences, USA.

A. Jøsang (2009). Subjective Logic, Draft Book.

A. Jøsang and S. Pope. Semantic Constraints for Trust Tansitivity.(2005). Proceedings of the Asia-Pacific Conference of Conceptual Modelling. Vol. 43, Australia.

A. Jøsang, R. Hayward, and S. Pope. (2006). Trust Network Analysis with Subjective Logic. In Proceedings of the Australasian Computer Science Conference, Vol. 48, Australia.

A. Jøsang, R. Ismail, and C. Boyd. (2007). A Survey of Trust and Reputation Systems for Online Service Provision. Decision Support Systems, 43(2):618-644.

Aberer, K and Despotovic, Z. (2001). Managing Trust in a Peer-2-Peer Information System. Proceedings of the 10th International Conference on Information and Knowledge Management, USA.

B. Christianson and W. S. Harbison. (2003). Why Isn't Trust Transitive? In Proceedings of the 6th International Conference on Information Fusion, 2003.

Bachrach, Y., A. Parnes et al. (2009). Gossip-based aggregation of trust in decentralized reputation systems. Autonomous Agents and Multi-Agent Systems. 19(2): 153-172.

Bharadwaj, K.K. and M.Y.H. Al-Shamri. (2009). Fuzzy computational model for trust and reputation systems. Electronic Commerce Research and Applications. 8(1): 37-47.

C. Ziegler. (2005). Towards Decentralized Recommender Systems. PhD Thesis, University of Freiburg, Germany.

Ding, X., Liu, B., & Yu, P. S. A, (2008). Holistic Lexicon-Based Approach to Opinion Mining. In the Proceedings of the Int. Conference on Web Search and Web Data Mining.

G. Zacharia, P. Maes (1999). Collaborative Reputation Mechanisms in Electronic Marketplaces. Proceedings of 32nd Hawaii International Conf on System Sciences.

Golbeck, J. (2006). Combining Provenance with Trust in Social Networks for Semantic Web Content Filtering. IPAW 2006: 101-108

Guha, R. V., Kumar, R., Raghavan, P., Tomkins, A., (2004). Propagation of trust and distrust. Proceedings of the 13th International World Wide Web Conference, USA, pp. 403-412.

J. B. Folkerts. (2005). A comparison of reputation-based trust management, MSc thesis, Rochester Institute of Technology, USA.

J. O'Donovan and B. Smyth. (2005). Trust in Recommender Systems. IUI'05, USA.

Kamvar, S., Schlosser, M. and Garcia-Molina, H. (2003). EigenRep: Reputation Management in P2P Networks. 12th International World Wide Web Conference.

L. Mui, M. Mohtashemi, and A. Halberstadt. (2002). A Computational Model of Trust and Reputation. In Proceedings of the 35th Hawaii International Conference on System Science.

L. Xiong. (2005). Resilient Reputation and Trust Management: Models and Techniques. PhD thesis, Georgia Institute of Technology, USA.

Levien, R. Attack-resistant trust metrics. (2004). Ph.D. thesis, University of California at Berkeley, USA.

M. Venkatraman, B. Yu, and M.P. Singh. (2000). Trust and Reputation Management in a Small-World Network. In 4th International Conference on Multi Agent Systems.

P. Resnick, R. Zeckhauser, R. Friedman, and K. Kuwabara. (2000). Reputation Systems. Communications of the ACM, 43(12):45–48.

Popescu, A.-M., & Etzioni, O. (1996). Extracting Product Features and Opinions from Reviews. In the Proceedings of Human Language Technology Conference, Canada.

Pujol, J. M., Sanguesa, R., Delgado, J. (2002). Extracting reputation in multi-agent system by means of social network topology. Proceedings of the first international joint conference on autonomous agents and multi-agent systems, Italy, pp. 467-474.

S. Marsh. (1994). Formalising Trust as a Computational Concept. PhD thesis, University of Stirling, 1994.

Sabater, J. and Sierra, C. (2005). Review on Computational Trust and Reputation Models. Artificial Intelligence Review, 2005 Vol.24, pp. 33-60.

Schillo, M., Funk, P. & Rovatsos, M. (2000). Using Trust for Detecting Deceitful Agents in Aritficial Societies. Applied Artificial Intelligence.

Sen, S. and Sajja, N. (2002). Robustness of Reputation-based Trust: Boolean Case. Proceedings of the First International Joint Conference on Autonomous Agents and Multi-Agent Systems, Italy.

Sundaresan, N. (2007). Online Trust and Reputation Systems. In 8th ACM Conference on Electronic Commerce.

Theo Dimitrakos. (2003). A Service-Oriented Trust Management Framework. International Workshop on Deception, Fraud, and Trust in Agent Societies, pp. 53-72.

Tian, C.-Q., Zou, S.-H., Wang, W.-D., & Cheng, S.-D. (2008). Trust model based on reputation for peer-to-peer networks. Journal on Communication, 29(4), 63-70.

Wang, L., Y.J.Guo, et al. (2009). A reputation-based trust evaluation model for P2P E-Commerce. International Journal of Distributed Sensor Networks. 5(1): 39-49.

Wang, Y., & Vassileva, J. (2007). A Review on Trust and Reputation for Web Service Selection. In the 27th International Conference on Distributed Computing Systems.

Xue, W., & Fan, Z. (2008). A New Trust Model based on Social Characteristic and Reputation Mechanism for the Semantic Web. In the Workshop on Knowledge Discovery and Data Mining.

Ziegler, C. and Golbeck, J. (2007). Investigating interactions of trust and interest similarity. Decision Support Systems 43(2): 460-475

Zou, Y., Gu, L., Li, G., Xie, B., & Mei, H. (2007). Rectifying Prejudicial Feedback Ratings in Reputation based Trust Management. In the IEEE International Conference on Services Computing.

11

Similarity-based Techniques for Trust Management

Mozhgan Tavakolifard
Centre for Quantifiable Quality of Service in Communication Systems (Q2S)
Department of Telematics (ITEM)
Norwegian University of Science and Technology
Norway

1. Introduction

A network of people having established trust relations and a model for propagation of related trust scores are fundamental building blocks in many of todayŠs most successful e-commerce and recommendation systems. Many online communities are only successful if sufficient mutual trust between their members exists. Users want to know whom to trust and how much to trust in the competence and benevolence of other community members in a specific application domain.

However, the web of trust is often too sparse to predict trust values between non-familiar people with high accuracy. Since, at least in large online communities, a user has experience with only a very small fraction of the other community members. Thus, very often there will be no trust relation to an intended new partner of an e-commerce transaction at all.

The process of building trust is hereby performed in two different ways. First, one can establish trust (or distrust) by gaining direct experience with another party. Of course, every positive event increases the assumed trustworthiness of the trustee while every negative one reduces it. Second, one can gain trust based on recommendations of third parties. If, e.g., Alice has high trust in Bob's ability to assess the trustworthiness of other people, Bob has similar trust in Claire's recommendations, and Claire considers David trustable based on her personal experience with him, then Alice gains also trust in David even if she has no or very limited knowledge of him at all. This form of propagated trust is called trust transitivity. Trust transitivity may provide additional information to alleviate the consequences of the sparsity and possible cold-start problems. Such approaches are helpful, provided that a complete trust path exists between the two users.

Based on the two forms of trust, a so-called web of trust between community members is created which is often used in recommender systems helping users of e-commerce applications to get an idea about the trustworthiness of their mostly personally unknown cooperation partners. Unfortunately, however, these webs of trust are often too sparse to be helpful in practice since — at least in large online communities — a user has experience with only a very small fraction of the other community members. Thus, very often there will be no trust relation to an intended new partner of an e-commerce transaction at all (Kim et al., 2008).

An alternative approach to the problem is advocated in this chapter. Based on collaborative filtering one can exploit the like-mindedness resp. similarity of individuals to infer trust to yet unknown parties which increases the trust relations in the web. For instance, if one knows that with respect to a specific property, two parties are trusted alike by a large number of different trusters, one can assume that they are similar. Thus, if one has a certain degree of trust to the one party, one can safely assume a very similar trustworthiness of the other one. In an attempt to provide high quality recommendations and proper initial trust values even when no complete trust propagation path or user profile exists, we propose TILLIT[1] (Trust Inference Links based on Like-minded Interaction Transitions) — a model based on combination of trust inferences and user similarity. The similarity is derived from the structure of the trust graph and users' trust behavior as opposed to other collaborative-filtering based approaches which use ratings of items or user's profile. We describe an algorithm realizing the approach based on a combination of trust inferences and user similarity, and validate the algorithm using a real large-scale data-set.

TILLIT enables to derive trust not only from direct experience and by transitive propagation but also from the similarity between users and vice versa. In particular, two users are considered similar if they either built akin trust relations to other users or if they are trusted very similarly by others. This can be used to propagate already known trust to new trust relations encompassing people similar to those of the yet known relationships. Thus, the web of trust can be augmented significantly.

In comparison with other approaches based on similarity, our work has the following differences:

- It intends to alleviate the sparsity problem in the web of trust matrix itself instead of the matrix of users rating items in the system. Since users have usually few items rated in common, the classic recommender system techniques are often ineffective and are not able to compute a user similarity weight for many of the users. Instead, exploiting the web of trust, it is possible to propagate trust better and to infer additional trust information about other users.
- It calculates the similarity from the structure of the web of trust and trust relations (the trust graph structure and trust values) instead of user-item ratings.
- It proposes methods to convert trust values to similarity measures and vice versa based on the TNA-SL model.

We conduct experiments on a large real dataset showing how our proposed solution increases the coverage (number of trust relations that are predictable) while not reducing the accuracy (the error of predictions). This is especially true for users who have provided few ratings (Tavakolifard et al., 2009).

The rest of this chapter is organized as follows: Section 2 presents a state-of-the-art survey of most popular approaches to deal with the sparsity problem and provide main directions along which research efforts have been done. In section 3 our proposed model is presented. Finally, Section 4 concludes the chapter and outlines some future issues concerning the applicability of the proposed method.

2. State of the Art

Most popular approaches proposed to deal with the sparsity problem include dimensionality reduction of the user-item matrix, application of associative retrieval techniques in the bipartite graph of items and users, item-based similarity instead of user-based similarity, and content-boosted collaborative filtering (see (Papagelis et al., 2005)). The dimensionality reduction approach addresses the sparsity problem by removing unrepresentative or insignificant

[1] "Tillit" is the Norwegian word for trust.

Paper	Web of trust	User-item ratings	rating-based similarity	profile-based similarity
(Papagelis et al., 2005)		x	x	
(Massa & Avesani, 2004)	x		x	
(Massa & Bhattacharjee, 2004)	x		x	
(Massa & Avesani, 2006)	x			
(Avesani et al., 2004)	x		x	
(Avesani et al., 2005)	x		x	
(Weng et al., 2006)	x			
(Lathia et al., 2008)	x			
(Gal-Oz et al., 2008)	x			
(O'Donovan & Smyth, 2005)		x	x	x
(Ziegler & Golbeck, 2007)		x		x
(Ziegler & Lausen, 2004)		x		x
(Golbeck, 2006)		x		x
(Golbeck & Hendler, 2004)		x		x
(Golbeck, 2005)	x			
(Bedi & Kaur, 2006)	x			
(Bedi et al., 2007)	x			
(Hwang & Chen, 2007)		x		
(Peng & Seng-cho, 2009)	x			
(Kitisin & Neuman, 2006)	x			
(Fu-guo & Sheng-hua, 2007)		x		x
(Peng & Seng-cho, 2009)	x			x
(Victor, De Cock, Cornelis & Teredesai, 2008)	x			
(Victor, Cornelis, De Cock & Pinheiro da Silva, 2008)	x			

Table 1. Categorization of the related work.

users or items so as to condense the user-item matrix. We briefly explain those which are based on trust management and similarity measurement and thus more closely resemble our work. Similarity-based approaches can be categorized in two groups: rating-based similarity and profile-based similarity.

Recently, several researches have suggested that the incorporation of a notion of trust into the standard collaborative filtering model can effectively solve the sparsity problem and thus provide better recommendations. A user can build his personalized web of trust by specifying those friends or users he trusts. The trust web can be constructed through the explicit trust ratings provided by users (Hwang & Chen, 2007). Table 1 indicates whether each related work is based on an explicit web of trust or the trust is derived from user-item ratings. In addition, this table shows which kind of similarity (rating-based or profile-based) is used.

In (Papagelis et al., 2005), authors explain how similarity can benefit from special characteristics of trust such as the ability to propagate along chains of trusted users; in this way similarity can support transitivity. They develop a model to establish trust between users by exploiting the transitive nature of trust. In their model they use ordinary measures of similarity taken from collaborative filtering to form the potential trust between the users which would be propagated in a similar way to the word-of-mouth scheme through a trust graph. Finally, by transforming the value back into similarity measure terms, it could be made appropriate for use in collaborative filtering algorithms. More specifically, for each pair of users they first calculate how similar they are, applying PearsonŠs correlation coefficient formula over the user-item ratings, and then they calculate the indirect trust between them. Next, this trust value is converted to a similarity metric using their formula. However, their model simply adopts similarity as trustworthiness. Hence, it still possesses the limitations of similarity-based collaborative filtering as discussed. The main contribution of this work is that a trust metric has been designed, which helps a user to quantify the degrees of trust it should place on others.

Massa et al. present in (Massa & Avesani, 2004) evidence that, by incorporating trust, recommender systems can be more effective than systems based on traditional techniques like collaborative filtering. They analyze the potential contribution of Trust Metrics in increasing the performances of Recommender Systems and proposed an architecture for trust-aware Recommender Systems. In this paper, it is proposed that a peer can establish trust on other peers through explicit trust statements and trust propagation. A trust model is built directly from users' direct feedbacks. This trust model is incorporated into the recommendation process for recommending various items (such as books, movie, music, software etc.) to on-line users. Users can express their personal web of trust by identifying those reviewers whose reviews and ratings are consistently found to be valuable. they argue that it is possible to predict trust in unknown users by propagating trust even there were no direct connection between them. However, it is not clear how a user quantify the degrees of trust when making trust statements. The authors show how the similarity measure, on average, is computable only against a very small portion of the user base and is, in most cases, a noisy and unreliable value because computed on few items rated in common by two users. Instead, trust-aware techniques can produce a trust score for a very high number of other users; the trust score of a user estimates the relevance of that users' preferences. In this paper, similarity is measured using PearsonŠs correlation coefficient on user-item ratings.

They also show, in their subsequent experiment (Massa & Bhattacharjee, 2004), that the incorporation of trust metric and similarity metric can increase the coverage of recommender systems while maintaining the recommendation accuracy. This work builds a trust model directly from trust data provided by users as part of the popular epinions.com service. A big limitation of the work in (Massa & Avesani, 2004) and (Massa & Bhattacharjee, 2004) is that the web of trust are built on binary relationships among users and the propagating trusts are computed simply based on the distances between them.

Massa and Avesani in (Massa & Avesani, 2006) analyze the relative benefits of asking new users either few ratings about items or few trust statements about other users for the purpose of bootstrapping a RS ability to generate recommendations. They run experiments on a large real world dataset derived from Epinions. com. The results clearly indicate that while traditional RS algorithms exploiting ratings on items fail for new users, asking few trust statements to a new user is instead a very effective strategy able to quickly let the RS generate many accurate items recommendations. The working hypothesis is that inviting users to elicit opinions on users (trust statements) rather than opinions on items allows to shorten the bootstrapping of RSs for cold start users. The benefits can be summarized as follows: (1) the number of trust statements needed from a new user for bootstrapping a Recommender System is much less than the number of rating on items; (2) while exploiting the few early ratings provided by a new user does not enable to generate recommendations, exploiting just few early trust statements allows to significantly increase the number of possible recommendations; (3) the accuracy of generated recommendations increases as well exploiting trust statements rather than ratings on items. The main contribution of this paper is the empirical proof of our hypotheses. The straightforward impact of this work is a new guideline for Recommender Systems design: a new user has to be invited to elicit few other users she trusts rather than to express her opinions on a pool of items.

Avesain et al. in (Avesani et al., 2004; 2005) apply the trust model into the ski mountaineering domain. They present a community-based website in which users can share their opinions about the snow conditions of different ski routes and also express their trust on othersŠ opinions. The trust score of a user depends on the trust statements of other users on him/her and their trust scores. However, the trust model requires the direct feedback of users and the effectiveness of the trust model on the skiing community has not been validated.

In (Weng et al., 2006) propose that peers predict the new items' ratings based on the recommendations of the peers that are trusted directly or indirectly. A trust metrics has been designed to help peers to determine the degrees of trust should be placed on others. The design of trust metrics also stimulates a novel method to make prediction, which is featured by the recommendation adjustment and pseudo-recommendation. It has been shown by the experimental results that the trust metrics and corresponding prediction making approach do improve the performance of traditional similarity-based collaborative filtering in terms of coverage, prediction accuracy and robustness.

A number of techniques for performing collaborative filtering from the point of view of a trust-management problem are outlined in (Lathia et al., 2008). In this work authors propose a variation of k-nearest neighbor collaborative filtering algorithm for trusted k-nearest recommenders. This algorithm allows users to learn who and how much to trust one another by evaluating the utility of the rating information they receive. They mainly address the problem of learning how much to trust rating information that is received from other users in a recommender system.

A model for computing trust-based reputation for communities of strangers is proposed in (Gal-Oz et al., 2008). The model uses the concept of knots, which are sets of members having high levels of trust in each other. Different knots typically represent different view points and preferences. The assumption underlying this knot-aware reputation model is that use of relatively small, but carefully selected, subsets of the overall community's reputation data yields better results than those represented by the full dataset.

In (O'Donovan & Smyth, 2005), O'Donovan and Smyth argue that profile similarity is just one of a number of possible factors that might be used to influence recommendation and prediction, and the reliability of a partner profile to deliver accurate recommendations in the past is another important factor, if a profile has made lots of accurate recommendation predictions in the past it can be viewed as more trustworthy than another profile that has made many poor predictions. They claim that the reliability of a user profile to deliver accurate recommendation in the past is an important factor for influencing recommendation and prediction. A user is viewed as more trustworthy if he has made more accurate predictions in the past than other users. The trust metrics are calculated at both the Item and Profile levels. Item Level trust is a representation for a producer's trustworthiness with respect to the recommendation of a specific item. Profile Level trust is a less fine-grained metric, representing a recommendation

producers trust as a whole, without respect to one specific item. For example, we might wish to refer to John's overall trustworthiness based on a series of different past recommendations. This score is simply an average over the Item Level trust scores for every item in the users profile. Essentially these metrics summarize the relative number of correct recommendations that a given user has made, according to a predefined error bound. They propose to modify the way that recommendation partners are generally selected or weighted during the recommendation process. They argue that profile similarity on its own may not be sufficient, that other factors might also have an important role to play. Specifically they introduce the notion of trust in reference to the degree to which one might trust a specific profile when it comes to make a specific rating prediction. They develop two different trust models, one that operates at level of the profile and one at level of the items within a profile. In both of these models trust is estimated by monitoring the accuracy of a profile at making predictions over an extended period of time. Trust then is the percentage of correct predictions that a profile has made in general (profile-level trust) or with respect to a particular item (item-level trust). They describe how this trust information can be incorporated into the recommendation process and demonstrate that it has a positive impact on recommendation quality. However, this system only uses a global trust metric and provides neither any personalization nor trust propagation. Ziegler and Lausen in (Ziegler & Lausen, 2004) mention that in order to provide meaningful results for recommender system applications, they expect notions of trust to clearly reflect user similarity. In this work, they provide empirical results obtained from one real, operational community and verify latter hypothesis for the domain of book recommendations. Ziegler and Golbeck in (Ziegler & Golbeck, 2007) experimentally prove that there exists a significant correlation between the trust expressed by the users and their profile similarity based on the recommendations they made in the system. This correlation is further studied as survey-based experiments in (Golbeck, 2006).
Golbeck et al. in (Golbeck & Hendler, 2004) describe an E mail filtering system based on trust ratings. The predicted trust of a user is given by a weighted average of her neighborsŠ trust ratings. They have shown that the weighted average metric can provide better results than other metrics.
Golbeck in (Golbeck, 2005) present FilmTrust, a website that uses trust in Semantic Web-based social networks, to create predictive movie recommendations. She show how these recommendations are more accurate than other techniques in certain cases, and discuss this as a mechanism of Semantic Web interaction. Within the FilmTrust website, trust in social networks has been used to personalize the user experience. Trust took on the role of a recommender system forming the core of an algorithm to create predictive rating recommendations for movies. The accuracy of the trust-based predicted ratings in this system is significantly better than the accuracy of a simple average of the ratings assigned to a movie and also the recommended ratings from a Person-correlation based recommender system.
In (Bedi & Kaur, 2006) a model that incorporates the social recommendation process is proposed. The trustworthy peers of the user become the recommender agents and suggest movies to the user according to the tastes of the user. The agents in our system also learn from their experience in dealing with the trustworthy peers and update the degree of trust on them. In the proposed system, they have tried to merge the advantages of the mechanical recommender system with the more humane recommendation process to make their recommendations trustworthy and useful for the user.
(Bedi et al., 2007) proposes the design of a recommender system that uses knowledge stored in the form of ontologies. The interactions amongst the peer agents for generating recommen-

dations are based on the trust network that exists between them. Recommendations about a product given by peer agents are in the form of Intuitionistic Fuzzy Sets specified using degree of membership, non membership and uncertainty. The presented design uses ontologies, a knowledge representation technique, instead of databases for creating annotated content for Semantic Web. Seeing the potential and popularity of ontologies among researchers, they believe that ontologies will be build and maintained in numerous knowledge domains for the Semantic Web and future applications. The presented recommender system uses temporal ontologies that absorb the effect of changes in the ontologies due to the dynamic nature of domains, in addition to the benefits of ontologies. A case study of tourism recommender system is chosen to generate the recommendations for the selection of destination, travel agents and the flight schedule. A comparison of the generated recommendations with the manual recommendations by peers establishes the validity of the presented recommender system.

In (Hwang & Chen, 2007) an improved mechanism to the standard collaborative filtering techniques by incorporating trust into collaborative filtering recommendation process is presented. They derive the trust score directly from the user rating data based on users' prediction accuracy in the past and exploit the trust propagation in the trust web. They investigate the effects of both the local trust metric and the global trust metric in the standard collaborative filtering recommendation. The global metric has shown to have an advantage over other approaches in prediction coverage. The local metrics provide more accurate recommendations than those provided by standard collaborative filtering technique. The overall performance of their trust-based recommender system is presented and favorably compared to other approaches. Experimental results verify that the incorporation of trust into collaborative filtering process can indeed improve the prediction accuracy while maintain satisfactory prediction coverage.

(Kitisin & Neuman, 2006) propose an approach to include the social factors e.g. user's past behaviors and reputation together as an element of trust that can be incorporated into the current recommender system framework and show their experiments in order to test their solution. Two computation models: expertise level and credit model are presented. The expertise model includes trust, reputation and past behaviors whereas the credit model represents the recommendation incentive. They propose using credits to help alleviate cold start problem and data sparseness.

In (Fu-guo & Sheng-hua, 2007) authors argue that items belonging to different topics need different trustworthy users to make recommendation, so topic-level trust will be more effective than profile-level trust in incorporating into the recommendation process. Based on this idea, they design a topic-level trust model which helps a user to quantify the trustworthy degree on a specific topic, and propose a new recommender algorithm by incorporating the new model into the mechanics of a standard collaborative filtering recommender system. Their proposed algorithm combines topic trust with profile similarity. The results from experiments based on Movielens dataset show that the new method can improve the recommendation accuracy of recommender systems.

(Peng & Seng-cho, 2009) is motivated by the need to provide recommendations about blog articles, so that bloggers/readers can find desired articles easily. Accordingly, this study proposes to exploit the trust relationships between bloggers and readers via explicit trust ratings to generate recommendations in a reliable and satisfactory way. Furthermore, rather than only using a single trust rating, this work presents a multi-faceted model that considers trust by dividing a general trust rating into multiple trust ratings for different types of blog articles, thus enabling trust relationships to be evaluated in a fine-grained manner. To help ease information overload in the blogosphere, this work proposes a trust-enhanced collaborative filtering approach that integrates multi-faceted trust based on article type and user similarity. An online blog article recommender system, called iTrustU, is also designed to evaluate the effectiveness of the proposed approach in terms of accuracy and quality of recommendations. Results demonstrate that the proposed integrated approach yields a significantly higher accuracy than traditional approaches, especially for cold-start users. In addition, analysis results indicate that trust and similarity among bloggers/readers have a significantly positive correlation in the blogosphere. Effective recommender systems can be achieved by exploiting trust relationships in a trust network. The proposed approach is applicable not only to the blogosphere, but also to online social communities when trust relationships already exist between users.

(Victor, De Cock, Cornelis & Teredesai, 2008) examines the problem of cold-start users in recommender systems and propose to connect the newcomer to an underlying trust network among the users of the recommender system which alleviates the so-called cold start problem. In this paper, they study the effect of guiding the new user through the connection process, and in particular the influence this has on the amount of generated recommendations. Experiments on a dataset from Epinions.com support the claim that it is more beneficial for a newcomer to connect to an identified key figure instead of to a random user.

In (Victor, Cornelis, De Cock & Pinheiro da Silva, 2008) the authors advocate the use of a trust model in which trust scores are (trust,distrust)-couples, drawn from a bilattice that preserves valuable trust provenance information including gradual trust, distrust, ignorance, and inconsistency. They pay particular attention to deriving trust information through a trusted third party, which becomes especially challenging when also distrust is involved.

In our work we provide an alternative approach to deal with the sparsity problem. We measure similarity based on the users' trust relationships, i.e. trust graph structure and trust values (in contrast to the other approaches which have used user-item ratings or profile similarity), and propose novel formulas to convert it to subjective logic opinions. The consideration of these similarities leads to extra information accessible for trust inferences.

3. TILLIT

In our model, we measure similarity based on the existing web of trust in a community using an iterative fixed-point algorithm on node-pair graphs introduced later in this section. As a method to describe the values of trust as well as its propagation we apply the TNA-SL model (Jøsang et al., 2006) which is based on the Subjective Logic (Jøsang, 2001). Our approach, however, would also work with other methods like (Abdul-Rahman & Hailes, 2000; Grandison & Sloman, 2002).

In subsection 3.1, we briefly explain the TNA-SL model as the background of our work. Our proposed model for trust inference is described in section 3.2.

3.1 Trust Network Analysis with Subjective Logic

for trust network analysis. TNA-SL uses the Subjective Logic (Jøsang, 2001) which enables to represent a specific belief calculus. There trust is expressed by a belief metric called opinion. An opinion is denoted by $\omega_B^A = (b, d, u, a)$ expressing the belief of a relying party A in the trustworthiness of another party B. The parameters b and d represent the belief resp. disbelief in B's trustworthiness while d expresses the uncertainty of A about to trust B or not. The three parameters are all probability values between 0 and 1 and fulfill the constraint $b + d + u = 1$. The parameter a is called the base rate, and determines how uncertainty shall contribute to the

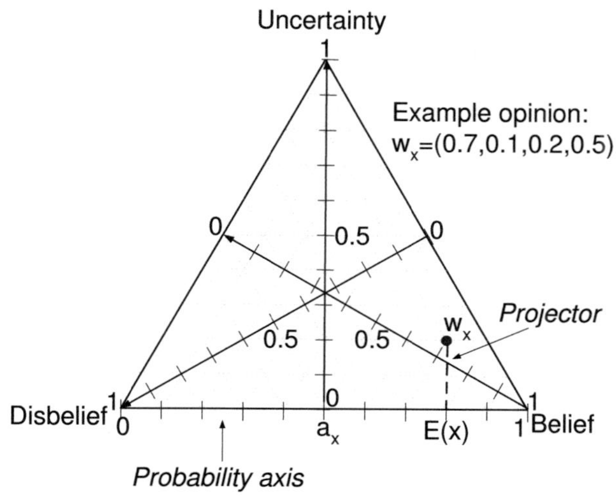

Fig. 1. Opinion triangle with an example opinion (Jøsang, 2001).

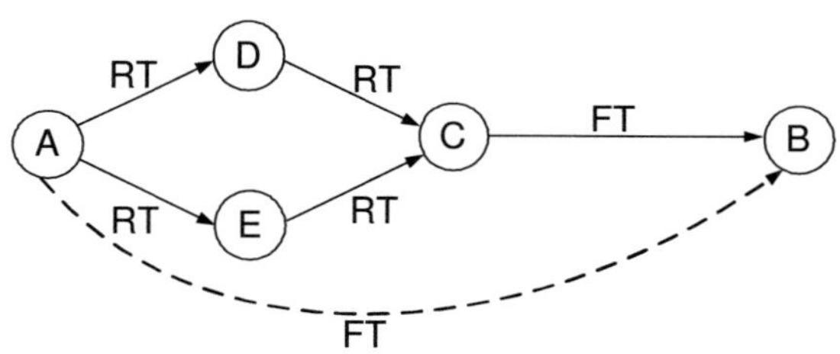

Fig. 2. Referral trust transitivity and parallel combination of trust paths.

opinion's probability expectation value which is calculated as $E(\omega_x^A) = b + au$. The opinion space can be mapped into the interior of an equal-sided triangle, where, the three parameters b, d, and u determine the position of the point in the triangle representing the opinion. Fig.1 illustrates an example where the opinion is $\omega_x = (0.7, 0.1, 0.2, 0.5)$.

Based on TNA-SL, there are two different types of trust relations: *functional trust* (FT) and *referral trust* (RT). The former concerns A's direct trust in B performing a specific task; the latter concerns A's trust in B giving a recommendation about someone else doing a task or in other words is the trust in the ability to refer to a third party. As mentioned in the introduction, the simplest form of trust inference is trust transitivity which is widely discussed in literature (Ding et al., 2005; Guha et al., 2004; Morselli et al., 2007; Quercia et al., 2007; Yang et al., 2002). That is, if A trusts B who trusts C, then A will also trusts C. A valid transitive trust path requires that the last edge in the path represents functional trust and that all other edges in the path represents referral trust. Referral trust transitivity and parallel combination of trust paths are expressed as part of TNA-SL model (figure 2) (Jøsang et al., 2006).

The discounting operator ($\otimes$) (Jøsang, 2002) is used to derive trust from transitive trust paths, and the consensus operator ($\oplus$) allows to combine parallel transitive trust paths. The trust network in figure 2 can then be expressed as

$$FT_B^A = ((RT_D^A \otimes RT_C^D) \oplus (RT_E^A \otimes RT_C^E)) \otimes FT_B^C$$

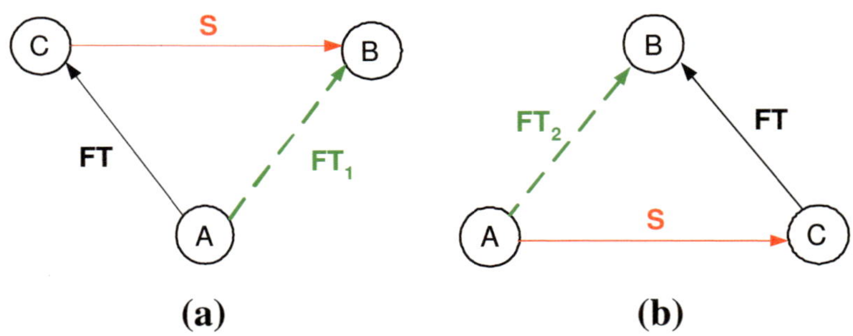

Fig. 3. (a) Similar trustees (b) Similar trustees.

While we consider TNA-SL and the Subjective Logic as a suitable fundament for our similarity model, it can be, as already mentioned, adapted to all trust management models enabling to combine referral and functional trust (e.g., (Abdul-Rahman & Hailes, 2000; Grandison & Sloman, 2002)).

3.2 The Proposed Model

Our model for the estimation how much trust A can place in B considers not only direct experience and recommendations but also similarities between agents with respect of trusting other agents or being trusted by other parties. The two kinds of similarities between trusters resp. trustees can be gradually expressed by triples very similar to the first three operands of the opinion quadruples such that we can use the consensus operator of the subjective logic for the trust value computation.

3.2.1 The Main Idea

If A has functional trust in C who is similar to B (they are *similar trustees*), then A can infer its functional trust to B ((Ding et al., 2005), see figure 3(a)).

Our similarity opinion is a special form of referral trust. It reflects that the akin trust evaluations of B and C by several other trusters are a kind of recommendation by these agents to A to treat B and C similarly. Thus, we see the discounting operator $\otimes$ as the correct mechanism to combine the similarity opinion between B and C with the functional trust of A in C in order to infer the functional trust of A in B:

$$FT1_B^A = S_B^C \otimes FT_C^A \tag{1}$$

As higher the similarity between B and C is, as closer the trust of A to B will equal to that between A and C. As lower this similarity is, as more uncertain A will be about whether to trust B or not.

If C has functional trust to B and A is similar to C (they are *similar trusters*), then A can also infer functional trust towards B ((Ding et al., 2005), see figure 3(b)).

This similarity opinion is discounted by the functional trust FT_B^C from C to B to form the new trust value.

$$FT2_B^A = S_C^A \otimes FT_B^C \tag{2}$$

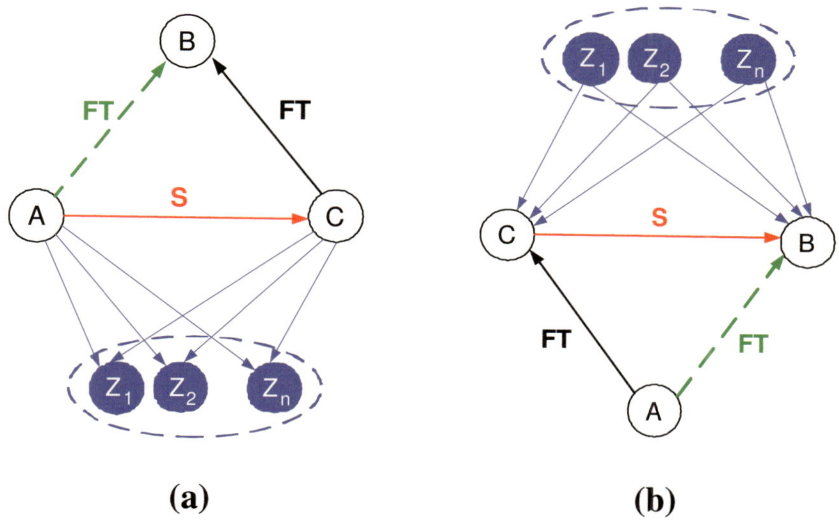

Fig. 4. (a) Similarly trusting (b) Similarly trusted.

Two trustees are similar if they are both similarly trusted by other agents Z_1, Z_2, ..., Z_n (figure 4(a)). This is an extension of TNA-SL in which it is not possible to infer any trust value of A towards B in a trust network.

We call C and A similar trusters if they have alike trust in several other agents Z_1, Z_2, ..., Z_n. In this case, if C has functional trust to a new agent B, then A can infer a functional trust to B (figure 4(b)). Again using TNA-SL alone, there is no way to infer a new trust value.

Similarly to Jøsang's way to define opinions, we use triples to describe similarity which enables us to consider uncertainty. In particular, the degree of similarity depends on the number n of agents Z_1, Z_2, ..., Z_n used for the computation reflecting that we are more certain about the similarity of two parties if they are trusted by a significant large number of other agents in an akin way.

The similarity opinion S_B^C from C towards B is the triple[2] (*similarity, non-similarity, uncertainty*). If $C = B$, the similarity opinion is defined to be $(1,0,0)$. Otherwise, it is calculated based on the measure $sim_{te}(C,B)$ of similarity between the two trustees C and B which is introduced in subsection 3.2.2:

$$S_B^C = \left(\frac{n \cdot sim_{te}(C,B)}{c+n}, \frac{n \cdot (1 - sim_{te}(C,B))}{c+n}, \frac{c}{c+n}\right) \tag{3}$$

c is a constant determining how fast uncertainty is replaced by assurance. As higher its value is, as more agents are needed to reduce the uncertainty value in favor of the similarity and non-similarity values. The similarity opinion fulfills the constraints that the sum of all three values is equal to 1.

Like (3), the similarity opinion S_C^A from A to C is calculated using the measure of similarity $sim_{tr}(C,A)$ between trusters which is also introduced in subsection 3.2.2:

$$S_C^A = \left(\frac{n \cdot sim_{tr}(C,A)}{c+n}, \frac{n \cdot (1 - sim_{tr}(C,A))}{c+n}, \frac{c}{c+n}\right) \tag{4}$$

[2] This metric is inferred from a metric for the trust value computation (Jøsang & Knapskog, 1998) by Jøsang and Knapskog.

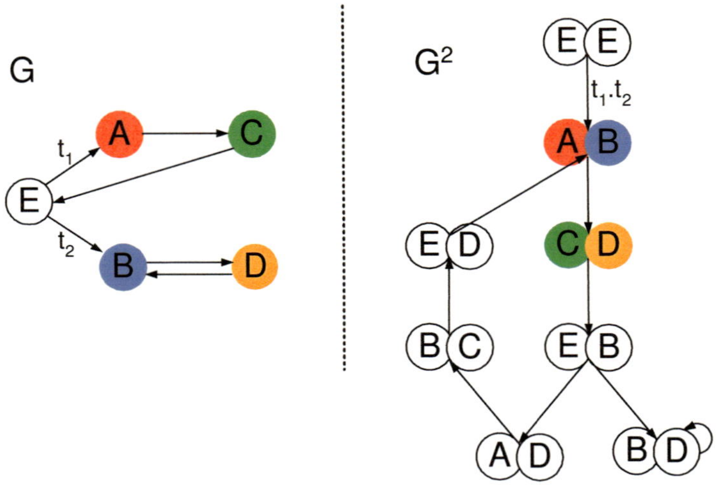

Fig. 5. Similarity measurement.

3.2.2 Similarity Calculation

In order to measure similarities, we model trusters, trustees, and trust relationships as a graph with nodes representing trusters and trustees and edges representing trust relations. The intuition behind our algorithm is that, *similar* trustees are related to *similar* trusters. More precisely, trusters A and B are similar if they are related to trustees C and D, respectively, and C and D are themselves similar. The base case is that each node is similar to itself. If we call this graph G, then we can form a node-pair graph G^2 in which each node represents an ordered pair of nodes of G as depicted in figure 5. A node (A, B) of G^2 points to a node (C, D) if, in G, A points to C and B points to D. Similarity scores are symmetric, so for clarity we draw (A, B) and (B, A) as a single node A, B (with the union of their associated edges) (Jeh & Widom, 2002).

We propose an iterative fixed-point algorithm on G^2 to compute similarity scores[3] for node-pairs in G^2. The similarity score for a node v of G^2 gives a measure of similarity between the two nodes of G represented by v. Scores can be thought of as flowing from a node to its neighbors. Each iteration propagates scores one step forward along the direction of the edges, until the system stabilizes (i.e., scores converge). Since nodes of G^2 represents pairs in G, similarity is propagated from pair to pair. Under this computation, two trustees are similar if they are trusted by similar trusters.

For each iteration k, iterative similarity functions $sim_{te,k}(*, *)$ for trustees and $sim_{tr,k}(*, *)$ for trusters are introduced. The iterative computation is started with $sim_{0,*}(*, *)$ defined as

$$sim_{0,*}(A, B) = \begin{cases} 1, & if\, A = B \\ 0, & if\, A \neq B \end{cases} \tag{5}$$

[3] An alternative approach to measure this similarity is to model an agent's mental structure as an ontology and using various methods proposed in our previous work (Tavakolifard et al., 2008a;b)

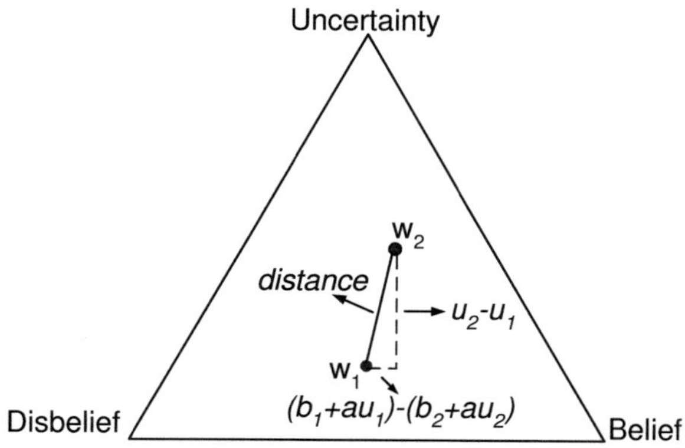

Fig. 6. The distance between opinions.

On the $(k+1)$-th iteration, $sim_{*,k+1}(*,*)$ is defined in special cases as

$$\begin{aligned} sim_{*,k+1}(A,B) &= 1, \quad if\, A = B \\ sim_{te,k+1}(A,B) &= 0, \quad if\, I(A) = \emptyset \; or \; I(B) = \emptyset \\ sim_{tr,k+1}(A,B) &= 0, \quad if\, O(A) = \emptyset \; or \; O(B) = \emptyset \end{aligned} \tag{6}$$

$I(A)$ is the set of in-neighbors of A while $O(A)$ specifies the set of A's out-neighbors. Individual in-neighbors are denoted as $I_i(A)$, for $1 \le i \le |I(A)|$, and individual out-neighbors are denoted as $O_i(A)$, for $1 \le i \le |O(A)|$. $sim_{te,k+1}(*,*)$ is computed from $sim_{tr,k}(*,*)$ in the general case as follows:

$$sim_{te,k+1}(A,B) = \frac{\sum_{i=1}^{n}\sum_{j=i}^{n} sim_{tr,k}\left(I_i(A),I_j(B)\right) \cdot (1 - \text{distance}(I_i(A),I_j(B),A,B))}{\sum_{i=1}^{n}\sum_{j=i}^{n} sim_{tr,k}\left(I_i(A),I_j(B)\right)} \tag{7}$$

and $sim_{tr,k+1}(*,*)$ is computed from $sim_{te,k}(*,*)$ in the general case as:

$$sim_{tr,k+1}(A,B) = \frac{\sum_{i=1}^{n}\sum_{j=i}^{n} sim_{te,k}\left(O_i(A),O_j(B)\right) \cdot (1 - \text{distance}(A,B,O_i(A),O_j(B)))}{\sum_{i=1}^{n}\sum_{j=i}^{n} sim_{te,k}\left(O_i(A),O_j(B)\right)} \tag{8}$$

Formulas (7) and (8) are alternately computed in iterations until the resulting similarity values sim_{tr} and sim_{te} converge.
The *distance* function is used to compare trust relations. $distance(A,B,C,D)$ expresses the difference between the trust from A, B to C, D. It averages the Euclidean distances between the trust values of A and C resp. B and D on the opinion triangle (see figure 1):

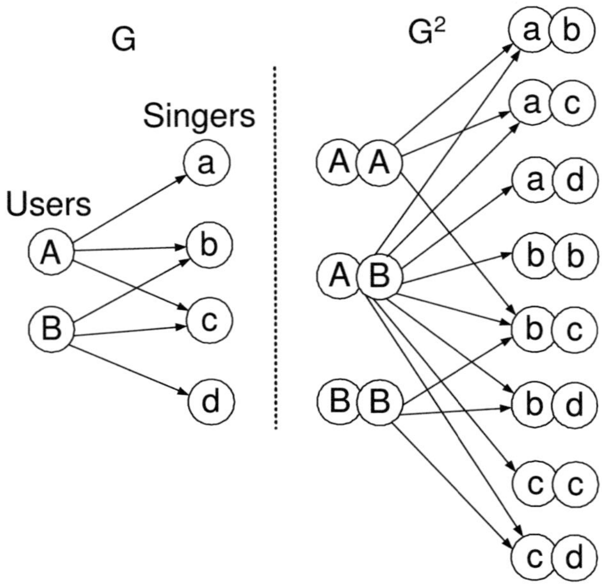

Fig. 7. Application Scenario

$$
\begin{aligned}
\text{distance}(A,A,C,D) &= \sqrt{(b_{AC}+\tfrac{1}{2}u_{AC}-b_{AD}-\tfrac{1}{2}u_{AD})^2+\tfrac{3}{4}(u_{AC}-u_{AD})^2} \\
\text{distance}(A,B,C,C) &= \sqrt{(b_{AC}+\tfrac{1}{2}u_{AC}-b_{BC}-\tfrac{1}{2}u_{BC})^2+\tfrac{3}{4}(u_{AC}-u_{BC})^2} \\
\text{distance}(A,B,C,D) &= \begin{cases} \tfrac{1}{2}(\sqrt{(b_{AC}+\tfrac{1}{2}u_{AC}-b_{BD}-\tfrac{1}{2}u_{BD})^2+\tfrac{3}{4}(u_{AC}-u_{BD})^2} \\ +\sqrt{(b_{AD}+\tfrac{1}{2}u_{AD}-b_{BC}-\tfrac{1}{2}u_{BC})^2+\tfrac{3}{4}(u_{AD}-u_{BC})^2}) \end{cases}
\end{aligned} \tag{9}
$$

For the sake of simplicity, all base rate values ($a_{AD}, a_{AC}, a_{BD}, a_{BC}$) are assumed to be $\frac{1}{2}$. The factor $\frac{3}{2}$ is used for the vertical axis to adapt the measures. Otherwise, the opinion triangle would be compressed and the distance between the points (0,1,0) and (0,0,1) would not be equal to one. Figure 6 illustrates the *distance* function graphically.

4. Conclusion and Future Work

In order to overcome sparseness of the web of trust, we consider users' similarity as a factor to derive trust connectivity and trust values. The main idea is that we account two persons similar if either a fair number of others have akin trust in them or if they themselves trust several other people alike. In the first case, every person who has trust in one of them can infer similar trust to the other one, at least as an estimated starting value. In the second case, a person may infer the trust value of a third party from other trusters similar to her. the results of our evaluation (Tavakolifard et al., 2009) lead to the expectation that the method TILLIT will increase the coverage of trust relationships significantly, and that the accuracy of the predicted additional will be fairly high as well.

We consider a similarity-based recommendation system for singers and songs as a good application example for our model. Normally, in systems like iTunes only the most popular

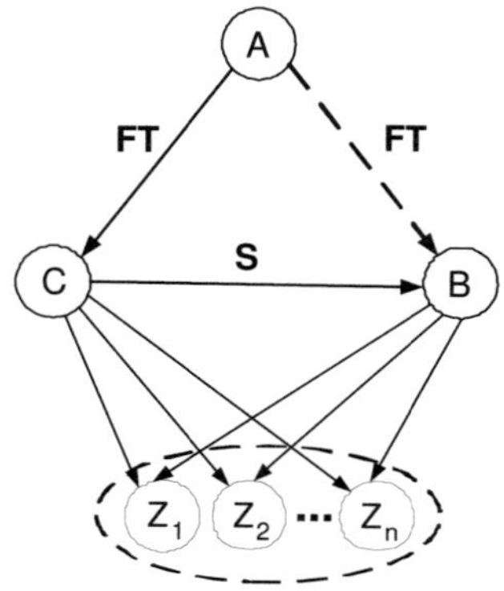

Fig. 8. Coupling: a trust propagation method.

songs or other songs of artists, of whom one already has bought songs, are advertised without any guarantee that one likes these songs as well. Using our approach, it is possible to find other customers who have an akin taste about music as the customer Alice reading the advertisements. Songs rated positively by these customers but not bought yet by Alice can be advertised to her since she will like them probably as well. This will make Alice more receptive to the advertisements.

We count all ratings of a buyer of songs of a particular singer to compute the trust value of that user to the singer by the metric mentioned before. A bipartite trust graph from users to singers can be formed based on these trust values (Figure 7). Then, (7) and (8) can be used to calculate similarity of singers and users respectively.

In the future, we aim to evaluate the accuracy of a whole recommender system that employs our proposed model. Furthermore, we assess the possibility of modeling some of other trust propagation methods using our approach. An example is transposition resp. reciprocity (Guha et al., 2004) assuming that A's trust in B causes B to develop also some level of trust towards A. Another propagation method is Coupling, in which A's trust in C propagates to B because C and B trust people in common (Guha et al., 2004). This propagation rule is depicted in figure 8. According to this rule we can use the similarity between trusters to propagate the trust in one trustee to another.

Moreover, one can use similarity in a complete different way. Trust is very specific and nobody trusting Bob as a good car mechanic will automatically trust him also in undertaking heart surgeries. But probably, he will be capable in repairing motorcycles. Thus, there is a large similarity between the domains of repairing cars and motorcycles but a very low one between both of these and medical surgery. We think to use trust relations in one domain to infer ones in similar domains and consider ontologies describing the degrees of similarity between the domains as a useful means. All-in-all, we are convinced, that the various forms of similarity are good vehicles to tackle the major problem of too sparse webs of trust in online communities.

5. References

Abdul-Rahman, A. & Hailes, S. (2000). Supporting trust in virtual communities, *Proceedings of the 33rd Hawaii International Conference, Volume 6*, IEEE Computer Society Press, Maui, Hawaii.

Avesani, P., Massa, P. & Tiella, R. (2004). Moleskiing: trust-aware decentralized recommender system, *1st Workshop on Friend of a Friend, Social Networking and the Semantic Web. Galway, Ireland.*

Avesani, P., Massa, P. & Tiella, R. (2005). A trust-enhanced recommender system application: Moleskiing, *Proceedings of the 2005 ACM symposium on Applied computing*, ACM New York, NY, USA, pp. 1589–1593.

Bedi, P. & Kaur, H. (2006). Trust based personalized recommender system, *INFOCOM Journal of Computer Science* **5**(1): 19–26.

Bedi, P., Kaur, H. & Marwaha, S. (2007). Trust based recommender system for the semantic web, *Proc. of the IJCAI07* pp. 2677–2682.

Ding, L., Kolari, P., Ganjugunte, S., Finin, T. & Joshi, A. (2005). Modeling and Evaluating Trust Network Inference, *Technical report*, MARYLAND UNIV BALTIMORE DEPT OF COMPUTER SCIENCE AND ELECTRICAL ENGINEERING.

Fu-guo, Z. & Sheng-hua, X. (2007). Topic-level Trust in Recommender Systems, *Management Science and Engineering, 2007. ICMSE 2007. International Conference on*, pp. 156–161.

Gal-Oz, N., Gudes, E. & Hendler, D. (2008). A Robust and Knot-Aware Trust-Based Reputation Model, *Proceedings of IFIPTM 2008 - Joint iTrust and PST Conferences on Privacy, Trust Management and Security*, Springer, pp. 167–182.

Golbeck, J. (2005). Semantic Web Interaction through Trust Network Recommender Systems, *Proc. of the ISWC05 Workshop on End User Semantic Web Interaction*, p. 2005.

Golbeck, J. (2006). Trust and nuanced profile similarity in online social networks, *Journal of Artificial Intelligence Research* .

Golbeck, J. & Hendler, J. (2004). Reputation network analysis for email filtering, *Proceedings of the First Conference on Email and Anti-Spam*, Vol. 44, pp. 54–58.

Grandison, T. & Sloman, M. (2002). Specifying and analysing trust for internet applications, *Proceedings of the 2nd IFIP Conference on E-Commerce, E-Business & E-Government (I3E)*, Kluwer Academic Publisher, Lisbon, pp. 145–Ű157.

Guha, R., Kumar, R., Raghavan, P. & Tomkins, A. (2004). Propagation of trust and distrust, *Proceedings of the 13th international conference on World Wide Web*, ACM Press New York, NY, USA, pp. 403–412.

Hwang, C. & Chen, Y. (2007). Using Trust in Collaborative Filtering Recommendation, *Lecture Notes in Computer Science* **4570**: 1052.

Jeh, G. & Widom, J. (2002). SimRank: a measure of structural-context similarity, *Proceedings of the eighth ACM SIGKDD international conference on Knowledge discovery and data mining*, ACM Press New York, NY, USA, pp. 538–543.

Jøsang, A. (2001). A Logic for Uncertain Probabilities, *International Journal of Uncertainty, Fuzziness and Knowledge-Based Systems* **9**(3): 279–311.

Jøsang, A. (2002). The consensus operator for combining beliefs, *Artificial Intelligence* **141**(1-2): 157–170.

Jøsang, A., Hayward, R. & Pope, S. (2006). Trust network analysis with subjective logic, *Proceedings of the 29th Australasian Computer Science Conference-Volume 48*, Australian Computer Society, pp. 85–94.

Jøsang, A. & Knapskog, S. J. (1998). A metric for trusted systems, *Proceedings of the 21st National Security Conference*, NSA.

Kim, Y., Le, M., Lauw, H., Lim, E., Liu, H. & Srivastava, J. (2008). Building a web of trust without explicit trust ratings, *Data Engineering Workshop, 2008. ICDEW 2008. IEEE 24th International Conference on*, pp. 531–536.

Kitisin, S. & Neuman, C. (2006). Reputation-based Trust-Aware Recommender System, *Securecomm and Workshops, 2006* pp. 1–7.

Lathia, N., Hailes, S. & Capra, L. (2008). Trust-Based Collaborative Filtering, *Proceedings of IFIPTM 2008 - Joint iTrust and PST Conferences on Privacy, Trust Management and Security*, Springer, pp. 119–134.

Massa, P. & Avesani, P. (2004). Trust-Aware Collaborative Filtering for Recommender Systems, *LECTURE NOTES IN COMPUTER SCIENCE* pp. 492–508.

Massa, P. & Avesani, P. (2006). Trust-aware Bootstrapping of Recommender Systems, *ECAI, Riva del Garda, Italy. Also available at: http://www. gnuband. org/papers/trustaware_bootstrapping_of_recommender_systems/[Last visit: 12.11. 2007]* .

Massa, P. & Bhattacharjee, B. (2004). Using Trust in Recommender Systems: An Experimental Analysis, *Trust Management: Second International Conference, ITrust 2004, Oxford, UK, March 29-April 1, 2004: Proceedings*, Springer.

Morselli, R., Bhattacharjee, B., Katz, J. & Marsh, M. (2007). Exploiting approximate transitivity of trust, *Broadband Communications, Networks and Systems, 2007. BROADNETS 2007. Fourth International Conference on*, pp. 515–524.

O'Donovan, J. & Smyth, B. (2005). Trust in recommender systems, *Proceedings of the 10th international conference on Intelligent user interfaces*, ACM New York, NY, USA, pp. 167–174.

Papagelis, M., Plexousakis, D. & Kutsuras, T. (2005). Alleviating the sparsity problem of collaborative filtering using trust inferences, *Proceedings of iTrust*, Springer, pp. 224–239.

Peng, T. & Seng-cho, T. (2009). iTrustU: a blog recommender system based on multi-faceted trust and collaborative filtering, *Proceedings of the 2009 ACM symposium on Applied Computing*, ACM New York, NY, USA, pp. 1278–1285.

Quercia, D., Hailes, S. & Capra, L. (2007). Lightweight Distributed Trust Propagation, *Data Mining, 2007. ICDM 2007. Seventh IEEE International Conference on*, pp. 282–291.

Tavakolifard, M., Herrmann, P. & Knapskog, S. (2009). Inferring trust based on similarity with tillit, *Proceedings of the Third IFIP WG 11.11 International Conference on Trust Management (IFIPTM 2009)*, Springer, West Lafayette, USA.

Tavakolifard, M., Knapskog, S. & Herrmann, P. (2008a). Cross-Situation Trust Reasoning, *Proceedings of The Workshop on Web Personalization, Reputation and Recommender Systems (WPRRSŠ08)*, IEEE Computer Society Press.

Tavakolifard, M., Knapskog, S. & Herrmann, P. (2008b). Trust Transferability Among Similar Contexts, *Proceedings of The 4th ACM International Workshop on QoS and Security for Wireless and Mobile Networks (Q2SWinet 2008)*, ACM.

Victor, P., Cornelis, C., De Cock, M. & Pinheiro da Silva, P. (2008). Gradual trust and distrust in recommender systems, *Fuzzy Sets and Systems* .

Victor, P., De Cock, M., Cornelis, C. & Teredesai, A. (2008). Getting Cold Start Users Connected in a Recommender SystemŠs Trust Network, *Computational Intelligence in Decision and Control 1* pp. 877–882.

Weng, J., Miao, C. & Goh, A. (2006). Improving collaborative filtering with trust-based metrics, *Proceedings of the 2006 ACM symposium on Applied computing*, ACM New York, NY, USA, pp. 1860–1864.

Yang, Y., Canberra, A., Brown, L., Wales, S., ADFA, A., Lewis, E. & Melbourne, V. (2002). W3 Trust Model: Evaluating Trust and Transitivity of Trust of Online Services, *International Conference on Internet Computing*, pp. 354–362.

Ziegler, C. & Golbeck, J. (2007). Investigating interactions of trust and interest similarity, *Decision Support Systems* **43**(2): 460–475.

Ziegler, C. & Lausen, G. (2004). Analyzing correlation between trust and user similarity in online communities, *Lecture notes in computer science* pp. 251–265.

12

An Information Filter for Intuitive and Simple Search

Sayaka Akioka[1], Hideo Fukumori[2] and Yoichi Muraoka[2]
[1] *The University of Electro-Communications*
Japan
[2] *Waseda University*
Japan

1.Introduction

Recent quick popularization of World Wide Web (WWW) has changed people's life; whenever people move into action, they probably go to the web first, and try to collect useful information. However, success and failure of this first step heavily relies on the queries they choose. That is, people will never run into any useful information without a set of expected keywords, which is a technical limitation of current information retrieval systems. In reality, many users find it difficult to form an appropriate set of queries to describe what exactly they are looking for.

In order to address this problem, this chapter proposes an information filter with the idea of kansei engineering. The approach expands the flexibility of an information filter, and has possibility to enable users to search items without specific queries, or helps users put their requirements into a concrete set of queries. The information filtering method described in this chapter does not necessarily provide "the very best one" result, however, promise to offer a user a certain set of "something like this" items. Our goal is to let users search information visually and sensuously, considering as many aspects as they need until they finally reach at the answer they were seeking, instead of helping users form a better set of queries.

"Kansei" is a Japanese vocabulary, and means psychological feeling or image of a product. Nagamachi founded kansei engineering as an activity to develop a new product by translating a customer's psychological needs and feeling (kansei) concerning it into design specifications (Nagamachi, 2006). Kansei engineering is widely used centering on the areas such as user interface (Berry et al., 2006; Klauser et al., 2007), music analysis (Kazama et al., 2006; Kamata et al., 2007), and virtual reality (Kaino et al., 2003).

Here, psychological feeling is often ambiguous, and hard to decide one solid expression for corresponding feeling. Therefore, kansei engineering often requires a questionnaire process in order to position a certain expression between two extreme impressions (for example, *large* and *small*), which is not a very appropriate way from the view of computational engineering. However, kansei engineering still has the potential to put flexibilities onto information retrieval or recommenders, if there exists a way to relate and position kansei expressions each other automatically, and map the relationships onto information on the web. Therefore, the rest of this chapter describes information filter as an application of kansei engineering including the methodology to replace the questionnaire process with more computational engineering way.

This chapter is organized as follows. Section 2 introduces kansei filter, and describes the methodology to build and apply kansei filter as information filter to WWW contents. In Section 3, we compared kansei filter with the conventional collaborative filter, and then we discuss the effect of kansei information filter in Section 4. Section 5 addresses related contributions regarding recommenders, and we conclude in Section 6.

2. Kansei Information Filter

A general methodology on application of kansei engineering to design activities is following.

1. Pick up kansei words regarding the vocabularies possibly related to the features or images of a target product. For example, if a designer of the product expects to give an impression such as *airly light*, one should pick up *heavy* and *light*.
2. Conduct questionnaires and let the examinees to grade the products in the measure of two extreme kansei words extracted in the previous step. For example, examinees are requested to locate the product somewhere between *light* and *heavy*, according to their impressions and images. Semantic differential is often used for the evaluation.
3. Based on the results through the questionnaires, a certain set of features and impressions is derived. The derivertives are feeded back to the product designer, and useful to be stocked as a part of the knowledge data base.
4. Repeat step 1 and step 3 as many as required, changing the set of kansei words and/or the design of the product if necessary. The set of steps repeats until the speculation of the product designer meets the results of the questionnaries.

The idea for kansei information filter, which is proposed in this chapter, is to utilize the knowledge database of kansei words as a part of information filter. More precisely, we employ the kansei database as an index of similarity of web documents or product descriptions. This section describes the details of kansei information filter as well as how to build up kansei database independent from questionnaires.

2.1 Kansei Map

Figure 1 is an example of kansei maps utilized in this chapter, and each document is scored according to these kansei maps for similarity measurements described in Section 2.2. In Figure 1, *wide* and *narrow* are the two extreme kansei words, and we call this map *wide-narrow* map. In order to generate kansei maps like the example shown in Figure 1, we execute a sequence of processes as follows.

1. Collect the web documents to process, and perform morphological analysis over the documents.
2. Extract adjectives, and find lexical and semantic synonyms, antonyms, and negatives utilizing dictionaries and/or other resources.
3. Relate extracted vocabularies and vocabularies from dictionaries each other, and build up kansei map candidates. Each set of related vocabularies becomes a kansei map candidate.

4. Match the kansei map candidates and kansei word definitions. The survival maps of the matching are adopted as information scoring base.

In the process above, we focus only on adjectives. As our purpose here is to build up kansei map, and kansei words express feeling or impression, so we simply rely only on adjectives and without loss of generality.

We also expand the level of classification from two levels to four levels. The original kansei word definition consists of pairs of two extreme vocabularies. Consequently, we match only the two extreme vocabulary pairs in step 4. However, in order to allow higher level of classification and flexibility, we fill the gap between the two extreme vocabularies with the help of lexical definitions.

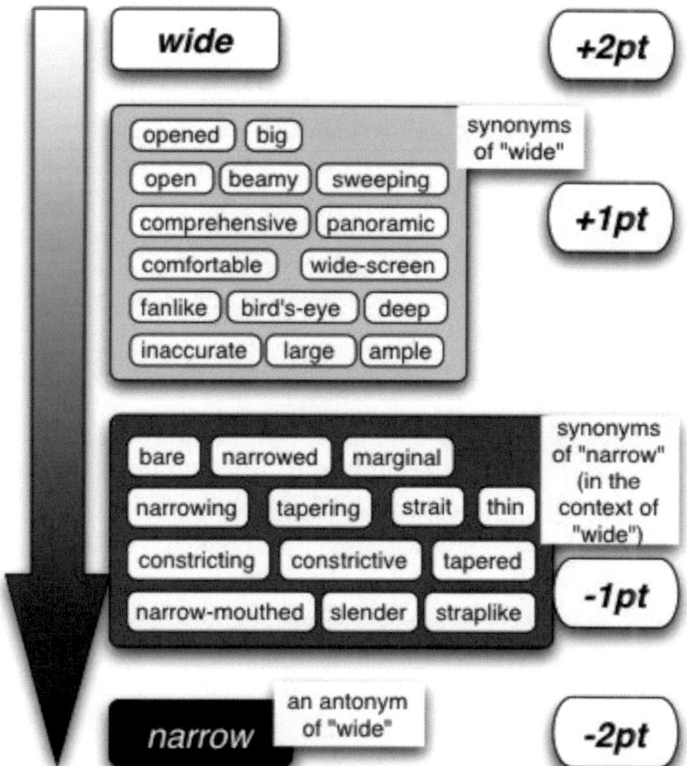

Fig. 1. An example of kansei map, and scoring according as similarity.

As shown in Figure 1, each kansei map classifies vocabularies into four levels according to direction and degree of expression on the kansei map. For example, in case of Figure 1, one opposite adjective "wide" scores two points, while the other opposite adjective "narrow" looses two points. Synonyms of "wide" scores one point, as those adjectives are semantically close to "wide". Similarly, synonyms of "narrow" loose one point, as these adjectives are semantically close to "narrow", but far from "wide".

2.1 Similarity Measurement

As a first step of the similarity measurement, we calculate information entropy for each document item. Let l be the score level on kansei map, and $l \in L = \{-2, -1, 1, 2\}$. We define information entropy of item x regarding scoring level l of map m (denoted as $H_{m,l}(x)$) as follows.

$$P_{m,l}(x,w) = \frac{n_x(m,l,w)}{n_x(m,l)} \tag{1}$$

$$H_{m,l}(x) = -\sum_{w} P_{m,l}(x,w) \log_2 P_{m,l}(x,w) \tag{2}$$

In equation (1), $n_x(m,l)$ represents total number of adjectives of level l on map m in the descriptions of item x, and $n_x(m,l,w)$ represents whether vocabulary w of level l on map m appears in the document item x or not. That is, $n_x(m,l,w)=1$ if vocabulary w appears, otherwise, $n_x(m,l,w)=0$.

If none of the vocabularies of level l on map m appears in the document x, $H_{m,l}(x)$ is defined as 0, as $P_{m,l}(x,w)=0$ for any vocabulary w. Although the definition is for descriptive purposes, this definition contains an intuitive sense. Under $P_{m,l}(x,w)=0$ for any vocabulary w at level l of map m, the item x has nothing to do with level l of map m. Therefore, the information entropy of the item x for level l of map m is also 0.

Once we define information entropy of items, mutual information is regarded as the measure of similarity. We denote mutual information between item x and y at level l on map m as $I_{m,l}(x;y)$. $I_{m,l}(x;y)$ is given as

$$I_{m,l}(x;y) = H_{m,l}(x) + H_{m,l}(y) - H_{m,l}(x,y) \tag{3}$$

Here, with adequately huge number of document items, the event of appearance of a vocabulary of a certain level on a certain map is consider to be random, and each event is independent each other. Therefore, joint entropy $H_{m,l}(x,y)$ is given as follows.

$$H_{m,l}(x,y) = H_{m,l}(x) \times H_{m,l}(y) \tag{4}$$

Now, note that $I_{m,l}(x;y)$ represents the similarity of item x and item y regarding the connectivity between items and map m at level l, however, does not represent the similarity between item x and item y itself. Larger $I_{m,l}(x;y)$ simply means item x and y relate to map m at level l with more similar level of connectivity. So, as a second stage, we consider similarity of items on the same map. We define the similarity of item x and item y on map m, denoted as $W_m(x,y)$, as

$$W_m(x,y) = \sum_{l \in L} s_l I_{m,l}(x;y) \tag{5}$$

where s_l represents the score at level l, shown in Figure 1. The situations $W_m(x,y)$ expresses are following.

- $W_m(x,y)=0$

  The two items have no relationship at any level of map m, or any meaningful relationship.

- $W_m(x,y)>0$

  The two items are similar and located in the positive area (around the original vocabulary or synonyms of the original vocabulary) in a large sense. If $W_m(x,y)$ is larger, the two items are plotted closer on the map.

- $W_m(x,y) < 0$
  The two items are similar and located in the negative area (around the antonyms or synonyms of the antonyms) in a large sense. If $W_m(x,y)$ is smaller, the two items are plotted closer on the map.

Finally, we consider the similarity between items across maps. We define the similarity of item x and item y, denoted as $W(x,y)$, as follows.

$$W(x,y) = \sum_{m \in M} |W_m(x,y)| \tag{6}$$

where M represents a set of kansei maps to consider. The larger $W(x,y)$ represents better similarity.

The contributions of the proposed algorithm are summarized as follows.

- Kansei map
  The vocabularies contained in the same kansei map comprehend the same context, semantic, and kansei. With kansei map, vocabularies are categorized into groups according to the mood the vocabulary has. For example, adjectives related to breadth are categorized into the same group.
- Scoring system
  The four-level scoring system direct vocabularies on a map according to the meaning the vocabulary has. For example, "wide" and "narrow" are recognized as a pair of opposite adjectives.
- Map level similarity
  The combination of mutual information and the scoring system vectorlizes documents ($W_m(x,y)$). The map level similarity not only measures the similarity between items, but also represents the mood (position on a kansei map) of the items.
- Map across similarity
  The map across similarity measure $W(x,y)$ allows cumulating as many maps as requested, but measures the similarity between items with only one measure.

3. Empirical Experiments

In this section, we examine kansei information filter through experiments with the actual data sets crawled from Yahoo! Shopping web services (Yahoo! Inc, 2009). We crawled the product data focusing on shoes, and extracted <summary> tags. A <summary> tag is defined at Yahoo! Product Search web service, and expected to contain a short description of the product. The XML document shown in Figure 2 is an example of the information that can be retrieved for a product item via Yahoo! Product Search web service.

3.1 Kansei filter construction

First, we processed morphological analysis over the 79,812 shoes products with the morphological analysis engine provided via LingPipe(Alas-I, Inc., 2009), for kansei map construction described in Section 2. In this experiment, we utilized Brown University Standard Corpus of Present-Day American English (Kucera et al., 1967) in Natural Language Toolkit (Loper et al., 2002; Natural Language Toolkit Projects, 2009), which is a well-utilized general-purpose corpus. After this first stage is completed, we obtained 91,093 kinds of adjectives.

Secondly, we referred the dictionary definitions to build up basic relationships among adjectives, and then matched those groups of adjectives with kansei word definitions by Nagamachi (Nagamachi, 1995). In the appendix of (Nagamachi, 1995), Nagamachi defined about 400 adjective pairs as kansei expressions. As lexical definitions, we utilized WordNet. WordNet defines words in its original fashion, different from general lexical definitions, but shares the basic idea with kansei engineering. WordNet categorizes words into sets of cognitive synonyms, called synsets, and each synset expresses a distinct concept. Synsets are connected each other based on conceptual semantic or lexical relations. We employed the definitions by WordNet in order to fill between the two extreme expressions with kansei engineering. Finally, we obtained a set of kansei maps with four levels of categorization, described in Section 2.


```
<Product type="Offer">
  <Offer ID="11085491">
    <Url>...</Url>
    <ProductName>...</ProductName>
    <Price>...</Price>
    <Thumbnail>...</Thumbnail>
    <ListImage>...</ListImage>
    <GridImage>...</GridImage>
    <Summary>
     These &lt;b&gt;Adidas&lt;/b&gt; AdiStar Trail 3
shoes have everything an athlete needs to stay on
their toes and in the game Stylish women&apos;s
running shoes are also durable This supportive
footwear is made to last
    </Summary>
    <Merchant id="1000264">...</Merchant>
    <Category>...</Category>
  </Offer>
</Product>
```


Fig. 2. An example for the product information available at Yahoo! Product Search web service.

4. Discussions

In this section, we take a close look on the representative four maps, which are hard-soft map, light-dark map, round-square map, and plain-fancy map. The expected effect for each map is as follows.

- Hard-soft map
  expressions for hardness of the materials, or taste of design.
- Light-dark map
  expressions for the colors of shoe products.

- Round-square map descriptions for the shape of toes.
- Plain-fancy map expressions for the overall impression, design, and concept of the shoe products.

Table 1 is the details of the four obtained maps. Each row represents each map, and each column represents the expression for each level respectively. The number in parentheses appears next to an adjective is the frequency of the appearance in the whole set of the product descriptions.

As shown in Table 1, both the synonyms of the original adjectives and the synonyms of the antonymous frequently appear in the descriptions as many times as, or even more frequently than the extreme expressions. This observation indicates that the information provider utilizes fine expressions to express the details or atmosphere of the products. That is, the simple matching method only with the extreme expressions causes the poor results such as missing the products with rich expressions, or failing to reflect the fine requirements by the users.

Even with the advantage of the maps shown in Table 1, the process of map production has a point to be improved. More specifically, some misplaced adjectives are observed from the view of the context expressed with the two extreme expressions, even though these adjectives are synonyms of the original adjectives or antonyms lexically. Better placement of adjectives will plot products more precisely on a map. However, the automatic way to eliminate those unsuitable expressions requires another evolution. Therefore, we reserve this improvement for the future work.

Original Adjective	Synonyms of the Original Adjective	Synonyms of the Antonymous Adjectives	Antonymous Adjective
hard(532)	ambitious(7), arduous(1), catchy(3), delicate(490), nasty(7), rocky(91), rugged(982), serious(339), tall(1087), troublesome(2), case-hardened(7), firm(529), unyielding(1), strong(347),indulgent(53), bad(48)	compressible(7), cushioned(12063), spongy(13), velvet(51), mellow(3), dull(9), gentle(77), little(494), low(2930), tender(22), mild(153), light(1289), easy(4908)	soft(7986)
light(1289)	lightweight(8490), airy(142), buoyant(30), pale(29), powdery(1), ablaze(11), bright(115), incandescent(3), luminescent(3), white(5800), loose(143), pure(396), easy(4908), ill(1), thin(921), temperate(4), frivolous(2), shallow(10)	black(7881), dusky(1), darkish(7)	dark(735)
round(4101)	full(7458)	squared(20),	square(431)

		aboveboard(2), wholesome(3), direct(205), conventional(43)	
plain(215)	obvious(9), bare(124), dry(1852), simple(835), solid-colored(1), pure(396), direct(205), unadorned(4), unattractive(1)	baroque(9), busy(108), dressy(402), elaborate(24), fanciful(11), fantastic(150), lacy(1), puff(1)	fancy(55)

Table 1. The four representative kansei maps. Each row represents each kansei map, and the number in the parentheses is the frequency of appearance across the product descriptions.

Figure 3 (case (a)) and Figure 4 (case (b)) are the plots of similarity measures on a particular item versus the other 49 items respectively. Figure 5 (case (a)) and Figure 6 (case (b)) are the plots of the same similarity measures on the same centering item versus the other 49 items, but in the different form. In both cases, if the absolute value is larger, the two items are more similar. At the same time, the positive similarity represents that the two items are similar in the flavor of one side of the map, while the negative similarity represents that those two items are similar in the flavor of the other side of the map, as described in Section 2.

Case (a) and case (b) are contrasting cases. For case (b), the plots are essentially located in the negative part, with a few exceptional cases. This is the result of the fact that the center item is located in the negative part of the map, and the other items are also similar in the same side of the map, or have no relationship with the center item. On the other hand, in case (a), the plots are distributed from the negative part to the positive part. As a matter of fact, the center item of case (a) is one of the exceptional in case (b). This type of similarity distribution should not appear logically, as this item has similarity equally to the other items across the map, which is not reasonable. The only reason for this observation is that the description for this center item contains expressions for all the levels of the map equally. So, if the description is correctly one-sided, the plot looks similar to case (a), and many of the 50 items actually showed this characteristic. The counter methodology for the cases such as case (b) is planned as future work.

5. Related Work

To the best of our knowledge, this is the first effort to apply kansei engineering to information filter. However, there are similar approaches utilizing WordNet applicable to information filter, as a contradictory approach to simple lexical mapping. The recent contributions are as follows. Varelas et al. propose an information retrieval model based on the semantic similarity among documents (Varelas et al., 2005). Sim developed information filtering agent utilizing the ontology provided by WordNet (Sim et al., 2004). Cao et al. built a dependency model relies on both co-occurrences of terms and definitions in WordNet (Cao et al., 2005). Zhang et al. presented an algorithm for noun phrase recognition, utilizing WordNet as well as other resources (Zhang et al., 2007).

The definitive difference between WordNet approach and kansei engineering approach is the underlying policy on map constructions. Cognitive synonyms (synsets) defined by WordNet are vocabularies related conceptually or lexically. That is, WordNet utilizes sense-to-sense and word-to-word relationships in order to break down the limitation of conventional lexical

mapping. Here, if there are two vocabularies sharing a hypernim or superordinate concept, the two expressions are recognized as sense-to-sense related vocabularies.
Kansei filter, proposed in this paper, stands one step ahead in the meaning of expression of concept. Our contribution aims to provide the methodology to bring more conceptual approach into information search or recommenders with kansei engineering. Kansei word definitions are pairs of opposite expressions. Especially for adjectives on valuations, kansei definitions for these adjectives are always pairs of an adjective and its negative, instead of its antonym. This feature of kansei engineering enables to construct more specific relationships, and boosts up the quality of information filtering.

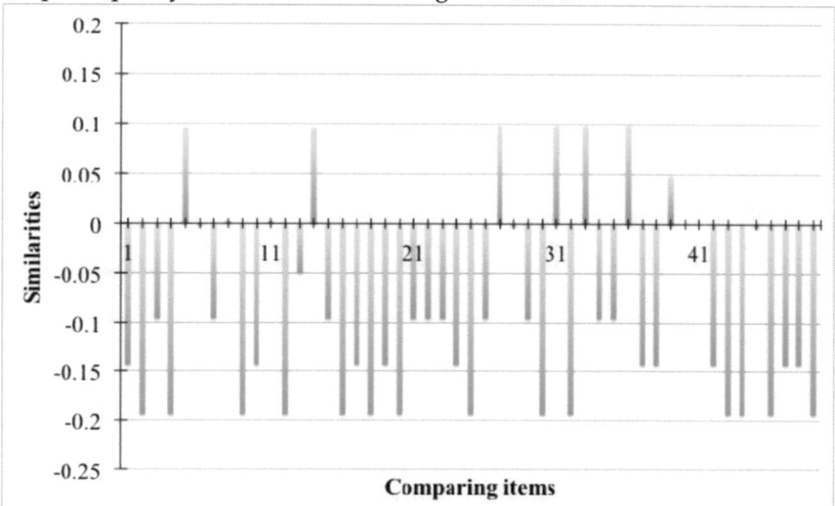

Fig. 3. Similarity measures with the other 49 items, centering on a particular item (case (a)).

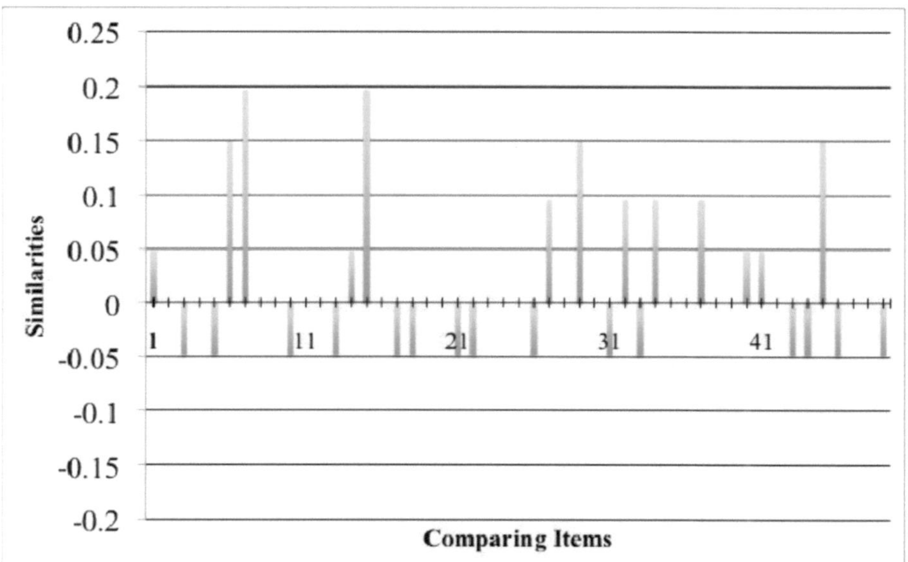

Fig. 4. Similarity measures with the other 49 items, centering on a particular item (case (b)).

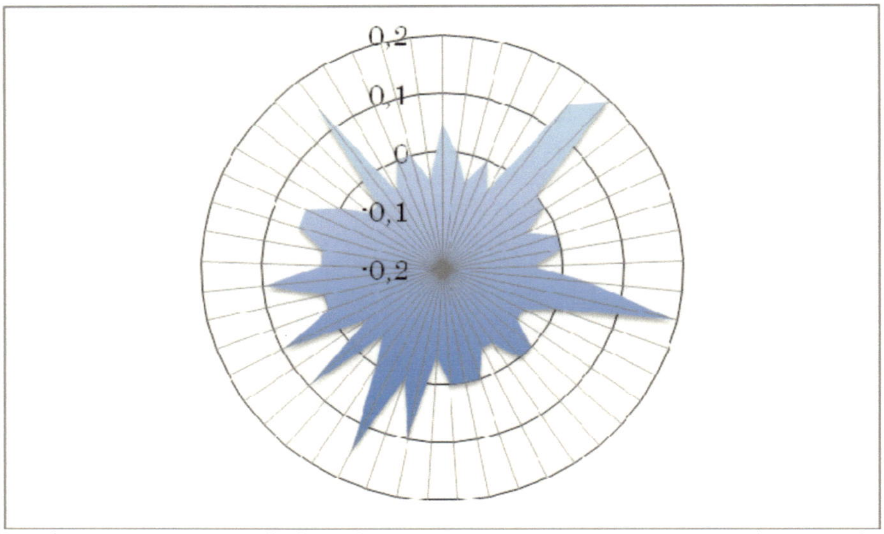

Fig. 5. Similarity measures with the other 49 items, centering on a particular item (case (a)). The same data set with Figure 3, however, in another form of plots.

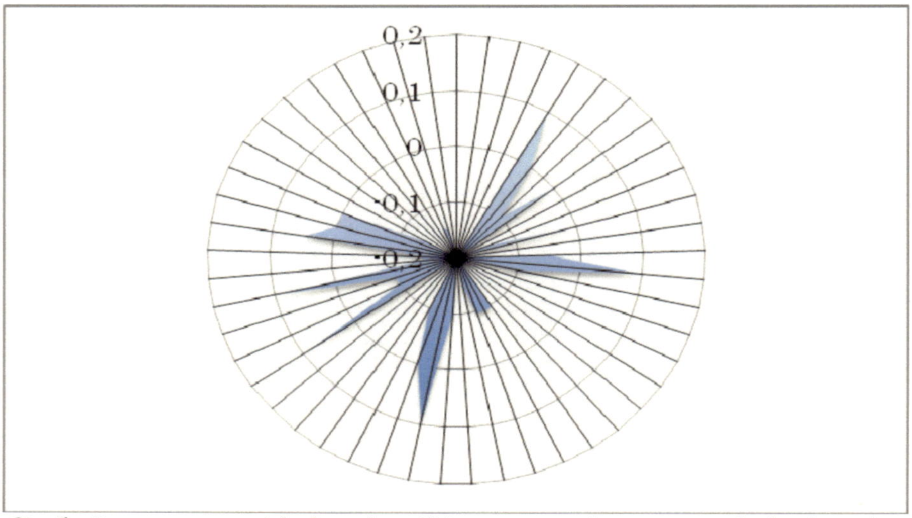

Fig. 6. Similarity measures with the other 49 items, centering on a particular item (case (b)). The same data set with Figure 4, however, in another form of plots.

6. Conclusions and Future Work

Recent quick spread of web services has change the style of information retrieving, and caused the explosive amount of information provided. Such situation requests a certain skill to obtain information effectively. Especially, ambiguous search is one of the major demands, however, such a service is known as one of the technical challenges.

In this paper, we proposed an information filter employed kansei engineering concept, in order to enable flexible filtering. Through the experiments with the actual data collected on the web, we verified that the concept of kansei filtering perform reasonably.
One of the unsolved problems is the methodology for the evaluation. Even though this paper successfully represented the flexibility and usefulness of information filter with kansei engineering, we have no clear way to measure the degree of satisfaction of users. The ideal benchmark set should be a set of data, such as product descriptions, evaluations by the users for the products, the history of purchases, and so on. We keep considering this problem for better justification.

7. References

Alias-I, Inc. (2009). LingPipe. http://www.alias-i.com/lingpipe

Berry, R.; Naemura, M.; Kobayashi, Y.; Tada, M.; Inoue, N.; Pisan, Y. & Edmonds, E. (2006). An Interface Test-bed for 'Kansei' Filters using the Touch Designer Visual Programming Environment. *Proceedings of 7thAustralian User Interface Conference (AUIC2006),* Vol. 50, pp. 173 - 176, ISSN 1-920682-32-5, Hobart, Australia, January 2006, Australian Computer Society, Darlinghurst, Australia

Cao, G.; Nie, J.-Y. &Bai, J. (2005). Integrating Word Relationships Into Language Models. *Proceedings of 28th Annual International ACM Conference on Research and Development in Information Retrieval (SIGIR2005),* pp. 298 - 305, ISSN 1-59593-034-5, Salvador, Braszil, August 2005, ACM, New York, USA

Fellbaum, C. (1998). *WordNet: An Electric Lexical Database,*ISBN 978-0262061971, May 1998, MIT Press, Cambridge, USA

Kaino, H. & Hagiwara, M. (2003). 3-D Virtual Space Creation System Reflecting User's Emotion by Interactive Evolutionary Method. *Proceedings of the Second International Conference on Entertainment Computing (ICEC2003),* pp. 1 - 6, Pittsburgh, USA, May 2003, Carnegie Mellon University, Pittsburgh, USA

Kamata, M. & Furukawa, K. (2007). Three Types of Viewers' Favourite Music Videos. *Proceedings of the International Conference on Advances in Computer Entertainment Technology (ACE2007),* pp. 196 - 199, ISBN 978-1-59593-640-0, Salzburg, Austria, June 2007, ACM, New York, USA

Kazama, M. & Shiizuka, H. (2006). Music Analysis in Consideration of Feelings. *Proceedings of 2006 International Conference on Game Research and Development (CyberGames2006),* pp.117 - 120, ISBN 86905-901-7, Perth, Australia, December 2006, ACM, New York, USA

Klauser, K. & Walker, V. (2007). It's About Time: An Affective and Desirable Alarm Clock. *Proceedings of 2007 International Conference on Designing Pleasure Products and Interfaces (DPPI2007),* pp. 407 - 422, ISBN 978-1-59593-942-5, Helsinki, Finland, August 2007, ACM, New York, USA

Kucera, H. & Francis, W. N. (1967). *Computational Analysis of Present-Day American English,*ISBN 978-0870571053, June 1967, Brown University Press, Providence, USA

Loper, E. & Bird, S. (2002). NLTK: The Natural Language Toolkit. *Proceedings of the ACL-02Workshop on Effective Tools and Methodologies for Teaching Natural Language Processing and Computational Linguistics,* Vol. 1, pp. 62 - 69, Philadelphia, USA, July 2002, ACL, Morristown, USA

Miller, G. A.; Fellbaum, C.; Tengi, R.; Wakefield, P.; Poddar, R.; Langone, H. & Haskell, B. (2009). WordNet: A Lexical Database for the English Language. http://wordnet.princeton.edu/

Nagamachi, M. (1995). *Kanseikougaku no Ohanashi,* ISBN 978-4-542-90186-5, July 1995, Japanese Standards Association, Tokyo, Japan (in Japanese)

Nagamachi, M. (2006). Kansei Engineering and Rough Sets Model. *Proceedings of 5th International Conference on Rough Sets and Current Trends in Computing (RTCS2006),* Vol. 4259, pp. 27 - 37, ISBN 3-540-47693-8, Kobe, Japan, November 2006, Springer, Berlin, Germany

Natural Language Toolkit Projects. (2009). Natural Language Toolkit. http://nltk.sourceforge.net/index.php/Main_Page

Sim, K. M. (2004). Toward an Ontology-enhanced Information Filtering Agent. *ACM SIGMOD Record,* Vol. 33, Issue 1, pp. 95 - 100, ISBN 0163-5808, March 2004, ACM, New York, USA

Yahoo! Inc. (2009). Documentation for Yahoo! Shopping Web Services: Product Search. http://developer.yahoo.com/shopping/V3/productSearch.html

Varelas, G.; Voutsakis, E. &Raftopoulou, P. (2005). Semantic Similarity Methods in WordNet and their Application to Information Retrieval on the Web. *Proceedings of 7th ACM International Workshop on Web Information and Data Management (WIDM2005),* pp. 10 - 16, ISBN 978-1595931948, Bremen, Germany, November 2005, ACM, New York, USA

Zhang, W.; Liu, S.; Yu, C.; Sun, C.; Liu, F. &Meng, W. (2007). Recognition and Classification of Noun Phrases in Queries for Effective Retrieval. *Proceedings of 16th Conference on Information and Knowledge Management (CIKM2007),* pp. 711 - 720, ISBN 978-1-59593-803-9, Lisbon, Portugal, November 2007, ACM, New York, USA

13

Skipping-Based Collaborative Recommendations inspired from Statistical Language Modeling

Geoffray Bonnin, Armelle Brun and Anne Boyer
LORIA – Nancy Université
France

1. Introduction

Due to the almost unlimited resource space on the web, efficient search engines and recommender systems have become a key element for users to find resources corresponding to their needs. Recommender systems aim at helping users in this task by providing them some pertinent resources according to their context and their profiles, by applying various techniques such as statistical and knowledge discovery algorithms.

Recommender systems are usually classified into content-based recommendation and collaborative filtering. Content-based recommendations (Balabanović & Shoham, 1997; Zhang et al., 2002) are performed by identifying resources similar to the ones a user appreciated, based on their content. One of the main limitations of these systems is that the efficiency is highly dependent on the domain. Indeed, it is very efficient for textual resources but not for resources such as pictures, videos, etc. Another limitation is that only resources similar to already rated resources can be recommended. Collaborative Filtering (Das et al., 2007; Goldberg et al., 1992), consists in recommending to users resources other users with similar tastes liked in the past. The content of the resources does not need to be considered, and the aforementioned limitations are not present. However, collaborative filtering has its own limitations, the most important being data sparsity and cold start (Park et al., 2006; Schein et al., 2002). Most of recommender systems only use ratings to predict if a user will appreciate some resource, and to provide recommendation lists by selecting the highest ratings predicted, or the most similar resources to resources a user already rated (Adomavicius & Tuzhilin, 2005). The quality of the recommendations may thus be enhanced by using other criteria.

Such a criterion is the context, which can be geographical, meteorological, social, cultural, etc. For instance, a user may like to eat his favorite dish at home but not in a restaurant, or at lunch but not at breakfast. The importance of using context for recommendations have been studied on a movie rating dataset in (Adomavicius et al., 2005). Among with the ratings, users were asked when, where and with whom the movie was seen. Results showed that using a combined form of a reduction-based collaborative filtering method to include contextual information in the model, the accuracy could be significantly outperformed compared to a standard memory-based collaborative filtering algorithm.

The order in which users consult or consume resources, which is referred to as sequences of consultations, is such a contextual criterion. For instance, one usually must have seen the first episodes of a television series to appreciate the last ones. In this chapter we focus on this particular form of context. The question is thus: how to take advantage of sequences to recommend the best possible resource?

The appropriateness of considering sequences is domain dependent: for instance, it seems of little help in domains such as on-line movie stores, in which user transactions are barely sequential; however it is especially appropriate for domains such as web navigation, which has a sequential structure. This was shown in (Zimdars et al., 2001), in which several techniques are used to transform sequences into a representation that can be used by traditional collaborative filtering algorithms. This representation makes the resulting model almost equivalent to a Markov model. A decision tree model has been used to perform tests on a browsing dataset. Results show a clear enhancement of the results using a sequential configuration instead of a classical collaborative filtering configuration.

Predicting future surfing paths is useful for many purposes such as web page research (Tan & Kumar, 2002), web page recommendations (Nakagawa & Mobasher, 2003), latency reduction (Schechter et al., 1998) or arrangement of the links among a website (Chi et al., 1998). That is why it has been widely studied. Such studies do not necessarily include ratings, for instance sequential patterns (Nakagawa & Mobasher, 2003) or Markov models (Borges & Levene, 2005; Deshpande & Karypis, 2004; Eirinaki & Vazirgiannis, 2007; Pitkow & Pirolli, 1999), although some other do (Trousse, 2000).

Web predictive modeling usually attempts to provide a tradeoff between accuracy, space and time complexity, and coverage (Deshpande & Karypis, 2004; Pitkow & Pirolli, 1999). However, few of these models possess features able to provide robustness to noise. Noise can occur when users do navigation mistakes, parallel navigations, open pages in new tabs, return to previous pages, etc. The amount of noise may vary depending on the domain. For instance, a website designed by an experimented webmaster usually induces less navigation mistakes than personal web pages within a web hosting service.

A study of statistical language modeling allowed us to notice that several similarities exist between web navigation and natural language (Boyer & Brun, 2007). Many statistical language models have been studied in the past decades with success, and most of them take into account the order of the words. We thus propose to draw inspiration from these models to compute recommendations.

We propose a new model inspired from the n-gram skipping model of statistical language modeling (Goodman, 2001) to compute recommendations in the frame of web navigation. This model exhibits several advantages: (1) It is robust to noise, (2) It has both a low time and a low space complexity while providing a full coverage, (3) Weighting schemes are used to alleviate the importance of distant resources, (4) A significant improvement of accuracy compared to state of the art models is provided.

In the first section, we will address the general issue of applying statistical language modeling to web navigation. The second section presents our Skipping-Based Recommender or SBR model. Tractability is then discussed in the third section, and robustness to noise in the fourth section. Last, we conclude the chapter.

2. Modeling Web Navigation as a Natural Language

In this section, we provide a detailed study of web navigation and natural language to explicit their similarities. We first provide an overview of web predictive modeling and natural language modeling. We then show similarities and differences between both domains, and present a discussion about which statistical language models seem to be the most appropriate for web navigation, and which adaptations seem necessary to maximize their efficiency for this domain.

2.1 Web Predictive Modeling

Recommending resources to users in the frame of web navigation is one of the most important tasks of web usage mining. Web usage mining can be defined as "the process of applying data mining techniques to the discovery of usage patterns from web data" (Srivastava et al., 2000). In this domain, recommending resources to users is referred to as predictive user modeling (Nakagawa & Mobasher, 2003) or predictive modeling (Pitkow & Pirolli, 1999).
The data processed usually consists in two sets: a set of distinct resources $R = \{r_1, ..., r_{|R|}\}$ and a set of sessions $S = \{s_1, ..., s_{|S|}\}$ where each s_i is a sequence of resources from R, *i.e.* $s_i = (\rho^i_1, ..., \rho^i_{|s_i|})$ with $\rho^i_j \in R$.
Two approaches are predominant: sequential patterns and Markov models. We thus present them in this section.

2.1.1 Sequential Patterns

One way of exploiting the order of past actions to predict future ones, is the use of sequential patterns (Agrawal & Srikant, 1995; Lu et al., 2005), which is the sequential form of association rules. Association Rules have been initially used for mining supermarket basket (Agrawal et al., 1993) to extract information about purchased items dependencies. An association rule is made up of items commonly purchased together in a transaction, where a transaction is a set of items.
An association rule is an expression of the form $X \rightarrow Y$, where X and Y are sets of items. X is called the antecedent and Y the consequent. An association rule means that, in one transaction, when users have purchased all resources in X then there is a high probability that they will purchase Y. Using association rules in the frame of web usage modeling thus enables to take into account non-ordered sets of resources in the history. Sequential patterns are more constrained than association rules due to the order taken into account. They thus represent more accurate information about user behavior. The sequences considered can be ordered lists of sets of resources (*e.g.* $(\{a,b\},\{c,d,e\})$). However in this chapter, we only focus on sequences of single resources (*e.g.* (a,b,c,d,e)).
Usually, the consequents considered in sequential patterns have a size of 1 (Nakagawa & Mobasher, 2003). So, a sequential pattern can be denoted by $X \circ Y$, where $X \circ Y$ is the concatenation of X and Y, X is a sequential antecedent of any size, and Y a consequent of size 1.
Both models are first built by browsing a training corpus and counting the sets of resources or sequences of resources. Then, during the recommendation step, all possible antecedents in current user's navigation history are compared to the antecedents in the model. If some antecedents match, then the corresponding consequents are recommended. However, several antecedents of different sizes may match the history, which raises the question of combining the rules. A score can be assigned to each consequent according to each corresponding matching antecedent. This can be done in several ways:

- Maximum confidence policy: only the rule having the highest confidence is used (Sarwar et al., 2000; Wang et al., 2005);
- Sum policy: the sum of the confidences is computed and associated to the corresponding consequents. Then, the consequent having the highest value is recommended (Kim & Kim, 2003);

- Maximum length policy: the rules having the longer antecedent are used to provide the recommendations (Nakagawa & Mobasher, 2003). This scheme is analogous to the all-k^{th}-order Markov model (*cf.* next section). It can be combined with maximum confidence policy or sum policy.

There are two types of sequential patterns: closed and open (Mobasher, 2007). Closed sequential patterns (Jianyong et al., 2007) identify contiguous sequences, while open sequential patterns (Ayres et al., 2002) identify non contiguous sequences. Looking for open sequences of unlimited sizes induces a huge amount of combinations. So the step of pattern discovery has to limit the size of the patterns to discover. Thus a sliding window with a fixed size is usually used during the pattern discovery step as well as during the recommendation step. However, the time complexity induced is still high. As they induce less combinations, the time complexity of closed sequential patterns is lower, but still high.
Space complexity can be reduced by integrating only the rules with a high *support* and *confidence* in the model. This was already the case for association rules, and was coped using the Apriori algorithm, which is an incremental algorithm (Agrawal et al., 1993). This algorithm has first been adapted to sequential patterns by (Srikant & Agrawal, 1996) and is referred to the Generalized Sequential Pattern algorithm or GSP algorithm. It is based on incremental pruning of low support and confidence patterns. Given a set of sessions $S = \{s_1, ..., s_{|S|}\}$, the support of a pattern $X \circ Y$ is defined as:

$$supp(X \circ Y) = |\{\sigma \in S | X \circ Y \subseteq \sigma\}|$$

where each σ is a subsequence of size D in S. The confidence of the sequential pattern $X \circ Y$ is defined as:

$$conf(X \circ Y) = \frac{supp(X \circ Y)}{supp(X)}$$

The algorithm first counts all sequences of size 1, and prunes the less frequent ones. It then builds sequences of size 2 using the remaining sequences of size 1, computes the corresponding counts and prunes the less frequent sequences. The algorithm continues until the sequences reach some maximum length. The supports thresholds used are usually the same whatever is the length of the considered sequence.
Selecting high confidence and support rules induces a lower space complexity and a higher accuracy; however, it induces a lower coverage of longer patterns too. Indeed, although a recommendation can always be provided using sequential patterns of size 1 (antecedent of size 0 and consequent of size 1), selecting few rules induces that longer antecedent match more rarely the previous user actions (Nakagawa & Mobasher, 2003).
In (Nakagawa & Mobasher, 2003), an empirical study comparing association rules, closed and open sequential patterns is provided. Results show that association rules and open sequential patterns are more suitable for short sessions and sites with a high degree of connectivity, while closed sequential patterns are more suitable for longer sessions. However the experiments have been done using small window sizes (3 and 4), and it is possible that higher window sizes lead to a different conclusion.

2.1.2 Markov models

Markov chains (Rabiner, 1989) model relationships between resources based on an independence assumption between past states and the present state. In the frame of web navigation they are used to predict the next resource according to the present state (the k previously

browsed resources), which is referred to as Markov models of order k or k^{th}-order Markov models. Although simple, Markov models provide surprisingly accurate recommendations. Markov models are built the same way sequential patterns are, *i.e.* by browsing a training corpus and counting sequences of resources of size $k+1$. The recommendation step is similar to the one of sequential patterns too: the previous actions are compared to the states in the model, and if some state matches, then the corresponding resource is recommended.
The use of Markov models usually involves a tradeoff between accuracy and coverage (Pitkow & Pirolli, 1999). Coverage is the percentage of cases where a state matching current history can be found in the model to recommend a resource. By pruning the less frequent elements, a better precision can usually be reached; however, the more elements are pruned, the less matching histories can be found during the recommendation step, which results in a lower coverage. Notice that contrary to sequential patterns, the number of possible states is low enough to perform a straightforward pruning, after having performed the training step.
Another way to enhance the accuracy is to increase the value of k. Indeed, a state having a higher length contains more information about user's past actions. However, above some value it becomes difficult to find a large enough training data to build the model. If the training dataset is too small, the resulting model will cover fewer cases and may even provide a lower accuracy; if a large enough training data can be found, the model may have a too high space complexity. That is why the length of the states is usually low.
One way to provide both accuracy and coverage is to use various Markov models having various orders. For example, one can try to provide a recommendation using a Markov model of order 3, and if no matching history can be found, try a Markov model of order 2, and so on, until a recommendation can be provided. In the worst case, a Markov model of order 0 is used, which corresponds to the overall probability of one single resource, without considering previous resources. Using such a scheme, a full coverage can be reached, while providing a good accuracy in the recommendations. This scheme is called the all-k^{th}-order Markov model (Pitkow & Pirolli, 1999), and is one of the best performing predictive models of the state-of-the-art. Notice that under the same pruning conditions, it is similar to closed sequential patterns.
Several studies have been done to cope with space complexity. In (Deshpande & Karypis, 2004), three pruning schemes are used to alleviate the state complexity: a support pruning scheme in which the same threshold is used for all of the Markov models, a confidence pruning scheme in which states are discarded if the difference of probability between the two most prominent resources is not statistically significant and an error pruning scheme using a validation dataset. (Borges & Levene, 2005) propose to transform first-order Markov models into a single model representing Markov models of variable orders by using cloning operations. This lowers time and space complexity while providing a full coverage and a good accuracy.
Instead of trying to deal with tradeoffs between accuracy, space and time complexity and coverage, some studies simply combine Markov models with some standard recommendation models to enhance the precision of the recommendations. In (Trousse, 2000), a case-based model is used to predict users' navigation behavior. The main feature of the model is the inclusion of past sequences in the cases, which is referred to as time-extended situations. Two sequential features are used to represent the cases. The first one corresponds to the last three browsed pages. The second is the sequence of the past pages having a high implicit rating. The main drawback of such a model is the coverage. Indeed, using the last three browsed pages is similar to the present states of a Markov model of order 3. As said previously, in such a case the number of possible states is generally high, and usually results in a low coverage. Besides,

a maximum coverage of 50% is reached in their experimentations. In (Eirinaki & Vazirgiannis, 2007), a PageRank-based model that includes a usage based personalization vector has been experimented. The personalization vector used is similar to a Markov model of order 1 whose transition values are computed according to websites' actual structures. Two variants of the model are put forward. The first one is called *l*-UPR (localized Usage-based PageRank) and consists in using current user's sessions to compute the personalization vector. The second is called *h*-UPR (hybrid Usage-based PageRank) and is a combination of the UPR model with a standard Markov model. In such a configuration, recommendations are based both on current users' usage data and actual website structure.

2.2 Statistical Language Modeling

The issue of Language Modeling is to compute the probability of a word w_i given its history $h = (w_1, ..., w_{i-1})$. The data processed usually consists in two sets: a set of distinct words called the vocabulary $V = \{v_1, ..., v_{|V|}\}$ and a set of sentences $S = \{s_1, ..., s_{|S|}\}$ where $s_i = (w^i_1, ..., w^i_{|s_i|})$ with $w^i_j \in V$. For complexity and feasibility reasons, the vocabulary is usually previously fixed.

As too long histories are computationally intractable, all existing statistical language modeling techniques assume some form of independence among different portions of the data. This results in approximated probabilities which can be calculated statistically using a training data (Rosenfeld, 2000). Surprisingly, statistical techniques have been shown to definitely perform better than linguistic rule-based techniques (Banko & Brill, 2001; Fleischman et al., 2003; Och & Ney, 2001).

The two predominant statistical models are the n-gram model and the trigger model, which are presented in the following.

2.2.1 n-gram model with skipping

Markov models are also used in the domain of statistical language modeling, in which they are referred to as n-gram models (an n-gram model is similar to a Markov model of order $n-1$). n-grams even represent the cornerstone of statistical language modeling (Rosenfeld, 2000).

As for web usage mining, in practice, $n = 3$ or 4, rarely 5. As well, the coverage problem is present too. An experiment performed in the 1970s by IBM puts forward this phenomenon. In this experiment, a text containing one thousand distinct words (the vocabulary) was divided into a training set of $1,500,000$ words and a test set of $300,000$ words. Then a trigram model built on the training set only covered 77% of the test set.

Many techniques have been used to enhance their efficiency, among which smoothing, clustering, mixture, etc. (Goodman, 2001). One of these improvements is skipping and is based on the fact that the larger the n-grams, the less matching histories can be found (due to the size of the training dataset). Skipping simply consists in not considering a resource: the resource is skipped. For example, given the sequence (a, b, x, y, z, c, d) and $n = 3$, instead of considering only contiguous raw triplets as (a, b, x) or (y, z, c) (as standard n-gram models), skipping allows to also consider triplets as (a, x, d), (a, b, c) or (b, c, d).

There are two ways of using skipping: by interpolating submodels (Goodman, 2001), and by merging the counts.

- Interpolation of submodels

The first way of using skipping consists in interpolating skipping submodels. For instance, the probability of a word w_i given the history h can be given by the following equation:

$$P(w_i|h) = \alpha P(w_i|w_{i-2}, w_{i-1}) + \beta P(w_i|w_{w-3}, w_{i-1}) + \gamma P(w_i|w_{i-3}, w_{i-2}) \quad (1)$$

where $0 \leqslant \alpha \leqslant 1, 0 \leqslant \beta \leqslant 1, 0 \leqslant \gamma \leqslant 1$ and $\alpha + \beta + \gamma = 1$. Using such a scheme thus allows to handle an over probability of a 4-gram-like model using trigram models, and to find more matching histories than would find a raw 4-gram model. The configuration corresponding to $P(w_i|w_{i-3}, w_{i-2})$ is also known as a distance-2 trigram, *i.e.* a long-distance n-grams with $n = 2$. Such models were studied in (Huang et al., 1993) and did not provide significant improvements. In (Goodman, 2001) however, it has been shown that skipping of trigrams (skipping involving 3 elements) represents a good technique to use if the training data is small. The interpolation of submodels has the advantage of allowing an accurate weighting of the respective skipping configurations. Indeed, as separate submodels are built, it is possible to estimate the importance and usefulness of each skipping configuration on the recommendation process. The major drawback of interpolating submodels is that it implies a larger number of n-grams. This last problem becomes worse when considering an even larger history: the larger the history, the larger the number of submodels.

- Merging the counts

The second way of using skipping is to merge all skipped n-grams occurrences so that they are all stored in the same list. This has the advantage of lowering the space complexity. For instance, given the training sequence (a, x, b, c, a, b, y, c), it is possible to detect three occurrences of the trigram (a, b, c). Such counts can then be stored in the same trigram counts in one single list. However, once stored in the list, it is impossible to determine if a n-gram has often been encountered in a contiguous configuration, or if it was almost always encountered in another particular skipping configuration. The interpolation of mixed submodels thus represents a more accurate modeling.

Another advantage of merging counts is that it allows some skipped n-grams of the model to be used by other skipping configurations. For example, given a trigram (a, b, c). It is possible that this trigram is found several times in some parts of the training data together with some noise resources x_i between a and b: (a, x_i, b, c). Then, when making recommendations, it is possible that a and b are found in the history before some other noise resource y: (a, b, y). In that case, during the training step, skipping is performed on the second resource (x_i) whereas during the recommendation step it is performed on the third (y), and the resource c can be recommended, which is not possible using the interpolation presented above. This feature is interesting because it induces a better coverage; however it represents a less accurate modeling of the data.

2.2.2 Trigger model

One of the first introduction of trigger models is (Rosenfeld, 1994). It was designed based on the observation that some information exists beyond the usual scope of contiguous n-grams. Trigger models are made up of highly correlated pairs of words, the first one being the trigger, and the second one the triggered word.

The selection of the trigger pairs is usually performed using the mutual information that measures the quantity of information provided by a trigger word A to a triggered word B. It is usually evaluated as follows:

$$MI(A,B) = p(A,B)\log\frac{p(B|A)}{p(B)} + p(A,\overline{B})\log\frac{p(\overline{B}|A)}{p(\overline{B})} + p(\overline{A},B)\log\frac{p(B|\overline{A})}{p(B)} + p(\overline{A,B})\log\frac{p(\overline{B}|\overline{A})}{p(\overline{B})} \quad (2)$$

where A denotes the presence of A, $\overline{A}$ denotes the absence of A, $P(A)$ the probability of A, $p(A,B)$ the probability that A and B are found together and $p(B|A)$ the conditional probability of B given A. This selection is usually performed using a fixed size sliding window.

Once the triggers have been selected, they are used to refine n-gram models (Chen & Chan, 2003; Rosenfeld & Huang, 1992). However, several triggers may match the history and have to be combined. This can be done in several ways that provide similar results : choosing only the trigger pair having the highest mutual information, adding the mutual information values of the trigger pairs, etc. (Rosenfeld & Huang, 1992).

As well, the way triggers are integrated in the n-gram model has to be determined. This can be done by using an interpolation, by enhancing the probabilities of the corresponding n-gram when a word is triggered, etc. (Rosenfeld & Huang, 1992).

Such models usually take into account only relationships between two words, although they can be applied to longer triggers, which could lead to more accurate models (for the same reason a higher order Markov model is more accurate). In (Chen & Chan, 2003) a model called the multi-word trigger model is studied. In this model, the triggering elements consist in pairs of words and here again, only the most correlated triplets of words are integrated using the mutual information. However, this did not lead to significant improvements.

2.3 Web navigation and Natural Language Similarities

In several points, web navigation predictive modeling is similar to statistical language modeling. This is particularly obvious when focusing on the respective corpus features.

- Words can be considered as being similar to resources (ignoring the content, just considering them as identifiers);
- Statistical language models use a vocabulary made up of words which can be viewed as being similar to the set of distinct resources of the web or a website.
- A sentence can be considered as being similar to a session;
- The presence of a word in a sentence depends on its previous words, as well as the consultation of a resource depends on the preceding resource consultations.
- Both domains provide large datasets that can be used to train statistical models.
- As can be noticed in the previous sections, both domains have been efficiently modeled using n-grams (n-gram models are equivalent to Markov models of order $n-1$). Thus both domains seem to allow a similar independence assumption.

Given these similarities, we can naturally think of exploiting statistical language modeling techniques for web recommendation. Statistical language modeling was studied far previously to web recommendation, and a lot of efficient models have been studied, it thus provides interesting perspectives.

However, two main differences exist between natural language and web navigation: (1) it is possible to have several web navigations overlapped, which would correspond to mixed sentences in natural language which does not exist, (2) natural language is governed by strong

constraints: each word and its localization in a sentence is important; navigation is less constrained and should be processed with more permissive models.
Thus statistical language modeling cannot be applied directly for web recommendation. Parallel navigations have to be handled. As the resources of one session can be relatively distant, the history considered should be longer than those of classical language modeling.
The second difference is problematic too. A more constrained corpus means that a light model can be build from it, and thus a less constrained data means that the resulting model is heavier. As the web contains a large number of resources, a rather light model would be welcome.
Hence, exploiting statistical language models induces an adjustment of the algorithms in order to provide a light and permissive model.

2.4 Exploiting statistical language modeling for web recommendation

In this section we discuss the exploitation of the aforementioned statistical language models for web usage mining. The goal is to find a model providing a high accuracy in the recommendations, a high coverage and a good robustness to noise while being tractable, which cannot be provided by classical statistical language modeling.
As previously said, using closed sequences (*e.g.* Markov models) makes it impossible to handle noise. One solution is to use open sequential patterns, but then the number of possible patterns is very high which leads to a high complexity.
A first possibility is the use of trigger models. Trigger models allow to consider distant elements, and only the most informative pairs are included in the model, which allows to discard noise. Indeed, if an element corresponds to noise, the impact of all other elements within the window will compensate its impact. The use of mutual information provides another interesting feature. Indeed, when using conditional probabilities, the most frequent resources are more likely to be recommended, although such resources may not be of major utility for a user. For instance, the home page of a website is usually the most visited one, but may not be the most interesting page to recommend to a user. Using the mutual information measure has a different effect of using conditional probabilities: the most frequent words are less likely to have a large mutual information value. However, as well as for natural language, they cannot be used alone. Indeed, a rare resource having a high correlation to a previous resource may be recommended, which may not be useful for a user.
Trigger models should thus also be combined with n-grams, as classically used in statistical language modeling in order to take advantage of both models. Such a configuration has been tested by (Pavlov et al., 2004). The models presented consist in mixtures of sub-models. In particular a bigram model (n-grams with $n = 2$) is combined with a trigger model. Both sub-models are interpolated using coefficients computed according the Expectation Maximization Algorithm (Dempster et al., 1977) on a validation set. Depending on the considered data, this algorithm may take too long to converge to an optimal solution. (Pavlov et al., 2004) thus propose to use a fast clustering algorithm based on users' navigation sequences. Using such a framework allows to take into account distant resources and to provide a high coverage while having a low time and space complexity. However, the use of a bigram model provides less accurate recommendations, and if the previous resource in the history is noise, then a bad recommendation is likely to be provided. This may not be compensated by the combination with a trigger model, as the mutual information may not be appropriate used alone, and should only be used as a complement.
An alternative is to use n-gram models with skipping. It allows distant resources to be taken into account, while using conditional probabilities. It is very close to open sequential pat-

terns; the main difference is that it is usually performed with a fixed value of n, and has a lower space and time complexity. The resulting model is thus tractable and robust to noise. Coverage depends on the considered data. With a fixed value of n, it is obvious that an n-gram model with skipping provides a better coverage than a raw n-gram model. Depending on the considered data and the value of n, it is possible that the coverage is not full, which can only be determined experimentally. An n-gram model with skipping was used in (Shani et al., 2005) to initialize a Markov Decision Process recommender system. When building the model, in addition to the raw n-gram counts, weighted occurrences of skipped n-grams are added to the counts. The skipping is performed only between the next to last and the last resource of the n-grams, and the occurrences are weighted according to an exponential decay scheme. This n-gram model has been compared to a dependency network based model in which the local distributions are probabilistic decision trees. Although these algorithms are among the most competitive, the skipping-based model reached better results. However, the skipping is applied only during the training step, which has been shown to provide less accurate recommendations (Bonnin et al., 2008).

A last possibility is to combine a trigger model with an n-gram model with skipping. To the best of our knowledge, such a configuration has never been studied in the frame of natural language. This is because the strong constraints of natural language make raw n-gram models very efficient, and they just need to be refined using distant information. However, as argued above, web navigation is far less constrained and the combination of both models provides an interesting alternative. Indeed, the complementarity of mutual information and conditional probabilities may even enhance the accuracy of the recommendations. In the following of this chapter we focus on the previous configuration (n-grams with skipping).

3. The Skipping-Based Recommender

As shown in the previous sections, predicting user behavior involves tradeoffs between complexity, predictive accuracy and coverage. Sequential patterns handle distance between the resources, but induce a huge number of sequences. The all-k^{th}-order Markov models, as to them, induce fewer sequences, lead to a high coverage, but still need a high storage space and do not allow distance between resources, which does not allow robustness to noise. In statistical language modeling the use of skipping in n-gram models is a way to benefit from the accuracy of n-gram models while handling distant resources as trigger models do, which leads to a high coverage and a low time and space complexity. Due to these advantages, the recommendation algorithm we propose is an n-gram model with skipping and is called the Skipping-Based Recommender or SBR.

When using skipping, the elements that can be skipped have to be determined and the size of the skipping has to be fixed. We thus present several possible skipping variants. We then present the weighting schemes we apply in order to alleviate the importance of distant resources. Last we describe the recommendation process of the SBR model.

3.1 Skipping Variants

In the skipping variants we study in this article, we consider that when an element can be skipped, the size of the skipping is limited to the size of the window used (similar to the sliding window used in association rules and Markov models).

3.1.1 Shani's skipping

The first skipping variant we study is the one used in (Shani et al., 2005). It consists in allowing skipping only for the last element of the n-grams, all other elements being contiguous.
For example, let $n = 3$, and the navigation sequence: (a,b,x,y,z,c,d) where (a,b,c,d) and (x,y,z) correspond to overlapping navigations. This variant allows to consider triplets as (a,b,y) or (a,b,c) and also raw triplets as (a,b,x) and (z,c,d). It is thus able to capture distant elements of a sequence if the last element corresponds to the continuance of a previously initiated navigation as for the triplet (a,b,c). The elements between (a,b) and c are here considered as elements of another navigation, but may also be considered as noise.
However, this skipping variant is not able to capture a navigation overlap if the two last elements correspond to the continuance of a previously begun navigation (a step after the previous configuration): for example, the triplet (b,c,d) cannot be handled as b and c are not contiguous.

3.1.2 Full skipping

The full skipping variant goes a step further by allowing skipping between all the elements of the n-gram. It makes the resulting model almost equivalent to sequential patterns, for instance the one proposed in (Nakagawa & Mobasher, 2003). The main difference is that the SBR model considers only sequences of size n while sequential patterns usually handle variable size patterns. This variant has several advantages. First, a high amount of n-grams is processed, which provides a better coverage. Second, this skipping captures parallel navigations, noise and approximate sequences, wherever these unexpected actions are, and whatever is their size. However, it can be viewed as a too permissive variant and the size of the model rapidly grows.

3.1.3 Enhanced skipping

We designed this new variant especially to take into account noise and parallel navigations without inducing a high complexity. The first variant can handle only noise in the last element. The second variant handles noise everywhere in the navigation, which may be too permissive. We propose here a variant that can be considered to be between both. It allows the consideration of two configurations simultaneously: skipping the last or the first element of the n-gram, which enables noise either in the first part of the n-gram, or in the last part, but not both.
For instance, given the previous example, it becomes possible to handle both cases (a,b,c) and (b,c,d) but not (a,x,c).

3.2 Weighting Schemes

We argue that skipped n-grams handled by the aforementioned skipping variants cannot be considered in the same way than raw n-grams (contiguous n-grams), and thus propose to weight them.
We present in this section several weighting schemes that can be used to take into account these skipped n-grams. Let d_i be the distance between the ith element and the last element of the trigram, and D the size of the window.
In order to show the benefits of weighting, we first propose to not use any weighting, as done for sequential patterns (Nakagawa & Mobasher, 2003). This weighting scheme is also similar to most of the trigger-based models: whatever is the distance between the elements of the n-

grams, they all have the same weight. In this case, the weighting scheme is referred to as the **No Weighting** scheme. The weight $w(d_1, ..., d_{n-1})$ of a given skipped n-gram is defined as:

$$w(d_1, ..., d_{n-1}) = \begin{cases} 1 & \text{if } d_1 \leq D \\ 0 & \text{else} \end{cases} \tag{3}$$

However, the recommendation impact of a skipped trigram should be lower than the one of a raw n-gram, due to the distance. We consider that the more a resource is distant, the more its influence is low, and the less the corresponding skipped n-gram is influencing. Thus, we propose to apply to a skipped n-gram a weight inversely proportional to the distance D. The following weight decreases linearly according to the distance. In this case, the weighting scheme is referred to as the **Linear Decay** weighting scheme. The weight becomes then:

$$w(d_1, ..., d_{n-1}) = \begin{cases} -\frac{d_1}{D} + 1 & \text{if } d_1 \leq D \\ 0 & \text{else} \end{cases} \tag{4}$$

Another way to perform this decrease is to decay exponentially the weight as proposed by (Shani et al., 2005). Using such a weighting scheme makes the value decrease faster. In this case, the weighting scheme is referred to as the **Single Exponential Decay** weighting scheme, and is defined as follows:

$$w(d_1, ..., d_{n-1}) = \begin{cases} 2^{-d_1} & \text{if } d_1 \leq D \\ 0 & \text{else} \end{cases} \tag{5}$$

This last scheme is sufficient for Shani's skipping variant. Indeed, only the last resource can be skipped, and it is not necessary to consider all the distances between the resources. In the enhanced and the full skipping variant however, other distances between the elements of a skipped n-gram may vary, and should be considered to compute the weightings. We thus propose to apply to skipped n-grams a weight that depends on the distance between each element of the n-grams and the resource to predict.

For example, applied to the sequence (a, b, x, y, z, c, d) with $n = 3$, triplets (a, b, d) and (a, c, d) should not have the same weight, even if the first element of both triplets is equidistant from the last element. Moreover the weight of (a, c, d) should be higher than the weight of (a, b, d) as the intermediate resource c is closer to d than b is. In this case, the weighting scheme is referred to as the **Multiple Exponential Decay** weighting scheme. The weight we propose to use is the following:

$$w(d_1, ..., d_{n-1}) = \begin{cases} \frac{1}{n-1} \sum_{i=1}^{n-1} 2^{-d_i} & \text{if } d_1 \leq D \\ 0 & \text{else} \end{cases} \tag{6}$$

Given the previous skipping variants and weighting schemes, the processing of recommendations can be done. The SBR model relies on the following steps:

Step 1: Training the model on a corpus to determine the counts of the n-grams

Step 2: Computing the probabilities of the n-grams based on their counts

Step 3: Running the model to recommend the pertinent resources to the active user given his/her stream of navigation

3.2.1 Training

In the training phase, raw n-grams and skipped n-grams are trained on the input data. The question now is how to mix the skipped n-grams and the raw n-grams. We propose to simply add the occurrences of skipped n-grams (weighted by the weighting schemes of the previous section) to the occurrences of raw n-grams (contiguous n-grams) as in (Chan & Goodman, 1998).

The weighted occurrences of the skipped n-grams are added to the counts of their corresponding raw n-grams. Algorithm 1 presents how these counts are computed when using the full skipping variant and $n = 3$. The count of the skipped trigram is denoted by $C(\rho_i, \rho_j, \rho_k)$.

Data: a set S of navigation sessions
Result: a list of trigrams associated with their occurrences

```
trigramlist ← ();
for each session s = (ρ1 ... ρ|s|) in S do
    for i ← 1 to |s| − 2 do
        for j ← i + 1 to min(i + D, |s| − 1) do
            for k ← j + 1 to min(j + 1 + D, |s|) do
                trigram ← (ρi, ρj, ρk);
                d1 ← k − i − 1;
                d2 ← k − j − 1;
                if trigram is in trigramlist then
                    C(ρi, ρj, ρk) ← C(ρi, ρj, ρk) + w(d1, d2);
                else
                    C(ρi, ρj, ρk) ← w(d1, d2);
                end
            end
        end
    end
end
```

Algorithm 1: Computing counts of trigrams with skipping using the full skipping variant

3.2.2 Computing the probabilities of the n-grams

Given the n-grams counts from the training phase, the conditional probabilities have to be computed. Let the n-gram $(\rho_{i-n+1}, ..., \rho_i)$. The probability of the resource ρ_i given $(\rho_{i-n+1}, ..., \rho_{i-1})$ is computed as follows:

$$P(\rho_i \mid \rho_{i-n+1}, ..., \rho_{i-1}) = \frac{C(\rho_{i-n+1}, ..., \rho_i)}{C(\rho_{i-n+1}, ..., \rho_{i-1})} \tag{7}$$

where $C(\rho_{i-n+1}, ..., \rho_i)$ is the count of the skipped n-gram $(\rho_{i-n+1}, ..., \rho_i)$.

3.2.3 Recommending

The recommendation step consists in predicting the next resource r_i given the $D - 1$ previous resources in the session $(\rho_{i-D+1}, ..., \rho_{i-1})$. For each resource in the set of distinct resources of the data $R = \{r_1, ..., r_{|R|}\}$, a score is computed according to each possible skipping state σ.

This score is a weighted form of the probability that at least one of the skipping states leads to resource r_j. The score is given by the following formula:

$$q(r_j, h) = 1 - \prod_{\sigma} \Big(1 - P(r_j \mid \sigma) \cdot w(d_1, ..., d_{n-1})\Big) \tag{8}$$

where $P(r_j|\sigma)$ is the probability of r_j given the skipping state σ, $w(d_1, ..., d_{n-1})$ the weighting of the skipping n-gram $(\sigma \circ r_j)$ according to the distances $d_1, ..., d_{n-1}$ between its elements. The skipping states σ considered depend on the skipping variant chosen.
For instance, if a user has browsed the following resources:

`388 401 55 359 325 369 381 368 366 60 72`

Then if the window size is $D = 10$, the resources considered are the following: `55, 359, 325, 369, 381, 368, 366, 60` and `72` (the 9 previous resources). If the skipping variant is the enhanced skipping and $n = 3$, than skipping states of size 2 have to be considered, thus $1 + 2 \times 7 = 15$ skipping states. These skipping states are presented in Figure 1.

⟨ 60,72 ⟩	⟨ 381,72 ⟩	⟨ 325,369 ⟩
⟨ 366,72 ⟩	⟨ 381,368 ⟩	⟨ 359,72 ⟩
⟨ 366,60 ⟩	⟨ 369,72 ⟩	⟨ 359,325 ⟩
⟨ 368,72 ⟩	⟨ 369,381 ⟩	⟨ 55,72 ⟩
⟨ 368,366 ⟩	⟨ 325,72 ⟩	⟨ 55,359 ⟩

Fig. 1. Example of skipping states obtained using the enhanced skipping variant for $n = 3$

Then, matching trigrams are searched in the model. The corresponding entries are weighted and included in the final recommendation list according to Equation (8).

The following sections study the performance of the model presented in this section.

4. Experimental setup

4.1 Corpus

Empirical studies are performed on two types of datasets. The first one is provided by the Crédit Agricole S.A. banking group[1], one of the main banks in France. Its employees use an Intranet interface containing workspaces, news, articles, etc. The bank provided us anonymized navigation client logs containing 3,391 distinct web pages (resources) browsed by 815 bank clerks during years 2007 and 2008. Using these logs we could extract a corpus of 123,470 consultations.
The second corpus is the CTI web server corpus of the DePaul University (`http://www.cs.depaul.edu`). It contains 69,471 consultations of 683 pages by 5,446 users during a two week period in April 2002 (*i.e.* about 170 consultations per day). The data has been cleaned and filtered by eliminating sessions of size 1 and low support page views.
The repartition of session sizes of both corpora are depicted in Figure 2. As can be seen, most of the sessions have a size below 10. The Crédit Agricole S.A. corpus has an average session size of 8.33 while the DePaul corpus has an average session size of 5.05.
In order to test the robustness to noise of our model, an increasing percentage of resources is randomly included in the corpora. These resources are extracted from the set of distinct

[1] Thanks to Jean-Philippe Blanchard

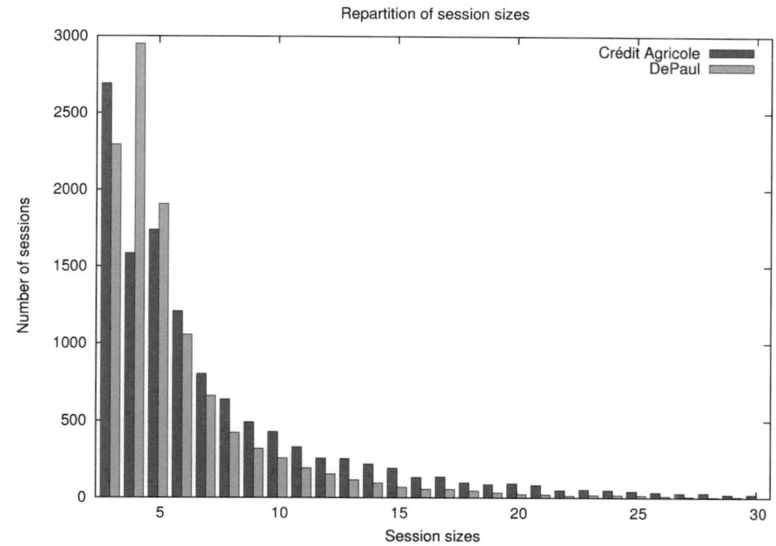

Fig. 2. Repartition of session sizes

resources (the vocabulary) of each corpus. Notice that noise was already present in the original corpora, but was not quantifiable.

Two extra processings have been applied to the data. The first is the elimination of sessions of size 1 (which was already performed on the DePaul corpus) and 2. This is because in the following, we compare our SBR model for $n = 3$ to state-of-the-art models, and wanted the same recommendation cases to be considered. The second is the division of the resulting corpora into training and test sets of 90% and 10% respectively.

4.2 Evaluation metrics

To evaluate the accuracy of our models, we used the Recommendation Score (RS). This metric evaluates the average pertinence of recommendation lists. For each history of the test corpus, a recommendation list of size m is built, containing the most probable resources according to the model. If the actual resource is in the list, the recommendation is pertinent (also called a hit). This metric thus calculates the percentage of pertinent recommendations; it is also called the hit-ratio (Jin et al., 2005; Pavlov et al., 2004). To complete the evaluations, we also provide the coverage, *i.e.* the percentage of cases where the model can recommend a resource. Running times and model sizes are provided too. All experiments have been performed on a 2.66GHz processor and 4GB memory computer. Running times have been obtained by running ten times each model and retaining the smallest ones.

4.3 Models

In the following, we compare our SBR model to state-of-the-art web predictive models. These models are a standard form of all-k^{th}-order Markov model and open sequential patterns.

The sequential patterns are built and selected according to the GSP algorithm and the combination of the antecedents is performed using the maximum length policy as done in (Nakagawa & Mobasher, 2003) together with the sum policy.

Recall that all-k^{th}-order Markov models are equivalent to closed sequential patterns. The only difference is that there is no need of the Apriori or GSP algorithm to filter the states.

5. Tractability

This section is dedicated to a theoretical and an empirical study of the tractability of the SBR model, the all-k^{th}-order Markov model and open sequential patterns.
Two aspects are considered: time and space complexity. As training can be performed off-line, only the time complexity of the recommendation step is studied.

5.1 Theoretical discussion

Theoretically, space complexity is dependent on the number of distinct elements N of the data considered. For instance, if a model has to store all encountered sequences of sizes 1 and 2, then the maximum number of elements to be stored is $N + N^2$.
Time complexity is dependent on the number of sequences that are considered in the history for each recommendation, and the time necessary to find a matching antecedent or state in the model.

5.1.1 Sequential patterns

- Space complexity:

Using sequential patterns, a huge number of sequences has to be stored. If N is the number of distinct elements and D the window size, the maximum number of elements to store is:

$$\sum_{k=1}^{D} N^k = N \cdot \frac{1 - N^D}{1 - N} = \mathcal{O}(N^D) \tag{9}$$

Using the GSP algorithm reduces space complexity; however it induces a lower coverage of longer patterns.

- Time complexity:

Open sequential patterns consider variable length open sequences in a window of size D. The last element of the pattern (the consequent) is always the rightmost element in the window. The number of combinations induced is thus:

$$\sum_{k=1}^{D-1} C_{D-1}^{k} = 2^{D-1} \tag{10}$$

The search of the corresponding patterns in the model, can be done in $\mathcal{O}(k)$ using a tree structure, where k is the length of the current pattern to be matched. The number of iterations of each recommendation is thus:

$$\begin{aligned}\sum_{k=1}^{D-1} \mathcal{O}(k) \cdot C_{D-1}^{k} &\leqslant \sum_{k=1}^{D-1} \mathcal{O}(D) \cdot C_{D-1}^{k} \\ &\leqslant \mathcal{O}(D) \sum_{k=1}^{D-1} C_{D-1}^{k} \\ &\leqslant \mathcal{O}(D) \cdot 2^{D-1} = \mathcal{O}(D \cdot 2^{D-1})\end{aligned} \tag{11}$$

5.1.2 All-k^{th}-order Markov models

- Space complexity:

The maximum number of elements induced using an all-k^{th}-order Markov model is the same as the one of sequential patterns. However, in practice considering contiguous patterns induces far less elements, and space complexity is lower. The difference depends on the size of the training data and on the number of distinct resources. As for sequential patterns, pruning the states can lower space complexity, as done in (Deshpande & Karypis, 2004), but may also induce a low coverage of longer sequences.

- Time complexity:

All-k^{th}-order Markov models have a lower complexity than sequential patterns. Indeed, as the patterns considered are contiguous, only D sequences are induced for each recommendation. Time complexity is thus:

$$\sum_{k=1}^{D} \mathcal{O}(k) = \mathcal{O}(D^2) \tag{12}$$

5.1.3 SBR model

- Space complexity:

The maximum number of elements induced using the SBR model is always lower than N^n, which is a quite lower upper bound than the ones of both previous models.

- Time complexity:

The complexity of our model depends on the skipping variant used. Using the full skipping variant, C_{D-1}^{k} sequences are induced for each recommendation, thus $\mathcal{O}(D^{n-1})$ if $n \leqslant \frac{D}{2}$, $\mathcal{O}(D^{D-n+1})$ if $\frac{D}{2} \leqslant n \leqslant D$, and $\mathcal{O}(D^{D/2})$ $\forall n \leqslant D$. As searching the states in a tree structure can be done in $\mathcal{O}(n)$, time complextity is thus:

$$\begin{array}{ll} \mathcal{O}(n \cdot D^{n-1}) & \text{if } n \leqslant \frac{D}{2} \\ \mathcal{O}(n \cdot D^{D-n+1}) & \text{if } \frac{D}{2} \leqslant n \leqslant D \\ \mathcal{O}(n \cdot D^{D/2}) & \forall n \leqslant D \end{array} \tag{13}$$

Shani's and the enhanced skipping variants reduce this number to $\mathcal{O}(n \cdot D)$.
Thus, depending on the value of n, the full skipping variant can have a high complexity. However, using low values of n such as 3 or 4 leads to acceptable complexities. For $n = 3$ and $D \geqslant 6$, the time complexity of the full skipping variant is $\mathcal{O}(D^2)$. As well, for $n = 4$ and $D \geqslant 8$, the time complexity of the full skipping variant is $\mathcal{O}(D^3)$. As using skipping allows to simulate a higher order model using a lower order model, the accuracy and coverage should be high.

5.2 Empirical comparison

In this section, experimental results of the three models are compared in terms of model sizes and computation time. In order to have comparable models, all support and confidence thresholds are set to 0. The size of the recommendation lists is set to 10. We chose this value for two reasons: (1) a user rarely takes into consideration resources recommended above this value (2) top-10 recommendation lists are widely used, which provides a direct comparison of the results. The size of the window is set to $D = 10$. The SBR is tested for a value of $n = 3$, and using the three aforementionned skipping variants: Shani's, enhanced and full. Results are shown in Table 1.

	DePaul		Crédit Agricole S.A.	
	size	time	size	time
SBR (Shani)	1.5 MB	14s	2.3 MB	3m05s
SBR (Enhanced)	2.6 MB	18s	4.1 MB	3m20s
SBR (Full)	5.3 MB	25s	8.1 MB	5m51s
AKO	3.3 MB	3m06s	8.3 MB	17m02s
SP	108.7 MB	1m08s	289.6 MB	10m50s

Table 1. Size and running time of the models

- Space requirements

We can first notice that using the SBR model with Shani's and the enhanced skipping variants provides the lowest model sizes on both corpora. On the Crédit Agricole S.A. corpus, the full skipping variant induces a larger model than the all-k^{th}-order Markov model. However, on the DePaul corpus, the size of the SBR model with the full skipping variant is slightly smaller than the one of the all-k^{th}-order Markov model.
The huge space complexity of sequential patterns is obviously verified: it is more than 20 times larger than all other models on the Crédit Agricole S.A. corpus, and more than 30 times larger on the DePaul corpus. So far, the SBR model and the all-k^{th}-order Markov model are almost equivalent.

- Running time

Surprisingly, the sequential patterns model ran faster than the all-k^{th}-order Markov model (1m08s *vs* 3m06s and 10m50s *vs* 17m05s). This is because the first one considers open sequences and contains far more elements (108.7 MB *vs* 3.3 MB and 289.6 MB *vs* 8.3 MB). Thus using sequential patterns, it is much more likely to find matching sequences and the model is able to provide top-10 recommendation lists after far less iterations. Indeed, the sequential patterns model we implemented use the maximum length policy. Using this policy, for each possible sequential pattern length, all combinations are considered in the window. If a sufficient number of recommendations is induced, then it is not necessary to continue the process using smaller sequential patterns. The same strategy is used for the all-k^{th}-order Markov model.
The running time of the SBR model is clearly below the ones of both other models. Using the full skipping variant, it ran more than four times faster than the sequential patterns on the DePaul corpus, and almost twice faster on the Crédit Agricole S.A. corpus. It thus represents the most tractable alternative. As could have been predicted, the most tractable skipping variants are Shani's and the enhanced skipping variants.

6. Robustness to noise

As discussed previously, the presence of noise in navigations can have dramatic effects on the recommendations. Our model is designed to be robust to noise. In this section we compare its features with the ones of all-k^{th}-order Markov models and open sequential patterns.

6.1 Theoretical discussion

In (Jianyong et al., 2007), it is argued that closed sequences are more appropriate for web navigation. The reasons put forward are that it provides more compact recommendation lists and that it is more efficient. Moreover, all-k^{th}-order Markov models are considered as being among the best performing models of the state-of-the-art. However, using closed sequences makes it impossible to ignore resources corresponding to noise. When the history does not match the model, it is then reduced step by step, until a resource can be recommended. After a reduction, the resource that is discarded is the one that is the more distant from the resource to recommend. So if any noise appears in a close past and no matching history can be found unless this resource is ignored, the history will be reduced until the resource is out of it. As a result, very few resources will be considered to compute the recommendations. Moreover, when the resource previously consulted is noise, no reliable recommendation can be provided. For these reasons, we think that using closed sequences, in particular all-k^{th}-order Markov models, is not the most appropriate configuration.

Open sequential patterns exhibits good characteristics that make them more robust to such problems. As all (2^{D-1}) possible open sequences in the past can be considered, if noise occurred in a recent past, longer sequences that does not include it can be considered to compute recommendations. It should be noticed that using such a scheme, most of the sequences induced are formed using distant resources. We think that such sequences may be less representative, as users rarely perform navigation mistakes, returns to previous pages or parallel navigations between each page consultation, and that most of contiguous consultations correspond to coherent transitions. Moreover, as the number of sequences induced is huge, it is not clear whether it is compensated by the accuracy provided.

The SBR model has several advantages concerning robustness to noise. First, all skipping states used to provide the recommendations are combined, and weighting schemes are used to alleviate the importance of distant resources. Moreover, using Shani's and the enhanced skipping variants, among the n elements of each n-gram, $n-1$ elements are always contiguous, which lowers the phenomenon of non coherent transitions. Last, it has low space and state complexities. It thus represents an even better candidate.

6.2 Empirical comparison

We are now interested in the empirical study of the robustness to noise of the models. Tests are performed on the Crédit Agricole S.A. and DePaul corpora in which 0%, 15% and 30% of noise is inserted. It should be noticed that when no noise is inserted, there is actually already some natural noise in the corpus. Thus, the 0% noise values below does not mean that there is no noise in the corpus, but that no additional noise was inserted. For this reason, we only inserted a maximum of 30% of noise.

We first focus on the determination of the best configuration of our SBR model. We then provide a comparison of the SBR model and the models of the state-of-the-art. Here again, the size of the recommendation lists is set to 10. Results are provided in terms of RS and coverage.

6.2.1 Skipping variants

This section is dedicated to the study of the SBR model. The two features studied are the skipping variant presented in section 3.1 and the weighting schemes presented in section 3.2. Figure 3 and Figure 4 show the RS obtained on the Crédit Agricole S.A. corpus and the DePaul corpus respectively.

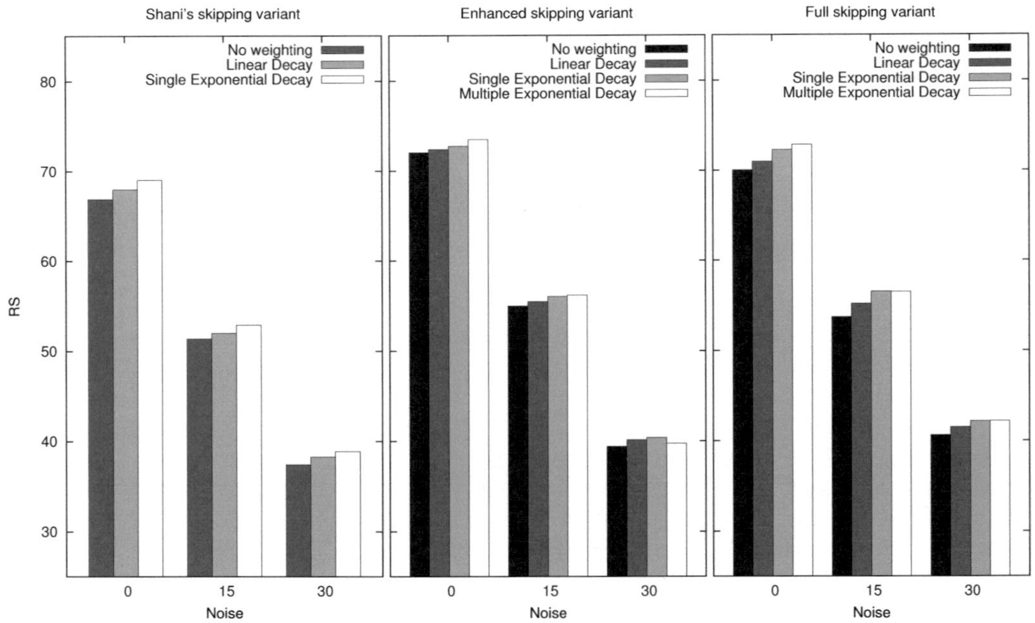

Fig. 3. Accuracy of the SBR model on the Crédit Agricole S.A. corpus according to the skipping variants and the weighting schemes proposed

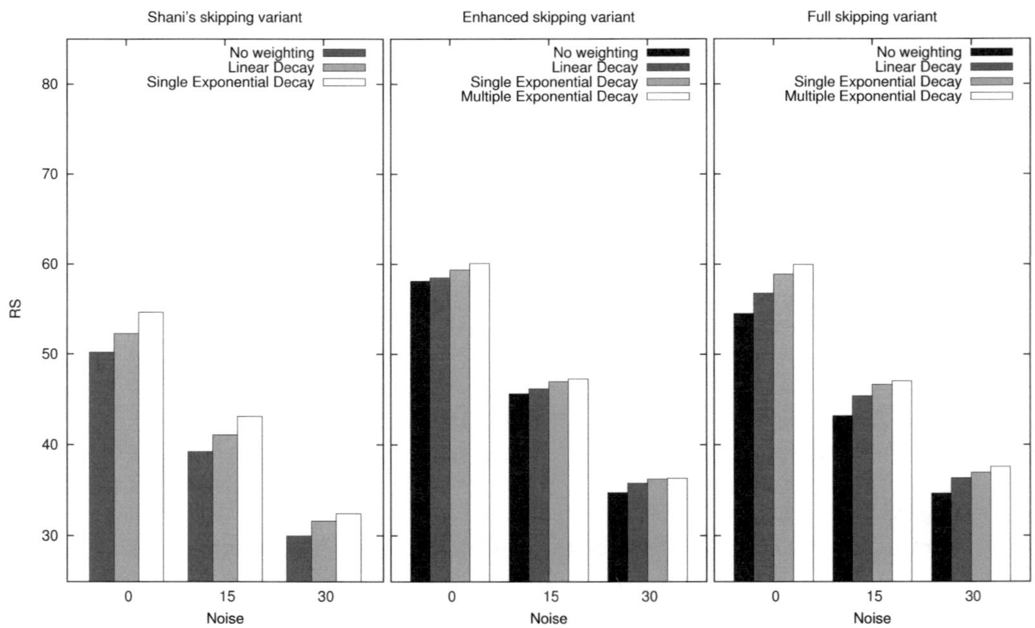

Fig. 4. Accuracy of the SBR model on the DePaul corpus according to the skipping variants and the weighting schemes proposed

We can first notice that Shani's skipping variant provides the lowest RS values on all 6 corpora. When no noise is inserted into the corpora, the enhanced and the full skipping variant provide similar results. When noise is inserted, the full skipping variant provides a slightly better RS. As our enhanced skipping variant is almost as accurate as the full skipping variant and has a lower complexity, it seems to be the best configuration.

Focusing on the weighting schemes, we can first notice that using no weighting provides almost always the lowest RS. When no noise is inserted, the Multiple Exponential Decay weighting scheme always provides the best results. When noise is inserted, it almost always provides the best results. It thus constitutes the best alternative.

So far, the best configuration of the SBR model is the enhanced skipping variant together with the Multiple Exponential Decay weighting scheme.

Focusing on Table 2 and Table 3, we can see that when no noise is inserted, all skippings reach an almost full coverage. When noise is inserted the enhanced and the full skipping variants provide the best coverages, which are similar. This thus confirms that the enhanced skipping variant we proposed is the best configuration.

Noise	0	15	30
Shani	98.8	89.5	84.5
Enhanced	99.5	95.9	93.6
Full	99.7	96.0	94.3

Table 2. Coverage of the SBR model on the Crédit Agricole S.A. corpus according to the skipping variants proposed

Noise	0	15	30
Shani	98.9	96.1	93.1
Enhanced	99.7	98.2	96.3
Full	99.8	98.3	96.4

Table 3. Coverage of the SBR model on the DePaul corpus according to the skipping variants proposed

6.2.2 Comparison to the state-of-the-art

This section is dedicated to the comparison of the robustness to noise of our SBR model to both state-of-the-art models. The configuration of the SBR model is the enhanced skipping variant together with the Multiple Exponential Decay Weighting scheme.

Results of the all-k^{th}-order Markov model and the sequential patterns are provided at optimal pruning thresholds. Notice that sequential patterns could not be used with support thresholds of 0, as moving to more noisy environment made the space requirements too huge for our computer, although it was possible using both other models.

Results are presented in Figure 5 and Figure 6. We can first notice that on the Crédit Agricole S.A. corpus, the best results are provided by the SBR model. When no noise is inserted, the SBR provides a significant enhancement compared to sequential patterns. This difference is

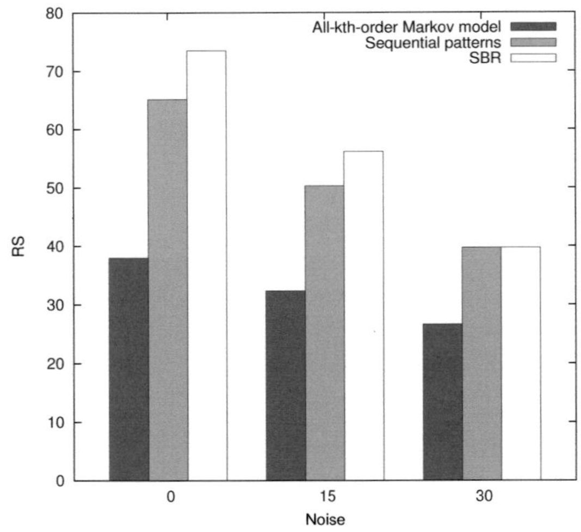

Fig. 5. RS of the models on the noisy Crédit Agricole S.A. corpora

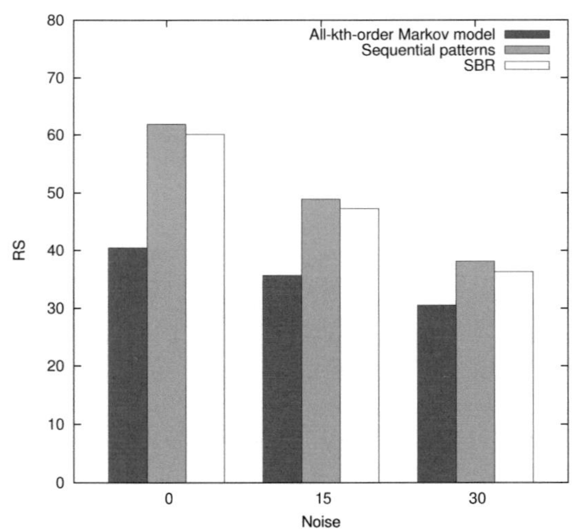

Fig. 6. RS of the models on the noisy DePaul corpora

lower when 15% of noise is inserted in the corpus. With 30% of noise, both models provide similar results.
On the DePaul corpus, sequential patterns provide slightly better results than the SBR model, whatever is the amount of noise inserted. As the SBR has lower time and space complexities, it constitutes a better choice.
The all-k^{th}-order Markov model provides the lowest accuracy, which confirms that using closed sequences provides less accurate results in a noisy environment. It should be noticed that this last model has a higher slope than both other. We think this shows that it is not able to handle long sequences and is more accurate using a lower maximum value of k. Indeed, the more noise is inserted in the model, the less long matching states are found, and thus the lower the length of the matching states. However, as this model provided a very lower accuracy, we did not study this phenomenon further.

7. Conclusion

In this chapter, we focused on sequence-based recommender systems. We first described related work and drew a parallel between natural language and Web navigation. We then decided to take advantage of statistical language models to perform recommendations in the frame of web navigation.
We proposed a new model called Sequence Based Recommender or SBR, that is based on an n-gram model and integrates skipping. This model has the advantage to take into account long histories while being tractable. Several skipping variant were proposed. As well, several weighting schemes were proposed to alleviate the importance of distant resources.
We provided theoretical and empirical studies of the tractability and robustness to noise of our model, compared to state-of-the-art models: all-k^{th}-order Markov models and sequential patterns. The empirical studies were performed on two browsing datasets. Results show that on both corpora, considering open sequences is more efficient than considering closed sequences. Furthermore, our model has been shown to represent the best alternative: it has the lowest time and space complexity, provides a better accuracy on one of the corpora and an accuracy comparable to the one of sequential patterns on the other one, while having a comparable coverage.

8. References

Adomavicius, G., Sankaranarayanan, R., Sen, S. & Tuzhilin, A. (2005). Incorporating contextual information in recommender systems using a multidimensional approach, *ACM Transactions on Information Systems* **23**(1): 103–145.

Adomavicius, G. & Tuzhilin, A. (2005). Toward the Next Generation of Recommender Systems: A Survey of the State-of-the-Art and Possible Extensions, *IEEE Transactions on Knowledge and Data Engineering* **17**(6): 734–749.

Agrawal, R., Imieliński, T. & Swami, A. (1993). Mining Association Rules between Sets of Items in Large Databases, *SIGMOD '93: Proceedings of the 1993 ACM SIGMOD international conference on Management of data*, pp. 207–216.

Agrawal, R. & Srikant, R. (1995). Mining Sequential Patterns, *ICDE'95: Proceedings of the International Conference on Data Engineering*, pp. 3–14.

Ayres, J., Flannick, J., Gehrke, J. & Yiu, T. (2002). Sequential Pattern Mining Using a Bitmap Representation, *KDD '02: Proceedings of the eighth ACM SIGKDD international conference on Knowledge discovery and data mining*, ACM, New York, NY, USA, pp. 429–435.

Balabanović, M. & Shoham, Y. (1997). Fab: Content-Based, Collaborative Recommendation, *Communications of the ACM* **40**(3): 66–72.

Banko, M. & Brill, E. (2001). Mitigating the paucity-of-data problem: Exploring the effect of training corpus size on classifier performance for natural language processing, *Human Language Technology Conference (HLT)*.

Bonnin, G., Brun, A. & Boyer, A. (2008). Using Skipping for Sequence-Based Collaborative Filtering, *IEEE/WIC/ACM International Conference on Web Intelligence and Intelligent Agent Technology*, pp. 775–779.

Borges, J. & Levene, M. (2005). Generating dynamic higher-order markov models in web usage mining.

Boyer, A. & Brun, A. (2007). Natural Language Processing for Usage Based Indexing of Web Resources, *29th European Conference on Information Retrieval (ECIR)*, Vol. 4425 of *Lecture Notes in Computer Science*, Fondazione Ugo Bordoni, Springer Berlin / Heidelberg, Rome, Italy, pp. 517–524.

Chan, S. & Goodman, J. (1998). An Empirical Study of Smoothing Techniques for Language Modeling, *Technical report*, Computer Science Group, Harvard University, Cambridge, Massachusetts.

Chen, Y. & Chan, K. (2003). Extended multi-word trigger pair language model using data mining technique, *IEEE International Conference on Systems, Man and Cybernetics*, pp. 262–267.

Chi, E., Pitkow, J., Mackinlay, J., Pirolli, P., Gossweiler, R. & Card, S. (1998). Visualizing the Evolution of Web Ecologies, *CHI '98: Proceedings of the SIGCHI conference on Human factors in computing systems*, ACM Press/Addison-Wesley Publishing Co., New York, NY, USA, pp. 400–407.

Das, A., Datar, M., Garg, A. & Rajaram, S. (2007). Google News Personalization: Scalable Online Collaborative Filtering, *WWW'07: Proceedings of the 16th International Conference on World Wide Web* pp. 271–280.

Dempster, A., Laird, N. & Rubin, D. (1977). Maximum Likelihood from Incomplete Data via the EM Algorithm, *Journal of the Royal Statistical Society. Series B (Methodological)* **39**(1): 1–38.

Deshpande, M. & Karypis, G. (2004). Selective Markov Models for Predicting Web Page Accesses, *Transactions on Internet Technology* **4**(2): 163–184.

Eirinaki, M. & Vazirgiannis, M. (2007). Web Site Personalization Based on Link Analysis and Navigational Patterns, *Transactions on Internet Technology* **7**(4): 21.

Fleischman, M., Hovy, E. & Echihabi, A. (2003). Offline Strategies for Online Question Answering: Answering Questions Before They Are Asked, *in* E. Hinrichs & D. Roth (eds), *Proceedings of the 41st Annual Meeting of the Association for Computational Linguistics*, pp. 1–7.

Goldberg, D., Nichols, D., Oki, B. & Terry, D. (1992). Using Collaborative Filtering to Weave an Information Tapestry, *Communications of the ACM* pp. 61–70.

Goodman, J. (2001). A bit of progress in Language Modeling (Extended Version), *Technical report*.

Huang, X., Alleva, F., Hwang, M. & Rosenfeld, R. (1993). An Overview of the SPHINX-II Speech Recognition System, *HLT '93: Proceedings of the workshop on Human Language Technology*, Association for Computational Linguistics, Morristown, NJ, USA, pp. 81–86.

Jianyong, W., Jiawei, H. & Li, C. (2007). Frequent Closed Sequence Mining without Candidate Maintenance, *IEEE Transactions on Knowledge and Data Engineering* **19**(8): 1042–1056.

Jin, X., Mobasher, B. & Zhou, Y. (2005). A Web Recommendation System Based on Maximum Entropy, *Proceedings of the International Conference on Information Theory: Coding and Computing*, pp. 213–218.

Kim, C. & Kim, J. (2003). A recommendation algorithm using multi-level association rules, *WI '03: Proceedings of the 2003 IEEE/WIC International Conference on Web Intelligence*, IEEE Computer Society, Washington, DC, USA, pp. 524–527.

Lu, L., Dunham, M. & Meng, Y. (2005). Mining Significant Usage Patterns from Clickstream Data, *7th International Workshop on Knowledge Discovery on the Web*, pp. 1–17.

Mobasher, B. (2007). *Data Mining for Web Personalization*, LNCS 4321 - Brusilovsky, P. and Kobsa, A. and Nejdl, W., chapter 3, pp. 90–135.

Nakagawa, M. & Mobasher, B. (2003). Impact of Site Characteristics on Recommendation Models Based On Association Rules and Sequental Patterns, *Intelligent Techniques for Web Personalization*.

Och, F. & Ney, H. (2001). Discriminative Training and Maximum Entropy Models for Statistical Machine Translation, *ACL '02: Proceedings of the 40th Annual Meeting on Association for Computational Linguistics*, Association for Computational Linguistics, Morristown, NJ, USA, pp. 295–302.

Park, S.-T., Pennock, D., Madani, O., Good, N. & DeCoste, D. (2006). Naïve Filterbots for Robust Cold-start Recommendations, *KDD '06: Proceedings of the 12th ACM SIGKDD international conference on Knowledge discovery and data mining*, ACM, New York, NY, USA, pp. 699–705.

Pavlov, D., Manavoglu, E., Pennock, D. & Giles, C. (2004). Collaborative Filtering with Maximum Entropy, *IEEE Intelligent Systems* **19**(6): 40–48.

Pitkow, J. & Pirolli, P. (1999). Mining Longest Repeating Subsequences to Predict World Wide Web Surfing, *USITS'99: Proceedings of the 2nd conference on USENIX Symposium on Internet Technologies and Systems*, pp. 139–150.

Rabiner, L. (1989). A Tutorial on Hidden Markov Models and Selected Applications in Speech Recognition, *Proceedings of the IEEE*, pp. 257–286.

Rosenfeld, R. (1994). *Adaptive Statistical Language Modeling: A Maximum Entropy Approach*, PhD thesis, Carnegie Mellon University, Computer Science Department.

Rosenfeld, R. (2000). Two Decades of Statistical Language Modeling: Where do we go from here?, *Proceedings of the IEEE* pp. 1270–1278.

Rosenfeld, R. & Huang, X. (1992). Improvement in Stochastic Language Modeling, *Speech and Natural Language*, San Mateo,CA, pp. 107–111.

Sarwar, B., Karypis, G., Konstan, J. & Riedl, J. (2000). Analysis of Recommendation Algorithms for e-commerce, *EC '00: Proceedings of the 2nd ACM conference on Electronic commerce*, ACM, New York, NY, USA, pp. 158–167.

Schechter, S., Krishnan, M. & Smith, M. (1998). Using Path Profiles to Predict HTTP Requests, *Computer Networks and ISDN Systems* **30**(1-7): 457–467.

Schein, A., Popescul, A., Ungar, L. & Pennock, D. (2002). Methods and Metrics for Cold-start Recommendations, *SIGIR '02: Proceedings of the 25th annual international ACM SIGIR conference on Research and development in information retrieval*, ACM, New York, NY, USA, pp. 253–260.

Shani, G., Heckerman, D. & Brafman, R. (2005). An MDP-Based Recommender System, *JMLR: The Journal of Machine Learning Research* pp. 453–460.

Srikant, R. & Agrawal, R. (1996). Mining Sequential Patterns: Generalizations and Performance Improvements, *EDBT '96: Proceedings of the 5th International Conference on Extending Database Technology*, Springer-Verlag, London, UK, pp. 3–17.

Srivastava, J., Cooley, R., Deshpande, M. & Tan, P. (2000). Web Usage Mining: Discovery and Applications of Usage Patterns from Web Data, *SIGKDD Explorations Newsletter* **1**(2): 12–23.

Tan, P. & Kumar, V. (2002). Discovery of Web Robot Sessions Based on their Navigational Patterns, *Data Mining Knowledge Discovery* **6**(1): 9–35.

Trousse, B. (2000). Evaluation of the Prediction Capability of a User Behaviour Mining Approach For Adaptive Web Sites, *In Proceedings of the 6th RIAO Conference - Content-Based Multimedia Information Access*.

Wang, Y., Li, Z. & Zhang, Y. (2005). Mining Sequential Association-Rule for Improving WEB Document Prediction, *ICCIMA '05: Proceedings of the Sixth International Conference on Computational Intelligence and Multimedia Applications*, IEEE Computer Society, Washington, DC, USA, pp. 146–151.

Zhang, Y., Callan, J. & Minka, T. (2002). Novelty and Redundancy Detection in Adaptive Filtering, *SIGIR '02: Proceedings of the 25th annual international ACM SIGIR conference on Research and development in information retrieval*, ACM, New York, NY, USA, pp. 81–88.

Zimdars, A., Chickering, D. M. & Meek, C. (2001). Using Temporal Data for Making Recommendations., *in* J. S. Breese & D. Koller (eds), *UAI*, Morgan Kaufmann, pp. 580–588.

14

Human Computation Games and Optimization of Their Productivity

Kuan-Ta Chen[1], Chien-Wei Lin[1], Ling-Jyh Chen[1] and Irwin King[2]
Institute of Information Science, Academia Sinica[1] Department of Computer
Science & Engineering, The Chinese University of Hong Kong[2]

Abstract

Web 2.0 technology enables people worldwide to collaborate over the Internet, a phenomenon known as social collaboration. While the incentives for social collaboration are primarily enthusiasm for a particular subject, building a reputation, or gaining a benefit by doing something in exchange for using services or downloading files, the emergence of human computation games has shown that the prospect of having fun can be a strong incentive for participants to actively engage in such collaboration. Among the human computation games, ESP game (ESP stands for Extrasensory Perception) is one of the most popular ones. To play an ESP game, two randomly matched players assign labels that appropriately describe an image provided by the system. It has been shown that the "outcomes" of ESP games have many useful applications, such as image-based CAPTCHA tests and semantic image searches.

In this chapter, we provide an overview of human computation games and present an analytical model for computing the utility of ESP games, i.e., the throughput rate of appropriate labels for given images. The model targets generalized games, where the number of players, the consensus threshold, and the stopping condition are variable. Via extensive simulations, we show that our model can accurately predict the stopping condition that will yield the optimal utility of an ESP game under a specific game setting. A service provider can therefore utilize the model to ensure that the hosted ESP games produce high-quality labels efficiently, given that the number of players willing to invest time and effort in the game is limited.

1. Introduction

The emergence of Web 2.0 has changed the way we solve problems. For example, when we encounter an unknown technical term, it is no longer necessary to consult an expert reference, such as an encyclopedia. Instead, Google and Wikipedia can often provide us with an overview of the term. If we are interested in a book, but we not sure whether it is worth buying, we can go to Amazon to review other readers' comments about it. Similarly, if we are planning a trip, we can visit travelers' help web sites, like Expedia and Orbitz to check which hotels are more comfortable and whether their service is satisfactory. The enhanced ability to share information in the Web 2.0 era can help people make countless decisions in everyday life.

Web 2.0 technology also enables people to collaborate in solving particular real-life problems over the Internet, a phenomenon known as *social collaboration.* One of the most famous examples is Wikipedia, where millions of contributors collaborate in compiling the most complete encyclopedia in the world. Another example can be found in content censoring, which is important for preventing the distribution of inappropriate material on websites that allow users to upload content freely. However, content censoring is labor-intensive for large-scale web services. *Social moderation systems* [1] provide an effective means of reducing the labor required by encouraging users to report inappropriate content. Such users may even become active moderators and develop a reputation in their respective communities. In another example, Internet users can now collaboratively decode the complicated texts of ancient books [8]. Previously, such tasks could only be performed by experts or highly customized OCR (optical character recognition) software. To summarize, with the help of Web 2.0 technology and appropriate designs to motivate people, any group of Internet users, who do not know each other, can combine their "computation power" to solve Al-hard problems. Because of this ability, the process is called *social computation* [2].

Web 2.0 technology enables people to collaborate in solving particular real-life problems over the Internet, a phenomenon known as *social collaboration.* One of the most famous examples is Wikipedia, where millions of contributors collaborate in compiling the most complete encyclopedia in the world. Another example can be found in content censoring, which is important for preventing the distribution of inappropriate material on websites that allow users to upload content freely. To summarize, with the help of Web 2.0 technology and appropriate designs to motivate people, any group of Internet users, who do not know each other, can combine their "computation power" to solve Al-hard problems. Because of this ability, the process is called *social computation* [2].

The key to the success of a social computation system lies in providing sufficient incentives for users to participate in the social collaboration process. The *incentives* provided by most social computation systems are enthusiasm for a particular subject, building a reputation, or even benefiting by doing something in exchange for using services or downloading files. However, it has been shown that the prospect of having *fun can be a strong incentive for people to actively participate in a social computation system.* In [4], Ahn and Dabbish proposed the ESP game, a real-time, web-based, two-player application. To play, in each round, the randomly matched players keep suggesting appropriate labels to describe an image until they achieve a *consensus,* i.e., both players suggest the same label. Since the players are randomly assigned and they cannot communicate, each player must "guess" the labels that his/her opponent will suggest. For this reason, the game is called *ESP (ExtraSensory Perception).* If the players achieve a consensus, the label they agree on is likely to be an appropriate description of the current image. Initially, the ESP game was proposed to acquire users' descriptions for a large set of images, which could then be applied in image-based CAPTCHA tests [3] and semantic image searches. It was later extended to collect users' definitions of the shape of a designated object [7]. The collected results were then used as training data for image understanding and object recognition research.

In [4], Ahn and Dabbish proposed the ESP game, a real-time, web-based, two-player application. To play, in each round, the randomly matched players keep suggesting appropriate labels to describe an image until they achieve a *consensus,* i.e., both players suggest the same label. If the players achieve a consensus, the label they agree on is likely to be an appropriate description of the current image.

In this chapter, our objective is to model the performance of the ESP game and optimize its utility by redefining the criteria for finishing a game. The ESP game proposed in [4] only allows two players to participate. Once they achieve a consensus, the current image is considered solved and the game continues with the next image. In our study, we consider a more generalized ESP game that incorporates the following extensions:

The number of players, n, can be greater than 2.

The consensus threshold, m, can be any positive integer that is not larger than n; that is, a label is considered a consensus decision if it is proposed by m out of n players.

The stopping condition, k, can be any positive integer; that is, an image is considered correctly labeled if k consensuses are reached.

In our framework for generalized ESP games, the game proposed by Ahn and Dabbish [4] corresponds to an instance where $n = 2$, $m = 2$, and $k = 1$. Hereafter, we use "ESP games" or "games" to refer to the proposed generalized version. As some variants of ESP games ask players to label audio clips instead of images, we use the term "puzzle" to denote the target object that players must label by consensus.

In our model, we assume that the number of appropriate labels for each puzzle is limited, and all remaining words are considered inappropriate. For example, to label an image containing a red car beside a river, "car," "river," "red" are considered appropriate or good. Other words are considered inappropriate or bad, even if there is a consensus among the players. For example, players may input typos like "cra," "rive," or "rde" by mistake, or words that are too vague or general, such as "picture," "photo," "sea" and still achieve a consensus occasionally. In such cases, we deem that the current game yields a bad label and the quality of the game's output is decreased.

We model the *utility* of generalized ESP games, i.e., the throughput rate of good labels for the puzzles and its relationship with the game's settings, i.e., the number of players, the consensus threshold, and the stopping condition. We find that a tradeoff exists between the efficiency of the consensus achieved and the quality of matched labels.

Given a fixed number of players and a specific consensus threshold, our model can predict the optimal stopping condition that will ensure the maximal possible utility for an ESP game.

Our contribution in this work is three-fold:

We present a generalized ESP game in which the number of players, the consensus threshold, and the stopping condition are variable.

We propose a probabilistic model that can predict the efficiency, quality, and utility of an ESP game based on the game's settings.

Via extensive simulations, we show that the proposed model can accurately predict the optimal stopping condition, which facilitates the maximal utility of a generalized ESP game. This feature can be used by game service providers to maximize the outcome of games, given that the number of players willing to invest time and effort in the game is limited.

The remainder of this chapter is organized as follows. In Section II, we review related works. We present our probabilistic model for generalized ESP games in Section III, and evaluate its performance via simulations in Section IV. Section V details the optimal stopping conditions predicted by our model. Then, in Section VII, we summarize our conclusions.

2. Related Work

Since Ahn and Dabbish first proposed the concept of the ESP game in [4], a number of social games based on similar ideas have been developed. In the ESP game, players are required to guess the same label for a given image provided by the system. Subsequently, Ahn et al. proposed `Peekaboom` [7], which does not require participants to submit appropriate descriptions for a given image. Instead, players must "circle" a certain object in the image based on a given description. The main difference between an ESP game and `Peekaboom` game is that, in an ESP game, the players guess *what* an image is but they describe *where* an object is in an image in `Peekaboom`.

`Verbosity` [6] collects so-called commonsense decisions of the game's two participants, where one participant acts as the Narrator and the other plays the Guesser. In the game, the Narrator must describe a secret word with a statement comprised of one of the predefined templates and a phrase given by the Narrator. The phrase input by the Narrator cannot include the secret word. The Guesser must guess the secret word based solely on the Narrator's statement. Once the latter makes a successful guess, the system will record the Narrator's statement and use it for further research on knowledge or commonsense reasoning and analysis.

A similar game called `Phetch` [5] is designed to capture users' natural language expressiveness about an image. In this game, a Describer is given a secret image and he/she helps one or more Seekers find the image by describing it with textual statements. The Seekers need to search for the image via an image search engine. Once any of the Seekers successfully identifies the image, the system will record the textual statements given by the Describer and use them as a corpus for research on natural language understanding.

Our work differs significantly from previous studies because we do not propose a new game to test the participants' knowledge. As the ESP game is an effective social computation platform that can "extract" users' knowledge during game play, we believe that it can be "optimized" in terms of "outcomes" through appropriate design. Thus, we focus on how to decide the game settings so that the system can derive more useful information given a fixed amount of resources, i.e., the number of participants. Via analytical modeling, we show that the utility of an ESP game can be maximized by choosing an appropriate stopping condition, i.e., the number of matches needed before a puzzle is considered solved.

3. Modeling of ESP Games

In this section, we describe the proposed probabilistic model for generalized ESP games. First we detail our assumptions and define the variables of the model. We then estimate the number of rounds required to solve a puzzle, as well as the number of good and bad labels suggested by participants before a puzzle is finally solved. Finally, based on our model, we evaluate the productivity of an ESP game by three characteristics, namely, efficiency, quality, and utility.

A. Assumptions

Our model of an ESP game is based on the following assumptions:

1) *Round-based play.* We assume that the game play is round-based rather than continuous. In each round, a player can only make one guess about the current

puzzle, and the system checks whether the players' guesses match at the end of each round.

2) *Independent guess.* For model tractability, we assume that subsequent guesses by a player are independent and identically distributed; that is, a player's current guess is not affected by his/her guesses in previous rounds. Although this assumption somewhat simplifies realistic user behavior, it does not affect the model's accuracy significantly. We discuss this point further in Section VI-A.

Good and bad words. We assume that the number of "good" labels for each puzzle is limited, so all remaining words are considered "bad", i.e., inappropriate. The good words are not known by the game system or the participants a priori. We assume that players will do their best to guess good words in the vocabulary. However, there is a possibility that they will fail to pick the right words; instead, they may make a guess from the bad vocabulary due to a spelling error, a memory error, a misunderstanding, or as a deliberate
ploy.

4) *Uniform guess.* How human beings conceptualize puzzles has yet to be statistically mod-eled. Therefore, we assume that players' guesses are drawn uniformly from both the good and bad vocabulary pools.

Name	Meaning
n	number of players
m	number of guesses required to reach a consensus
k	number of tags required to solve a puzzle
v_{good}	size of the good vocabulary
V_{bad}	size of the bad vocabulary
d	total size of the vocabularies
$prob_{good}$	probability of choosing good words in a round
$prob_{bad}$	probability of choosing bad words in a round

Table 1. Variable definitions

In our model, we assume that n players participate in a game. In addition, the consensus threshold is set to m, and the stopping condition is set to k. For a certain puzzle, the size of the good vocabulary is denoted by $v_{goo(i}$, while that of the bad vocabulary is denoted by v_{bad}. Thus, the total number of words that players can choose from is $d = v_{good} + v_{bad}$. The probability that a player will guess a word in the good vocabulary is $prob_{good}$; and the probability that a player will guess a bad word is $prob_{bad}$, which is equal to $1 - prob_{good}$. The variables used in the model are summarized in Table I.

B. Time Required to Solve Puzzles

We begin by modeling the number of rounds required to solve a puzzle, i.e., how many rounds it takes to satisfy the specified stopping condition k. The terms "consensus" and "match" are used interchangeably to indicate that a label has been proposed by m players, and denote the label as a *matched label.* In addition, we define a discrete random variable, S, to represent the number of rounds needed to solve a puzzle, and write the probability mass function of S as follows:

$fs(s)$ = Pr(a puzzle is solved in the s_{th} round) = Pr(no. of matches > k in the s_{th} round),

which is equivalent to

Pr (no. of matches > k in the first s rounds) – Pr (no. of matches > k in the first $(s - 1)$ rounds). We assume the probability that exactly i matches will occur in the first s rounds is $P(i;\ s)$, and that the i matches will comprise i_{good} matches from good words and i_{bad} matches from bad words. The number of good matches, i_{good}, must be in the range 0 and $min(i,v_{good})$, and $i_{good} + i_{bad}$ i.

Now we focus on computing the probability of i_{good} matches in the first s rounds. On average, each player in the first s rounds proposes $s_{good} = s \bullet prob_{good}$ good words and $s_{bad} = s \bullet prob_{bad}$ bad words. A match in the first s rounds indicates that at least m players propose the same label in a total of $n \bullet s$ guesses. Moreover, if the matched label is a good word, then the match indicates that at least m players propose that label in a total of $n \bullet s_{good}$ guesses.e can model the probability of one good match occurring in the first s rounds as

$$\begin{aligned}&\Pr(\text{one good match in the first } s \text{ rounds})\\&= P_{good}(1)\\&= 1-\sum_{q=0}^{m-1}\binom{n \bullet s_{good}}{q}\left(\frac{1}{v_{good}}\right)^{q}\left(1-\frac{1}{v_{good}}\right)^{n \bullet s_{good}-q}\end{aligned} \tag{1}$$

Next, we model the probability of i_{good} good matches occurring in the first s rounds. The i_{good} good matches indicate that i_{good} words have been matched, but the remaining $v_{good} - i_{good}$ good words have yet to be matched. Thus, we have a total of C''^{sood} combinations of matched labels. The probabilities of the combinations are equivalent because each word has an equal probability, l/v_{good}, of being selected.herefore, the probability of i_{good} good matches in the first s rounds can be computed by

$$\begin{aligned}&P_{good}\left(i_{good}\right)\\&= C_{i_{good}}^{v_{good}} P_{good}(1)^{i_{good}}\left[1-P_{good}(1)\right]^{v_{good}-i_{good}}.\end{aligned} \tag{2}$$

Similarly, the probability of i_{bad} bad matches in the first s rounds can be computed by

$$\begin{aligned}&P_{bad}\left(i_{bad}\right)\\&= C_{i_{bad}}^{v_{bad}} P_{bad}(1)^{i_{bad}}\left[1-P_{bad}(1)\right]^{v_{bad}-i_{bad}}.\end{aligned} \tag{3}$$

Combining Eq. 2 and Eq. 3, we can derive the probability of i matches in the first s rounds as

$$P(i;s) = \sum_{i_{good}=0}^{\min(i,v_{good})} P_{good}\left(i_{good}\right)P_{bad}\left(i_{bad}\right),$$

where i_{good} must be in the range 0 and $min(i,v_{good})$ and the sum of i_{good} and i_{bad} must be i. After rewriting the probability mass function of S, the number of rounds needed to solve a puzzle becomes

$$f_s(s) = \sum_{q=1}^{s} f_s(q)$$
$$= \left[1 - \sum_{i=0}^{k-1} P(i;s)\right] - \left[1 - \sum_{i=0}^{k-1} P(i;s-1)\right].$$

Finally, we obtain the expected number of rounds needed to solve a puzzle as follows:

$$E(s) = \sum_{s=1} s \bullet f_s(s).$$

C. Number of Matches

In the above subsection, we consider that how many rounds are required for players to achieve consensus on k different labels. Next, we model the composition of the matched labels, i.e., how many good labels and bad labels are matched. First, we derive the expected number of good matches. If we assume that the puzzle is solved in the s_{th} round; then, on average, $n \bullet s_{good}$ guesses will be made by n players, and each of the guesses will be drawn from the v_{good} good words.e treat the question of whether a certain word is a match or not as a Bernoulli event, where "success" indicates that the label is matched and "fail" indicates a non-match. The probability of a good label being matched in the first s rounds is shown in Eq. 1. Consequently, the sum of the Bernoulli random variable of each good word will be a binomial random variable with a success probability equal to Eq. 1. It can be computed as

$$\sum_{v_i \in V_{good}} I(v_i \text{ matched}), \tag{4}$$

where V_{good} denotes the set of good words, and $I(\cdot)$ denotes the indicator function. Let $N_{good}(s)$ be the expected value of Eq. 4, i.e., the expected number of good matches in the first s rounds. The value can be derived by $N_{bad}(s)$, the expected number of bad matches in the first s rounds, can be derived similarly by

$$N_{good}(s) = v_{good} \bullet P_{good}(1)$$
$$= v_{good} \left\{ 1 - \left[\sum_{q=0}^{m-1} \binom{n - s_{good}}{q} \right] \left(\frac{1}{v_{good}} \right)^{q} \times \left(1 - \frac{1}{v_{good}} \right)^{n \bullet s_{good} - q} \right] \right\}.$$

Note that both $N_{good}(\text{-})$ and $N_{bad}(\text{-})$ are functions of S, the number of rounds required to solve a puzzle. In other words, for puzzles that require a different number of rounds to find a solution, the expected number of good matches and bad matches will also be different.Efficiency, Quality, and Utility Here we explain how we evaluate the productivity of an ESP game. We define *the efficiency of an ESP game as the rate that labels are matched for the given images.Ifthe* number of participants remains the same, higher efficiency indicates that

the system is more "productive" given the same amount of resources. Thus, we consider game settings that lead to higher efficiency as more desirable.n addition, we define *the quality of an ESP game as the proportion of good labels among all the matched labels.* Higher quality indicates that the matched labels are more likely to be appropriate descriptions of the target puzzle. Thus, we naturally seek game settings that yield high-quality matched labels.However, there is often a trade-off between efficiency and quality in a real system because configurations that yield higher efficiency often lead to lower quality; conversely, settings that yield higher quality may impact on the level of efficiency. For this reason, we define *the utility of an ESP game as the product of the game's efficiency and quality.* This definition enables us to explain utility as *the throughput rate ofgood labels produced by an ESP game.*
Based on the probabilistic model presented in this section, we can write the formula of the efficiency, quality, and utility of an ESP game as follows:

$$\begin{aligned} Efficiency &= \frac{E\left(N_{good}(s)+N_{bad(S)}\right)}{E(s)}; \\ Quality &= \frac{E\left(N_{good}(s)\right)}{E\left(N_{good}(s)+N_{bad}(s)\right)}; \\ Utility &= \frac{E\left(N_{good}(s)\right)}{E(s)}. \end{aligned} \tag{5}$$

Name	Default value	Name	Default value
n	**2**	d	**1000**
m	**2**	$prob_{good}$	**0.8**
$^{v}{}_{good}$	**20**	$prob_{bad}$	**1 -** $prob_{good}$
V_{bad}	^{d} $^{v}{}_{good}$	T	**10000**

Table 2. Default values of variables

4. Model Validation

In this section, we describe the simulations used to validate our model. After explaining the simulation setup, we compare the utility computed by our model with that derived in the simulations. The effects of various game parameters on the game's utility are also considered.

A. Simulation Setup

We designed our simulator based on the rules of ESP games. In each round, there are n players, each of which randomly selects a good word with probability $prob_{good}$, and a bad word with probability $prob_{bad}$. At the end of each round, the simulator checks the number of matches to determine whether the current puzzle has been solved. If m matches are found, all the players' guesses are erased to simulate that the participants are trying to solve a new puzzle; otherwise, the simulator just advances to the next round. The simulator assumes the number of puzzles is infinite, and that there are always n players ready to participate in a game. The simulations end after running for T rounds, no matter how many puzzles have been solved. We then compute the average efficiency, quality, and utility of the matches based on the time taken to solve each puzzle and the number of good and bad matches recorded during the simulations.

To investigate the accuracy of our model under different settings, we change the parameters and observe whether the simulated quantity of good and bad matches is identical to or close to that computed by our analytical model. Specifically, we change the four major variables, i.e., the number of players, n; the consensus threshold, m; the size of the good vocabulary, v_{good}; and the probability that the players will guess a good word, $prob_{good}$. When evaluating the effect of one variable, the other three are set to their default values, as shown in Table II. Moreover, when we adjust the consensus threshold, we set the number of players at 20, as the consensus threshold must be no greater than the number of players.

B.Validation by Utility Curves

Although we have defined three key characteristics of an ESP game, namely, the efficiency, quality, and utility, we only validate the accuracy of our model by a game's utility. This is because the magnitude of the utility depends on the efficiency and the quality; thus, the utility is unlikely to be correct if the values of the other two characteristics are incorrect. Since our objective is to optimize the utility of ESP games by changing the game settings, the model's accuracy in predicting a game's utility should be examined more carefully.

In the following, we investigate how the utility of an ESP game changes under different stopping conditions, k. As shown in Fig. 1, the utility reaches its maximum when $n = 2$ and $k = 10$. As the number of participants increases, the shapes of the utility curves change slightly, and the optimal stopping condition shifts slightly to the lower k values. The concave shape of the utility curve indicates that, as k increases, there should be a tradeoff between the efficiency and quality of ESP games such that the utility curve is not monotonic. To demonstrate the tradeoff between efficiency and quality, we plot the values of all three characteristics in Fig. 2. Clearly, the game's efficiency increases as k increases, while its utility decreases. The utility reaches the highest point when k is around 15.

We now consider the effects of the other parameters on the utility curves of ESP games, and check the correspondence between the results derived by our model and those of the simulations. The effects of the consensus threshold, the size of the good vocabulary, and the probability that players will guess a good word are investigated. However, because of space limitations, Fig. 3 only shows the effect of the consensus threshold. For all the parameters, the utility curves computed by our model are very close to those derived by the simulations. We observe that the consensus threshold and the size of the good vocabulary have a strong effect on the optimal stopping condition, while the number of participants and the probability of choosing good words have relatively little effect.

C.Effect of Game Settings

We now examine the effect of various game settings on the game's utility. The relationships between the utility and different game parameters are shown in Fig. 4. Figure 4(a) shows that if more players participate in a game simultaneously, the matching rate of good words increases faster than linearly, as the number of guess-pairs grows quadratically. In contrast, if the consensus threshold is raised, as shown in Fig. 4(b), the game's utility declines exponentially, but the quality of the matched results increases. The size of the good vocabulary also has a substantial impact on the game's utility. Figure 4(c) shows that the utility gradually decreases as the size of the good vocabulary increases because of the lower probability that two participants will guess the same good word. Finally, as expected, the game's utility increases linearly as the probability of guessing good words rises. Note that, in all the graphs, the utility scores computed via simulations and by our model match closely, which demonstrates the accuracy of our analytical model.

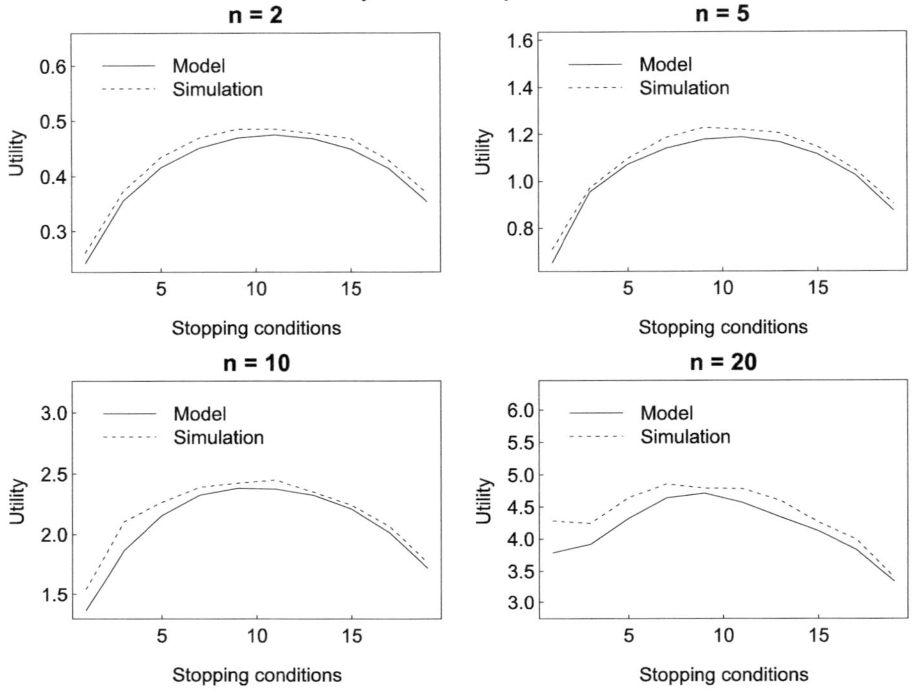

Fig. 1. The relationships between utility and stopping conditions under different n.

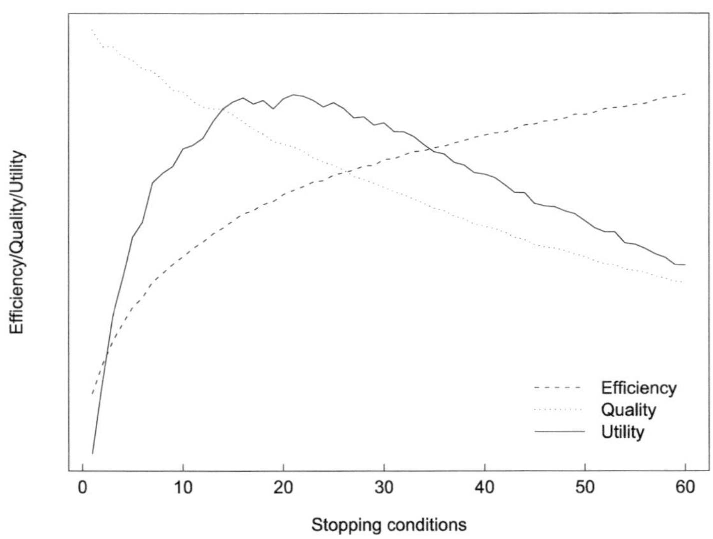

Fig. 2. The relationships between efficiency, quality, and utility in an ESP game.

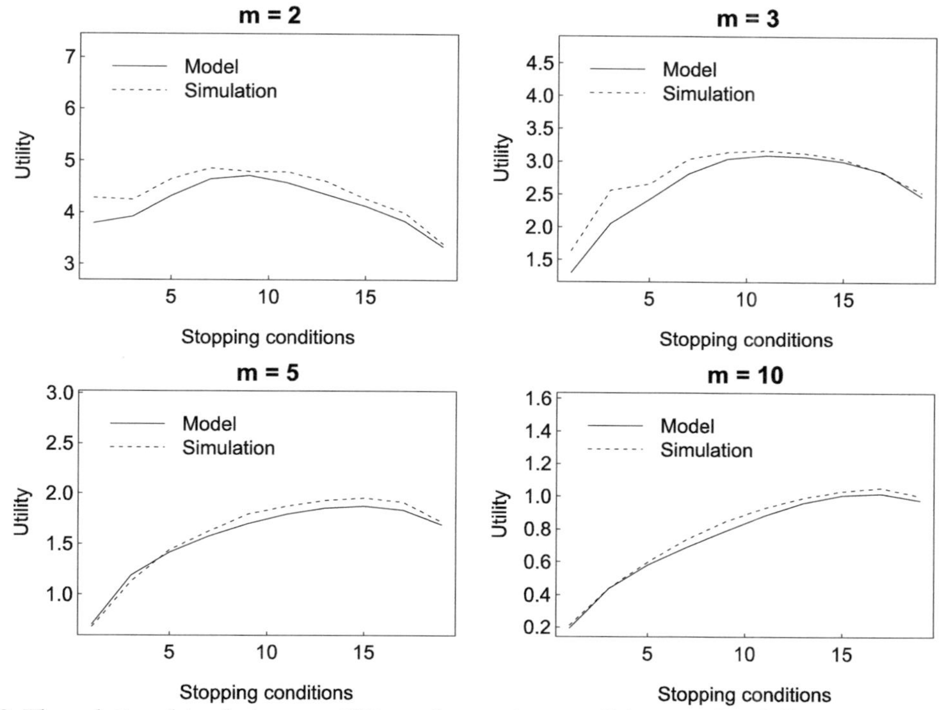

Fig. 3. The relationships between utility and stopping conditions under different m.

5. Optimal Stopping Conditions

In this section, we focus on how to set the stopping condition to maximize an ESP game's utility. We explain the derivation of the optimal stopping conditions, and discuss how they change under different configurations. In addition, we examine how our optimization method improves the game's utility.

A. Computation

The utility equation of our model (Eq. 5) is a discontinuous function, so we cannot obtain its optimal point by differentiating the function with respect to the stopping conditions. Therefore, we derive it in a numerical way. From Section IV-B, we know that the utility function that takes the stopping condition, k, as the only parameter is a unimodal function. In addition, the domain

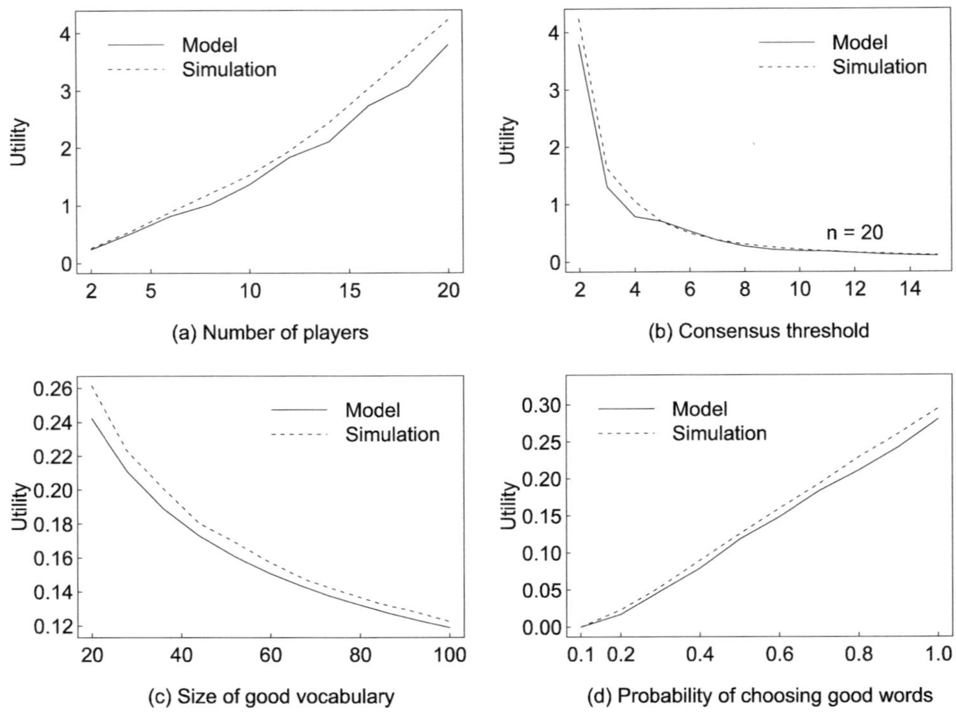

Fig. 4. The effect of other parameters on utility.

of *k* is a positive integer, which is usually small (less than 100 in most of our scenarios). Thus, we use an exhaustive search to find the maximum utility within a reasonable range, say, from 1 to 200. In our implementation, this exhaustive search process takes only a few seconds on a commodity PC.

B. Effect of Parameters

Here, we consider the effect of different parameters on the optimal stopping conditions. Interestingly, the number of participants does not affect the optimal stopping conditions, as shown in Fig. 5(a). This is reasonable because the probability of good matches and bad matches remains the same regardless of the number of players, which only affects the rate of label matching. The consensus threshold, on the other hand, affects the optimal stopping conditions significantly when it increases, as shown in Fig. 5(b).

This behavior can be explained by the occurrence probability of good matches relative to that of bad matches. Raising the consensus threshold makes label matching more difficult; however, the advantage is that matching bad labels will become relatively more difficult than matching good labels. Therefore, when the consensus threshold increases, the matching rate of good labels will grow faster than that of bad labels; consequently, the optimal stopping condition is deferred to allow more good words to be matched before finishing the puzzle.

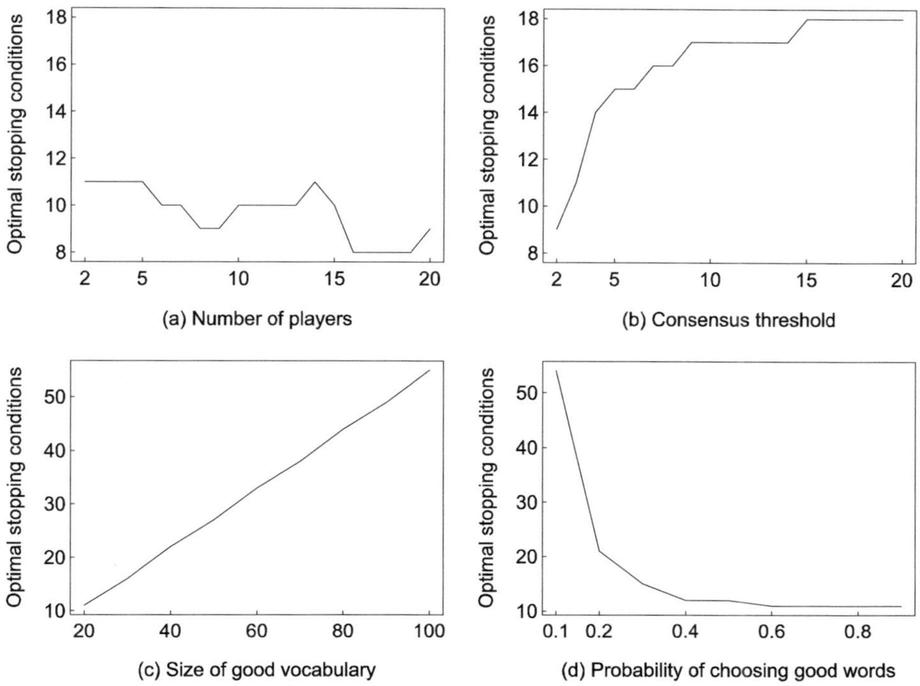

Fig. 5. The effect of the parameters on the optimal stopping conditions

The size of the good vocabulary and the probability of choosing good words have similar impacts on the optimal stopping conditions. Both increasing the number of good words and reducing the probability of choosing good words increase the optimal stopping conditions because they make matching good labels more difficult. Thus, a relatively late stopping condition is required in order to increase the proportion of good matches.

C. Benefit of Optimization

To demonstrate how optimization improves the game's achieved utility, we examine the gain derived by adopting the optimal stopping condition suggested by our model. We define the *utility gain* as the ratio of the utility of an optimized game to that of a simple ESP game, i.e., with the stopping condition set to 1.

The relationships between the utility gain and various game parameters are shown in Fig. 6. We observe that, the optimization achieved by adopting the optimal stopping condition generally provides a utility boost that is 2 or more times higher than that of the simple ESP game. Even if we consider a more conservative scenario, where only two participants play the game and the consensus threshold is set to 2, the utility gain will be around 2, assuming the number of good words is 20 and the probability of choosing good words is 0.8. Moreover, the utility gain increases rapidly as either the consensus threshold or the size of the good vocabulary increases. The utility gain is only significantly lower than 2 when the number of participants is much higher than 2. However, we can still achieve a utility gain of around 1.3, even the number of players is as high as 20. These findings demonstrate that the utility optimization provided by our analytical model can generally provide twice as much utility as a non-optimized game, which stops immediately after a label has been matched.

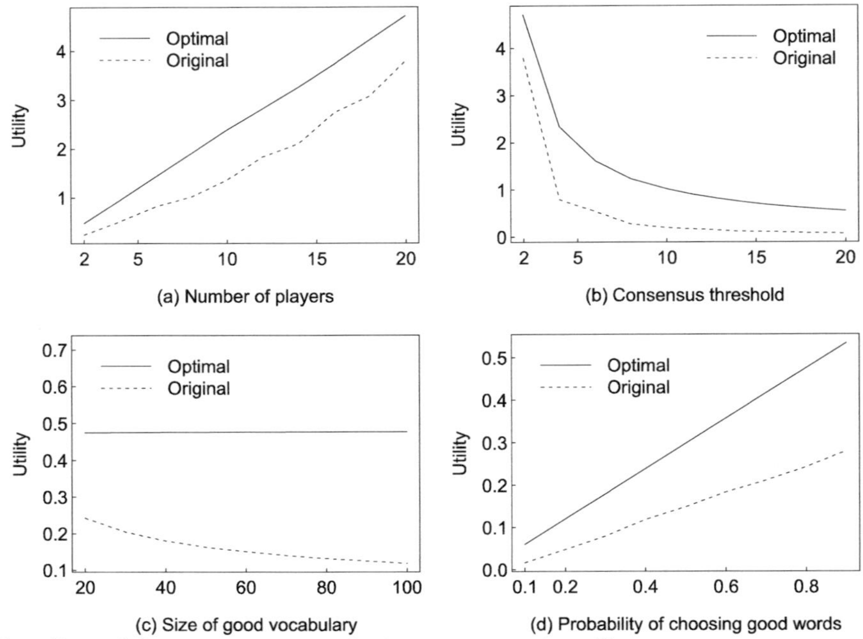

Fig. 6. The effect of the parameters on the improvement in utility

6. Discussion

In this section, we discuss the effects of the assumptions used by our analytical model and some issues that may occur when applying our optimization technique in real-life ESP games.

A. Model Assumptions

One major assumption of our analysis is that the guesses made by each player are independent of each other. in practice, players remember what labels they have already used and avoid submitting duplicate guesses. However, considering the "memory" effect would make the analytical modeling too complicated to manage. Thus, we adopt the independent guess assumption and examine its impact on the model's accuracy by simulations.

To demonstrate that our model provides a reasonable solution for utility optimization, we show the optimal utility achieved by different models and simulations respectively in Fig. 7. Because we do not actually construct an ideal model that takes the memory effect into consideration, we compute its output by simulations. On the graph, the three curves in the figure represent the optimal utility achieved by the ideal model, by our model with the independent guess assumption, and by simple games in which k is set to 1. The results show that both models yield much higher utility than the simple games. Even though our model does not provide as high utility as the ideal model, the games that adopt the stopping condition suggested by our model still achieve near optimal utility. In view of the complexity of modeling with the memory effect, we consider that our independent guess assumption is a reasonable tradeoff between the model's computational complexity and the degree of optimization we are pursuing.

Another assumption of our model is that players uniformly guess words in the vocabulary pool. In practice, players may guess according to some preferences. For example, they may prefer to guess more common, shorter words first, or guess more specific words first, because they think a particular strategy would lead to consensus more quickly. Players' strategies in prioritizing their label choices may significantly impact the outcome of an ESP game. In addition, the situation becomes more complex when players with different strategies are assigned to the same game. Thus, we leave the modeling of players' strategies for choosing words to a future work.

B. Choice of Parameters

To put our model to real use, we must first address the problem of how to choose the model's parameters, especially the size of the good vocabulary and the probability that players will guess a good word. We believe that these parameters could be measured *empirically* from reallife observations. Specifically, one can take the average number of labels on which there has been a consensus in a large number of games as the size of the good vocabulary. Accordingly, one can compute the probability that players will guess a good word by the ratio of guesses that fall into the set of the good vocabulary. While the parameters may be different due to the types of puzzles and the composition of the participants, an empirical choice of parameters like this would be the most appropriate way to achieve accurate modeling results and thereby optimize the utility of games.

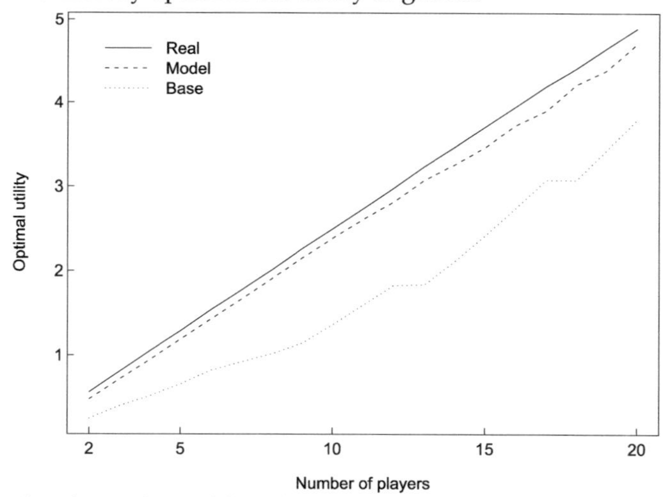

Fig. 7. The optimal utility achieved by ideal modeling, independent modeling, and simple games without optimization.

7. Conclusion

We have proposed a generalized ESP game in which the number of players, the consensus threshold, and the stopping condition are variable. In addition, we have presented an analytical model that computes the efficiency, quality, and utility of an ESP game given the game's settings. Via extensive simulations, we show that by applying the optimal stopping condition predicted by our model, the game's utility will be usually be at least 2 times higher than that of a non-optimized game. This feature can be leveraged by game service providers to improve the utilization of finite player efforts in order to maximize both the efficiency and quality of the matched labels.

8. References

[1] C. Lampe and P. Resnick, "Slash (dot) and burn: distributed moderation in a large online conversation space," *Proceedings of the 2004 conference on Human factors in computing systems,* pp. 543-550, 2004.

[2] D. Stork *et al.,* "The Open Mind Initiative," *IEEE Expert Systems and Their Applications,,* vol. 14, no. 3, pp. 19-20, 1999.

[3] L. von Ahn, M. Blum, N. Hopper, and J. Langford, "CAPTCHA: Using hard AI problems for security," in *Proceedings of Eurocrypt.* Springer, 2003.

[4] L. von Ahn and L. Dabbish, "Labeling images with a computer game," *Proceedings of the SIGCHI conference on Human factors in computing systems,* pp. 319-326, 2004.

[5] L. von Ahn, S. Ginosar, M. Kedia, and M. Blum, "Improving Image Search with PHETCH," *Acoustics, Speech and Signal Processing, 2007. ICASSP 2007. IEEE International Conference on,* vol. 4, 2007.

[6] L. von Ahn, M. Kedia, and M. Blum, "Verbosity: a game for collecting common-sense facts," *Proceedings of the SIGCHI conference on Human Factors in computing systems,* pp. 75-78,2006.

[7] L. von Ahn, R. Liu, and M. Blum, "Peekaboom: a game for locating objects in images," *Proceedings ofthe SIGCHI conference on Human Factors in computing systems,* pp. 55-64,2006.

[8] L. von Ahn, B. Maurer, C. McMillen, D. Abraham, and M. Blum, "reCAPTCHA: Human-based character recognition via web security measures," *Science,* vol. 321, no. 5895, p. 1465,2008.

15

Web Intelligence for the Assessment of Information Quality: Credibility, Correctness, and Readability

Johan F. Hoorn and Teunis D. van Wijngaarden
VU University Amsterdam
Netherlands

1. Introduction

There is a shift in the use of the Internet at the cost of traditional media to access scientific information. By mere frequency of exposure, the information of Web sites seems 'more true' than the usually heavily reviewed and editorially controlled scientific venues (cf. Johnson & Kaye, 1998). In addition, the bulk of users are non-expert in a particular field (e.g., health, finance) but nevertheless use the first links Google shows to make decisions that affect their lives. Most users do not verify the information they find. Quality labels are overlooked or have little meaning to the non-expert user. A strong selection criterion for non-expert users is the readability of a site and scientific papers are not known for being easy in that respect. Speed before accuracy seems to be the doctrine for Web engineers, designers, and users alike but we wish to turn that principle around by proposing an intelligent Web service that assesses the quality of information by combining Web-page credibility through Google's PageRank algorithm, informational correctness through text mining, and over 200 formulas for readability measurement; everything under one button, rendering one simple graphical output in a 3D space.

Compared to the traditional media such as newspapers, radio, or television, its de-central nature makes the Internet non-selective in who takes the floor. Flanagin and Metzger put it like this: "Whereas newspapers, books, magazines, and television all undergo certain levels of factual verification, analysis of content, and editorial review, by and large Internet information is subject to no such scrutiny." Editorial functions now fall upon the shoulder of the media consumer (Flanagin & Metzger, 2000). Certain traditional media try to survive by maintaining a digital counterpart on the Web (e.g., the Washington Post).

The Internet provides information for the public at large and people can individually access that information without the interference of a third party such as a teacher, journalist or other expert. Nowadays, the Internet is used for information seeking more than books, television, or newspapers (Flanagin & Metzger, 2001). Web publishing happens on a global scale and bypasses the traditional media gate-keepers such as publishing houses. Sites that provide means to shape content in a collaborative way are, for example, YouTube[1] (a movie Web site) and Wikipedia[2] (an online encyclopedia). Web-based content management systems such as Joomla![3] make Web publishing all too easy. Not a lot of technical skills are needed, for instance, to install the software, but even this can be left to specialized Web design bureaus. There are almost no boundaries, except that illegal information (e.g., porn or cracked software) can be prohibited by law.

Reality is that not many people verify information (Flanagin & Metzger, 2000). They trust the information found on the Internet, although it depends on what the user is planning to use that information for (Rieh & Belkin, 1998). In reviewing the literature, Johnson and Kaye found that young adults trust the Internet more then other media (Johnson & Kaye, 1998).

Health information is particularly wanted (Fox, 2005) and people judge, interpret, and use that information without consulting a physician (cf. self-medication), which may have considerable repercussions if done in the wrong way. Research actually shows quite some variety in the quality of health Web sites (Griffiths et al., 2005). Griffiths and Christensen evaluated the quality of health Web sites while looking at site ownership and editorship. They found that for only 40% of the sites, health professionals were involved in editing (Griffiths & Christensen, 2005).

Consumers in the early years deemed the Web as credible as traditional media (Flanagin & Metzger, 2000). Only recently, some cracks in this image occurred but not to a large extent (Flanagin & Metzger, 2007). One could argue that with the growth of the Web as indicated by the number of hosts (Internet Systems Consortium, 2007; Ministy of Economic Development of New Zealand, 2003), users became experienced and should be streetwise by now with respect to credibility of the information source. The opposite is true, however: People perceive their most used or preferred medium as the most credible source (Johnson & Kaye, 1998). Heavy users verify information the least (Flanagin & Metzger, 2000). This is in line with the repeatedly confirmed finding in cultivation theory that mere-exposure to media determines the way people look at the world (e.g., Morgan, in press).

In other words, ripe and green are made known to the world and the world consumes this information without much critique. In particular heavy users may conceive of the Internet as the most credible of all media, a problem that in the near future – the younger generations – can only become more severe.

The main question, then, is how to discern good quality information from bad quality information. In 2005, *Nature* published a Korean research paper about the cloning of a dog (Lee, et al., 2005) that in 2006, was compromised because one of the authors admitted that the results were faked.[4] Thus, highly credible sources (*Nature*) may pass on incorrect information (fake data).

Information *correctness* is one of the trickiest things to verify because it touches upon our deepest epistemic beliefs. What is 'true' in religion may not be 'true' in science or vice versa. The source of information could give a clue. That is, a university professor may be regarded as more of an expert than a lay person. Yet, professors can be wrong and lay people are sometimes right, so *credibility* may be an indicator but is not definitive. In addition, a

[1] http://www.youtube.com
[2] http://www.wikipedia.org
[3] http://www.joomla.org
[4] http://www.smm.org/buzz/blog/lies_in_korean_stem_cell_research

biochemical publication about leukemia in *The Lancet* may be correct and credible, but will be ignored by the non-expert audience because to them it is not *readable*.

In this chapter, we attempt to develop a measurement tool that helps people in determining the quality of an information Web site by indicating the estimated correctness of information, the estimated credibility of the source, and the readability of the text. We will stumble upon many hurdles and try to take them anyways in the hope that our attempts are thought-provoking enough to inspire a new generation of information-quality assessment tools.

2. Information quality

Quality of information seems to be a container term. In this section, we attempt to conceptualize 'correctness,' 'credibility,' and 'readability,' which supposedly contribute to information quality. We argue that correctness is an aspect of the information, credibility of the source, and readability of the user's level of expertise.

2.1 Conceptualization

Quality is often mentioned in health-related contexts and pertains to the actual content of a Web site in terms of correctness, readability, and completeness (e.g., Price & Hersh, 1999; Griffiths et al., 2005). The word quality is often used to indicate correctness or accuracy of information but then again, correctness is used interchangeably with credibility. In our view, this indicates that quality should be decomposed into a number of quality indicators. Moreover, that correctness and credibility may be highly related concepts but that they are not the same.

Flanagin and Metzger define credibility in terms of believability, accuracy, trustworthiness, bias, and completeness of information (Flanagin & Metzger, 2000). In comparing political Web sites with traditional media, Johnson and Kaye (1998) measured credibility as believability, fairness, accuracy, and depth (completeness). Credibility is also indicated by a Web site's domain, i.e. .com or .gov (Treise et al., 2003; Rieh & Belkin, 1998).

Credibility seems to be indicated by status and appearance factors of the source rather than correctness of information, although the latter does contribute. To measure credibility, for example, Flanagin and Metzger asked Internet users to indicate whether they checked the author of a Web site, whether contact information was provided, what the author's qualifications and credentials were, what the author's goals/objectives with the published information were, if the information itself was current, if other sources were available for validation, if there was a stamp of approval or recommendation, if the information was an opinion or fact and if the information was complete and comprehensive (Flanagin & Metzger, 2000). In other words, credibility is a surrogate for correctness of information, probably because it is easier to check and somehow is related to correctness.

If this is so, many aspects that are mentioned to indicate credibility actually indicate correctness. Accuracy and completeness are aspects of information correctness whereas believability, trustworthiness, and bias are aspects of credibility.

Quality was also indicated by readability. Readability can be approached from two sides, whether the text is easy enough that it can be accessed by lay people or whether lay people have enough reading skills to understand a text. This division is visible in the type of readability formulas available on the market. The Flesh (1948) reading ease score is a typical example of the first and estimates how easy a text is. Its successor, the Flesh Grade Level, estimates the school grade a reader should have to be able to read a certain text. All readability measures use text properties such as syllables and sentence length to estimate a score (Hartley et al., 2004) but it is hard to decide whether such text properties indicate readability seen as reading 'ease' or as 'appropriate to the reading level of the user.'

The confusion of terms points at quite some conceptual overlap. Just like credibility and correctness may be positively correlated, readability and correctness may be negatively correlated. An explanation of a disease may be incomplete, whereas for the sake of readability certain omissions in the story may be desired. In other words, a validation of concepts and a verification of the strength of their distinctive power are most wanted.

Table 1 provides the items that in our view indicate correctness, credibility, and readability. We regard credibility an aspect of the source and correctness an aspect of the message. If readability is connected to reading level, it is an aspect of the user. Credibility is indicated by reliability, believability, trustworthiness, bias of information, and fairness (Rieh & Belkin, 1998; Flanagin & Metzger, 2000; Johnson & Kaye, 1998). Correctness is indicated by accuracy, completeness, and depth (Price & Hersh, 1999; Griffiths, et al., 2005). Readability (whether ease or level) is indicated by, among others, number of syllables and sentence length (e.g., Flesh, 1948; Hartley et al., 2004).

Aspect of source	**Credibility** • Reliability • Believability • Trustworthiness • Bias of information • Fairness	Flanagin and Metzger (2000) Johnson and Kaye (1998)
Aspect of message	**Correctness** • Accuracy • Completeness • Depth	Price and Hersh (1999) Griffiths et al. (2005)
Aspect of receiver (i.e. level)	**Readability** • Number of syllables • Sentence length	Flesch (1948) Hartley et al. (2004)

Table 1. The three dimensions of information quality and some of their indicators

In sum, information quality appears to be a container concept that ranges from believability to readability. Correctness of information comes closest to what one may regard as 'the truth.' Credibility of the source indicates how seriously the content should be taken. Readability, then, is a compound of reading ease and reading level.

3. Quality assessment

In the early days of the Internet, quality of Web sites was verified by hand. In a later stage, the user was helped by automated protocols such as AQA (Automated Quality

Assessment). Later advances made use of Google PageRank or required a semi-automatic reviewing effort as observed in the Wikipedia community.

3.1 Evaluating Web sites by hand

Over the years, assessment methods such as checklists helped experts and novices alike to evaluate Web sites by hand. For instance, the Health Information Technology Institute of Mitretek Systems, Inc. made a list of criteria that consumers could use to assess the quality of Health Web sites (Price & Hersh, 1999). DISCERN was another rating tool for health Web sites (Charmock, et al., 1999). According to Griffiths and Christensen (2005), three studies investigated the relationship between DISCERN ratings and scientific quality rated by experts and two of them found a significant relation.

The Health on the Net Foundation developed a set of principles called the Net Code of Conduct (Price & Hersh, 1999). Web sites can voluntarily comply with these principles and express their commitment through a logo. Price and Hersh (1999) proposed to have experts review Web sites and publish the reviews on the Web. Again, the site's commitment can be expressed through an examination logo. Another option is a portal with references to good quality Web sites.

The questions with these approaches are whether the user should do a checklist for each site and which list they should use? There are many logos around, but what are they worth? Checklists and logos relate to the credibility of a source, not to its contents. Who reviews the reviewer? Internet is a volatile medium - who reevaluates whether information is still up-to-date?

3.2 Early tooling

Eysenbach and Diepgen (1998) attempted to label the quality of health information by attaching metadata to each document. They argued that not only the authors should provide metadata but third parties such as rating services should do so as well. Browsers could use that metadata to filter out pages that do not meet personal quality criteria as predefined by the user. These authors concluded that an "agreed formal international standard for medial publication on the internet, enforced by appropriate peer or government organisations" was not realistic. Nevertheless, they argued for at least a standard for the labeling of health-related information. In addition, Eysenbach and Diepgen (1998) proposed that the "potential of computers to determine indirect quality indicators by means of automatic (mathematical) methods" should be explored.

Price and Hersh (1999) employed two engines to search for user-requested information. The outcomes were merged, downloaded, analyzed, the resulting URLs scored, and listed for the user. These criteria were used to assess quality in terms of relevance, credibility, absence of bias, content, currency, and value of links. The tool yielded a ranked list of URLs, but the researchers stated that evaluations remained necessary to verify that highly ranked pages were indeed more credible and that non-experts were able to use the tool. Moreover, the authors did not provide many details on the working of the tool. Although they posited that automatic analyses of Web pages for quality indicators is feasible and useful, they also stated that it is easier to identify indicators for undesirable Web pages than it is to identify indicators of high quality (Price & Hersh, 1999).

Automated Quality Assessment (AQA) as developed by Griffiths et al. (2005) consisted of six steps: Target Web sites were downloaded using web crawler software, the pages were aggregated with arbitrary pages, a previously learned relevance query was processed over the collection, a previously learned quality query was processed in the same way, site relevance and quality scores were computed and normalized, and the overall site score was computed. The relevance feedback-technique was used to learn the queries:

> A complex query consisting of weighted terms (words and phrases), is automatically generated by comparing the term frequency distributions of sets of relevant and irrelevant documents. (...) The resulting query is used by a text retrieval system to derive relevance scores for documents. (Griffiths et al., 2005)

Griffiths et al. (2005) did the same for the quality query. These authors claimed to be the first that made a customized automated tool for identifying the evidence-based quality of health information that focuses on accuracy rather than reliability. They stated that the tool is useful for quality portal maintainers to do the first selection. Their research focused on depression Web sites. To use AQA for other health topics requires a new training procedure. According to the authors, limitations of AQA are that it can be spammed (Web site owners can include terms that lead to high scores) and that the focus is solely on treatment information (Griffiths et al., 2005).

3.3 Google PageRank – indicating credibility

The Google PageRank algorithm (Brin & Page, 1998) is the central formula that ranks URLs found by Google's search engine.[5] The number is not the position in Google, but reflects the 'importance' of the page. The PageRank algorithm is based on graph theory. The Internet is represented as a directional graph (Figure 1), with every page being a node. Every link from page to page is represented by an arrow such that an incoming link is depicted as an incoming arrow.

The PageRank of page A is based on the PageRank of pages that link to page A. The more pages with a high PageRank link to A, the higher A's PageRank becomes. The assumption is that the height of Google PageRank indicates the importance of a page.

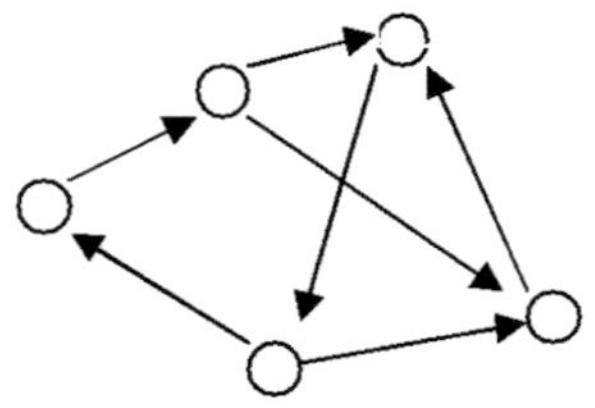

Fig. 1. Directional graph representing Internet links and targets

Chen et al. (2007) used an algorithm based on Google PageRank to assess the relative importance of all publications in the *Physical Review* family of journals from 1893 to 2003.

[5] http://www.google.com

They claimed that Google PageRank did better than simply counting the number of citations:

> We suggest that the Google number Gi of paper I (...) is a better measure of importance than the number of citiations alone in two aspects: (i) being cited by influential papers contributes more to the Google number than being cited by unimportant papers; (ii) being cited by a paper that itself has few references gives a larger contribution to the Google number, than being cited by a paper with hundreds of references. (Chen et al., 2007)

Griffiths and Christensen (2005) asserted that for consumers, Google PageRank was "as strong an indicator of evidence-based quality as DISCERN." Altogether, Google PageRank seems to provide a good indication of a Web site's credibility. We cannot regard PageRank as an indicator of information correctness, because PageRank processes hyperlinks and not contents.

3.4 Wikipedia – attaining correctness

Wiki software,[6] as developed by Ward Cunningham in 1995, allows anyone to edit a Web site from within the browser (Web-based) with a simple markup language for collaborative content creation. Wikipedia is an online encyclopedia based on the wiki principle. The English version of Wikipedia contains more than 2 million articles.[7]

The open way of content creation and editing raised questions with Stvilia, Twidale, Gasser & Smith (2005) as to why people bother to contribute at all, what the quality of the product is, and why people would trust and use it? Why does the project not disintegrate into anarchy? How is the project organized, and how do the processes change over time?

For our purposes, we would like to focus on the way Wikipedia treats information correctness. What technical facilities and social constraints are built into wiki and Wikipedia to improve and maintain the accuracy and verity of information?

3.4.1 Wikipedia's correctness

A CNET headline in December 2005 ran "Study: Wikipedia as accurate as Britannica" (Terdiman, 2005). The article referred to an investigation by *Nature* (Giles, 2005), claiming that Wikipedia came close to the traditional *Encyclopedia Britannica* in terms of accuracy. *Encyclopedia Britannica* responded that the *Nature* publication was wrong (Nature, 2006), but *Nature* still defends her findings (ibid.).

3.4.2 Vandalism on Wikipedia

Wikipedia can repair malicious edits such as mass deletion of content in a median time of 2.9 minutes (Viégas et al., 2007; Viégas et al., 2004). Because of the vandalism issue, certain pages are protected against changes. Semi-protected pages cannot be edited by anonymous and newly registered users.[8] Fully protected pages can only be edited by administrators.

---

[6] http://en.wikipedia.org/wiki/Wiki

[7] Based on their own statistics. See http://en.wikipedia.org/wiki/Main_Page

[8] http://en.wikipedia.org/wiki/Category:Semi-protected

Protection of a page must be requested on the talk pages and can be refused, "especially if they [the requests] are controversial, do not comply with Wikipedia policies, or do not have evidence of consensus."[9]

3.4.3 Featured articles

Wikipedia provides a list of featured articles that contains the best Wikipedia has to offer, according to the community (Figure 2 shows a screenshot). On the Wikipedia Web site, featured content is described as follows:

> These are the articles, pictures, and other contributions that showcase the polished result of the collaborative efforts that drive Wikipedia. All featured content undergoes a thorough review process to ensure that it meets the highest standards and can serve as an example of our end goals.[10]

Peer reviewed material has to comply with the following criteria:[11]

- 'well written'
- 'comprehensive', in a sense that it does not neglect major facts and details
- 'factually accurate', that is: verifiable against reliable sources to be supported with citations and references
- 'neutral', without bias
- 'stable', what means that there are no significantly changes from day to day
- following style guidelines (e.g., having a lead, using the right markup tags)
- having images where they are appropriate, with captions and acceptable copyright status
- of appropriate length, meaning staying focused

Users can nominate an article for receiving the featured status. Before a user nominates an article, s/he is asked to post it on a special page that solicits for peer review. A featured article can also be nominated to be denied its status.

In a way, the list of featured articles is a portal to the high quality content that Price and Hersh (1999) were looking for. The quality is assessed by peers who use a checklist (the criteria). Unlike other checklists mentioned earlier in this chapter, the Wikipedia assessment process is different in that no individual consumer or expert evaluates the page, but a group of people.

[9] http://en.wikipedia.org/wiki/Category:Wikipedia_protected_edit_requests
[10] http://en.wikipedia.org/wiki/Wikipedia:Featured_content
[11] http://en.wikipedia.org/wiki/Wikipedia:Featured_article_criteria

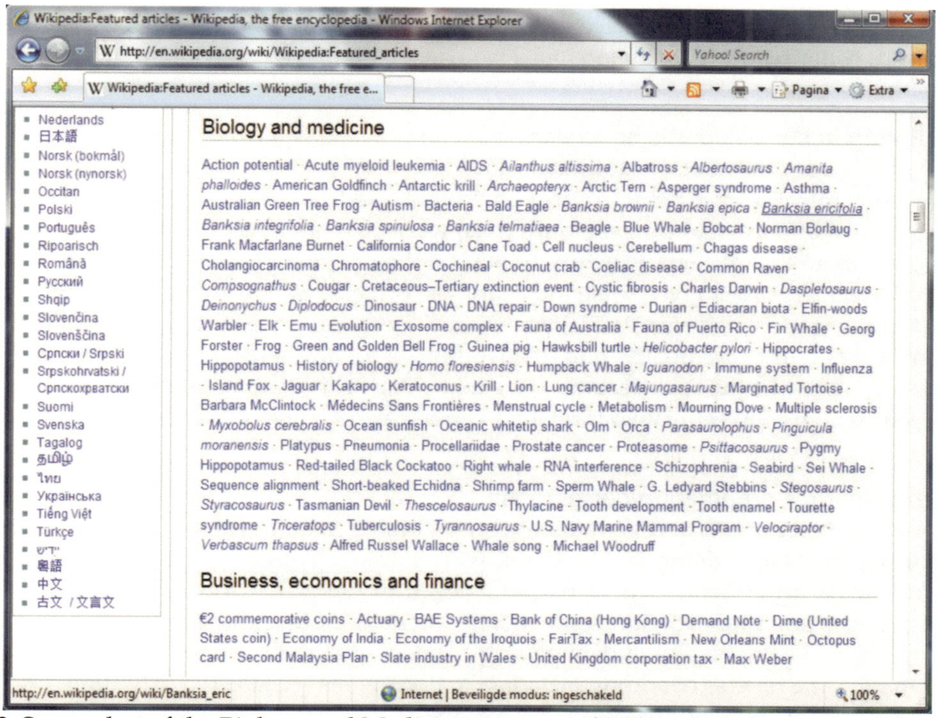

Fig. 2. Screenshot of the Biology and Medicine category of Wikipedia´s featured articles

The Wikipedia criteria fit in nicely with our concepts of credibility, correctness, and readability. That featured articles are as unbiased as possible, refer to verifiable sources, and show copyright status of images pertains to our notion of credibility. That featured content should be comprehensive, factually accurate, and stable (no significant changes from day to day), in our view, would indicate correctness of information. Readability, then, would be indicated by following style guidelines, being well written, using appropriate images (plus captions), and having appropriate length (focused).

3.4.4 Discussion pages

Wikipedia provides so called talk pages, which discuss the quality of a page. Talk pages can be attached to every page in Wikipedia. In addition, people can also post questions or can ask for additional information (Stvilia et al., 2005). Organized and readable discussions on talk pages add to the quality of Wikipedia content (Viégas et al., 2007; Stvilia et al., 2005).
Stvilia et al. (2005) analyzed the content of 60 discussion pages of featured articles and identified ten types of quality problems that Wikipedia users mentioned. There were problems with accessibility, accuracy, authority, completeness, complexity, consistency, informativeness, relevance, verifiability, and volatility. They noted that quality assessments "… are often relative to a particular community's cultural and knowledge structures. … If the user is not aligned with those structures, his or her claim of the existence of an IQ problem may not be shared by the rest of the community and get rejected" (Stvilia et al., 2005). These authors further reported that featured pages had better discussion pages

attached to it than randomly selected (non-featured) pages. The discussions were better organized, better readable, and more polls were used (Stvilia et al., 2005).

3.4.5 Fitting in the Wikipedia approach

Wikipedia is certainly not an automatic tool but does provide the community with the means to control correctness, source credibility, and readability. The correctness of information is of particular interest to this chapter, as we can already define credibility and readability in a more automatic way. Checking a Web page for Wikipedia contents (i.e. the featured articles) at least gives some indication of correctness. Featured articles will be close to *Britannica*, are checked for vandalism, comply with strong quality criteria (not merely correctness but also credibility and readability), and are constantly scrutinized in the discussion pages. In the next section, we explore the way to automate the check-up with reviewed content so to estimate information correctness of a given Web page.

3.5 Text mining – automating correctness

Data mining, text mining, and Web mining are emerging fields in computer science, biology, and chemistry. Data mining is concerned with extracting useful information from huge amounts of (semi) structured data that are stored in databases. Text mining is a specific technique to extract information from unstructured texts, in particular, natural language. Web mining is a combination of data mining and text mining in relation to the Web. In fact, text mining is the reverse of adding metadata to documents (cf. labeling in Section 3.2).

Metadata add structured information that make a document easier to handle for a computer, whereas text mining makes the computer capable of handling unstructured data. For instance, STEMWAY is a text mining tool that was capable of extracting a general model out of a host of stem cell documents (Park et al., 2005). TAKMI (Text Analysis and Knowledge Mining) is a text mining tool for the identification of patterns in questions received by helpdesk call-centers (Nasukawa & Nagano, 2001). These tools have one thing in common: They provide a way to represent (or convert) textual data into structured knowledge.

For our quality assessment tool, text mining could help in establishing a measure for information correctness. For a given topic, a tool such as STEMWAY or TAKMI could extract a general model from the scientific literature. This becomes a reference ontology against which individual Web pages found by the user are tested.

> An ontology is an explicit specification of a conceptualization. (…) When the knowledge of a domain is represented in a declarative formalism, the set of objects that can be represented is called the universe of discourse. This set of objects, and the describable relationships among them, are reflected in the representational vocabulary with which a knowledge-based program represents knowledge. Thus, we can describe the ontology of a program by defining a set of representational terms. In such an ontology, definitions associate the names of entities in the universe of discourse (e.g., classes, relations, functions, or other objects) with human-readable text describing what the names are meant to denote, and formal axioms that constrain the interpretation and well-formed use of these terms. (Gruber, 1993)

The World Wide Web Consortium (W3C) provides a number of languages to represent ontologies,[12] with OWL being one of the strongest Web ontology languages. A free tool to create an OWL ontology is Protégé by Stanford Medical Informatics.[13] Through text mining Protégé creates the ontology without the help of its human user.

Once the computer created a reference ontology, the knowledge of an individual Web article can be structured through text mining. The difference or tension between the reference ontology and the knowledge structure extracted from an individual paper indicates the level of correctness: The smaller the difference, the more complete and correct the Web text is. For the user, this difference could be translated into a percentage that the found article is correct.

To date, text mining tools are not as exact as hand-curated data (Rebholz-Schumann et al., 2005). Parsing natural language such as negations is still a challenge (Briscoe & Carroll, 2002; Pyysalo et al., 2004; Stavrianou et al., 2007). In the bag-of-words approach, however, negations are treated as part of the same knowledge structure because they share the same set of keywords as affirmative statements (Nasukawa & Nagano, 2001). Also rich vocabularies are harder to process than texts with limited contexts (ibid.) but "it is only a matter of time and effort before we are able to extract facts automatically" (Rebholz-Schumann et al., 2005).

3.6 Readability – multiple measures

Information may come from a highly credible source and be correct, but if a user cannot read it, the source will not be used. Readers may not have the proper level of expertise or the text is written in an obscure style.

In the area of readability formulas, many competitors exist. "By the 1980s, there were 200 formulas and over a thousand studies published on the readability formules attesting to their (…) validity." (DuBay, 2004). Often mentioned in the literature is the reading ease formula of Flesch (1948). It became the most widely used and one of the most tested and reliable formulas (DuBay, 2004; Chall, 1974; Klare, 1963). This formula uses two variables: the number of syllables and the number of sentences in a 100-word sample (DuBay, 2004).

Readability formulas should be considered rough estimates because they count linguistic forms and not content. The words 'computer' and 'freedom' are of the same length - and therefore not treated differently by formulas - but the latter word is more complex because it is an abstraction with an enormous political bias. In addition, the formulas do not account for infographics, multimedia, or any other explanatory medium besides text.

Hartley et al. (2004) evaluated the readability of magazine articles about science and compared them to articles in the field of psychology and history. They found that science articles have the shortest sentences and the highest Flesch scores. They did the same comparison with other genres, from scholarly journals to magazines and in most of the cases the same difference was found: Science is shorter (Hartley et al., 2004). In knowing, however, that most non-experts cannot read science, the abstract quality and use of formulas in scientific texts puts up a hurdle not acknowledged by a readability formula. Another unexpected finding by Hartley et al. (2004) was that passive voice does not necessarily make a text less readable.

---

[12] www.w3c.org

[13] www.protégé.stanford.edu

Readability formulas are based on counting text properties. Common text editors usually offer a Flesh reading ease score together with text statistics such as number of characters, words, and sentences. Surprisingly, however, automated Flesch measures sometimes vary between different tools (Hartley et al., 2004; Harris, 1996; Mailloux, et al., 1995; Sydes & Hartley, 1997). Because we want to use readability measures for relative comparisons only, this is not a problem as long as we use the same tool for all Web sites.

4. A combination of techniques

We would like to design an intelligent service that assesses the quality of information of Web pages. In this section, we suggest to estimate credibility through Google's PageRank algorithm and informational correctness through text mining. Readability may be indicated by an all-inclusive variable of over 200 available formulas. The analyses could be brought under one button, outputting a position of the Web page in a 3D graphical space.

Google PageRank can be used to calculate a *credibility value*. In line with Brin and Page (1998), Chen et al. (2007), and Griffiths and Christensen (2005), we believe that Google PageRank performs better than simply counting the number of citations in scientific journals. The importance of a Web page is reflected in the number of incoming and outgoing links. The more links point at you, the higher your rank number.

To validate this claim, we suggest creating a psychometric scale that has the following items on it, as derived from Flanagin and Metzger (2000) and Johnson and Kaye (1998): reliable, believable, trustworthy, unbiased, and fair. In employing this scale, let users rate the credibility of a large range of information Web-pages. After scale analysis, make a rank order of pages according to their level of estimated credibility. Also make a rank order for these Web pages according to Google PageRank and according to a traditional citation index. Then calculate the Spearman rho statistic between the paired rank orders of user-rated credibility vs. PageRank as well as user-rated credibility vs. citation index. The measure (PageRank or citation index) that shows the least difference with the rated-credibility ranking is the most indicative measure. The closer rho approaches 1, the higher the correlation between paired rankings. In other words, rho also indicates in how far the best measure is still away from human assessment of credibility. Credibility rating through psychometric scales should be a community effort and we could use wiki technology to do so.

To assess *correctness* of information of a Web page, we could employ AQA (Griffiths et al., 2005, Section 3.2). However, the AQA procedure is quite difficult because it takes six steps and uses multiple software programs. Also, the queries must be learned. AQA was designed and tested for depression Web sites and we do not know whether it will be successful in other fields of health or science. Therefore, we wish to try for a more generic approach.

We envision a repository of reference ontologies that relate to each lemma in, for example, the *Encyclopedia Britannica Online*. For each lemma, text mining of the relevant scientific literature supplemented with featured articles in Wikipedia provides the general pattern or semantic structure (cf. the stem cell model of Park et al., 2005) that a given Web page should provide about a topic. The difference or tension between the reference ontology and the specific page indicates the accuracy (are the proper concepts used in the proper relations?) and completeness of the page (is everything there?). This could count as the automatically generated *correctness value*.

To validate the correctness value, a psychometric scale should be made that has the following items on it as derived from Price and Hersh (1999), Griffiths, et al. (2005), and the Wikipedia criteria for featured articles: comprehensive, factual, stable, accurate, complete, and with depth. With this scale, users rate the correctness of a large number of information Web-pages. After scale analysis, the scale values can be regressed on the difference between reference ontologies and specific pages (the automatic correctness values) to permit the prediction of the most probable values of user-rated correctness. The higher the regression weights, the more the automatically extracted correctness value is indicative for human-rated correctness.

With respect to *readability*, we want to dodge the problem of arbitrarily selecting one of the readability scores. We suggest using multiple formulas so to keep from ignoring important aspects emphasized by other measures. This means that certain formulas should be automated first and that the final score is a compound of all measures. Then the body text should be assessed, that is, text satellites such as headings, sub headings, lengthy quotations, references, and other peripheral data should be discarded in the analysis (Hartley et al., 2004; Stavrianou et al., 2007). This could be done by the user but it would be better to fully automate this procedure.

Many of the available formulas seem to indicate a valid aspect of readability (DuBay, 2004). However, each readability formula makes estimations on a different scale (Figure 3, left box), so that for a compound *readability score*, we need to calculate the normalized mean or a z-score.

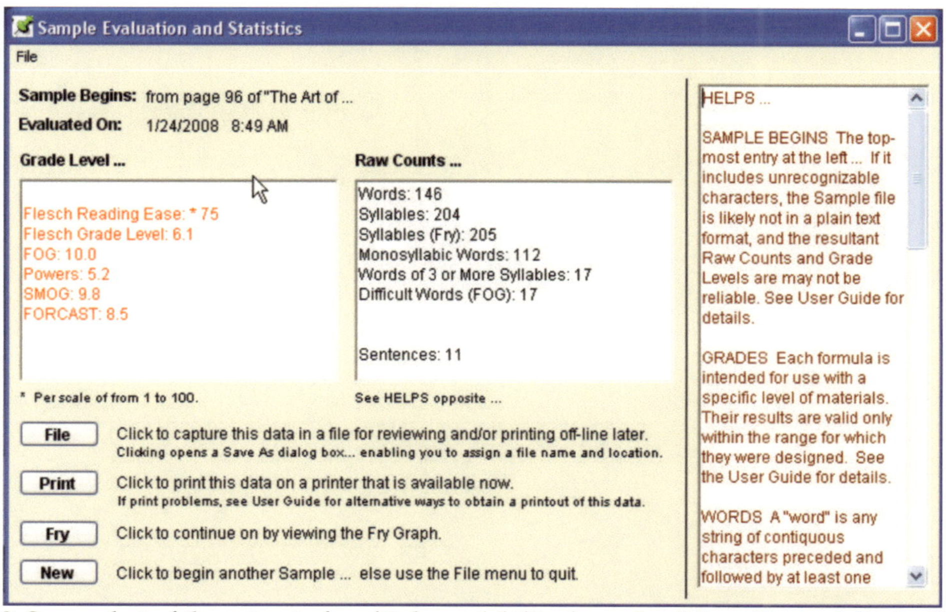

Fig. 3. Screenshot of the output of multiple readability formulas (Micro Power & Light Co.)[14]

[14] http://www.micropowerandlight.com/readability-formula-scores-screen.html

For validation purposes, a psychometric scale should be devised that follows the style guidelines for Wikipedia's featured articles: well written, appropriate images, appropriate length, and focus. Users score the readability of a number of body texts using this scale. After scale analysis, regression of the scale values on the normalized mean scores can be used to estimate user-rated readability given the automatically calculated normalized-mean readability. The higher the regression weights, the more the normalized mean is indicative for human-rated readability.

If we follow Hartley et al. (2004), the system should calculate readability for the body text, skipping text satellites such as headings and images. This restriction will mitigate the regression weights because 'appropriate images' (and captions) is one of the items on the psychometric readability scale.

As a standard, the measure yields a general readability score but this could be fine-tuned to the user's reading skills by calibrating the system first. At first use, the user could do a readability test after which the system always provides a score that is relative to the user's benchmark value.

In all, the browser could have an interface button that triggers the assessment of the information quality of an open Web page. Such a tool should be capable of positioning, for instance, a published but later on retracted paper as credible but incorrect (e.g., Lee, et al., 2005). Wikipedia featured articles will probably be positioned as correct, readable, and somewhat credible and a patient's blog as readable, somewhat correct but not too credible (Figure 4).

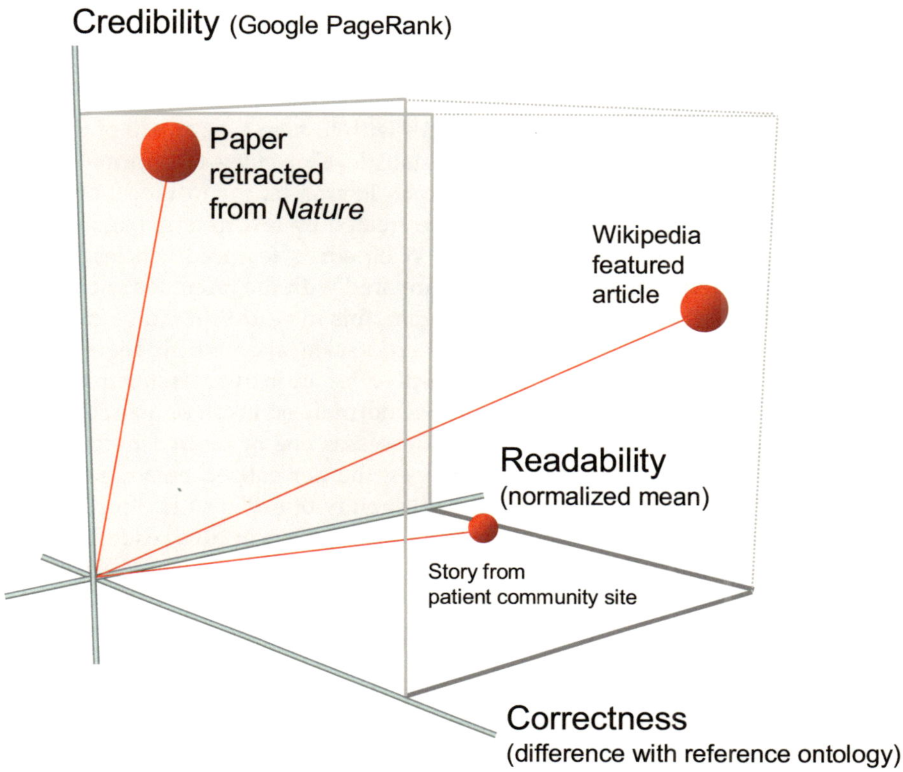

Fig. 4. Impression of a 3D space that positions Web pages on the axes of credibility, correctness, and readability

5. Conclusions

The Internet offers a vast amount of information that can be accessed and used by everyone who is online without much guidance. Heavy users such as young people judge the first hits Google offers at face value. Particularly in health issues, following the wrong advice may cause serious damage. The main question is how to separate good quality information from the bad. One could perhaps read the scientific journals but unless you are a specialist in a certain field, science is not particularly readable for non-experts.

Several methods were proposed to distinguish information quality. Checklists, quality stamps, logos, and automated quality assessment are useful tools but are either labor-intensive or simply overlooked by the non-expert. A genuine contribution would be to have an intelligent widget in the browser interface that automatically assesses the information quality of a Web site and presents the evaluation result in one easy-to-grasp representation (a number, a graph, thumbs up or down, or any other qualifier).

We observed that in the earlier approaches, difficulties were insidious in the definition of information quality as well as in the boundaries of its underlying concepts such as credibility and correctness. Such confusion is bound to render quality estimates that are not in sync with human judgment. In this chapter, we have attempted to decompose quality into three main parts and have argued to measure them with novel Web technologies.

Credibility of the source should be assessed by Google PageRank and validated by comparing the resulting rank order of Web pages with human assessment of those pages on a psychometric scale, using the Spearman rho statistic. *Correctness* of information should be assessed by creating reference ontologies for each lemma in, for instance, the *Encyclopedia Britannica Online*. Reference ontologies could be created by text mining (e.g., STEMWAY or TAKMI) the relevant scientific literature and Wikipedia's featured articles. The semantic structure of a given Web page could then be compared with the reference ontology, yielding a difference value that indicates correctness. Again, this measure should be confronted with user assessment of correctness on a psychometric scale after which regression analysis shows whether automated estimates are predictive for human assessment of information correctness. *Readability* should be indicated by the normalized mean or a z-score for the 200+ readability measures that each in its own right assesses one or more aspects of readability (e.g., ease or grade level). In a regression analysis, the normalized mean or z-score should have predictive power for the user-estimated readability of texts as rated on a psychometric scale. Reading-level calibration could be done by letting the user do a readability test at first use (the personal readability benchmark). We realize that the readability method is a bit crude but easy to implement. In addition to the usual variables in text complexity measurement, we could look at sets of participle perfectum, embedding, priority placement, jargon, etc.

Most of what we suggested is technically feasible. A possible bottleneck lies in the state-of-the-art of text mining and ontology modeling. Stavrianou et al. (2007), for example, explain that the distribution of terms that make up a semantic structure varies across text types (e.g., abstracts, articles, or collections of articles). Word sense disambiguation is a challenge in free text (ibid.). Lastly, the text properties that need to be analyzed may vary with different text types (ibid.). Thus, modeling ontologies is not to be underestimated. The status of the technique as is may be insufficient to use instantly. Quality sometimes lies in subtle things, which a model may not perceive. Over time, the models should develop greater detail and the scope of the model should become clearer. As a cross-validation, we could look at the number of sources that provide the same information, which may indicate the acceptance of information. This could also be done cross-lingual to ensure that no duplicates are counted.

As far as we can see, a concept analysis of notions such as information quality, correctness, and credibility is new in this area. The separation between correctness as an aspect of the message and credibility as an aspect of the source is important because 'truth' is not the same as 'reputation.' To validate computer-generated estimates against human assessment on psychometric scales is a novelty in the area but important to judge whether the system is anywhere near a proper judgment. The use of text mining to create ontologies is already explored but to use ontologies as a reference to assess the correctness of a free text is a new idea. In addition, we are the first to suggest a democratic measure (all voices count) of readability instead of arbitrarily opting for, at best, a handful of measures. The same goes for the combination of all readability estimates into one measure instead of losing the overview with a host of readability scores that are all measured on a different scale. Compiling all three measures into one 3D graphic that can be generated by one button click would create a new intelligent Web service for search engines to support decisions on

information quality. Shortcomings of the present chapter are that nothing is tested yet and that there are still issues left in the domain of text mining tools.
What needs to be done, then, is to perform a large scale survey among users to scrutinize the concepts of information quality, correctness, credibility, and readability and to test the convergent and divergent validity of their indicators (e.g., believability, accuracy, depth). In addition, a large number of reference ontologies needs to be created, which will urge to look into a number of problems in text mining such as word sense disambiguation and the type of text properties that needs to be analyzed. If all is set, user studies should test the results of the automated measures against user ratings.

6. Acknowledgements

We kindly thank Piek Vossen for reviewing an earlier draft of this chapter.

7. References

Brin, S. & Page, L. (1998). The Anatomy of a Large-Scale Hypertextual Web Search Engine, *Proceedings of the Seventh International Conference on World Wide Web, 7*, pp. 107-117, Brisbane, Australia, April 1998, *Computer Networks and ISDN Systems,* Vol. 30, No.1-7, (April 1998) 107-117, ISSN: 0169-7552.

Briscoe, T. & Carroll, J. (2002). Robust Accurate Statistical Annotation of General Texts, *Proceedings of the Third International Conference on Language Resources and Evaluation,* pp. 1499-1504, Las Palmas, Gran Canaria, May 2002, Canary Islands, Spain: European Language Resources Association.

Chall, J. S. (1958). *Readability: An appraisal of research and application.* Columbus, OH: Ohio State University Press. Reprinted 1974. Epping, Essex, England: Bowker Publishing Company.

Charmock, D.; Shepperd, S.; Needham, G. & Gann, R. (1999). DISCERN: an instrument for judging the quality of written consumer health information on treatment choices. *J. Epidemiol. Community Health , 53*, pp. 105-111, ISSN: 0143-005X.

Chen, P.; Xie, H.; Maslov, S. & Redner, S. (2007). Finding scientific gems with Google's PageRank algorithm. *Journal of Informetrics,* Vol. 1, No. 1 (January 2007), pp. 8-15, ISSN: 1751-1577.

DuBay, W. H. (2004). *The Principles of Readability.* Retrieved October 04, 2007, from Impact Information: Plain Language Services:
http://www.impactinformation. com/impactinfo/readability02.pdf

Eysenbach, G. & Diepgen, T. L. (1998). Towards quality management of medical information on the internet: evaluation, labelling, and filtering of information. *BMJ,* Nov 1998, pp. 1496-1502, ISSN: 09598138.

Flanagin, A. J. & Metzger, M. J. (2001). Internet use in the contemporary environment. *Human Communication Research ,* Vol. 27, No. 1, pp. 153-181, ISSN: 1468-2958.

Flanagin, A. J. & Metzger, M. J. (2000). Perceptions of Internet Information Credibility. *Journalism and Mass Communication Quarterly,* Vol. 77, No. 3, pp. 515-540, ISSN:1077-6990

Flanagin, A. J. & Metzger, M. J. (2007). The role of site features, user attributes, and information verification behaviors on the perceived credibility of web-based information. *New media & society,* Vol. 9, No. 2, pp. 319-342, ISSN: 1461-7315.

Flesch, R. (1948). A new readability yardstick. *Journal of Applied Psychology,* Vol. 32, No. 3, pp. 221-223, ISSN: 0021-9010.

Fox, S. (2005). *Health Information Online.* Retrieved September 11, 2007, from PEW Internet & America Life Project: http://www.pewinternet.org/pdfs/PIP_Healthtopics_May05.pdf

Giles, J. (2005). Internet encyclopedias go head to head. *Nature,* Vol. 438, No. 15, pp. 900-901, ISSN: 0028-0836.

Griffiths, K. M. & Christensen, H. (2005). *Website Quality Indicators for Consumers.* Retrieved September 11, 2007, from Journal of Medical Internet Research: http://www.pubmedcentral.nih.gov/articlerender.fcgi?artid=1550688

Griffiths, K. M.; Tang, T. T.; David, H. & Helen, C. (2005). *Automated Assesment of the Quality of Depression Websites.* Retrieved September 11, 2007, from Journal of Medical Internet Research: http://www.pubmedcentral.nih.gov/articlerender.fcgi?artid =1550680

Gruber, T. R. (1993). *A Translation Approach to Portable Ontology Specifications.* Retrieved October 15, 2007, from TomGruber.org: http://tomgruber.org/writing/ontolingua-kaj-1993.pdf

Harris, R. (1996). Variation among style checkers in sentence measurement. *TEXT Technology,* Vol. 6, No. 2, pp. 80-90.

Hartley, J.; Sotto, E. & Fox, C. (2004). Clarity across the disciplines: an analysis of texts in the sciences, social sciences, arts and humanities. *Science Communication,* Vol. 26, No. 2, pp. 188- 210, ISSN: 1824-2049.

Internet Systems Consortium. (2007). *ISC Internet Domain Survey.* Retrieved October 20, 2007, from Internet Systems Consortium: http://www.isc.org/index.pl?/ops/ds/

Johnson, T. J. & Kaye, B. K. (1998). Cruising Is Believing?: Comparing Internet and Traditional Sources on Media Credibility Measures. *Journalism and Mass Communication Quarterly,* Vol. 75, No. 2, pp.325-340, ISSN:1077-6990.

Klare, G. R. (1963). *The Measurement of Readability.* Ames, Iowa: Iowa State University Press.

Lee, B.; Kim, M.; Jang, G.; Oh, H.; Yuda, F.; Kim, H. et al. (2005). Dogs cloned from adult somatic cells. *Nature,* Vol. 436, No. 7051, pp. 641-641, ISSN: 1476-4687.

Mailloux, S. L.; Johnson, M. E.; Fisher, D. G. & Pettibone, T. J. (1995). How reliable is computerized assessment of readability? *Computers in nursing* , Vol. 13, No. 5, pp. 221-225, ISSN: 0736-8593. Ministy of Economic Development of New Zealand. (2003). *6. Size of the Internet | Statistics on Information Technology in New Zealand: updated to 2003.* Retrieved October 20, 2007, from Ministry of Economic Development: http://www.med.govt.nz/ templates/MultipageDocumentPage____9980.aspx

Morgan, M. (in press). Cultivation analysis, In: *The SAGE Handbook of Media Processes and Effects,* R. L. Nabi & M. B. Oliver, (Eds.), xx-xx, SAGE, ISBN, Thousand Oaks, CA

Nasukawa, T. & Nagano, T. (2001). Text analysis and knowledge mining system. *IBM Systems Journal,* Vol. 40, No. 4, pp. 967-984, ISSN: 0018-8670.

Nature (2006). Britannica attacks... and we respond [Editorial]. *Nature, 440,* 582. DOI: 10.1038/440582b. Retrieved April 7, 2009 from http://www.nature.com/nature/journal/v440/n7084/full/440582b.html

Park, H. S.; Kim, M. K.; Choi, E. J. & Seol, Y. S. (2005). Text Mining from Categorized Stem Cell Documents to Infer Developmental Stage-Specific Expression and Regulation Patterns of Stem Cells, In: *Lecture Notes in Computer Science: Natural Language Processing and Information Systems, Vol. 3513/2005,* pp. 353-356, Springer Berlin/Heidelberg, ISBN 978-3-540-26031-8.

Price, S. L. & Hersh, W. R. (1999). Filtering Web pages for quality indicators: an empirical approach to finding high quality consumer health information on the World Wide Web, *Proceedings of AMIA Symposium,* pp. 911-915, Washington, DC, November 1999.

Pyysalo, S.; Ginter, F.; Pahikkala, T.; Koivula, J. & Boberg, J. (2004). Analysis of link grammar on biomedical dependency corpus targeted at protein-protein interactions, *Proceedings of the International Joint Workshop on Natural Language Processing in Biomedicine and Its Applications,* pp. 15-21, Geneva, Switzerland, August 2004.

Rebholz-Schumann, D.; Kirsch, H. & Couto, F. (2005). Essay: Facts from Text - Is Textmining Ready to Deliver. *PLoS Biology,* Vol. 3, No. 2, pp. 188-191, ISSN: 1545-7885.

Rieh, S. Y. & Belkin, N. J. (1998). Understanding Judgment of Information Quality and Cognitive Authority in the WWW, In: *ASIS 98: Information access in the global information economy. Proceedings of the 61st Annual Meeting of the American Society for Information Science,* pp. 279-289, ISSN: 0044-7870, Pittsburgh, PA, October 1998, Medford, NJ: Information Today.

Stavrianou, A.; Andritsos, P. & Nicoloyannis, N. (2007). Overview and semantic issues of text mining. *ACM SIGMOD Record,* Vol. 36, No. 3, pp. 23-34, ISSN: 0163-5808.

Stvilia, B.; Twidale, M. B.; Gasser, L. & Smith, L. C. (2005). Information quality in a community-based ecyclopedia. In: S. Hawamdeh (Ed.), *Knowledge Management: Nurturing Culture, Innovation, and Technology - Proceedings of the 2005 International Conference on Knowledge Management,* pp. 101-113, ISBN 978-981-256-556-3, North Carolina, October 2005, Charlotte, NC: World Scientific Publishing Company.

Sydes, M. & Hartley, J. (1997). A thorn in the Flesch: Observations on the unreliability of computer-based readability formulae. *British Journal of Educational Technology,* Vol. 28, No. 2, pp. 143-145, ISSN: 1467-8535.

Terdiman, D. (2005). Study: Wikipedia as accurate as Britannica. *CNET News.* Retrieved Oct. 1, 2007 from http://www.news.com/2100-1038_3-5997332.html

Treise, D.; Walsh-Childers, K.; Weigold, M. F. & Friedman, M. (2003). Cultivating the Science Internet Audience: Impact of Brand and Domain on Source Credibility for Science Information. *Science Communication,* Vol. 24, No. 3, pp. 309-332, ISSN: 1552-8545.

Viégas, F. B.; Wattenberg, M.; Kriss, J. & Van Ham, F. (2007). Talk Before You Type: Coordination in Wikipedia. *40th Annual Hawaii International Conference on System Sciences,* pp.78-78, ISBN: 0-7695-2755-8, Waikoloa, Big Island, Hawaii, January 2007, IEEE Computer Society 2007.

Viégas, F.; Wattenberg, M. & Dave, K. (2004). Studying Cooperation and Conflict between Authors with history flow Visualizations. *Proceedings of SIGCHI 2004*, pp. 575-582, ISBN: 1-58113-702-8, Vienna, Austria, April 2004, ACM New York, NY, USA.

16

Overview of the Relational Analysis approach in Data-Mining and Multi-criteria Decision Making

Julien Ah-Pine
Xerox Research Centre Europe
France

Jean-François Marcotorchino
Thales Communications
France

1. General scope

In this chapter we introduce a general framework called the Relational Analysis approach and its related contributions and applications in the fields of data analysis, data mining and multi-criteria decision making. This approach was initiated by J.F. Marcotorchino and P. Michaud at the end of the 70's and has generated many research activities. However, the aspects of this framework that we would like to focus on are of a theoretical kind. Indeed, we aimed at recalling the background and the basics of this framework, the unifying results and the modeling contributions that it has allowed to achieve. Besides, the main tasks that we are interested in are the ranking aggregation problem, the clustering problem and the block seriation problem. Those problems are combinatorial ones and the computational considerations of such tasks in the context of the RA methodology will not be covered. However, among the list of references that we give throughout this chapter, they are numerous articles that the interested reader could consult to this end.

In order to introduce the Relational Analysis approach (denoted "RA" in the rest of the document), let us first introduce several problems that one could encounter in the data analysis field. To this end, let us consider a data table concerning a set of N objects $\mathbb{O} = \{O^1, \ldots, O^i, \ldots, O^N\}$ described by a set of M variables $\mathbb{V} = \{V^1, \ldots, V^k, \ldots, V^M\}$. These data can be represented using a $(N \times M)$ feature matrix denoted T given by the following eq. (2); $\forall i = 1, \ldots, N; k = 1, \ldots, M$:

$$T_{ik} = \quad V_i^k = \text{Numerical value assigned to object } O^i \text{ according to } V^k \quad (1)$$

$$T = \begin{array}{c} \\ O^1 \\ O^2 \\ \vdots \\ O^i \\ \vdots \\ O^N \end{array} \begin{array}{c} \begin{array}{cccccc} V^1 & V^2 & \dots, & V^k & \dots & V^M \end{array} \\ \begin{pmatrix} V_1^1 & V_1^2 & \dots & V_1^k & \dots & V_1^M \\ V_2^1 & V_2^2 & \dots & V_2^k & \dots & V_2^M \\ \vdots & \vdots & \vdots & \vdots & \vdots & \vdots \\ V_i^1 & V_i^2 & \dots & V_i^k & \dots & V_i^M \\ \vdots & \vdots & \vdots & \vdots & \vdots & \vdots \\ V_N^1 & V_N^2 & \dots & V_N^k & \dots & V_N^M \end{pmatrix} \end{array} \tag{2}$$

Depending on the nature of the features of T, we can list the different following problems tackled in the data analysis field and related domains:

- The variables in $\mathbb{V}$ can correspond to M criteria that give M different rankings on the objects $\mathbb{O}$. In that case, the objects could be N different alternatives. Then, one can be interested in finding a consensual ranking that "sums up" these M different rankings in order to determine the best (the most consensual) alternative[1]. This task is known as the ranking aggregation problem and it can be encountered in other domains, than data analysis, such as social choice theory, multi-criteria decision making or multi-agent systems.
- The variables in $\mathbb{V}$ can be categorical[2] variables. In that case, one can be motivated by discovering patterns among the set of objects $\mathbb{O}$. In other words, one would want to find a partition such that objects belonging to the same cluster have high similarities and objects belonging to different clusters have low similarities. This problem, known as the clustering problem, is studied in statistical data analysis, and data-mining fields and it has many applications such as customer relationship management, text mining or web data clustering for instance.
- Finally, one could also be interested in finding a bi-partition which simultaneously decompose both sets $\mathbb{O}$ and $\mathbb{V}$. In that context, a bicluster is the association of a cluster of objects and a cluster of variables. This task is known as the biclustering or block seriation problem and it is studied notably in gene-mining or in group technology problems for example.

The previously mentioned problems are often modeled and solved by means of different approaches. One of the main advantages of the method presented here, is that it allows to synthesize in a unique formal way, all those different data analysis tasks, as particular cases of a general model. In the RA framework, those different problems can be formalized as binary relations aggregation problems. Departing from the feature matrix T, the different aforementioned tasks, can be seen as finding a consensual binary relation that aggregates and summarizes a set of individual binary relations (the variables) encoded through T.

We briefly give in the what follows some illustrative examples:

- When the variables $V^k; k = 1, \dots, M$, are numerical criteria, they induce M different rankings $\mathcal{R}^k; k = 1, \dots, M$, on the set of alternatives $\mathbb{O}$. These rankings are order relations (partial or total orders) and the solution we look for is a consensual relation $\mathcal{R}$ (a total order for example) that fits "as good as possible", the M individual rankings.

[1] The alternative that is ranked first in the consensual ranking.
[2] And more generally, numerical variables.

- When the variables $V^k; k = 1, \ldots, M$, are categorical features, the latter induce M different partitions $\mathcal{R}^k; k = 1, \ldots, M$, of the set of objects. Clustering those objects can thus be seen as looking for a consensual partition (or an equivalence relation) $\mathcal{R}$, that sums up the M individual partitions.
- When the feature matrix T consists of $0/1$ values such as indicator tables that encode categorical variables, the biclustering problem amounts to determine a bi-partition of objects and categories. This problem can also be interpreted as the search for a consensual relation $\mathcal{R}$. This kind of relation is called a "block seriation" relation.

The RA approach uses algebraic concepts related to binary relations in order to turn the previously mentioned problems into binary relations aggregation problems. Basically, if we denote by $\mathcal{R}^k$ the binary relation associated to a variable V^k, then all aforementioned problems could be seen as a particular instance of the following problem:

$$\max_{\mathcal{R}} \text{Aggreg}(\mathcal{R}^1, \ldots, \mathcal{R}^k, \ldots, \mathcal{R}^M; \mathcal{R}) \tag{3}$$

where Aggreg is an aggregation procedure.

One of the main characteristics of the RA methodology is to use pairwise comparisons matrices similar as adjacency matrices in order to represent binary relations. We will see that the representation of binary relations through that coding has many properties. The second principle of the RA approach consists in using a criterion called "the Condorcet's criterion" as a global measure of consensus. This criterion has its origins in mathematical social sciences and was first studied in its literal form by A. de Condorcet in 1785. This criterion is nothing but a voting criterion, which was applied first to the ranking aggregation problem. It was shown that this criterion satisfies many axioms in the context of social choice theory. The Condorcet's criterion was, then, extended to the partitions aggregation problem. Therefore it can be interpreted as a partitioning criterion as well. The RA approach notably contribute to show that the ranking aggregation problem and the clustering one were particular cases of a unique model, as we will show in the next paragraphs.

The rest of this chapter is organized as follows. In section 2, we basically recall some key properties of the RA approach: the individual relational matrices, that represent individual binary relations; the collective relational matrix, that aims at aggregating the individual binary relations in a simple yet efficient way; the relational properties of binary relations that can be expressed as linear inequalities or equalities using relational matrices; and the general expression of the Condorcet's criterion.
In section 3, 4, 5, we respectively detail the applications of the RA approach in ranking aggregation problems, clustering problems, and block seriation problems. Particularly, in the RA framework, all these problems are modeled using the same formalism, based on integer linear programming.
Recently, "Correlation Clustering" (CC) problems were proposed in (6). This setting tackles the clustering problem from a graphic point of view and has many relationships with different concepts underlined in the RA approach. Indeed, the partitioning criterion used in the CC approach is very similar to the Condorcet criterion. Moreover, the linear program used by this approach for modeling the clustering problem (see for example (15), (22), (18)), is the same as in the RA method. Accordingly, we also introduce in section 6, other results of interest obtained in the clustering field by using the RA method in order to strengthen the graphical and the linear programming point of views for addressing clustering problems.

2. Introduction to the Relational Analysis approach

We first recall some previous contributions concerning the analysis of relational data, that is to say, data which have particular structures such as binary relations: order relations, equivalence relations or graph relations in general. There has been a growing interest for such kinds of data since the end of the 70's.

Concerning order relations, Condorcet's work opened up the mathematical field of decision making in the social sciences (14). In France, A. de Condorcet's work got a particular interest in the 80's, rediscovered and updated by J.F. Marcotorchino and P. Michaud (36), (40), B. Monjardet, J.P. Barthélémy and B. Leclerc (8), (26)... In the USA, we can also mention the Nobel Prize's laureate, K.J. Arrow who has contributed to the social choice theory (5) and also the book of Kemeny and Snell (23) in mathematical sciences as well.

Concerning equivalence relations (categorical data), since this type of data has been mostly studied by statisticians and data analysts, it is an other set of contributors which has to be quoted. We can firstly mention S. Régnier (46), I.C. Lerman (27) and J.F. Marcotorchino and P. Michaud (37), on the french side. Apart from french researchers, we can particularly mention H.T. Zahn's work (52) as well as B. Mirkin's work, see (42) for example.

Obviously, this is not an exhaustive reference list of scientists who have contributed to this area. We have only mentioned some main papers that are closely related to the approach proposed by the RA framework: an approach that we are just going to introduce now.

The RA methods, presented here, are mainly the approaches, studied and developed by J.F. Marcotorchino and P. Michaud and colleagues. Their work is essentially based upon the study of relational data from the graph theory, the statistical and the integer linear programming standpoints (36), (41).

First of all, let us recall basic definitions about binary relations.

A binary relation $\mathcal{R}$ on two sets of objects $\mathbb{O}$ (the domain) and $\mathbb{D}$ (the codomain[3]), is a triple $(\mathbb{O}, \mathbb{D}, G(\mathcal{R}))$, where $G(\mathcal{R})$ called the graph of the relation $\mathcal{R}$, is a subset of the Cartesian product $\mathbb{O} \times \mathbb{D}$. If we have $(O^i, D^j) \in G(\mathcal{R})$, then we say that object O^i is in relation with object D^j for the relation $\mathcal{R}$. This will be denoted by $O^i \mathcal{R} D^j$.

We can also associate to $\mathcal{R}$, its complement which is a binary relation denoted by $\overline{\mathcal{R}}$ and which is the subset of the cartesian product $\mathbb{O} \times \mathbb{D}$ such that $(O^i, D^j) \notin G(\mathcal{R})$.

When $\mathbb{D} = \mathbb{O}$, we will talk about binary relations on a single set $\mathbb{O}$. This particular kind of binary relations is of interest and it will be referred as $(\mathbb{O}, G(\mathcal{R}))$.
There exist different properties that a binary relation $(\mathbb{O}, G(\mathcal{R}))$ can satisfy. Among all those relational properties, the most useful ones are given in Table 1.
Those properties allow us to characterize the type of a binary relation $(\mathbb{O}, G(\mathcal{R}))$. We have the following definitions:

[3] For a real continuous quantitative variable, $\mathbb{D}$ could equal $\mathbb{R}$ for example; for a categorical variable, $\mathbb{D}$ could be the set of categories of this variable.

Relational property	Logical definition
Reflexivity	$O^i \mathcal{R} O^i \quad \forall O^i \in \mathbb{O}$
Irreflexivity	$O^i \overline{\mathcal{R}}^k O^i \quad \forall O^i \in \mathbb{O}$
Symmetry	$O^i \mathcal{R} O^{i'} \Rightarrow O^{i'} \mathcal{R} O^i \quad \forall (O^i, O^{i'}) \in \mathbb{O}^2$
Asymmetry	$O^i \mathcal{R} O^{i'} \Rightarrow O^{i'} \overline{\mathcal{R}}^k O^i \quad \forall (O^i, O^{i'}) \in \mathbb{O}^2 : O^i \neq O^{i'}$
Transitivity	$O^i \mathcal{R} O^{i'} \wedge O^{i'} \mathcal{R} O^{i''} \Rightarrow O^i \mathcal{R} O^{i''} \quad \forall (O^i, O^{i'}, O^{i''}) \in \mathbb{O}^3$
Totality	$O^i \mathcal{R} O^{i'} \vee O^{i'} \mathcal{R} O^i \quad \forall (O^i, O^{i'}) \in \mathbb{O}^2 : O^i \neq O^{i'}$

Table 1. Relational properties for $(\mathbb{O}, G(\mathcal{R}))$

- A preorder is a binary relation that is reflexive and transitive.
- A strict total order is a binary relation that is irreflexive, asymmetric, transitive and total.
- An equivalence relation is a binary relation that is reflexive, symmetric, and transitive.

After recalling briefly, basic concepts inherent to binary relations, we now present how the RA approach copes with such data structures.

The first principle of the RA methodology amounts to represent binary relations as pairwise comparisons matrices, called "relational matrices", which are made of $0/1$ values.
Let $(\mathbb{O}, G(\mathcal{R}))$ be a binary relation on a single set $\mathbb{O}$, where $\#\mathbb{O} = N$. Then in the RA method, we represent this binary relation by its $(N \times N)$ relational matrix[4] X where, $\forall i, i' = 1, \ldots, N$:

$$X_{ii'} = \begin{cases} 1 & \text{if } O^i \mathcal{R} O^{i'} \\ 0 & \text{otherwise} \end{cases} \tag{4}$$

Using the RA formalism, we can easily define the relational matrix $\overline{X}$, associated to the complement of the relation $(\mathbb{O}, G(\mathcal{R}))$. Indeed, we have, $\forall i, i' = 1, \ldots, N$:

$$\overline{X}_{ii'} = 1 - X_{ii'} \tag{5}$$

[4] In graph theory those matrices are adjacency matrices but in the case of particular binary relations, these matrices have special properties as we will see later.

In the block seriation problems, we are no longer faced with relations on the same set, as previously done, but we will consider, in that case, binary relations on two different sets $(\mathbb{O}, \mathbb{D}, G(\mathcal{R}))$.
For clarity reasons, we will use other notations for that type of binary relations. Suppose that, $\#\mathbb{O} = N$ and $\#\mathbb{D} = P$; then the relational matrix that represents the binary relation is the $(N \times P)$ binary matrix Z, where, $\forall i = 1, \ldots, N; j = 1, \ldots, P$:

$$Z_{ij} = \begin{cases} 1 & \text{if } O^i \mathcal{R} D^j \\ 0 & \text{otherwise} \end{cases} \tag{6}$$

The representation of binary relations by using pairwise comparison matrices allows to express the relational properties as linear equations. This is a strong property of the RA formalism. We give in Table 2, the linear equations related to the relational properties already presented in Table 1.

Relational properties	Linear equations using the relational matrix
Reflexivity	$X_{ii} = 1 \quad \forall i = 1, \ldots, N$
Irreflexivity	$X_{ii} = 0 \quad \forall i = 1, \ldots, N$
Symmetry	$X_{ii'} = X_{i'i} \quad \forall i, i' = 1, \ldots, N$
Asymmetry	$X_{ii'} + X_{i'i} \leq 1 \quad \forall i, i' = 1, \ldots, N : i \neq i'$
Transitivity	$X_{ii'} + X_{i'i''} - X_{ii''} \leq 1 \quad \forall i, i', i'' = 1, \ldots, N$
Totality	$X_{ii'} + X_{i'i} \geq 1 \quad \forall i, i' = 1, \ldots, N : i \neq i'$

Table 2. Relational properties as linear equations in the RA formalism for $(\mathbb{O}, G(\mathcal{R}))$ binary relations

The second principle of the RA approach is the use of Condorcet's criterion as an association and consensus criterion. This criterion is based upon a similarity or association measure between objects, and a dissimilarity or non association measure between the same items as well.

Let us call respectively, A and $\overline{A}$, the matrices associated to relation[5] and to non relation[6] between pairs of objects. Then the Condorcet's criterion applied to binary relations on a single set is given as follows:

$$\text{Condorcet}(A, \overline{A}, X) = \sum_{i=1}^{N} \sum_{i'=1}^{N} \left(A_{ii'} X_{ii'} + \overline{A}_{ii'} \overline{X}_{ii'} \right) \tag{7}$$

For the case of binary relations on two different sets[7], we have:

$$\text{Condorcet}(A, \overline{A}, Z) = \sum_{i=1}^{N} \sum_{j=1}^{P} \left(A_{ij} Z_{ij} + \overline{A}_{ij} \overline{Z}_{ij} \right) \tag{8}$$

As we can see, the Condorcet's criterion is a quite "logical" criterion: it measures the total agreements ("positive" and "negative" agreements) between two relations. Likewise, the greater the values of A_{ij} and $\overline{A}_{ij}$, the more likely objects O^i and D^j should be in relation from a consensus standpoint.

3. The ranking aggregation problem

The ranking aggregation problem consists in looking for a consensual ranking (or order relation) on a set of objects (or alternatives) that summarizes a set of individual rankings (or a set of several criteria). This problem was firstly mathematically addressed by A. de Condorcet (14) in the context of voting theory and decision making. Historically, it is the first background of the RA approach and the first consistent foundation of such a theoretical framework.

The first aspect of this task consists in aggregating individual rankings in a natural manner. Indeed, suppose that we have items who are described by two real continuous quantitative variables such as their height (in centimeters) and their weight (in kilograms). These two real continuous quantitative variables induce a ranking among the items (the smallest to the tallest for example). How can we compute a consensual ranking that could efficiently summarize the rankings given by the height and the weight ?

In statistics, suppose we want to measure a central trend for the variable "height", it is then possible to compute the mean of this variable for instance. While computing the mean, we have to sum up the heights over all the items and we divide the obtained value by N. Here, the addition is possible because we aggregate "centimeters with centimeters". On the contrary, it is not obvious to aggregate for each item, his height and his weight. Indeed, it is a non sense to add centimeters with kilograms. Thus, how could we proceed to aggregate both variables ?

In order to answer this question, the RA suggests to compute the relational matrices associated to the individual rankings induced by the real continuous quantitative variables. Let us

---

[5] For two objects O^i and $O^{i'}$, this measure gives the "strength" of the relation $O^i \mathcal{R} O^{i'}$.

[6] For two objects O^i and $O^{i'}$, this measure gives the "strength" of the relation $O^i \overline{\mathcal{R}} O^{i'}$.

[7] In the case of two different sets, A_{ij} gives the "strength" of the relation $O^i \mathcal{R} D^j$ and $\overline{A}_{ij}$ gives the "strength" of the relation $O^i \overline{\mathcal{R}} D^j$.

suppose that we have M real continuous quantitative variables denoted by $V^k; k = 1, \ldots, M$. Let V_i^k be the value assigned to item O^i with respect to variable V^k. Then, for each variable, we can associate its following relational matrix:

$$C_{ii'}^k = \begin{cases} 1 & \text{if } V_i^k \le V_{i'}^k \\ 0 & \text{otherwise} \end{cases} \tag{9}$$

For example we build up a relational matrix as follows:

$$\begin{array}{|c|c|} \hline & V^k \\ \hline O^1 & 0.5 \\ O^2 & 0.2 \\ O^3 & 0.6 \\ O^4 & 0.9 \\ \hline \end{array} \rightarrow \begin{array}{c} \\ O^1 \\ O^2 \\ O^3 \\ O^4 \end{array} \begin{array}{c} \begin{array}{cccc} O^1 & O^2 & O^3 & O^4 \end{array} \\ \begin{pmatrix} 1 & 0 & 1 & 1 \\ 1 & 1 & 1 & 1 \\ 0 & 0 & 1 & 1 \\ 0 & 0 & 0 & 1 \end{pmatrix} \end{array} \tag{10}$$

Considering the M individual relational matrices, the relation aggregation procedure becomes possible: it is just given by the sum over all the individual relational matrices. By doing so, we define the collective relational matrix also called the "collective Condorcet's matrix", denoted $\mathbf{C}$. The general term of the latter matrix is given by:

$$\mathbf{C}_{ii'} = \sum_{k=1}^{M} C_{ii'}^k = \begin{cases} \text{Nb of variables for which } O^i \\ \text{has a lower rank than } O^{i'} \end{cases} \tag{11}$$

Similarly, we can also define the collective relational matrix $\overline{\mathbf{C}}$ related to the aggregation of the M individual relational matrices $\overline{C}^k$ where:

$$\overline{\mathbf{C}}_{ii'} = \sum_{k=1}^{M} \overline{C}_{ii'}^k = \begin{cases} \text{Nb of variables for which } O^i \\ \text{has not a lower rank than } O^{i'} \end{cases} \tag{12}$$

This aggregation process that we have just introduced, gives a partial answer to the initial problem represented by eq. (3). It gives a subsequent process for aggregating order relations in a natural manner. But now that we have aggregated the different rankings, how can we determine a consensual ranking $\mathcal{R}$ that agrees as much as possible with the M individual rankings ?

In the RA methodology, the consensus ranking is the one that maximizes the Condorcet's criterion where $A_{ii'} = \mathbf{C}_{ii'}$ and $\overline{A}_{ii'} = \overline{\mathbf{C}}_{ii'}$:

$$\text{Condorcet}(A, \overline{A}, X) = \sum_{i=1}^{N} \sum_{i'=1}^{N} \left(\mathbf{C}_{ii'} X_{ii'} + \overline{\mathbf{C}}_{ii'} \overline{X}_{ii'} \right) \tag{13}$$

Replacing $\overline{X}_{ii'}$ with $1 - X_{ii'}$ and selecting only the part of the criterion which is dependent on X, we then have the following Condorcet's criterion:

$$\text{Condorcet}(\mathbf{C}, \overline{\mathbf{C}}, X) = \sum_{i=1}^{N} \sum_{i'=1}^{N} \left(\mathbf{C}_{ii'} - \overline{\mathbf{C}}_{ii'} \right) X_{ii'} \tag{14}$$

This means that O^i should have more chances ot have a lower rank than $O^{i'}$ in the consensus ranking[8], if the number of variables that give a lower rank to O^i than to $O^{i'}$ is greater or equal than the number of variables that give a higher rank to O^i than to $O^{i'}$.

If we suppose, moreover, that there is no missing rank value among the individual rankings, then we have: $\overline{\mathbf{C}}_{ii'} = M - \mathbf{C}_{ii'}$. If we take into account this expression in eq. (14), then we obtain the following simplified Condorcet's criterion:

$$\text{Condorcet}(\mathbf{C}, X) = \sum_{i=1}^{N}\sum_{i'=1}^{N}\left(\mathbf{C}_{ii'} - \frac{M}{2}\right) X_{ii'} \tag{15}$$

In the particular case where we do not have any missing value, the consensual ranking will more likely give to O^i a rank lower than to $O^{i'}$[9], provided that the number of variables or criteria which ranked O^i before $O^{i'}$ is greater or equal to the simple majority.

If we simply apply the previous rule we will observe a paradoxical situation most of the time. Indeed, aggregating order relations using the simple majority decision rule does not guarantee to obtain an order relation as a solution[10]. This is the famous "Condorcet's paradox", which states that if a majority of voters prefer "i" to "j" and a majority of voters prefer "j" to "k", it could happen that a majority of voters prefer "k" to "i", thus violating the transitivity condition. Consequently the real problem, we want to solve is now based upon the following key question: how can we determine the strict total order relation that maximizes the Condorcet's criterion ? This problem is unfortunately not so simple, since it is an NP-hard problem (51). Without any algorithmic process, it would need a complete enumeration of all the $N!$ possible solutions to get the final result (by the way, just for N=70, notice that 70!≈ 1.2^{100}). Thanks to the RA approach we can solve the ranking aggregation problem, through an integer (0/1) linear programming approach. Furthermore, it is also possible to use a simpler model, based upon binarity relaxation scheme by considering $0 \leq X_{ii'} \leq 1$. In that case, we could use continuous linear programming technique and the "dual of dual process" described in (36).

According to Table 1, the use of pairwise comparisons matrices allows to turn the relational properties, characterizing an order relation, into linear constraints. Furthermore, once we are given A and $\overline{A}$, we can see that the Condorcet's criterion is a linear objective function with respect to X, the solution we are looking for. As a result, we can model the ranking aggregation problem by maximizing a linear consensus criterion subject to linear constraints. Hence, we can get the exact optimal solution using an integer linear programming solver as mentioned beforehand and as described in (36), (41), (39):

$$\begin{array}{lll} & \max_X \text{Condorcet}(A, \overline{A}, X) & \\ & \text{wrt} & \\ X_{ii'} \in \{0,1\} & & \text{(binarity)} \\ X_{ii'} + X_{i'i} \leq 1 & \forall i, i' = 1, \ldots, N : i \neq i' & \text{(asymmetry)} \\ X_{ii'} + X_{i'i} \geq 1 & \forall i, i' = 1, \ldots, N : i \neq i' & \text{(totality)} \\ X_{ii'} + X_{i'i''} - X_{ii''} \leq 1 & \forall i, i', i'' = 1, \ldots, N & \text{(transitivity)} \end{array} \tag{16}$$

[8] ie $X_{ii'} = 1$.
[9] ie $X_{ii'} = 1$.
[10] That is to say: irreflexive, asymmetric, total and transitive.

We have presented the general model to solve the ranking aggregation problem using the RA methodology. In eq. (16), X must respect the linear constraints of a strict and total order, but other types of order relations could also be modeled in a similar way. The interested reader could find in (41), (2), other relational properties and their associated linear equations (in terms of the RA formalism).
Other works, related to the ranking aggregation problem, can be found in (4), (21), (47) or (7) for example. In those papers, the ranking aggregation problem, which is also referred as the "median linear ordering problem" or shortly the "linear ordering problem"; is treated from a combinatorial optimization viewpoint. For a study of the complexity of problems like relations aggregation, see (51) for instance.

Among the different contributions in ranking aggregation problems, for which RA approach was used as a basic concept, special attention must be paid to the results obtained by S. Ghashghaie in (17). In this work, it is shown that statistical association criteria for comparing rankings such as Goodman and Kruskal, Somers, Kendall, Deuchler and Kim; differ from the Condorcet's criterion, just by slight changes. We can also mention the following reference too (19), where the author provides a theoretical and axiomatic comparison of Condorcet's criterion against other aggregation criteria.

4. The clustering problem

The RA methodology is still valid when we want to consider other relations and aggregation problems than the ranking aggregation task.

From an algebraic point of view, we can observe that the only difference between a linear order and an equivalence relation mainly consists in replacing the asymmetry property with the symmetry one. From this observation, J.F. Marcotorchino and P. Michaud extended the integer linear programming that solve the rank aggregation problem to the similarities aggregation problem (41), (37). Hence, we get the second main application of the RA methods in data analysis: modeling the clustering of categorical data problem as an integer linear program.

Suppose that we have at our disposal $(N \times N)$ matrices A and $\overline{A}$ of pairwise similarities and dissimilarities between pairs of objects that we want to cluster. Then we can use the Condorcet's criterion as a clustering function similarly as for the ranking aggregation:

$$\begin{aligned} \text{Condorcet}(A, \overline{A}, X) &= \sum_{i=1}^{N} \sum_{i'=1}^{N} \left(A_{ii'} X_{ii'} + \overline{A}_{ii'} \overline{X}_{ii'} \right) \\ &= \sum_{i=1}^{N} \sum_{i'=1}^{N} \left(A_{ii'} - \overline{A}_{ii'} \right) X_{ii'} + \sum_{i=1}^{N} \sum_{i'=1}^{N} \overline{A}_{ii'} \end{aligned} \tag{17}$$

If we consider the part of eq. (17) which is only a function of X, we can notice that maximizing the Condorcet's criterion in the clustering task, consists in putting[11] objects O^i and $O^{i'}$ in the same cluster[12] if their measure of similarity $A_{ii'}$ is higher than their measure of dissimilarity $\overline{A}_{ii'}$.

[11] In condition to satisfy the relational properties of an order relation see eq. (18).
[12] ie $X_{ii'} = 1$.

Given A and $\overline{A}$, then looking for a partition which is represented by a relational matrix X and which aims at maximizing the Condorcet's criterion, can be obtained by means of integer linear programming (41), (37), (32), (31).

$$\begin{array}{lll} & \max_X \text{Condorcet}(A, \overline{A}, X) & \\ & \text{wrt} & \\ X_{ii'} \in \{0,1\} & & \text{(binarity)} \\ X_{ii} = 1 & \forall i = 1, \ldots, N & \text{(reflexivity)} \\ X_{ii'} - X_{i'i} = 1 & \forall i, i' = 1, \ldots, N : i \neq i' & \text{(symmetry)} \\ X_{ii'} + X_{i'i''} - X_{ii''} \leq 1 & \forall i, i', i'' = 1, \ldots, N & \text{(transitivity)} \end{array} \quad (18)$$

This model is particularly adapted for clustering objects, described by categorical variables[13]. Hence, the same aggregation method introduced beforehand for dealing with orders relation can be applied here as well.

Suppose that we have M categorical variables denoted by $V^k; k = 1, \ldots, M$, and let denote by V_i^k the class of V^k assigned to object O^i. Then each variable induce an equivalence relation on the objects. As a result, we can associate to each V^k a relational matrix C^k:

$$C^k_{ii'} = \begin{cases} 1 & \text{if } V_i^k = V_{i'}^k \\ 0 & \text{otherwise} \end{cases} \quad (19)$$

For instance, we can get the following relational matrix:

$$\begin{array}{|c|c|} \hline & V^k \\ \hline O^1 & \text{blue} \\ O^2 & \text{brown} \\ O^3 & \text{brown} \\ O^4 & \text{blue} \\ \hline \end{array} \quad \rightarrow \quad \begin{array}{c} \\ O^1 \\ O^2 \\ O^3 \\ O^4 \end{array} \begin{array}{c} \begin{array}{cccc} O^1 & O^2 & O^3 & O^4 \end{array} \\ \begin{pmatrix} 1 & 0 & 0 & 1 \\ 0 & 1 & 1 & 0 \\ 0 & 1 & 1 & 0 \\ 1 & 0 & 0 & 1 \end{pmatrix} \end{array} \quad (20)$$

Just by considering the M individual relational matrices, we can, as for order relations, aggregate equivalence relations by summing up the individual relational matrices. We then define the collective relational matrix which general term is given by:

$$\mathbf{C}_{ii'} = \sum_{k=1}^{M} C^k_{ii'} = \left\{ \begin{array}{l} \text{Nb of variables for which } O^i \text{ and } O^{i'} \\ \text{are in the same cluster} \end{array} \right. \quad (21)$$

We can also define the collective relational matrix $\overline{\mathbf{C}}$ related to the aggregation of the individual relational matrices $\overline{C}^k$ where:

$$\overline{\mathbf{C}}_{ii'} = \sum_{k=1}^{M} \overline{C}^k_{ii'} = \left\{ \begin{array}{l} \text{Nb of variables for which } O^i \text{ and } O^{i'} \\ \text{are not in the same cluster} \end{array} \right. \quad (22)$$

Similarly to the previous section, if we take $A = \mathbf{C}$ and $\overline{A} = \overline{\mathbf{C}}$ and if we replace $\overline{X}_{ii'}$ with $1 - X_{ii'}$ then we first obtain:

$$\text{Condorcet}(\mathbf{C}, \overline{\mathbf{C}}, X) = \sum_{i=1}^{N} \sum_{i'=1}^{N} \left(\mathbf{C}_{ii'} - \overline{\mathbf{C}}_{ii'}\right) X_{ii'} \quad (23)$$

[13] However, in section 6, we will consider the case where objects are described by real continuous quantitative variables.

Secondly, if we suppose that there is no missing value then we have, $\overline{\mathbf{C}}_{ii'} = M - \mathbf{C}_{ii'}$, and the following simplified Condorcet's criterion:

$$\text{Condorcet}(\mathbf{C}, X) = \sum_{i=1}^{N}\sum_{i'=1}^{N}\left(\mathbf{C}_{ii'} - \frac{M}{2}\right)X_{ii'} \tag{24}$$

Maximizing the Condorcet's criterion in order to cluster categorical data, amounts to highly consider to put O^i and $O^{i'}$ in the same cluster[14] of the consensus partition[15], if the number of variables considering that O^i and $O^{i'}$ are in the same cluster is higher than the number of variables considering that O^i and $O^{i'}$ are not in the same cluster. Moreover, if there is no missing value then it is equivalent to say that O^i and $O^{i'}$ are more likely in the same cluster of the consensual partition, if the number of variables indicating that O^i and $O^{i'}$ are in the same cluster is greater or equal to the simple majority $\frac{M}{2}$ of the total number of variables.

Here, it is worth mentioning that the integer linear program given in eq. (18) does not require as an "a priori" hypothesis, the knowledge of the expected number of clusters of the partition we are looking for. This is quite an attractive and interesting property of the RA approach in the clustering context: the number of clusters obtained solving eq. (18) is an optimal inherent value according to Condorcet's criterion.

There are other related problems of the clustering task that have been studied when using the RA formalism. We quote here some references[16]. In (13), the RA approach is used for studying binary relations over triples of objects. This work led to the definition of association and partitioning criteria for heterogeneous data. In (10), an application in computational linguistics is proposed and particularly for the automatic building of synonyms dictionaries. We can also mention other theoretical contributions from (8), (45), or (50) for example.

More recently, the "Correlation Clustering" (CC) method has been proposed by G. Bansal and al in (6). The similarity matrix, considered here, is built up as follows: we put 1 if objects O^i and $O^{i'}$ are considered as similar and -1 otherwise. In terms of the notations presented in this chapter, this corresponds to the particular case where $A_{ii'} = 1$ if O^i and $O^{i'}$ are similar and $\overline{A}_{ii'} = 1$ if they are not. In (15), the linear program used for approximating the clustering problem is equivalent to eq. (18) except that the unknown relational matrix is $\overline{X}$ with general term $\overline{X}_{ii'} = 1 - X_{ii'}$. This latter representation leads to a distance relation which is irreflexive, symmetric and which satisfies the "triangle inequality" which is the exact dual of the transitivity property[17]. In a recent work, L. Labiod (25) has studied the possible connections between the CC methods, the N-Cuts methods and other clustering functions and the RA approach. Accordingly, his conclusions corroborate the fact that the Condorcet's criterion is a central and focal concept.

[14] In condition to satisfy the relational properties of an equivalence relation see eq. (18).

[15] ie $X_{ii'} = 1$.

[16] But we will show in section 6 other main results obtained by using the RA formalism.

[17] If X satisfies the transitivity inequality given in eq. (18), then it is easy to see that *overlineX* satisfies the triangle inequality: $\overline{X}_{ii''} \leq \overline{X}_{ii'} + \overline{X}_{i'i''}$.

5. The block seriation problem

Let us consider the case where we have as an input, a $(N \times P)$ $0/1$ indicator table $\mathbf{K}$. Then in its original form, the problem of seriation consists in finding two permutations, the first one τ, corresponding to a permutation of the rows of $\mathbf{K}$, and the other one σ, corresponding to a permutation of the columns of $\mathbf{K}$; such that a dense structure "appears" along the diagonal of the permuted K'. A simple example is given below:

$$\mathbf{K} = \begin{matrix} \\ O^1 \\ O^2 \\ O^3 \\ O^4 \\ O^5 \\ O^6 \\ O^7 \end{matrix} \begin{pmatrix} D^1 & D^2 & D^3 & D^4 & D^5 & D^6 & D^7 & D^8 & D^9 \\ 1 & 0 & 0 & 1 & 0 & 0 & 1 & 0 & 0 \\ 1 & 0 & 0 & 0 & 1 & 0 & 0 & 1 & 0 \\ 1 & 0 & 0 & 1 & 0 & 0 & 1 & 0 & 0 \\ 0 & 1 & 0 & 0 & 1 & 0 & 0 & 1 & 0 \\ 0 & 1 & 0 & 0 & 1 & 0 & 0 & 1 & 0 \\ 0 & 0 & 1 & 0 & 1 & 0 & 0 & 0 & 1 \\ 0 & 0 & 1 & 0 & 0 & 1 & 0 & 0 & 1 \end{pmatrix}$$

$$\downarrow (\tau, \sigma) \tag{25}$$

$$\mathbf{K}' = \begin{matrix} \\ O^1 \\ O^3 \\ O^2 \\ O^4 \\ O^5 \\ O^6 \\ O^7 \end{matrix} \begin{pmatrix} D^1 & D^4 & D^7 & D^2 & D^8 & D^5 & D^3 & D^6 & D^9 \\ 1 & 1 & 1 & 0 & 0 & 0 & 0 & 0 & 0 \\ 1 & 1 & 1 & 0 & 0 & 0 & 0 & 0 & 0 \\ 1 & 0 & 0 & 0 & 1 & 1 & 0 & 0 & 0 \\ 0 & 0 & 0 & 1 & 1 & 1 & 0 & 0 & 0 \\ 0 & 0 & 0 & 1 & 1 & 1 & 0 & 0 & 0 \\ 0 & 0 & 0 & 0 & 0 & 1 & 1 & 0 & 1 \\ 0 & 0 & 0 & 0 & 0 & 0 & 1 & 1 & 1 \end{pmatrix}$$

In a more general perspective, let suppose that we have two $(N \times P)$ matrices, A and $\overline{A}$, such that A_{ij} gives the "strength" of the relation $O^i \mathcal{R} D^j$ and $\overline{A}_{ij}$ gives the "strength" of the relation $O^i \overline{\mathcal{R}} D^j$, $\forall i = 1, \ldots, N; j = 1, \ldots, P$. For example, considering the previous example, we can take $A_{ij} = \mathbf{K}_{ij}$ and $\overline{A}_{ij} = 1 - \mathbf{K}_{ij}$.

Let us moreover denote by $P = P^1 \cup \ldots \cup P^k \cup \ldots P^\kappa$ and $Q = Q^1 \cup \ldots \cup Q^k \cup \ldots Q^\kappa$, two partitions with regards to the set of objects $\mathbb{O}$ and the set of descriptors $\mathbb{D}$. These two partitions have the same number of clusters κ. Then, the block seriation problem can be reshaped under the maximization of the following criterion:

$$F(\kappa, P, Q) = \sum_{k=1}^{\kappa} \left(\sum_{\substack{O^i \in P_k \\ D^j \in Q_k}} A_{ij} + \sum_{\substack{O^i \in P_k \\ D^j \notin Q_k}} \overline{A}_{ij} \right) \tag{26}$$

We can see that the solution $\kappa = 3$; $P^1 = \{O^1, O^3\}, P^2 = \{O^2, O^4, O^5\}, P^3 = \{O^6, O^7\}$ and $Q^1 = \{D^1, D^4, D^7\}, Q^2 = \{D^2, D^8, D^5\}, Q^3 = \{D^3, Dv, O^9\}$; is the triple that maximizes the criterion considering the example given in eq. (25).

We can therefore define the two following assignment matrices:

$$P_{ik} = \begin{cases} 1 & \text{if } O^i \text{ belongs to } P^k \\ 0 & \text{otherwise} \end{cases} \tag{27}$$

$$Q_{jk} = \begin{cases} 1 & \text{if } D^j \text{ belongs to } Q^k \\ 0 & \text{otherwise} \end{cases} \tag{28}$$

Using those assignment matrices, the problem can be re-stated as follows:

$$\begin{array}{c} \max_{\kappa,P,Q} F(\kappa,P,Q) = \sum_{k=1}^{\kappa}\left(\sum_{i=1}^{N}\sum_{j=1}^{P} A_{ij}P_{ik}Q_{jk} + \sum_{i=1}^{N}\sum_{j=1}^{P}\overline{A}_{ij}P_{ik}(1-Q_{jk})\right) \\ \text{wrt} \\ \begin{array}{ll} P_{ik} \in \{0,1\} & \forall i = 1,\ldots,N; k = 1,\ldots,\kappa \\ Q_{jk} \in \{0,1\} & \forall i = 1,\ldots,N; k = 1,\ldots,\kappa \\ \sum_{k=1}^{\kappa} P_{ik} = 1 & \forall i = 1,\ldots,N \\ \sum_{k=1}^{\kappa} Q_{jk} = 1 & \forall j = 1,\ldots,P \end{array} \end{array} \tag{29}$$

There are $N + P$ linear constraints but the criterion that we have to maximize is quadratic according to $P_{ik}Q_{jk}$ thus we cannot use integer linear programming solvers.

But, considering the criterion given in eq. (29), one can distribute the sum over k into the brackets and introduce the following variable (33), (35):

$$\begin{array}{rcl} Z_{ij} & = & \sum_{k=1}^{\kappa} P_{ik}Q_{jk} \\ & = & \begin{cases} 1 & \text{if } O^i \text{ and } D^j \text{ belong to the same block} \\ 0 & \text{otherwise} \end{cases} \end{array} \tag{30}$$

For example, according to this variable, the optimal solution corresponding to the example given previously is the following one (to be clear we give this solution according to permutations τ and σ):

$$Z = \begin{array}{c} \\ O^1 \\ O^3 \\ O^2 \\ O^4 \\ O^5 \\ O^6 \\ O^7 \end{array} \begin{array}{c} \begin{array}{ccccccccc} D^1 & D^4 & D^7 & D^2 & D^8 & D^5 & D^3 & D^6 & D^9 \end{array} \\ \begin{pmatrix} 1 & 1 & 1 & 0 & 0 & 0 & 0 & 0 & 0 \\ 1 & 1 & 1 & 0 & 0 & 0 & 0 & 0 & 0 \\ 0 & 0 & 0 & 1 & 1 & 1 & 0 & 0 & 0 \\ 0 & 0 & 0 & 1 & 1 & 1 & 0 & 0 & 0 \\ 0 & 0 & 0 & 1 & 1 & 1 & 0 & 0 & 0 \\ 0 & 0 & 0 & 0 & 0 & 0 & 1 & 1 & 1 \\ 0 & 0 & 0 & 0 & 0 & 0 & 1 & 1 & 1 \end{pmatrix} \end{array} \tag{31}$$

For instance we can see that the first block constituted of $(P^1; Q^1)$ is given by $(\{O^1, O^3\}; \{D^1, D^4, D^7\})$ and all terms of Z corresponding to the Cartesian product $\{O^1, O^3\} \times \{D^1, D^4, D^7\}$ are assigned 1.

The $(N \times P)$ binary matrix Z is interpreted as a relational matrix associated to a binary relation on two sets $\mathbb{O}$ and $\mathbb{D}$. The important facts are that this approach firstly allows us to have a criterion that is independent from κ and which is linear according to Z, and secondly, it is possible to express the relational properties of this particular relation using linear equations.

These linear equations were given in (33):

$$
\begin{array}{ll}
\sum_{j=1}^{P} Z_{ij} \geq 1 & \forall i = 1,\ldots,N \\
\sum_{i=1}^{N} Z_{ij} \geq 1 & \forall j = 1,\ldots,P \\
\left\{\begin{array}{l}
Z_{ij} + Z_{i'j} + Z_{ij'} - Z_{i'j'} \leq 2 \\
Z_{ij} + Z_{i'j} + Z_{i'j'} - Z_{ij'} \leq 2 \\
Z_{ij} + Z_{ij'} + Z_{i'j'} - Z_{i'j} \leq 2 \\
Z_{i'j} + Z_{ij'} + Z_{i'j'} - Z_{ij} \leq 2
\end{array}\right. & \forall i = 1,\ldots,N
\end{array}
\tag{32}
$$

These four latter constraints are called "impossible triads": "at the crossing of two rows and two columns of Z, one cannot get a "1" value three times". More precisely, let us suppose that for the optimal solution, $Z_{ij} = 1$, that is to say, O^i and D^j are in the same block. If furthermore, $Z_{ij'} = 1$ and $Z_{i'j'} = 1$ then we must also have $Z_{i'j} = 1$. In other words, if O^i is in the same block as D^j and $D^{j'}$, and if $O^{i'}$ is in the same block as D^j then $O^{i'}$ should be in the same block as D^j.

Using the binary relation formalism, we can see that we can also obtain the relational matrix Z by means of integer linear programming solver:

$$
\begin{array}{c}
\max_Z \text{Condorcet}(A, \overline{A}, Z) \\
\text{wrt}
\end{array}
$$

$$
\begin{array}{lll}
Z_{ij} \in \{0,1\} & & \text{(binarity)} \\
\left\{\begin{array}{l}
\sum_{j=1}^{P} Z_{ij} \geq 1 \\
\sum_{i=1}^{N} Z_{ij} \geq 1
\end{array}\right. & \begin{array}{l}\forall i = 1,\ldots,N \\ \forall j = 1,\ldots,P\end{array} & \text{(assignment)} \\
\left\{\begin{array}{l}
Z_{ij} + Z_{i'j} + Z_{ij'} - Z_{i'j'} \leq 2 \\
Z_{ij} + Z_{i'j} + Z_{i'j'} - Z_{ij'} \leq 2 \\
Z_{ij} + Z_{ij'} + Z_{i'j'} - Z_{i'j} \leq 2 \\
Z_{i'j} + Z_{ij'} + Z_{i'j'} - Z_{ij} \leq 2
\end{array}\right. & \begin{array}{l}\forall i, i' = 1,\ldots,N \\ \forall j, j' = 1,\ldots,P\end{array} & \text{(impossible triads)}
\end{array}
\tag{33}
$$

Let us recall that the Condorcet's criterion under its general form, is given as follows:

$$
\text{Condorcet}(A, \overline{A}, Z) = \sum_{i=1}^{N} \sum_{j=1}^{P} \left(A_{ij} Z_{ij} + \overline{A}_{ij} \overline{Z}_{ij} \right) \tag{34}
$$

If $A = \mathbf{K}$, $\mathbf{K}$ being an indicator table, commonly used in categorical data analysis, then the block seriation model given in eq. (33) gives rise to a biclustering method for this type of table. In this particular case, we have $\overline{A}_{ij} = 1 - \mathbf{K}_{ij}$ and by replacing $\overline{Z}_{ij}$ with $1 - Z_{ij}$, we obtain the following simplified Condorcet's criterion:

$$
\text{Condorcet}(\mathbf{K}, Z) = \sum_{i=1}^{N} \sum_{j=1}^{P} \left(\mathbf{K}_{ij} - \frac{1}{2} \right) Z_{ij} \tag{35}
$$

We have highlighted the RA approach for biclustering tasks in the particular case of $0/1$ data type but, the proposed method can be straightforwardly extended to other types of data such as real continuous quantitative data. In that case, matrices A and $\overline{A}$[18] are required.

Block seriation models, through their relational formalism, have generated many research works, both for theoretical and practical purposes. We can quote as an illustrative example C. Bédécarax's Phd Thesis (9) where is defined a more general framework called "quadri-decomposition". From that general model, the above mentioned clustering problems[19] are in fact structural derivatives. Besides, "quadri-decomposition" modeling was successfully applied to the automatic building of dictionaries in computational linguistics see (10). Furthermore, in order to take into account large amount of data, several heuristics have been developed and the interested reader could consult (43) for such algorithms and also (16) for an application to production management optimization.

6. Other results of the RA method in the context of clustering problems

In the analysis of equivalence relations, the RA approach has allowed other interesting contributions.

The first one, concerns the study of numerous "association criteria" crossing categorical variables[20] such as Belson, Lerman, χ^2 of Tchuprow, Jordan, Rand and Janson and Vegelius indexes for instance. Suppose that we have at our disposal two categorical variables V^k and V^l with respectively p_k and p_l categories. Then the previous association criteria are basically defined using the $(p_k \times p_l)$ contingency table $\mathbf{n}^{kl}$ where $\forall(u,v) \in \{1,\ldots,p_k\} \times \{1,\ldots,p_l\}$:

$$\mathbf{n}^{kl}_{uv} = \begin{cases} \text{Nb of objects that have both category } D^u \text{ of } V^k \\ \text{and category } D^v \text{ of } V^l \end{cases} \tag{36}$$

Relational matrices C^k and C^l are an other type of coding for categorical variables. Following some previous contributions from M.G. Kendall (24), J.F. Marcotorchino in (28), (29), (30), (31), developed correspondence or transfer formulas that allow to express the association criteria using relational matrices C^k and C^l. Some of the main correspondence formulas are given below:

$$\sum_{u=1}^{p_k}\sum_{v=1}^{p_l}(\mathbf{n}^{kl}_{uv})^2 = \sum_{i=1}^{N}\sum_{i'=1}^{N} C^k_{ii'}C^l_{ii'} \tag{37}$$

$$\sum_{u=1}^{p_k}(\mathbf{n}^{kl}_{u.})^2 = \sum_{i=1}^{N}\sum_{i'=1}^{N} C^k_{ii'} \tag{38}$$

The reformulation of association criteria into the RA formalism, allows us to model coefficients like Belson, Rand, χ^2 of Tchuprow, Janson and Vegelius..., as particular cases of a general Coefficient, which is nothing but a simple variant of Bravais-Pearson's correlation coefficient $\Delta(C^k, C^l, f, \mu^k, \mu^l)$ see (28), (38), (44), (2), (3).

The RA formalism has allowed to get a deeper understanding of the main differences between several association criteria: in fact, the latent differences between the above mentioned association criteria can be expressed, according to 3 parameters (f, μ^k, μ^l):

18 $\overline{A}$ could be taken from A.

19 ie clustering $\mathbb{O}$ or $\mathbb{D}$ or both.

20 Two way contingency tables analysis.

- f is a function that transforms the general term of each relational matrix[21]
- μ^k is a central trend (playing the role of a mean) corresponding to C^k
- μ^l is a central trend (playing the role of a mean) corresponding to C^l

In order to illustrate those results, we give as an example, the different formulations of the χ^2 of Tchuprow criterion:

$$\text{Tchuprow}(V^k, V^l) = \frac{\sum_{u,v} \frac{1}{\mathbf{n}^{kl}_{u.}\mathbf{n}^{kl}_{.v}} \left(\mathbf{n}^{kl}_{uv} - \frac{\mathbf{n}^{kl}_{u.}\mathbf{n}^{kl}_{.v}}{N}\right)^2}{\sqrt{(p_k-1)(p_l-1)}} \quad (39)$$

$$= \frac{\sum_{i,i'} \left(\frac{C^k_{ii'}}{C^k_{i.}} - \frac{1}{N}\right)\left(\frac{C^l_{ii'}}{C^l_{i.}} - \frac{1}{N}\right)}{\sqrt{\sum_{i,i'} \left(\frac{C^k_{ii'}}{C^k_{i.}} - \frac{1}{N}\right)^2 \sum_{i,i'} \left(\frac{C^l_{ii'}}{C^l_{i.}} - \frac{1}{N}\right)^2}} \quad (40)$$

where $C^k_{i.} = \sum_{i'} C^k_{ii'}$ gives the number of objects that belong to the same cluster[22] of O^i according to V^k. Here, the parameters (f, μ^k, μ^l) corresponding to the χ^2 of Tchuprow is $(f(C_{ii'}) = C_{ii'}/C_{i.}, \mu^k = 1/N, \mu^l = 1/N)$. Another example is the (modified) Rand index, which can also be expressed using this general coefficient Δ: it is linked to the particular coefficient given by $(f(C_{ii'}) = C_{ii'}, \mu^k = 1/2, \mu^l = 1/2)$.

Concerning the relational expression of association criteria, we can also quote the "Maximal Association model" defined in (32) and (48) which aims at defining partitioning criteria by aggregating association criteria between relations and X. More precisely, suppose that we have M relational matrices[23], $C^k; k = 1, \dots, M$, and we want to find out a consensual equivalence relation X. Furthermore, we can use a particular association criterion $\Delta(C^k, X, f, \mu^k, \mu^l)$ in order to measure the correlation between a given partition C^k and an unknown consensus partition X. Then, one can consider to find the X that maximizes[24] the following partitioning criterion[25]:

$$\sum_{k=1}^{M} \Delta(C^k, X, f, \mu^k, \mu^l) \quad (41)$$

We can see that the Maximal Association model for partitions gives many solutions to the initial problem given by eq. (3), that we want to address.
Moreover these association criteria, can be interpreted as similarity measures between categorical variables. As a result, one can use those measures to partition categorical variables and apply these results in a dimension reduction purpose. This question has been investigated in the context of the RA framework in (1).

[21] For example, among the transformation functions that occurred in the relational formalism, Torgerson's transformation is the one related to the Belson criterion.
[22] ie the number of objects that have the same category of O^i according to V^k.
[23] Derived from M categorical variables.
[24] Most of the association criterion's numerators given by particular $\Delta(C^k, X, f, \mu^k, \mu^l)$ lead to linear partitioning criteria according to X and can then be used with integer linear programming.
[25] With respect to the linear equations given in eq. (18).

The second contribution in data analysis that is worth noticing is related to the measure of similarity between objects. The approach developed in (11), (12), called "regularized similarity" consists in giving automatic weights to the initial variables according to particular models of weighting, among them let us quote: the logical, the statistical and the probabilistic models.

One can represent a set of M categorical variables using the $(N \times P)$ indicator matrix $\mathbf{K}$ where $P = \sum_{k=1}^{M} p_k$. This matrix is a binary one and we have, $\forall i = 1, \ldots, N; \forall j = 1, \ldots, P$:

$$\mathbf{K}_{ij} = \begin{cases} 1 & \text{if object } O^i \text{ is in the category}^{26}\ D^j \\ 0 & \text{otherwise} \end{cases} \tag{42}$$

We have previously defined $\mathbf{C}_{ii'}$ according to a logical approach in terms of equivalence relations aggregation. We can also have a more geometrical approach since we have:

$$\mathbf{C}_{ii'} = \sum_{j=1}^{P} \mathbf{K}_{ij}\mathbf{K}_{i'j} = \langle \vec{O^i}, \vec{O^{i'}} \rangle \tag{43}$$

where $\vec{O^i} = (\mathbf{K}_{i1}, \ldots, \mathbf{K}_{ij}, \ldots, \mathbf{K}_{iN})$ and $\langle .,. \rangle$ is the canonical scalar product.
From a geometrical standpoint, the regularized similarity method amounts to exhibit a diagonal metric, for which the diagonal weights are computed from the categorical variables. The regularized similarity of type α denoted by $A^{\alpha}_{ii'}$ is given by:

$$A^{\alpha}_{ii'} = \sum_{j=1}^{P} \alpha_j \mathbf{K}_{ij}\mathbf{K}_{i'j} \tag{44}$$

For instance, "statistical regularized similarity", defined in (11), gives higher weights to infrequent categories and reciprocally, very low weights to those frequent categories. In this particular case, we have actually $\alpha_j = 1/\mathbf{K}_{.j}$. We can observe that the model supposes that if two objects have a rare category in common then their similarity should be higher than if their shared category were frequent.

This particular similarity measure is related to the χ^2 metric used in Correspondence Factor Analysis methods (20). We can mention here, the following paper (34), where the latent link between the RA method and Factor Analysis methods is explained.
Basically, the Condorcet's criterion, while we use the statistical regularized similarity, becomes highly related to "Inertial criteria". More precisely, J.F. Marcotorchino showed that the Condorcet's criterion associated to the similarity matrix of general term $A^{\alpha}_{ii'}$, and the dissimilarity matrix of general term $\overline{A}^{\alpha}_{ii'} = \frac{A^{\alpha}_{ii} + A^{\alpha}_{i'i'}}{2} - A^{\alpha}_{ii'}$, is the non trivial partitioning criterion strongly relevant to the family of criteria based upon inertia or "variance". This result led to the design of a full methodology called "Relational Factor Analysis method" (34) that consists in coupling the representations of clusters in terms of "bubbles", resulting from the RA[27] method, with the projection of objects on a 2D space obtained after applying the Factor Analysis method. Both approaches complement each other, because they maximize a quite equivalent criterion.

[27] With the statistical regularized similarity.

The third contribution that we can mention finally, is based on the extension of the RA method which is well-designed for clustering categorical data, to deal with objects described by real continuous quantitative variables. Indeed, we can notice that similarity measures can be expressed through scalar products or in a general manner by kernels. Then if we take $A_{ii'} = \langle \vec{O}^i, \vec{O}^{i'} \rangle$ and $\overline{A}_{ii'} = \frac{\langle \vec{O}^i, \vec{O}^i \rangle + \langle \vec{O}^{i'}, \vec{O}^{i'} \rangle}{2} - \langle \vec{O}^i, \vec{O}^{i'} \rangle$ which is equal to $\frac{1}{2}||\vec{O}^i - \vec{O}^{i'}||$, we have the following simplified Condorcet's criterion:

$$\text{Condorcet}(A, X) = \sum_{i=1}^{N} \sum_{i'=1}^{N} \left(\langle \vec{O}^i, \vec{O}^{i'} \rangle - \frac{1}{2} \left(\frac{\langle \vec{O}^i, \vec{O}^i \rangle + \langle \vec{O}^{i'}, \vec{O}^{i'} \rangle}{2} \right) \right) X_{ii'} \qquad (45)$$

Following previous results given in (34), we can show that the criterion based upon the inertial difference can be expressed using the RA formalism as follows:

$$\begin{aligned} \mathbb{IB}(X) - \mathbb{IW}(X) \quad = \quad & \tfrac{2}{N} \textstyle\sum_{i=1}^{N} \sum_{i'=1}^{N} \left(\langle \vec{O}^i, \vec{O}^{i'} \rangle - \frac{1}{2} \left(\frac{\langle \vec{O}^i, \vec{O}^i \rangle + \langle \vec{O}^{i'}, \vec{O}^{i'} \rangle}{2} \right) \right) \left(\frac{X_{ii'}}{X_{i.}} \right) \\ & - \tfrac{1}{N^2} \textstyle\sum_{i=1}^{N} \sum_{i'=1}^{N} \langle \vec{O}^i, \vec{O}^{i'} \rangle \end{aligned} \qquad (46)$$

$\mathbb{IB}(X)$ is the "between classes inertia" related to a partition represented by its relational matrix X, $\mathbb{IW}(X)$ is the "within classes inertia[28]" and $\langle ., . \rangle$ is a scalar product (kernel).

In the formula (46), if we look at the subpart depending on X, we can observe that the main difference between Condorcet's criterion and the inertial difference criterion resides in the fact that the first one does not weight the general term $X_{ii'}$, whereas the second one integrates a weight[29], $1/X_{i.}$, to the general term $X_{ii'}$.

Finally, by considering eq. (46) and the integer linear program described in eq. (18) we can thus extend the RA approach for clustering problems to the more general case of objects described by real continuous quantitative variables.

7. Acknowledgments

Part of this work was supported by Cap Digital (french business cluster in the digital content creation and knowledge management area)

8. References

[1] Abdallah, H.: Application de l'analyse relationnelle pour classifier descripteurs et modalités en mode discrimination. Ph.D. thesis, University of Pierre and Marie Curie (Paris 6, France) (1996)

[2] Ah-Pine, J.: Sur des aspects algébriques et combinatoires de l'analyse relationnelle. Ph.D. thesis, University of Pierre and Marie Curie (Paris 6) (2007)

[3] Ah-Pine, J., Marcotorchino, J.F.: Statistical, geometrical and logical independences between categorical variables. In: Proceedings of Applied Stochastic Models and Data Analysis, Chania Crete, 2007 (2007)

[4] Arditti, D.: Un algorithme de recherche d'un ordre induit par des comparaisons par paires. Note technique CNET, Paris, France (1982)

[28] See (49) for example for the definition of these quantities using euclidean distances.

[29] Which consists in dividing by the number of objects that belong to the same cluster as O^i.

[5] Arrow, K.J.: Social choice and individual values 2nd ed. Wiley, New-York (1963)
[6] Bansal, N., Blum, A., Chawla, S.: Correlation clustering. In: IEEE Symposium on Foundations of Computer Science (FOCS) (2002)
[7] Barthélémy, J.P., Guenoche, A., Hudry, O.: Median linear orders: heuristics and a branch and bound algorithm. European Journal of Operational Research **41**, 313–325 (1989)
[8] Barthélémy, J.P., Monjardet, B.: The median procedure in cluster analysis and social choice theory. Mathematical social sciences **1**, 235–267 (1991)
[9] Bédécarrax, C.: Classification automatique en analyse relationnelle: la quadri-décomposition et ses applications. Ph.D. thesis, University of Pierre and Marie Curie (Paris 6, France) (1989)
[10] Bédécarrax, C., Warnesson, I.: Relational analysis and dictionnaries. In: Proceedings of Applied Stochastic Models and Data Analysis, pp. 131–151. Wiley, London, New-York (1989)
[11] Benhadda, H.: La similarité régularisée et ses applications en classification automatique. Ph.D. thesis, University of Pierre and Marie Curie (Paris 6, France) (1998)
[12] Benhadda, H., Marcotorchino, J.F.: Introduction à la similarité régularisée en analyse relationnelle. Revue de statistique appliquée **46** (1998)
[13] Chah, S.: Nouvelles techniques de codage d'association et de classification. Ph.D. thesis, University of Pierre and Marie Curie (Paris 6, France) (1986)
[14] Condorcet, M.J.A.: Essai sur l'application de l'analyse à la probabilité des décisions rendues à la pluralité des voix. Paris (1785)
[15] Demaine, E., Immorlica, N.: Correlation clustering with partial information. In: International Workshop on Approximation Algorithms for Combinatorial Optimization (APPROX), Princeton, New Jersey (2003)
[16] Garcia, H., Proth, J.M.: Group technology in production management. Applied Stochastic Models and Data Analysis **1**, 25–34 (1985)
[17] Ghashghaie, S.: Agrégation relationnelle des données ordinales: généralisation de critères d'association. Ph.D. thesis, University of Pierre and Marie Curie (Paris 6, France) (1990)
[18] Gionis, A., Mannila, H., Panayiotis, T.: Clustering aggregation. ACM Transactions on Knowledge Discovery from Data **1** (2007)
[19] Giraud, S.: Comparaison de règles d'agrégation d'ordres et études de règles multicritères d'aide à la décision. Ph.D. thesis, University of Pierre and Marie Curie (Paris 6, France) (1985)
[20] Greenacre, J.: Theory and applications of correspondence analysis. Academic Press (1984)
[21] Grötschel, M., Jünger, M., Reinelt, G.: A cutting plane algorithm for the linear ordering problem. Operations research **32**, 1195–1220 (1984)
[22] Joachims, T., Hopcroft, J.: Error bounds for correlation clustering. In: Proceedings of the 22nd international conference on Machine learning (2005)
[23] Kemeny, J.G., Snell, J.L.: Mathematical models in the social sciences. MIT Press, Boston (1972)
[24] Kendall, M.G.: Rank correlation methods. Griffin Londres (1970)
[25] Labiod, L.: Contribution au formalisme relationnel des classifications simultanées de deux ensembles. Ph.D. thesis, University of Pierre and Marie Curie (Paris 6, France) (2008(forthcoming))
[26] Leclerc, B., Monjardet, B.: Latticial theory of consensus. In: W. Barnett, H. Moulin,

M. Salles, N.E. Schofield (eds.) Social Choice, Welfare, and Ethics, pp. 145–160. Cambridge University Press (1995)
[27] Lerman, I.C.: Classification et analyse ordinale de données. Dunod, Paris (1981)
[28] Marcotorchino, J.F.: Utilisation des comparaisons par paires en statistiques des contingences i. Etudes du Centre scientifique IBM France, Paris **F069** (1984)
[29] Marcotorchino, J.F.: Utilisation des comparaisons par paires en statistiques des contingences ii. Etudes du Centre scientifique IBM France, Paris **F071** (1984)
[30] Marcotorchino, J.F.: Utilisation des comparaisons par paires en statistiques des contingences iii. Etudes du Centre scientifique IBM France, Paris **F081** (1985)
[31] Marcotorchino, J.F.: Cross association measures and optimal clustering. In: Proceedings in Computational statistics, pp. 188–196. Physica-Verlag Heidelberg (1986)
[32] Marcotorchino, J.F.: Maximal association theory as a tool of research. In: W. Gaul, M.e. Schader (eds.) Classification as a tool of research, pp. 275–288. North Holland Amsterdam (1986)
[33] Marcotorchino, J.F.: An unified approach to the block seriation problems. Applied Stochastic Models and Data Analysis **3** (1987)
[34] Marcotorchino, J.F.: L'analyse factorielle relationnelle: parties i et ii. Etudes du CEMAP, IBM France, Paris **MAP-03** (1991)
[35] Marcotorchino, J.F.: Seriation problems: an overview. Applied stochastic models and Data Analysis **7**, 139–151 (1991)
[36] Marcotorchino, J.F., Michaud, P.: Optimisation en analyse ordinale des données. Masson Editions, Paris (1979)
[37] Marcotorchino, J.F., Michaud, P.: Heuristic approach of the similarity aggregation problem. Methods of operation research **43**, 395–404 (1981)
[38] Messatfa, H.: Unification relationnelle des critères et structures optimales des tables de contingences. Ph.D. thesis, University of Pierre and Marie Curie (Paris 6, France) (1989)
[39] Michaud, P.: Opinions aggregation. In: New trends in data analysis and applications, pp. 5–27. North Holland Amsterdam (1983)
[40] Michaud, P.: Condorcet: A man of the avant-garde. Applied stochastic models and Data Analysis **3**, 173–189 (1987)
[41] Michaud, P., Marcotorchino, J.F.: Optimisation en analyse de données relationelles. In: Data Analysis and informatics. North Holland Amsterdam (1980)
[42] Mirkin, B.G.: Approximation problems in space of binary relations and analysis of non quantitative characteristics. Automatics and remote control (russian) **9**, 51–61 (1974)
[43] Mutel, B., De Guio, R., Bouzid, L.: Application of relational analysis techniques to production data structuring. In: Proceedings of Applied Stochastic Models and Data Analysis, Granad, Spain, pp. 493–507 (1991)
[44] Najah Idrissi, A.: Contribution à l'unification de critères d'asociation pour variables qualitatives. Ph.D. thesis, University of Pierre and Marie Curie (Paris 6, France) (2000)
[45] Owsinski, J.W.: Optimization in clustering: an approach and other approaches. Control and cybernetics **15**, 107–114 (1986)
[46] Régier, S.: Sur quelques aspects mathématiques des problèmes de classification automatique. ICC Bulletin **4**, 175–191 (1965)
[47] Reinelt, G.: The linear ordering problem: algorithms and applications. Research and Exposition in Mathematics **8** (1985)
[48] Saporta, G.: About maximal association criteria in linear analysis and in cluster analysis.

In: H.H.e. Bock (ed.) Classification and related methods of Data Analysis, pp. 541–550. North Holland Amsterdam (1988)

[49] Saporta, G.: Probabilités, analyse des données et statistiques (2nd édition). Technip, Paris (2006)

[50] Schader, M., Tüshaus, U.: Analysis of qualitative data: a heuristic for finding a complete preorder. In: H.H.e. Bock (ed.) Classification and related methods of Data Analysis, pp. 341–346. North Holland Amsterdam (1988)

[51] Wakabayashi, Y.: On the complexity of computing medians of relations. Resenhas IMEUSP **3**, 323–349 (1998)

[52] Zahn, C.T.: Approximating symmetric relations by equivalence relations. SIAM Journal of applied mathematics **12**, 840–847 (1964)

17

Representative-based Protocol for Multiple Interdependent Issue Negotiation Problems

Katsuhide Fujita
Nagoya Institute of Technology
Japan

Takayuki Ito* and Mark Klein
Massachusetts Institute of Technology
U.S.A.

1. Introduction

Multi-issue negotiation protocols represent an important field in the multi-agent systems study. In fact, negotiation covers many aspects of our lives has led to extensive research in the area of automated negotiators, that is, automated agents capable of negotiating with other agents in a specific environment include e-commerce, large scale argument on worldwide problem(Malone & Klein, 2007), collaborative design for cars and so on. Even though there has been a lot of previous work in this area ((Bosse & Jonker, 2005; Faratin et al., 2002; Fatima et al., 2004; Lin & Chou, 2003)) most have dealt exclusively with simple negotiations involving independent multiple issues. Many real-world negotiations, however, are complex negotiation and involve interdependent issues. When designers work together to design a car, for example, the value of a given carburetor is highly dependent on which engine is chosen. We study on the multiple interdependent issues negotiation using automated agent with nonlinear utility function reflected on the real-world negotiations.

The Bidding-based Negotiation Protocol is high performance on multi interdependent issues negotiation(Ito et al., 2007). In bidding based protocol, agents generate bids by sampling and searching their utility functions, and the mediator finds the optimum combination of submitted bids from agents. However, the bidding-based negotiation protocol has two main issues. **1) Privacy:** Existing works have not yet been concerned with agents' private information. Agents' private information should not be revealed excessively because agents who reveal much utility information are brought to a disadvantage. For example, suppose that several companies collaboratively design and develop a new car model. If one company reveals more utility information than other companies, the other companies can know more of that company's utility information. As a result, the company is brought to a disadvantage in the next negotiations. Furthermore, it is dangerous to reveal utility information explicitly as an aspect of security. **2) Scalability for the number of agents:** The bidding-based negotiation protocol is not a high scalability for the number of agents. In the bidding based negotiation protocol, the mediator needs to find the optimum combination of submitted bids from agents. However,

*Visiting from Nagoya Institute of Technology

the computational complexity in finding the solution is too large. The number of agent's bids was limited in the exiting work(Ito et al., 2007). Limiting bids have caused low optimality and high failure rate for agreements.

For resolving privacy issues, we define an agent's **revealed area**, which represents the amount of his/her revealed utility space. The revealed area can numerically define which agents are cooperative and which are not. Additionally, the mediator can understand how much of the agent's private information has been revealed in the negotiation.

Moreover, we propose the **representative-based protocol** that is high scalability for the number of agents and considering the agent's private information. In our protocol, we first select representatives who revealed their utility space more than the others. These representatives reach an agreement on some alternatives and, propose the alternatives to the other agents. Finally, the other agents can express their own intentions on agreement or disagreement. In this protocol, agents who revealed more private utility information can have a greater chance to be representatives who will attend to reach an agreement on behalf of the other agents. Namely, although agents tend not to reveal their private information, they have an incentive to reveal their private information in order to be representatives.

The representative-based protocol has been inspired by the parliamentary systems in England, Canada, Australia, Japan, etc. in which representatives are making an agreement on behalf of other people. In a situation in which a lot of people have to make an agreement, it is quite difficult to directly reflect all members' opinions. If we try to do so, it takes much time and energy, and is not scalable. Although voting is one option, it is well known that voting could have paradoxical results (Arrow, 1970).

We expand our mechanism to be multi-round by using the Threshold Adjustment Protocol (Fujita et al., 2007). The multi-round mechanism improves the failure rates and achieve fairness in terms of the revealed area. This means that the amounts of the revealed areas are almost the same among agents. Further, representative mechanism can prevent the unfair solutions that can exist in the original Threshold Adjustment Protocol.

The representative-based protocol drastically reduces the computational complexity. This is because only representative agents mainly try to reach a consensus. The experimental results demonstrate that our protocol reduces the failure rate in making agreements, and it is scalable on the number of agents compared with existing approaches. We also demonstrate that our protocol reduces the revealed area compared with existing work. Furthermore, we investigate the detailed effect of the representative selection method in our protocol. We call the selection method in which agents who reveal a larger utility area are selected as representatives RAS. In the experiments, we compare RAS with the selection method in which representative agents are randomly selected (RANDOM).

The remainder of the paper is organized as follows. First, we describe a model of non-linear multi-issue negotiation and an existing work's(Ito et al., 2007) problems. Second, we define the revealed area and proposed the new negotiation mechanism. Third, we describe the multi-round negotiation protocol. Fourth, we present an experimental assessment of this protocol. Finally, we describe related work and draw conclusions.

2. Negotiation Using Complex Utility Space

2.1 Complex Utility Model

We consider the situation where n agents want to reach an agreement. There are m issues, $s_j \in S$, to be negotiated. The number of issues represents the number of dimensions of the utility space. For example, if there are 3 issues, the utility space has 3 dimensions. The issues are not

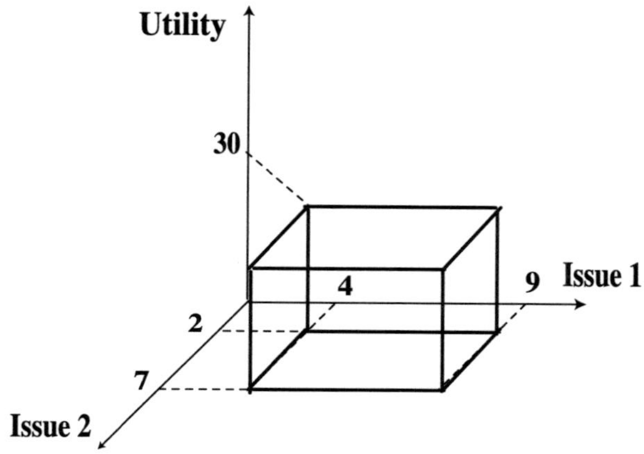

Fig. 1. Example of A Constraint

"distributed" over agents. The agents are all negotiating over a contract that has N (e.g. 10) issues in it. All agents are potentially interested in the values for all N issues. An issue s_j has a value drawn from the domain of integers $[0, X]$, *i.e.*, $s_j \in [0, X]$. A discrete domain can come arbitrarily close to a real domain by increasing the domain size. As a practical matter, very many real-world issues that are theoretically real (delivery date, cost) are discretized during negotiations. Our approach, furthermore, is not theoretically limited to discrete domains. The deal determination part is unaffected, though the bid generation step will have to be modified to use a nonlinear optimization algorithm suited to real domains.

A contract is represented by a vector of issue values $\vec{s} = (s_1, ..., s_m)$.

An agent's utility function is described in terms of constraints. There are l constraints, $c_k \in C$. Each constraint represents a region with one or more dimensions, and has an associated utility value. A constraint c_k has value $w_i(c_k, \vec{s})$ if and only if it is satisfied by contract $\vec{s}$. Figure 1 shows an example of a binary constraint between issues 1 and 2. This constraint has a value of 30, and holds if the value for issue 1 is in the range $[4, 9]$ and the value for issue 2 is in the range $[2, 7]$. Every agent has its' own, typically unique, set of constraints.

An agent's utility for a contract $\vec{s}$ is defined as $u_i(\vec{s}) = \sum_{c_k \in C, \vec{s} \in x(c_k)} w_i(c_k, \vec{s})$, where $x(c_k)$ is a set of possible contracts (solutions) of c_k. This expression produces a "bumpy" nonlinear utility space, with high points where many constraints are satisfied, and lower regions where few or no constraints are satisfied. This represents a crucial departure from previous efforts on multi-issue negotiation, where contract utility is calculated as the weighted sum of the utilities for individual issues, producing utility functions shaped like flat hyper-planes with a single optimum. Figure 2 shows an example of a nonlinear utility space. There are 2 issues, *i.e.*, 2 dimensions, with domains $[0, 99]$. There are 50 unary constraints (*i.e.*, that relate to 1 issue) as well as 100 binary constraints (*i.e.*, that inter-relate 2 issues). The utility space is, as we can see, highly nonlinear, with many hills and valleys.

We assume, as is common in negotiation contexts, which agents do not share their utility functions with each other, in order to preserve a competitive edge. It will generally be the case, in fact, that agents do not fully know their desirable contracts in advance, because each own utility functions are simply too large. If we have 10 issues with 10 possible values per

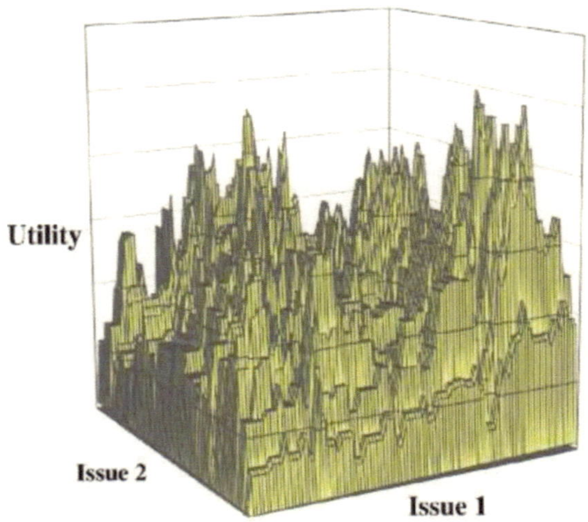

Fig. 2. A Complex Utility Space for a Single Agent

issue, for example, this produces a space of 10^{10} (10 billion) possible contracts, too many to evaluate exhaustively. Agents must thus operate in a highly uncertain environment.
Finding an optimal contract for individual agents with such utility spaces can be handled using well-known nonlinear optimization techniques such a simulated annealing or evolutionary algorithms. We cannot employ such methods for negotiation purposes, however, because they require that agents fully reveal their utility functions to a third party, which is generally unrealistic in negotiation contexts.
The objective function for our protocol can be described as follows:

$$\arg\max_{\vec{s}} \sum_{i \in N} u_i(\vec{s}) \tag{1}$$

Our protocol, in other words, tries to find contracts that maximize social welfare, *i.e.*, the total utilities for all agents. Such contracts, by definition, will also be Pareto-optimal.

2.2 Existing Biding-based Protocol

In the existing work(Ito et al., 2007), agents reach an agreement based on the following steps. We call this **basic bidding-based mechanism**.
[Generate bids] Each agent samples its utility space in order to find high-utility contract regions. A fixed number of samples are taken from a range of random points, drawing from a uniform distribution. Note that, if the number of samples is too low, the agent may miss some high utility regions in its contract space, and thereby potentially end up with a sub-optimal contract.
There is no guarantee, of course, that a given sample will lie on a locally optimal contract. Each agent, therefore, uses a nonlinear optimizer based on simulated annealing (Russell & Norvig, 2002) to try to find the local optimum in its neighborhood. Figure 3 exemplifies this concept. In this figure, a black dot is a sampling point and a white dot is a locally optimal contract point.

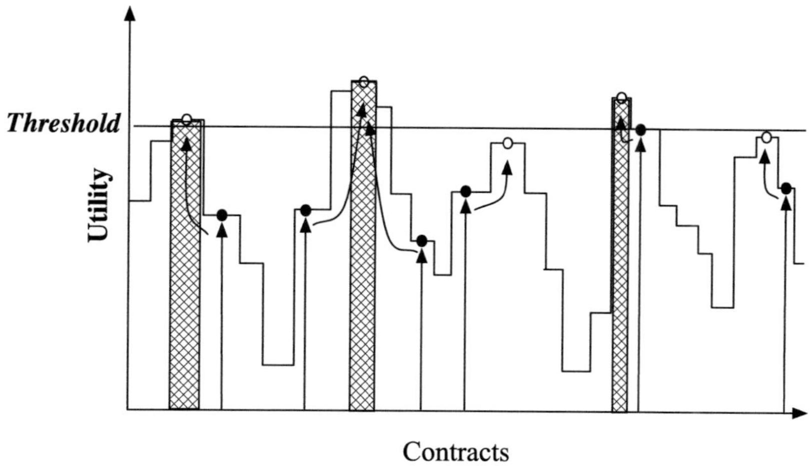

Fig. 3. Example of Generating the Bids

Num. of agents	Limit of bids	Num. of agents	Limit of bids
2	2530	7	9
3	186	8	7
4	50	9	6
5	23	10	5
6	13		

Table 1. Limitation of the bids

For each contract $\vec{s}$ found by adjusted sampling, an agent evaluates its utility by summation of values of satisfied constraints. If that utility is larger than the reservation value δ **(threshold)**, then the agent defines a bid that covers all the contracts in the region that have that utility value. This is easy to do: the agent need merely find the intersection of all the constraints satisfied by that $\vec{s}$.

[Find the Solutions] In negotiation, there is a mediator who takes the middle position. The mediator identifies the final contract by finding all the combinations of bids, one from each agent, that are mutually consistent, *i.e.*, that specify overlapping contract regions (Figure 4) [1]. If there is more than one such overlap, the mediator selects the one with the highest summed bid value (and thus, assuming truthful bidding, the highest social welfare).

2.3 Problems on Scalability and Privacy

Computational complexity in finding the solutions exponentially increases according to the number of bids since it is a combinatorial optimization calculation. For example, if there are 10 agents and each agent have 20 bids, the number of bids is 20^{10}. To make our negotiation

[1] A bid has an acceptable region. For example, if a bid has a region, such as [0,2] for issue 1, [3,5] for issue 2, the bid is accepted by a contract point (1,4), which means issue1 takes 1, issue2 takes 4. If a combination of bids, i.e. a solution, is consistent, there are definitely overlapping region. For instance, a bid with regions (Issue 1,Issue 2) = ([0,2],[3,5]), and another bid with ([0,1],[2,4]) is consistent.

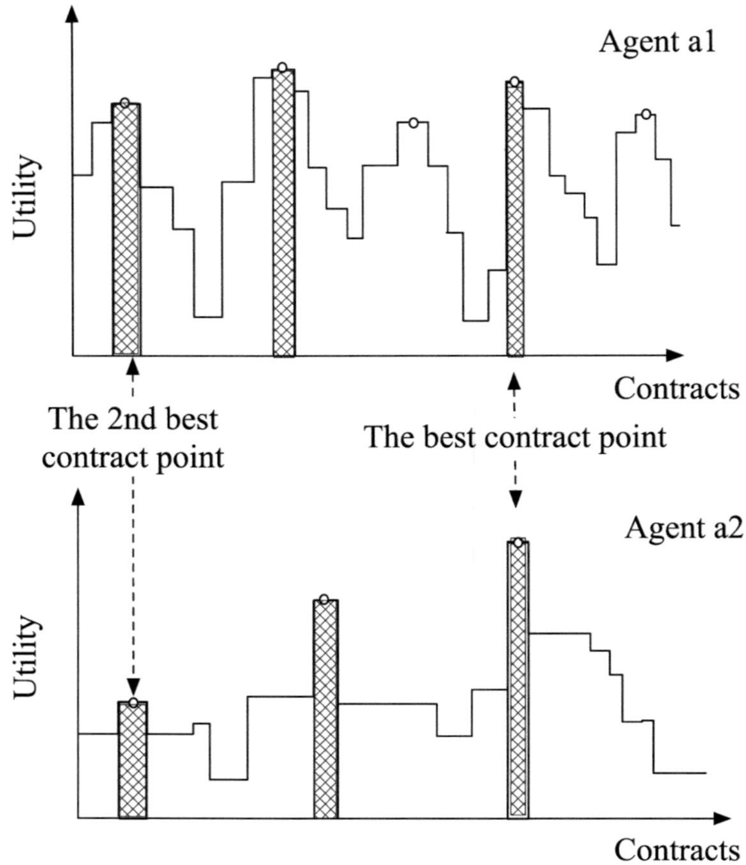

Fig. 4. Find solutions

mechanism scalable, it is necessary to reduce the computational complexity to find the solutions.

In order to handle the computational complexity, in the basic bidding-based protocol (Ito et al., 2007), we limited the number of bids for each agent. The concrete number of bids in this limitation was $\sqrt[N]{6,400,000}$. This number came from our experimental calibration in 2005. But, even though CPUs are faster now, the limitation number does not differ so much because this is an exponential problem. Table 1 shows the limitation numbers of bids in one agent. The limitation number of bids quickly drops by increasing the total number of agents. Because of the limitation of bids, the failure rate in finding agreements quickly increases along with increasing the number of agents. When the number of agents is 5 and the number of issues is 7, we observed experimentally that the failure rate is around 40%. In fact, there is a strong trade-off between just increasing the number of total bids and finding good quality solutions. Thus, increasing the number of total bids is not an effective approach for finding good quality agreements.

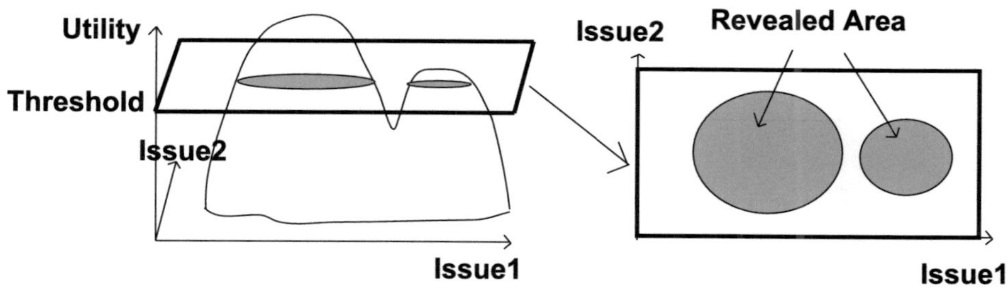

Fig. 5. Revealed Area

Thus, it is necessary to build another mechanism that will find higher quality solutions without limiting the bids. Our mechanism proposed in this paper is highly scalable. The other issue with existing protocols is that they are not concerned with privacy or security in the utility spaces. Even in a collaborative situation among people, it is normal to keep one's own utility space unopened as long as one is not asked to do otherwise. Our new mechanism will achieve such a situation by defining the **revealed area** in utility spaces.

3. Multi-Round Representative-based Protocol based on Revealed Private Information

3.1 Revealed Area for Agent

We focus on the amount of private information agents revealed in the negotiation. We employ **revealed area** as the measure of the amount of revealed utility space. Figure 5 shows an intuitive example of a revealed area. The revealed area is defined as an agent's possible contract points that are revealed in his utility space on his/her threshold.

For an agent, it is important for him/her to know how much his/her private information is revealed compared with the other agents. The mediator can judge whether an agent is cooperative or not cooperative based on his amount of revealed private information.

We use the **threshold** that is employed in generating bids as the measure of adjusting agents' revealed area. It is difficult to adjust the revealed area directly because agents have complex utility space. So, we consider adjusting their threshold to adjust their revealed area. Threshold is employed for an agent to generate his/her bids based on utility values above the threshold. Threshold was originally adopted for adjusting the number of bids. However, in this paper, we utilize threshold also for determining an agent's revealed area while handling complex utility space.

3.2 Representative-based Protocol

Representative-based protocol consists of three steps. The first step is to select the representative agents **(Step1)**. The second step is to find solutions, and propose them to the other agents **(Step2)**. The third step is to respond to the agreement by the other agents **(Step3)**.

We assume each agent uses a reservation value for determining whether to "agree" or "disagree" with representative agents. Actually, for practical application, the reservation value can be determined by a human user. Thus, the reservation value is a constant number that is not changed in negotiation. The reservation value is set as lower or the same value as the threshold described in the previous subsection. This protocol consists of following steps.

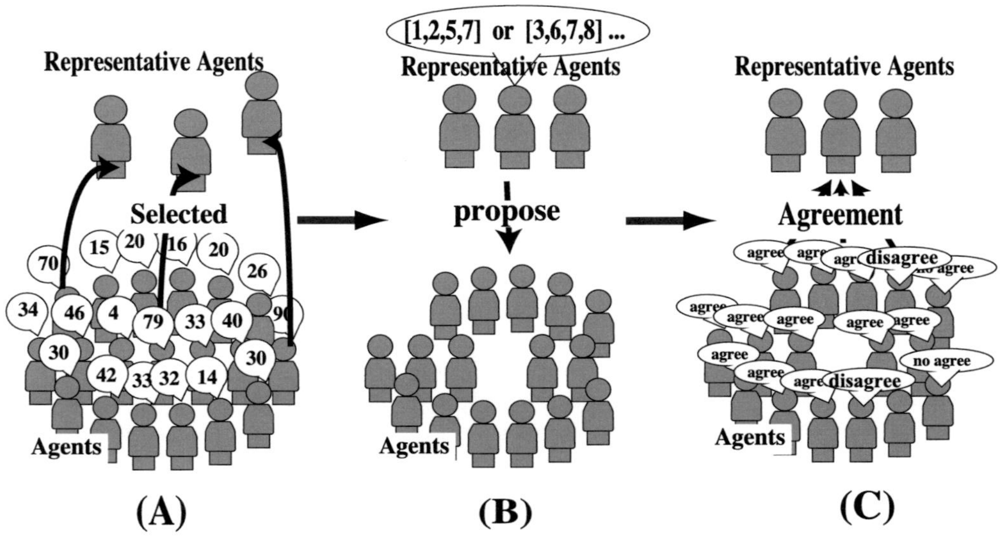

Fig. 6. Representative-based Protocol

[Step1: Selection of the Representative Agents] Representative agents are selected based on the amount of their revealed area as shown in Figure 6 (A). First, each agent submits how much he can reveal his utility to the mediator. Namely, each agent submits the numeric value of the amount of his possible revealed area. The mediator selects the representative agents who could reveal a large area. We call this selection method RAS.

[Step2: Proposing by the Representatives] Representative agents find the solutions and propose to the other agents as shown in Figure 6 (B). First, representative agents find the solutions. They employ a breadth-first search with branch cutting to find solutions. (from line 3 to line 14 in representative_protocol())

Next, the representative agents ask to the other agents whether they will "agree" or "disagree". Step 2 is repeated until all the other agents agree or the solutions representatives found are rejected by the other agents.

[Step3: Respond to the agreement by the other agents] The other agents receive the solution from representatives. Each of them will determine whether he/she "agrees" or "disagrees" with the solution (agreement) as shown in Figure 6 (C). First, the other agents receive the solution from the representative agents. Then, they judge whether they will "agree" or "disagree" with the solution. Each agent judges based on whether the solution's utility is higher than his/her reservation value or not.

Steps 1, 2 and 3 can be captured as Algorithm 12 and Algorithm 2:

This protocol is scalable for the number of agents. In representative protocol, combinatorial optimization only occurs in the negotiation among representative agents. In fact, the computational complexity for asking unrepresentative agents increases only linearly and is almost negligible. Thus, the computational complexity is drastically reduced compared with the existing mechanism.

Finally, we call the trade-off for an agent between revealing a large amount of utility space and being a representative agent. Representative agents have advantages in being able to

Algorithm 1 representative_protocol(B)

B: A set of bid-set of each agent
(B=$\{B_0, B_1, ..., B_n\}$, a set of bids from agent i is $B_i = \{b_{i,0}, b_{i,1}, ..., b_{i,m_i}\}$)
RB:A set of bid-set of each representative agent
(RB=$\{RB_0, RB_1, ..., RB_m\}$, a set of bids from representative agent i is $RB_i = \{rb_{i,0}, rb_{i,1}, ..., rb_{i,l_i}\}$)
SC: A set of solution-set of each representative agent
(SC=$\{SC_0, SC_1, ..., SC_n\}$, a set of bids from agent i is $SC_i = \{sc_{i,0}, sc_{i,1}, ..., sc_{i,m_i}\}$)

$RB := select\_representative(B)$
$SC := RB_0, i := 1$
while $i <$ *the number of representative agents* **do**
  $SC' := \emptyset$
  for $s \in SC$ **do**
    for $rb_{i,j} \in RB_i$ **do**
      $s' := s \cup rb_{i,j}$
    end for
  end for
  if s' is consistent **then**
    $SC' := SC' \cup s'$
  end if
  $SC := SC', i := i + 1$
end while
while $i < |SC|$ **do**
  if $ask\_agent(SC_i)$ is true & SC_i Utility is maximum **then**
    return SC_i
  else
    return No Solution
  end if
end while

Algorithm 2 ask_agent(SC)

select_representative() is a method for performing Step 1
Th: A reservation value of each agent (Th=$\{Th_0, Th_1, ..., Th_n\}$)

while $i <$ *the number of agents* **do**
  if $SC'sUtility < Th_i$ **then**
    return **false**
  else
    $i := i + 1$
  end if
end while
return **true**

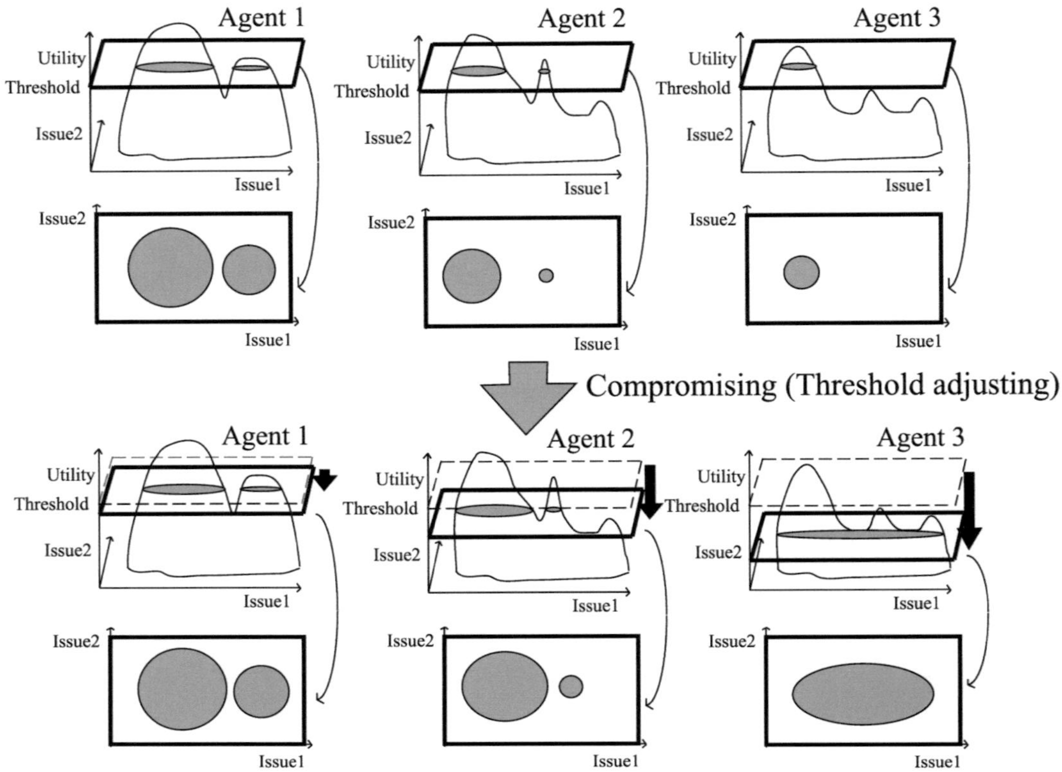

Fig. 7. Threshold Adjusting Process

propose the alternatives to the other agents and disadvantages in the need to reveal larger utility spaces. Unrepresentative agents have advantages in keeping their utility hidden and disadvantages in responding based on the representatives' agreement.

3.3 Threshold Adjusting Mechanism

We extend our protocol to multi-round negotiation based on the threshold adjusting method (Fujita et al., 2007) in order to make the number of times to be representative agents fair. The total amount of revealed utility space for each agent is almost the same by the threshold adjustment mechanism.

The main idea of the threshold adjusting mechanism is that if an agent reveals a larger area of his utility space, then he should gain an advantage. On the other hand, an agent who reveals a small area of his utility space should adjust his threshold to agree with others. The threshold values are changed by each agent based on the amount of revealed area. If the agent decreases the threshold value, then this means that he reveals his utility space more.

This mechanism is repeated until an agreement is achieved or all agents refuse to decrease the threshold. Agents can decide whether to decrease the threshold or not based on their reservation value, i.e., the minimum threshold. The reservation value is the limitation that of what the agent can reveal. This means that agents have the right to reject the request to decrease their threshold if the request decreases the threshold lower than the reservation value.

Figure 7 shows an example of the threshold adjusting process among 3 agents. The upper figure shows the thresholds and the revealed areas before adjusting the threshold. The bottom figure shows the thresholds and the revealed areas after adjusting the threshold. In particular, in this case, agent 3 revealed a small amount of his utility space. The amount of agent 3's revealed utility space in this threshold adjustment is the largest among these 3 agents. The exact rate of the amount of utility space revealed and the amount of threshold decreased is defined by the mediator or the mechanism designer.
The threshold adjusting mechanism is shown as Algorithm 3:

Algorithm 3 threshold_adjustment( )

Ar: Area Range of each agent ($Ar = \{Ar_0, Ar_1, ..., Ar_n\}$)
representative_protocol(): representative-based protocol explained in previous section.

loop
    $i := 1, B := \emptyset$
    while $i < |Ag|$ **do**
        bid_generation_with_SA(Th_i,V,SN,T,B_i)
    end while
    $maxSolution$:= representative_protocol(B)
    if find $maxSolution$ **then**
        break loop
    else if all agent can lower the threshold **then**
        $i := 1$
        $SumAr := \Sigma_{i \in |Ag|} Ar_i$
        while $i < |Ag|$ **do**
            $Th_i := Th_i - C * (SumAr - Ar_i)/SumAr$
            $i := i + 1$
        end while
    else
        break loop
    end if
end loop
return $maxSolution$

4. Experiment Results

4.1 Setting of Experiment

We conducted several experiments to evaluate the effectiveness of our approach. In each experiment, we ran 100 negotiations between agents with randomly generated utility functions. In the experiments on optimality, for each run, we applied an optimizer to the sum of all the agents' utility functions to find the contract with the highest possible social welfare. This value was used to assess the efficiency (*i.e.*, how closely optimal social welfare was approached) of the negotiation protocols. To find the optimum contract, we used simulated annealing (SA) because exhaustive search became intractable as the number of issues grew too large. The SA initial temperature was 50.0 and decreased linearly to 0 over the course of 2500 iterations. The initial contract for each SA run was randomly selected.

In terms of privacy, the measure is the range of revealed area. Namely, if an agent reveals one point on the grid of utility space, this means he lost 1 privacy unit. If he reveals 1000 points, then he lost 1000 privacy units.
We also analyze the representative selection method in our protocol. The representative selection method has remained an important research point. We call the selection method in which agents who reveal a larger utility area are selected representatives (**RAS**), and the random selection method in which representatives are randomly selected (**RANDOM**). To investigate the detailed effects of RAS, we assume RANDOM is the general basis for comparison.
The parameters for our experiments were as follows:

- Domain for issue values is $[0,9]$.
- Constraints: 10 unary constraints, 5 binary constraints, 5 trinary constraints, etc. (a unary constraint relates to one issue, a binary constraint relates to two issues, and so on).
- The maximum value for a constraint: $100 \times (Number\ of\ Issues)$. Constraints that satisfy many issues thus have, on average, larger weights. This seems reasonable for many domains. In meeting scheduling, for example, higher order constraints concern more people than lower order constraints, so they are more important for that reason.
- The maximum width for a constraint: 7. The following constraints, therefore, would all be valid: issue 1 = $[2,6]$, issue 3 = $[2,9]$ and issue 7 = $[1,3]$.
- The number of samples taken during random sampling: $(Number\ of\ Issues) \times 200$.
- Annealing schedule for sample adjustment: initial temperature 30, 30 iterations. Note that it is important that the annealer not run too long or too 'hot' because then each sample will tend to find the global optimum instead of the peak of the optimum nearest the sampling point.
- The threshold agents used to select which bids to make start with 900 and decrease until 200 in the threshold adjusting mechanism. The protocol without the threshold adjusting process defines the threshold as 200. The threshold is used to cut out contract points that have low utility.
- The amount of the threshold is decreased by $100 \times (SumAr - Ar_i)/SumAr$. $SumAr$ means the sum of all agents' revealed area. Ar_i means agent i's revealed area.
- The limitation on the number of bids per agent: $\sqrt[n]{6,400,000}$ for N agents. It was only practical to run the deal identification algorithm if it explored no more than about 6,400,000 bid combinations, which implies a limit of $\sqrt[n]{6,400,000}$ bids per agent, for N agents.
- The number of representative agents is 2 in the representative-bsed protocol.
- The number of issues is 3.

In our experiments, we ran 100 negotiations in every condition. Our code was implemented in Java 2 (1.5) and run on a core 2 duo processor iMac with 1.0 GB memory on the Mac OS X 10.4 operating system.

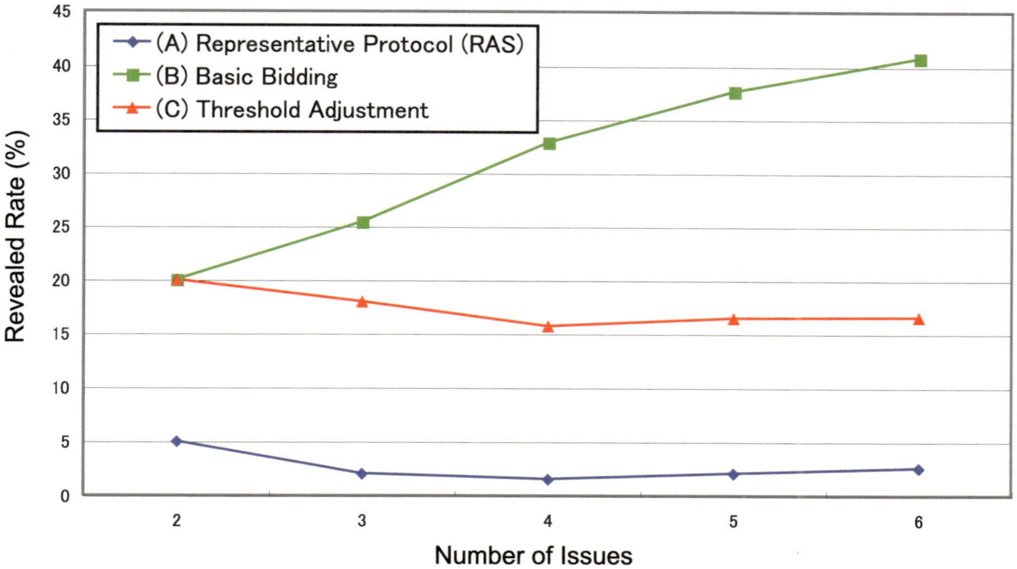

Fig. 8. Revealed Rate

4.2 Experimental Results

Figure 8 shows the revealed rate of 3 comparable protocols. The number of agents is 3. (A) is the proposed protocol that is a multi-round negotiation with the representative protocol the selection method is RAS. (B) is the basic bidding-based mechanism without threshold adjustment explained in Section 2. (C) is the protocol with threshold adjustment.

In (B), the revealed rate increases as the number of issues increases. This means that if we do not use the threshold adjustment, agents need reveal their utility space too much more than the other protocols. On the other hand, in (A) and (C), the revealed rate decreases as the number of issues increases. When we compare (A) with (C) the revealed rate of the representative protocol is less than the mechanism with threshold adjustment. There are two reasons for this. First, the representative protocol finds the solutions earlier than the threshold adjustment mechanism. Second, in the threshold adjustment most agents need to reveal their utility space. On the other hand, only representative agents reveal their utility spaces. Essentially, the representative protocol proposed in this paper drastically decreases the revealed rate compared with the other two protocols.

The next experimental results show our negotiation protocol is sufficiently scalable on the number of agents. Figure 9 shows the optimality when agents reach an agreement when the number of agents is from 2 to 100. In this experiment, we assume agents have a shared utility area that is agreeable for them. This is because when the number of agents becomes large, it is quite hard to find an agreement point by using any negotiation protocols and it could be impossible to compare optimality. To create a common area, first, agents' utility space is randomly generated. Then, a common area whose value is more than an agent's threshold is randomly generated. The results demonstrated that the optimality is more than 80% in all cases. Although the high optimality came from the above common area assumption, scalability of our new protocol is ensured by this experiment.

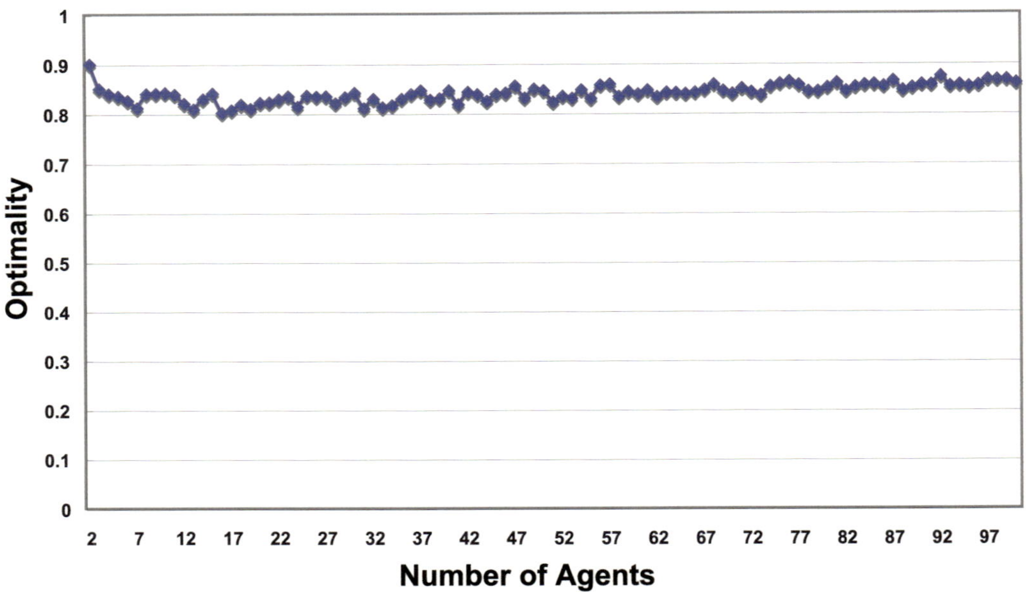

Fig. 9. Scalability on number of agents

Figure 10 shows the failure rate in finding solutions in the three protocols. (A) is the proposed protocol that is a multi-round negotiation with the representative protocol the selection method is RAS. (B) is the representative-based protocol with the representative protocol the selection method is RANDOM. (C) is the basic bidding-based mechanism without threshold adjustment explained in Section 2. Even if the number of agents increases, (A) is almost 0. On the other hand, (C) shows a drastic increase over 5 agents. This is because the bid limitation for computing winner determination starts when there are 5 agents. Also, for more than 5 agents, the existing mechanism fails to find solutions. Furthermore, (A) and (B) show that RAS improves the failure rate more than RANDOM. Thus, the representative protocol with the selection method is RAS has better failure rates.

Figure 11 shows a comparison on optimality rate among (A), (B) and (C). Comparing (A) and (C), the difference of optimality is small, and around 0.05 at most. This difference comes from the fact that since the representative-based protocol tends to find the solutions at an early stage, it might miss better solutions. Furthermore, (A) and (B) show that RAS is higher optimality than RANDOM. The reason for this is that more solutions are found in representatives who have large revealed area. Thus, the representative protocol with the selection method is RAS has better optimality rates.

Figure 12 shows the variance of the number of times to be representative agents in (A) and (D). The fairness of the number of times to be representative agents is defined as the variance of the number of times to be representative agents for each agent. Comparing (A) with (D), the deviation of the (A) is much lower than that of (D). Thus, RAS can achieve fair opportunity on the number of times to be representative agents.

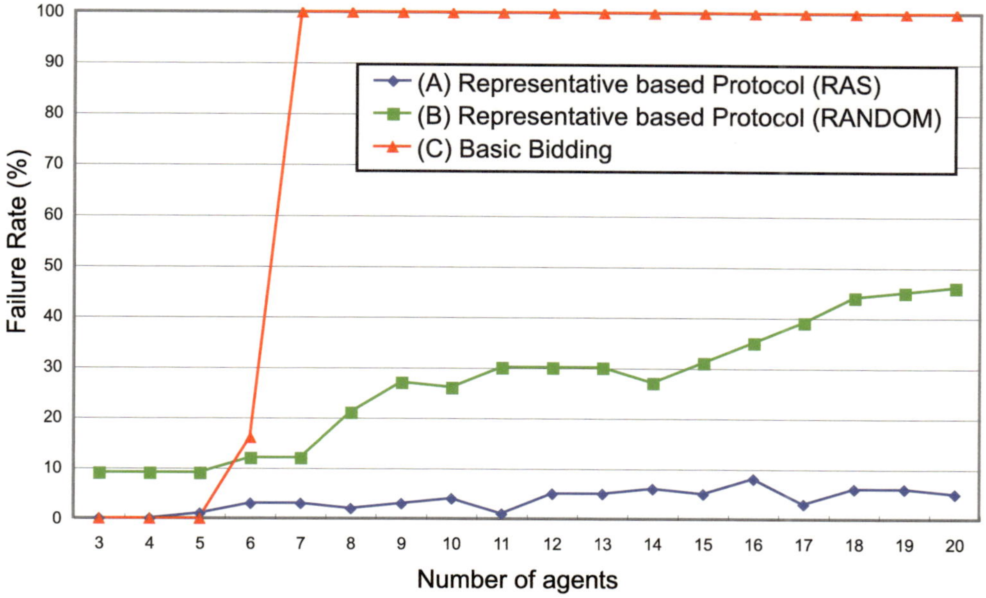

Fig. 10. Failure Rate

5. Related Work

Most previous work on multi-issue negotiation (Bosse & Jonker, 2005; Faratin et al., 2002; Fatima et al., 2004) has addressed only linear utilities. Recently some researchers have been focusing on more complex and non-linear utilities. (Lin & Chou, 2003) does not describe what kind of utility function is used, nor does it present any experimental analyses. It is therefore unclear whether this strategy enables sufficient exploration of the utility space. (Barbuceanu & Lo, 2000) presents an approach based on constraint relaxation. However, there is no experimental analysis and this paper presents only a small toy problem with 27 contracts. (Luo et al., 2003) modeled a negotiation problem as a distributed constraint optimization problem. This paper claims the proposed algorithm is optimal, but does not discuss computational complexity and provides only a single small-scale example.

(Klein et al., 2003) presented a protocol, based on a simulated-annealing mediator, that was applied with near-optimal results to medium-sized bilateral negotiations with binary dependencies. The work presented here is distinguished by demonstrating both scalability and high optimality values for multilateral negotiations and higher order dependencies. (Lai, Li & Sycara, 2006; Lai, Sycara & Li, 2006) also presented a protocol for multi-issue problems for bilateral negotiations. (Robu & Poutre, 2006; Robu et al., 2005) presented a multi-item and multi-issue negotiation protocol for bilateral negotiations in electronic commerce situations. (Fatima et al., 2007) proposed bilateral multi-issue negotiations with time constraints. These studies were done from very interesting viewpoints, but focused on just bilateral trading or negotiations.

(Shew & Larson, 2008) proposed multi-issue negotiation that employs a third-party to act as a mediator to guide agents toward equitable solutions. This framework also employs an agenda

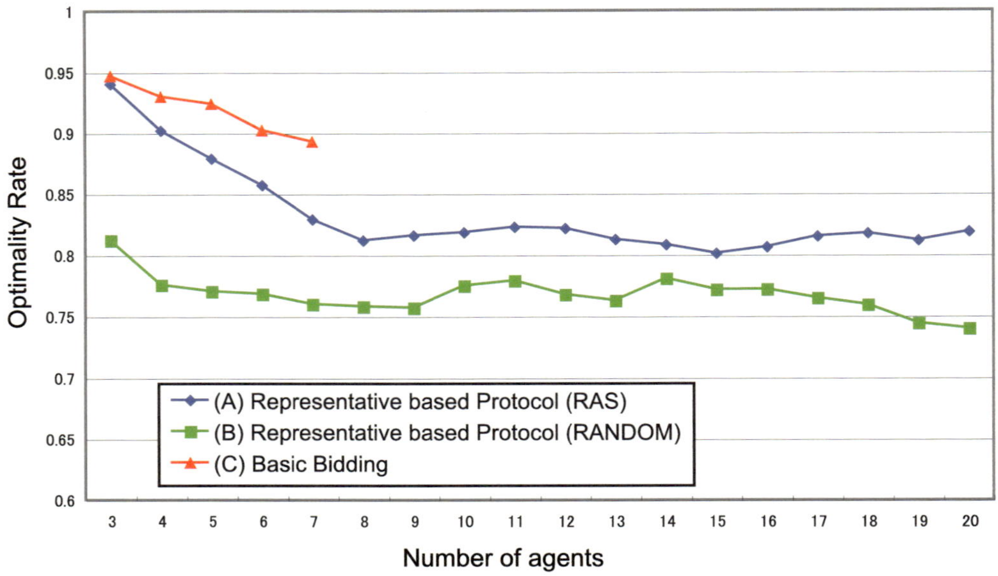

Fig. 11. Comparison on Optimality

that serves as a schedule for the ordering of issue negotiation. Agendas are very interesting because agents only need to focus on a few issues.

(Hindriks et al., 2008) proposed a checking procedure to mitigate this risk and show that by tuning this procedure's parameters, outcome deviation can be controlled. These studies reflect interesting viewpoints, but they focused on just bilateral trading or negotiations.

6. Conclusion

In this paper, we proposed a multi-round representative-based protocol in very complex negotiations among software agents. The representative-based protocol could always make agreements if the number of agents was large. It was important for agents to make agreements without revealing their private information in the negotiation. This proposed protocol could reach an agreement while revealing agents' utility space as little as possible. The experimental results demonstrated that the representative-based protocol could reduce the amount of private information that is required for an agreement among agents, and the failure rate in this mechanism was almost 0. Furthermore, we compared RAS with RANDOM in the experiments. The failure rate in RAS was lower than RANDOM.

In terms of possible future work, in a real parliamentary system, the representatives (in theory) have done their best to model the utility functions of the people they represent, so the solutions that satisfy the representatives are likely to be good for (the majority of) the people they represent. In the approach described in the paper, the representative's utility functions are purely idiosyncratic to them, so the solutions that the representatives like may be different from the solutions that are best for the other agents. Changing representatives in the mluti round negotiation helps to support this. The changing mechanism proposed here is a simple one. Thus investigating changing mechanisms are possible future work.

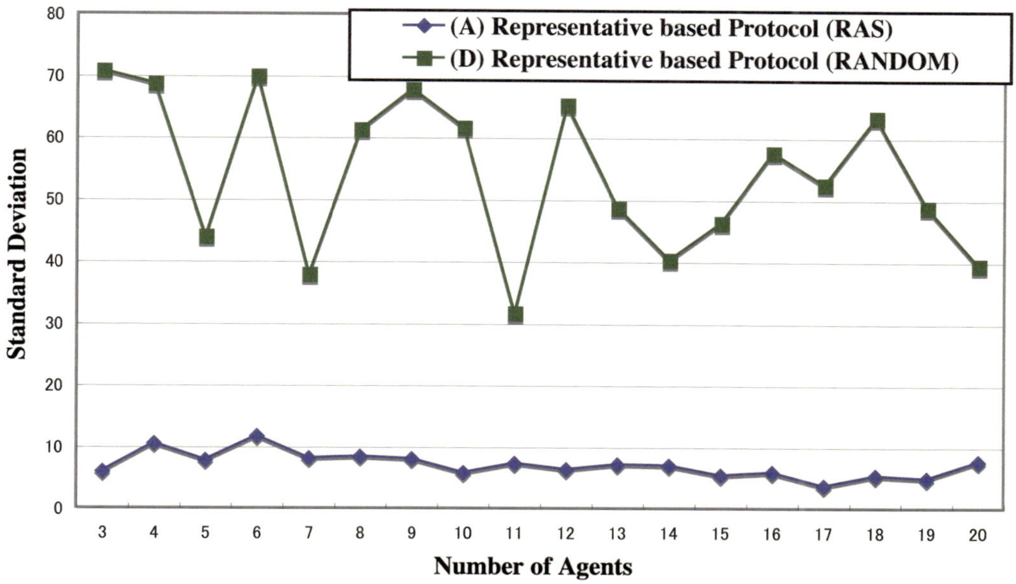

Fig. 12. Variance of the number of times to be representative agents

7. References

Arrow, K. J. (1970). *Social Choice and Individual Values*, Yale Univ. Press.

Barbuceanu, M. & Lo, W.-K. (2000). Multi-attribute utility theoretic negotiation for electronic commerce, *In Proceedings of the International Workshop on Agent-mediated Electronic Commerce (AMEC2000)*, pp. 15–30.

Bosse, T. & Jonker, C. M. (2005). Human vs. computer behaviour in multi-issue negotiation, *In Proceedings of 1st International Workshop on Rational, Robust, and Secure Negotiations in Multi-Agent Systems (RRS-2005)*, pp. 11–24.

Faratin, P., Sierra, C. & Jennings, N. R. (2002). Using similarity criteria to make issue trade-offs in automated negotiations, *Artificial Intelligence*, pp. 142:205–237.

Fatima, S. S., Wooldridge, M. & Jennings, N. R. (2004). Optimal negotiation of multiple issues in incomplete information settings, *In Proceedings of Third International Joint Conference on Autonomous Agent and Multi-Agent Systems (AAMAS-2004)*, pp. 1080–1087.

Fatima, S. S., Wooldridge, M. & Jennings, N. R. (2007). Approximate and online multi-issue negotiation, *In Proceedings of th 6th Inernational Joint Conference on Autonomous Agents and Multi-agent Systems (AAMAS-2007)*, pp. 947–954.

Fujita, K., Ito, T., Hattori, H. & Klein, M. (2007). An approach to implementing a threshold adjusting mechanism in very complex negotiations: A preliminary result, *In Proceedings of The 2nd International Conference on Knowledge, Information and Creativity Support Systems (KICSS-2007)*.

Hindriks, K., Jonker, C. & Tykhonov, D. (2008). Avoiding approximation errors in multi-issue negotiation with issue dependencies, *In Proceedings of The 1st International Workshop on Agent-based Complex Automated Negotiations (ACAN-2008)*.

Ito, T., Hattori, H. & Klein, M. (2007). Multi-issue negotiation protocol for agents : Exploring nonlinear utility spaces, *In Proceedings of 20th International Joint Conference on Artificial Intelligence (IJCAI-2007)*, pp. 1347–1352.

Klein, M., Faratin, P., Sayama, H. & Bar-Yam, Y. (2003). Negotiating complex contracts, *Group Decision and Negotiation* **12**(2): 58–73.

Lai, G., Li, C. & Sycara, K. (2006). A general model for pareto optimal multi-attribute negotiations, *In Proceedings of The 2nd International Workshop on Rational, Robust, and Secure Negotiations in Multi-Agent Systems (RRS-2006)*.

Lai, G., Sycara, K. & Li, C. (2006). A decentralized model for multi-attribute negotiations with incomplete information and general utility functions, *In Proceedings of The 2nd International Workshop on Rational, Robust, and Secure Negotiations in Multi-Agent Systems (RRS-2006)*.

Lin, R. J. & Chou, S. T. (2003). Bilateral multi-issue negotiations in a dynamic environment, *In Proceedings of the International Workshop on Agent-mediated Electronic Commerce (AMEC2003)*.

Luo, X., Jennings, N. R., Shadbolt, N., Leung, H. & Lee, J. H. (2003). A fuzzy constraint based model for bilateral, multi-issue negotiations in semi-competitive environments, *Artificial Intelligence* **148**: 53–102.

Malone, T. W. & Klein, M. (2007). Harnessing collective intelligence to address global climate change, *Innovations Journal* **2(3)**: 15–26.

Robu, V. & Poutre, H. L. (2006). Retrieving the structure of utility graphs used in multi-item negotiation through collaborative filtering of aggregate buyer preferences, *In Proceedings of The 2nd International Workshop on Rational, Robust, and Secure Negotiations in Multi-Agent Systems (RRS-2006)*.

Robu, V., Somefun, D. J. A. & Poutre, J. L. (2005). Modeling complex multi-issue negotiations using utility graphs, *In Proceedings of the 4th International Joint Conference on Autonomous Agents and Multi-Agent Systems (AAMAS 2005)*.

Russell, S. J. & Norvig, P. (2002). *Artificial Intelligence : A Modern Approach*, Prentice Hall.

Shew, J. & Larson, K. (2008). The blind leading the blind: A third-party model for bilateral multi-issue negotiations under incomplete information, *In Proceedings of The 1st International Workshop on Agent-based Complex Automated Negotiations (ACAN-2008)*.

18

Object-oriented Semantic and Sensory Knowledge Extraction from the Web

Shun Hattori
*Geosphere Research Institute of Saitama University**
Japan

1. Introduction

Automatic knowledge extraction from such a very large document corpus as the Web is one of the hottest research topics in the domain of Artificial Intelligence and Database technologies. This chapter introduces my object-oriented and the existing methods to extract semantic (e.g., hyponymy and meronymy) and sensory (e.g., visual and aural) knowledge from the Web, and compares them by showing several experimental results. My object-oriented semantic knowledge extraction is based on property inheritance(s) and property aggregation, and repeatedly improves the extracted results of both hyponymy and meronymy relations. Meanwhile, my object-oriented sensory knowledge extraction is improved by utilizing the extracted hyponymy and meronymy relations. Finally, this chapter introduces my Sense-based Object-name Search (SOS) to enable users to identify the concrete name of a target object which they do not know only by inputting its hyponym (class-name) and some sensory descriptions, as an application system to utilize the Web-extracted semantic and sensory knowledge.

2. Concept Hierarchy Extraction from the Web

Concept hierarchies, such as hyponymy (is-a) and meronymy (has-a) relations between words, are very fundamental as semantic knowledge for various natural language processing systems. For example, query expansion in information retrieval (Hattori, Tezuka, Ohshima, Oyama, Kawamoto, Tajima & Tanaka, 2007; Hattori et al., 2006; Mandala et al., 1998), question answering (Fleischman et al., 2003), machine translation, object information extraction by text mining (Hattori, Tezuka & Tanaka, 2007), and so forth. Also, I have been developing Sense-based Object-name Search (SOS) for a name-unknown object by its class-name (e.g., "bird") and feature descriptions (e.g., "blue wings") as one of the application systems that utilize hyponymy relations (e.g., isa("kingfisher", "bird") $=1$) as a basic knowledge (Hattori & Tanaka, 2009).

While the WordNet (2009) (Miller et al., 1990) and Wikipedia (2009) (Völkel et al., 2006) etc. are being manually constructed and maintained as lexical ontologies at the cost of much time and effort, many researchers have tackled how to extract concept hierarchies from very large corpora of text documents such as the Web not manually but automatically (Caraballo, 1999; Hearst, 1992; Kim et al., 2006; Morin & Jacquemin, 2004; Ruiz-Casado et al., 2007; Sanderson &

---

*Presently with School of Computer Science, Tokyo University of Technology.

Croft, 1999; Shinzato & Torisawa, 2005). However, their methods are mostly based on lexico-syntactic patterns as sufficient but not necessary conditions of concept hierarchies. Therefore, they can achieve high precision but only low recall when using stricter patterns (e.g., "x such as y"), or they can achieve high recall but only low precision when using looser patterns (e.g., "y is a/an x").

To achieve high recall and not low precision, I first propose a basic method to extract hyponymy relations (i.e., subordinate concepts for a target concept) from the Web based on single "Property Inheritance" from the target concept to its hyponym candidate as a necessary and sufficient condition of hyponymy (Hattori et al., 2008).

Next, I try to make my basic method more robust by two approaches: not single but "Multiple Property Inheritances" and "Property Aggregation" (Hattori & Tanaka, 2008). The former approach is to utilize the other semantic relations surrounding the subordinate relation (hyponymy) between a target concept and its hyponym candidate, i.e., superordinate relations (hypernymy) and coordinate relations (including synonymy and antonymy), and to improve a weighting of hyponymy extraction by using multiple property inheritances not only from the target concept to its hyponym candidate but also between the other pairs of concepts (e.g., from a hypernym of the target concept to its hyponym candidate and/or from the target concept to a coordinate concept of its hyponym candidate). The latter approach is to improve a weighting of property (meronymy) extraction by using property aggregation to each target concept from its typical hyponyms.

The remainder of this section is organized as follows. Section 2.1 introduces my basic hyponymy extraction based on single "Property Inheritance". Section 2.2 and 2.3 describe my improved hyponymy extraction based on "Multiple Property Inheritances" and "Property Aggregation" respectively. Section 2.4 shows several experimental results to evaluate my proposed hyponymy extractions.

2.1 Hyponymy Extraction based on Single Property Inheritance

I introduce my basic method to extract hyponymy relations (i.e., subordinate concepts for a target concept) from the Web not only by using lexico-syntactic patterns as sufficient but not necessary conditions of hyponymy but also by using single "Property Inheritance" as its necessary and sufficient condition (PI-based hyponymy extraction as shown in Fig. 1).

Basic Assumption

Let C be the universal set of concepts (words). I assume that a concept $y \in C$ is a hyponym of a concept $x \in C$ if and only if the set of properties that the concept y has, $P(y)$, completely includes the set of properties that the concept x has, $P(x)$, and the concept y is not equal (equivalent) to the concept x:

$$\mathrm{isa}(y, x) = 1 \Leftrightarrow P(y) \supseteq P(x) \text{ and } y \neq x, \tag{1}$$

$$P(c) = \{p_i \in P |\, \mathrm{has}(p_i, c) = 1\}, \tag{2}$$

where P stands for the universal set of N properties,

$$P = \{p_1, p_2, ..., p_N\}, \tag{3}$$

and $\mathrm{has}(p_i, c) \in \{0, 1\}$ indicates whether or not a concept $c \in C$ has a property $p_i \in P$,

$$\mathrm{has}(p_i, c) = \begin{cases} 1 & \text{if a concept } c \text{ has a property } p_i, \\ 0 & \text{otherwise.} \end{cases} \tag{4}$$

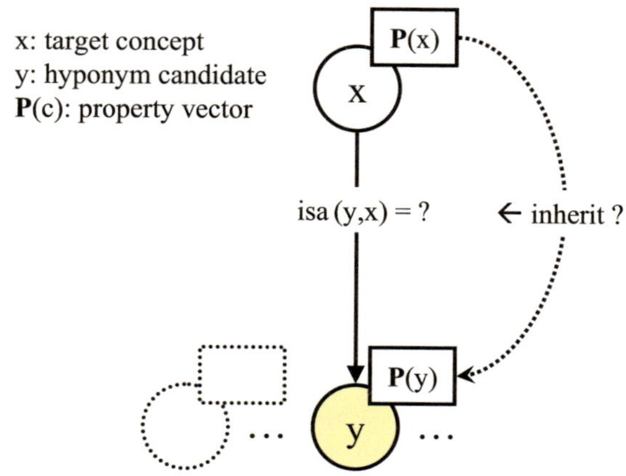

Fig. 1. Hyponymy and single property inheritance from a target concept x to its hyponym candidate y (PI-based).

In other words,

$$\text{isa}(y,x) = \begin{cases} 1 & \text{if } \sum_{\forall p_i \in P} \text{has}(p_i,x) \cdot \text{has}(p_i,y) = \sum_{\forall p_i \in P} \text{has}(p_i,x) \cdot \text{has}(p_i,x), \\ & (\text{ i.e., } \mathbf{P}(x) \cdot \mathbf{P}(y) = \mathbf{P}(x) \cdot \mathbf{P}(x)\ ) \\ 0 & \text{if } \sum_{\forall p_i \in P} \text{has}(p_i,x) \cdot \text{has}(p_i,y) < \sum_{\forall p_i \in P} \text{has}(p_i,x) \cdot \text{has}(p_i,x), \\ & (\text{ i.e., } \mathbf{P}(x) \cdot \mathbf{P}(y) < \mathbf{P}(x) \cdot \mathbf{P}(x)\ ) \end{cases} \tag{5}$$

$$\mathbf{P}(c) = (\text{has}(p_1,c), \text{has}(p_2,c), ..., \text{has}(p_N,c)). \tag{6}$$

It is very essential for hyponymy extraction based on the above assumption of hyponymy and property inheritance to calculate the binary value $\text{has}(p_i,c) \in \{0,1\}$ for any pair of a concept $c \in C$ and a property $p_i \in P$ accurately. However, it is not easy, and I can use only the continuous value $\text{has}^*(p_i,c) \in [0,1]$ in the below-mentioned method. Therefore, I suppose that the ratio of the number of properties that a concept $y \in C$ inherits from a target concept $x \in C$ to the number of properties that the target concept x has,

$$\frac{\sum_{\forall p_i \in P} \text{has}^*(p_i,x) \cdot \text{has}^*(p_i,y)}{\sum_{\forall p_i \in P} \text{has}^*(p_i,x) \cdot \text{has}^*(p_i,x)}, \tag{7}$$

can measure how suitable the concept y is for a hyponym of the target concept x, as an approximation of whether or not the concept y is a hyponym of the target concept x, $\text{isa}^*(y,x)$. And then, the concept y would be considered to be a hyponym of the target concept x when the ratio is enough near to one (or greater than a threshold value), while the concept y would be considered to be not a hyponym of the target concept x when the ratio is not near to one (or less than a threshold value).

Method

When a target concept $x \in C$ is given, my basic hyponymy extraction based on single property inheritance executes the following three steps to extract its hyponyms from the Web. First, a set of candidates for its hyponyms, $C(x)$, is collected from the Web as exhaustively as possible. Second, the continuous value $\text{has}^*(p_i, c)$ for each pair of a property $p_i \in P$ and a concept c (the target concept x or its hyponym candidate $y \in C(x)$) is calculated by using Web search engine indices. That is, the property vector of each concept c, $\mathbf{P}^*(c)$, is obtained,

$$\mathbf{P}^*(c) = (\text{has}^*(p_1, c), \text{has}^*(p_2, c), ..., \text{has}^*(p_N, c)). \tag{8}$$

Last, the continuous value $\text{isa-PI}_n^*(y, x)$ for each pair of the target concept x and its hyponym candidate $y \in C(x)$ is calculated based on single inheritance of the top n typical properties of the target concept x to its hyponym candidate y, and then a set of its top k hyponym candidates ordered by their weight would be outputted to the users.

Step 1. Hyponym Candidate Collection

A set of hyponym candidates of the target concept, $C(x)$, is collected from the Web as exhaustively as possible and enough precisely. If $C(x)$ is set to the universal set of concepts, C, its recall always equals to 1.0 (the highest value) but its precision nearly equals to 0.0 (too low value). Meanwhile, if $y \in C(x)$ is collected from some sort of corpus of documents by using too strict lexico-syntactic pattern such as "y is a kind of x", its precision is enough high but its recall is too low in most cases. Therefore, I use not too strict but enough strict lexico-syntactic pattern of hyponymy to collect the set. Any noun phrase y whose lexico-syntactic pattern "y is a/an x" exists at least once in the title or summary text of the top 1000 search results by submitting a phrase "is a/an x" as a query to Yahoo! Web Search API (2008) is inserted into $C(x)$ as a hyponym candidate of the target concept x.

Step 2. Property Extraction

Typical properties (meronyms) p_i of each concept c (the target concept x or its hyponym candidate $y \in C(x)$) are extracted as precisely as possible from the Web by using an enough strict lexico-syntactic pattern "c's p_i" as a sufficient condition of meronymy. The continuous value $\text{has}^*(p_i, c)$ of a property p_i for each concept c is defined as follows:

$$\text{has}^*(p_i, c) := \frac{\text{df}([\text{"}c\text{'s } p_i\text{"}])}{\text{df}([\text{"}c\text{'s"}])}, \tag{9}$$

where $\text{df}([q])$ stands for the number of documents that meet a query condition q in such a corpus as the Web. In the after-mentioned experiments, I calculate it by submitting each query to Yahoo! Web Search API (2008).
Note that $\text{has}^*(p_i, c)$ is not a binary value $\{0, 1\}$ but a continuous value $[0, 1]$, so $\text{has}^*(p_i, c)$ cannot indicate whether or not a concept c has a property p_i but it is supposed to indicate how typical the property p_i is of the concept c.

Step 3. Hyponym Candidate Weighting

To filter out noisy hyponym candidates of the target concept, my basic hyponymy extraction based on single Property Inheritance, i.e., how many properties a hyponym candidate

$y \in C(x)$ inherits from the target concept x, assigns the following continuous weight to each hyponym candidate:

$$\text{isa-PI}_n^*(y,x) := \frac{\sum\limits_{\forall p_i \in P_n(x)} \text{has}^*(p_i,x) \cdot \text{has}^*(p_i,y)}{\sum\limits_{\forall p_i \in P_n(x)} \text{has}^*(p_i,x) \cdot \text{has}^*(p_i,x)}, \tag{10}$$

where $P_n(x)$ stands for a set of the top n typical properties of the target concept x ordered by their weight $\text{has}^*(p_i,x)$ that is calculated in Step 2.
Note that if $n = N$, i.e., $P_n(x) = P_n(y) = P$, I cannot decide which x or y is subordinate to the other because of $\text{isa-PI}_n^*(y,x) = \text{isa-PI}_n^*(x,y)$. So, I must set n to a number which is less than N. In the after-mentioned experiments, I use 1 to 20 as n to evaluate its effect.
Meanwhile, an existing hyponymy extraction based on lexico-Syntactic Patterns defines the following weighting:

$$\text{isa-SP}(y,x) := \text{df}([\text{"}y \text{ is a/an } x\text{"}]). \tag{11}$$

I use it as a baseline to validate my proposed hyponymy extractions in the after-mentioned experiments.

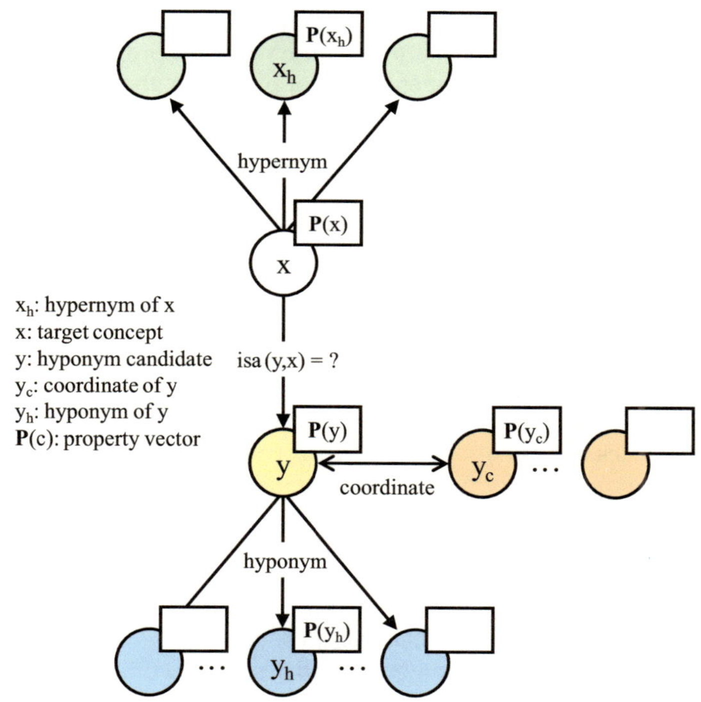

Fig. 2. Surrounding concepts in hyponymy extraction based on property inheritance.

2.2 Hyponymy Extraction based on Multiple Property Inheritances

My previous hyponymy extraction is based on single property inheritance from a target concept to a hyponym candidate. One approach to make it more robust is to utilize the other semantic relations surrounding the subordinate relation (hyponymy) $\text{isa}(y, x)$ between the target concept x and the hyponym candidate y, i.e., superordinate relations (hypernymy) and coordinate relations (including synonymy and antonymy), as shown in Fig. 2. I propose a improved method to extract hyponymy relations (i.e., subordinate concepts for a target concept) from the Web based on not single but "Multiple Property Inheritances".

Basic Assumption

I assume that if a concept $y \in C$ is a hyponym of a concept $x \in C$, then the set of properties that the concept y has, $P(y)$, completely includes not only the set of properties that the concept x has, $P(x)$, but also the set of properties that x's hypernym x_h has, $P(x_h)$, and the concept y is not equal (equivalent) to the concept x:

$$\text{isa}(y, x) = 1 \Leftrightarrow P(y) \supseteq P(x) \text{ and } P(y) \supseteq P(x_h) \text{ and } y \neq x, \tag{12}$$

$$x_h \in \text{Hypernym}(x),$$

where $\text{Hypernym}(x)$ stands for a set of superordinate concepts (hypernyms) of a concept x. I also assume that if a concept $y \in C$ is a hyponym of a concept $x \in C$, then not only the set of properties that the concept y has, $P(y)$, but also the set of properties that y's coordinate concept y_c has, $P(y_c)$, completely includes the set of properties that the concept x has, $P(x)$, and the concept y is not equal (equivalent) to the concept x:

$$\text{isa}(y, x) = 1 \Leftrightarrow P(y) \supseteq P(x) \text{ and } P(y_c) \supseteq P(x) \text{ and } y \neq x, \tag{13}$$

$$y_c \in \text{Coordinate}(y, x),$$

where $\text{Coordinate}(y, x)$ stands for a set of coordinate concepts of a concept y sharing a concept x as their superordinate concept.

Method

When a target concept $x \in C$ is given, my improved hyponymy extraction based on multiple property inheritances executes the following four steps to extract its hyponyms from the Web. First, a set of candidates for its hyponyms, $C(x)$, is collected from the Web as exhaustively as possible. Second, hypernyms of the target concept, x_h, or coordinate concepts of each hyponym candidate, y_c, is extracted from the Web as precisely as possible. Third, the continuous value $\text{has}^*(p_i, c)$ for each pair of a property $p_i \in P$ and a concept c is calculated by using Web search engine indices. Last, the continuous value $\text{isa-PIH}^*_n(y, x)$ or $\text{isa-PIC}^*_n(y, x)$ for each pair of the target concept x and its hyponym candidate $y \in C(x)$ is calculated based on multiple property inheritances not only from the target concept x to its hyponym candidate y but also from x's hypernym x_h to its hyponym candidate y or from the target concept x to y's coordinate concept y_c as shown in Fig. 3 or 4.

Step 1. Hyponym Candidate Collection

(Just all the same as Step 1 in Section 2.1.)

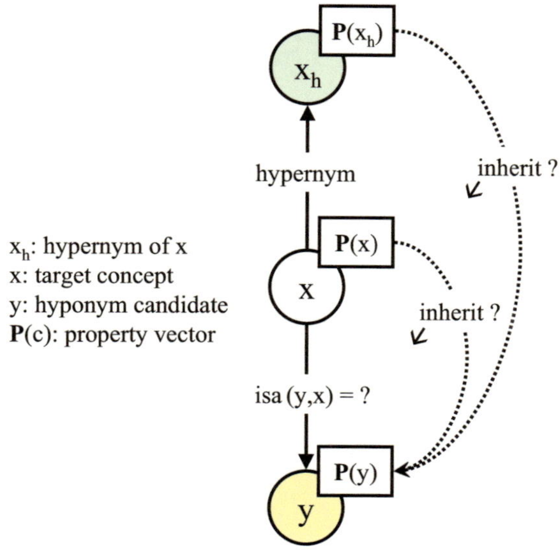

Fig. 3. Hyponymy and multiple property inheritances from not only a target concept x but also its superordinate concept (hypernym) x_h to its subordinate candidate y (PIH-based).

Step 2. Hypernym or Coordinate Extraction

There are some methods to extract hypernymy or coordinate relations (Ohshima et al., 2006). Because my improved method requires at least one hypernym of the target concept or one coordinate term of each hyponym candidate as precisely as possible, I use not recall-conscious but precision-conscious extraction. A hypernym x_h of the target concept x is extracted by using stricter lexico-syntactic pattern "x_h(s) such as x(s)" than "x is a/an x_h", and a coordinate term y_c of a hyponym candidate $y \in C(x)$ is extracted by using a pair of enough strict lexico-syntactic patterns "y or y_c" and "y_c or y" (Hattori, Tezuka, Ohshima, Oyama, Kawamoto, Tajima & Tanaka, 2007).

Step 3. Property Extraction

(Just all the same as Step 2 in Section 2.1.)

Step 4. Hyponym Candidate Weighting

A weight for each hyponym candidate y of the target concept x is defined based on two Property Inheritances not only from the target concept x to the hyponym candidate y but also from a Hypernym x_h of the target concept to the hyponym candidate y:

$$\text{isa-PIH}_n^*(y,x) := (1-\alpha)\cdot\text{isa-PI}_n^*(y,x) + \alpha\cdot\text{isa-PI}_n^*(y,x_h), \tag{14}$$

where $\alpha \in [0,1]$ stands for a certain combination parameter.
Another weight is also defined based on two Property Inheritances not only from the target concept x to the hyponym candidate y but also from the target concept x to a Coordinate concept y_c of the hyponym candidate:

$$\text{isa-PIC}_n^*(y,x) := (1-\beta)\cdot\text{isa-PI}_n^*(y,x) + \beta\cdot\text{isa-PI}_n^*(y_c,x), \tag{15}$$

where $\beta \in [0,1]$ stands for a certain combination parameter.

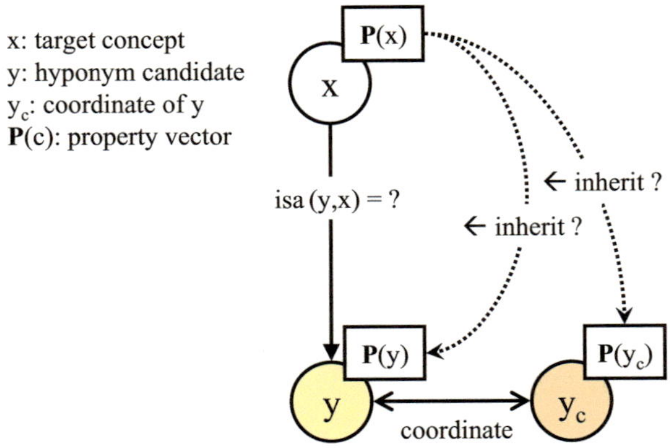

Fig. 4. Hyponymy and multiple property inheritances from a target concept x to not only its subordinate candidate y but also y's coordinate concept y_c (PIC-based).

2.3 Meronymy Refinement based on Property Aggregation

Another approach to make my hyponymy extraction based on "Property Inheritance(s)" more robust is to improve a method of property extraction (Step 2 in Section 2.1 and Step 3 in Section 2.2). I propose a improved method to extract hyponymy relations (i.e., subordinate concepts for a target concept) from the Web by adding "Property Aggregation" as a necessary and sufficient condition of hyponymy.

Basic Assumption

Let $Y \subset C$ be a set of concepts. I assume that all concepts of $\forall y \in Y$ are hyponyms of a concept $x \in C$ if and only if the product set of any set of properties that the concept y has, $\bigcap P(y)$, completely includes the set of properties that the concept x has, $P(x)$, and the set of concepts Y does not include the concept x:

$$\forall y \in Y, \ \ \mathrm{isa}(y,x) = 1 \Leftrightarrow \bigcap_{\forall y \in Y} P(y) \supseteq P(x) \text{ and } x \notin Y. \tag{16}$$

In other words,

$$\mathrm{has}(p_i, x) = \begin{cases} 1 & \text{if } \sum\limits_{\forall c \in C} \mathrm{isa}(c,x) \cdot \mathrm{has}(p_i, c) = \sum\limits_{\forall c \in C} \mathrm{isa}(c,x), \\ 0 & \text{if } \sum\limits_{\forall c \in C} \mathrm{isa}(c,x) \cdot \mathrm{has}(p_i, c) < \sum\limits_{\forall c \in C} \mathrm{isa}(c,x). \end{cases} \tag{17}$$

It is also essential for property extraction based on the above assumption of meronymy and property aggregation to calculate the binary value $\mathrm{isa}(c,x) \in \{0,1\}$ for any pair of concepts accurately. However, it is not easy, and I can use only the continuous value $\mathrm{isa}^*(c,x)$ in the below-mentioned method. Therefore, I suppose that the ratio

$$\frac{\sum\limits_{\forall c \in C} \mathrm{isa}^*(c,x) \cdot \mathrm{has}^*(p_i, c)}{\sum\limits_{\forall c \in C} \mathrm{isa}^*(c,x)}, \tag{18}$$

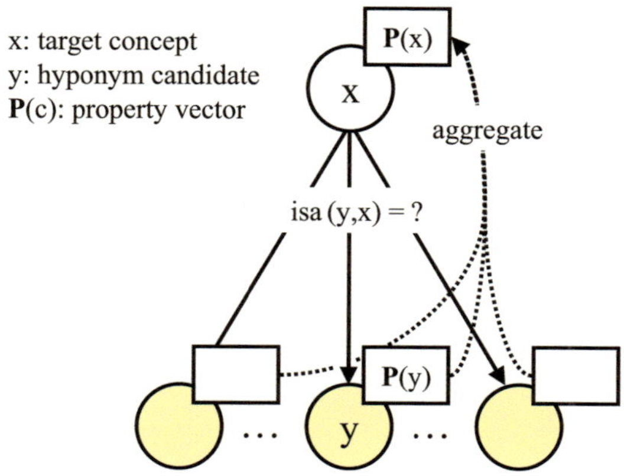

Fig. 5. Meronymy and property aggregation from a set of hyponym candidates y to a target concept x (PIA-based).

can measure how suitable a property p_i is for a concept x, as an approximation of whether or not the concept x has the property p_i, $\text{has}^*(p_i, x)$.

Method

When a target concept $x \in C$ is given, my improved hyponymy extraction based on property inheritance(s) and property aggregation executes the first step and repeats the other steps cyclically to extract its hyponyms from the Web. First, a set of candidates for its hyponyms, $C(x)$, is collected. Second, the continuous value $\text{has}^{*(0)}(p_i, c)$ for each pair of a property $p_i \in P$ and a concept c is calculated by using Web search engine indices. That is, the typical properties of each concept c (the target concept x or its hyponym candidate $y \in C(x)$) are extracted. Third, the continuous weight $\text{isa-PIA}_n^{*(0)}(y, x)$ for each pair of the target concept x and its hyponym candidate $y \in C(x)$ is calculated based on property inheritance from the original property vector of the target concept x, $\mathbf{P}^{(0)}(x)$, to the original property vector of its hyponym candidate y, $\mathbf{P}^{(0)}(y)$. Next, only the property vector of the target concept x, $\mathbf{P}^{(1)}(x)$, is recalculated based on property aggregation from its hyponym candidates with their weights, and the continuous weight $\text{isa-PIA}_n^{*(1)}(y, x)$ for each pair of the target concept x and its hyponym candidate y is re-calculated based on property inheritance from the new property vector of the target concept x, $\mathbf{P}^{(1)}(x)$, to the original property vector of its hyponym candidate y, $\mathbf{P}^{(0)}(y)$. Subsequently, the method repeats several times in the same way. Finally, a set of its top k hyponym candidates ordered by their weight would be outputted to the users.

Step 1. Hyponym Candidate Collection

(Just all the same as Step 1 in Section 2.1.)

Step 2. Property Extraction and Improvement

Typical properties (meronyms) p_i of each concept c (the target concept x or its hyponym candidate $y \in C(x)$) are extracted and repeatedly improved based on property aggregation. The

0-th (original) continuous weight of a property p_i for each concept c (i.e., how typically a concept c has a property p_i) is defined by using the document frequency of the lexico-syntactic pattern "c's p_i" just as Step 2 in Section 2.1:

$$\text{has}^{*(0)}(p_i, c) := \frac{\text{df}([\text{"}c\text{'s } p_i\text{"}])}{\text{df}([\text{"}c\text{'s"}])}. \tag{19}$$

The $m \in \{1, 2, ...\}$-th continuous weight of a property p_i for only the target concept x is defined as follows:

$$\text{has}^{*(m)}(p_i, x) := (1-\gamma) \cdot \text{has}^{*(m-1)}(p_i, x) + \gamma \cdot \frac{\sum_{y \in C(x)} \text{isa-PIA}_n^{*(m-1)}(y, x) \cdot \text{has}^{*(0)}(p_i, y)}{\sum_{y \in C(x)} \text{isa-PIA}_n^{*(m-1)}(y, x)}. \tag{20}$$

where $\gamma \in [0, 1]$ stands for a certain combination parameter.

Step 3. Hyponym Candidate Weighting

My improved hyponymy extraction based on Property Inheritance and Aggregation assigns the $m \in \{0, 1, 2, ...\}$-th weight to each hyponym candidate y just as Step 3 in Section 2.1:

$$\text{isa-PIA}_n^{*(m)}(y, x) := \frac{\sum_{p_i \in P_n^{(m)}(x)} \text{has}^{*(m)}(p_i, x) \cdot \text{has}^{*(0)}(p_i, y)}{\sum_{p_i \in P_n^{(m)}(x)} \text{has}^{*(m)}(p_i, x) \cdot \text{has}^{*(m)}(p_i, x)}, \tag{21}$$

where $P_n^{(m)}(x)$ stands for the m-th set of the top n typical properties of a concept x ordered by their weight $\text{has}^{*(m)}(p_i, x)$ that is calculated in Step 2. Note that

$$\text{isa-PIA}_n^{*(0)}(y, x) = \text{isa-PI}_n^{*}(y, x). \tag{22}$$

2.4 Experiment

I show several experimental results to evaluate my proposed methods of extracting hyponymy relations (i.e., subordinate concepts for a target concept) from the Web based on "Property Inheritance(s)" and "Property Aggregation" by comparing them with a traditional lexico-syntactic pattern based hyponymy extraction.

First, I applied my basic hyponymy extraction based on single Property Inheritance (i.e., $\text{isa-PI}_n^{*}(y, x)$ defined in Section 2.1) and a traditional one based on such a lexico-Syntactic Pattern as "y is a/an x" (i.e., $\text{isa-SP}(y, x)$ defined in Section 2.1) to 25 kinds of target concepts as follows.

Animals: "amphibian", "bird", "fish", "mammal", and "reptile".

Plants: "flower", "fruit", "herb", "tree", and "vegetable".

People: "actor", "novelist", "prime minister", "singer", and "soccer player".

Products: "furniture", "magazine", "musical instrument", "stationery", and "vehicle".

Places: "capital city", "hot spring resort", "shrine", "temple", and "world heritage site".

Fig. 6 compares my PI-based and the SP-based hyponymy extractions with regard to the average of area under PR (Precision-Recall) curve (Davis & Goadrich, 2006) for all of 25 concepts. My PI-based hyponymy extraction is almost completely superior to the SP-based one, and gains the most, +0.0586 (+11.75%), when $n = 17$.
Fig. 7 and Table 1 show the average PR curves and the recall per precision by my PI-based ($n = 17$) and the SP-based hyponymy extractions respectively. My PI-based hyponymy extraction is almost superior to the SP-based one, but is sometimes a little inferior in the high recall range (about from 0.9 to 1.0). My PI-based hyponymy extraction cannot salvage any candidate concept c whose df(["c's"]) is equal to zero as a hyponym of a target concept. For example, most scientific names such as "panthera leo" and "allium cepa" cannot be salvaged, while most common names such as "lion" and "onion" corresponding to them can be salvaged. Therefore, I could refine my proposed extractions if I can utilize the equivalent relations between scientific names and their common names in some handcrafted databases or automatically extract the equivalent relations from the Web.

	Precision							
	0.80	0.75	0.70	0.65	0.60	0.55	0.50	0.45
SP-based	0.0000	0.0000	0.0000	0.0083	0.0294	0.2649	0.7511	1.0000
PI-based ($n = 17$)	0.0088	0.0305	0.0883	0.2160	0.4441	0.6659	0.8195	1.0000

Table 1. Recall per precision by SP-based and PI-based hyponymy extractions.

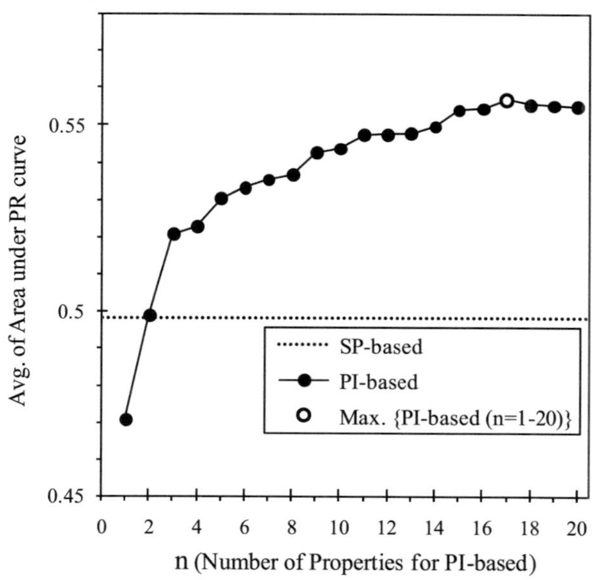

Fig. 6. Area under precision-recall curve by Syntactic Pattern (SP) based vs. single Property Inheritance (PI) based hyponymy extractions.

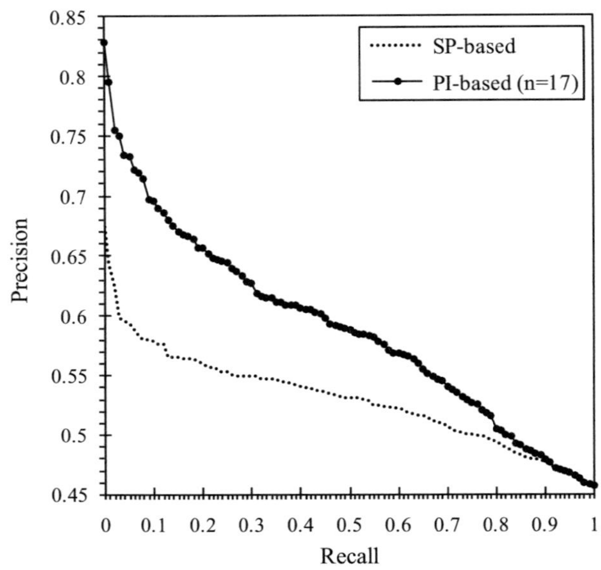

Fig. 7. Average precision-recall curves by Syntactic Pattern (SP) based vs. single Property Inheritance (PI) based hyponymy extractions.

Second, I also applied my improved hyponymy extractions based on "Multiple Property Inheritances" not only from a target concept x to its hyponym candidate y but also from a Hypernym x_h of the target concept to the hyponym candidate y (i.e., isa-$\text{PIH}_n^*(y, x)$ defined in Section 2.2), and not only from a target concept x to its hyponym candidate y but also from the target concept x to a Coordinate concept y_c of the hyponym candidate (i.e., isa-$\text{PIC}_n^*(y, x)$ defined in Section 2.2) to the same 25 kinds of target concepts.

Fig. 8 compares my improved PIH-based and my basic PI-based hyponymy extractions with regard to average of area under PR curve per combination parameter α. Note that my basic PI-based hyponymy extraction is equivalent to my improved PIH-based one when $\alpha = 0.00$. Unfortunately, my improved PIH-based hyponymy extraction is almost inferior to my basic PI-based one. Therefore, I should not take into account the additional property inheritance from a hypernym x_h of a target concept x to its hyponym candidate y.

Fig. 9 and 10 compare my improved PIC-based and my basic PI-based hyponymy extractions with regard to average of area under PR curve per combination parameter β and per number of properties n respectively. Note that my basic PI-based hyponymy extraction is equivalent to my improved PIC-based one when $\beta = 0.00$. Fortunately, my improved PIC-based hyponymy extraction is superior to my basic PI-based one and gains the most, +0.0073 (+1.31%), and it is almost completely superior to the SP-based one and gains the most, +0.0659 (+13.22%), when $n = 17$ and $\beta = 0.40$. And Fig. 9 shows that I should not set the combination parameter β too great, i.e., take into account too much the additional property inheritance from a target concept x to a coordinate concept y_c of its hyponym candidate y.

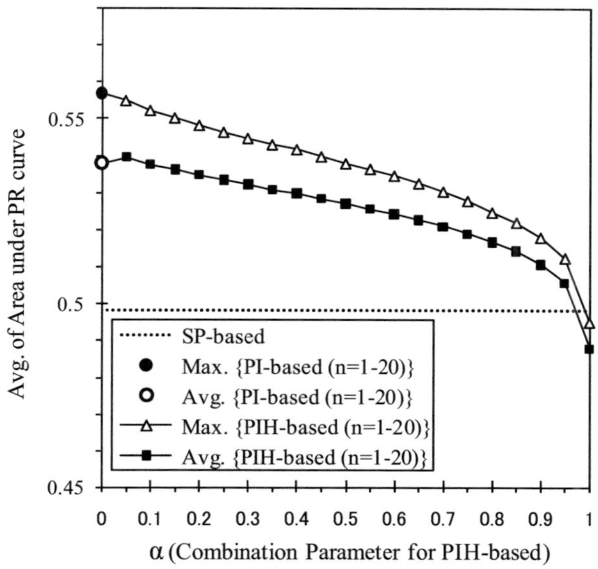

Fig. 8. Average of area under precision-recall curve per α by single Property Inheritance (PI) based vs. multiple Property Inheritances with Hypernym (PIH) based hyponymy extractions.

Subsequently, I also applied my improved hyponymy extraction based on both single Property Inheritance and Property Aggregation (i.e., isa-PIA$_n^{*(m)}(y, x)$ defined in Section 2.3) to the same 25 kinds of target concepts.
Fig. 11 and 12 compare my improved PIA-based and my basic PI-based hyponymy extractions with regard to average of area under PR curve per combination parameter γ and per number of repeats m respectively. Note that my basic PI-based hyponymy extraction is equivalent to my improved PIA-based hyponymy extraction when $\gamma = 0$. My improved PIA-based hyponymy extraction is superior to my basic PI-based one and gains the most, +0.0071 (+1.28%), and it is superior to the SP-based one and gains the most, +0.0657 (+13.18%), when $n = 17$, $\gamma = 0.45$, and $m = 1$. But it is slightly inferior to my improved PIC-based one.
Last, I also applied my combined hyponymy extraction based on both multiple Property Inheritances with Coordinate and Property Aggregation (PICA), i.e., by combining both my PIC-based and PIA-based methods, to the same 25 kinds of target concepts. Fortunately, my combined PICA-based hyponymy extraction is the best among my proposed ones. It is superior to my basic PI-based one and gains the most, +0.0222 (+3.99%), and it is superior to the SP-based one and gains the most, +0.0808 (+16.21%), when $n = 4$, $\beta = 0.30$, $\gamma = 0.90$, and $m = 11$.
Fig. 13 shows the average PR curves for all of 25 concepts by my basic PI-based ($n = 17$), my improved PIC-based ($n = 17$, $\beta = 0.40$), my improved PIA-based ($n = 17$, $\gamma = 0.45$, $m = 1$), and my combined PICA-based ($n = 4$, $\beta = 0.30$, $\gamma = 0.90$, $m = 11$) hyponymy extractions. My combined PICA-based hyponymy extraction is almost the best in the low recall range (about from 0.00 to 0.65), while my improved PIC-based hyponymy extraction is almost the

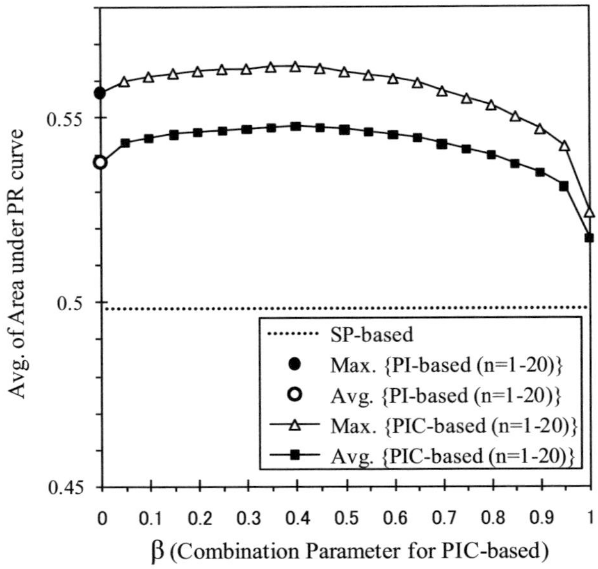

Fig. 9. Average of area under precision-recall curve per β by single Property Inheritance (PI) based vs. multiple Property Inheritances with Coordinate (PIC) based hyponymy extractions.

best in the high recall range (about from 0.65 to 0.90). In the future, I try to make more robust hyponymy extraction in the whole recall range by sampling from both worlds (PICA-based and PIC-based).

Table 2 summarizes the experimental results for comparison of my proposed hyponymy extractions. They show that my basic hyponymy extraction based on single property inheritance (PI-based) is superior to a traditional hyponymy extraction based on such a lexico-syntactic pattern as "*y* is a/an *x*", that one of my improved hyponymy extractions based on multiple property inheritances (not PIH-based but PIC-based) is superior to my basic PI-based one as well as the traditional SP-based one, that my improved hyponymy extraction based on both property inheritance and property aggregation (PIA-based) is superior to my basic hyponymy extraction based on only property inheritance but is slightly inferior to my improved PIC-based one, and that my combined hyponymy extraction based on both multiple property inheritances with coordinate and property aggregation (PICA-based) is superior to the others. As future directions, I have to invent a method for parameter optimization, and I will tackle how to construct time-dependent and/or space-dependent concept hierarchies for context-aware applications in mobile and ubiquitous computing environments.

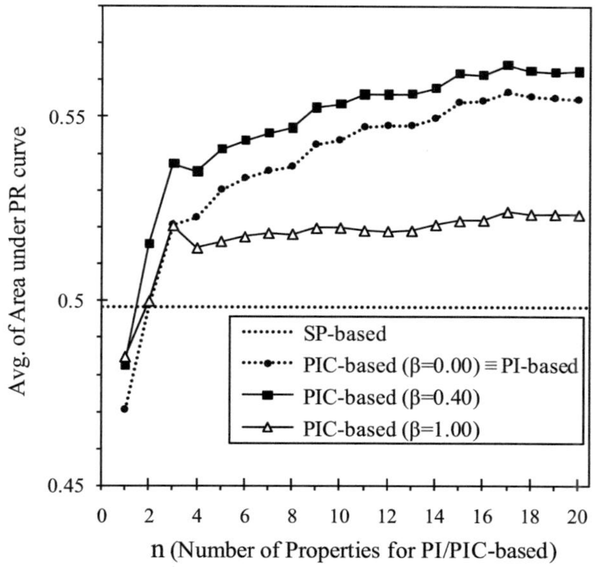

Fig. 10. Average of area under precision-recall curve per n by single Property Inheritance (PI) based vs. multiple Property Inheritances with Coordinate (PIC) based hyponymy extractions.

3. Visual Description Extraction from the Web

Sensory knowledge of objects, such as visual descriptions/images and audio descriptions/clips, is very useful for us in various situations. For example, object-name search by sensory information when we encounter a name-unknown species of bird, insect, or plant and want to know its concrete name to search the Web for its more detail documents in mobile and ubiquitous computing environments, and sensory information search by object-name when we visit a unacquainted area and want to know the appearance information of navigated landmarks rather than their concrete names in car/walk navigation systems (Fig. 14). One approach to solve these problems is to manually construct databases of relationships between object-names and their sensory information. There are already good databases for only specific domains (e.g., pictorial books of only animals or plants), but they are not general.

	AuPR	vs. SP-based	vs. PI-based
SP-based	0.4984	————	————
PI-based (n=17)	0.5570	+0.0586(+11.75%)	————
PIC-based (n=17, β=0.40)	0.5643	+0.0659(+13.22%)	+0.0073(+1.31%)
PIA-based (n=17, γ=0.45, m=1)	0.5641	+0.0657(+13.18%)	+0.0071(+1.28%)
PICA-based (n=4, β=0.30, γ=0.90, m=11)	0.5792	+0.0808(+16.21%)	+0.0222(+3.99%)

Table 2. Comparison of my proposed hyponymy extractions with regard to area under precision-recall curve (AuPR).

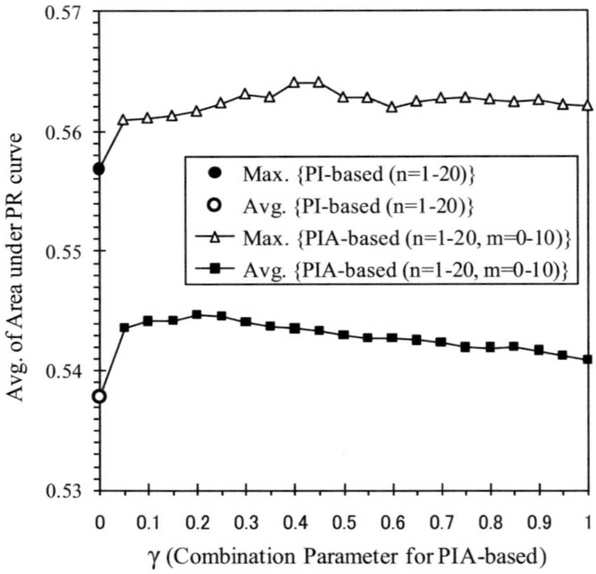

Fig. 11. Average of area under precision-recall curve per γ by Property Inheritance (PI) based vs. Property Inheritance and Aggregation (PIA) based hyponymy extractions.

By mining the Web as another approach, I try to construct much larger database for general objects from various domains.

This section introduces my visual description extraction to extract typical appearance descriptions for each target object-name from the Web by using text mining techniques and concept hierarchy knowledge, i.e., hyponymy (is-a) and meronymy (has-a) relations (Hattori, Tezuka & Tanaka, 2007). Section 3.1 analyzes and models lexico-syntactic patterns of visual appearance descriptions. Section 3.2 describes my visual description extraction in detail. Section 3.3 shows several experimental results to evaluate my proposed visual description extraction.

3.1 Pattern Analysis and Modeling

There are the following lexico-syntactic patterns of appearance descriptions for a target object, which consisting of its concrete object-name (e.g., "kingfisher"), visual-modifiers, and class/component-names:

1. "(visual-modifier) (object-name)"
   - e.g., "beautiful kingfisher"
2. "(object-name) is/are (visual-modifier)"
   - e.g., "kingfisher is very pretty"
3. "(object-name) is a/an (visual-modifier) (class-name)"
   - e.g., "kingfisher is a small bird"

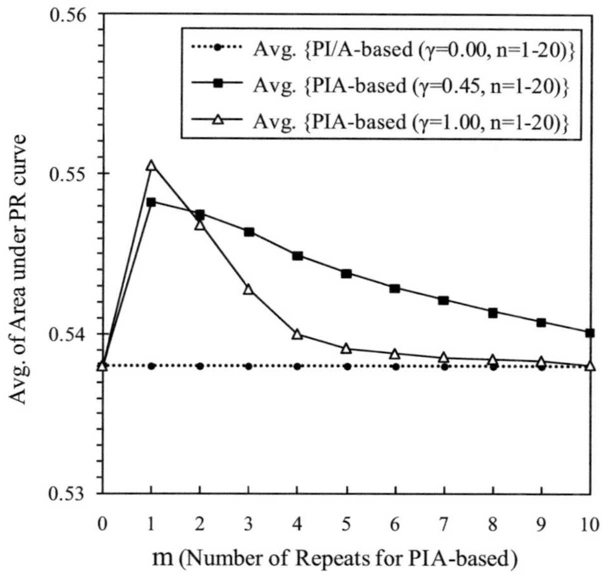

Fig. 12. Average of area under precision-recall curve per m by Property Inheritance (PI) based vs. Property Inheritance and Aggregation (PIA) based hyponymy extractions.

4. "(object-name) is a/an (class-name) with (visual-modifier) (component-name)"
   - e.g., "kingfisher is a bird with brilliantly colored feathers"
5. "(object-name) has/have (visual-modifier) (component-name)"
   - e.g., "kingfisher has a large beak"

I have formalized the most simplified model of an *appearance* description for a general object, as a triplet of the name of *object* itself, a name of its *class* or *component*, and a *visual modifier* describing its visual characteristic:

$$appearance = (object,\ \ visual\text{-}modifier,\ \ class/component). \tag{23}$$

For example, a sentence "A kingfisher is a small bird." can be simplified to one triplet of an object-name, a visual modifier, and a modified class-name of the object, (kingfisher, small, bird). For another example, a sentence "A kingfisher has a short blue tail and a long bill." can be simplified to three triplets of an object-name, a visual modifier, and a modified component-name of the object, (kingfisher, short, tail), (kingfisher, blue, tail), and (kingfisher, long, bill). This model is based on the observation that an object is usually perceived as an aggregation of components with specific visual characteristics. If the visual modifier describes the whole of the object itself, such as in the case of "A kingfisher is colorful.", then the class would be the name of the object itself, that is, the simplified triplet would be (kingfisher, colorful, kingfisher).

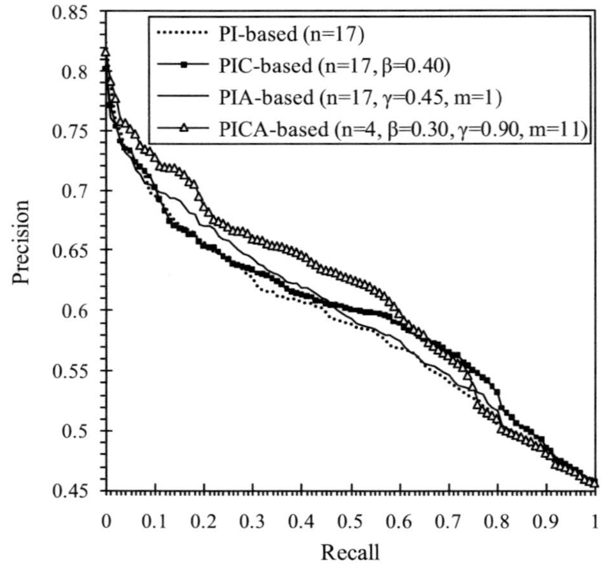

Fig. 13. Average precision-recall curves by Property Inheritance (PI) based vs. Property Inheritances with Coordinate (PIC) based vs. Property Inheritance and Aggregation (PIA) based vs. Property Inheritances with Coordinate and Aggregation (PICA) based hyponymy extractions.

3.2 Method

I describe in detail a method to extract typical appearance descriptions for each target object-name by mining a very large corpus of documents such as the Web. The goal of my proposed method is to collect a set of pairs (*visual* v_i, *class/component* c_i) that correctly describes the appearance of the given object o. I call these pairs, *V-C pairs,*

$$o \Longrightarrow \{(v_1, c_1), (v_2, c_2), ..., (v_n, c_n)\}. \tag{24}$$

Moreover, I also aim to rank these *V-C pairs* in the order of some weight w_i, which indicates the suitability of each *V-C pair* as an appearance description of the target object o,

$$o \Longrightarrow \{(v_1, c_1, w_1), (v_2, c_2, w_2), ..., (v_n, c_n, w_n)\}. \tag{25}$$

When a object-name o is given, my proposed method executes the following three steps and then outputs its typical appearance descriptions as several *V-C pairs* ordered by their weight.

Step 1. Visual Modifier Dictionary Construction

I have manually collected a set of visual modifiers as a basic data set for my proposed method. It consists of 617 words that describe color, shape, size, and surface material of objects. The composition of the set is shown in Table 3. The dictionary contains many (maybe too many) words referring to size, such as "short", "long", "small", "big", "high", "low", "many", "much", "few", and "little". Although they are important for describing the appearance in some occasions, they have also caused some noise in the results.

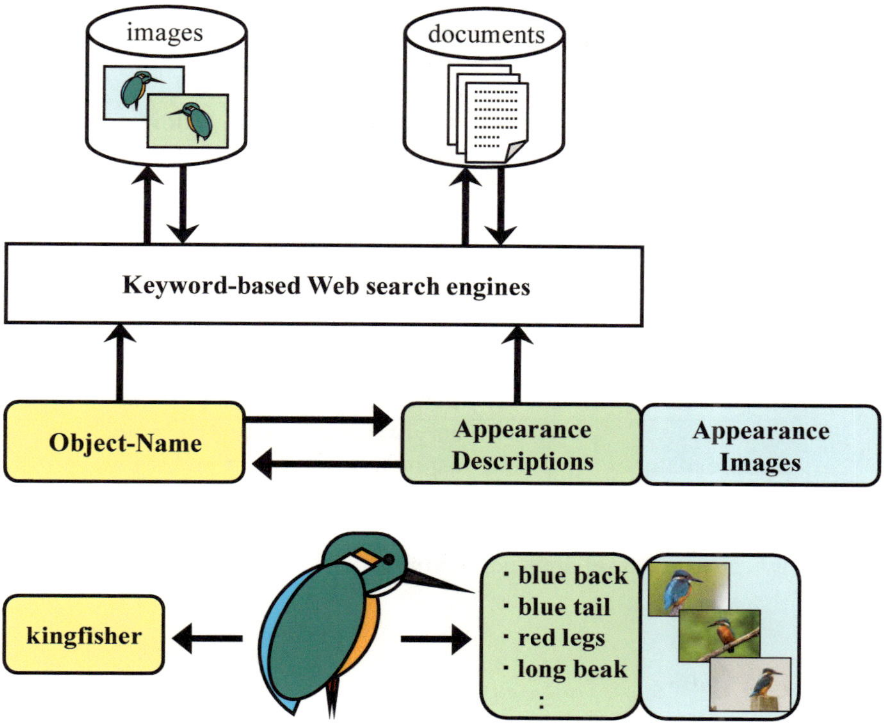

Fig. 14. Conversion between object-names and appearance descriptions/images.

Step 2. Class/Component-Name Collection for Visual Modifiers

To collect the names of classes/components for a target object, first, my proposed method crawls Web pages described about only the target object, by submitting the name of the target object as a query to Google Web Search (2007) which is a conventional keyword-based Web search engine. To make the search results more accurate for the target object, my system retrieves only Web pages that contain the name of the target object o in the title, by submitting not ["o"] but [`intitle:`"o"] as a query to Google Web Search. Henceforth, I use $D(o)$ as the set of crawled documents relevant to each target object-name o obtained from D, the set of all documents of a corpus such as the Web.

Next, the parser scans through the collected Web pages and finds phrases that contain a visual modifier in the dictionary. Words that immediately follow a visual modifier in the crawled Web documents are considered as candidates for class/component-names of the target object. There are, however, many irrelevant words on the candidate list. I apply the following ranking techniques to refine the results.

Type	Number	Examples
Color	192	aeruginous, amber, amethyst, antique, apricot, ..., wheat, white, wine, wisteria, yellow
Shape	143	antisymmetric, aquiline, arc, asymmetric, ..., vertical, wavy, wedge-shaped, winding
Texture	119	abrasive, allover, argyle, banded, belted, ..., veined, velvety, watermarked, wet, zebra-stripe
Size	53	abundant, average, big, bold, brief, broad, ..., thick, thin, tiny tremendous, trivial, vast, wide
Surface material	110	acrylic, adobe, alloy, aluminum, asphalt, bamboo, ..., vinyl, waxy, wire, wood, wooden, woolly
Total	617	

Table 3. Manually-constructed set of visual modifiers.

Step 3. V-C Pair Weighting

After obtaining a mixture of good and bad pairs of Visual modifier and Class/Component-name (*V-C pairs*), my system evaluates their weight to offer the users them ranked according to their significance for the target object. I present four kinds of weighting methods.

Simple weighting is a very simple approach that evaluates each weight of a *V-C pair* (v_i, c_i) for the target object o by the number of Web documents in $D(o)$ that contain the adjacent phrase "v_i c_i" (i.e., a visual modifier v_i immediately followed by a class/component c_i):

$$\text{weight}_o^{simple}(v_i, c_i) := \text{df}_o([\text{"}v_i\ \ c_i\text{"}]), \tag{26}$$

where $\text{df}_o([\text{"}p\text{"}])$ stands for the number of Web documents within $D(o)$ that contain a phrase p, i.e, by submitting [`intitle:`"o" & "p"] as a query to Google Web Search. Because the weighting method considers a word that frequently appears after a visual modifier to be a class/component-name automatically (maybe too illogically), it is vulnerable to a compound word that starts with a visual modifier but is not an appearance description of the target object, e.g., "high school" and "yellow pages". Therefore, the below weighting methods try to cope with this problem.

Summation based weighting is a more refined approach that evaluates each weight of a *V-C pair* (v_i, c_i) for the target object o by multiplying the simple weight by the significance of a class/component c_i for the target object o:

$$\text{weight}_o^{sum}(v_i, c_i) := \text{weight}_o^{simple}(v_i, c_i) \cdot \text{weight}_o(c_i), \tag{27}$$

$$\text{weight}_o(c_i) := \sum_{v_j \in V} f_o(v_j, c_i), \tag{28}$$

$$f_o(v_j, c_i) := \begin{cases} 1 & \text{if } \mathrm{df}_o([\text{"}v_j \;\; c_i\text{"}]) > t^{sum}, \\ 0 & \text{otherwise.} \end{cases} \tag{29}$$

where t^{sum} stands for a threshold value, which I set to 1. $f_o(v_j, c_i)$ is a boolean function that indicates whether or not there is a meaningful co-occurrence as the phrase "v_j c_i" in the crawled Web documents $D(o)$ for the target object o, and $\text{weight}_o(c_i)$ means that the number of variations of visual modifiers that have a meaningful co-occurrence with a candidate class/component c_i of the target object in $D(o)$.

Syntactic Pattern based weighting is to filter the above-mentioned problematical *V-C pairs* by using a lexico-syntactic pattern "c_i is/are v_i":

$$\text{weight}_o^{sp}(v_i, c_i) := \begin{cases} \text{weight}_o^{sum}(v_i, c_i) & \text{if } \dfrac{\mathrm{df}([\text{"}c_i \text{ is/are } v_i\text{"}])}{\mathrm{df}([\text{"}v_i \;\; c_i\text{"}])} > t^{sp}, \\ 0 & \text{otherwise.} \end{cases} \tag{30}$$

where t^{sp} stands for a threshold value, which I set to 10^{-4}, and df(["p"]) stands for the number of documents that contains the phrase p within D, the set of all the documents of a corpus, not just the sampled documents $D(o)$ (i.e., by submitting ["p"] to Google Web Search). The formula is based on an observation for a set phrase "v_i c_i" that df(["v c"]) is too great but df(["c_i is/are v_i"]) is too small or nearly equal to 0. For example, in the case of (kingfisher, red, legs), both "legs are red" and "red legs" appear with a high frequency in all the documents and maybe also in D("kingfisher"). Therefore, this *V-C pair* (red, legs) is considered as an appearance description in general. On the other hand, although the phrase "high school" appears at a certain high rate in D("kingfisher"), this *V-C pair* (high, school) is not considered as an appearance description in general because of low frequency of the phrase "school is high", and thus should not always be considered as an appearance description of the target object "kingfisher".

Concept Hierarchy based weighting is to restrict c_i of a *V-C pair* (v_i, c_i) to the target object-name o, its class-name (hyponym) or component-name (meronym) by utilizing concept hierarchy knowledge:

$$\text{weight}_o^{ch}(v_i, c_i) := \begin{cases} \text{weight}_o^{simple}(v_i, c_i) & \text{if } c_i \text{ is the object } o\text{, its class or component,} \\ 0 & \text{otherwise.} \end{cases} \tag{31}$$

3.3 Experiment

I show several experimental results to evaluate my proposed method of extracting typical appearance descriptions for a target object-name from the Web. I performed experiments on a set of 20 kinds of target object-names, consisting of four typical categories that the users might encounter in their daily lives. Each set has five objects as follows.

Birds: "Jungle Myna", "Kingfisher", "Shoebill", "Snowy Owl", and "Sun Conure".

Flowers: "Edelweiss", "Japanese Cherry", "Lavender", "Lily of the Valley", and "Sunflower".

Products: "InterCityExpress", "PS3", "TGV", "ThinkPad", and "Wii".

Landmarks: "Big Ben", "Leaning Tower of Pisa", "Statue of Liberty", "Taj Mahal", and "Tokyo Tower".

I applied the above-mentioned four kinds of weighting methods to obtain typical appearance descriptions appropriate for the 20 kinds of target object-names.

Fig. 15 to 18 compares the four kinds of weighting methods with regard to the top *k* average precision for each category. These graphs illustrate that the Concept Hierarchy (CH) based weighting is substantially better than the others. Note that the top *k* average precision for products is much worse than the other categories.

Last, Fig. 19 compares the four kinds of weighting methods with regard to the top *k* average precision in the total for all categories. The graph also illustrates that the Concept Hierarchy (CH) based weighting is substantially better than the others and keeps about 0.70 average precision in the top 10 ranks. So, concept hierarchy knowledge (e.g., extracted from the Web in Section 2) is very useful for appearance description extraction from the Web as well as the other natural language processing systems.

As one future direction, I will have to evaluate the recall as well as the precision of my proposed weighting methods. Because only the top *k* average precision of the Syntactic Pattern (SP) based weighting becomes obviously lower when *k* becomes greater, the SP-based weighting seems to be unable to achieve higher recall than the other weighting methods.

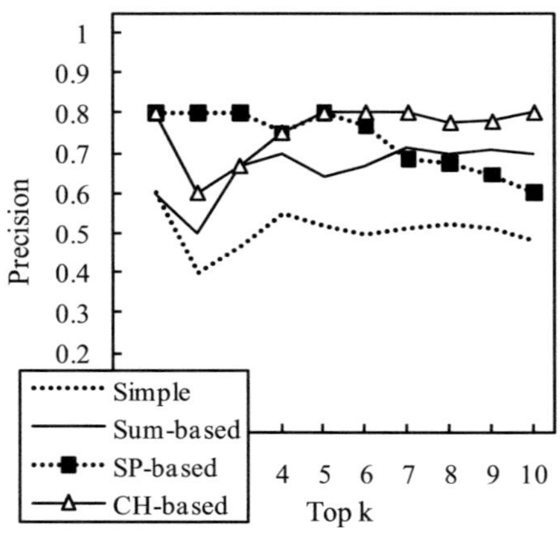

Fig. 15. Top *k* precision of visual description extraction for five birds.

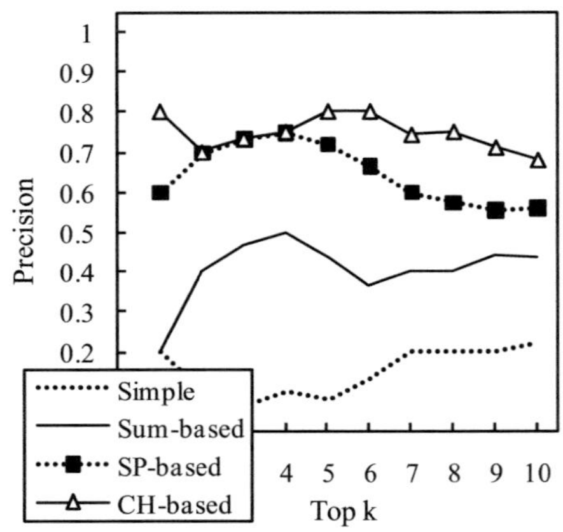

Fig. 16. Top *k* precision of visual description extraction for five flowers.

4. Application: Sense-based Object-name Search

This section introduces my Sense-based Object-name Search (SOS) to enable users to identify the concrete name of a target object which they do not know only by inputting its hyponym (class-name) and some sensory descriptions, as an application system to utilize the Web-extracted semantic and sensory knowledge.

When we move around in the real world such as town or nature, we usually encounter various real objects (e.g., products/buildings or animals/plants) and want information about some among them. In recent years, with the advances in mobile/ubiquitous computing devices and mobile Web search engines, we have become able to search the Web for information anywhere at any time in our daily lives.

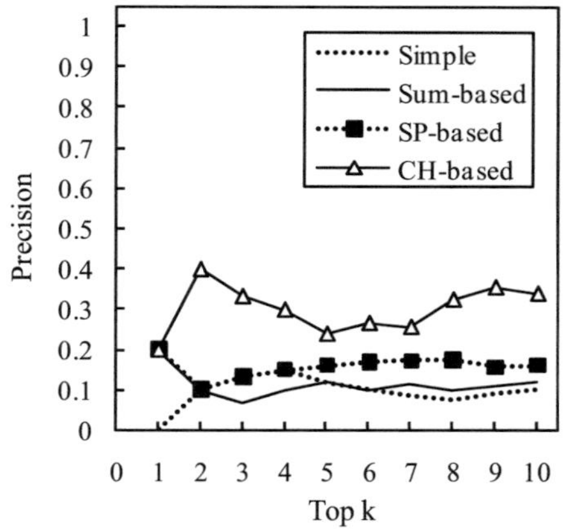

Fig. 17. Top k precision of visual description extraction for five products.

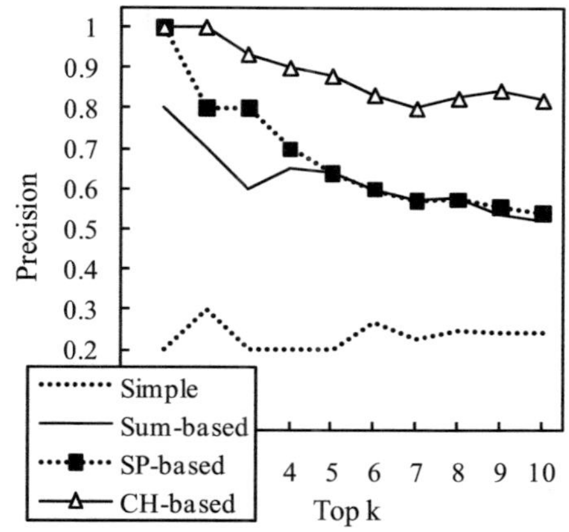

Fig. 18. Top k precision of visual description extraction for five landmarks.

When we search the Web for information about a target object by submitting a keyword-based query to such a conventional Web search engine as Google and Yahoo!, the precision and recall of the search results depend a great deal on whether or not we have known exactly the concrete name of the target object. If we know the concrete name of the target object, we could get not bad search results only by submitting it without any modification to a mobile Web search engine. However, we do not always know the concrete name of any target object that we have encountered in the real world and wanted information about. If we do not know the concrete name of the target object, we have no alternative but to compose a keyword-based query by its ambiguous features except its concrete object-name. For example, its class-name (i.e., hypernym), its visual appearance (e.g., color or shape), and its spatio-temporal information (e.g., place or season). And we could not get enough good search results only by submitting its class-name, visual appearance and/or spatio-temporal descriptions to the same mobile Web search engine.

Let's suppose that two users encounter a beautiful bird at a riverside and want to search the Web for information about the target bird (shown in Fig. 20). If one of them knows exactly "Kingfisher" which is a concrete name of the bird, she could get good (possibly not bad) search results only by submitting a concrete query ["Kingfisher"]. Meanwhile, if the other user does not know the concrete name of the bird, he might have no alternative but to compose an ambiguous query ["blue bird"] by its class-name "bird" and its visual appearance "blue". And he would get too bad search results which rarely include information about the target bird named by "Kingfisher" only by submitting the ambiguous query, because there are various kinds of not only blue birds but also objects except "Kingfisher". The precision of our keyword-based Web search results depends a great deal on whether or not we have known exactly the concrete name of a target object.

Therefore, for a mobile user trying to search the Web for information about the target object whose concrete name s/he has not known, an object-name search that helps her/him to identify the concrete name of the target object by its ambiguous features is one of the most essential services for mobile/ubiquitous Web searches. Meanwhile, there have been many researches

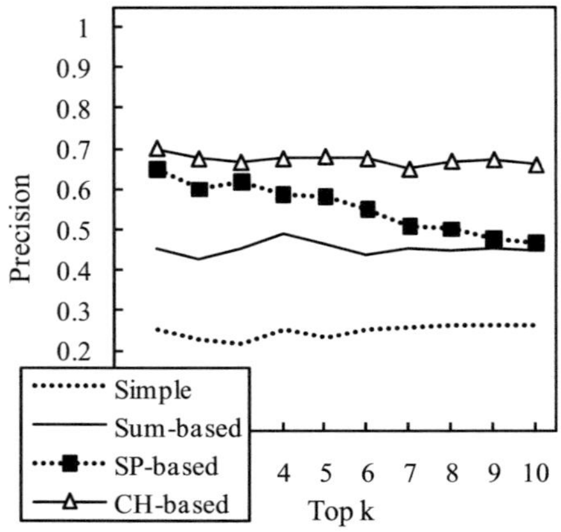

Fig. 19. Top *k* precision of visual description extraction for twenty general objects.

on Generic Object Recognition that recognizes a target object in its photographs with its category name (Duygulu et al., 2002), and the accuracy has improved greatly. But it is still very difficult to recognize the target object with its concrete name.

I have been developing an object-name search system by a class-name, visual appearance and/or spatio-temporal descriptions (Hattori & Tanaka, 2009), as the first step to Sense-based on Object-name Search (SOS). When the user inputs a class-name, visual appearance and/or real-world context descriptions, my proposed system executes the following three steps to return not only concrete object-names ranked by her/his specification but also their typical images, visual appearance and spatio-temporal descriptions. First, my system converts from the user-given class-name to its concrete object-names by using Web-extracted semantic knowledge in Section 2. Second, each concrete object-name is assigned some kind of weight to, which is calculated by co-occurrence frequency of the object-name with the user-given descriptions in the Web. Next, sensory knowledge such as typical appearance descriptions of concrete object-names ranked by their weight is extracted from the Web in Section 3. And then the user can also modify her/his original specification repeatedly by using their typical features as a useful reference. Finally, the user could identify more concrete name of the target object by its ambiguous features, and get better search results by submitting the concrete object-name as a keyword-based Web query than by submitting its ambiguous features.

5. Conclusion

Automatic knowledge extraction from such a very large document corpus as the Web is one of the hottest research topics in the domain of Artificial Intelligence and Database technologies. This chapter has introduced my object-oriented and the existing methods to extract semantic (e.g., hyponymy and meronymy) and sensory (e.g., visual and aural) knowledge from the Web, and compares them by showing several experimental results. My object-oriented semantic knowledge extraction is based on property inheritance(s) and property aggregation, and repeatedly improves the extracted results of both hyponymy and meronymy relations. Meanwhile, my object-oriented sensory knowledge extraction is improved by utilizing the ex-

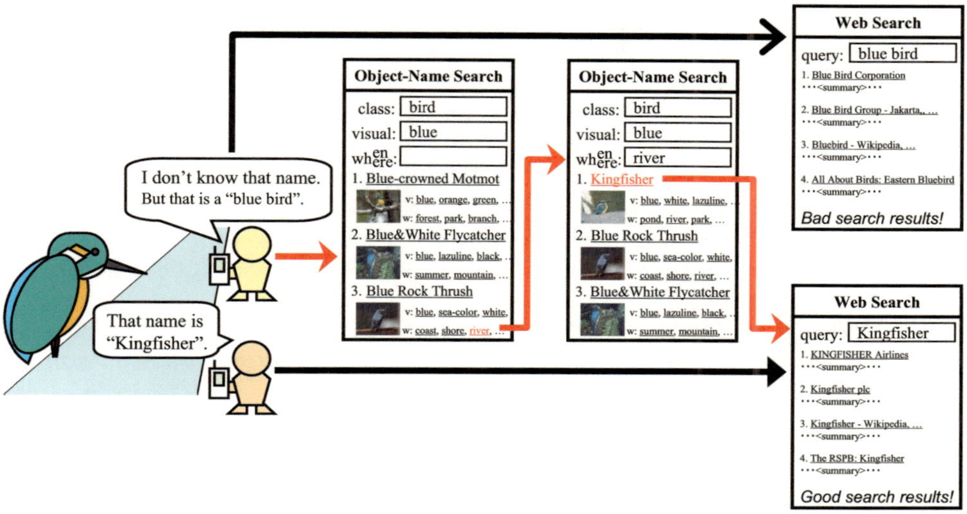

Fig. 20. Sense-based object-name search by a class-name, visual appearance and/or spatio-temporal descriptions.

tracted hyponymy and meronymy relations. The effectiveness of my proposed object-oriented approach for object-knowledge extractions from the Web has been shown by several experimental results. Finally, this chapter has introduced my Sense-based Object-name Search (SOS) to enable users to identify the concrete name of a target object which they do not know only by inputting its hyponym (class-name) and some sensory descriptions, as an application system to utilize the Web-extracted semantic and sensory knowledge.

6. References

Caraballo, S. A. (1999). Automatic construction of a hypernym-labeled noun hierarchy from text, *Proceedings of the 37th annual meeting of the Association for Computational Linguistics on Computational Linguistics (ACL'99)*, pp. 120–126.

Davis, J. & Goadrich, M. (2006). The relationship between precision-recall and ROC curves, *Proceedings of the 23rd ACM International Conference on Machine learning (ICML'06)*, pp. 233–240.

Duygulu, P., Barnard, K., de Freitas, J. F. G. & Forsyth, D. A. (2002). Object recognition as machine translation: learning a lexicon for a fixed image vocaulary, *Proceedings of the 7th European Conference on Computer Vision (ECCV'02) - Part IV, LNCS Vol.2353*, pp. 97–112.

Fleischman, M., Hovy, E. & Echihabi, A. (2003). Offline strategies for online question answering: answering questions before they are asked, *Proceedings of the 41st Annual Meeting of the Association for Computational Linguistics (ACL'03)*, pp. 1–7.

Google Web Search (2007). `http://www.google.com/`.

Hattori, S., Ohshima, H., Oyama, S. & Tanaka, K. (2008). Mining the Web for hyponymy relations based on property inheritance, *Proceedings of the 10th Asia-Pacific Web Conference (APWeb'08), LNCS Vol.4976*, pp. 99–110.

Hattori, S. & Tanaka, K. (2008). Extracting concept hierarchy knowledge from the Web based on property inheritance and aggregation, *Proceedings of the 7th IEEE/WIC/ACM International Conference on Web Intelligence (WI'08)*, pp. 432–437.

Hattori, S. & Tanaka, K. (2009). Object-name search by visual appearance and spatio-temporal descriptions, *Proceedings of the 3rd International Conference on Ubiquitous Information Management and Communication (ICUIMC'09)*, pp. 63–70.

Hattori, S., Tezuka, T., Ohshima, H., Oyama, S., Kawamoto, J., Tajima, K. & Tanaka, K. (2007). ReCQ: real-world context-aware querying, *Proceedings of the 6th International and Interdisciplinary Conference on Modeling and Using Context (CONTEXT'07), LNAI Vol.4635*, pp. 248–262.

Hattori, S., Tezuka, T. & Tanaka, K. (2006). Activity-based query refinement for context-aware information retrieval, *Proceedings of the 9th International Conference on Asian Digital Libraries (ICADL'06), LNCS Vol.4312*, pp. 474–477.

Hattori, S., Tezuka, T. & Tanaka, K. (2007). Mining the Web for appearance description, *Proceedings of the 18th International Conference on Database and Expert Systems Applications (DEXA'07), LNCS Vol.4653*, pp. 790–800.

Hearst, M. A. (1992). Automatic acquisition of hyponyms from large text corpora, *Proceedings of the 14th International Conference on Computational Linguistics (COLING'92)*, pp. 539–545.

Kim, H., Kim, H., Choi, I. & Kim, M. (2006). Finding relations from a large corpus using generalized patterns, *International Journal of Information Technology* **12**(7): 22–29.

Mandala, R., Tokunaga, T. & Tanaka, H. (1998). The use of WordNet in information retrieval, *Proceedings of the COLING-ACL Workshop on Usage of WordNet in Natural Language Processing Systems*, pp. 31–37.

Miller, G. A., Beckwith, R., Felbaum, C., Gross, D. & Miller, K. J. (1990). Introduction to WordNet: an online lexical database, *International Journal of Lexicography* **3**(4): 235–312.

Morin, E. & Jacquemin, C. (2004). Automatic acquisition and expansion of hypernym links, *Computers and the Humanities* **38**(4): 363–396.

Ohshima, H., Oyama, S. & Tanaka, K. (2006). Searching coordinate terms with their context from the Web, *Proceedings of the 7th International Conference on Web Information Systems Engineering (WISE'06), LNCS Vol.4255*, pp. 40–47.

Ruiz-Casado, M., Alfonseca, E. & Castells, P. (2007). Automatising the learning of lexical patterns: an application to the enrichment of WordNet by extracting semantic relationships from Wikipedia, *Data & Knowledge Engineering* **61**(3): 484–499.

Sanderson, M. & Croft, B. (1999). Deriving concept hierarchies from text, *Proceedings of the 22nd Annual International ACM SIGIR Conference on Research and Development in Information Retrieval*, pp. 206–213.

Shinzato, K. & Torisawa, K. (2005). Automatic acquisition of hyponymy relations from HTML documents, *Japanese Journal of Natural Language Processing* **12**(1): 125–150.

Völkel, M., Krötzsch, M., Vrandecic, D., Haller, H. & Studer, R. (2006). Semantic wikipedia, *Proceedings of the 15th International Conference on World Wide Web (WWW'06)*, pp. 585–594.

Wikipedia (2009). `http://www.wikipedia.org/`.

WordNet (2009). `http://wordnet.princeton.edu/`.

Yahoo! Web Search API (2008). `http://api.search.yahoo.co.jp/`.

19

Pinpoint Clustering of Web Pages and Mining Implicit Crossover Concepts

Makoto HARAGUCHI and Yoshiaki OKUBO
IST, Hokkaido University
JAPAN

1. Introduction

In this chapter, we present our Top-N methods for extracting clusters of documents which have originated from the article (Haraguchi, 2002). We first discuss a method for pinpoint clustering of Web pages by pseudo-clique search (Haraguchi & Okubo, 2006; Okubo et al., 2005) and then a method for finding implicit page groups (clusters) represented as formal concepts (Li et al., 2008).

A huge collection of documents including pages over the Web has been considered as an information source of knowledge. One of the core tasks of *Information Retrieval* (*IR*) is to effectively find useful and important documents from such a collection. For this purpose, many retrieval engines compute *ranks* of documents and show them in the order of their ranks (Page et al., 1999; Salton & McGill, 1983). Highly ranked documents are easily checked by users, while documents ranked lower are rarely examined. Any retrieval system based on document ranking has its own ranking scheme. So, even potentially interesting documents are sometimes ranked lower and are therefore actually hidden and invisible to users. In this sense, we might be missing many useful documents. If we can make such hidden significant documents visible, our chance to obtain valuable information and knowledge can be enhanced.

The standard approach to cope with this problem is to use the techniques of *clustering* (Gan et al., 2007) by which we classify various documents into several clusters of similar documents. We pick up a few clusters that seem to be relevant, and then examine them in details to look for interesting documents. However, if the number of clusters is small, clusters tend to be larger ones involving even non-similar documents, and are hard to be examined. Conversely, if we have many clusters, it is also hard to check every cluster, although each cluster is smaller and involves only similar documents. Thus, it is not an easy task to have an adequate method for controlling the number of clusters.

This has motivated us to investigate a new clustering method, *Pinpoint Clustering*, by which we can efficiently extract *only nice clusters*. We have developed some strategy in (Haraguchi & Okubo, 2006; Okubo et al., 2005) for finding only Top-N number of clusters of similar documents with respect to their evaluation values reflecting the ranks of documents in them.

In the framework, the document similarity is evaluated with the help of *Singular Value Decomposition*(SVD) (Strang, 2003). We first extract semantic correlations among terms by applying SVD to the term-document matrix generated from a corpus with a specific topic. Then, given a set of ranked Web pages to be clustered, we evaluate potential similarities among

them based on the semantic correlations of terms, with the standard cosine measure for document vectors. Based on the similarities, we draw edges among similar documents to form a (weighted) undirected graph of documents. An algorithm has been designed as an extension of branch-and-bound *maximum clique search algorithms* (Fahle, 2002; Tomita & Seki, 2007) to find Top-N *pseudo-cliques* as clusters of documents. As is shown in Section 3, we verify that the algorithm can find clusters in which lowly ranked documents appear in them together with highly ranked documents contributing toward raising the whole evaluation of clusters.
However, it has already been pointed out in the area of *conceptual clustering* (Hotho et al., 2003; Hotho & Stumme, 2002) that as long as the similarity of documents is derived from the cosine measure for vector representation, it is generally difficult to understand the meaning of clusters (cliques in this case) by means of feature terms. In our case of finding interesting documents with lower ranks, the detected lower ranked documents together with highly ranked documents in one cluster are in fact similar vectors. However, it is always difficult to judge if the former and the latter share the same meaning or not. In other words, the conceptual classes they belong to may differ. In order to avoid such a conceptually indistinct argument, a method for finding Top-N clusters based on *formal concepts* in *Formal Concept Analysis* (*FCA*) (Ganter & Wille, 1999; Ganter et al., 2005) has been investigated (Haraguchi & Okubo, 2007; Li et al., 2008; Okubo & Haraguchi, 2006). Based on these our studies, we also discuss in this chapter a problem of mining *implicit Web page groups* from the data in the form of page-term relationship. In other words, our target page group is a relatively smaller set X of pages that has an intentional definition that "X is a set of pages that have every term in a feature term set A". Then a formal concept is a pair of X, called the *extent* of concept, and its term set A, called the *intent*.

Such an implicit concept will be useful in discovering *"Crossover Group of Pages"* for instance. Suppose we have several concepts with their extents of large numbers of pages so that they are visible by applying standard effective mining engines as (Han et al., 2007; Lakhal & Stumme, 2005; Uno et al., 2004; Wang et al., 2003) for instances. These pages are not necessarily connected by links, as we consider here a page-term relationship only. Suppose furthermore those groups are extensionally far away. There may be no overlapping. Even for such a case, there exists a possibility for two minor groups, each from each major group, of sharing common important feature terms. From a viewpoint of *FCA*, the union of the minor groups appears as a part of the concept defined from the common terms (see Figure 1). When the concept is minor with relatively smaller extent, the concept is worth examining to check if some invisible interconnection among the parent major groups occurs via the minor one. Those implicit concepts are also hard to be found by *clustering* (Gan et al., 2007). To detect implicit extents with smaller size, we are forced to have a large number of smaller clusters. It is actually unpractical for users to check them all. Without category labels to pages, or almost equivalently without using prior clustering, we show in Section 5.3 that our algorithm succeeds in finding several interesting implicit concepts beyond several distinct categories.

As is well known, each intent of concept just corresponds to a *closed itemset* of an association rule (Bastide et al., 2000). Many nice algorithms (Han et al., 2007; Lakhal & Stumme, 2005; Uno et al., 2004; Wang et al., 2003) for finding frequent closed itemsets have been developed successfully. However, since our targets are non-frequent, we cannot apply them at least directly.

A similar problem about potentially implicit page groups has been already conceived as *"implicitly defined communities"* (Zhang et al., 2006). The implicitly defined communities have too specific interests and are generally difficult to be identified via Web portals or centers in the

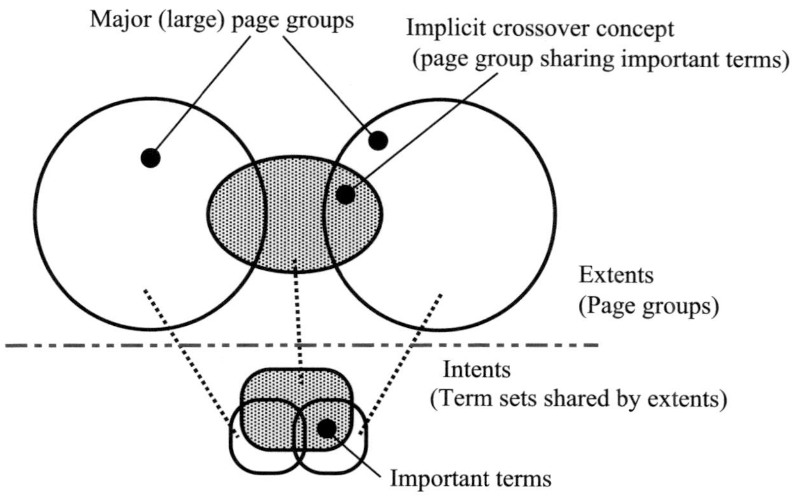

Fig. 1. Crossover Concept

bipartite graph (bigraph). Consequently the number of such communities is large. The situation will be worse when we consider a bigraph representing page-term relationships with a higher density. We are, therefore, required to have more effective miner for detecting implicit concepts under some constraints. In this sense, ours is an instance of *Constrained Mining* (Boulicaut & Jeudy, 2005).

For this purpose, we present in this chapter a revised version of the Top-N algorithm (Okubo & Haraguchi, 2006). Both of them try to enlarge extents as long as their intents are longer patterns to some extent. In other words, since too much smaller extents are out of our concerns, we maximize the extent size under the constraint about the corresponding intent's size. The algorithms are basically based on a depth-first and branch-and-bound search method (Tomita & Seki, 2007) with a pruning rule to cut off candidate concepts whenever their over-estimated evaluation values are less than the tentative Top-N values already detected.

In this chapter, to cope with large scale data and to reflect user's interests, we firstly improve the ability to enumerate possible solution concepts based on a *dynamic ordering technique*, and then introduce additional *space constraints*. A similar ordering strategy is also used in (Bayardo Jr., 1998; Burdick et al., 2001) to find longer itemsets using a *set enumeration tree*. In that case, however, no special expansion rule to avoid duplication is needed, while ours needs an expansion rule to skip duplications. Another important technique to improve the efficiency of pattern miners is a preprocessing method for concise representation (Wang et al., 2003) of dataset. However, our Top-N algorithm accesses only a part of whole data by the branch-and-bound pruning. For this reason, we here do a direct depth-first search without applying prior data analysis. A miner that searches for longer patterns (called *colossal patterns*) has been also proposed in (Zhu et al., 2007). It is based on some bias to avoid hopeless search for longer patterns, while we introduce some *space constraints* under which ours keeps the ability to enumerate every solution satisfying the constraints.

We introduce the constraints of three kinds. The first one defines a starting extent that must include positive example pages. The second one requires for an extent not to cover any negative example pages. The positive and negative examples are also used in (Murata, 2003; 2000) to discover Web communities, given an Web bigraph consisting of centers and fans, where the communities are found by enlarging initial page groups guided by best-first search heuristics. Our Top-N method is also considered as an enlargement process. However, it is complete in the sense that it finds every solution page group under the constraints.

Although we allow to use negative examples, users seem not to be aware of target pages or concepts and their counterparts as well. For this reason, we introduce the third constraint in addition to positive and negative examples. The third one is for realizing searches with an upper bound concept whose intent is just a set of terms given by user. The constraint contributes for accelerating the search and for keeping the interestingness of the result to some extent, as we see in Section 5.3.

In a word, our constrained search can respond within 10 seconds for 10,000 pages with 1,200 terms, given an adequate set of constraints. Thus, the algorithm can run in an interactive mining environment for analyzing search results and for realizing implicit page groups connecting major groups. This will motive us to search Web from a different point of view represented by implicit concepts.

The remainder of this chapter is organized as follows. In the next section, we introduce some basic terminologies used throughout this chapter. Section 3 discusses a method for pinpoint clustering of Web pages by pseudo-clique search. An interesting cluster with higher and lower ranked pages is also presented. In Section 4, we turn our attention from clique-based clusters to formal concept-based clusters. In Section 5, we discuss our method for finding implicit groups of pages. We describe our problem specification and discuss an efficient algorithm for the problem. We show some concrete examples of interesting page groups including a crossover concept. Computational performance of our algorithm is also presented. In the final section, we conclude this chapter with a summary and an important future direction.

2. Preliminaries

We introduce in this section some terminologies used throughout this chapter.

A *simple graph* is denoted by $G = (V, E)$, where V is a set of *vertices* and $E \subseteq V \times V$ a set of (undirected) *edges*. For any vertices $v, v' \in V$, if $(v, v') \in E$, v is said to be *adjacent* to v'. If any pair of vertices $v, v' \in V$ $(v \neq v')$ are adjacent each other, then G is said to be *complete*. For a vertex $v \in V$, the set of vertices adjacent to v is denoted by $N_G(v)$, that is, $N_G(v) = \{v' \mid v' \in V \wedge (v, v') \in E\}$. The size of $N_G(v)$, $|N_G(v)|$, is called the *degree* of v in G. It is often referred to as $degree_G(v)$. If it is clear from the context, they are simply denoted by $N(v)$ and $degree(v)$, respectively. If each vertex $v \in V$ is assigned a positive weight, the graph is called a *weighted graph*. The weight of v is referred to as $w(v)$. For a vertex set $V' \subseteq V$, the weight of V', denoted by $w(V')$, is simply defined as the sum of individual weights, that is, $w(V') = \sum_{v \in V'} w(v)$. In this chapter, we are concerned with a weighted graph unless stated otherwise.

For a graph $G = (V, E)$, a complete subgraph of G is called a *clique* in G. We simply refer a clique as the set of vertices by which it is induced. For cliques C and D in G, if $C \subset D$, then D is said to be an *extension* of C. For a clique C in G, if there exists no extension of C, then C is said to be *maximal*. A maximal clique with the largest size is especially called a *maximum clique*.

Let $\mathcal{O}$ be a set of *objects* (or individuals) and $\mathcal{F}$ a set of *features* (or attributes). For a binary relation $R \subseteq \mathcal{O} \times \mathcal{F}$, a triple $< \mathcal{O}, \mathcal{F}, R >$ is called a *formal context*. If $(x, f) \in R$, we say that

the object o has the feature f. Then, for an object $o \in O$, the set of features associated with o is denoted by $F_R(o)$, that is, $F_R(o) = \{f \in \mathcal{F} \mid (o,f) \in R\}$.
Given a formal context $< \mathcal{O}, \mathcal{F}, R >$, for a set of objects $X \subseteq \mathcal{O}$ and a set of features $Y \subseteq \mathcal{F}$, we define two mappings $\varphi : 2^{\mathcal{O}} \rightarrow 2^{\mathcal{F}}$ and $\psi : 2^{\mathcal{F}} \rightarrow 2^{\mathcal{O}}$ as follows:

$$\begin{aligned} \varphi X &= \{f \in \mathcal{F} \mid \forall o \in X, f \in F_R(o)\} = \bigcap_{o \in X} F_R(o) \quad \text{and} \\ \psi Y &= \{o \in \mathcal{O} \mid Y \subseteq F_R(o)\}. \end{aligned}$$

That is, the former computes the set of features shared by every object in o. The latter, on the other hand, returns the set of objects with Y.
Based on these mappings, for a set of objects $X \subseteq \mathcal{O}$ and a set of features $Y \subseteq \mathcal{F}$, a pair of X and Y, (X, Y), is called a *formal concept* (or simply concept) under the formal context if and only if $\varphi X = Y$ and $\psi Y = X$, where X and Y are called the *extent* and the *intent* of the concept, respectively. From the definition, it is easy to see that $\psi\varphi X = X$ and $\varphi\psi Y = Y$. That is, a formal concept is defined as a pair of *closed* sets of objects and features under the mappings. Thus, the compound mappings, $\psi\varphi$ and $\varphi\psi$, define *closure operators*.
For a set of objects X, we can *uniquely* obtain a formal concept defined as $(\psi\varphi X, \varphi X)$. Dually, $(\psi Y, \varphi\psi Y)$ is a formal concept uniquely defined for a set of features Y.
Let (X, Y) and (X', Y') be formal concepts. If $X \subseteq X'$ (or $Y \supseteq Y'$), then we say (X, Y) *precedes* (X', Y') and denote it by $(X, Y) \preceq (X', Y')$. Under the ordering, the set of formal concepts in a formal context forms a lattice, called a *concept lattice*.

3. Pinpoint Clustering of Web Pages with Pseudo-Clique Search

In this section, we discuss a method of finding useful clusters of Web pages which are significant in the sense that their contents are similar or closely related to ones of higher-ranked pages (Haraguchi & Okubo, 2006; Okubo et al., 2005). Since we are usually careless of pages with lower ranks, they are unconditionally discarded even if their contents are similar to some pages with high ranks. We try to extract such hidden pages together with significant higher-ranked pages as a cluster.
In order to obtain such clusters, we first extract semantic correlations among terms by applying *Singular Value Decomposition*(SVD) to the term-document matrix generated from a corpus w.r.t. a specific topic. Based on the correlations, we can evaluate potential similarities among Web pages from which we try to obtain clusters. The set of Web pages is represented as a weighted graph G based on the similarities and their ranks. Our clusters can be found as *pseudo-cliques* in G. We present an algorithm for finding Top-N weighted pseudo-cliques. Our experimental result shows that quite valuable clusters can be actually extracted according to our method.

3.1 Semantic Similarity among Web Pages

In order to find clusters of Web pages, we have to measure similarities among Web pages. For the task, we follow a technique in *Information Retrieval*(IR) (Salton & McGill, 1983).
Let $\mathcal{D}$ be a set of documents and $\mathcal{T}$ the set of terms appeared in $\mathcal{D}$. We first remove too frequent and too infrequent terms based on $\mathcal{T}$. The set of remaining terms, called *feature terms*, is denoted by $\mathcal{T}^*$. Supposing $|\mathcal{T}^*| = n$, each document $d_i \in \mathcal{D}$ can be represented as an n-dimensional document vector $\boldsymbol{d_i} = (tf_{i1}, \ldots, tf_{in})^T$, where tf_{ij} is the frequency of the term $t_j \in \mathcal{T}^*$ in the document d_i. Thus, $\mathcal{D}$ can be translated into a *term-document matrix* $(\boldsymbol{d_1}, \ldots, \boldsymbol{d_{|\mathcal{D}|}})$.

For the term-document matrix, we apply *Singular Value Decomposition*(SVD) in order to extract correlations among feature terms (Moens, 2000).
An $m \times n$ matrix A can be decomposed by applying SVD as $A = U\Sigma V^T$, where U and V are $m \times m$ and $n \times n$ orthogonal matrices, respectively. Each column vector in U (V) is called a left (right) singular vector. Σ is an $m \times n$ matrix of the form

$$\Sigma = \left[\begin{array}{ccc|c} \sigma_1 & & O & \\ & \ddots & & O_{r\times(n-r)} \\ O & & \sigma_r & \\ \hline & O_{(m-r)\times r} & & O_{(m-r)\times(n-r)} \end{array}\right],$$

where $rank(A) = r$ ($r \leq \min\{m, n\}$) and σ_i is called a *singular value*. First r left singular vectors $\boldsymbol{u_1}, \ldots, \boldsymbol{u_r}$ correspond to a orthonormal basis and define a new subspace of the original one in which column vectors of A exist, where the $m \times r$ matrix $(\boldsymbol{u_1}, \ldots, \boldsymbol{u_r})$ is denoted by U_r.
Let us assume the matrix A is a term-document matrix generated from a set of documents. Intuitively speaking, by applying SVD to A, we can capture *potential but not presently evident* correlations among the terms. Highly semantically correlated terms give a base vector $\boldsymbol{u_i}$ and define a dimension corresponding to a compound term. Such new base vectors define a new subspace based on compound terms. For documents not in A, therefore, if they are projected on the subspace, we can find similarity among them based on the semantic correlations among terms captured from the original documents in A.
In order to take such semantic similarities of Web pages into account, we prepare a *corpus* of documents written about some specific topic. Then by applying SVD to the term-document matrix generated from the corpus, we obtain a subspace reflecting semantic correlations among terms in the corpus. Let U_r be the orthonormal basis defining the subspace. In IR, we do not always use r left singular vectors. A part of them, that is, $U_k = (\boldsymbol{u_1}, \ldots, \boldsymbol{u_k})$ $(k < r)$ is usually used for *approximation*. Such an approximation with U_k is called *Latent Semantic Indexing* (LSI) (Kowalski & Maybury, 2000).
Besides the corpus, with some keywords related to the corpus topic, we retrieve a set of Web pages $\mathcal{P}$ from which we try to obtain clusters. Using the same feature terms for the corpus, each document $p_i \in \mathcal{P}$ is represented as a vector $\boldsymbol{p_i} = (tf_{i1}, \ldots, tf_{in})^T$, where tf_{ij} is the frequency of the feature term t_j in p_i. Then each Web page $\boldsymbol{p_i}$ is projected on the subspace as

$$\boldsymbol{p_i^r} = U_r^T \boldsymbol{p_i}.$$

A similarity between Web pages p_i and p_j, denoted by $sim(p_i, p_j)$, is defined based on the standard *cosine measure*, that is,

$$sim(p_i, p_j) = \frac{\boldsymbol{p_i^r} \cdot \boldsymbol{p_j^r}}{\| \boldsymbol{p_i^r} \| \times \| \boldsymbol{p_j^r} \|}.$$

3.2 Finding Clusters of Web Pages by Top-N Pseudo-Clique Search

3.2.1 Graph Representation of Web Pages

Let $\mathcal{P}$ be a set of Web pages from which we try to extract clusters. In order to find our clusters, $\mathcal{P}$ is represented as an undirected weighted graph G.

Assume we computed the semantic similarities among pages in $\mathcal{P}$ according to the procedure just discussed above. Let δ be a similarity threshold. Each page $p_i \in \mathcal{P}$ corresponds to a vertex in G. For any Web pages $p_i, p_j \in \mathcal{P}$, if $sim(p_i, p_j) \geq \delta$, then they are connected by an edge. Furthermore, we assign a weight to each vertex (page) based on its rank, where a higher-ranked page is assigned a larger weight. The weight of a page p is referred to as $w(p)$.

3.2.2 Top-N Weighted Pseudo-Clique Problem

Our cluster of similar pages can be obtained as a weighted *pseudo-clique* in the graph G. In fact, we obtain only nice clusters by extracting maximal weighted pseudo-cliques whose evaluation values are in the top-N. Before giving the problem description, we first define the notion of pseudo-cliques.

Definition 1. (Pseudo-Clique)
Let $\mathcal{C} = \{C_1, \ldots, C_m\}$ be a class of maximal cliques in a graph. $pseudo(\mathcal{C}) = \cup_{C_i \in \mathcal{C}} C_i$ is called a *pseudo-cliques* with the overlap degree $overlap(\mathcal{C})$ which is defined as $overlap(\mathcal{C}) = \min_{C_i \in \mathcal{C}} \left\{ \left| \cap_{C_j \in \mathcal{C}} C_j \right| / |C_i| \right\}$, where $\bigcap_{C_j \in \mathcal{C}}$ is called the *core*. Moreover, its *size* and *weight* (evaluation value) are given by $|pseudo(\mathcal{C})|$ and $w(pseudo(\mathcal{C})) = \Sigma_{v \in pseudo(\mathcal{C})} w(v)$, respectively. Note here that the weight of pseudo-clique is not restricted to the sum of vertex weights. Any monotone weight under the set inclusion can be accepted. ■

Our problem of finding Top-N weighted pseudo-cliques is defined as follows.

Definition 2. (Top-N Weighted Maximal τ-Valid Pseudo-Clique Problem)
Let G be a graph and τ a threshold for overlap degree. The *Top-N Weighted Maximal τ Pseudo-Clique Problem* is to find any maximal pseudo-clique in G such that its overlap degree is greater than or equal to τ [1] and its weight is in the top N. ■

3.2.3 Computation of Top-N Weighted Pseudo-Cliques

Let $G = (V, E)$ be an weighted graph we are concerned with. In our search, for a clique Q in G, we try to find a τ-valid pseudo-clique $\tilde{C}$ whose core is Q.
Let $cand(Q)$ be the set of vertices v adjacent to any vertex in Q, that is, $cand(Q) = \{v \in V \mid \forall w \in Q \quad (v, w) \in E\}$. Then, we can easily observe that for any pair of cliques Q and Q' in G such that $Q \subseteq Q'$, $cand(Q) \supseteq cand(Q')$ and $w(Q) + w(cand(Q)) \geq w(Q') + w(cand(Q'))$ hold. Note here that the weight of a pseudo-clique with the core Q is *at most* $w(Q) + w(cand(Q))$. Therefore, a simple theoretical property can be easily observed.

Observation1 : Let Q be a clique. Assume we already have *tentative* Top-N maximal pseudo-cliques and the minimum weight of them is w_{min}. If $w(Q) + w(cand(Q)) < w_{min}$ holds, then for any Q' such that $Q' \supset Q$, there exists no pseudo-clique with the core Q' whose weight is in the top N.

Assume that a τ-valid pseudo-clique $\tilde{C}$ contains a clique Q as its core. $\tilde{C}$ can be obtained as the union of any maximal clique C such that $Q \subset C$ and $|Q|/|C| \geq \tau$. It should be noted here that for such a clique C, there exists a maximal clique D in $G(cand(Q))$ such that $Q \cup D = C$, where $G(cand(Q))$ is the subgraph induced by $cand(G)$. That is, finding any maximal clique D in $G(cand(Q))$ such that $|Q|/(|Q| + |D|) \geq \tau$ is sufficient to obtain the pseudo-clique $\tilde{C}$. Although one might claim that such a task is quite expensive from the computational point of view, we can observe some theoretical properties from which pruning rules can be derived.

[1] Such a pseudo-clique is said to be τ-*valid*.

Observation2 : For a clique Q in G, let us assume that we try to find a τ-valid pseudo-clique $\tilde{C}$ whose core is Q. For a clique D in $G(cand(Q))$, if $|D| > (\frac{1}{\tau} - 1) \cdot |Q|$, then any extension (superset) of D is useless for obtaining $\tilde{C}$.

Observation3 : For a clique Q, $Q \cup cand(Q)$ is a τ-valid maximal pseudo-clique with the core Q, if

- $(\frac{1}{\tau} - 1) \cdot |Q| \geq k$ holds, where k is an upper bound of the maximum clique size in $G(cand(Q))$ and
- for any $v \in cand(Q)$, its degree in $G(cand(Q))$ is less than $|cand(Q)| - 1$.

Upper bounds for the maximum clique size have been widely utilized in efficient depth-first branch-and-bound algorithms for finding maximum cliques (Fahle, 2002; Tomita & Seki, 2007). The literature (Fahle, 2002) has argued that the (*vertex*) *chromatic number* χ can provide the tightest upper bound. However, since identifying χ is an NP-complete problem, approximations of χ are usually computed (Fahle, 2002; Tomita & Seki, 2007).
Based on the above observations, Top-N τ-valid weighted pseudo-cliques can be extracted with a *depth-first hybrid search*. For each core candidate Q, its surroundings are explored by finding maximal cliques in $G(cand(Q))$. In the search for core candidates, we can enjoy a pruning based on Observation1. In the surroundings search, a pruning based on Observation2 can be applied. Furthermore, for some core candidates, our surroundings search can be skipped based on Observation3. More precise description of our algorithm is found in (Haraguchi & Okubo, 2006).

3.3 Experimental Results

In this section, we present our experimental results. The main purpose of this experimentation is to confirm that we can actually obtain a useful cluster of Web pages consisting of higher-ranked pages and any other similar (or related) pages with lower ranks. Our system has been implemented in C language and run on a PC with Xeon-2.40 GHz CPU and 512MB memory.

3.3.1 Datasets and Graph Construction

In order to capture semantic correlations among terms, we have prepared a Japanese corpus constructed from 100 Web pages written about "Hokkaido". These pages have been manually selected and only visible texts on them have been manually gathered. After an application of *Morphological Analysis*, we have obtained 2,224 nouns appeared in the corpus. Nouns with frequencies more than 1,000 and less than 2 have been removed from them. The remaining 211 nouns were regarded as feature terms. Applying SVD to the term-document matrix constructed from the corpus, we have obtained a new 98-dimensional subspace.
Besides the corpus, we have retrieved 829 (Japanese) Web pages by Google with the keywords "Hokkaido" and "Sightseeing". We have tried to extract significant clusters from these pages. Each Web page has been first represented as a document vector w.r.t. the original feature terms and then projected on the 98-dimensional subspace in order to capture potential similarities among pages. For any pair of pages, then, we have evaluated the similarity between them based on the cosine measure. Under the setting of $\delta = 0.95$, we have constructed a weighted graph G from the pages. That is, if the angle between two pages is less than or equal to about 18.2 degree, then they are connected by an edge. The numbers of vertices and edges are 829 and 798, respectively. Each page (vertex) d has been assigned a weight defined as $w(d) = 1/rank(d)^2$. As has been stated in the previous section, although we can define

Page Rank	Subject
11th	Index page for travel information maintained by a local travel agency in Hokkaido (especially, for travels in Hokkaido)
382th	Index page for travel information maintained by a famous newspaper company (for domestic and overseas travels)
416th	An article on a private BBS for travels
797th	Information about smorgasbords enjoyable at a hotel in Hokkaido
798th	Information about smorgasbords enjoyable at another hotel in Hokkaido
826th	Page for hotel awards in a famous travel site

Table 1. The 11th significant cluster

various weights according to ranks of pages, we have currently adopted the reciprocal of the rank squared. The reason why we prefer this measure is as follows:

- It is sensitive to difference of ranks in higher range of ranks.
- On the other hand, in lower range, page weights are hardly affected by difference of ranks.

From the characteristics, a clique containing higher-ranked pages is likely to be extracted even if its size is relatively small. Since we can often expect higher-ranked pages are significant, such a phenomenon would be desirable. On the other hand, we are usually careless of lower-ranked pages. In other words, difference of weights among lower-ranked pages would be unimportant for us. In this sense, a likelihood of extracting pseudo-cliques should not be sensitively affected by weights of pages with lower ranks. The above measure would be reasonable from this viewpoint as well.

3.3.2 Example of Extracted Interesting Cluster

We have tried to extract Top-15 weighted 0.8-pseudo cliques in the graph constructed above. Among the extracted clusters (pseudo-cliques), the authors especially consider that the 11th cluster is quite interesting.

The cluster consists of 6 Web pages. Table 1 shows their ranks assigned by Google and subjects. In the authors' opinion, their contents are considered to be very similar in the sense that all of them give us some information about accommodations in Hokkaido, especially information about hotels and foods. The 11th and 382th pages are index pages for travel information and we can make reservations for many hotels via the pages. The 416th page is an article in a private BBS site for travels. The article reports on a private travel in Hokkaido and provides an actual and valuable information about a hotel and enjoyable foods in "Furano" [2]. The 797th and 798th personal pages give us the names of two hotels serving smorgasbords in Hokkaido. The 826th page tells us several hotels which were the most popular or were most frequently reserved in 2004.

Thus, the pages in the 11th cluster are closely related each other and give us quite valuable information. When we try to make travel plans for sightseeing in Hokkaido, we would often care about hotels and foods as important factors. In such a case, the cluster will be surely helpful for us.

Needless to say, we can find clusters of Web pages by *exact* clique search. In that case, however, the above 11th cluster can never be obtained. The cluster as a pseudo-clique consists of two

[2] "Furano" is one of the most famous sightseeing areas in Hokkaido.

exact maximal cliques: $\{11^{th}, 382^{nd}, 797^{th}, 798^{th}, 826^{th}\}$ and $\{382^{nd}, 416^{th}, 797^{th}, 798^{th}, 826^{th}\}$. In the exact case, the former can be ranked as 11th, whereas the latter cluster as 343rd. It should be noted that the 416th page will be invisible unless we specify a large N for Top-N. However, it would be impractical to specify such a large N because many clusters are undesirably extracted. Although 416th page has valuable contents as mentioned above, we will lose a chance to browse it.

In case of pseudo-clique search, the 343rd exact cluster can be absorbed into the 11th cluster to form a pseudo-clique. In other word, the 343rd cluster can be drastically raised its rank. As the result, 416th page can become visible by just specifying a reasonable N.

Thus, our chance to get significant lower-ranked pages can be enhanced with the help of pseudo-cliques. This is a remarkable advantage brought by pseudo-cliques.

3.3.3 Computational Performance of Pseudo-Clique Search

Our experimental result also shows that the pruning rules presented in the previous section are very effective. The number of cores actually examined was 69,981 and our pruning based on the tentative minimum weight were invoked at 40,801 nodes of them. Moreover, the maximal clique searches were skipped at 31 nodes. Thus, the pruning rules can be applied very frequently in our search. As the result, the total computation time was just 0.847 second.

As we have experienced, an IR system often retrieves over hundreds of thousands of Web pages. Therefore our graph constructed from gathered Web pages would have a large number of vertices in more practical situation. In general, however, our graph tends to be quite sparse. Therefore, it is expected that our algorithm can still work well even in such a practical case.

From the experimental result, the authors consider that our pseudo-clique search would be a promising approach to finding significant clusters of Web pages.

4. From Clique-Based Clusters to Formal Concept-Based Clusters

As has been shown just above, we can extract an interesting cluster of Web pages with pseudo-clique search. In the area of *conceptual clustering* (Hotho et al., 2003; Hotho & Stumme, 2002), however, it has been pointed out that as long as the similarity of documents is based on the cosine measure for vector representation, it is generally difficult to understand the meaning of clusters (cliques in this case) by means of feature terms. In our case of finding interesting documents with lower ranks, the detected lower ranked documents together with highly ranked documents in one cluster are in fact similar vectors. However, it is always difficult to judge if the former and the latter share the same meaning or not. In other words, the conceptual classes they belong to may differ. In order to avoid such a conceptually indistinct argument, we have made an informal constraint on the clusters to be obtained as follows:

> *The notion of relevance or interestingness depends only on a conceptual class of documents, not dependent on particular instance documents. Then the clusters we have to find must be concepts of documents that can be definable by means of feature terms.*

As the primary data for a document set is a document-term relationship, we have adopted the notion of *Formal Concept Analysis* (FCA) (Ganter & Wille, 1999; Ganter et al., 2005). Thus, if some higher-ranked documents and lower-ranked ones share a set of terms, they could form the extent of a formal concept, that is, a conceptual cluster of documents.

It is well known that formal concepts can be computed by finding maximal *bipartite cliques* of a bipartite graph or equivalently by finding *closures* of documents or terms. Therefore, keeping the evaluation scheme for extents as clusters of documents, it can be a strategy to find only

Top-N extents by using some very fast enumeration algorithm, *LCM* (Uno et al., 2004) for instance, for finding all the closures.

The problem for such an approach is however that the number of possible extents is still large. Particularly, there exist a numerous number of extents of concepts whose corresponding intents are very smaller set of terms. For smaller intents we have, the extents tend to be larger sets of documents and to involve documents with less similarity. In other words, the quality of those extents becomes worse. For the reason, we have tried to find only Top-N extents w.r.t. the same evaluation schema for clusters, keeping the quality of their intents (Haraguchi & Okubo, 2007; Okubo & Haraguchi, 2006). The method is summarized as follows:

Evaluation on Extents

Extents of formal concepts are evaluated by some *monotone function*. The evaluation becomes higher, as the extents grow as sets of documents, and as each document in them shows higher rank.

Graph Formation under Static Quality Control on Intents

Two documents are judged similar if they share at least a given number of common terms. We draw an edge between any similar two documents, and form a weighted undirected graph of documents, where each document is assigned a weight based on its rank. It should be noted here that any extent with enough quality of intent is always a clique in the graph.

Extent Search under Dynamic Quality Control

To enumerate only Top-N extents (that is, closures of documents), our algorithm adopts again a branch-and-bound method, where

Candidate Closures of Documents: a list of candidate top-N closures is always kept,

Branch-and-Bound Pruning due to Monotone Evaluation: for any search node, a closure of documents, whose evaluation value can never become larger than the minimum of those candidates, we cut off the nodes below, and

Dynamic Quality Control: for any search node whose corresponding intent has less number of feature terms than a given lower bound, we also cut off the nodes below.

Clearly the two pruning rules are safe in the sense that we never miss any of Top-N extents satisfying the requirements.

In the graph formation process, we can exclude document pairs *in advance* which are never included in any extent with enough quality of intent. Furthermore, a theoretical property of cliques can provide us several *upper-bounds* of evaluation values for extents. For example, we can obtain a tight upper-bound with a *sequential approximate coloring* (Fahle, 2002; Tomita & Seki, 2007). Based on the bounds, we can prune many useless extents which are never in Top-N. Thus, the clique search-based approach enables us to efficiently find Top-N extents.

5. Finding Implicit Groups of Web Pages as Constrained Top-N Formal Concepts

In this section, we present a method for finding relatively smaller therefore more implicit groups of Web pages as formal concepts and discuss an effective depth-first mining algorithm for them (Li et al., 2008). The algorithm is based on a dynamic ordering method depending on each search node and some search tree expansion rules. Moreover it is designed so as to find Top-N implicit concepts subject to the size restriction and some space constraints reflecting user's interests.

5.1 Problem Specification

For a given formal context $< \mathcal{O}, \mathcal{F}, R >$, we suppose $\mathcal{O}$ and $\mathcal{F}$ represent the set of pages (documents) and a set of their feature terms, respectively. Then, the set of terms possessed by every page in $X \subseteq \mathcal{O}$ is denoted as φX. Conversely, ψA is a set of pages with every term in $A \subseteq \mathcal{F}$. The actual construction of φ and ψ from Web pages is described in Section 5.3.
The only fact remarked here is that φX and ψA are an intent and an extent for any set $X \subseteq \mathcal{O}$ and $A \subseteq \mathcal{F}$, respectively. Since a formal concept is defined as a pair of extent X and its corresponding intent φX, we identify the concept with its extent (or its intent).
We suppose in addition a pair of monotone evaluation functions $eval_{\mathcal{O}}$ and $eval_{\mathcal{F}}$ such that $eval_{\mathcal{O}}(X_1) \leq eval_{\mathcal{O}}(X_2)$ whenever $X_1 \subseteq X_2$ and $eval_{\mathcal{F}}(A_1) \leq eval_{\mathcal{F}}(A_2)$ if $A_1 \subseteq A_2$. Their most simple forms are set sizes which we assume simply in this chapter. Another forms of *eval* can be found in (Haraguchi & Okubo, 2006) including rank information of Web pages.
Now, our problem of finding implicit concepts is described as follows:

Definition 3. (Top-N Implicit Concept Problem)
For a formal context $< \mathcal{O}, \mathcal{F}, R >$,

Objective: Enumerate every solution extent X with top N evaluation value $eval_{\mathcal{O}}(X)$, where they must be subject to the followings:

Length Constraint (required): Given $\delta > 0$, $eval_{\mathcal{F}}(\varphi X) \geq \delta$ for excluding larger X.

Space Constraints (option): X must satisfy

- **(POS)** $S^+ \subseteq X$ for an example page set S^+,
- **(NEG)** $S^- \cap X = \phi$ for a negative page set S^-, and
- **(SUB)** $X \subseteq \psi K$ for a relevant term set K. ■

5.2 Efficient Computation of Implicit Concepts

5.2.1 Basic Search Strategy

Given a formal context $\mathcal{C} =< \mathcal{O}, \mathcal{F}, \mathcal{R} >$, for each formal concept under $\mathcal{C}$, there always exists a set of objects $X \subseteq \mathcal{O}$ such that $\psi\varphi X$ and φX correspond to the extent and the intent of the concept, respectively. Therefore, by applying the mappings φ and ψ to each set of objects $X \subseteq \mathcal{O}$, we can completely obtain all of the concepts under $\mathcal{C}$.
From the monotonicity of the evaluation function $eval_{\mathcal{F}}$, a simple theoretical property can be observed. Let X_i and X_j be sets of objects in $\mathcal{O}$ such that $X_i \subseteq X_j$. Then, $eval_{\mathcal{F}}(\varphi X_i) \geq eval_{\mathcal{F}}(\varphi X_j)$. As a direct consequence, a pruning rule is available in our search. That is, for a set of objects $X \subseteq \mathcal{O}$, if $eval_{\mathcal{F}}(\varphi X) < \delta$, then there is no need to examine any superset of X. Therefore, our search for finding target concepts can be performed in *depth-first manner* with the simple pruning.
During our search, we maintain a list which stores Top-N concepts already found. That is, the list keeps *tentative* Top-N concepts. For a set of objects $X \subseteq \mathcal{O}$, we check whether $eval_{\mathcal{F}}(\varphi X) \geq \delta$ holds or not. If it holds, then $(\psi\varphi X, \varphi X)$ becomes a concept satisfying the length constraint under δ and the tentative Top-N list is adequately updated for the concept. Then a child of the extent φX, $\varphi X \cup \{x\}$, is generated by expanding the extent with an object $x \in \mathcal{O} \backslash \varphi X$ and the same procedure is recursibly performed for the child. If $eval_{\mathcal{F}}(\varphi X) < \delta$, we can immediately backtrack to examine another search branches. Starting with the initial X of the empty set, the procedure is iterated in depth-first manner until no X remains to be examined.

When common terms of Z appear as terms shared by W (that is, $\varphi Z \subseteq \varphi W$), we here say that Z *implies* W and write as $Z \to W$. Then, the extent of a concept is defined as a set X such that $X = \{x \mid X \to \{x\}\}$. That is, the extent is closed under (object) implication, and is called a *closure* (or *closed set*). Similarly, intent A of terms is similarly defined using (attribute) implication (Ganter & Wille, 1999).
The constraint (POS) is requiring $I = \{z \mid S^+ \to \{z\}\} \subseteq X$. Hence S^+ defines the starting extent I in our depth-first search. The constraint (SUB) assigns an upper bound closure ψK, and is equivalent to $K \subseteq \varphi X$ meaning that X must have every term in K which users show their interests. By (POS) and (SUB), a sublattice with I and ψK as the least and the greatest closures, respectively, is formed. When (POS) is not presented, S^+ is just the bottom extent of whole concept lattice. Similarly, we treat other constraint types in the same manner when they are not explicitly presented.

5.2.2 Dynamic Ordering in Expansion Process

Although we are allowed to restrict the search space by the constraints, it is a key to have an effective enumeration method of concepts when the optional constraints are not presented explicitly or when the data in the form of page-term relationship scales up. For this reason, we introduce a *dynamic ordering of candidates* and a search tree expansion rule customized to it.

Definition 4. (Candidate Page)
Let X be a present extent consistent with the given constraints. Then, a page $x \notin X$ is called a *candidate* at X if the enlarged extent, $\psi\varphi(X \cup \{x\}) = \{z \mid X \cup \{x\} \to \{z\}\}$, still satisfies the constraints. ∎

Some candidate z at X cannot be a candidate at $\psi\varphi(X \cup \{x\})$ if $\{w \mid X \cup \{x, z\} \to \{w\}\}$ violates the constraints. Thus the sequence of candidate sets is monotonically decreasing as we add new candidates to the closure extents.

Dynamic Candidate Ordering: For a present extent X and its candidate x, x is a branch to form the next extent. We arrange candidates x in the increasing order of the sizes of term sets $\varphi(X \cup \{x\})$. The ordering is locally fixed at each X. So we denote it as $\prec_X$.

When the candidate x is actually chosen at X, another y s.t. $X, x \to y$ is included together with x into the next closure. As x has smaller term set at X, it has more chances to imply such additional y. This helps us to form larger next closures earlier.

5.2.3 Prunings with Right and Left Candidates

Now, based on the dynamic ordering strategy, we expand our search tree. The root node is $\{z \mid S^+ \to \{z\}\}$. The procedure expands tree nodes in the depth-first manner by selecting a candidate at each node according to the dynamic ordering. The sequence of chosen candidates $c_1, ..., c_k$ represents the path from the root to the extent $\{z \mid S^+ \cup \{c_1, ..., c_k\} \to \{z\}\}$. Thus a path with S^+ is just a generator (Lakhal & Stumme, 2005) of the extent. Unlike a set enumeration tree, some control to avoid duplicated generations of the same extents is needed, as there exist several generators for the same extents. For this reason, we classify candidates into two types. One is called a *right candidate* used for expansion. The other is called a *left candidate* used for checking the duplication. Suppose we have a series of extents $X_k = \{z \mid S^+ \cup \{c_1, ..., c_k\} \to \{z\}\}$, where c_k is a chosen candidate at X_{k-1} to form X_k. That is, $X_k = \{z \mid S^+ \cup X_{k-1} \cup \{c_k\} \to \{z\}\}$. Then a candidate r at X_k is called a left candidate, given a chosen candidate c_{k+1} at X_k to form X_{k+1}, if $r \in \{c_1, \cdots, c_k\}$ or $r \prec_{X_{k+1}} c_{k+1}$.

With the help of right and left candidates, we can enjoy the following prunings in our search process.

Inverse Implication Pruning: For a present extent X and its right candidate r, if $X \cup \{r\} \rightarrow \ell$ holds for some left candidate ℓ at X, we need not take the branch by r.

Branch-and-Bound Pruning: For a present X and a right candidate r, we skip the branch by r whenever the evaluation value of $(X_r = \{w \mid X \cup \{r\} \rightarrow \{w\}\}) \cup \{\text{right candidate at } X_r\}$ by $eval_{\mathcal{O}}$ is less than the minimum of the current top N values. When the number of values stored is less than N, this rule is void.

The algorithm repeats the tree expansion on a path in a depth-first manner, using the above pruning rules, and goes back to its parent node to try another right candidate at the parent node, whenever the remaining right candidate set becomes empty.

5.3 Experimental Results

We present here our experimental results. Our system has been implemented in JAVA and run on a PC with Dual-Core AMD Opteron processor 2222 SE and 16GB main memory.

5.3.1 Dataset

In our experimentation, we have tried to extract Top-N clusters from a dataset called *BankSearch*.
The dataset *BankSearch* has been released as a benchmark for Web document clustering (Sinka & Corne, 2002). It consists of Web documents (HTML sources) in 11 categories, *"Commercial Banks"*, *"Building Societies"*, *"Insurance Agencies"*, *"Java"*, *"C/C++"*, *"Visual Basic"*, *"Astronomy"*,*"Biology"*, *"Soccer"*, *"Motor Sport"* and *"Sport"*. The total number of documents is $11,000$ ($1,000$ documents for each category).
As a preprocess, we have first converted each HTML source into a plane text by removing HTML tags. From the text documents, adjectives and adverbs in `WordNet` (Fellbaum, 1998) have been eliminated. Furthermore, we have removed a set of stopwords as well. After *Stemming Process* with Porter stemmer (Porter, 1980), we have selected $1,223$ words as feature terms by removing too frequent and too infrequent ones. That is, each document can be represented as a 1223-dimensional vector. It should be emphasized here that the category informations never appears in the documents as features explicitly.

5.3.2 Extracted Clusters

We present here some clusters we have actually extracted based on our method.
Given a Web page,

`http://www.vbsquare.com/files/association/,`

as a positive example, we have tried to find Top-3 concepts under $\delta = 50$. As an example, a concept

```
({ http://www.vbsquare.com/files/association/,
   http://www.vbsquare.com/registry/tip471.html,
   http://www.vb-helper.com/links.htm,
                ⋮
   http://www.vbsquare.com/databases/dbclass/,
   http://www.vbsquare.com/databases/learndb/,
```

`http://www.vbsquare.com/mouse/context/` },
{ `API, component, resource, ... tips, VB, graphic` })

consisting of 35-pages has been extracted. All of the pages are related to resource links, tutorials and stories on *Visual Basic*. They belong to the same category assigned in (Sinka & Corne, 2002). It should be noted here that our method never uses the information about the categories explicitly. Our clusters are extracted based on only terms appearing in Web pages. Thus, without the category information, our method can extract clusters which are consistent with the known categories.

Given two Web pages,

`http://www.citibank.com/uk/portal/consumer/helpdesk/tc/tc1.htm` and
`http://vbtechniques.com/useragreement.asp`,

and two terms, `claim` and `Internet`, as positive examples and relevant terms, respectively, we have tried to find Top-1 concepts under $\delta = 50$, then obtained a concept

```
({ http://www.citibank.com/uk/portal/
                consumer/helpdesk/tc/tc1.htm,
   http://vbtechniques.com/useragreement.asp,
   http://www.hrbs.co.uk/cashisatandcapply.htm,
                    ⋮
   http://www.hrbs.co.uk/panthertandconline.htm,
   http://www.hrbs.co.uk/rewardsixtandcapply.htm,
   http://www.lloyds.com/un/en/
                termsandconditions/category/article/ },
 { claim, Internet, accept, ...
         law, condition, reason, right, term, transfer })
```

consisting of 22-pages. These pages are concerned with contracts and terms of agreement. Furthermore, since they belong to different categories, *"Commercial Banks"*, *"Visual Basic"*, *"Building Society"* and *"Insurance Agency"*, we consider that it is a concrete example of crossover concepts actually obtained with our method.

Thus, our Top-N method has an ability to flexibly extract various concepts reflecting our interests represented as positive example and relevant terms.

5.3.3 Computational Performance

Finding Formal Concepts by Closed Itemset Miners:

As has been mentioned previously, formal concepts can be obtained by any closed itemset miner, e.g. `LCM` (Uno et al., 2004). Such a system is, however, not always helpful for finding our Top-N formal concepts satisfying some constraints. More concretely speaking, in order to find our Top-N formal concepts, a closed itemset miner must first enumerate frequent closed itemsets including our targets and then choose the targets from them. However, the miner often enumerates a huge number of frequent closed itemsets, taking long computation time.

Figure 2 shows the computation time by `LCM` and the number of frequent closed itemsets under various minimum support thresholds (*minsup*) for the *BankSearch* dataset, regarding each feature term as an item. The figure tells us that for lower *minsup* values, extracting Top-N concepts with `LCM` would be impractical from the viewpoint of its computation time

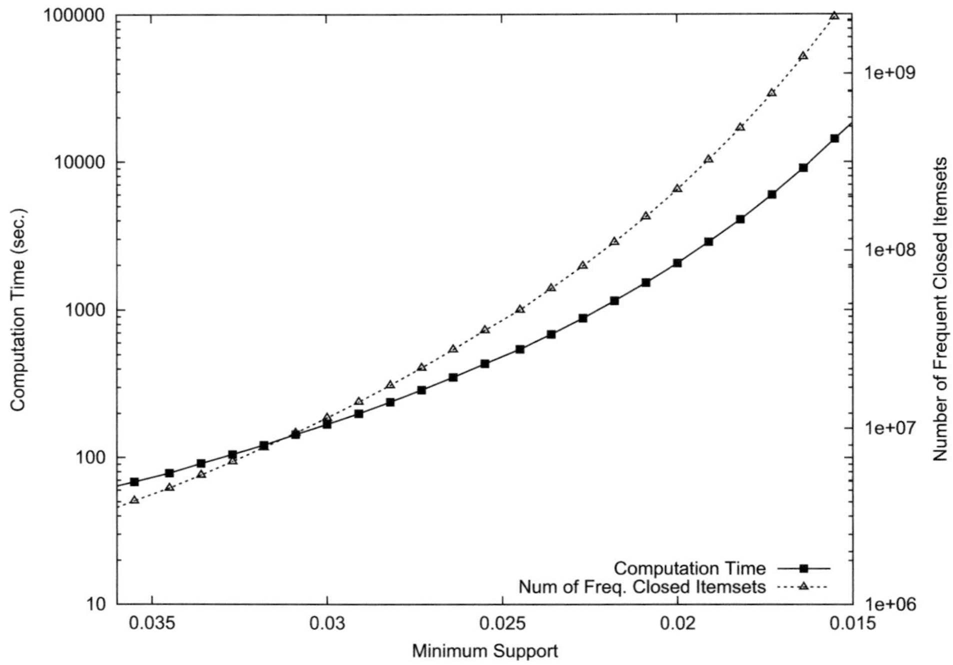

Fig. 2. Computation Time by LCM and Number of Frequent Closed Itemsets

and output size. For example, the setting of $minsup = 0.015$ forces us to extract all concepts consisting of at least 165 documents. Therefore, any smaller concepts (say, below a hundred) can never be obtained with the help of closed itemset miners in practice. More concretely speaking, the extent of each concept just presented above consists of 35-pages and 22-pages, respectively. In order to obtain the former concept with a *minsup*-based closed itemset miner like LCM, therefore, we have to set $minsup = \frac{35}{11000} = 0.003$. For the latter, $minsup = \frac{35}{11000} = 0.002$. Needless to say, our targets are out of range for which such a miner can compute. Thus, our Top-N method can extract targets actually intractable for *minsup*-based itemset miners. This is a remarkable advantage of our Top-N method.

Effectiveness of Positive Examples, Relevant Terms and Dynamic Ordering:
Since positive examples and relevant terms restrict the search space, our computational cost can be reduced. In addition, our dynamic ordering on candidate expansions also achieves improvement in computation time. For the same positive examples and relevant terms, their effectiveness is verified in Figure 3. In the figure, we can easily observe that they are quite effective in improving our computational efficiency. We can enjoy significant improvement with them. Although the positive examples can solely provide a great reduction of computation time, the relevant terms bring us further drastic improvement. Particularly, for lower δ-values, the ratio of computation time with only examples to those with both examples and relevant terms is above 100. It is highly expected that the larger our dataset becomes, the greater difference we will observe. Thus, our method would be promising even for large-scale datasets.

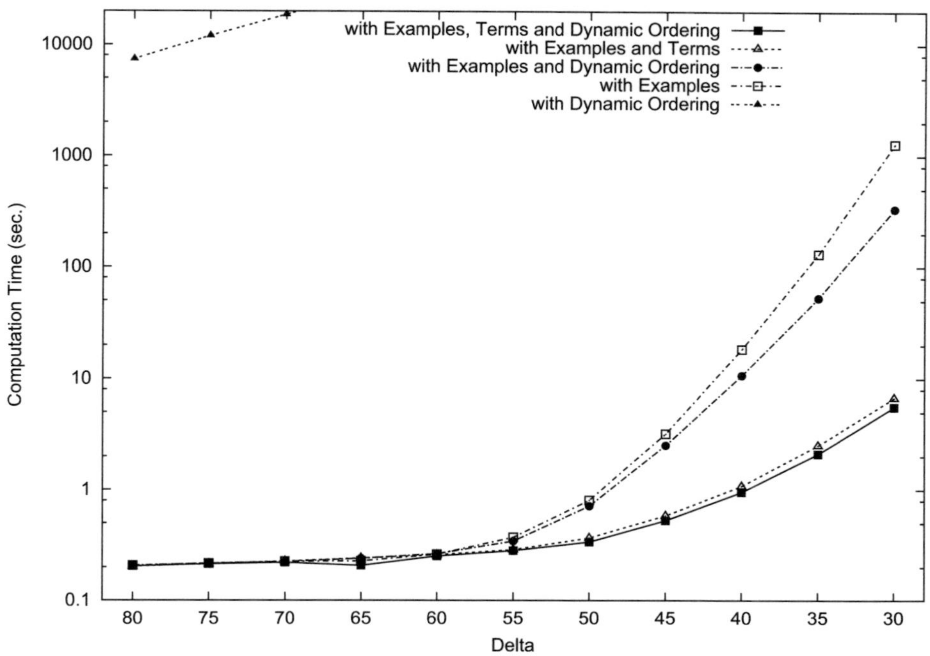

Fig. 3. Computation Time with Positive Examples, Relevant Terms and Dynamic Ordering

6. Conclusion

In this chapter, we presented our Top-N methods for extracting clusters of Web pages, especially, a method for pinpoint clustering of Web pages by pseudo-clique search and a method for finding implicit page groups represented as formal concepts.

In our pinpoint clustering, we first extract semantic correlations among terms by applying SVD to the term-document matrix generated from a corpus w.r.t. a specific topic. Based on the correlations, we can evaluate potential similarities among Web pages from which we try to obtain clusters. The set of Web pages is represented as a weighted graph G based on the similarities and their ranks. Then our clusters are extracted as *pseudo-cliques* in G. Our experimental results showed that a valuable cluster can be actually extracted according to our method.

Turning our attention from clique-based clusters to formal concept-based clusters in order to make our clusters more meaningful, we discussed an effective depth-first mining algorithm for finding relatively smaller therefore more implicit groups of Web pages as formal concepts. The algorithm is based on a dynamic ordering method depending on each search node and some search tree expansion rules. Moreover it was designed so as to find Top-N implicit concepts subject to the size restriction and some space constraints reflecting user's interests. Our experimental results showed that our Top-N algorithm succeeds in finding less frequent (crossover) concepts under some space constraints.

In order to have more effective method under more vague constraints, we are planning to define the notion of crossover concepts more directly and to design more efficient and accurate procedure under the help of clustering of pages allowing outliers (Gan et al., 2007).

7. References

Bastide, Y.; Pasquier, N.; Taouil, R.; Stumme, G. & Lakhal, L. (2000). Mining Minimal Non-Redundant Association Rules Using Frequent Closed Itemsets, *Proceedings of the 1st International Conference on Computational Logic - CL'00*, LNCS 1861, pp. 972–986, ISBN 3540677976, London, U. K., July, 2000, Springer, Berlin.

Bayardo Jr., R. J. (1998). Efficiently Mining Long Patterns from Databases, *Proceedings of the 1998 ACM SIGMOD International Conference on Management of Data*, pp. 85–93, ISBN 0-89791-995-5, Washington, D. C., U. S. A., June, 1998, ACM Press, New York.

Burdick, D.; Calimlim, M. & Gehrke, J. (2001). MAFIA: A Maximal Frequent Itemset Algorithm for Transactional Databases, *Proceedings of the 17th International Conference on Data Engineering - ICDE'01*, pp. 443–452, ISBN 0-7695-1001-9, Heidelberg, Germany, April, 2001, IEEE Computer Society Press, Washington, D. C.

Boulicaut, J. & Jeudy, B. (2005). Constraint-Based Data Mining, *The Data Mining and Knowledge Discovery Handbook 2005*, pp. 399–416, Springer, ISBN 978-0387244358, Berlin.

Fahle, T. (2002). Simple and Fast: Improving a Branch-and-Bound Algorithm for Maximum Clique, *Proceedings of the 10th European Symposium on Algorithms - ESA'02*, pp. 485 – 498, LNCS 2461, ISBN 978-3540441809, Rome, Italy, September, 2002, Springer, Berlin.

Fellbaum, C. (1998). *WordNet - An Electronic Lexical Database*, Fellbaum, C. (Ed.), The MIT Press, ISBN 978-0262061971, Cambridge.

Gan, G.; Ma, C. & Wu J. (2007). *Data Clustering – Theory, Algorithms, and Applications*, SIAM, ISBN 978-0898716238, Philadelphia.

Ganter, B. & Wille, R. (1999). *Formal Concept Analysis - Mathematical Foundations*, Springer, ISBN 978-3540627715, Berlin.

Ganter, B.; Stumme, G. & Wille, R. (2005). *Formal Concept Analysis – Foundations and Applications*, Ganter, B., Stumme, G. and Wille, R. (Eds.), LNAI 3626, Springer, ISBN 978-3540278917, Berlin.

Han, J.; Cheng, H.; Xin, D. & Yan, X. (2007). Frequent pattern mining - current status and future directions, *Data Mining and Knowledge Discovery*, Vol. 15, No. 1, pp. 55–86, ISSN 1384-5810.

Haraguchi, M. & Okubo, Y. (2007). An Extended Branch-and-Bound Search Algorithm for Finding Top-*N* Formal Concepts of Documents, *New Frontiers in Artificial Intelligence*, JSAI 2006 Conference and Workshops, Tokyo, Japan, June 5-9, 2006, Revised Selected Papers, pp. 276 – 288, LNCS 4384, Springer, ISBN 978-3540699019, Berlin.

Haraguchi, M. & Okubo, Y. (2006). A Method for Pinpoint Clustering of Web Pages with Pseudo-Clique Search, *Federation over the Web*, International Workshop, Dagstuhl Castle, Germany, May 1 - 6, 2005, Revised Selected Papers, pp. 59 – 78, LNAI 3847, Springer, ISBN 978-3540310181, Berlin.

Haraguchi, M. (2002). Concept Learning Based on Optimal Clique Searches, *JSAI SIG Report*, pp. 63 – 66, SIG-FAI-A202-11, Fukuoka, Japan, December, 2002, JSAI, Tokyo (in Japanese).

Hotho, A.; Staab, S. & Stumme, G. (2003). Explaining Text Clustering Results Using Semantic Structures, *Proceedings of the 7th European Conference on Principles of Data Mining and*

Knowledge Discovery - PKDD'03, pp. 22 – 26, LNAI 2838, ISBN 3-540-20085-1, Cavtat-Dubrovnik, Croatia, September, 2003, Springer, Berlin.

Hotho, A. & Stumme, G. (2002). Conceptual Clustering of Text Clusters, *Proceedings of the Machine Learning Workshop - FGML'02*, pp. 37 – 45, Hannover, SIG of German Informatics Society.

Kowalski, G. J. & Maybury, M. T. (2000). *Information Storage and Retrieval Systems: Theory and Implementation (Second Edition)*, Kluwer Academic Publishers, ISBN 978-0792379249, Dordrecht.

Lakhal, L. & Stumme, G. (2005). Efficient mining of association rules based on formal concept analysis, *Formal Concept Analysis – Foundations and Applications*, Ganter, B., Stumme, G. and Wille, R. (Eds.), pp. 180–195, LNAI 3626, Springer, ISBN 978-3540278917, Berlin.

Li, A.; Haraguchi, M. & Okubo, Y. (2008). Implicit Groups of Web Pages as Constrained Top-*N* Concepts, *Proceeding of the 2008 IEEE/WIC/ACM International Conference on Web Intelligence and Intelligent Agent Technology Workshops*, pp. 190 – 194, Sydney, Australia, December, 2008, IEEE Computer Society Press, Washington, D. C.

Moens, M-F. (2000). *Automatic Indexing and Abstracting of Document Texts*, Kluwer Academic Publishers, ISBN 978-0792377931, Dordrecht.

Murata, T. (2003). Discovery of Web Communities from Positive and Negative Examples, *Proceedings of the 6th International Conference on Discovery Science - DS'03*, LNAI 2843, pp. 369 – 376, ISBN 978-3540202936, Sapporo, Japan, October, 2003, Springer, Berlin.

Murata, T. (2000). Discovery of Web Communities based on the Co-Occurrence of Reference, *Proceedings of the 3rd International Conference on Discovery Science - DS'00*, LNCS 1967, pp. 65 – 75, ISBN 978-3540413523, Kyoto, Japan, December, 2000, Springer, Berlin.

Okubo, Y. & Haraguchi, M. (2006). Finding Conceptual Document Clusters with Improved Top-N Formal Concept Search, *Proceedings of the 2006 IEEE/WIC/ACM International Conference on Web Intelligence - WI'06*, pp. 347 – 351, ISBN 0-7695-2747-7, Hong Kong, China, December, 2006, IEEE Computer Society Press, Washington, D. C.

Okubo, Y.; Haraguchi, M. & Shi, B. (2005). Finding Significant Web Pages with Lower Ranks by Pseudo-Clique Search, *Proceedings of the 8th International Conference on Discovery Science - DS'05*, pp. 346 – 353, LNAI 3735, ISBN 978-3540292302, Singapore, October, 2005, Springer, Berlin.

Page, L.; Brin, S.; Motwani, R. & Winograd, T. (1999). *The PageRank Citation Ranking: Bringing Order to the Web*, http://dbpubs.stanford.edu/pub/1999-66.

Porter, M. F. (1980). An Algorithm for Suffix Stripping, *Program: Electronic Library and Information Systems*, Vol. 14, No. 3, pp. 130 – 137, ISSN 0033-0337.

Salton, G. & McGill, M. J. (1983). *Introduction to Modern Information Retrieval*, Mcgraw-Hill College, ISBN 978-0070544840, Boston.

Sinka, M. P. & Corne, D. W. (2002). A Large Benchmark Dataset for Web Document Clustering, *Soft Computing Systems: Design, Management and Applications*, Series of Frontiers in Artificial Intelligence and Applications, Vol. 87, pp. 881 – 890, `http://www.pedal.reading.ac.uk/banksearchdataset/`, ISBN 978-1586032975.

Strang, G. (2003). *Introduction to Linear Algebra*, 3rd Edition, Wellesley-Cambridge Press, ISBN 978-0961408893, Massachusetts.

Tomita, E. & Seki, T. (2007). An Efficient Branch-and-Bound Algorithm for Finding a Maximum Clique with Computational Experiments, *Journal of Global Optimization*, Vol. 37, No. 1, pp. 95 – 111, ISSN 0925-5001.

Uno, T; Kiyomi, M. & Arimura, H. (2004). LCM ver. 2: Efficient Mining Algorithm for Frequent/Closed/Maximal Itemsets, *Proceedings of IEEE ICDM'04 Workshop on Frequent Itemset Mining Implementations - FIMI'04*, http://ftp.informatik.rwth-aachen.de/Publications/CEUR-WS/Vol-126/.

Wang, J.; Han, J. & Pei, P. (2003). CLOSET+: Searching for the Best Strategies for Mining Frequent Closed Itemsets, *Proceedings of the 9th ACM SIGKDD International Conference on Knowledge Discovery and Data Mining - KDD'03*, pp. 236 – 245, ISBN 978-1581137378, Washington, D. C., U. S. A., August, 2003, ACM Press, New York.

Zhang, Y.; Yu, J. & Hou, J. (2006). *Web Communities - Analysis and Construction*, Springer, ISBN 978-3540277378, Berlin.

Zhu, F,; Yan, X.; Han, H.; Yu, P. S. & Cheng, H. (2007). Mining Colossal Frequent Patterns by Core Pattern Fusion, *Proceedings of the 23rd International Conference on Data Engineering - ICDE'07*, pp. 706 – 715, ISBN 1-4244-0803-2, Istanbul, Turkey, April, 2007, IEEE Computer Society Press, Washingon, D. C.

20

Intelligent Agents for Automatic Service Composition in Ambient Intelligence

Maria J. Santofimia, Francisco Moya, Felix J. Villanueva,
David Villa and Juan C. Lopez
Universidad de Castilla-La Mancha
Spain

1. Introduction

The Ubiquitous Computing concept was first defined by Mark Weiser in (Weiser, 1995), referring to a new computing era where electronic devices merge with the background, becoming invisible, in such a way that people could make use of those devices in an unconsciously way, focusing just on their needs and not in the interaction.

One decade later, the IST Advisory Group first states the concept of Ambient Intelligence (Ducatel et al., 2001), which lying on the ubiquitous computing paradigm, refers to those environments where people are surrounded by all kind of intelligent intuitive devices, capable of recognising and responding to their changing needs. In these contexts, people perceive the surrounding as a service provider that satisfies their needs or inquiries in a seamless, unobtrusive, and invisible way.

These computing paradigms set a frame of reference, characterised by being mainly concentrated on releasing mechanisms that gather information about users, match behavioural patterns, or predict user actions, requirements and needs (Costa et al., 2007) (Cugola & Picco, 2006) (Issarny et al., 2005) (Prete & Capra, 2008). Nevertheless, the Ambient Intelligence paradigm is meant to consider users as constituent parts of the context, although in most solutions presented to date, users are considered in isolation. In this regard, extending the user-centered view, in order to encompass the context services and purposes, arises as key requirements for systems in Ambient Intelligence.

It soon becomes apparent the need for a multidisciplinary approach capable of addressing all the emerging challenges. One of these fields is concerned with the communication support. The heterogeneity of the context devices, as well as their dinamism, impose high demands upon the middleware platform, that it is now responsible for abstracting the technological peculiarities. It is then possible to provide a common and well-known set of communication interfaces. These interfaces are described in terms of a semantic model, that can be easily shared and translated into different languages, so that in can be used by the rest of involved technologies (intelligent agents and reasoning engine). Finally, and probably the most important part of the provided solution, refers to the context-awareness, in charge of understanding the context. This requires some approach that resembles human behaviour in regard to its ability to deal with information of an imprecise nature, ambiguous, and of a questionable retrievability, but also capable of making decisions based on this partial information. To this

end, involving intelligent agents, seems to be an effective approach when resembling human behaviours.
Accordingly, this work presents a comprehensive approach towards Ambient Intelligence, making special emphasis on the role played by the intelligent agents, as the key element orchestrating the overall solution.

2. Background Information

This section basically describes the background information behind the combined proposal presented here as an approach towards Ambient Intelligence.

2.1 Service Oriented Architecture

The service concept, regarding the Service-Oriented paradigm, is coupled to whatever the resource (distributed object, agents, or basic web services, for example), in such a way that one service is created for each available resource. This paradigm identifies two types of services: the basic and composite ones. The former are the services directly offered by devices, while the later are composed of basic service aggregations, which result in more complex services.
Service-Oriented Architectures (SOAs) support the development of highly adaptable systems, capable of adding, removing and replacing the constituent services of the system. Commercial standards developed with this purpose in mind already exist, such as Web Services. However, despite the achieved success , composition is currently a subject of study for ongoing research and is still far from a mature stage.
Most of the Service Oriented Architecture (SOA) systems for Ambient Intelligence simply pursue the system reconfigurability or adaptability, placing the responsibility to do this on the middleware framework. Obviously, these systems cannot take decisions out of the prefixed behaviours, set beforehand, neither can they tackle unforeseen circumstances, requirements and needs. Therefore, instead of trying to describe the responses to all the likely scenarios, it is more effective to enumerate the main goals that the system has to achieve or maintain, along with the basic mechanisms available to this end. The service composition paradigm provides the foundations for generating new services that fulfill new needs or requirements. However, in the context of Ambient Intelligence, this task should be automatically accomplished, relieving the user from dictating the basic services involved in the composition.

2.2 Approaches towards Automatic Service Composition

The most relevant approaches intended to provided systems for Ambient Intelligence with the capability to automatically compose services are described underneath:

- Configuration files: The first attempt to provide some sort of dynamism was based on the adaption concept. This proposal was intended to provide architectures with adaption capabilities by means of configuration files. These architectures counted on some features that could be customised in order to select the components loaded at startup time. This approach allows a limited level of dynamism, far from what an adaptive middleware should be, since the main features are placed at the middleware kernel and could not be changed. Therefore, rather than adaptive middlewares they should be considered customisable middlewares, supporting just a fixed group of cases.
- Reflection: As a second attempt, after the use of configuration files, reflectiveness appeared as the solution to add some dynamism support to middlewares. This proposal advocates for a middleware core with a minimal set of services installed in devices.

By means of reflective mechanims, applications can obtain from the middleware the context information, and use it to tune the middleware behaviour.

- Reflection and metadata: The next stage in this evolution is based on the combination of reflection and metadata, aimed at developing adaptive and context-aware applications. This approach is mainly based on policies, that is, the use of a set of primitives aimed at describing how the context might change and how these changes are to be treated. Since conflicts among policies may arise, a solution based on a micro-economic approach was proposed in order to handle this conflicts.
- Externalization: Although reflective middleware services do support configurability, by supporting replacement and assembly of components in reaction to changes, the reality was that most of them assumed a basic backbone of fixed services. The externalization approach advocates for a middleware architecture that explicitly externalises the state, the logic, and the internal structure of middleware services, in such a way that the system can be updated, upgraded, or changes its configuration without requiring user intervention.
- Policies: This approach proposes the use of profiles, where the associations between services and policies applied to these services are described. Profiles are passed down to the middleware, and whenever a service is invoked, the middleware consults the profiles of the application that requests it. The profile determines which policy can be applied in the current context, depending on the state of the requested resource, thus relieving the application from performing these steps.
- Web Services: Among all these different approaches towards service composition, Web Services have been by far the most popular. This XML-based approach allows the specification of web services that can be dynamically loaded according to the requests. A service is specified by means of a service abstract interface and the non-functional properties associated with the service. This approach provides a set of Service Repositories containing information about local and remote service repositories.
- Ontologies: Finally, it has to be pointed out that nowadays, the use of ontologies is gaining great attention. Among all the ongoing proposals on these field, domain ontologies is one of the most relevant, and is intended to model the domain knowledge and provide semantics to service description. The capability to express semantic relations among services is quite useful in guiding the composition process.

2.3 Intelligent Agents

The motivation behind the use of an agent-based approach is founded on the possibility to describe agents as goal-oriented entities, on the basis of the BDI model presented in (Bratman, 1987), and developed in (Rao & Georgeff, 1991) as an approach to model rational agents, using three basic mental attitudes, such as beliefs, desires and intentions.

Nonetheless, different approaches to implement the intelligent agents can be found in literature (Wooldridge, 2000): Logic based architectures (deductive agents), reactive architecture (reactive agents), layered architectures (hybrid agents), and practical reasoning architectures (the aforementioned Belief-Desire-Intention agents). Among these alternatives, the Belief-Desire-Intention model (BDI) has proved to be a powerful framework for building rational agents.

The BDI model of decision making is intended to reproduce the process carried out when people make decisions in order to achieve a certain goal. The main characteristic of the BDI

model lies on the significance conceded to beliefs, desires, and intentions involved in rational actions. Therefore, those systems that grant importance to these attitudes over any other, are often referred to as BDI-architectures. Beliefs are the information agents hold about the world, which is not necessarily accurate. This information might change as a result of new perceptions or the execution of intentions. Desires or goals refer to those tasks that, in an ideal world, the agent would like to accomplish. Intentions are those desires that agents are committed to accomplish.
The Jadex framework (Pokahr et al., 2005) provides an agent-oriented reasoning engine that also supports the development of rational agents. In spite of using formal logic descriptions, Jadex proposes the use of two commonly known languages, such as Java and XML. The BDI agent is modeled by mapping the concepts of beliefs into Java objects, while desires and intentions are mapped into procedural recipes coded in Java that the agent carries out in order to achieve a goal.

3. The Architecture Foundations

Having an accurate semantic model seems essential for an architecture intended to support Ambient Intelligence contexts. This semantic model is shared with the agent-based platform and the reasoning system, supporting cooperation among them. Figure 1 depicts the overview of the proposed solution to support Ambient Intelligence contexts. The different technologies proposed are intended to tackled the challenges arising in such contexts. Therefore, the middleware module is in charge of managing the services deployed in the context, basically by supporting the communication with the services. Furthermore, the intelligent agents interact with the environment, not only by gathering information but also by accomplishing actions by means of actuators. Furthermore, in order to be context-aware, the role played by the reason-

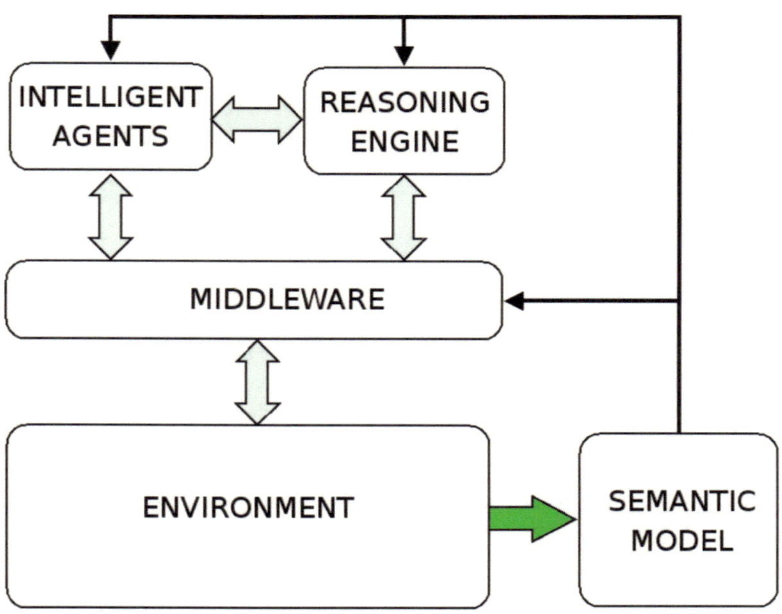

Fig. 1. A comprehensive view of the propose architecture.

ing engine fulfills this purpose by reasoning about the information gathered by the intelligent agents.
However, these three modules need to be connected in order to cooperate towards supporting the Ambient Intelligence contexts. To this end, the semantic model supposes this linking element, that is common to all the modules of the architecture and provides a way of communicate them.

3.1 The semantic model for Ambient Intelligence

Ambient Intelligent contexts are characterised for being highly dynamic and heterogeneous in terms of provided services, existing users and devices. In such scenarios it is hard to accomplish a thorough description of the context information and pretend it to be up to date along the time. For such reason, it is preferable to provide the architecture with the capability to describe the context on the basis of a semantic model injecting meaning to the context information.
Once the importance of an accurate semantic model has been stated, next step consists of selecting the right approach to undertake the model description, and among the many different approaches (Strang, 2004), ontologies are a widely accepted technique to accomplish semantic descriptions, in terms of the relevant entities of the domain and the relationships established among them. There exist several formalisms for representing ontologies, however, the Web Ontology Language (OWL), (encoded as a RDF/XML) is widely used and supported with tools such as Protégé (BMIR, 2009) that simplifies the tedious task of describing an ontological model.
Nevertheless, the graphical models that can be derived from the ontology, using Protégé or any other tool, are commonly poor, and relationship others than "is-a" are hard to catch at a glance. Considering that ontologies simply state entities and relationships among entities, resort to the Entity-Relationship (E-R) diagram seems to provide a more understandable graphical representation, as it can be seen in figure 2.
The semantic model here presented has been intentionally designed to support automatic service composition, and for this reason, services are semantically described by means of specifications, which at the same time are made of properties. These specifications, as it will be explained later, are intended to support the reasoning process that leads the service composition. Furthermore, this semantic model also describes services in terms of the actions the service performs, and the object over which such actions are accomplished. Each action is performed on an object, therefore, services are described as a set of actions performed over certain objects. For instance, an authentication service, performs the action of authenticate over the object of domain user type.
The benefits of using such a semantic model, rather than a simple service taxonomy, as the one provided by UpnP, for instance, lays in the fact that taxonomies do not consider relationships others than "`has a`" or "`is a`". On the contrary, the proposal stated by the AMIGO project, using a declarative language for semantic service specification, accomplish a thorough description of the context and all the elements and services involved in it. However, the semantic model provided, for being so specific, does not suffice to support automatic service composition, but a simple service aggregation, that is, there is no new functionality inferred from existing services.
The main strength of the semantic model, here proposed, lays in its simplicity. This simplicity eases the process of semantically describe any element of the context, without missing any detail. Furthermore, in order to not to miss these details, the `specification` concept is in-

troduced to the model, which encompass all the particularities of services, objects, and devices of an specific domain, adopting the shape of properties.

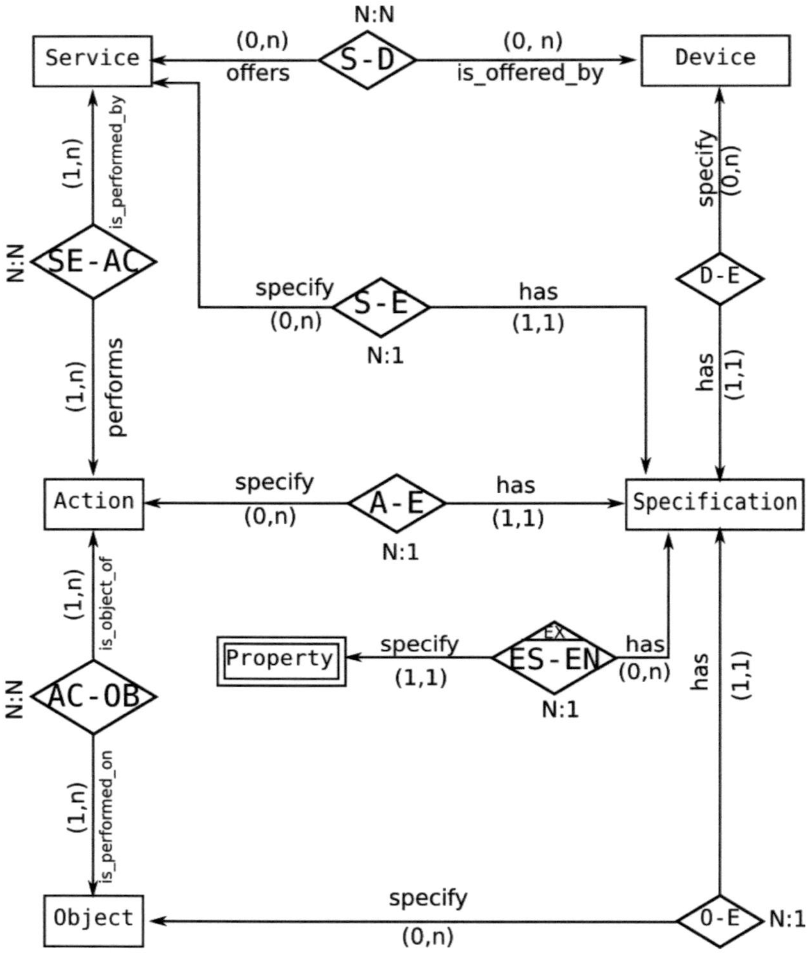

Fig. 2. Entity-Relationship Model for an Ambient Intelligent system.

3.2 The Middleware framework

The role played by the middleware architecture is essential in simplifying and abstracting the complexity and heterogeneity of both, network and device technologies. However, middlewares for traditional environments made some simple assumptions, such as high bandwidth, reliable connectivity, fixed network topology or hardware capabilities, that do not correspond themselves to the reality of an Ambient Intelligence environment.

Middlewares deployed in Ambient Intelligence contexts are used to deal with data generally based on physical parameters, such as temperature, distance, or position. Most of the times, this information is retrieved from sensors, located all along the environment, connected by means of Wireless Sensor Networks (WSN). These sensors are usually hidden so as to keep users unaware of their presence. At the same time, many heterogeneous devices might act as consumers of this data, such as X10 or EIB, or some others for multimedia support such as HAVi or MHP. Moreover, it is a middleware role to provide common services such as a basic service discovery, event management, resource management, etc. All these requirements, imposed by the Ambient Intelligence context peculiarities, demand a fully equipped middleware framework capable of integrating heterogeneous devices in a transparent way, and transmit them the adopted semantic model as a way of homogenising the interaction with these services and devices.

This work proposes a combination of intelligent agents and a reasoning engine in order to handle the dynamism, ambiguity, and uncertainty of Ambient Intelligence. It should be noticed that the middleware framework is an essential component of the system, since it provides the groundings for the intelligent agents.

Therefore, from a layered perspective, the architecture proposed here rests on top of a powerful middleware framework, that provides the upper layers with the structure, tools and services required to successfully accomplish their tasks. A deep description of the middleware framework details is out of the scope of this work, nonetheless, the most relevant issues are detailed underneath.

This middleware framework, known as DOBS (Distributed Object Based Services), takes the form of distributed object based services. Figure 3 depicts the key components and services of the framework at the core of its great potential.

The **DOBS interfaces** basically standardise the way how services are modelled and con-

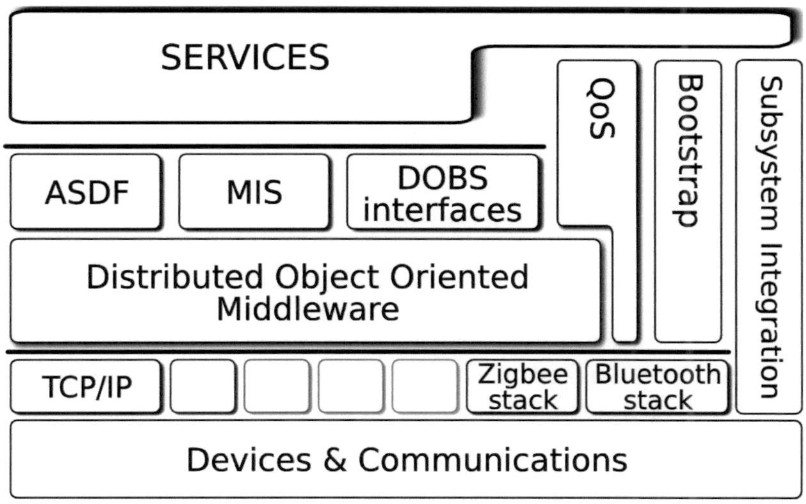

Fig. 3. DOBS framework overview.

trolled. The fact that these interfaces are derived from the semantic model makes them well known and common to all services and modules of the considered architecture. Therefore, it simplifies the way how services are accessed and controlled.

Apart from a common set of interfaces the middleware framework also provides a set of commonly used functionalities, such as the *service discovery, bootstrap service, security mechanisms,* and so forth. **Integration subsystems** work as technological bridges, allowing a seamless integration of services from different technologies. So far, subsystems for UPnP, X10, and Bluetooth service integration are currently available.

Finally, the **model information system (MIS)**, based on the aforementioned semantic model, is intended to provided a common nomenclature to services that eases the understanding and reasoning task carried out in the upper layers.

4. Intelligent Agents Supporting Automated Service Composition

The underlying idea behind the work here described, is to provide the appropriate combination of technologies and the right semantic model, capable of allowing systems for Ambient Intelligence contexts to exhibit an autonomous behaviour, driven by a set of objectives that are to be achieved, satisfied, or maintained. Furthermore, these systems are also expected to be proactive and to foresee curses of actions that lead them to the expected situations or objectives. If necessary, these systems resort to other systems, also deployed in the context, establishing a collaboration or cooperation pattern that leads to the final objectives.

In the seeking of the best approach to satisfy these requirements, an agent-based solution turns out to be the most compelling mean to this end. The motivation behind this choice is twofold. Firstly, given the service oriented character of the middleware framework, the agent-based approach can be easily fit into the framework, adopting the shape of yet another middleware service. Secondly, autonomy and pro-activity features are inherent to agents. In addition to this, the BDI model of agency provides the goal-oriented character, required by the architecture here proposed. However, an agent based approach needs to be enacted with some other low level capabilities, that provides the agent system with a transparent way of communicating with other elements of the context, and controlling the sensors and actuators of the context, as well as an homogeneous access method to all the services deployed in the context. These are too specific capabilities that are generally overlooked by agent frameworks, that delegate the responsibility of providing such capabilities to the middleware framework. Entrusting these low level capabilities to the middleware layer, allows the multi-agent system to remain unaware of the implementation details, giving rise to a modular design.

Nevertheless, the middleware platform does not suffice to cope with the uncertainty, ambiguity, and imprecision of the context information managed by Ambient Intelligence systems. These features state a new demand, as it is the understanding of what is happening in the context, so that this contextual information can be enclosed and get rid of the ambiguity. In this regard, a reasoning engine is revealed as the key element of the overall architecture, since it makes use of the information gathered and endows it with the semantic meaning that supports the reasoning process. Among the many different approaches supporting the reasoning process, for its simplicity and easy integration, this work resorts to a rule-based reasoning engine, known as CLIPS.

The following subsections undertake a thorough description of the agent layer, and the role it plays in the overall architecture. Some implementations details are offered so as to understand how the combination of the multi-agent system, the middleware layer, and the reasoning engine manage to deal with the arisen requirements of an Ambient Intelligence context.

4.1 The Multi-Agent Service Composer System (MASCS)

The proposed multi-agent system solution consists of three intelligent agents: the *Manager*, the *Retriever*, and the *Actor*, described in terms of their beliefs, desires and intentions, as BDI agents. However, since a JADEX implementation is used, this information is translated into beliefs, plans and goals, proper for each application context.

The *Manager* agent plays the role of the context supervisor, and to this end, it strongly depends

on interactions with the middleware platform, so as to communicate with services in a transparent way. The sort of interactions established with the middleware platform are mainly based on an event channel approach.
Services are characterised by the sort of *interface* they implement. Basically, services can be *active services* when they publish their state whenever a change occurs. Sensor services are a good example of active services. The other type of services are the *reactive services* which are capable of answering to the requests published in an event channel. Therefore, considering that services are univocally identified by means of the proxy concept (ZeroC, 2008), and the fact that knowing the implemented interface supposes an univocal way of identifying the methods that can be invoked over the services.
The manager agent is also committed to assure a minimum level of system functionality, overcoming the lack of services, service failures or disappearance. In this endeavour, the manager agent has a set of context goals that are to be maintained or achieved. Whenever the context conditions fail to fulfil the ideal state, the manager agent gets engaged on returning to the *ideal* state. First step consists of launching the *Retriever* and the *Actor* agent, that get noticed of the cause that lead to this undesirable situation.
The retriever agent is basically in charge of gathering the appropriate context information, used in the reasoning process. Therefore, the semantic model and the context information have to be translated into rules, although the difference between using a XML language or the CLIPS language is minimum. Finally, the context objectives or intentions are expressed as rules, stating a set of actions, that according to the current state are capable of leading the context to the envisage state.
The selected actions are carried out by the *Actor* agent, which is in charge of translating into method invocations the semantic action inferred by the rule-based reasoning engine.
Sometimes the inferred semantic actions involve some sort of composition, since there are no basic services capable of providing such functionality. Therefore, when a service composition is required in order to perform the inferred semantic action, the actor agents takes the role of a *planner*, and using an approach based on the hierarchical task network (HTN)(Amigoni et al., 2005), it manages to generate a plan that leads to the composite service. The plan is composed of basic actions that are to be performed over specific objects.

4.2 Integration of the Reasoning Engine

The domain specific knowledge also needs to be provided to the architecture so as to capture the peculiarities of the different contexts where the architecture can work. Once again this knowledge needs to be translated into OWL and combined with the semantic model describing the architecture. Despite its great relevance, this knowledge does not suffice to support the reasoning and inference task on itself, since the reasoning capabilities of the intelligent agents are mainly constrained to their plans and goals, having to resort to an external reasoning engine to achieve broader reasoning capabilities.
Among the different approaches supporting the reasoning task, such as those based on domain logic, ontologies, or declarative languages, an approach based on the combination of a semantic model and a rule-based system that adopt the same semantic model, largely bears the context reasoning and understanding demanded by the composition task. Provided with this knowledge, a rule-based reasoning engine holds enough information to understand the capabilities of the services, as well as to infer new capabilities out of the raw ones.
The ontology classes are mapped into CLIPS classes, while the relationships of the semantic

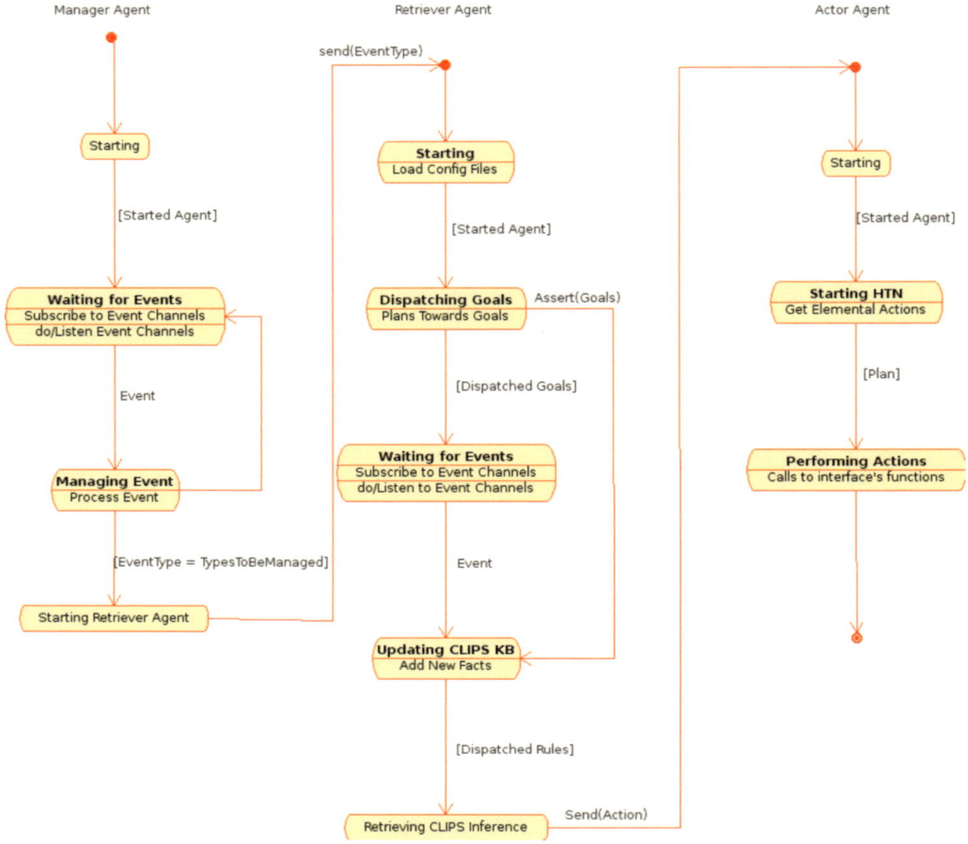

Fig. 4. State Diagram for the Multi-Agent System

model are managed as properties in the ontology, and slots of the CLIPS classes. For instance, the following listing confronts the OWL and the CLIPS definitions for the *action* entity.

Listing 1. OWL code for the *action* class

```
<owl:Class rdf:about="#Action">
    <rdfs:subClassOf rdf:resource="http://www.w3.org/2002/07/owl#Thing"/>
    <rdfs:subClassOf>
      <owl:Restriction>
        <owl:someValuesFrom rdf:resource="#Specification"/>
        <owl:onProperty>
          <owl:ObjectProperty rdf:about="#has-a-specification"/>
        </owl:onProperty>
      </owl:Restriction>
    </rdfs:subClassOf>
```

```
      <rdfs:subClassOf>
        <owl:Restriction>
          <owl:someValuesFrom rdf:resource="#Object"/>
          <owl:onProperty>
            <owl:ObjectProperty rdf:ID="action-is-performed-on-object"/>
          </owl:onProperty>
        </owl:Restriction>
      </rdfs:subClassOf>
      <rdfs:subClassOf>
        <owl:Restriction>
          <owl:onProperty>
            <owl:ObjectProperty rdf:about="#is-part-of-service"/>
          </owl:onProperty>
          <owl:someValuesFrom rdf:resource="#Service"/>
        </owl:Restriction>
      </rdfs:subClassOf>
    </owl:Class>
```

Listing 2. CLIPS code for the *action* class

```
        (defclass ACTION
          (is-a USER)
          ;(create-accessor write)
          (slot ID
                  (type SYMBOL)
                  (allowed-symbols action-$?))
          (slot has-a-specification
                  (allowed-symbols specification-$?)
                  (default ?NONE))
          (multislot action-is-performed-on-object
                  (allowed-symbols object-$?)
                  (default ?NONE))
          (multislot is-part-of-service
                  (allowed-symbols service-$?)
                  (default ?NONE)))
```

The Protégé tool provides an utility to automatically generates the CLIPS code out of the RDF/XML ontology description, what simplifies the migration of the semantic model to the reasoning engine.
Regarding the implementation details, CLIPS provides an extensive API in C language. Nevertheless, it is easily used from the agents plans, written in Java, thanks to the Java Native Interface framework, also provided by CLIPS. Therefore, the integration of the reasoning system with the intelligent agent platform is almost straightforward, and can be reduced to call to the API functions.

5. A case study

Surveillance contexts are one of those fields where Ambient Intelligence systems can be of great help. Nevertheless, this is far from being a reality, and at the moment, these systems require human supervision when making important decisions or when wise reactions are expected from them. An ideal Ambient Intelligence system, instead of being constrained to a

fixed set of possible reactions, it is supposed to actively anticipate and make decisions under whatever the circumstances. This section draws on a simplified case study for depicting the important advances that could be achieved by implementing the proposal here presented.
The surveillance context considered for this case study is constrained to a building. It counts on several devices, such as cameras, presence, noise and light sensors, among some. These devices are placed all around the building, with the intention of supervising the activity of the critical areas. This case study considers a restricted access corridor, where an alarm arises as a result of an unauthorised presence. Along this corridor, three presence sensors can be encountered, as well as two cameras focusing the entrance of the rooms, located at the two ends of the corridor.
Founded on figure 4 that describes the state diagram for the multi-agent system, the first step accomplished by the manager agent, once started, consists on subscribing to certain event channels, where services publish their state and answer to requests. This is to say that, when the presence sensor changes its state to *activated*, as result of a person breaking into a restricted access area, the sensor service sends a message to the event channel, publishing its new state. This message is then received by the manager agent, that interprets this message as an *unauthorised presence alarm*, and gets into the state of dealing with an *unauthorised presence state*. The manager starts and notifies the retriever agent, which afterwards establishes the new context objectives, as well as the plans to achieve them, as it can be seen in the following code, relating to the retriever agent description, using the JADEX nomenclature.

Listing 3. Some of the most relevant goals and plans for the *Retriever* agent

```

  <!--
      ********************************
      ******** List of goals **********
      ********************************
    -->

    <!-- O1. Find out the intrusion intention -->
    <achievegoal name="discover_intentions">
      <creationcondition>$beliefbase.event.isTYPEUNAUTHORISEDPRESENCE()<
          /creationcondition>
      <contextcondition>$beliefbase.intruders.isSTATEONRUNNING()</
          contextcondition>
      <targetcondition>$beliefbase.intruders.getIntruderHasAimObjective
          ()!=null</targetcondition>
    </achievegoal>

    <!-- O2. Intruder identification -->
    <achievegoal name="intruder_identification">
      <creationcondition>$beliefbase.event.isTYPEUNAUTHORISEDPRESENCE()<
          /creationcondition>
      <contextcondition>$beliefbase.intruders.getIdentification.equals(
          null)</contextcondition>
      <targetcondition>$beliefbase.intruders.getIdentification()!=null</
          targetcondition>
    </achievegoal>

    <!-- O3. Damages caused during intrusion -->
    <maintaingoal name="caused_damages" recur="true"
```

```
                    recurdelay="2000">
      <creationcondition>$beliefbase.event.isTYPEUNAUTHORISEDPRESENCE()<
          /creationcondition>
      <maintaincondition>$beliefbase.intruders.isSTATEONRUNNING()</
          maintaincondition>
    </maintaingoal>

    <!-- O4. Stop the intruder -->
    <performgoal name="stop_intruder" retry="true" exclude="never">
      <creationcondition>$beliefbase.event.isTYPEUNAUTHORISEDPRESENCE()<
          /creationcondition>
      <contextcondition>$beliefbase.intruders.isSTATEONRUNNING()</
          contextcondition>
    </performgoal>

    <!-- O5. Mantain the safety of the environment -->
    <performgoal name="keep_safe" retry="true" exclude="when_failed">
      <parameter name="intruder" class="Intruder">
        <bindingoptions>$beliefbase.intruders</bindingoptions>
      </parameter>
      <unique/>
      <!-- Create a new goal when new intruder is seen and
           the agent isnt already keeping environment safe. -->
      <creationcondition>$beliefbase.event.isTYPEUNAUTHORISEDPRESENCE()<
          /creationcondition>
      <!-- Suspend the goal when the intruder has been caught. -->
      <contextcondition>$beliefbase.intruders.isSTATEONRUNNING()</
          contextcondition>
      <!-- The goal will be dropped when the intruder has vanished. -->
      <dropcondition>$beliefbase.intruder==null</dropcondition>
    </performgoal>
    <achievegoalref name="df_deregister">
      <concrete ref="dfcap.df_deregister"/>
    </achievegoalref>

  </goals>


  <!--
      ********************************
      ******** List of plans *********
      ********************************
    -->
  <plans>
    <!-- Plan to get the route followed by the intruder -->
    <plan name="get_route">
      <body class="GetRoutePlan"/>
      <trigger>
        <goal ref="discover_intentions"/>
        <goal ref="stop_intruder"/>
      </trigger>
    </plan>

    <!-- Plan intended to obtain likely vulnerabilities -->
    <plan name="get_vulnerability">
```

```
        <body class="GetVulnerabilityPlan"/>
        <trigger>
          <goal ref="discover_intentions"/>
        </trigger>
      </plan>

     <!-- Plan intended to obtain images from the intruders -->
      <plan name="get_snapshot">
        <body class="GetSnapshotPlan"/>
        <trigger>
          <goal ref="intruder_identification"/>
        </trigger>
      </plan>

     <!-- Plan intended to sucess in the intruder face recognition -->
      <plan name="face_recognition">
        <body class="FaceRecognitionPlan"/>
        <trigger>
          <goal ref="intruder_identification"/>
        </trigger>
      </plan>

      <!-- Plan intended to gathered the damages -->
      <plan name="get_damage">
        <body class="GetDamagePlan"/>
        <trigger>
          <goal ref="caused_damages"/>
        </trigger>
      </plan>
    </plans>
```

Among the goals driving the agent behaviour, the first one is intended to discover the intruder aim, thought of as the building place where the intruder is going to. The plans provided to achieve the goal of `discoverintentions` are the ones referred as `GetRoutePlan` and `GetVulnerabilityPlan`. The first plan is meant to obtain the route that the intruder is following, as an attempt to provide the guards with this route information so that intruders can be more easily caught up. The second plan seeks for keeping an updated list of the likely objectives, in such a way that depending on the relative importance of an objective, and the proximity of the intruder, this plan provides the guards with an ordered list of the likely objectives of the intrusion.

Here the domain specific knowledge, modeled using an E-R diagram, as depicted in figure 5 is combined with the semantic model proposed for the system and depicted in figure 2. In order to provide the reasoning system with all this semantics, concepts and their relationships of the domain specific knowledge are coded as CLIPS classes, and slots.

Therefore, the context objectives that are likely to be a target of intrusion attacks are mapped into the `Objective` CLIPS classes, and ranked according to their subjective importance. Here, the retriever agent is constantly asserting the feedbacks of the intruder position, using to this end the information gathered from the contextual sensors and services. The faculty to gather or request the appropriate services in order to keep track of the intruder is founded on the ability to distinguish those services that implement the action of *detect* or *sense* `persons` or *objects*. Since all the services deployed in the system are described in terms of the actions

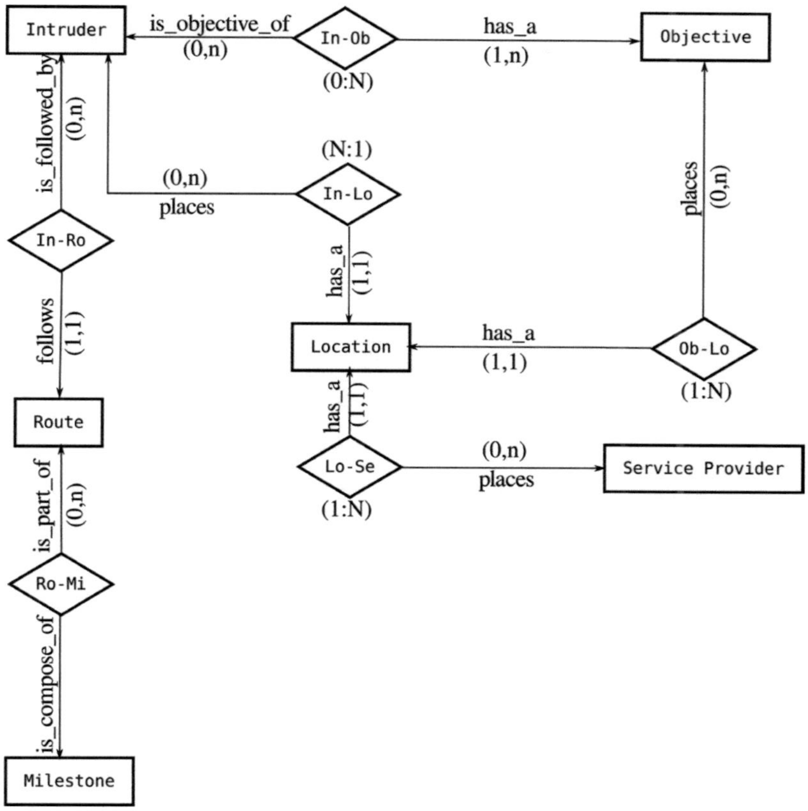

Fig. 5. Entity-Relationship Diagram for the Unauthorised Presence State Domain

they can accomplish and the objects on which these actions are preformed, the retriever agent launches the plan in charge of retrieving updated information of the intruder location, by subscribing to all those channels where services deployed at the current intruder location publish their state.

The plan intended to discover the route followed by the intruder shows a particular case of service composition, rather than a simple service combination that basically joins service functionalities. This is the case of a video camera service, used as a presence sensor, if combined with a service of face detection, in such a way that if a face is detected, presence can be inferred.

Selecting those services that at a certain location provide specific functionalities, as for this example would be *detecting people*, suffices to the actor agent to make some inquiries about these services state, either by subscribing to the appropriate channels or by direct method invocation, since the implemented interfaces are determined by the type of service.

```
(defmessage-handler INTRUDER get-location()
        (do-for-all-instances ((?serv SERVICE))
        (if (eq (send ?serv in-the-same-area ?self:x ?self:y) TRUE) then
        (bind ?action ?serv:service-consits-of-action)
        (bind ?object ?serv:service-consits-of-object)
```

```
        (if (> (str-index ?action detect) 0) then
                (if (> (str-index ?object person) 0) then
                        (bind ?selected-service ?serv)))
        (printout t "The service "  ?serv:ID "detects presence in the
            area where the intruder was last located"))
```

6. Conclusions and future works

This work has presented a novel approach towards Ambient Intelligence, mainly supported on the benefits derived from the Automated Service Composition, achieved by means of a multi-disciplinary approach, that combines an omnipresent semantic model with a middleware platform and a reasoning engine, orchestrated all this by a set of intelligent agents. As constituent components of a broader architecture, these are integrated in a middleware platform that provides them with the groundings to support their endeavours towards intelligent environments.

Nevertheless, this proposal does not represent a silver bullet to achieving self-managed systems, since the main drawback encountered when trying to develop systems for Ambient Intelligent lies on the vast amount of domain specific knowledge required when supporting systems for Ambient Intelligence contexts. Despite the availability of reasoning tools capable of dealing with domain knowledge, they reveal futile without the common sense knowledge support. However, this approach claims to solve many of the more common shortcomings of approaches intended to cope with Ambient Intelligence. Further research efforts are to be dedicated to the automation the of workflow generation just as accomplishing an extensive domain knowledge modelling by means of a common-sense framework as OpenCyc (Cycorp, 2008a)(Cycorp, 2008b).

7. Acknowledgments

This work has been funded by the European Regional Development Fund, the Regional Government of Castilla-La Mancha, the Spanish Ministry of Science and Innovation, and the Spanish Ministry of Industry under grants PAI08-0234-8083 (RGrid), TEC2008-06553 (DAMA), and CENIT Hesperia.

8. References

Amigoni, F., Gatti, N., Pinciroli, C. & Roveri, M. (2005). What planner for ambient intelligence applications?, *IEEE Transactions on Systems, Man, and Cybernetics, Part A* **35**(1): 7–21.

Bratman, M. E. (1987). *Intention, Plans, and Practical Reason*, Harvard University Press, Cambridge, MA.

Costa, P., Coulson, G., Mascolo, C., Mottola, L., Picco, G. P. & Zachariadis, S. (2007). A reconfigurable component-based middleware for networked embedded systems, *Int. Journal of Wireless Information Networks* **14**(2).

Cugola, G. & Picco, G. P. (2006). Reds: a reconfigurable dispatching system, *SEM '06: Proceedings of the 6th international workshop on Software engineering and middleware*, ACM, New York, NY, USA, pp. 9–16.

Cycorp, I. (2008a). The cyc project home page. Available online at: `http://www.cyc.com`. Retrieved on December 10th, 2008.

Cycorp, I. (2008b). The opencyc project home page. Available online at: `http://www.opencyc.org`. Retrieved on December 10th, 2008.

Ducatel, K., Bogdanowicz, M., Scapolo, F., Leijten, J. & Burgelman, J. C. (2001). Istag: Scenarios for ambient intelligence in 2010, *Technical report*, ISTAG.

Issarny, V., Sacchetti, D., Tartanoglu, F., Sailhan, F., Chibout, R., Levy, N. & Talamona, A. (2005). Developing ambient intelligence systems: A solution based on web services, *Automated Software Engg.* **12**(1): 101–137.

Pokahr, A., Braubach, L. & Lamersdorf, W. (2005). Jadex: A bdi reasoning engine, *in* J. D. R. Bordini, M. Dastani & A. E. F. Seghrouchni (eds), *Multi-Agent Programming*, Springer Science+Business Media Inc., USA, pp. 149–174. Book chapter.

Prete, L. D. & Capra, L. (2008). Mosca: seamless execution of mobile composite services, *ARM '08: Proceedings of the 7th workshop on Reflective and adaptive middleware*, ACM, New York, NY, USA, pp. 5–10.

Rao, A. S. & Georgeff, M. P. (1991). Modeling rational agents within a BDI-architecture, *in* J. Allen, R. Fikes & E. Sandewall (eds), *Proceedings of the 2nd International Conference on Principles of Knowledge Representation and Reasoning (KR'91)*, Morgan Kaufmann publishers Inc.: San Mateo, CA, USA, pp. 473–484.

Weiser, M. (1995). The computer for the 21st century, pp. 933–940.

Wooldridge, M. J. (2000). *Reasoning about Rational Agents*, The MIT Press, Cambridge, Massachusetts.

ZeroC, I. (2008). Ice home page. Available online at: `http://www.zeroc.com/`. Retrieved December 20th, 2008.

21

Exploring the bee hive metaphor as a model for problem solving: search, optimisation, and more

Pavol Navrat, Anna Bou Ezzeddine,
Lucia Jastrzembska and Tomas Jelinek
Slovak University of Technology, Faculty of Informatics and Information Technologies,
Ilkovicova 3, SK-842 16 Bratislava
Slovakia

1. Introduction

One of the great challenges attracting researchers of various disciplines has been the question: how to solve it? Problem solving has been an important topic of research e.g. in artificial intelligence and many remarkable results have been achieved there. However, the challenge is too complex that only one discipline, or one paradigm, or one approach can prevail.

Within artificial intelligence, there has been a natural tendency to relate somehow artificial problem solvers to human ones: either in the way they behave, or in the way they actually do it. However, nature seems to offer a much broader wealth of inspiration. Among other sources of inspiration, social insects seem to play a distinct role. Indeed, their behaviour is interesting not only individually, but also in a collective, or a colony, or a swarm.

From among the kinds of social insects, ants have gained perhaps the biggest attraction of problem solving researchers. Their ability to solve classes of optimisation tasks with a help of pheromones has become infamous. Only relatively recently, other kinds of social insects began to draw attention of researchers. We shall devote our attention to honey bees (apis mellifera). Honey bees are relative newcomers, although the very idea of taking inspiration from a bee hive model to represent knowledge for a knowledge based system can be traced back to 1986 (Bullock, 1986). We are interested in taking inspiration from honey bees for devising of approaches to problem solving and in particular to automated, or computer based problem solving.

Behaviour of honey bees is a subject of study of other disciplines, in particular of biologists. Their studies have proven to be extremely useful (Beekman, 2007), (Biesmeijer, 2001), (Bonabeau, 1996), (Camazine, 1991), (Selley, 1991), (Zhang, 2006). Without them, we would not have the underlying knowledge on how honey bees behave in nature. From the problem solving perspective, much of the research has been concentrated on the optimisation task, perhaps in reference to the success of ant colonies (Karaboga, 2005), (Pham, 2006), (Teodorovic, 2005), (Tovey, 2005), (Wong, 2008).

We venture to identify one additional new dimension for the problem solving: the web. It brings new challenges, since it poses new kinds of problems. We had a great wealth of information before the web. But now we have a great, and probably even a greater wealth of information instantly retrievable. Therefore, we identify web problem solving as another grand theme of research.

The rest of this chapter is structured as follows. First, we take a look at self-organization in biological systems. Next, we deal briefly with approaches to bee hive modelling. We mention at least some approaches in related work. Then we present our bee hive model. As a special issue, we devote a section to web page evaluation. We continue with presenting our experiments with web story tracking and with optimisation. Another concept we experiment with is hierarchy. We conclude with some comments on possible future works.

2. Self - Organization in Biological Systems

Social insects rank a key position in the field of artificial life, especially because of relative simplicity of behaviour of an individual as opposed to their complex collective behaviour. Colonies of social insects are able to develop means for solving problems collectively. Complexity of these tasks exceeds any individual problem solving ability. They can solve tasks without central direction, without existence of ahead given fixed structures, although the existence of expressive internal whirrs.

Ants are among the social insects that have been studied most intensively in both the social biology and computing literature. Ants have an ability to produce structures, which change dynamically. They can find the shortest way from a source of food to their nest without using the sight. They can adapt to changes of environment. For example they can find a new shortest way in case that the old one cannot be used any more because it has become barricaded off by a barrier. The main means that ants use to form and maintain the connection is a pheromone mark. Ants secrete certain amount of pheromones. When moving, they prefer direction, which is marked by a higher number of them. In this case, ants which had chosen the shorter path reconstruct the new path more quickly than the ones which had chosen the longer one. The shorter path obtains more pheromones per unit of time.

The apprehension of emergent abilities of ants´ colony, in particular of the collective behaviour of a colony was an inspiration for proposing new distributive computing methods. This is the case not only for ants, but for other kinds of social insects, too. Bees in case of searching the nectar due to using air lines do not have the possibility to mark their way as ants. So bees pass the information to each other about the source distance of nectar by dance.

In 1973, Austrian zoologist Karl Ritter von Frisch was awarded the Nobel prize for discovery of the language of dancing bees (Gadakar, 1996). If the source is situated near the bee hive, a bee dances a circular dance, which does not include information about the direction of nectar. If the source is in a greater distance, bees encode the information about direction and distance of the source into dance, too. The dance begins to elongate and acquire the shape of the number eight.

We shall assume that the waggle dance is a means of communicating a food source. The dancer lets know not only distance and direction of the food source. Duration of dancing is influenced by the quality of the source.

3. Bee hive modelling

In (Selley, 1991), authors have demonstrated experimentally that a decision of a bee in a process of searching for nectar is based on limited information acquired from the visited sources. Despite the simplicity of bee's individual behaviour, the hive is able to select the best source of nectar. It is selected by following certain way of dancing for a better source and by possibly abandoning the source of a lower quality.

The authors performed an interesting experiment designed to investigate how a hive (a system of bees) chooses between the sources. Experiment was performed in a desert. In the vicinity of a colony, there were placed two nectar sources, one of them 400 m to the north, the other one 400 m to the south. 12 bees were trained to fly to the north source, 15 other bees to the south source. The sources were of different quality and the experiment lasted from 8.00 am till 4.00 pm. The south one was better (sugar concentration of 2.5 units) than the north one (1.0 units) initially. At noon, however, the sources were swapped so the concentration of sugar was changed, too.

Empirical observation showed that number of bees foraging for the better source was increasing in time, whereas number of bees foraging for the worse source remained low. After having swapped the sources, the situation changed, too. The north one - it is the one that has become the better one in the afternoon - started to be visited by more and more bees. The south one – the worse one now - started to lose visitors as more and more foragers were abandoning it.

The result of the simulation of the experiment is showed in Fig. 1.

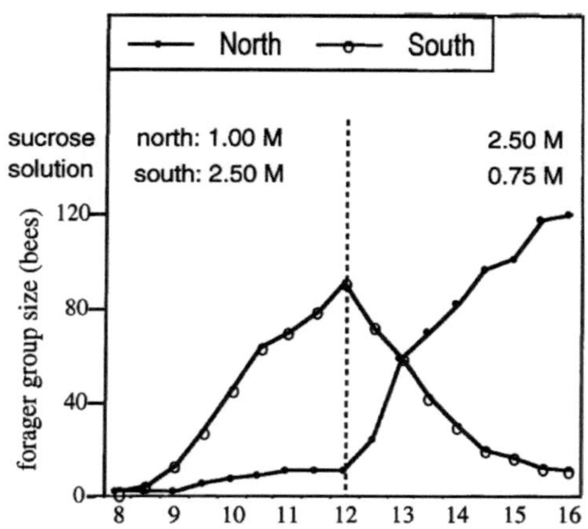

Fig. 1. Result of the experiment aimed at investigating how colonies choose among nectar sources (Seeley, 1991).

4. Related work

In (Camazine, 2003) authors deal with description of self organization of a honey bee system. Bees select the best source of nectar with a help of simple rules. They fly out to their surround and look for nectar, which is essential for their survival.

When a bee finds a food source, it flies back to the bee hive and brings the information about the source.

Having returned to the hive, a bee has the following options:
-to stay with the food source and keep on retrieving it without attempting to allure other bees,
-to attempt to allure other bees for the food source, to pass information about it, doing all that by a dance that encodes the direction, quality and distance from the source.,
-to abandon the source and expose herself to be allured by some other bee, which propagates presumably a better source (with a higher concentration of sugar).
Next, we briefly present and comment a selection of works in which authors describe behaviour of bees and attempt to use the metaphor of bees for acquiring information. In many of such works, a swarm of bees is viewed symbolically as a multiagent system. One of the main problems in these systems is the way how agents communicate with each other. In case of bees, it is hypothesized that dance is the primary, if not the only way of communication. Agents have neither a global view of the state of the world nor in particular a view of the state of the problem being solved. They see only locally. The system, however, is able to take into account also constraints, which single agents do not apprehend because of local nature of their view. The agents are forced to cooperate in a rational way. One of the possible ways of cooperation among agents without an explicit communication is making use of the swarm intelligence (Bonabeau, 1999), (Vries, 1998).
In (Vries, 1998), authors deal with modelling of bees collectively looking for collecting nectar. Individually oriented simulation is constructed to simulate collective behaviour of bees in time of foraging. Each bee follows the same set of behavioural rules. The aim was to build up a simulation model, which would achieve similar results as those presented in (Selley, 1991).
In (Camazine, 1991), a mathematical simulation describing dynamical interaction among bees in the process of carrying nectar from two sources is presented.
On the ground of the mathematical model of (Camazine, 1991), a prototype of multi-agent recommending system was proposed in (Lorenzi, 2005A) and presented in (Lorenzi, 2005B), (Lorenzi, 2005C). They make use of the bee hive metaphor. They built up also on works of (Schafer,2001) and (Resnick, 1994) applying different approaches to solving problems. This question was elaborated in (Lorenzi, 2004), too. They generalized the model of (Camazine, 1991) by allowing more than two sources of food. However, their model assumes there are as many bees as there are sources. In the next Section, we present our enhancement of this model.

5. Bee hive model

We took an initial inspiration from the model of (Lorenzi, 2005A, B) who in turn were inspired by (Camazine, 1991).
The way bees communicate among themselves in nature contributes to formation of their collective intelligence, called also swarm intelligence. We believe that swarm intelligence has a potential to nurture new ideas that could ameliorate research approaches to various open problems.
Our model (Navrat, 2006A) uses a preset number of bees to find the best of the sources by evaluating them and using social interaction to agree upon the best source. The mechanism of interaction is shown in Fig. 2.

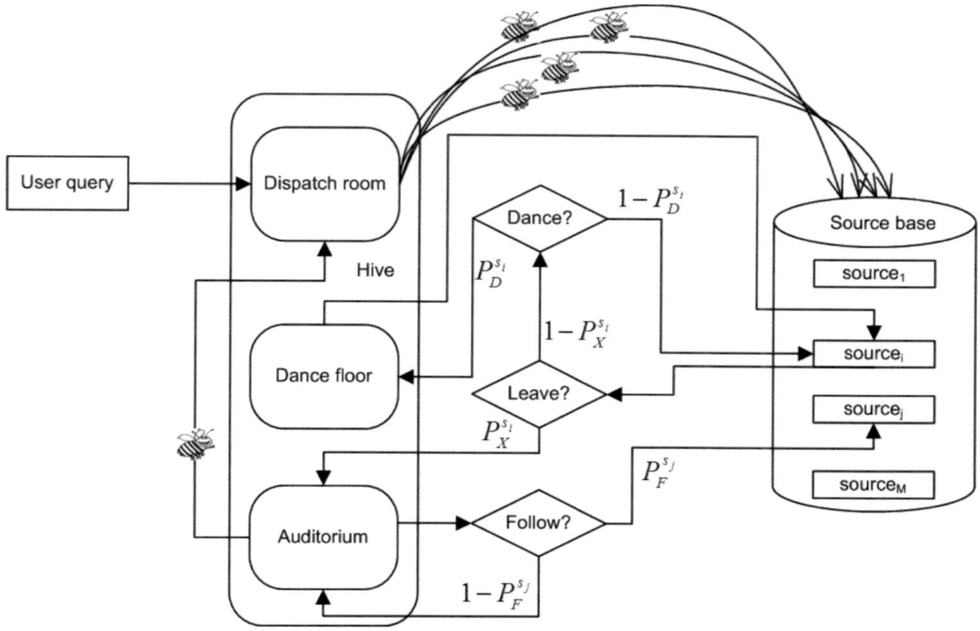

Fig. 2. The bee hive comprises of the dispatch room, dance floor and auditorium.

We enhanced the model by a dispatch room, bringing additional flexibility to it.
The dispatch room is a place where addresses of the food sources are available. The information exchange among individual bees is the most important part of the collective knowledge sharing. Communication among bees about the quality of nectar sources takes place in a dancing area, i.e. the dance floor by performing and observing the waggle dance. The auditorium is a place where bees are able to watch dancers on the dance floor.
Parameters of our model are the following:
N (BIOR+BISB) - Number of bees in the hive (BIOR - bees in the observing room - observers, BISB - bees in the source base - foragers),
MDT - Maximal dancing time - maximal time the bee can stay on the dance floor,
OT - Observing time - maximal time a bee can spend in the auditorium,
ERR - Error of source quality evaluation.

5.1 Mechanisms of the model

When the user inputs a search query, the bees leave the dispatch room and they are randomly assigned to the sources. After a bee has collected enough data at the source to be able to evaluate it, she returns to the hive and makes a decision whether to stay with the source, or to abandon it. The probability of staying with the source is set to be equal to the quality q of the visited source, assuming that q is expressed as a number within <0, 1>.
If a bee decides to stay with the source, it makes another decision, whether to keep on foraging, or to start dancing for the source. Again, the probability of deciding to dance is set to be equal to the quality of the source. If the bee decides to start dancing for the source, it moves to the dance floor and starts dancing. Length of a dance depends on the parameter (MDT) and quality q of the source (MDT*q). The better the source is, the longer time the bee

dances. The bees that decide not to dance, return to the same sources they visited before and continue foraging.

If a bee decides to abandon the source, she moves into the auditorium to watch the dancing bees, for a period of time that depends on the parameter OT. She then considers the sources being propagated at the dance floor by the dancing bees. The chance of choosing a propagated source is equal to the number of bees dancing for the propagated source divided by the total number of dancing bees. If a bee fails to choose from the propagated sources within the observation time, she transfers into the dispatch room and receives some randomly assigned source. This is important, because if we have fewer bees than sources, we need a mechanism to find and subsequently propagate sources without the need of bees assigned to them in the beginning.

A more detailed elaboration of the mechanism of our model can be found in (Navrat, 2006B).

5.2 Experiments with parameters of model

Various experiments were accomplished alike in (Selley, 1991), with monitoring of actual settings of system new parameters.

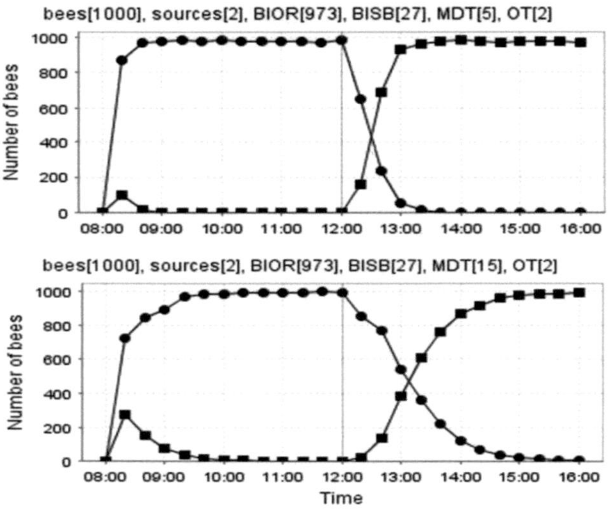

Fig. 3. Experiments with parameter MDT.

By increasing the parameter MDT, dynamics of the system was observed to decrease. When bees dance longer, expectancy of alluring other bees becomes higher. From among the allured bees inevitably some bees will later go dancing, too. As a consequence, with a constant total number of bees in the hive, there remain less bees to amass around the best source. The hive's ability to yield a decisive outcome gets slower – see Fig. 3.

By decreasing the parameter OT dynamics of the system increases. When the time is very short (i.e., values are near the zero), frequent behaviour variances of system occur, because bees often take off at random sources, see Fig. 4.

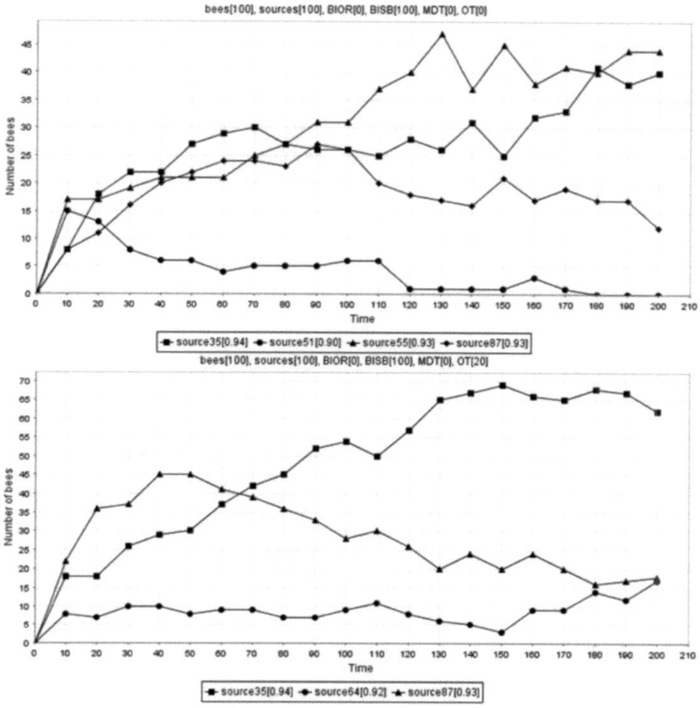

Fig. 4. Experiment with parameter OT, x axis represents time, y axis represents number of bees.

More experiments with parameters of the model were documented in (Navrat, 2007 A) and (Navrat, 2008).

6. Web pages evaluation

Relevance of particular web page is subjective from the user's point of view. Each user has different interests and knowledge. There are algorithms to determine relevancy of a particular web page based on properties of the web represented as a graph. In this graph, vertices represent web pages and edges represent interconnections (links) between pages.

Page rank algorithm (Page, 1998) can by considered a simulation of an imaginary user that accidentally chooses various links on the web. After each click the user decides if he continues. The probability of requesting another random page is called damping factor d. Many studies discussed the problem of appropriate values of damping factor. Generally this factor is assumed to have value approximately 0.85 (Page, 1998).

The universal formula of PageRank calculation according to (Page, 1998) is:

$$PR(p_i) = 1 - d + d \sum_{p_j \in M(p_i)} \frac{PR(p_j)}{L(p_j)} \tag{1}$$

where p_i is page, of which PageRank value is computed, $M(p_i)$ is set of pages referring to page p_i and $L(p_j)$ is number of outgoing links from page p_j.

For calculation of sufficiently exact PageRank value of each page, several iterations are required. During each iteration the PageRank of every page in the collection is recomputed. Number of iterations depends on the number of pages in the collection and on the complexity of interconnections among particular pages.

In Fig. 5, web pages are represented by vertices denoted A, B, etc and links between them are represented by orientated edges.

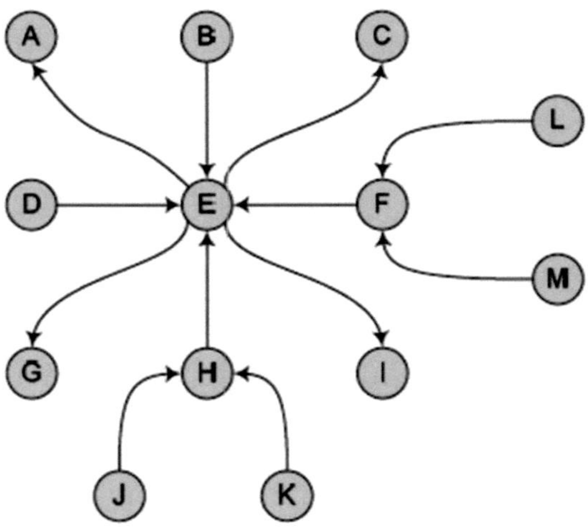

Fig. 5. A simple graph expressing interconnections of web pages.

PageRank values of pages must be computed iteratively. For example, value of the page E cannot be determined without knowing values of the pages B, D, F, and H. Of course, in order to determine values of these pages, values of still other pages may need to be known (i.e., computed). Conversely, value of the page E is needed to compute values of the pages A, C, G, I.

Let us contemplate about using bees to perform the above described evaluations. The bees would benefit from a slight modification of their behaviour. When a bee flies to the source E (page or vertex E), she evaluates quality of the source, i.e she determines a preliminary PageRank value of E denoted as PR(E). At the same time she knows that to compute PR(E) more precisely, values of PR(D), PR(B), PR(F) and PR(H) must be known.

If the source E has a high quality, the bee probably goes in the dance floor and dances there. Our idea is that she will not dance attempting to allure other bees for the source E. She dances to allure other bees for one of the sources that refer to source E. The choice of the source will be random with an even assignment of choice probability to each of the pages that are sources of links pointing to E. In this case the bee would try to attract other bees to come to sources, for which she needs to calculate PR of the vertex she visited. The bee would fly back to the source E after finishing dancing, whereby if she would succeed to attract the other bees to fly to source D, B, F or H, the bee on the source E could determine PR(E) more accurately. There is a high probability for the bee to fly to the dance floor again and dancing there for one of the sources D, B, F or H, in the case that the quality of the source is high enough also after its actualization. The whole cycle is repeated and PR (E) gradually approaches its theoretical value.

Computing PageRank values of all the pages (represented by vertices) proceeds in a similar way.

Experiments published in (Navrat, 2008) show that employing bees to compute PageRank values is comparable, in many cases even faster than a standard iterative procedure.

7. Web story

Finding and reading most relevant and up to date articles requires continuously observing all the new sources for updates of stories one is interested in. It also includes discovering new data sources. All this can be problematic if not impossible for a human, so a system capable of doing these tasks might be helpful.

We propose to use a focused crawler to download relevant pages. We took an inspiration for constructing the crawler from nature, particularly from the social behaviour of honey bees.

The field of focused crawlers is not new. Early concepts of such crawlers include best-first, fish search (De Bra, 1994) and shark search (Hersovici, 1998) algorithms. In late 90's the term focused crawler was introduced in (Chakrabrati, 1999).

Even the use of focused crawler for online search is not new. In the system called Fetuccino (Ben-Shaul, 1999) the authors tried to solve the classic problem of web search with an offline database, viz. the problem that the pages returned may have changed since they were indexed into the database. They called the classical web search as static search and enhanced it by dynamic search. A dynamic search was an approach to revisit the pages at the time of searching after the results from static search had been obtained. The results were then updated according to the dynamic search and provided to the user.

There have been attempts to propose nature inspired algorithm for focused crawling. For example, the focused Ant Crawling Algorithm (Dziwinski, 2008), for hypertext graph crawling is claimed to be better than the Shark-Search crawling algorithm.

Another example of using online search is the agent InfoSpider (Menczer, 1999). The authors based this agent on previous work on adaptive agents (Menczer, 1998). In (Pant, 2004) and (Menczer, 2000) the autors used adaptive agents, too. Another area related to our work is story tracking. In (Pouliquen, 2008) there is published an approach of handling information overflow by clustering similar articles into stories.

7.1 Modified bee hive model

We chose the model (Fig. 2) and specified the behaviour of the bee outside the hive (Navrat, 2007 B). The web page was used as the source and the aim of the hive was to find the most relevant pages and thus focus the search for new pages into the more promising areas. When a bee flies outside the hive to a source (web page), she estimates its quality (relevancy) as q. With the probability q she stays with the current page, or with the probability 1−q she follows one of the links on the page to visit some new source. Then she will with the probability q fly back to the hive with her current source or with the complementary probability stay outside the hive and search for better sources. The bee cannot stay outside the hive forever, therefore we used the concept of energy taken from (Menczer, 1999). Every time the bee visits some source, the energy will increment by the quality of the source (non relevant source has zero quality) and decrement by the specified parameter. If the bee has no more energy (energy <= 0) she will return to the hive regardless of other conditions.

7.2 Bees scouts or recruits

While performing the experiments with this behaviour we encountered a problem with discovering of few relevant sources where the bees could start the search. We again found inspiration in nature (Biesmeijer, 2001) and in the failed follower hypothesis (Beekman, 2007). The foraging bees fall within one of two categories - scouts or recruits. Scouts search for food independently regardless of the other bees. Recruits are bees that have been allured by a dance of some other bee. Under the failed follower hypothesis the scouts are failed followers. It means that if a bee does not find a dancing bee to follow, she will become a scout and search for food on her own. As a result, if the food is scarce, the probability of finding a dancing bee is low and more bees become scouts. If there is plenty of food, there will be more dancing bees and consequently more bees become recruits. We managed to accommodate this hypothesis with our original model without even the need of modifying it.

7.3 Story tracking

We assume that aim of on-line search is not to retrieve some single information, the aim is to find a relevant set of pages which would create a story. It is supposed to be used on sites containing frequently changing or added information.

One of excellent applications is for headline stories. An example of such a headline story are elections. We present a case study of tracking the story of the recent presidential elections in Slovakia.

The aim of the case study was to explore if the algorithm can track a story being in development. We chose the second round of presidential elections in Slovakia.

The search started from two Slovak news portals www.sme. sk and www.pravda.sk. During the experiment our system discovered 4615 different pages from various domains, 742 of them had above zero quality. 217 pages could be marked as relevant to its content. From the 217 pages marked as relevant, only 85 had informative character.

Our system was able to track the story back to its immediate origins and beyond, the oldest article was published in February 2009.

We divided the real story of presidential elections in Slovakia into five parts and inspected how many pages the bees were able to find (Table 1).

We can conclude that the system was able to follow the story on the day of the elections. Moreover, it was able to track the story back.

Story part	Number of found pages
First leg of elections	12
Campaign before the second leg	28
The day of elections (second leg)	30
Announcement of the results	9
The reactions	6

Table 1. Parts of coverage of presidential elections in Slovakia 2009

This is a simple system for tracking a developing story that is based on a model of a bee hive. We performed a case study that demonstrates the way how our proposed system works. From the case study we can conclude the following:
- the system is able to collect relevant pages,
- it can monitor the story being developed during the search,
- it can reconstruct the story backwards in time.

8. Optimisation based on a social behaviour of honey bees

The bee behaviour inspired various researches. Their interests are basically: modelling of bees' behaviour, or constructing algorithms inspired by bees' behaviour.
Our hypothesis is that the behaviour the bees show might be an instructive inspiration to develop a model of solving problems from a suitable class. More specifically, having developed a model of a bee hive that can work as a kind of search engine (Navrat, 2008), we propose to investigate a bee hive as a possibly useful metaphor for optimisation.
We took an inspiration from a popular model described in (Pham, 2006). It has been successfully applied to optimisation of mathematical functions. This algorithm has good results in terms of number of evaluations of the optimized function needed to achieve the required result.
Another bee inspired algorithm is described in (Wong, 2008). The authors successfully applied their algorithm to the travelling salesman problem. Other algorithms from the area of optimisation using the bee metaphor are Bee Colony Optimisation (Teodorovic, 2005) and Abstract Bee Colony (Karaboga, 2005).
In this part we will describe a specialization of our model (Navrat, 2006A) to optimisation of mathematical functions.
This model is very general and does not define the behaviour of the bee outside the hive. It means that before applying the model to specific problems this behaviour has to be defined.
This generality brings an opportunity to fine-tune the behaviour of the algorithm to the specific needs of the problem domain without the need to modify the basic behaviour of the hive. The bee hive metaphor can be thus used for such different tasks as on-line web search or function optimisation.
We proposed a behaviour of a bee outside the hive for the case of optimizing mathematical functions. Sources in this case are different vectors of values of function arguments.

8.1 New parameters of the model

We introduce two new parameters for the model to suit the optimisation task.

Parameter Step size: Bees outside the hive can visit more than one source before returning to the hive. When the bee flies from source to source she adds a random number from the interval <−stepSize, +stepSize > to each argument of the function.
Parameter Energy: Using this parameter was inspired by (Menczer, 1999). It is the energy of the bee acting outside the hive. When the bee runs off her spare energy, she has to return to the hive without (inspecting, bringing) any source.

8.2 Source quality evaluation

There are two main aspects in the field of evaluating the quality of the source for this model: use of ranking and mapping all values of optimized function from $< -\infty,\infty >$ to $< 0, 1 >$.
Since the proposed model is able to work only with values within range $< 0, 1 >$ and the functions have their functional values (in general) in range $< -\infty, \infty >$, we need a function which can map every function value into the range. Assume this function is Map(x). The function must satisfy the three conditions stated in the equations (2), (3) and (4).

$$\forall x, y \in R : x < y \Leftrightarrow Map(x) < Map(y) \tag{2}$$

$$\forall x, y \in R : x > y \Leftrightarrow Map(x) > Map(y) \tag{3}$$

$$\forall x, y \in R : x = y \Leftrightarrow Map(x) = Map(y) \tag{4}$$

For example, the function shown in the formula 5 satisfies these conditions.

$$Map(x) = \frac{1}{\pi}\left(arctg(x) + \frac{\pi}{2} \right) \tag{5}$$

When looking for a global maximum, the formula is used as it is, when looking for a global minimum, the formula 1− Map(x) is to be used. The function is not linear. However, it is not an issue, because the model uses ranking. The specific formula we used is shown in (6),

$$rank = \frac{1}{1 - NB} * ((1 - \varepsilon) * P + \varepsilon - NB) - k \tag{6}$$

where NB is the number of bees, ϵ is a small constant (we have used 0.001), P is position in the ordered list of qualities and k is an empirical constant which safeguards the quality not to be 1. If the quality would be 1 the bee would propagate the corresponding source with 100% probability, i.e. with certainty and the algorithm would be too greedy. We have used k = 0.2.

8.3 Results of experiments

For these experiments, we used as the underlying model of the hive the one described in Fig. 2 superimposed by the modification described in 8.1 to optimize a set of benchmarking functions. These functions' parameters are stated in the Table 2. These data were taken from (Pham, 2006). In Table 3 there are shown results of applying our proposed algorithm to the benchmarking functions as well as results of other commonly used stochastic optimisation algorithms which were previously published in (Pham, 2006).

ID	Function name	Interval	Global optima
1	Rosenbrock 2D	[-1.2, 1.2]	X(1,1) F=0
2	Rosenbrock 2D	[-10,10]	X(1,1,1,1) F=0
3	Goldstein & Price	[-2,2]	X(0,-1) F=3
4	Martin & Gaddy	[0,10]	X(5,5) F=0
5	Rosenbrock 4D	[-1.2, 1.2]	X(1,1,1,1) F=0
6	De Jong	[-2.048, 2.048]	X(1,1) F=3905.93
7	Branin	[-5, 10]	X(-22/7, 12.275) X(22/7, 2.275) X(66/7, 2.475) F=0.3977272
8	Hyper Sphere	[-5.12, 5.12]	X(0,0,0,0,0,0) F=0

Table 2. Functions and their parameters as subjected to the experiments

ID	S	NS	GA	ANT	BA	BHM
1	10780	4508	10212	6842	631	**2409**
2	12500	5007	*****	7505	2306	**16019**
3	*****	*****	5662	5330	999	**6773**
4	*****	*****	2844	1688	526	**645**
5	21177	3053	*****	8471	28529	**68249**
6	*****	*****	10160	6000	868	**6699**
7	*****	*****	7325	1936	1655	**1822**
8	*****	*****	15468	22050	7113	**17152**

Table 3. Experimental results given as an average from 100 iterations
S: Simplex Method, NS: Stochastic Simulated Annealing Optimisation Procedure, GA: Genetic Algorithm, ANT: Ant Colony System, BA: Bees' Algorithm, BHM: Our proposed Bees' Algorithm, *****: not available data.

9. Hierarchy of bee hives

There are algorithms which utilize some sort of hierarchy. For example the Hierarchical Subpopulation Particle Swarm Optimisation Algorithm (Chuan, 2007) uses a hierarchy of particles to solve the problem with premature convergence of the algorithm. It isolates better solutions from those worse ones into different hierarchy levels.
The concept of hierarchy was studied also in (Cerny, 2000). Cerny used a simple example of a hierarchical problem: there is a hexagon shaped picture composed of other hexagons and the goal is to find a symmetrical shape composed of these pictures. To accomplish this task the author used a simple Simulated Annealing without hierarchy.
Our concept of hierarchy is mostly based on the paper of (Cerny, 2000). Our model of the bee hive is divided into two parts - the hive and the bees. We described two conditions a bee must satisfy to cooperate with the hive. The first condition is that a bee must be able to take a source. The second condition is that a bee must be able to return a source. The fulfilling of the conditions implies that we can consider the hive as a more complex bee, but still the bee.

The hierarchy is constructed in Fig. 6 as follows: in higher, non ground levels, a hive is a host to other hives, whereas only at the ground level, a hive is host to true bees.

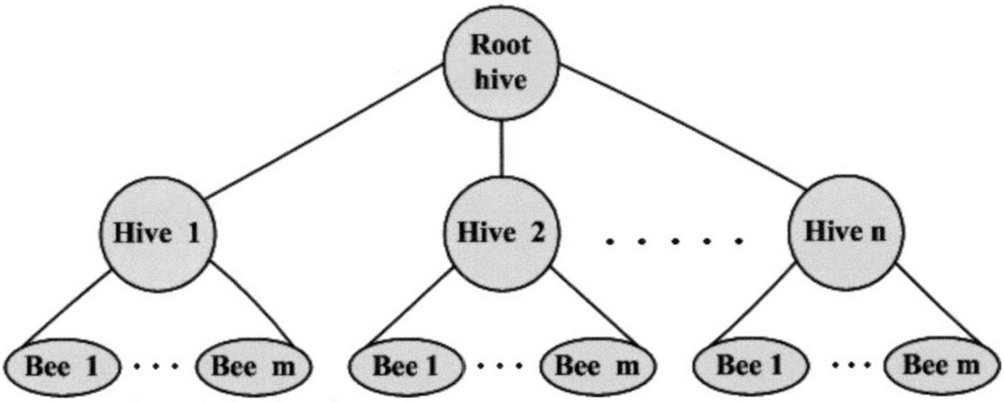

Fig. 6. An outline of a bee hive hierarchy

Higher level hive is thanks to our design still a hive, since it works as a hive, albeit it hosts other hives, but they in turn are designed to act as bees. The rationale behind our design is to give higher level hives a capability to influence behaviour of lower level hives (without the need to know whether it is a bee or a hive).

9.1 Experiments based on hierarchy

Cerny in (Cerny, 2000) contemplated an experiment to find a symmetrical shape. We employed the above described model and actually conducted a series of experiments. Accumulated results of them are in Fig. 7 showing 9 runs of the experiment in a row. As one can see in Fig. 7, each run except of the first one produced symmetrical solutions.

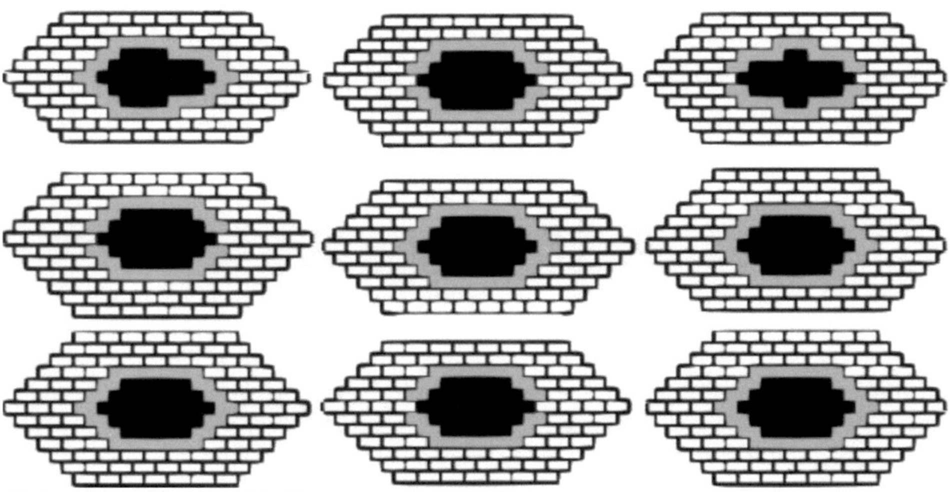
Fig. 7. Experiments aimed to form a symmetrical shape

10. Conclusion and future work

Bee hive metaphor has recently been attracting researchers who investigate methods of problem solving, although early attempts can be traced one or even two decades ago. A bee hive is a complex system composed of bees whose behaviour in turn can by sufficiently approximately described in very simple terms. There are several approaches to do it. We mention some and provide a slightly more detailed treatise of one of them, viz. the one we have proposed and continue to investigate.

However, no matter what is the particular approach, there have been achieved sufficiently solid results to support the claim that the bee metaphor is an attractive alternative that deserves further study. In particular, several works attempt to propose a method of optimisation based on a suitably defined model of a bee hive. Despite the fact that at least in some cases, results comparable to other optimisation approaches have been achieved, it is not clear if optimisation is going to become the kind of application that kills all possible doubts on the potential of the metaphor. Comparing to ants, bees do not work with pheromones, so in effect they do not have available any memory to store even the simplest kinds of data. Although there were some attempts to apply the concept of pheromones to bees, the important thing to be noted is that bees have instead a mechanism of dynamic remembering realised by their dancing. The key question is not to view this as a possible limitation of the bee hive metaphor, but rather as a unique feature.

Leaving the task of optimisation aside, it is not clear if the up to now research has already found the killer application for the bee hive. For example, we have investigated web search, symmetry formation and developing story tracking on the web. The results that we achieved are quite promising, but further research is required before any definitive conclusions can be made.

11. References

Baykasoglu, A. & Özbakır, L. & Tapkan, P. (2007). Artificial Bee Colony Algorithm and Its Application to Generalized Assignment Problem. In: *Felix T. S. Chan and Manoj Kumar Tiwari (Eds.): Swarm Intelligence: Focus on Ant and Particle Swarm Optimisation,* ISBN 978-3-902613-09-7, pages 532, December 2007, Itech Education and Publishing, Vienna, Austria.

Beekman, M. & Gilchrist, A.L. & Duncan, M. & Sumpter, D.J.T. (2007). What makes a honeybee scout? *Behavioral Ecology and Sociobiology*: 61:pages 985- 995, 2007.

Ben-Shaul, I. & Herscovici, M. & Jacovi, M. & Maarek, Y. S. & Pelleg, D. & Shtalhaim, M. & Soroka, V. & Ur, S. (1999). Adding support for dynamic and focused search with Fetuccino. In *Proceedings of the Eighth international Conference on World Wide Web (Toronto, Canada).* P. H. Enslow, Ed. Elsevier North-Holland, New York, NY, pages 1653-1665.

Biesmeijer, J.C. & de Vries, H. (2001). Exploration and exploitation of food sources by social insect colonies: a revision of the scout-recruit concept. *Behavioral Ecology and Sociobiology,* 49(2-3), pages 89-99, 2001.

Bonabeau, E. & Thraulaz, G. & Dorigo, M. (1999). Swarm Intelligence: From Natural to Artifcial Systems. *Oxford University Press,* 1999.

Bullock, H.E. & Dey, P. & Reilly, K.D. (1986) A "Bee Hive" Model For Heterogeneous Knowledge In Expert Systems, *ACM 1986*, pages 417–417.

Camazine, S. & Sneyd, J. (1991) A model of collective nectar source selection by honey bees: Self-organization through simple rules. *Journal of Theoretical Biology*, 149(4):pages 547-571, 1991.

Camazine, S. & Deneubourg, J.L. & Franks, N.R. & Sneyd, J. & Theraulaz, G. & Bonabeau, E. (2003). Self-organization in Biological Systems. *Princeton University Press*, 2003.

Cerny, V. (2000). Searching for the Best Model of the World: from Simulated Annealing to Hierarchical Systems (in Slovak), *IRIS Bratislava* , pages 27 - 44, 2000.

Chakrabarti, S. & Berg, M. & Dom, B. (1994). Focused crawling: a new approach to topic-specific Web resource discovery (1999). *Computer Networks*, Amsterdam, Netherlands: 1999.

Chuan, L. & Quanyuan, F. (2007). A Hierarchical Subpopulation Particle Swarm Optimisation Algorithm, In *Proc.: ISKE-2007 Proceedings, Advances in Intelligent Systems Research*, October 2007.

De Bra, P. & Houben, G.J. & Kornatzky, Y. & Post, R. (1994). *Proccedings of RIAO 94* , pages 481-493, 1994.

Dziwinski, P. & Rutkowska, D. (2008). Ant Focused Crawling Algorithm. In: *L. Rutkowski et al. (Eds.): ICAISC 2008*, LNAI 5097, pages 1018-1028, 2008.

Gadagkar, R. (1996). The Honeybee Dance-Language Controversy. Robot Bee Comes to the Rescue. *Journal Resonance*, Springer India, in co-publication with Indian Academy of Sciences, Volume 1, number 1/January 1996.

Gheorghe, M. & Holcombe, M. & Kefalas, P. (2001). Computational Models of Collective Foraging. *Biosystems, Volume 61, Issues 2-3, 8 July 2001*, pages 133-141.

Hersovici, M. & Jacivi, M. & Maarek, Y.S. & Pelleg, D. & Shtalhaim, M. & Ur, S. (1998). The shark-search algorithm - An application: Tailored Web site mapping. *Proceedings of the seventh international conference on World Wide Web 7*, 1998.

Karaboga D. (2005). An Idea Based on Honey Bee Swarm For Numerical Optimisation, Technical Report-TR06. *Erciyes University, Engineering Faculty*, Computer Engineering Department 2005.

Lemmens, N. & de Jong, S. & Tuyls, K. & Nowe, A. (2008). Bee Behaviour in Multi-agent Systems (A Bee Foraging Algorithm). In: *K. Tuyls et al: Adaptive Agents and Multi-Agent Systems III.* Adaptation and Multi-Agent Learning, LNCS 4865, Springer, 2008, pages 145-156.

Lorenzi, F. & Ricci, F. (2004). Case-based reasoning and recommender systems. *Technical report, IRST* 2004.

Lorenzi, F. & Sherer dos Santos, D. & Bazzan, A.L.C. (2005A). Case-based Recommender Systems: a unifying view. In *LNCS/LNAI State-of-the-Art Survey book on Intelligent Techniques in Web Personalization*, 2005.

Lorenzi, F. & Sherer dos Santos, D. & Bazzan, A.L.C. (2005B). Case-based recommender systems inspired by social insects. In *XXV Congresso da Sociedade Brasileira de Computacao*, 22-29 jul 2005.

Lorenzi, F. & Sherer dos Santos, D. & Bazzan, A.L.C. (2005C). Negotiation for task allocation among agents in case-based reccommender systems: a swarm - intelligence approach . In *IJCAI-05 Workshop on Multi-Agent Information Retrieval and Recomander Systems*. Edinburgh, pages 23-27, 2005.

Menczer, F. & Belew, R. K. (1998). Adaptive Information Agents in Distributed Textual Environments. *Agents*, 1998: pages 157-164.

Menczer, F. & Monge, A. E. (1999). Scalable Web Search by Adaptive Online Agents: An InfoSpiders Case Study. *Intelligent Information Agents, Springer*, 1999.

Menczer, F. & Belew, R. K. (2000). Adaptive Retrieval Agents: Internalizing Local Context and Scaling up to the Web. *Machine Learning Journal* 39 (2/3): pages 203-242, 2000.

Navrat, P. (2006 A). Bee Hive Metaphor for Web Search. *Communication and Cognition-Artificial Intelligence* Vol 23, N° 1-4, 2006, pages 15-20.

Navrat, P. & Kovacik, M. (2006 B). Web search engine as a bee hive. *IEEE/WIC/ACM International Conference on Web Intelligence, Hong Kong*, pages 694-701, 2006.

Navrat, P. & Kovacik, M. & Bou Ezzeddine, A. & Rozinajova, V. (2007 A). Information retrieval using honey bees. In *Znalosti 2007, Ostrava*, pages 63-74, 2007.

Navrat, P. & Jastrzembska, L. & Jelinek, T. & Bou Ezzedine, A. & Rozinajova, V. (2007 B). Exploring Social Behaviour of Honey Bees Searching on the Web, In *Proc.: 2007 IEEE/WIC/ACM International Conference on Web Intelligence and Intelligent Agent Technology - Workshops*, pages 21 – 25, 2007.

Navrat, P. & Kovacik, M. & Bou Ezzeddine, A. & Rozinajova, V. (2008). Web search engine working as a bee hive. *Web Intelligence and Agent Systems. An International Journal Volume 6, Number 4*, pages 441-452, 2008.

Page L. & Brin S. (1998). The Anatomy of Large-Scale Hypertextual Web Search Engine. *Computer Networks and ISDN Systems*, 30 (1-7): pages 107-117, 1998.

Pant, G. & Srinivasan, P. & Menczer, F. (2004). Crawling the Web. *Web Dynamics*, 2004: pages 153-178, 2004.

Pham, D.T. & Ghanbarzadeh, A. & Koc, E. & Otri, S. & Rahim S. & Zaidi M. (2006). The Bees - A Novel Tool for Complex Optimisation Problems. *In Innovative Production Machines and Systems*, 2006.

Pouliquen, B. & Steinberger, R. & Deguernel, O. (2008). Story tracking: linking similar news over time and across languages Coling 2008: *Proceedings of the workshop on Multi-source Multilingual Information Extraction and Summarization*, pages 49–56 Manchester, August 2008.

Resnick, P. & Iacovou, N. & Suchak, M. & Bergstrom, P. & Riedl, J. (1994). An open architecture for collaboretive _filtering of netnews. *In Proceedings ACM Conference on Computer-Supported Cooperative Work*, pages 175-186, 1994.

Selley, D. & Camazine, S. & Sneyd, J. (1991). Collective decision-marking in honey bees: How colonies choose nectar sources. *Behavioral Ecology and Sociobiology*, 28: pages 277-290, 1991.

Schafer, J.B. & Konstan, J.A. & Riedl, J. (2001). E-commerce recommendation applications. *Data Mining and Knowledge Discovery*, 5(1/2): pages 115-153, 2001.

Teodorovic, D. & Dell' Orco, M. (2005). Bee Colony Optimisation: Cooperative Learning approach to Complex Transportation Problems, In *Proc.:16th Mini - EURO Conference and 10th Meeting of EWGT*. Poznan 2005.

Tovey, C.A. (2004). The Honey Bee Algorithm. A Biologically Inspired Approach to Internet Server Optimisation, *Engineering Enterprise* (Spring 2004), pages 13–15.

Visscher, K. & Camazine, S. (1999). Collective Decisions and Cognition in Bees, *Nature 397* (1999), page 400.

Vreis, H. & Biesmeijer, J.C. (1998). Modelling collective foraging by means of individual behaviour rules in honey-bees. *Behav Ecol Sociobiol* 44: pages 109-124, 1998.

Walker, R.L. (2007). Purposive Behavior Of Honeybees As The Basis Of An Experimental Search Engine. *Soft Computing*, 11: pages 697-716.

Wong, Li-Pei & Chi Yung Puan & Malcolm Yoke-Hean Low & Chin Soon Chong (2008). Bee Colony Optimisation algorithm with Big Valley landscape exploitation for Job Shop Scheduling problems. *Winter Simulation Conference 2008*: pages 2050-2058.

Zhang, S. & Schwarz, S. & Pahl, M. & Zhu, H. & Tautz, J. (2006). Honeybee Memory: A Honeybee Knows What To Do And When. *Journal of Experimental Biology*, 209, pages 4420-4428.

Combining pervasive computing with activity recognition and learning

Patrice C. Roy[1], Bruno Bouchard[2],
Abdenour Bouzouane[2] and Sylvain Giroux[1]
[1]*DOMUS Laboratory, Université de Sherbrooke, (Canada)*
[2]*LIAPA Laboratory, Université du Québec à Chicoutimi, (Canada)*

1. Introduction

Today, networks, microprocessors, memory chips, smart sensors and actuators are faster, more powerful, cheaper and smaller than ever. Chips are all around, invading everyday objects. Wireless networks enable to easily connect them. Everyday objects can then propose innovative and unexpected interactions (Ullmer & Ishii, 2000). Clothes will transport one's profile to reconfigure his environment according to his preferences (Abowd et al. 1997). Lamps will help people finding lost objects (Vergnes et al., 2005). Interactive portraits will reflect at distance the mood and health state of one's beloved relatives (Mynatt et al., 2001). This new technologically enhanced environment will enable finding novel solutions to help people in their everyday life, such as elders that suffer from cognitive deficit and have many difficulties to carry out their activities of daily living (Pigot et al., 2003). Most of these people wish to stay at home, where they feel comfortable and safe, as long as possible. The governments aim to help them for social reasons as well as economical ones. However, keeping cognitively impaired people at home involves many risks that are necessary to control. In order to do that, the physical and human environment must be specifically designed to compensate the cognitive impairments and the loss of autonomy (Ramos et al., 2008).

Combining pervasive computing with techniques from artificial intelligence (AI) greatly increases the acceptance of the pervasive assisted living and makes it more capable of providing a better quality of life in a non-intrusive way, where elderly people, with or without disabilities, could clearly benefit from this concept. From the computational perspective, there is a natural association between them. However, research addressing smart environments has in the past largely focused on network and hardware oriented solutions. AI-based techniques (planning and action theory, ontological and temporal reasoning, etc) that promote intelligent behaviour have not been examined to the same extent (Augusto & Nugent, 2006), although notable exceptions can been found in the domain of activity recognition for healthcare. Prior work has been done to use sensors to recognize the execution status of particular types of activities, such as hand washing (Mihailidis et al., 2007), meal preparation (Barger et al., 2002), and movements around town (Liao et al., 2004). Additionally, several projects have attempted to do more general activity recognition, using radio frequency identification (RFID) tags attached to household objects and gloves (Philipose et al., 2004). At DOMUS and LIAPA labs, we investigate theory and praxis of activity recognition for cognitive assistance. Most theoretical and long term approaches are based on hierarchical task Markovian model (Bauchet & Mayers, 2005; Pigot et al., 2008), Bayesian networks (Charniak & Goldman, 1993), and lattice-based models (Bouchard et al., 2007) enhanced with probabilities (Roy et al., 2009) to recognize activities of daily living (ADLs) and to anticipate erroneous behaviours classified according to cognitive errors (Bouchard et al., 2008).

This chapter will investigate in details the challenging key issues that emerge from research in the field of activity recognition under the context of smart environment. We will clearly describe the specific functional needs inherent in cognitive assistance for effective activity recognition and then we will present the fundamental research works that try addressing this problem in such context. This chapter is more of a survey and an analysis of existing works that have been studied for potential integration into our laboratories, rather than a focused evaluation report. Our objective is to identify gaps in the capabilities of current techniques and to suggest the most productive lines of research to address this complex issue. The chapter is organized as follows. Section 2 presents the foundations that characterize the problem of activity recognition and position it in the context of smart environments. Section 3 draws a detailed portrait of the learning techniques for activity recognition that exist, and presents their forces and weakness in our specific context. Finally, we conclude this chapter with perspectives and future challenges of this fascinating issue.

2. Activity recognition

Activity recognition aims to recognize the actions and goals of one or more agents from a series of observations on the agent's actions and the environmental conditions (Kautz et al., 2003). Due to its many-faceted nature, different fields may refer to activity recognition as plan recognition. The problem of plan recognition has been an active research topic for a long time (Carberry, 2001) and still remains very challenging. The recognition problem corresponds to a fundamental question: how can we predict the behaviour of an observed or communicating agent, so that this prediction can be then used for task coordination, cooperation, assistance, etc.? From that definition, the expression *activity recognition* refers to the fact that one supposes the existence of an activity structure (i.e. a set of actions ordered in time) chosen at start by the acting entity (for instance a patient), which constitutes the result that the observing agent (for instance a smart environment) seeks to recognize. By referring to the literacy on the subject, one can realize that this vision of the problem is a historical heritage from the first expert systems, which was originally used to resolve *planning* issues (Waern & Stenborg, 1995). The *planning* problem also constitutes a well-known challenge in the AI community, which can be considered as the inverse of activity recognition (Russell & Norvig, 2003). This difficulty consists, for an agent, to identify a sequence of actions (a plan) which, at the end of its execution, will allow the agent to achieve a pursued goal (Georgeff, 1987). For instance, an agent in a manufacturing environment can sense information from the environment and plan an action sequence in order to improve the manufacturing control system effectiveness (Merdan et al, 2006). Therefore, the problem of recognizing an activity can be seen as the inverse operation, in which another agent that does not know the planned objective has the task to identify the goal of the actor agent by inferring, from the observed actions, the possible on-going activities set. According to (Cohen et al., 1982) and (Geib & Goldman, 2005), activity recognition can be characterized by the relationship that exists between the observed agent and its observer. This relationship allows dividing activity recognition into three different categories. Each of these recognition types makes a particular presumption about the existing relationship between the observing agent and the actor entity, which will guide the recognition process.

2.1 Intended activity recognition

In a context of *intended recognition*, one supposes that the agent explicitly knows that it is been observed and therefore, that it adapts deliberately its behaviour to perform its activity in a manner that will facilitate the recognition process of the observer (Kautz, 1991). Consequently, this form of recognition presumes a direct cooperative effort on behalf of the observed entity. This category of recognition was introduced by (Cohen et al., 1982). His goal was to position the activity recognition problem within the particular context of natural language processing, in which he worked at the time. Some researchers supposed, based on the cooperative assumption of this category, that the observer agent could directly ask the actor in case of uncertainty, in order to get clarifications on the on-going task (Lesh et al., 1998). From a pervasive assisted living viewpoint, it is unrealistic to position the problem of recognizing activities in a context of intended recognition. For instance, in the case of trying to assist an Alzheimer's patient in his every day tasks, it is clearly difficult to make any assumption about the capacity of the patient to sustain a cooperative effort by adapting his behaviour in order to positively influence the recognition process. Moreover, we cannot let the system to ask an observed patient for clarifications in case of uncertainty, because this action would result in an increased cognitive charge on behalf of the patient, which is unsuitable in a context of cognitive assistance.

2.2 Adversarial activity recognition

The second category, named *adversarial recognition*, has been introduced by (Geib & Goldman, 2005) as a corollary of the first category, the intended recognition. In this type of recognition, rather than presuming that the observed agent will positively contribute to the recognition process, one supposes that the actor agent will likely attempt to spoil the process in a competitive gesture on its behalf (Mao & Gratch, 2004). In other terms, the actor agent considers the observer agent as an enemy and therefore, it will voluntarily try to perform actions that are incoherent with its goals in order to lead the observer to infer false conclusions about its behaviour. This type of recognition suits better to a military context (Heinze et al., 1999) or to context where competitive agents are deployed inside video games to challenge a human player (Albrecht et al., 1998). However, this type of recognition does not fit well in pervasive assisted living context of cognitive assistance. Even if we need to take into account the fact that a cognitively impaired patient will likely perform activities in an erroneous way, as it is commonly the case in adversarial context to misguide the observer, these errors are not performed deliberately. They are rather the consequence of the patient's symptoms and not the result of a well-planned stratagem to compromise the recognition process.

2.3 Keyhole activity recognition

The last category, named *keyhole recognition*, characterizes the assumption that an agent does not really know that it is been observed and thus, it will not attempt to influence the recognition process or to misguide the observer conclusions (Cohen et al., 1982). With this category, Cohen wanted to define a generic frame for activity recognition, in which one make a supposition of a neutral cooperative effort on behalf of the acting agent. Hence, Cohen made an analogy, from which the name of the category emanates, with a person being observed, inside a room, through the keyhole of the door, so that this person acts in the room naturally without worrying about being observed and without trying to help or compromise the on-going recognition process. We can position the activity recognition problem, from an assisted living point of view, in this category that suits better to the context of cognitive assistance, in which we certainly cannot presume the collaboration nor the deliberate nuisance of the patient (Bouchard, 2006).
The theory of keyhole plan recognition, on which we are working, tries to establish a formalization of this behavioural prediction. It is usually based on a probabilistic-logical inference engine for the construction of hypotheses about the possible plans, and on a matching process linking the observations with some plans included in a library or a model of activities related to the application domain. This library is an ontology of activity patterns that the observed agent can potentially carry out. At each observation of an action occurrence, the recognition agent tries to build hypotheses based on the knowledge described in this ontology. Since there can be many possible plans that can explain the observations, and thus the behaviour of the observed agent, the challenge is then to disambiguate these concurrent hypotheses. The researchers at DOMUS and LIAPA labs are exploring the following representation models to attack this issue.

2.3.1 Lattice-Based Model

The lattice plan recognition model tries to address the recognition issue by using lattice theory and Description Logics (DL) (Baader et al., 2007), which transforms the plan recognition problem into a classification issue. Description logics are a well-known family of knowledge representation formalisms that may be viewed as fragments of first-order logic. The main strength of DL is that they offer considerable expressive power going far beyond propositional logic, although reasoning is still decidable. The proposed model (Bouchard et al., 2007) provides an adequate basis to define algebraic tools used to formalize the inferential process of ADL recognition for Alzheimer's patients. To summarize, our approach consists of developing a model of minimal interpretation for a set of observed actions, by building a plan lattice structure as shown in the Figure 1. In this model, an intention schema characterizes the uncertainty related to the anticipated patient's behaviour. This schema corresponds to the lower bound of the lattice and is used to extract the anticipated incoherent plans, which are not pre-established in the knowledge base, that the patient may potentially carry out as a result of the symptoms of his disease. However, it is not sufficient to be able to disambiguate the relevant hypotheses. Therefore, the addition of a probabilistic quantification on the lattice structure (Roy et al., 2009) is an interesting and effective alternative, in the sense that it makes it possible to combine the symbolic approach for hypotheses construction with a probabilistic inferential process. The symbolic recognition agent filters the hypotheses by passing only a bounded lattice recognition space to the probabilistic inference engine, instead of considering the whole set of plans included in the ontology of the activities, as the classical probabilistic approaches usually do. The probabilistic quantification that we propose is based on samples of observation frequencies obtained at the end of a training period while the system learns the usual routines of the patient. This knowledge allows us to create a profile of the patient that offers a relevant basis to accurately estimate the probabilities of possible ongoing plans.

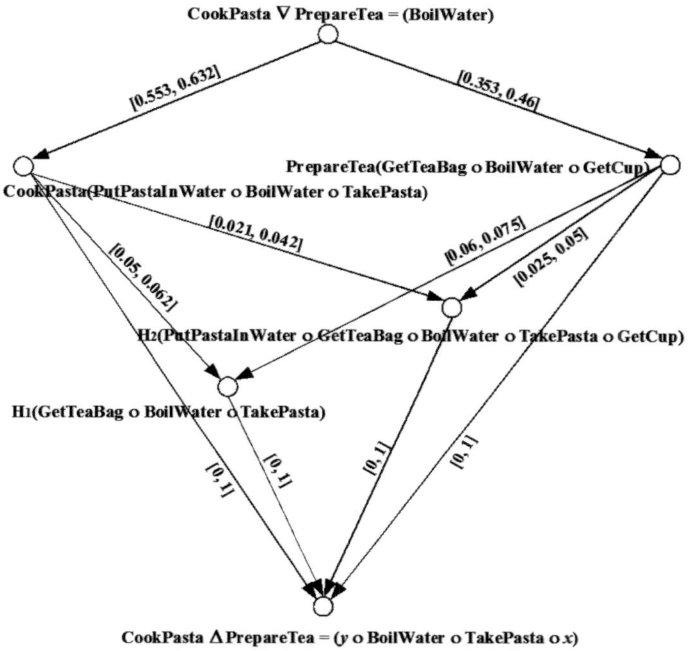

Fig. 1. A plan lattice structure that models two activities: cooking pasta and preparing tea.

This approach was implemented and tested in the DOMUS experimental smart home infrastructures, where we have simulated different scenarios based on 40 low-level actions and 10 activities of daily living. Each of these activities corresponds to a common kitchen task (cooking cake, cooking pasta, making tea, etc.) sharing several actions with some other activities, in order to create a realistic context where plans can be interleaved and can lead to many different kinds of planning errors (realization, initiation, sequence, completion, etc). The observation's frequencies of the erroneous and coherent behaviours are based on the frequencies described in the study of Giovannetti et al. (Giovannetti et al., 2002), done on 51 patients suffering from neurodegenerative diseases, which include the Alzheimer's disease. The results clearly show that the model recognizes all of the interleaved plans and realization type errors, and 70% of the sequence type errors. These results are promising, as all these recognized hypotheses were not pre-established in the knowledge base; they were dynamically generated in the recognition space, according to the initial identified possible plans set. However, our approach is limited by the fact that the first observed action is assumed to be correct (no errors) and coherent with the patient's goal. The problem is that in some scenarios that we simulated, the patient started by performing an action that he was only supposed to carry out in a later stage. This limitation explains the 30% of unpredicted sequence errors and also explains why our system has trouble predicting initiation errors. In another hand, we have also experimented the approach in concrete case by extending the system named COACH (Bouchard et al., 2008; Mihailidis et al., 2007), a cognitive aide for Alzheimer's patients that actively monitors an user attempting a handwashing task and offers assistance in the form of task guidance (e.g., prompts or reminders) when it is most appropriate. When an Alzheimer's patient is performing the handwashing activity, the system gets as observations a set of state variables obtained using cameras, such as the patient's hand location, the tap position (open or closed), etc., in order to determine the completion status of the task according to a previously handcrafted model. If the completion status of the task regresses or does not evolve for a certain period of time, the system will compute the best possible solution to achieve the task and will try to guide the person until the next activity step.

2.3.2 Hierarchical task model

Several investigators have highlighted the importance on representing hierarchically structured complex activities with dynamic probabilistic model. For instance, in Pigot et al. (Pigot et al., 2008) and Bauchet et al. (Bauchet & Mayers, 2005), the recognition process is based on a model of activities where tasks are described using hierarchical structure as shown in the following figure.

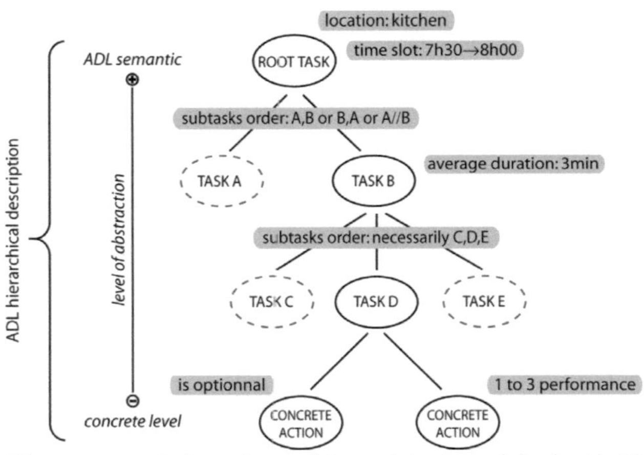

Fig. 2. ADL recognition process is based on a hierarchical model of activities.

The model includes two types of task's nodes: goal of the occupant and the method to complete it. Leaves are methods of terminal tasks, which mean an atomic way to realize a concrete goal. Similar approaches can be found in hierarchical task network planning. However, this hierarchical model does not consider the set of subtasks as a predefined sequence, since there are numerous ways to realize an activity for a given method. Instead of generating all plausible sequences, rules are defined to generalize, for a given method, the criteria of integration of subtasks: partial or total sequence, repetition and/or necessity constraint. Breaking those rules should be considered as an improper activity completion. To monitor the proper completion of activities, temporal information is introduced for tasks nodes. This deals with the average time needed to realize the task, and the time slot of completion. The validation of these constraints during task realization is done according to

the *Epitalk* approach, a tutoring architecture used for generating advisor agents (Paquette et al., 1996). Each adviser manages a local model of the activity based on a hierarchical Markov model of the patient's habits by using an episodic memory. The activity is considered as an episode incorporating information on the method used for task completion, on right time slots, locations, sequences of subepisodes, frequencies of the observed activities, and so on. Hence, the adviser agent is both responsible to recognize a precise subtask and to provide assistance related to this task. The leaves of the model are connected to the IO events server and are fed by low-level events triggered by the sensors. A bottom-up traversal of the hierarchy aggregates information to provide for a larger view of what is going on.
The main characteristics of this model are that the plan recognition and the production of pieces of advice are combined into a single walk through the adviser tree. The principle is simple: each time a sensor triggers an event, it sends it to the corresponding terminal advisers. Then a bottom-up spreading is activated as follows: (i) each adviser (terminal or non-terminal) processes the information, either to issue local advice or to update a local model of the activity being observed, (ii) the adviser transmits to its direct father any information it considers relevant. This scheme is applied recursively for all advisers of the tree, terminal or non-terminal, until the root adviser is reached. Terminal advisers receive information directly from the host system, in particular sensors, whereas non-terminal advisers receive information from advisers below them in the hierarchy. This model, compared to previous works, allows a more effective description of ADLs for cognitive assistance. Despite the good results that has shown in real case assistance scenarios, the system appears to be somewhat limited owing to the fact that it is only able to monitor one specific ADL and the assistance agent react after the user error. This model constitutes the base component of the *Archipel* system (Bauchet et al., 2008) developed at DOMUS lab. Archipel is a context-oriented framework for cognitive assistance and has been applied to meal preparation. Its objectives are to promote ADLs completion for people with cognitive impairments, to foster their functional autonomy and their quality of life, and to exploit context-awareness and to use resources in the environment for assistance. A framework integrating four axis was implemented: knowledge representation, man-machine interfaces, ADL monitoring and ADL assistance.

2.3.3 Bayesian networks and Markovian models

In general, Bayesian networks are the principal technology used for performing activity recognition (Pollack, 2005). A typical approach is that taken in the Barista system (Patterson et al., 2007), which is a fine-grained ADL recognition system that uses object IDs to determine which activities are currently executed. It uses radiofrequency identification (RFID) tags on objects and two RFID gloves that the user wears in order to recognize activities in a smart home. The system is composed of a set of sensors (RFID tags and gloves) that detects object interactions, a probabilistic engine that infers activities with observations from the sensors, and a model creator that allows creating probabilistic models of activities from, for instance, written recipes. The activities are represented as sequences of activity stages. Each stage is composed of the objects involved, the probability of their involvement, and, optionally, a time to completion modelled as a Gaussian probability distribution. The activities are converted into Dynamic Bayesian Networks (DBN) by the probabilistic engine. By using the current sub-activity as a hidden variable and the set of objects seen and time elapsed as observed variables, the engine is able to probabilistically estimate the activities from sensor data. It was able to identify the specific on-going activity with recognition accuracy higher than 80%, which is very impressive. This approach is able to identify the currently carried out ADL in a context where activities can be interleaved. However, this approach does not take into account the erroneous realization of activities, because the result of the activity recognition is the most plausible on-going ADLs.

Following the traces of works on Bayesian approaches, another branch of scientists (Boger et al., 2006; Patterson et al., 2005) recently proposed to define the activity recognition process by using Hidden Markov Models (HMM) formalism (Rabiner, 1990). This type of approach tries to represent the library of the observing agent with a set of discrete possible states. These states aim to characterize all the possible configurations of the smart environment, assuming that these configurations are not directly observable but can only be evaluated from inputs given by sensors. A stochastic model specifies and quantifies the dynamic that bound the transition between those states. The structure of the HMM is defined as a tuple (S, Obs, A, B, π), where S is the set of all possible states of the environment, Obs is the set of observable inputs given by sensors, A (actions) is the probability transition matrix between states, B is the probability matrix that links inputs from sensors with environment states, and π defines the *a priori* probability of each state at the beginning of the recognition process, when there is no input.

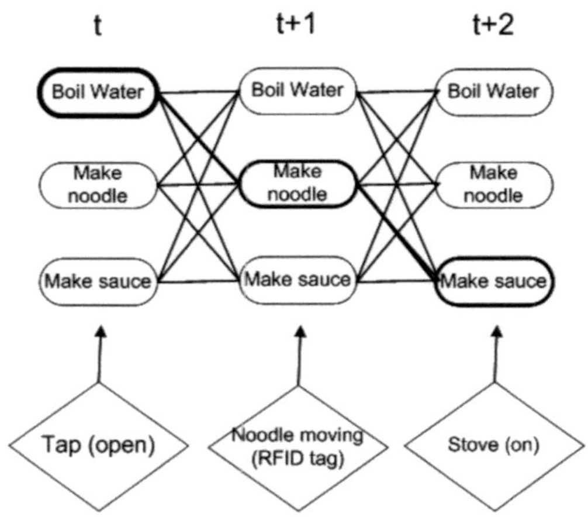

Fig. 3. Simple HMM for activity recognition in a smart environment.

Figure 3 shows an example of such HMM, where S = {"*Boil water*", "*Make noodle*", "*Make sauce*"}, defining that the environment can be in three possible states: (1) the person is putting water to boil, (2) the person is making noodle, (3) the person is preparing sauce. In this example, we have three sensors, one on the tap, one on the noodle box and one on the stove. The probability of getting an input from the tap while being in the state "*Boil water*" could be, for instance, very high. Same thing with the noodle box sensor and "*Make noodle*", and the stove sensor and "*Make sauce*". Knowing the *a priori* probability of each state defined in π, and the probabilities matrix A and B, the Viterbi algorithm (Forney, 1973) is used to estimate the most likely sequence of states that fit best with the sequence of observations. For instance, if the tap sensor came on at time t, the noodle box RFID tag indicates it is moving at time $t+1$, and the stove sensor came on at time $t+2$, the most likely inferred states

sequence could be "*Boil water*", "*Make noodle*", "*Make sauce*". This sequence could then be linked with the corresponding activity, which could be here "*Prepare Spaghetti*".
At the end, it is clear that several limitations restraint the use of probabilistic models for recognizing activities in a context of ambient intelligence (AmI). The first problem is the complexity of calculations, notably with Bayesian's networks, at the time of the propagation in the network, mainly observed when the network's size is large. Most of these calculations are somewhat blind because the probabilities of all possible hypotheses are evaluated, even the one of irrelevant activities. Moreover, the estimation of the prior probabilities is a difficult and important task, because the probabilistic inference's precision depends on this estimation. In addition, the probabilistic distribution in the plan library must remain uniform. Therefore, when a new activity is added to the library, the probabilistic distribution must be re-evaluated in order to stay uniform. This constitutes a clear limitation in a context where one wishes to learn new behaviours coming from a patient. Furthermore, the result of the recognition consists of the most likely plan (activity) to be carried out, which constitutes a problem in a context where multiple activities can be performed in an interleaved or an erroneous way.

2.4 Context-awareness and activity recognition

When humans interact with each others, they are able to use implicit situational information, or context, in order to increase the efficiency of the interaction. In order to improve the effectiveness of computational services offered by smart home technologies, the context must be taken into account by the computing devices. Since the activity recognition process uses the current and previous situations of the environment to infer the behaviour of its occupant, contextual information must be retrieved from the environment sensors. There exist several definitions of the context concept. In (Schilit & Theimer, 1994), a context is defined as the location, identities of nearby individuals and objects, and changes to those objects. In (Dey, 2001), a context is defined as any information that can be used in order to characterize the situation of an entity, which can be a person, place, or object that is considered relevant to the interaction between an user and an application, including the latter themselves. Systems that use or infer on contexts to provide contextual services are denoted to be context-awareness. One of the earlier definitions of a context-aware system is given in (Schilit & Theimer, 1994), where a context-aware system is a system that adapts itself according to its location of use, the set of nearby objects and people, and the changes to those objects over time. In (Dey, 2001), a context-aware system uses context in order to provide relevant information and/or services to the user, where relevancy depends on the user's task.
There exist several models of context-aware systems. The approach of (Zhang et al., 2005) uses a layered model (*context stack*) to represent context-aware systems. The lowest level is the *context acquisition layer*, where context in raw data is acquired from the ubiquitous sensors. The second level is the *context representation layer*, where raw data are converted into an understandable and readable format according, for instance, to a context ontology. The next level, the *context aggregation layer*, aggregates contexts from distributed sensors in order to form a centralized context database, which allows to provide functionalities of a knowledge base and to store previous contexts. The fourth layer is the *context interpretation layer*, which uses reasoning/learning techniques to deduce implicit high-level context from explicit low-level context. Finally, the *context utilization layer* allows to context-aware

services to use low and high-level contexts to adjust their behaviours. The model of (Ailisto et al., 2002) also subdivides context-aware systems into five layers. The lowest level is the *physical layer*, where sensors and objects in the environment produce output in a raw format. The next layer is the *data layer*, where objects produce processed data according to low-level sensors data. The third layer is the *semantic layer*, where data are transformed into a format where inference services can be applied. The fourth level, the *inference layer*, uses information from the semantic level and inference rules to make guesses on what the user is doing and what kind of services he might want. The last level, the *application layer*, uses the inferred context in order to plan a service task. In the activity recognition perspective, a context can be seen as raw data from the environment sensors in a particular situation or as an interpretation of the sensors data according to a knowledge representation language. Since the environment is partially observable, a context can be associated to a particular environment state or to a subset of possible environment states. The actions, activities or behaviours of the occupant inferred from the context can be seen as high-level contexts. By using hypotheses associated with those high-level contexts, a context-aware assistant application can plan and provide support tasks to the user if the situation requires it.

3. Learning for activity recognition

Another avenue of attack on the activity recognition problem is to apply learning techniques. These techniques seek to identify patterns from the observed actions set, in order to build a predictive model of the observed agent behaviour. A great number of these learning recognition approaches are based on probabilistic methods. For instance, Liao et al. (Liao et al., 2004) proposed a hierarchical Bayesian learning model for a person moving through a transportation network in an urban environment. This model aims to recognize and predict the future person's location and his transportation mode. This probabilistic learning technique is based on Rao-Blackwellised particle filters (Doucet et al., 2000), a variant of Bayes filters for estimating the state of a dynamic system. The main motivation for Liao's work is the development of a personal guidance system that will help cognitively impaired individuals to move safely and independently in their community. From this point of view, a significant contribution of these works is to provide a way to detect user errors and deviations from common routines by using a model-selection approach (Liao et al. 2004). This new feature, called by the authors novelty detection, is based on using two parallel stochastic models and on comparing the likelihood of the learned hierarchical model with a prior model. This method is interesting, as it gives a concrete means to the system to know when an assistance action would be required. The limitation of this model-selection approach is that, even if it recognizes the patient's new behaviour, it is still unable to determine if it corresponds to a coherent new routine or to an erroneous performance of a known plan. Moreover, this approach does not allow distinguishing between the different kinds of activity errors and is unable to evaluate the significance of the person's deviation. Wilson and Philipose (Wilson & Philipose, 2005) have proposed a method for estimating how well an elder performs day-to-day activities and for suggesting to him some ways to enhance his performance. This method is based on a HMM and on the well-known Viterbi algorithm which is an algorithm used to find the most likely sequence of hidden states in a HMM, incorporating the notion of edit distance. When an elder person has failed in the completion of an activity, this method evaluates his performance, according to a set of correct examples performed and rated by a human professional, and finds the closest successful solution by computing the edit distance between the elder's performed action sequence and the learned examples. The strength of this approach is the capacity to evaluate precisely how bad the performance of the person's erroneous activity is, and also to propose an adapted correcting solution based on this specific erroneous performance. The main disadvantage of the method is that it cannot anticipate the possible abnormal behaviour of the patient, what is exactly what we try to do.

3.1 Non-probabilistic Learning

Regarding non-probabilistic learning techniques, Lent (Lent & Laird, 2001) have worked on a general framework for learning-by observation systems based on inductive learning algorithms such as the C4.5 decision-tree learning (Quinlan, 1993). This approach tries to mimic human behaviour and models acquiring knowledge from observation as a machine-learning problem. The problem of this approach is how to manage the observations containing a great deal of noise. The observations of the human's behaviour consist of the sensor inputs, the human operator selections, and the actions performed to achieve these operators. Usually, these methods are effective in a deterministic environment, and if the agent's tasks were changed slightly, the decision trees would have to be relearned from a new set of observations. Tambe (Tambe et al., 2000) has conducted some experiments, using a C4.5 decision-tree approach, on building an agent for helping user scheduling meetings based on observation learning of transfer decision making between a human and his agent. This agent fails to address the adjustable autonomy challenge in a team context, due to the fact that in this kind of logically based learning approaches, the generalization of learned rules might lead to inferring inconsistent behaviour (in this case, the agent incorrectly cancelled a meeting because it over-generalized from training examples).

3.2 Applying Learning Techniques to ADL Recognition

Over the last few years, a great amount of work has used learning approaches, mostly probabilistic ones, to address the problem of ADL recognition for cognitively impaired patients. In their assisted cognition project (Patterson et al., 2002) have developed Activity Compass, a cognitive aide for early-stage Alzheimer's patients. This system is based on the learning recognition model described in (Liao et al., 2004). In his work, Patterson directly addresses the issue of incoherent behaviour recognition and proposes to identify the Alzheimer's patient plans that are incomplete or improperly formed, by matching them to the closest learned pattern. Cook's team in their MavHome project (Singla et al., 2008) argues that if one can successfully recognize ADL initiation and completion in the context where the activity is incomplete or the resident may switching between tasks, then one can use the technologies to perform automatic assessment of an individual's well being and provide the foundation for reminder-based interventions. They designed algorithms that probabilistically identify the activity while it is performed, as well as identify steps that are missing. They employ a HMM augmented with temporal information to automatically learn the initiation and completion of ADLs. They demonstrate by showing an overall accuracy of 88.63% that this temporal information improves activity recognition performance on real-world task as performed in their smart home testbeds. Once again, theses approaches cannot distinguish the different types of patient's deviations and needs a long training period to be efficient. Moreover, the patient's habits may change from time to time, according to new experiences, the hour of the day, his physical and psychological condition, etc. Therefore, the patient's routines must be constantly re-learned and an adaptation period is required by the system.

4. Ongoing and future work

The new development towards pervasive assisted living will stimulate the research in many fields of artificial intelligence, such as multi-agent approach as development paradigm for this open and hardly dynamic environment. Since forty years, artificial intelligence has not ceased to being used on a large scale through expert system applications, web search agent, etc. If the internet devoted the advent of the conventional planetary networks, the next evolution, that will support the development of the artificial intelligence, relates to new challenging issues concerning how a network of agents will be deployed within our natural living environment, and how each of these artificial agents, in the sense of multi-agent systems, will be represented according to the following ambient capacities: (i) ubiquity which means that the agent must be able to interact with an embarqued heterogeneous electronic devices by using pervasive computing, (ii) context-awareness based on ontological reasoning to detect the localization and the implication of objects and inhabitants in daily activities, (iii) natural interaction for communicating intuitively with occupant through a personalized multimodal interface, and finally (iv) intelligence based on activity recognition and machine learning in order to predict the behaviour of the inhabitant in the case of assisted living allowing cognitive assistance and as well as stimulation for avoiding the rejection of such new technology. Hence, the question concerns the integration of these four characteristics within any objects of everyday life. For instance, if the door of the refrigerator is open, the associated ambient agent must be able to have an idea on the behaviour of the person, such as this opening is under the context of meal preparation while it communicates in an opportunistic way with other objects of the habitat, for example, the cooker's ambient agent. The stimulation for closing the door because of memory loss can be done through an intuitive interaction (game) between the refrigerator's ambient agent and the occupant with disabilities, explaining the concept of the door closed. This new concept of ambient agent will ineluctably impose a capital evolution, for instance, in the assisted living. As a contribution, this chapter investigated in details the challenging key issues related to the development of ambient agents in smart environment, under the context of activity recognition, by defining the notion of activity recognition in the context of AmI, and by presenting a survey and an analysis of existing works on activity recognition that have been studied for potential integration into our respective laboratories. This chapter allows one to identify gaps in the capabilities of current techniques and to give hints on the most productive lines of research to address this complex issue. We raised numerous research challenges that need to be addressed for understanding the domain and enabling ambient multi-agent recognition systems for cognitive assistance to operate effectively.

5. References

Abowd, G.D.; Dey, A.K.; Orr, R. & Brotherton J.A. (1997). Context-awareness in wearable and ubiquitous computing, *Proceedings of the 1st International Symposium on Wearable Computing (ISWC '97)*, pp. 179-180, Cambridge, USA, October 13-14, 1997.

Ailisto, H.; Alahuhta, P.; Haataja, V.; Kylloenen, V. & Lindholm, M. (2002). Structuring context aware applications: Five-layer model and example case, *Proceedings of the Workshop on Concepts and Models for Ubiquitous Computing*, pp.1-5, Goteborg, Sweden.

Albrecht, D.W.; Zukerman, D.W. & Nicholson, A.E. (1998). Bayesian Models for Keyhole Plan Recognition in an Adventure Game. *User Modeling and User-Adapted Interaction*, Vol.8, No.1-2, pp. 5-47.

Augusto, J.C. & Nugent, C.D. (2006). *Designing Smart Homes: The Role of Artificial Intelligence, State of the Art Survey, vol. LNAI 4008*, Springer-Verlag, 2006.

Baader, F.; Calvanese, D.; McGuinness, D.L.; Nardi, D. & Patel-Schneider, P.F. (2007). *The Description Logic Handbook: Theory, Implementation, and Applications. Second Edition*, Cambridge University Press.

Barger, T.; Alwan, M.; Kell, S.; Turner, B.; Wood, S. & Naidu, A. (2002). Objective remote assessment of activities of daily living: Analysis of meal preparation patterns, *Medical Automation Research Center*, University of Virginia Health System, Charlottesville.

Bauchet, J.; Giroux, S.; Pigot, H.; Lussier-Desrochers, D. & Lachapelle Y. (2008). Pervasive Assistance in Smart Homes For People with Intellectual Disabilities: A Case Study on Meal Preparation. *IJARM*, Vol. 9, pp. 53-65.

Bauchet, J. & Mayers, A. (2005). Modelisation of ADLs in its Environment for Cognitive Assistance, *Proc. of the 3rd International Conference on Smart homes and health Telematic, ICOST'05*, pp.3-10, Sherbrooke, Canada.

Boger, J.; Hoey, J.; Poupart, P.; Boutilier, C.; Fernie, G. & Mihailidis, A. (2006). A Planning System Based on Markov Decision Processes to Guide People with Dementia Through Activities of Daily Living. *IEEE Transactions on Information Technology in BioMedicine*, Vol.10, No.2, pp.323-333.

Bouchard, B. (2006). *Un modèle de reconnaissance de plan pour les personnes atteintes de la maladie d'Alzheimer basé sur la théorie des treillis et sur un modèle d'action en logique de description*, Ph.D. Thesis, University of Sherbrooke, Canada, 268 pages.

Bouchard, B.; Bouzouane, A. & Giroux, S. (2007). A Keyhole Plan Recognition Model for Alzheimer's Patients: First Results, *Applied Artificial Intelligence: An International Journal*, Vol.22, No. 7, pp. 623–658.

Bouchard, B.; Roy, P.C.; Bouzouane, A.; Giroux, S. & Mihailidis, A. (2008). Towards an extension of the COACH task guidance system: Activity recognition of alzheimer's patients. *ECAI'08 3rd Workshop on Artificial Intelligence Techniques for Ambient Intelligence (AITAmI'08)*, pp. 16-20, Patras, Grece.

Carberry, S., Techniques for plan recognition, (2001). *User Modeling and User-Adapted Interaction*, Vol.11, No.1–2, pp. 31–48.

Charniak, E. & Goldman, R.P. (1993). A Bayesian model of plan recognition. *Artificial Intelligence*, Vol.64, No.1, pp.53-79.

Cohen, P.R.; Perrault, C.R. & Allen, J.F. (1982). Beyong question answering, in *Strategies for Natural Language Processing*, Lehnert, W.G. & Ringle, M.H. eds., Lawrence Erlbaum Associates, Hillsdale, NJ.

Dey, A.K. (2001). Understanding and Using Context. *Personal and Ubiquitous Computing*, Vol.5, No.1, pp.4-7.

Doucet, A.; Freitas, N.; Murphy, K. & Russell, S. (2000). Rao-Blackwellised particle filtering for dynamic Bayesian networks. *Annual Conference on Uncertainty in Artificial Intelligence (UAI'00)*, pp. 176–183.

Forney, G.D. (1973). The Viterbi algorithm. *Proc. of IEEE*, Vol.61, No.3, pp. 268–278.

Heinze, C.; Goss, S.; Lloyd, I. & Pearce, A. (1999). Plan Recognition in Military Simulation : Incorporating Machine Learning with Intelligent Agents. *Proc. of IJCAI-99 Workshop on Team Behaviour and Plan Recognition*, pp. 53–64.

Geib, C. & Goldman, R. (2005). Partial Observability and Probabilistic Plan/Goal Recognition, *Proc. of the IJCAI-05 workshop on Modeling Others from Observations (MOO-05), Int. Joint Conference on Artificial Intelligence*, pp.1–6.

Georgeff, M.P. (1987). Planning, *Annual Review of Computer Science*, Vol.2, pp. 359-400, Annual Reviews, Palo Alto, California.

Giovannetti, T.; Libon, D.J.; Buxbaum, L.J. & Schwartz, M.F. (2002). Naturalistic action impairments in dementia, *Neuropsychologia*, Vol.40, No.8, pp.1220–1232.

Kautz, H. (1991). A Formal Theory of Plan Recognition and its Implementation, in: *Reasoning About Plans*, Allen, J.; Pelavin, R. & Tenenberg, J. eds., pp.69-125, Morgan Kaufmann, San Mateo, CA.

Kautz, H.; Etzioni, O.; Fox, D. & Weld, D. (2003). *Foundations of assisted cognition systems.* Tech. Rep. CSE-02-AC-01, University of Washington.

Lent, M. and Laird, J.E. (2001). Learning Procedural Knowledge Through Observation, *Proceedings of the 1st international conference on Knowledge capture*, pp.179-186, Victoria, British Columbia, Canada.

Lesh, N.; Rich, C. & Sidner, C.L. (1998). *Using plan recognition in Human-Computer Collaboration, TR-98-23*, Mitsubishi Electric Research Lab (MERL).

Liao, L.; Kautz, H. & Fox, D. (2004). Learning and inferring transportation routines. *Proceedings of the 19th National Conference on Artificial Intelligence (AAAI)*, pp.348-353, San Jose, California.

Merdan, M.; Kordic, V.; Zoitl, A. & Lazinica, A. (2006) Knowledge-based Multi-agent Architecture, *Proc. of the International Conference on Computational Intelligence for Modelling Control and Automation and International Conference on Intelligent Agents, Web Technologies and Internet Commerce (CIMCA-IAWTIC'06)*, pp.1-6, Sydney, Australia.

Mao, W. & Gratch, J. (2004). *Decision-Theoric Approach to Plan Recognition. Technical Report ICT-TR-01-2004*, Institute for Creative Technologies (ICT).

Mihailidis, A.; Boger, J.; Canido, M. & Hoey, J. (2007). The use of an intelligent prompting system for people with dementia, *Interactions*, Vol. 14, pp.34-37.

Mynatt, E.D.; Rowan, J.; Craighill, S. & Jacobs, A. (2001). Digital family portraits: Supporting peace of mind for extended family members. *Proc. of the ACM Conference on Human Factors in Computing Systems (CHI 2001)*, pp. 333-340, Seattle, Washington, ACM Press.

Paquette, G.; Pachet, F.; Giroux, S. & Girard, J. (1996). Epitalk, generating advisor agents for existing information systems. *Artificial Intelligence in Education,* Vol.7, No.3-4, pp.349-379.

Patterson, D.J.; Etzioni, O. & Kautz, H. (2002). The Activity Compass. *Proc. of the 1st Int. Workshop on Ubiquitous Computing for Cognitive Aids*, pp.1-3, Gothenberg, Sweden.

Patterson, D.J.; Fox, D.; Kautz, H.A. & Philipose, M. (2005). Fine-Grained Activity Recognition by Aggregating Abstract Object Usage, *Proc. of the IEEE International Symposium on Wearable Computers*, pp.1–8, Osaka, Japan.

Patterson, D.J.; Kautz, H.A. ; Fox, D. & Liao L. (2007) Pervasive computing in the home and community. In: *Pervasive Computing in Healthcare*, Bardram, J.E.; Mihailidis, A. & Wan, D. (Eds.), pp.79–103, CRC Press, Boca Raton, FL.

Philipose, M.; Fishkin, K.P.; Perkowitz, M.; Patterson, D.J.; Hahnel, D.; Fox, D. & Kautz H., (2004). Inferring Activities from Interactions with Objects, *IEEE Pervasive Computing,* Vol.3, No.4, pp. 50-56.

Pigot, H.; Lussier-Desrochers, D.; Bauchet, J.; Lachapelle, Y. & Giroux, S. (2008). A Smart Home to Assist in Recipe Completion. In: *Technology and Aging, Assistive Technology Research Series, vol. 21*, Mihailidis, A.; Kautz, H.; Boger, J. & Normie, L., Eds., pp.35-42, IOS Press, Amsterdam.

Pigot, H.; Mayers, A. & Giroux, S. (2003). The intelligent habitat and everyday life activity support, *Proc. Int. Conf. in Simulations in Biomedicine,* pp.507-516, Slovenia.

Pollack, M.E. (2005). Intelligent Technology for an Aging Population: The Use of AI to Assist Elders with Cognitive Impairment, *AI Magazine*, Vol.26, No.2, pp.9–24.

Quinlan, J.R. (1993). *C4.5: Programs For Machine Learning,* Morgan Kaufmann, San Mateo, CA.

Ramos, C.; Augusto, J.C. & Shapiro, D. (2008). Ambient Intelligence: the Next Step for Artificial Intelligence, *IEEE Intelligent Systems*, Vol. 23, No. 2, pp.5-18.

Rabiner, L.R. (1990). A tutorial on hidden Markov models and selected applications in speech recognition. *IEEE* Vol.77, No.2, pp.267–296.

Roy, P.C.; Bouchard, B.; Bouzouane, A. & Giroux, S., (2009). A hybrid plan recognition model for Alzheimer's patients: interleaved-erroneous dilemma, *Web Intelligence and Agent Systems (WIAS): An Int. Journal*, Vol.7, No.4, pp.1-23, (to appear).

Russell, S. & Norvig, P. (2003). *Artificial Intelligence: A Modern Approach, 2nd edition*. Prentice-Hall, Englewood Cliffs, NJ.

Schilit, B.N. & Theimer, M.M. (1994). Disseminating active map information to mobile hosts. *IEEE Network*, Vol.8, No.5, pp.22-32.

Singla, G.; Cook, D. & Schmitter-Edgecombe, M. (2008). Incorporating temporal reasoning into activity recognition for smart home residents. *Proceedings of the AAAI Workshop on Spatial and Temporal Reasoning*, pp.1-9.

Tambe, M.; Pynadath, D.V.; Chauvat, N.; Das, A. & Kaminka, G.A. (2000). Adaptive agent integration architectures for heterogeneous team members. *International Conference on MultiAgent Systems*, pp. 301–308.

Ullmer, B. & Ishii H. (2000). Emerging frameworks for tangible user interfaces. *IBM Systems Journal,* Vol.39, No.3-4, pp.1-15.

Vergnes, D.; Giroux, S. & Chamberland-Tremblay, D. (2005). Interactive assistant for activities of daily living. *3rd International Conference on Smart Homes and Health Telematics, ICOST 2005,* pp.229-236, July 4-6, Sherbrooke, Canada.

Waern, A. & Stenborg, O. (1995). Recognizing the plans of a replanning user. *IJCAI-95 Workshop on The Next Generation of Plan Recognition Systems*, pp.113-118, Montréal, Canada.

Wilson, D. & Philipose, M. (2005). Maximum a posteriori path estimation with input trace perturbation: algorithms and application to credible rating of human routines. *Nineteenth International Joint Conference on Artificial Intelligence (IJCAI'05)*, pp.895-901, Edinburgh, Scotland, UK.

Zhang, D.; Gu, T. & Wang, X. (2005). Enabling Context-aware Smart Home with Semantic Technology. *International Journal of Human-friendly Welfare Robotic Systems*, Vol.6, No.4, pp1-14.

Intelligent Agents in Extreme Conditions – Modeling and Simulation of Suicide Bombing for Risk Assessment

Zeeshan-ul-hassan Usmani[1] , Fawzi Alghamdi[2] and Daniel Kirk[3]
Florida Institute of Technology
USA

1. Introduction

Intelligent agents in extreme conditions is an attempt to use agent based simulation to save lives, predict the outcome of catastrophic events like suicide bombing, and model the behavior of crowd in emergency situations. This work is set to implement, test, analyze and measure intelligent agents' behavior and its consequences under extreme conditions like suicide bombing through multi-agent simulation.

Suicide bombing has become one of the most lethal and favorite modus operandi of terrorist organizations around the world. It claims 48% of the casualties, while only 3% of all terrorist attacks can be classified as suicide bombing attacks. On average, there is a suicide bombing attack somewhere in the world on every 6th day that claims 13.4 lives (on average) per attack (Usmani a, 2009). While various attempts have been made to assess the impact of explosions on structures, little has been done on modeling the impact of a blast wave for an individual or a crowd. There is no tool exist to determine the impact of explosion as a function of crowd dynamics, and explosive characteristics. And there is not a single method available to map the blast overpressure to human injuries that is calibrated against the real-life victims' data. All of the existing estimates and pressure-lethality curves are based on experiments on pigs, sheep, and data collected from stationary sensors without any consideration of blockage and 3D environment.

Explosion modeling is a complicated task that requires the knowledge of physical properties of explosions, projectiles and debris, chemical properties of explosive materials and their reactions, complex details of simulating gaseous and combustion flows with boundary conditions, complex coding for blast waves and fragmentation models, know-how of computational fluid dynamics, and the overall impact of explosions on humans and structures supported by experimental and theoretical studies. This work explains the physics, explosive models, mathematics and the assumptions we need to create such a simulation. The work also describes human shields available in the crowd with partial and full blockage in both two dimensional and three dimensional environments.

A virtual simulation tool (BlastSim) has been developed which is capable of assessing the impact of crowd formation patterns and their densities on the magnitude of injury and number of casualties during a suicide bombing attack. Results indicated that the worst crowd formation is Zig-Zag (e.g., street) where 30% crowd can be dead and 45% can be injured, given typical explosive carrying capacity of a single suicide bomber. Row wise crowd formation was found to be the best for reducing the effectiveness of an attack with 18% crowd in lethal zone and 38% in injury zones. For a typical suicide bombing attack, we can reduce the number of fatalities by 12%, and the number of injuries by 7% by simply following the recommendations in this chapter. Simulation results were compared and validated by the real-life incidents and found to be in good agreement. Line-of-sight with the attacker, rushing towards the exit, and stampede were found to be the most lethal choices both during and after the attack. These findings, although preliminary, may have implications for emergency response and counter terrorism.

2. Literature Review

Suicide bombing is an operational method in which the very act of the attack is dependent upon the death of the perpetrator (Pape, 2005). The world is full of unwanted explosives, brutal bombings, accidents, and violent conflicts, and there is a need to understand the impact of these explosions on one's surroundings, the environment, and most importantly on human bodies. There is a growing need and interest in treating explosion related injuries in emergency rooms, a phenomenon traditionally only considered to be present in the emergency units of battlefields. From 1980 to 2001 (excluding 9/11/01) the average number of deaths per incident for suicide bombing attacks was 13. This number is far above the average of less than one death per incident across all types of terrorist attacks over the same time period (Harrison, 2004). In Israel, from November 2000 to November 2003 the average number of deaths per incident was 31.4 (Harrison, 2006). From 2006 to 2007 the average number of deaths in Pakistan was 14.2 (Usmani a, 2009). Suicide bombers, unlike any other device or means of destruction, can think and therefore detonate the charge at an optimal location with perfect timing to cause maximum carnage and destruction. Suicide bombers are adaptive and can quickly change targets if forced by security risk or the availability of better targets. Suicide attacks are relatively inexpensive to fund and technologically primitive, as IEDs can be readily constructed.

A significant progress has been made in the modeling and simulation of explosion and blast waves in last two decades (Pritchard *et. al.*, 1999, Lester, *et. al.*, 2004, Clutter, *et. al.*, 2006). However, the majority of work (Redlins, 1977, HJertager, 1982, Ettouney, 2001) follows a trend of capabilities and limitations mainly influence by their requirements in industry and non-civil settings. For example, none of the models (Cates & Samuels, 1991, Baker, *et. al.* 1998, Baker, *et. al.* 1994, Berg, 1985, Arntzen, 1982, Usmani c, *et. al.*, 2009, Usmani d, *et. al.*, 2009, Usmani e, *et. al.*, 2009) have considered the open space scenarios like markets and streets for simulating explosion effects. Another important parameter missed by almost all existing models is the plotting of multiple explosions, as witnessed recently by multiple suicide bombers in Iraq and Pakistan (Usmani a, 2009).

Most of the models have also neglected the effects of the negative phase, reflection waves, and blockage shields by living and non-living objects, crowd density, projectiles and debris, different explosives, and the scenario visualization in a 3D environment. Blast/FX (Fertal & Leone, 2000) stands out to be the best available explosion model for testing and evaluation of blast loading, but it is also based on empirical studies on sheep and pigs. There is an acute need of explosion effects model based on human data. While the models work well in general, collectively they lack the following characteristics, much needed for real-life risk assessment and emergency planning in case of events like terrorism and suicide bombing:

1. Require too much computing and time resources when implemented with complex geometries and scenarios
2. Need special hardware and software to execute
3. Need a subject matter expert to tune the constants for new and different situations
4. Do not consider blockage and obstacles in a three dimensional environment
5. Lack the capability to work with different kinds of explosives
6. Do not consider crowd formations, density and demographics
7. Have no experimental data with humans
8. None of the models provide a direct mapping of over-pressure to human injuries
9. Provide no capability of new equation plug-in and algorithms
10. Provide no venue for the assessment of sensitivity analysis due to change in explosive characteristics
11. None of the models have considered the negative phase and reflection waves
12. None of the models have considered crowd formation and topologies

Resolution of these issues is needed for real-life risk assessment and emergency planning, and to develop a comprehensive model of a suicide bomber attack. Our model (BlastSim) is rightly filling the gap and providing exactly what is missing.

Few researchers have also focused on developing psychological profiles of suicide bombers, understanding the economical logic behind the attacks (Gupta & Kussum, 2005, Harrison, 2004, Harrison, 2006), explaining the strategic and political gains of these attacks, their role in destabilizing countries (Azam, 2005, Ganor, 2000), and the role of bystanders in reducing the casualties of suicide bombing attacks (Harrison, 2006, Kress, 2004). The specifics of the actual crowd formation and orientation of the bomber with respect to the crowd has not been examined. The presented simulation examines variables such as the number and arrangement of people within a crowd for typical layouts, the number of suicide bombers, and the nature of the explosion including equivalent weight of TNT and the duration of the resulting blast wave pulse for both 2D and 3D environments. The goals of the analysis are to determine optimal crowd formations to reduce the deaths and/or injuries of individuals in the crowd, to determine what architectural and geometric changes can reduce the number of casualties and injuries, and what is the correlation between variant crowd densities and formations with the weight and pulse duration of the explosives? The main objective of our research is to explore and identify crowd formation precautions that when followed will minimize the number of deaths and injuries during a suicide bombing attack.

3. Modelling Overview

Authors have developed a framework to predict the damage of a suicide bombing attack as illustrated in Figure 1. The main goal of our research is to define a general blast wave explosion model to predict and estimate the damage for such incidents. The proposed model will be a total turn-key solution for emergency response management, casualty prediction, classification of injuries, and will provide a safe distance matrix to event managers and security officials. The model will be general enough to make it unclassified (thus avoiding misuse) and specific enough to give an educated guess for the outcome.

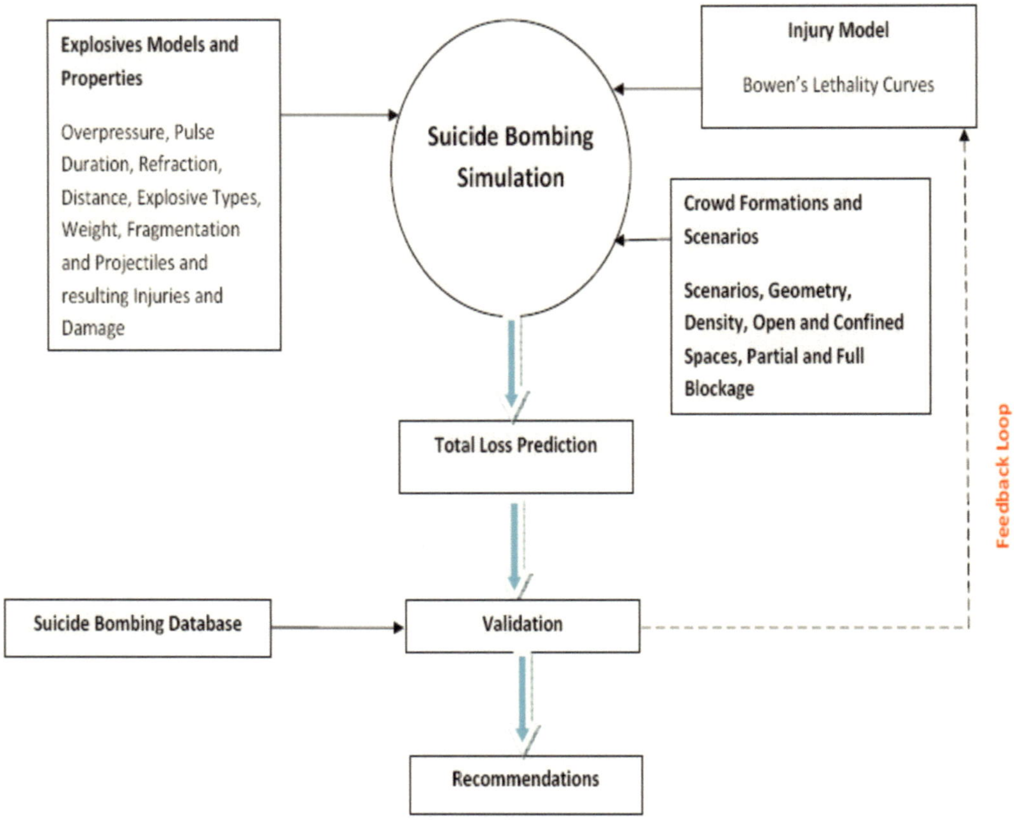

Fig. 1. Components of the suicide bombing model

The effects of an explosion are contingent upon various factors, such as: explosive type (i.e. TNT, RDX, C4, AN etc.), explosive weight (pounds) and results overpressure (pressure-per square inch PSI), ignition source and criteria, crowd density (number of people per square meter), crowd demographics (i.e. age, gender, weight, height), pulse duration (milliseconds), and reflection waves, blockage ratios (percentage), size, shape, location, and number of obstacles, projectiles, debris and fragments, and shape of the explosive carrier. A suicide bombing model and simulation should consider all of the aforementioned factors. Furthermore, the model should be easy to use, contain appropriate physics, be able to work with different scenarios, blockage ratios, injury matrices, and different ambient conditions without special time consuming tuning of parameters. The model should also have sufficient numerical accuracy to allow realistic representation of geometry and explosive strength. It should be easy to configure, and run in a short amount of time.

Some of these requirements are contradictory. For example, a complex model will require too many resources and time if it truly contains appropriate physics and complex geometries. Consequently, a good model should allow for a tradeoff between time, resources, physics, geometry and the resulting output. Sometimes there is a need of faster results to be able to save lives, and sometimes there are scarce resources to distribute for various purposes. A good model should be flexible enough to use in a diverse set of situations with varying requirements. Our proposed framework is fulfilling this gap by providing faster results while taking care of all required characteristics of a good model.

4. Explosive Model

In order to model the effects of an explosion on a given crowd formation, it is essential to properly model the deleterious properties of the blast waves themselves. A conventional bomb generates a blast wave that spreads out spherically from the origin of the explosion. The strength of the blast wave decreases exponentially with distance (Irwin, 1999, FEMA 2004). Although the physics of blast waves are complex and nonlinear, a wave may be broadly characterized by its peak overpressure (pressure above atmospheric) and the duration of the positive phase of the blast event, as shown in Figure 2. Based on those two quantities, the intensity of the blast wave can be assessed and exposure threshold limits can be determined, although this only applies to a specific scenario. Enhanced-blast explosive devices, in contrast, can have more damaging effects, and cause a greater proportion of blast injuries than conventional devices. In an enhanced-blast device, a primary blast disseminates the explosive and later triggers a secondary explosion. The high-pressure wave then radiates from a much larger area, prolonging the duration of the over pressurization phase, thus increasing the total energy transmitted by the explosion.

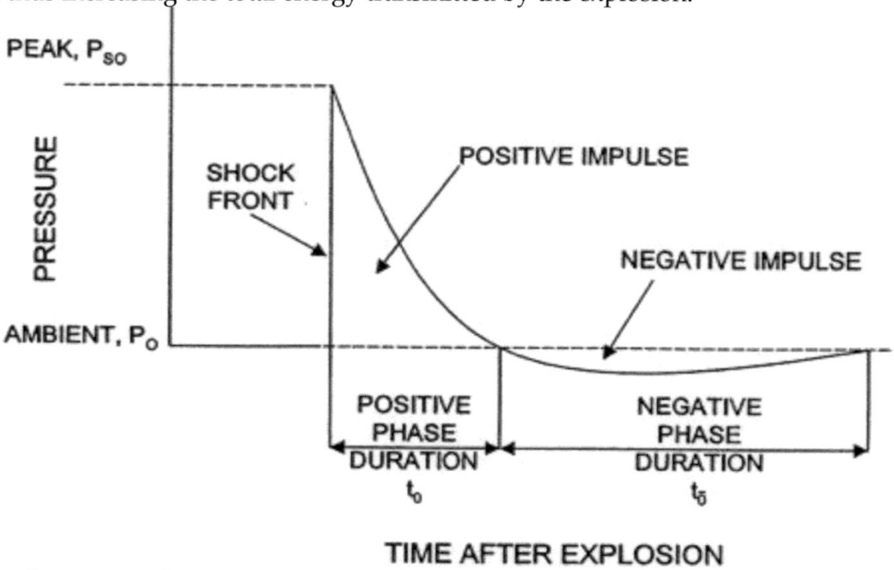

Fig. 2. Blast wave showing positive and negative phase durations. Such waves may be characterized by the peak overpressure and duration of the positive phase

Depending on the type of explosive and the proximity to the target, the positive phase duration can vary between a few microseconds up to several milliseconds (Kinney & Graham, 2985). Injury correlations as a function of peak overpressure and duration have been developed for various organs, such as the eardrums and lungs, as well as probability of fatality curves for humans in various orientations to the blast wave. Impulse, which is the force-time product of the blast wave, is also important to consider, as two profiles with identical peak overpressure and duration can have different total impulses. Studies on blast-related injuries have shown that both the peak overpressure and duration of the positive phase, which correlate to the overall impulse, each contribute to the magnitude of injury experienced by a victim.

A simulation which seeks to study the impact of a suicide bomber on casualty rates and injuries related to crowd formation must be able to adequately model the influence of peak overpressure, duration, and impulse of the explosion; the next few paragraphs discuss blast modeling and the assumptions made in the simulation.

Experimental and theoretical means have been used to obtain important parameters associated with blast waves. A theoretical analysis for peak overpressure utilizes the same mathematical approach as for a planar shock wave, but includes the effects of spherical divergence and the transient nature of the blast event (Cooper, 1996, Kinney and Graham, 1985). As an example, values for the peak overpressure generated in a standard atmosphere for the blast wave generated by a one pound spherical charge of TNT are shown in Figure 3. At distances far from the center of an explosion, a blast wave behaves like a sound wave in that its energy-distance relation follows an inverse square law. The intensity of sound energy, however, is proportional to the square of sound pressure, so that a simple inverse relation between peak overpressure and distance is sufficiently great that the blast wave overpressure approaches zero.

Also shown in Figure 3 is the peak overpressure that would be expected at various distances had the energy been released by one pound point source of TNT. It can be seen by comparing the two curves that the effect of the explosive charge is to initially spread out the energy and so to reduce the peak overpressure to some appreciable distance from the center of the explosion - around 5 charge diameters. At intermediate distances, the large amounts of gas produced from the TNT become evident in the peak overpressure curve. At greater distances, losses due to dissociation and ionization become evident in the point source and act to reduce the energy available so that observed peak overpressure is somewhat less than that from TNT with the same energy release. This demonstrates that although knowing the total energy release is important, it is inadequate to completely describe the blast event.

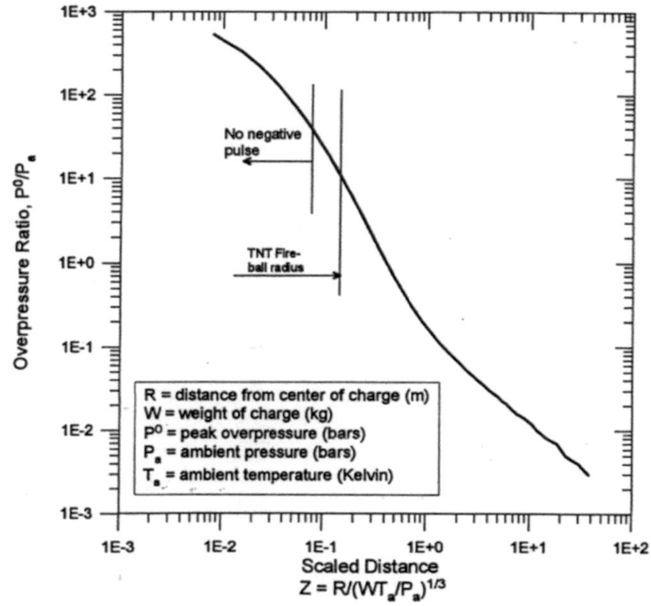

Fig. 3. Peak overpressure ratio versus scaled distance, adopted from (Kinney & Graham, 1985)

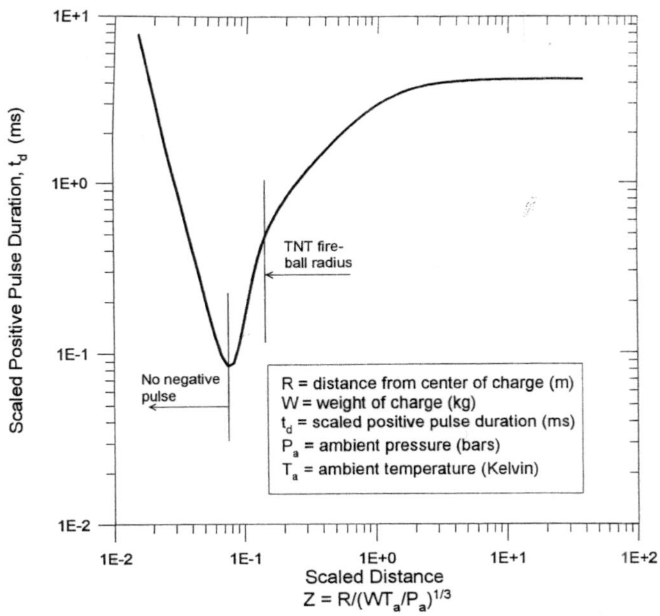

Fig. 4. Scaled positive pulse duration versus scaled distance, adopted from (Kinney & Graham, 1985)

The data depicted in Figure 3 and 4 applies for any weight of TNT through an energy-weight scaling law. Two explosions can be expected to give identical blast wave peak overpressures at distances which are proportional to the cube root of the respective energy release. For example, to produce a given blast overpressure at twice a given distance requires eight times the explosive energy release. The following scaling law is used (Cooper, 1996), which also allows for compensation in different atmospheric pressures (Pa) and temperatures (Ta):

$$Z = \frac{R}{(WT_a/P_a)^{1/3}} \tag{1}$$

The energy release factor is contained in the ratio $(R/WT_aP_a)^{1/3}$, where W is the energy release, or amount of TNT in kilograms, in the explosion to be described, R is the distance in feet, T_a is the ambient temperature in Kelvin and P_a is the ambient pressure in bars. By using this scaling law, the distance at which a given peak overpressure is produced by a reference explosion may be scaled up or down to provide a corresponding distance for other explosions. Different explosives can be considered by modifying the overpressure versus distance history or by utilizing data specific to the explosive composition.

The time duration of a blast wave must also be considered because the magnitude of injury depends in part on how long the damaging forces are applied. Because of the relationship between the speed associated with the initial shock front and the changing local speed of sound as the blast wave propagates, the duration of the blast wave increases with distance from the center of the explosion, and reaches a limiting maximum value (and ultimately vanishes) as the shock front degenerates into a sound wave. To model duration increase as a function of distance from the origin of the explosion, the digitized data of Figure 4 has been used, where the distance is scaled as for Figure 3, and the curve in Figure 4 gives the corresponding scaled positive pulse duration in a given time.

Impulse is also an important aspect of the damage-causing ability of the blast, and may become a controlling factor for short duration, small yield explosives. The significant portion of the impulse is associated with the positive phase. The decay of blast overpressure does not follow a typical logarithmic decay relation, because the overpressure drops to zero in finite time (Kinney & Graham, 1985). A quasi-exponential form for pressure in terms of a decay parameter α, and of a time t, which is measured from the instant the shock front arrives, can be given as (Cooper, 1996):

$$p = p_0\left(1 - \frac{t}{t_d}\right)e^{\frac{-\alpha t}{t_d}} \tag{2}$$

Where p is the instantaneous overpressure at time t, p_0 the maximum or peak overpressure observed when t is zero, and, t_d is the time duration. The decay parameter is also a measure of intensity of the shock system. Equation (2) may also be used in the simulation if the decay parameter α is specified, for example, to determine the evolution of the positive phase duration as a function of distance from the explosive center.

5. Injury Model

In order to tie together the influence of peak overpressure and duration to injury and fatality probability, a series of data curves were utilized. Figure 5 shows the fatality curves predicted for a 70-kg man applicable to free-steam situations where the long axis of the body is perpendicular to the direction of blast wave propagation.

Specifying the amount of TNT, using the scaling law of equation (1), and the overpressure versus distance curve of Figure 3, then allows for the calculation of the peak overpressure at any distance away from the explosive origin. Using this peak overpressure and the increasing duration given by the digitized dataset of Figure 4 a new duration of the blast wave can be calculated at any distance away from the explosion. Using these two pieces of information and injury or fatality probability curves, such as Figure 5, an estimate of the injury or fatality levels at any location of the explosion can be calculated for various crowd formations.

Injuries that occur as a result of explosions can be grouped into several broad categories, as primary, secondary and tertiary injuries. Primary injuries caused by the direct result of pressure wave impacting and travelling through the body; it includes rupture of tympanic membranes, pulmonary damage, rupture of hollow viscera. Secondary injuries result from flying debris that damage body; it includes penetrating trauma and fragmentation injuries. Tertiary blast injuries results from victim's body being thrown by blast wind, and then impacting stationary object; it includes crushing injuries and blunt trauma, penetrating or blunt trauma, fractures and traumatic amputations. And miscellaneous blast injuries are caused by flame and chemicals that includes burns, asphyxia, and exposure to toxic inhalants

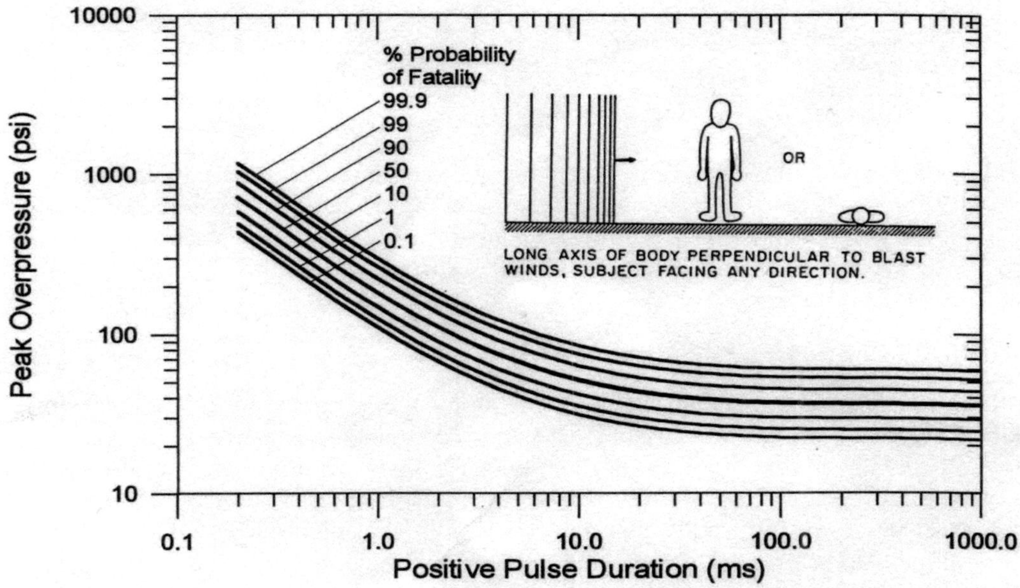

Fig. 5. Fatality curves as a function of blast wave peak overpressure and positive pulse duration (Cooper, 1996).

The exact explosive mass used in suicide attacks is hard to determine. However, it is possible to give some general indications of the overall level of injuries to be expected based on the size of an explosion, the number of participants and crowd formation. Large trucks typically contain 25,000 pounds or more of TNT equivalent, and vans typically contain 5,000 to 25,000 pounds. Small automobiles can contain 50 to 5,000 pounds of TNT equivalent. A briefcase bomb is about 50 pounds, and a suicide bomber wearing a vest belt generally carries up to 30 pounds of TNT equivalent (Air Force, 2004).

The preliminary results described in this paper are based on a division of the blast area into six zones: three for lethality, and three for injuries. Lethal zone #1 results in a 99% probability of death, lethal zone #2 results in a 50% probability of death, and the zone #3 results in a 1% probability of death. Similarly, injuries are divided into three zones. Injury zone #1 includes people who get 60 PSI or more overpressure, zone #2 refers to more than 40 and less than 60 PSI overpressure, and zone #3 for more than 20 and less than 40 PSI overpressure. In general, 60 PSI results in severe injuries such as missing body parts, amputation, brain or heart rupture, or Abbreviated Injury Score (AIS) 3. PSI of 40 usually results in the rupture of air-filled organs like lungs and kidney or AIS 2, and 20 PSI is usually responsible for minor bruises and ear-drum rupture or AIS 1. Persons below the range of 20 PSI are generally unharmed (Irwin, 1999).

Lethal Zones	**No Blocker**	**Partial Blocker**	**Full Blocker**
#1	Death 99%	Death 99%	Death 50%
#2	Death 50%	Death 1%	Unharmed
#3	Death 1%	Unharmed	Unharmed
Injury Zones			
#1	Injured 60 PSI	Injured 40 PSI	Injured 20 PSI
#2	Injured 40 PSI	Injured 20 PSI	Unharmed
#3	Injured 20 PSI	Unharmed	Unharmed

Table 1. Full and partial blockers impact

Table 1 provides the details of the respective impacts of the full and partial blockers on the lethal and injury zones. For example, a person within the 50% lethality zone blocked by a full blocker will be unharmed, on the other hand, the same person blocked by a partial blocker will be downgraded to lethal zone 3 (1% probability of death).

6. Crowd Formation – Full and Partial Blockers

Blockage or shields present in a crowd can play an important role in the event of an explosion. Even a person providing a blockage in the line-of-sight between another person and an explosion can actually save the later person's life by absorbing most of the shrapnel or by consuming part of the blast wave overpressure. Spatial distribution of individuals in a crowd can therefore significantly alter the casualty toll. Thus different crowd formations can yield different outcomes with the same amount and type of explosive, even when the average distance to the bomber between two different crowd configurations is identical.

This section introduces 2D and 3D models for finding the exact number of full and partial blockers between each person and the point of explosion. Persons in the line of sight between a given target and the blast point are termed *full blockers*. Blockers who are not in the line of sight, but whose body width covers some part of the body of the person from the blast projectiles, is referred as a *partial blocker*. For example, imagine a person of 4 feet standing in front of a 6 feet 10 inches person, or a person standing next to another. These persons, while not covering another person completely, can provide partial blockage.

To the best of our knowledge, this study is the first to consider partial blockers in blast wave simulation. Figure 6 presents the blockage model for 2D. Each person in the area is modeled by a vertical line segment, where the mid-point of the vertical line represents the position of the person, and the length represents their width.

Each line in the model is represented by the coordinates of its two end points. The line between the mid-point of the target and the blast point is called the *line-of-sight*. Each target is also represented by a vertical line called the *body-width-line*. The triangle, whose base is the body-width-line of the target and the blast point, is termed the *blast triangle*.

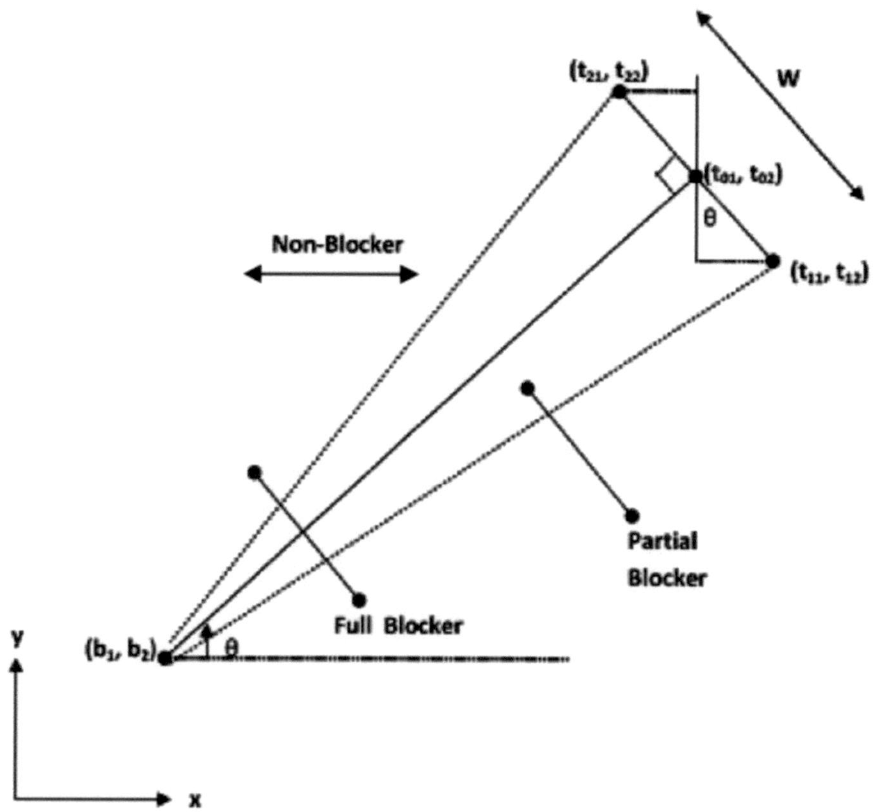

Fig. 6. Full, partial and no blockers in 2D

The line segment between the blast point (b_1, b_2) and the center of the target (t_1, t_2) is constructed and its slope is calculated. Assuming all people face towards the blast, the body-width-line of the target will be perpendicular to the line of sight. The slope of this line is the negation of the slope of the line of sight. Using simple coordinate geometry, one can easily determine the end points of the body-width-line of the target ((x,y):(z,w)) given the mid-point of the line (t_1,t_2), the body width and the slope of the line. Given the end points of the body-width-line of the target, one can easily construct the two other sides of the blast triangle. All other people's body-width-line is assumed to have the same slope as the slope of the body-width- line of the target. Taking this slope, the position coordinate, and the width, it is trivial to determine the end points of the body-width-line of each person.

It is also worth noting that all infinite slopes are approximated by $\pm 1\times 10^6$. To determine the blockage, one has to determine if the body-width-line (representing a person) is intersecting with either the line-of-sight or the sides of the blast triangle. If a body-width-line is intersecting the line of sight, the person represented by this line is taken as full blocker. Otherwise, if it intersects with either side of the blast triangle, the person will be considered a partial blocker. Figure 6 shows full and partial blockers, and other individuals that do not provide any blockage at all (non-blockers).

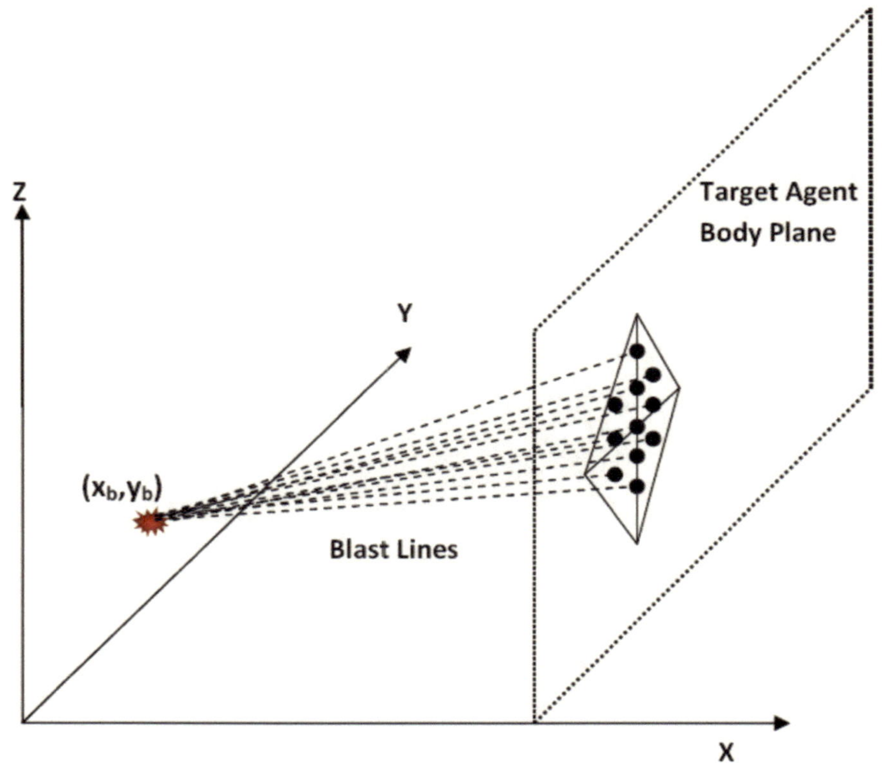

Fig. 7. Percentage of partial blocking in 3D

To find blockers in three-dimensions, a Cartesian(x-y-z) plane is used as a reference to the distribution of agents. Each agent is modeled by a four sided polygon whose dimensions are determined by their height and width. These polygons are made to lie parallel to the y-z plane to reduce the computational overhead. Figure 7 illustrates the concept.

There are four planes which enclose the cone whose vertex is the point of explosion and whose base is the four sided polygons modeling an agent. The cone referred to as the blast cone and the enclosing planes are referred to as blast cone planes. The plane containing this polygon is called the agent body plane and the polygon is called the agent body polygon. The four line segments extending from the bomb position and the corner points of the polygon are called the blast lines.

The algorithm consecutively considers each agent as a target, and checks if any other agent is interfering with it from the blast point. A blocker is referred to as a *full blocker* if its' four-sided polygon intersects the line of sight between the explosion and the target agent. An agent is referred to ask a *Partial* Blocker if it is not a full blocker, but its' four-sided polygon intrudes into the blast cone. To check if an agent is intruding into the blast cone, first the smallest distance between the line of sight and the blast lines from the position point of the agent and the explosion is calculated. If this distance is less than half of the width of the agent, the line crosses the body plane between the polygon sides and the agent is considered a blocker. If the line is the line of sight, the agent is a full blocker and if the line is only one of the blast lines, it is a partial blocker. If the smallest distance from each of the lines obtained is greater than half the width of the agents then it is not a blocker at all.

To check if an agent is intruding into the blast cone, first we find the smallest distance between the line of sight and the blast lines from the position point of the agent and the bomb. If this distance is less than half of the width of the agent, the line apparently crosses the body plane between the polygon sides and the agent will be considered as a blocker. If the line is the line of sight, it will be the full blocker and if the line is one of the blast lines, it will be considered as a partial blocker. If the smallest distance from each of the lines obtained is greater than half of the width the agent it is not a blocker.

If an agent is a partial blocker, the percentage of blockage can also be determined. This is done by constructing additional lines that extend between the target agent body plane in the polygon area and the point of explosion. The percentage of lines crossing the body plane between the sides of the polygon is used as the percentage of the partial blockage, as shown in Figure 7.

7. Suicide Bombing Database

As part of this research we have compiled a real-life bombing and injuries database from the actual records of the suicide bombing incidents in Pakistan from November 15, 1995 to April 18, 2009. During that time there was a total of 169 suicide bombing incidents in 42 cities of Pakistan that left 2,327 dead and 5,410 injured. This study compiled the records of the patients in most of these attacks from the hospitals, which include patients' medico-legal reports, X-Rays, ECGs, PSTD profiles, injury types and characteristics. The database also contains blast characteristics (explosive type, weight, shape, fragmentation signatures, and temperature of the day), crowd characteristics (crowd density, gender, age ratio, weight, and the distance from the bomber with +- 2 feet of error). To the best of our knowledge, this database is the first of its' kind one of its kinds in the blast research on human body.

8. Simulation Tool Development

The simulation is being programmed in Visual C#. Visual C# was utilized due to its extensive library of graphics and geometry functions (to generate the Cartesian grid with agents). The explosive range is determined by the explosive weight. By using the scaling law as described in Eq. 1, and the TNT overpressure versus scaled distance data of Figure 3 and 4, it is easy to calculate the exact overpressure received by each agent at particular locations given the weight and type of explosive. Specific simulation inputs are the number of individuals and bombers in the vicinity, explosive characteristics (type, weight, fragmentation etc.), and crowd formation (topology, gender, height, width, weight etc). Additionally the arrival time of the explosive pressure front to travel from the point of explosion to any given location may also be calculated.

The work has only considered primary and direct injuries. Persons who are directly in the line-of-sight with an explosion will absorb the effects, and thus act as a shield for person(s) behind them. Direct injuries mean injuries caused by the bomb's blast wave overpressure during the explosion, and not by fire or debris (pieces of furniture or glass). The simulation has, however, incorporated the effects of stampede. Stampede usually occurs when a large number of people start running towards the same direction and surpass the capacity of flow from that particular channel.

The work has also considered mostly "open space" scenarios to serve as the basis for our crowd formation types (e.g., mosques, streets, concerts etc.). The types of injury caused by overpressure depend on whether overpressure occurs in open air or within buildings. In the later case the type of injuries also depends on whether the explosion causes collapse of a building or other structure. There are numerous objects to consider in closed environments that can either increase the casualty/injury toll (primarily by working as flying debris) or decrease the toll by providing a shield to humans. Closed environments also need to entertain reflection waves. A blast wave can amplify in closed environments by reflection and reduced ventilation. Ventilation, reflection waves, and non-human objects are out of scope of this work.

There are two types of formations user can choose from - random formations and user created scenarios, like circles, zigzags, rectangular etc to represent real-life settings like cafeteria, mosques, concerts etc. - to estimate the outcome of an attack for a particular crowd formation. Figure 8 shows few examples of crowd formations, and Figure 9 shows the display after the blast is simulated.

The simulation takes care of beam and line-of-sight adjustments in cases of uneven surfaces (e.g., concert stage, mosque or shopping mall). To date, this work has not considered physical objects (like walls, trees, furniture etc.) as obstacles, or a means to harm people. A suicide bomber is a pedestrian in all cases and the explosion does not originate from a moving vehicle. The reason for choosing a suicide bomber location in almost all cases (except in a zigzag formation) on the entrance or exit gate was based upon recent attacks in Iraq, Israel and Pakistan where suicide bombers detonated their bombs at the gates of mosques and restaurants (Johnson, 2005).

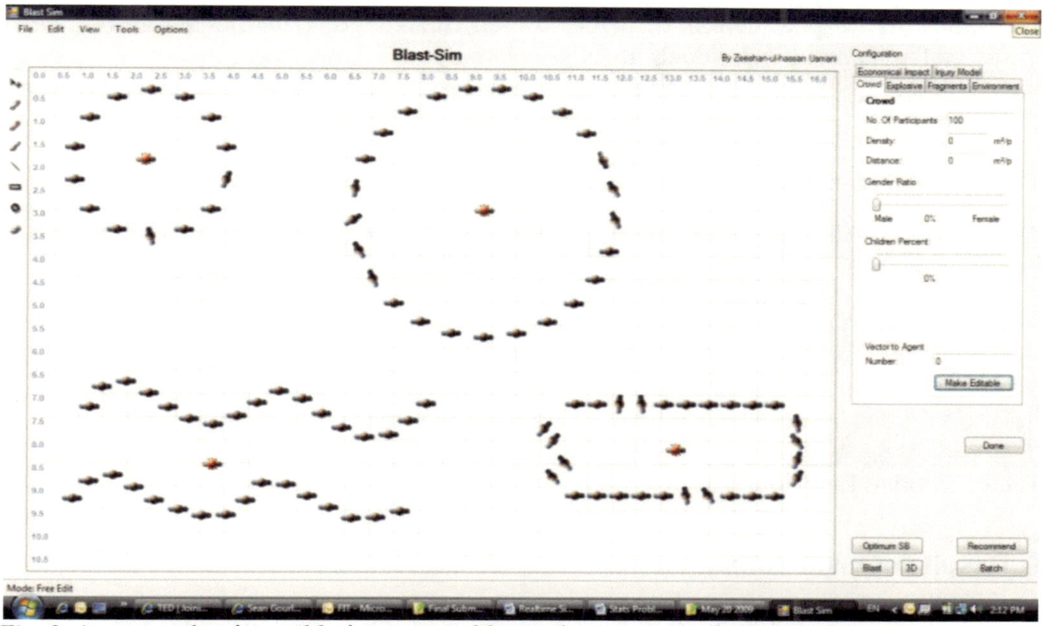

Fig. 8. An example of possible formations like circle, zigzag, and rectangular

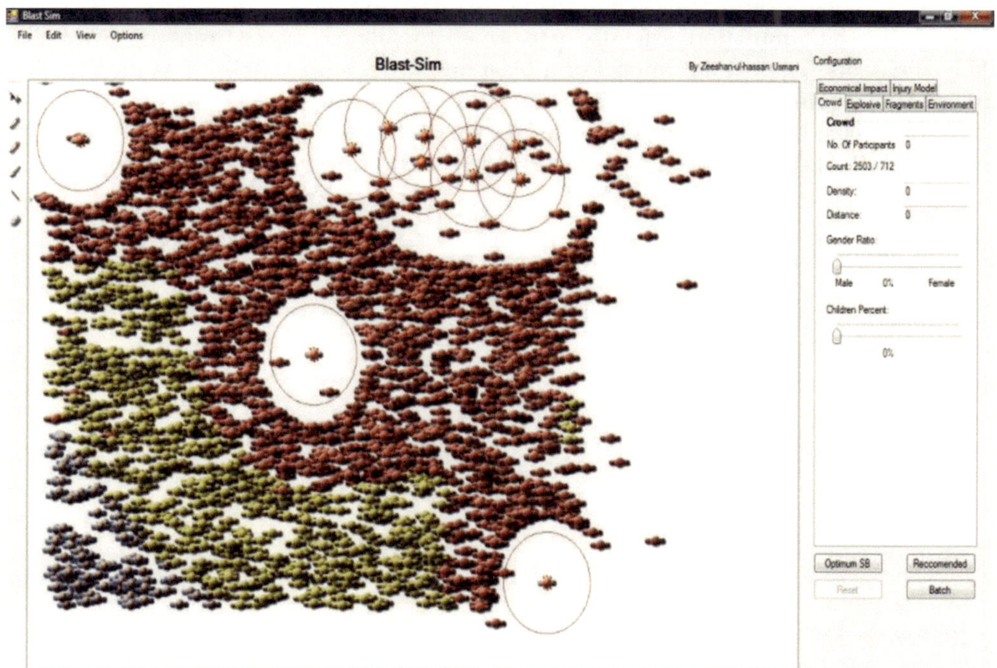

Fig. 9. Simulation screen after the blast

The simulation display depicts casualties by red colored icons, injuries in green colored icons, and unharmed individuals in blue colored icons. Thus, there are three states of victims after the blast: dead, injured and unharmed (but in panic and contributing to stampede).

The simulation can run in three different models, as presented in Table 2:

Models	Description
Model 1 (M1)	Basic simulation of a blast wave without blockage (full or partial) in 2 dimensions.
Model 2 (M2)	Simulation with full and partial blockage in 2 dimensions
Model 3 (M3)	Full simulation with partial and full blockage in 3 dimensions (incorporating the height and width of the agents).

Table 2. Models Description

9. Results and Validation

The average case scenario has been simulated for all of the models (M1, M2, and M3). The weight of the explosives used in the simulation ranged from 1 to 30 lbs. The number of participants ranged from 20 to 100 and the pulse duration ranged from 0.5 milliseconds to 2 milliseconds. The simulation was also performed for bigger crowds ranging from 500 to 1000 participants. The overall impact of a blast on participants stabilized as the number of participants increased, as shown in Figure 10. For example, the average number of participants in the lethal zone was 11, with 20 total participants (55%), and 185 with 500 total participants (37%). These findings are consistent with Moshe Kress findings (Kress, 2004).

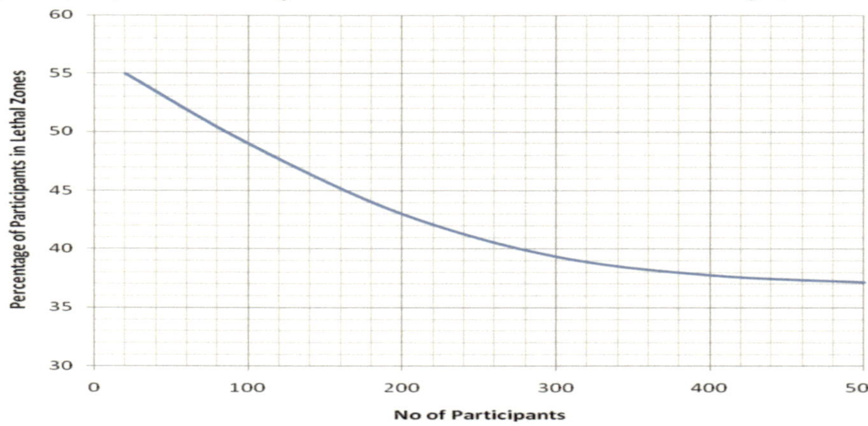

Fig. 10. Percentage of participants killed in the lethal zone vs. number of participants in the lethal zone. For this example, the bomber is carrying 30 lbs of TNT, which corresponds to a lethality radius (without blockage) of 37.5 feet. The results are based on 200 simulations with random crowd distributions.

The simulation was performed for different example crowd formations with the same number of participants and weight of explosives. The height, weight and the number of participants were exactly the same for each run for all three models. Figure 11 shows the average results of 200 simulation runs for each crowd formation with different explosive mass, pulse duration and number of participants. The expected output for the model M1 was an upper bound or least conservative, since there is no blockage available to people in the crowd, so the model should report more injuries and deaths. For M2 the expected output was a lower bound of the results or most conservative, since in two-dimensions anyone in the line-of-sight can provide blockage, thus minimizing the impact of blast wave overpressure to the people behind the shields. While the expectations for the model M3 results were in between M1 and M2, it should be lower than M1 since it is providing blockage shields to the crowd and it should be greater than M2 due to its three-dimensional capabilities. For example, a child standing in front of an adult person in 2D simulation can provide the full blockage while he will be providing only partial blockage in 3D simulation model.

Figure 11 summarizes the findings of the percentages of the people in the lethal and injury zones with given crowd formations. Each set of three bars in Figure 11 represents a crowd formation. It is clear to see that model M2 with blockers results in a fewer number of dead and injured people than M1 (without blockers), while M3 has the higher number of death and injuries as compared to M2. M3 is more realistic due to its three-dimensional capabilities. The simulation was also performed using 40 and 50 lbs of explosives (though it is uncommon to see a pedestrian suicide bombing attack of that magnitude). The relationship between the increase in the percentage of casualties and injuries with the amount of explosive is observed to be piecewise linear. This relationship is logical since augmenting the explosive material will increase the overpressure pounds per square inch (psi) in the vicinity.

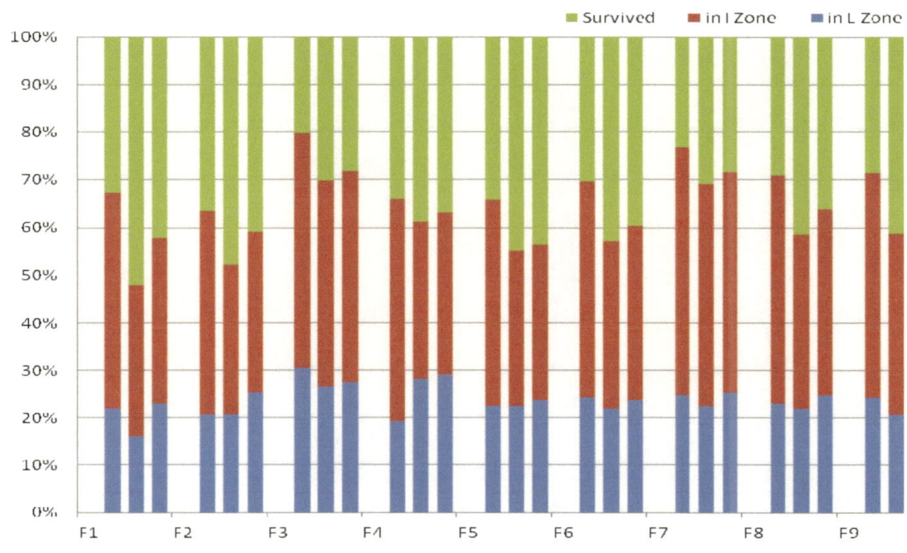

Fig. 11. Casualties and crowd formations

The average deadliest crowd formation for casualties was found to be the zigzag scenario, where 30% of participants were in the lethal zone and 45% in the injury zone. Row wise crowd formations were found to be the best for reducing the effectiveness of an attack, with on average 18% of the crowd in the lethal zone and 38% in the injury zone. Thus by only changing the way a crowd forms, one can reduce deaths by 12% and injuries by 7%, on average. This is really useful where one has control to form the crowd, like in airports by placing them in queues. One of the reasons for the dramatic change in casualties is that in row wise formations there are fewer people in the direct line-of-sight with the bomber and more people also provide the blockage to others.

To validate our results and to see how close they are with real-life incidents, the results were compared against a database of every single suicide bombing attack in Pakistan from 2000 to 2009 that fits the open-scenario criterion (Johnson, 2005). Figure 12 shows a comparison of the average number of persons killed and injured in all of the simulation runs against the suicide bombing attacks in Pakistan. The real-life averages come from mostly open-space scenarios with a single pedestrian suicide bomber. For the sake of consistency, the database excluded the suicide bombing attacks in close environments like buses or with multiple suicide bombers, or ones carried out with the help of an automobile.

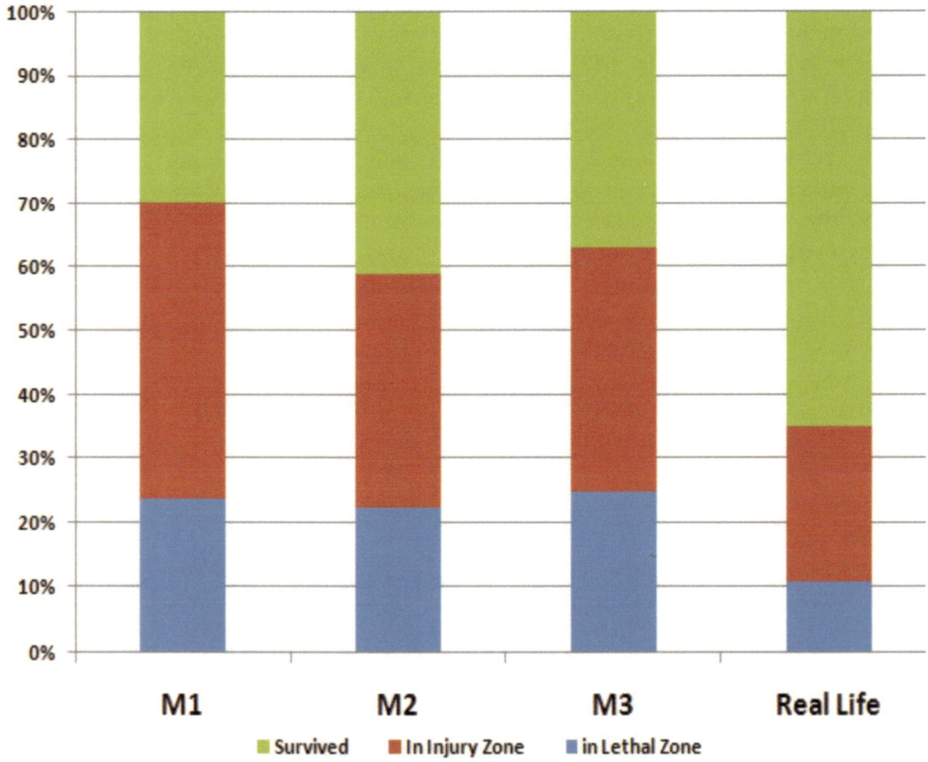

Fig. 12. Models comparison with the real-life database of suicide bombing incidents in Pakistan

Clearly, the model M3 with blockers is more close to real-life results than M1 with no blockers and M2 of blockers in 2D. The average injury per fatality ratio in real-life incidents is 2.18, that is, for every dead person there are 2.18 injured people. The number is pretty much consistent in the history of the modern world, where there are 2.6 injuries per fatality in Vietnam War, 2.8 in the Korean War, 1.8 in the World War I, and 1.6 in the World War II. Simulation models, on the other hand, had produced 1.9 injuries per fatality in M1, 1.6 for M2, and 1.54 for M3. This can be explained as follows: First the current simulation does not count for secondary and tertiary blast injuries by fire, debris, fragmentation and shrapnel. Second, the current simulation only accounts for TNT explosive, while in the real-life instances there are quite a few mixtures of explosives being used. As examples, note an RDX and TNT mixture in the recent suicide bombing attack in Pakistan that claimed the life of former Prime Minister Benazir Bhutto, and the mixture of Ammonium Nitrate and RDX in Oklahoma City bombings. Third, the simulation is not giving the exact number of dead and injured people; instead it is gives the number of people in the lethal and injury zones based on their probabilities of death and injury. For example, a person in lethal zone 3 with 1% chances of being dead is most likely to be injured and not dead, similarly a person in Injury zone 3 with 20 PSI can be unharmed.

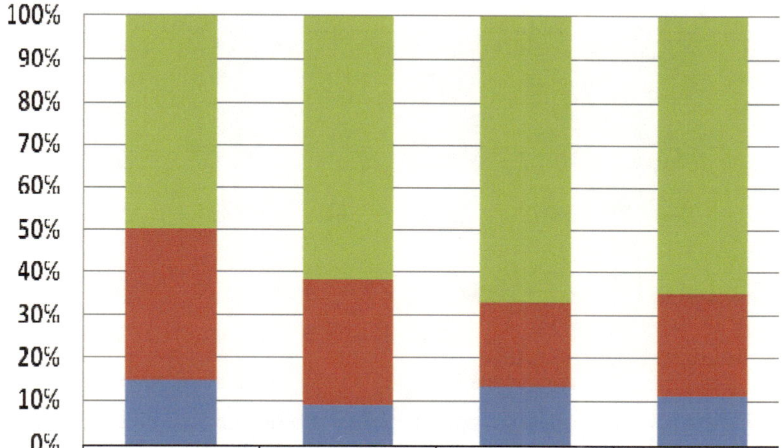

	M1%	M2%	M3%	Real Life %
Survived	50	62	67	65
Injiury Zone	35	29	20	24
Lethal Zone	15	9	13	11

Fig. 13. Model comparison with injury and lethal levels 1

There are demographical, environmental and physical characteristics as well, that play an important role in the overall toll. For example, an infant next to a fire cracker can die while a muscular six and half foot person with 250 lbs of weight can survive a 1 pound TNT explosion. The simulation yields more realistic results with the incorporation of non-human shields, reflection waves, secondary and tertiary blast injuries and physical characteristics. However, simulation at current stage can provide a good upper bound, lower bound, and

medium estimates of the number of dead and injured for emergency preparedness, triage of patients, and the required number of medical and ambulance facilities for such an event.
The simulation was performed against the real-life results with persons only in Lethal Zone 1 (99% probability of death) and Injury Zone 1 (60 PSI). These models will be referred to as optimized models from the point forward. Figure 13 portrays the findings of this comparison.

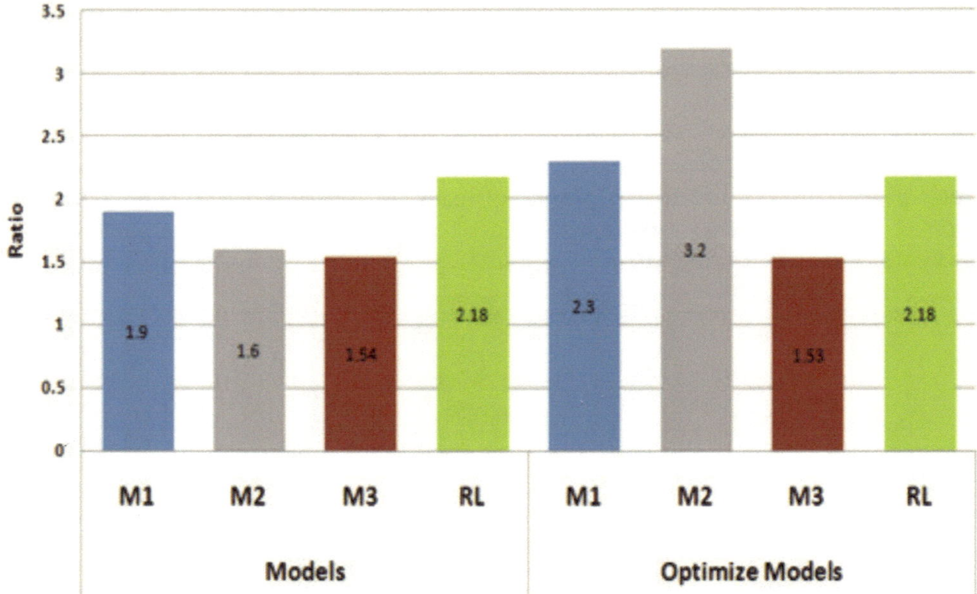

Fig. 14. Injury per fatality ratios

Figure 14 shows a comparison of injury per fatality count. Here models have provided 2.3 injuries per fatality in M1, 3.2 for M2 and 1.53 for M3. The number of deaths is higher in M1, lower in M2, and more close to real life in M3.
The results are in good agreement for the death count but are off slightly for injury counts. Beside the aforementioned reasons, one of the reasons for this difference can be totally political, where governments tend to show the manipulated figures to minimize the aftereffects (for example, riots, revenge etc) by victim supporters or a huge outcry in the home state. For example, 4,000 soldiers have been killed in Iraq so far since the invasion of the country by US forces in October 2003. Media have only concentrate on the dead, while little has known about the more than 250,000 injured soldiers. An injured soldier costs at least three times more than a dead soldier economically to the country, according to one estimate the cost is 10.1 million dollar for injured, and 3.7 million dollar for a dead soldier (Stiglitz, 2008). The government has to pay disability and social security allowances, and it is a loss of one worker from the labor force. Thus a loss of one statistical value of life, and the injured also need a caretaker, therefore another loss of the statistical value of life. According to the recent work by the authors, the cost of human life only for US soldiers in the Iraq comes to 14.8 billion dollar (Usmani b *et. al.*, 2009), readers are referred to the authors website www.FindMyWorth.com for further information. Given the current geo-political

conditions of the world and the US ongoing war in Iraq and Afghanistan, it is more necessary than ever to examine and employed the technologies to reduce the rate of injured and dead. Another reason for the gap in the number of injured might be the level of injuries - a victim who has a minor injury and was able to walk may not have been included in the actual count of the injuries in the real life events.

The sensitive analysis for all of the models was also performed. M1 or the basic model results are the same as M2 2D model without blockage. And the M2 2D models without blockage results are similar to the results of M3 3D model without blockage. The results suggest using the M1 basic model if there is no need to consider the blockage. M1 can also give an upper bound of body count. If blockage has to be considered, the results suggest using M2 2D model, since the M3 3D models contribution is statistically insignificant if only considering the blockage in the crowd. On the other hand, 3D demands more computational power and resources. M3 3D should be used when there is a need of blockage with uneven surfaces like stages or stadiums, and when the user has to work on bomb fragments, shrapnel, projectiles, and secondary and tertiary blast injuries. The 3D model is more realistic when used with the majority of blast characteristics. For the simple estimates M2 2D model is as good as 3D, while the M1 basic model can be used for quick estimation of the required number of medical and emergency management facilities.

Announcing the threat of suicide bombing in the crowd can only make the condition and the causality toll much worse. People will panic and thus increase the possibility of more victims in the line-of-sight with the suicide bomber than before. People will also try to rush towards the exit gates (thus coming closer to a bomber in the majority of cases), and there will be high chances of a stampede.

10. Conclusion and Future Work

There are a number of lessons one can learn from the analysis of this suicide bombing simulation. For example, one can reduce the number of fatalities by 12% and the number of injuries by 7% by switching the crowd formation from zigzag to row-wise formation styles. Doing this reduces the minimum average distance of each person in the crowd with the bomber. For example, a blast may yield more casualties in a heavily dense crowd with fewer people than a least dense crowd with more people. The topological impact highly depends on the minimum average distance of a person from the bomber in near-field scenarios. Blockage can only play a minimum role when a person is close enough to the bomber with respect to explosive characteristics. To avoid a stampede in possible crowd formations, one could arrange more exit points than normally available. Suggestions can also be made for architectural design changes in the buildings to reduce the count. For example by placing entrance and exit gates X feet away from the main venue, victims can be reduced by Y% (the values depends on environment, crowd information and the weight of explosive). The results can also help planning for post-disaster management. For example, how many ambulances and doctors one will need if something like this should happens to a given crowd or how to direct the crowd to behave or run towards particular exits by announcing it through loudspeakers. In the light of these findings, the crowd can be manipulated in real-life by imposing formation guidelines like queues at the airport or by placing chairs in particular orders that will block the line-of-sight with of any perspective attacker.

There is an acute shortage of accurate data for many other variables and conditions that are pertinent to such an attacks (e.g. was a bomber running or standing? Carrying methods for the explosive, Weight of the explosive). It makes it difficult to validate the numbers of the simulation results with actual events. Also the simulation assumed continuous uniform distribution for the people, which is the least preferred distribution, but realistic in this case due to unknown real distribution). If that assumption is eliminated, it will have very little effect on the overall simulation results since the simulation is only calculating the blast overpressure (at this stage) from the origin of the explosion to the agent. In any case the agent will receive overpressure proportional to its distance from the bomber.
The simulation and findings are limited in that they only incorporate primary injuries. Future plans are to add secondary effects (e.g., injuries by fire, debris, etc.) so as better approximate the real world environment and provide more valid comparisons with the data of suicide bombing attack aftermaths (Usmani a, 2009). The flexibility to create a user defined crowd formation with variable number of entrances and exits will be added in the future. This paper provides an interesting direction for future research to take in investigating the catastrophic event of the suicide bomber attack in hopes of making the world a safer place.

11. References

Arntzen, B. J. (1982). Modeling of turbulence and combustion for simulation of gas explosions in complex geometries, Dr. Ing. Thesis, Norges Tekniske-Naturvitenskapelige Universitet, Trondheim, Norway

Air Force (2004), U.S. Air Force Installation Force Protection Guide

Azam, Jean-Paul (2005), "Suicide-bombing as inter- generational investment", Public Choice. Springer. 122, pp (177-198)

Berg, A. C. van den (1985), The Multi-Energy Method - A Framework for Vapour Cloud Explosion Blast Prediction Journal Hazardous Materials 12: pp (1-10)

Baker, Q. A., Tang, M. J., Scheier, E. A., and Silva, G. J. (1994), Vapor Cloud Explosion Analysis, AIChE Loss Prevention Symposium, Atlanta, GA

Birkby, P., Cant, R. S., and Savill, A. M. (1997), Initial HSE Baffled Channel Test Case Results with Refined Combustion and Turbulence Modelling 1st Milestone Report on the HSE Research Contract Research at Cambridge University under Agreement No. HSE/8685/3278

Baker, Q. A., Doolittle, C. M., Fitzgerald, G. A., and Tang, M. J. (1998), Recent developments in the Baker-Strehlow VCE Analysis Methodology Process Safety Progress 17(4): pp (297-301)

Cates, A. T., and Samuels, B. (1991), A Simple Assessment Methodology for Vented Explosions Journal of Loss Prevention in the Process Industries 4: pp (287-296)

Cooper, Paul W. (1996), Explosive Engineering, Wiley-VCH

Clutter, J. K, , Mathis, J. T, and Stahl, M. W. (2006), Modeling Environmental effects in the Simulation of Explosion Events, International Journal of Impact Engineering

Ettouney, M. (2001), Is Seismic Design Adequate for Blast?, Society of American Military Engineers National Symposium on Comprehensive Force Protection, Charleston, S.C.

Fertal, Martin and Leone, Kelly (2000): Applications of Blast/FX, An Explosive Effects Analysis Software Tool", IEEE 34th Annual 2000 International Carnahan Conference on Security Technology, Ottawa, ON, Canada

FEMA (2004), Explosive Blast Manual, Section 4.1. Federal Emergency Management Association Press

Ganor, Boaz (2000), The Rationality of the Islamic Radical Suicide Attack Phenomenon, Countering Suicide Terrorism, Institute of Counter Terrorism

Gupta, Dipak K. & Mundra, Kusum (2005), "Suicide Bombing as a Strategic Weapon: An Empirical Investigation of Hamas and Islamic Jihad. Terrorism and Political Violence", 17, pp (573-598).

Hjertager, B. H. (1982), Numerical Simulation of Flame and Pressure Development in Gas Explosions SM study no. 16, University of Waterloo Press, Ontario, Canada, pp (407-426)

Harrison, Mark (2004), The Immediate Effects of Suicide Attacks, University of Warwick

Harrison, Mark (2006), Bombers and Bystanders in Suicide Attacks in Isreal 2000 to 2003, Studies in Conflict and Terrorism. 29, pp (187-206)

Irwin, R. J., Lerner, M. R., Bealer, J. F., Mantor, P. C., Brackett, D. J., and Tuggle, D. W. (1999), Shock after blast wave injury is caused by a vagally mediated reflex, Journal of Trauma, Volume 47, pp (105-110)

Johnson, D. L (2005), Overpressure Studies with Animals and Man: Nonauditory Damage Risk Assessment for Simulated 155mm Self-Propelled Howitzer Blast. Final Report for U.S. Army Medical Research and Material Command, Fort Detrick, Maryland.

Kinney, Gilbert & Graham, Kenneth (1985), Explosive Shocks in Air, 2nd Sub edition. Springer

Kress, Moshe (2004), "The Effect of Crowd Density on the Expected Number of Casualties in a Suicide Attack", Wiley Periodicals

Lester, David, Yang, Bijou & Lindsay, Mark (2004), Suicide Bombers: Are Psychological Profiles Possible?, Studies in Conflict and Terrorism. 27, pp (283-295)

Pritchard, D. K., Lewis, M. J., Hedley, D., and Lea, C. J. (1999), Predicting the effect of obstacles on explosion development HSL Report No. EC/99/41 - CM/99/11

Pape, Robert A. (2005), Dying to Win: The Strategic Logic of Suicide Terrorism, Random House, New York, NY

Radlins, J. S. P., (1977), Physical and Pathophysiological Effects of Blast, Journal of Royal Naval Scientific Service, Volume 29

Stiglitz, Joseph E., and Bilmes, Linda J. (2008), The Three Trillion Dollar War – The True Cost of the Iraq Conflict, W. W. Norton & Company, New York, NY

Usmani (a), Zeeshan-ul-hassan (2009), Suicide Bombing - National Survey of Pakistan, FIT@Blast Center of Defense Modeling and Simulation, working paper

Usmani (b), Zeeshan-ul-hassan, Puri. Talal, and Kirk. Daniel (2009), How Much a Programmer Worth? - Introducing Personal Worth Indicator, The 2009 International Conference on Software Engineering Research and Practice (SERP' 09), Las Vegas, NV

Usmani (c), Zeeshan-ul-hassan, Alghamdi, Fawzi, and Kirk Daniel, (2009), Numerical Solutions of Explosion Modeling with CFD, The 2009 International Conference on Scientific Computing (CSC'09), Las Vegas, NV

Usmani (d), Zeeshan-ul-hassan, Alghamdi, Fawzi, and Kirk, Daniel (2009), A Survey of Empirical/Co-Relation Models for Explosion Modeling, The 2009 International Conference on Scientific Computing (CSC'09), Las Vegas, NV

Usmani (e), Zeeshan-ul-hassan, Alghamdi, Fawzi, and Kirk, Daniel (2009), A Mediocre Choice - Phenomenological Models for Blast-wave Modeling, The 2009 International Conference on Scientific Computing (CSC'09), Las Vegas, NV